STUDENT DEVELOPMENT IN COLLEGE

STUDENT DEVELOPMENT IN COLLEGE

Theory, Research, and Practice

SECOND EDITION

Nancy J. Evans
Deanna S. Forney
Florence M. Guido
Lori D. Patton
Kristen A. Renn

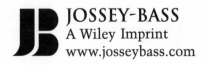
JOSSEY-BASS
A Wiley Imprint
www.josseybass.com

Published by Jossey-Bass
A Wiley Imprint
989 Market Street, San Francisco, CA 94103–1741—www.josseybass.com

Jossey-Bass books and products are available through most bookstores. To contact Jossey-Bass directly call our Customer Care Department within the U.S. at 800-956-7739, outside the U.S. at 317-572-3986, or fax 317-572-4002.

Jossey-Bass also publishes its books in a variety of electronic formats. Some content that appears in print may not be available in electronic books.

Library of Congress Cataloging-in-Publication Data
Evans, Nancy J., 1947-
  Student development in college : theory, research, and practice / Nancy J. Evans...[et al.]. — 2nd ed.
     p.   cm.
  Includes bibliographical references and index.
  ISBN 978-0-7879-7809-9 (cloth)
     1. College student development programs—United States.   2. College students—United States—Psychology.
  LB2343.4.E88 2010
  378.1′98—dc22
                                                                                2009033974

Printed in the United States of America
SECOND EDITION
HB Printing   10 9 8 7 6 5 4 3

The Jossey-Bass
Higher and Adult Education Series

CONTENTS

FIGURES AND EXHIBIT

Figures

Exhibit

We dedicate this book to those who teach and those who
learn and those who make student development happen:

To college students,
yearning for self-discovery and insights about the world.
To master's students in student affairs preparation programs,
seeking awareness and teaching us about taking risks.
To doctoral students,
conducting student development inquiry and challenging us to view
the world differently.
To students' parents,
watching in awe as their children transform into mature adults.
To faculty,
teaching student development but first learning and living it
themselves.
To practitioners,
designing programs and facilitating college student growth.
To administrators,
creating and supporting policy to promote student development.
To student development theorists,
giving us insight into the complexity of students' lives.

THE AUTHORS

Nancy J. Evans is a professor in the Department of Educational Leadership and Policy Studies at Iowa State University, where she teaches in the master's program in higher education–student affairs. She holds a B.A. in social science from Potsdam State College, an M.Ed. in higher education from Southern Illinois University, an M.F.A. in theatre from Western Illinois University, and a Ph.D. in counseling psychology from the University of Missouri. She taught previously at Penn State University, Western Illinois University, and Indiana University. Her previous student affairs experience includes positions in counseling centers, student activities, and residence life.

Evans is a former president of the American College Personnel Association (ACPA), former editor of ACPA's Books and Media Board, an ACPA Senior Scholar Emeritus, and a recipient of ACPA's Contribution to Knowledge, Voice of Inclusion, and Annuit Coeptis Senior Professional awards. At Iowa State, she has received both the Superior Research and Superior Teaching Medallions from the College of Education.

Evans is the author of publications on the impact of the campus environment on student development, particularly focusing on nondominant student populations, especially lesbian, gay, bisexual, and transgender students and students with disabilities. Her most recent work is related to social justice in higher education.

◆ ◆ ◆

Deanna S. Forney is a professor of college student personnel in the Department of Educational and Interdisciplinary Studies at Western Illinois University (WIU). She earned a B.A. from Gettysburg College, an M.A. from Pennsylvania State University, and an M.A. and a Ph.D. from the University of Maryland, College Park. Prior to becoming a faculty member at WIU, she was a student affairs practitioner at several institutions.

Forney has been elected an American College Personnel Association (ACPA) Senior Scholar and a National Association of Student Personnel Administrators Faculty Fellow. She is a past chair of ACPA's professional preparation commission. She has served on the editorial board of the *Journal of College Student Development* and on ACPA's Books and Media Board.

Forney has published several articles and book chapters. She is the senior editor of *Using Entertainment Media in Student Affairs Teaching and Practice*. She has also given numerous conference presentations and consulted with several institutions. Forney is a recipient of ACPA's Diamond Honoree and Annuit Coeptis awards and a corecipient of the Measurement and Evaluation in Counseling Research Award. She has also received the University of Maryland Department of Counseling and Personnel Services's distinguished alumni award and WIU's Faculty Excellence and Professional Achievement awards.

◆ ◆ ◆

Florence M. Guido (formerly Guido-DiBrito) has been an associate professor of higher education and student affairs leadership at the University of Northern Colorado for the past eleven years. Prior to this position, she taught at the University of Northern Iowa and held several leadership positions in student affairs, including dean of students. She holds a B.A. in art history from Briarcliff College, an M.A. in college student personnel administration from Ball State University, and a Ph.D. in educational leadership (emphasis in higher education administration) from Texas A&M University.

Guido is the first female recipient of both ACPA's junior and senior Annuit Coeptis awards. She has served on the editorial boards of the *Journal of College Student Development* and the *NASPA Journal*. Her numerous journal articles and book chapters address such topics as diversity development, ethnic identity, Mexican male students and social class, college women students, Latina students, traditional and new paradigm leadership, women's leadership, management and career development, and leadership and loyalty. She has included her images in photo-ethnographic research with Alicia Chávez on higher education culture in northern New Mexico. Her photographs were the first to accompany a scholarly article in the *NASPA Journal*, and her photograph appears on the cover of this book.

◆ ◆ ◆

Lori D. Patton is an assistant professor of higher education in the Department of Educational Leadership and Policy Studies at Iowa State University. She earned a B.S. in speech communication from Southern Illinois University at Edwardsville, an M.A. in college student personnel from Bowling Green State University, and a Ph.D. in higher education administration from Indiana University. She has held positions in residence life, Greek affairs, multicultural affairs, admissions, academic support, and student activities.

Patton is involved in the American College Personnel Association (ACPA), recently serving on the governing board as the director of equity and inclusion, the National Association of Student Personnel Administrators, Association for the Study of Higher Education, and American Educational Research Association. She has been recognized as an ACPA Emerging Scholar and has received the ACPA Annuit Coeptis Emerging Professional Award.

Patton's publications have appeared in leading student affairs journals. Her research examines access, equity, and racial injustice in the academy, with a particular focus on the experiences of African American college students. Patton recently coedited a volume of New Directions for Student Services, *Responding to the Realities of Race*. She also serves on the *Journal of College Student Development* editorial board.

◆ ◆ ◆

Kristen A. Renn is associate professor of higher, adult, and lifelong education at Michigan State University. She earned a bachelor's degree from Mount Holyoke College, an Ed.M. from Boston University, and a Ph.D. in higher education from Boston College. Renn worked in student activities before becoming assistant dean of student life at Brown University. She did policy analysis for the Massachusetts Board of Higher Education and began her faculty career at Southern Illinois University–Carbondale.

Renn is associate editor for international research and scholarship of the *Journal of College Student Development* and served on its editorial board, as well as that of the *NASPA Journal*. She was a longtime member of the leadership team of NASPA's Gay, Lesbian, Bisexual, and Transgender Knowledge Community and is the recipient of NASPA and ACPA awards for her research on biracial students and lesbian, gay, bisexual, and transgender student leaders (LGBT).

Renn's research focuses on identity in higher education. Her four books and numerous articles and book chapters describe research on mixed-race students, LGBT students, women in higher education, and new professionals in student affairs.

PREFACE

When we wrote the preface to the first edition of *Student Development in College*, we began with the sentence, "Our student populations and the developmental issues they confront are more diverse and complex than ever in the history of higher education." This statement is even more the case twelve years later. Increasing numbers of students of color; gay, lesbian, and bisexual students; transgender students; older students; students from lower socioeconomic backgrounds; students of different faith backgrounds; immigrants; and students who identify in many other ways are now enrolled in colleges and universities in the United States.

The student development theory that we included in the first edition of *Student Development in College* is inadequate to understand and work effectively with students of the twenty-first century. We offer this second edition to introduce a broader range of theory that we view as useful in working with today's college students. Although many of the theories we discussed in the 1998 edition are included in this edition, we now label these approaches "foundational theories," in the sense that later theorists have built on and moved beyond them in an attempt to more inclusively and completely explain the process of student development. In addition, newer integrative theories that look at student development in a more holistic way are included, as are social identity theories that we believe are critical for understanding diverse student populations.

This second edition of *Student Development in College*, like the first, will help student affairs practitioners understand the developmental challenges facing college students within the cognitive, intrapersonal, and interpersonal domains, independently and in combination. It will also provide them with knowledge of factors contributing to development in these domains. Most important, it will assist student affairs professionals in designing individual, group, and institutional approaches to work more effectively with students at various developmental levels and to facilitate student growth. As a result of reading this book, practitioners should have a better understanding of the overall needs of college students and strategies for meeting these needs.

In addition, this second edition will provide scholars with a comprehensive and inclusive overview of the most important student development theories and related research, including new approaches with which they may not be familiar, particularly related to social identity development. As such, the book should serve as an important review and critique of foundational and cutting-edge literature in the field. It will be a helpful resource in the design of future research.

We certainly advocate reading original sources of theory, but given the explosion of literature related to student development, reading every original source is not viable, especially for individuals who are unfamiliar with the topic. Our goal is to provide an introduction, overview, and evaluation of the theories we believe are helpful in understanding and working with students, with the hope that readers will expand the depth of their knowledge by reading the work of theorists they find particularly interesting and useful.

This edition has been written for individuals involved in student affairs work in higher education and students in college student affairs graduate programs. It will be valuable to individuals with no background in student development theory who wish to obtain a comprehensive understanding of this area, as well as individuals who wish to update their knowledge. It will be particularly helpful for practitioners who work directly with students, such as student activities advisors, residence life coordinators, academic advisors, career counselors, multicultural educators, and counseling center staff, as well as individuals who supervise frontline staff and are responsible for program design and administration. University faculty interested in learning more about student development and applications of student development theory in classroom and advising settings will also find the book useful. That examples are drawn from a variety of institutional settings gives this book broad appeal.

Student Development in College is designed to provide a comprehensive, in-depth review of the major student development theories as they relate to student affairs and educational practice. Because of space limitations, not all theories could be included. The theories selected for inclusion represent a range of philosophical and methodological perspectives, are frequently cited in the educational literature, and lend themselves to use in educational settings.

Some theories that were popular in the early history of the student development movement, such as the work of Roy Heath, Douglas Heath, and Jane Loevinger, remain valuable because of the ideas they introduced, but they are rarely referred to today as the basis of research and practice. As in the first edition, we refer to these theories in the historical overview to acknowledge the role they played. Because of space limitations and after much struggle, we deleted chapters on the typology theories of Isabel Myers and John Holland from the second edition. Although these theories have much utility in student affairs practice and have been extensively researched, they are not truly developmental in nature. In Chapter Two, we present these approaches as a way to look at individual differences in relation to student development and encourage readers to seek out fuller descriptions of these helpful theories. Theories that we did not address in the first edition, including James Fowler's theory of spiritual development and Robert Kegan's model of self-evolution, have seen a surge of popularity as other authors, in these cases, Sharon Parks and Marcia Baxter Magolda, respectively, have based exciting new work on the principles they introduced. As such, we examined these older theories in this new edition to provide an introduction to the newer work that they have generated.

Another group of theories, including models of multiple identities as well as many of the newer racial and ethnic identity models, showed great promise in 1998 but had not yet been tested to any great extent. They have now been used extensively and as a result warrant significant attention today.

Finally, there are new theories that have been introduced since 1998 that have had a major influence on our understanding of students and must therefore also be included. These include Roger Worthington and his colleagues' work on heterosexual identity development, Brent Bilodeau's theory of transgender identity development, and Kristen Renn's ecological model of multiracial identity. We freely admit that our personal biases have entered into the selections we made and that we were not all of one mind regarding selections. We believe, however, that the theories we have chosen to include will provide a comprehensive grounding for the practice of intentional student development in higher education.

The result, as might be predicted, is a much more comprehensive and longer book. To adjust for coverage of more theories, we have eliminated sections on assessment and included relevant material on that topic under research or application. We have also strictly limited discussion of research to studies within higher education settings and those directly validating the theory being addressed. It was also much harder to organize this edition of the book into parallel chapters.

Although we attempted to maintain a format similar to that of the first edition, which included for each theory a discussion of its development, the basic concepts associated with the theory, assessment techniques, related research, applications of the theory to student affairs practice, and a critique, in many cases it was necessary to deviate a bit from this structure to cover particular topics in this edition. Many chapters, for instance, include coverage of several theories on a similar topic. This is particularly the case with the newer theories. In some of these chapters, discussion of development, research, and application examines work related to all theories in that chapter as a whole. If we had attempted to cover one theory per chapter, the book would have over fifty chapters, certainly not a viable solution. As in the first edition, particular attention has been paid to the applicability of various approaches to diverse student populations and diverse settings. Case studies and practical examples have been included to assist readers to better understand the theoretical concepts being discussed and to see their utility in the daily practice of student affairs work.

The chapters in Part One examine the concept of student development and explore meanings attached to it in student affairs literature and practice. We also outline the historical context of student development (Chapter One) and discuss the role of theory and the uses of student development theory in student affairs practice (Chapter Two).

Part Two introduces the foundational theories of student development, representing the psychosocial, cognitive-structural, and learning style approaches that comprise most of the first edition. Chapter Three introduces Erik Erikson's psychosocial identity theory and the theories of two individuals who built on his work, James Marcia and Ruthellen Josselson. Chapter Four presents an overview of Arthur Chickering's theory of psychosocial development, focusing particularly on his revised theory, developed in collaboration with Linda Reisser. In Chapter Five, we introduce William Perry's cognitive structural approach, which examines the intellectual and ethical development of college students. Chapter Six focuses on moral development, a specific component of cognitive structural development that deals with how people make decisions that affect their lives and the lives of others. We review the pioneering work of Lawrence Kohlberg, followed by an examination of James Rest's neo-Kohlbergian theory and Carol Gilligan's alternative explanation of moral development. In Chapter Seven, we present several other important cognitive structural theories that built on Perry's work, including Mary Belenky and her colleagues' study of women's intellectual development, Baxter Magolda's original research on epistemological development of men and women, and the reflective judgment model of Patricia King and Karen Kitchener. In Chapter Eight we examine David Kolb's theory of experiential learning that helps us understand learning style differences among students.

Part Three introduces four integrative approaches to student development, only one of which—Nancy Schlossberg's transition theory—was included in the first edition of this book. These approaches take a holistic view of development and offer a more comprehensive understanding of the overall developmental experience. Chapter Nine includes an overview of various ecological approaches to student development, particularly the increasingly important work of Urie Bronfenbrenner. In Chapter Ten we review Kegan's theory of self-evolution and Baxter Magolda's breakthrough work on self-authorship, which builds on Kegan's work. Chapter Eleven introduces theories of faith and spirituality—increasingly important topics for many students. The theories we examine are those of Fowler and Parks. Chapter Twelve covers Schlossberg's transition theory, which remains valuable.

We present a greatly expanded discussion of social identity development in Part Four. Chapter Thirteen introduces concepts associated with social identity development, particularly privilege and oppression, as well as multiple identity models that examine the interconnections of social identities. In Chapter Fourteen, we discuss the meaning of race, principles of critical race theory, and a number of racial identity development models, including the general model of Derald W. Sue and David Sue, the black identity model of William Cross and Peony Fhagen-Smith, the white racial identity models of Janet Helms and Wayne Rowe and his colleagues, Jean Kim's model of Asian American identity development, Bernardo Ferdman and Plácida Gallego's model of Latino identity development, and Perry Horse's examination of how race is viewed in American Indian communities. Chapter Fifteen, in turn, reviews the separate concepts of ethnic identity development and acculturation and looks at various models, including Jean Phinney's model of ethnic identity, Vasti Torres's Latino identity model, acculturation models that explain the experience of American Indians and Asian Americans; and womanist and Caribbean identity models that speak to the ethnic experience of black Americans. Chapter Sixteen introduces numerous models of multiracial identity development that have become increasingly important as more interracial couples have children. We give particular attention to the ecological models of Maria Root and Renn. Sexual identity development models are discussed in Chapter Seventeen. In addition to an expanded discussion of the gay and lesbian identity development theories of Vivienne Cass and Anthony D'Augelli, we have added Ruth Fassinger's approach to this topic and Worthington and his colleagues' examination of heterosexual identity development. Another new addition, gender and gender identity, is the focus of Chapter Eighteen. These two concepts are examined along with Sandra Bem's gender schema and Bilodeau's model of transgender identity development.

To conclude the book, in Part Five we again include a chapter on integrating theoretical approaches to create intentional developmental environments (Chapter Nineteen). Examples using several theories and models in a comprehensive manner should help readers pull together previously presented material in an inclusive and concrete way. In Chapter Twenty, we conclude with an examination of the state of the art of student development theory and provide recommendations for future research and more intentional application of student development theory.

In conceptualizing this second edition of *Student Development in College,* once again our goal was to provide a user-friendly introduction to student development theory that would also challenge readers to explore the topic in more depth. In addition, we intend the book to serve as an update for individuals who wish to learn more about recently introduced theories of student development. As student affairs professionals and other educators work together to enhance the learning environment on college campuses, they will find that an understanding of student development theory is essential. We hope that this book will again make a meaningful contribution to this knowledge base.

ACKNOWLEDGMENTS

Many people have contributed to this work in significant ways. First, we thank David Brightman and Erin Null, our editors at Jossey-Bass. David has provided support, encouragement, and an occasional kick in the butt during this process. His continuing enthusiasm about this book and his faith in our ability to pull it off has meant more to us than he realizes. Erin's insightful feedback has certainly improved the quality of this book. We also thank David and Erin's assistant at Jossey-Bass, Aneesa Davenport, who has provided helpful and timely responses to all of our technical questions.

In addition, each of us has particular individuals to thank who have supported our efforts.

Nancy Evans first and foremost thanks her partner, Jim Trenberth, for his incredible support and assistance through the entire process of writing this book. In so many tangible ways, from meal preparation to computer support to photocopying articles at the library to providing much-needed backrubs and ice cream, he has been there every step of the way. Nancy seriously doubts that this book would have been completed without his contributions and his incredible ability to say and do the right thing at the right time to keep her going.

Nancy also thanks her friends and mentors Harry Canon and the late Ursula Delworth for their ongoing support and faith in her abilities. In addition to her coauthors, former students and valued colleagues Ellen Broido and Bob Reason have been wonderful sounding boards over the years in which this book has been in progress. Several former and current Iowa State students have made important tangible and intangible contributions to this project, especially Jessica Ranero, Alissa King, Juan Guardia, Nina Grant, Robyn Cooper, Karly Schmidt, and Todd Herriott. Finally, individuals whose scholarly work has greatly influenced Nancy's thinking about students, student development, and the role of student affairs in higher education deserve acknowledgment as well. They include Tony D'Augelli, Marcia Baxter Magolda, Kristen Renn, Heidi Levine, Susan Jones, Jamie Washington, and Vernon Wall.

Dea Forney acknowledges the positive impact that her students in the graduate program at Western Illinois University continue to have in stimulating her thinking about student development theory. In particular, she thanks those students who have served as teaching assistants for the student development theory course that she teaches: Anthony Bettendorf, Kendrick Schetter, Sarah Cunningham, Meagen Scholl, Zachary Nicolazzo, Benjamin Parks, Nicole Remy, and Melina Strohman. Their enthusiasm and insight have been a joy as she has worked with them to prepare future reflective practitioners.

Flo Guido finds it difficult to believe that Nancy, Dea, and she began their initial discussion of the first edition of *Student Development in College* about thirteen years ago. All three of them were teaching student development theory with little for a text and a course packet that rivaled the length of *Moby Dick*. More than ten years later, no one could conceive of so many different ways to conceptualize student development. Undertaking such a hefty task meant others helped her do her part. So the first people to whom gratitude is bestowed are Nancy and Dea. Lori and Kris stepped in and helped out; she extends her gratefulness to both of them. Their outstanding work has strengthened the manuscript.

Flo also thanks the graduate students in Higher Education and Student Affairs Leadership (HESAL) at the University of Northern Colorado, who taught her so much about college students and their development. HESAL students Patty Armfield and Chris Linder could not have been more eager, helpful research assistants. A special thanks to the spring 2008 Advanced Student Development class members—Ashley Hartmann, Erin Medina, Marianne Price, and Kristen Kushmider—who read early chapter drafts and offered excellent feedback. Thanks to students and former students who walk a developmental path and offer their continuous support: Patrick Clarke, Jody Donovan, Dean Kennedy, Kelly Kirven, Pam Moreno, Jeffrey Powell, Samantha Ortiz-Schriver, Scarlett Ponton de Dutton, and Samilyn Story, to name a few. In addition, heartfelt gratitude is extended to colleagues who challenge her and still extend constant support: Alicia Chávez, James Wallace, Sherry Gutman, Yvonna Lincoln, Stan Carpenter, Jane Fried, and Vasti Torres. And finally, thanks to her sister,

Antoinette Guido Browning, and friend Lisa Seyler, who are always willing to help, no questions asked.

And finally, *grazie* to the two people in her life who believe in the power of education, helped her spend much of her life in the academy as a student-teacher, and instilled in her the desire to do the right thing: her parents, Toni and Cosmo. The legacy left to their family will live in the hearts of Guidos for generations to come.

Lori Patton thanks God for the numerous and unending blessings that she has received, many times undeservingly. She is also thankful for the undying support of her family. She thanks Tobias for loving her and helping her to sustain the belief that she can do anything. She thanks Shaun, Chayla, Michelle, Ontario, and Leah for reminding her what true friendship means and for lending their ears every time she either wanted to share a new theoretical discovery or retreat from theory so that she could return to it with a fresh perspective. She is grateful to the many students who willingly share their experiences in the student development courses and continuously inspire her to value the opportunity to teach theory. She acknowledges her graduate teaching assistants, whose invaluable assistance has helped her to be successful and in turn role-model the behavior that they will need to exhibit as they prepare the next generation of student affairs educators. Finally, she thanks Nancy for her encouragement and belief that she could make a significant contribution to this book by inviting her to collaborate with such outstanding scholars in the field of student affairs.

Kristen Renn thanks her students and colleagues at Michigan State, who provide fertile ground for asking important questions about what student development is, how we can use it to improve educational practice, and how we can best study it. Advising dissertations written by Brent Bilodeau, Philip Strong, Jennifer Hodges, and Jody Jessup-Anger provided especially deep opportunities for learning more about theories of gender, gender identity, and human ecology. Kristen thanks mentor Karen Arnold, who led the way into deep thinking about student development from multiple disciplinary perspectives. She also thanks Nancy Evans for inviting her into the writing of this book; it has been a challenging and rewarding process to work from the inside on creating a resource intended for broad use by an important audience. Finally, Kristen thanks her partner, Melissa McDaniels, for her patience, good humor, and unflagging support.

STUDENT DEVELOPMENT IN COLLEGE

PART ONE

UNDERSTANDING AND USING STUDENT DEVELOPMENT THEORY

Regina is about to begin her master's program in student affairs administration. In addition to maintaining a 3.5 grade point average and running track, Regina was active as an undergraduate in student government and the Association for Multicultural Understanding (AMU). When she decided early in her senior year that a career in business was not for her, the AMU advisor suggested that she think about student affairs administration. Regina had never heard of this profession, but she enjoyed the college environment and thought that the work her advisor did was important. She wanted to have the same kind of impact on others as he had had on her. So she investigated various preparation programs and ended up with an offer from one of the best programs in the country, along with an assistantship in multicultural student affairs. Needless to say, she is excited but also a little scared.

Regina is hoping that the course in student development theory for which she is registered will give her some clues as to how to approach the students with whom will be working. After her orientation to the office, all she knows is how to use the phone system, what her e-mail address is, and who the other people in her division are. No one has provided much guidance as to the issues students are facing or how to go about addressing them. At this point, all she has to go on is her own experience as an undergraduate, and she is bright enough to know that students at this large research university might have different concerns from her and her peers who attended a historically black college.

In preparation for her first class, Regina pages through her student development theory text. There are so many theories! How will she ever learn them all? Will she be able to use all these concepts meaningfully in her work? Regina is feeling overwhelmed.

◆ ◆ ◆

As Regina has intuitively discovered, understanding student development is crucial to being an effective student affairs educator. The growth and development of students is a central goal of higher education, and student affairs professionals play an integral role in its achievement. To accomplish this goal, educators must be familiar with an extensive literature base focusing on student development and be able to use relevant concepts and ideas effectively in their daily interactions with students. In addition, program planning and policy development are both enhanced when student development concepts are used as a guide. Becoming knowledgeable about student development requires serious study, including critical analysis and evaluation of theory and research.

Part One sets the stage for examining student development by introducing a number of concepts to provide a context for the study of specific student development theories presented later in the book. Although some of this material may seem abstract at first reading, we encourage readers to refer back to the text of Part One when exploring later chapters. In Part Five we will revisit many of these ideas in the process of examining the use of theory in practice and considering the current state of the student development knowledge base.

In Chapter One, we present various definitions of the term *student development* and clarify the numerous ways in which the concept has been applied. To provide historical background and a sense of how and why student development became the foundation of the student affairs profession, we trace the evolution of the student development approach. We then provide an overview of the theories examined in the book, introduce the concept of paradigms, and discuss their influence on student development theory and research.

In Chapter Two, we discuss the role of theory in practice, provide suggestions for evaluating the potential utility of specific theories, and examine the role of research and evaluation in the development of theory. We also make a case for linking theory to practice, examine the challenges and benefits in doing so, and explore how to use theory in a responsible manner. The interactionist paradigm, which stresses the importance of considering the interaction of person and environment, is introduced. Factors in the college environment that facilitate development are then explored, followed by a brief review of typology theories that focus on individual difference. As a prelude to examining the theories in the following parts of the book, we provide a series of cautions to keep in mind when using theory and a reminder that theory must be used in a holistic way to be most effective. Chapter Two concludes with our response to critics of student development theory.

The wealth of knowledge that now exists about what happens to students in college is gratifying and exciting. We hope that Regina—and our other readers—will embark as eager explorers on their journey of discovery.

CHAPTER ONE

DEFINITIONS AND HISTORICAL ROOTS OF STUDENT DEVELOPMENT

From the paternalistic faculty authority figure who supervised Harvard students in 1636 to the contemporary student affairs professional who uses developmental theory to understand and enhance students' personal growth and learning, student development has always existed in some form as a goal of educators. But what development consists of and factors that contribute to it have been contested topics throughout the course of history.

Some scholars argue that students, regardless of the era in which they lived and studied, are basically similar. For example, a scholar of medieval higher education (Haskins, 1957) believed that human development "remain[s] much the same from age to age and must so remain as long as human nature and physical environment continue what they have been. In his relations to life and learning the medieval student resembled his modern successor far more than is often supposed" (p. 93). Other writers would object vehemently to Haskins's position, arguing that rapidly changing conditions within society have created dramatically different circumstances for students across time and location and that student development must be considered in light of these changing scenarios (see Woodard, Love, & Komives, 2000). The expectations, needs, and developmental issues of a fifteen-year-old, upper-class white male student attending Harvard in the 1700s preparing for a clergy vocation were certainly different from those of a first-generation Laotian American woman attending a community college in the early twenty-first century and aspiring to become a dental hygienist. Many argue that to be considered "developed" in each instance looks vastly different. These differences are reflected in the assumptions of student development theorists, based on the societal conditions and thinking of the periods in which they wrote and their own belief systems (McEwen, 2003a).

This chapter provides an overview of the ways in which student development has been defined in the literature and examines the origins and evolution of major student development theories created in the second half of the twentieth century and beginning of the twenty-first century. The chapter ends with a discussion of the influence of paradigms on student development theory and research.

Definitions of Student Development

Student development is a term that is used extensively in student affairs practice. Professionals talk about "facilitating student development," offices are titled "Student Development," and graduate students study "student development theories." Student development is almost universally viewed as a good thing. Parker (1974), however, criticized student affairs professionals for attaching vague and nonspecific meanings to this term and suggested that for many, it has become a catchphrase with no direct application to their work. What exactly is meant, then, by the phrase, "student development"?

In 1967, Sanford defined *development* as "the organization of increasing complexity" (p. 47). He saw development as a positive growth process in which the individual becomes increasingly able to integrate and act on many different experiences and influences. He distinguished development from *change*, which refers only to an altered condition that may be positive or negative, progressive or regressive; and from *growth*, which refers to expansion but may be either favorable or unfavorable to overall functioning. Rodgers (1990c) defined *student development* as "the ways that a student grows, progresses, or increases his or her developmental capabilities as a result of enrollment in an institution of higher education" (p. 27). This definition guides the discussion of student development in this book.

Student development, Rodgers (1990c) noted, is also a philosophy that has guided student affairs practice and served as the rationale for specific programs and services since the profession's inception. He summed up this philosophy as "concern for the development of the whole person" (p. 27).

A related application of the term *student development* is programmatic in nature. Rodgers (1990c) stated that it is what student affairs professionals do to encourage learning and student growth. In a frequently quoted definition that reflects this perspective, Miller and Prince (1976) suggested that student development is "the application of human development concepts in postsecondary settings so that everyone involved can master increasingly complex developmental tasks, achieve self-direction, and become interdependent" (p. 3).

Rodgers (1990c) also noted that the term *student development* has been used to categorize theory and research on adolescent and adult development. This body of literature includes psychosocial, cognitive-structural, integrative, and social identity perspectives discussed in this book. These theories expand Sanford's (1967) definition of *development* by identifying specific aspects of development and examining factors that influence its occurrence. Developmental theory should respond to four questions (Knefelkamp, Widick, & Parker, 1978):

1. What interpersonal and intrapersonal changes occur while the student is in college?
2. What factors lead to this development?
3. What aspects of the college environment encourage or retard growth?
4. What developmental outcomes should we strive to achieve in college?

Student development theory provides the basis for the practice of student development. Knowledge of student development theory enables student affairs professionals to identify and address student needs, design programs, develop policies, and create healthy college environments that encourage positive growth in students. Because student development theories focus on intellectual growth as well as affective and behavioral changes during the college years, they also encourage partnerships between student affairs professionals and faculty to enhance student learning and maximize positive student outcomes.

A Brief History of the Student Development Movement

Early in the twentieth century, the relevance of the newly organized disciplines of psychology and sociology to the collegiate environment became apparent. Psychological theorists such as Freud, Jung, and later Skinner examined human behavior through a lens different from the theologians who earlier espoused the fostering of Christian moral character as a goal for educators in the colleges of the eighteenth and nineteenth centuries (Upcraft & Moore, 1990). As the scientific study of human development evolved, the academy responded by hiring student personnel workers who were viewed as human development specialists (Nuss, 2003). At first, they focused on vocational guidance; however, the tumultuous events of the mid-twentieth century prompted significant changes in the student personnel profession and how the profession viewed student development. Influences that contributed to this renewed focus on students were an embryonic student affairs field, the psychology of individual differences, and the need for institutions, particularly during the Great Depression of the 1930s, to place students in the world of work (Nuss; Rhatigan, 2000).

The 1920s Guidance Movement

In the 1920s, the vocational guidance movement began in earnest as colleges and universities graduated students who increasingly sought occupational security in business and industry. Credited with initiating the vocational guidance movement (Rhatigan, 2000), Frank Parsons (1909) was the first to articulate a "match" between personal characteristics and particular occupations to determine the "best fit" for individuals in the work environment. For the next forty years, vocational guidance in higher education (and elsewhere) rested on this premise.

Taking more interest in vocational preparation than developing themselves in a holistic way (Arbuckle, 1953), students in the early 1920s sought practical knowledge to propel them into the work world. At the same time, higher education and industry joined to create new knowledge and train new workers.

In reaction to student demand for work preparation and industry demand for applied research, an alarm was sounded by critics who believed that the economic ties between industry and higher education had to be severed in order to preserve academic freedom and integrity (Veblen, 1918/1946). At the same time, pragmatic philosophers, who asserted that optimal learning occurs when students' rational and emotional selves are integrated (see Carpenter, 1996; Rhatigan, 2000), alerted educators to the need to make education more than just vocational preparation. Combined, these latter two forces created a moral imperative for higher education to address students' multidimensional needs rather than focusing exclusively on vocational preparation.

The Student Personnel Point of View: 1937 and 1949

In 1925, representatives from fourteen institutions of higher education met to discuss vocational guidance problems. World War I was over, and increased enrollments left educators scrambling for ways to evaluate students and their needs.

From 1925 to 1936, data concerning students were collected at numerous institutions. Several specialized assessment tools, such as personality rating scales, were developed to examine students' ability and performance (American Council on Education, 1937/1994a). The culmination of these efforts was the American Council on Education's 1937 statement, the "Student Personnel Point of View" (SPPV). This landmark report recognized the proud history of higher education's commitment to "the preservation, transmission, and enrichment of the important elements of culture" produced in the forms of "scholarship, research, creative imagination, and human experience" (p. 67.) The report went on to assert that educators must guide the "whole student" to reach his or her full potential and contribute to society's betterment. In short, the statement was a reminder to the higher education community that in addition to the contributions of research and scholarship, the personal and professional development of students was (and remains) a worthy and noble goal.

In 1949, the American Council on Education (1949/1994b) revised the 1937 SPPV statement to include an expanded delineation of the objectives and goals of student affairs administration. Returning to the late nineteenth-century focus on the psychology of individual differences, the document called for faculty, administrators, and student personnel workers to encourage the development of students and recognize their "individual differences in backgrounds, abilities, interests and goals" (p. 110). Furthermore, the influence of World War II was reflected in the document's call for more attention to democratic processes and socially responsible graduates.

Early Student Development Theory and Research

The 1960s saw the beginning of significant changes in student affairs and higher education as the country faced nearly a decade of social turmoil brought on by the Vietnam War and the civil rights and women's movements. No longer were students primarily upper- and upper-middle-class white males. Women, veterans, and students of color from all social class backgrounds were enrolling in college in increasing numbers, and student affairs administrators sought information about their needs and perspectives. They first turned to psychologists (for example, Erikson, 1950, 1968; Piaget, 1952) for information about human development that would help them to understand the students with whom they were working. Social psychologists and sociologists, such as Kurt Lewin (1936), contributed knowledge of group dynamics and the effect of the environment on human interaction. In time, theorists such as Nevitt Sanford (1967), Douglas Heath (1968), Roy Heath (1964), and Kenneth Feldman and Theodore Newcomb (1969) began focusing specifically on the experiences of students in college.

Nevitt Sanford. Psychologist Nevitt Sanford was one of the first scholars to address the relationship between college environments and students' transition from late adolescence to young adulthood (Strange, 1994). He brought forth two insights about the process of development—cycles of differentiation and integration, and balancing support and challenge—that continue to be influential concepts when considering student development (Evans, 2003; P. King, 1994; Moore & Upcraft, 1990). Differentiation and integration are evident when students learn about their own personality characteristics and understand how these characteristics shape their individual identities (Sanford, 1962). Support and challenge are evident when students try to lessen the tension produced by the collegiate environment and succeed to the extent that environmental support is available (Sanford, 1967). Sanford's concepts are discussed further in Chapter Two.

Douglas Heath. Douglas Heath's (1968) theory, based on his study of male undergraduates at Haverford College, focused on the concept of maturity and described factors that contribute to the maturation process. He identified characteristics of a mature person and described the path by which a person moves from "immature" to "mature" ways of functioning (Widick, Parker, & Knefelkamp, 1978a). D. Heath suggested that maturation occurs along five growth dimensions in four areas: intellect, values, self-concept, and interpersonal relationships. He identified the following growth dimensions: becoming better able to represent experience symbolically, becoming allocentric or other-centered, becoming integrated, becoming stable, and becoming autonomous (Widick et al., 1978a). D. Heath (1977) posited that the environment is influential in either facilitating or inhibiting development along these dimensions. Widick et al. (1978a) noted that while Heath's work is not specific enough to guide practice, it does suggest "outcomes of an ideal educational experience" (p. 90).

Roy Heath. Based on a longitudinal study of the experiences of undergraduate men at Princeton during the 1950s, Roy Heath (1964) introduced a typology theory that focused on how individual differences affect students' progress toward maturity. He suggested that two dimensions must be considered when examining development: ego functioning and individual style. He defined ego functioning as "the manner in which the self interacts with the world, achieves its satisfaction, and defends itself from threats to its survival" (1973, p. 59). Individuals are hypothesized to move through three levels of maturity as they progress to an idealized state that Heath called "a Reasonable Adventurer." Individual style or type refers to "the manner in which the individual regulates the 'dynamic tension' between the inner, instinctual, feeling self and the outer, more rational self" (Knefelkamp, Parker et al., 1978, p. 94). Individual style is posited to influence how the person proceeds through the levels of maturity to become a Reasonable Adventurer. While Heath's model is important in stressing individual difference as a factor to consider in development, it does not provide a clear picture of factors that contribute to movement through the levels of maturity (Knefelkamp, Parker, et al., 1978).

Kenneth Feldman and Theodore Newcomb. Sociologists during the 1960s also examined the impact of college on students (see Feldman & Newcomb, 1969). Recognizing how the environment shapes a student's development, some researchers focused on the interpersonal world of college students, specifically the effects of peer groups (Newcomb & Wilson, 1966). In an exhaustive summary of research on college students, Feldman and Newcomb (1969) delineated the impact of peer group influence on individual students. They noted that peer groups help students accomplish family independence, facilitate the institution's intellectual goals, offer emotional support and meet needs not met by faculty, provide contact with and practice for interacting with others who are unlike the student, reinforce student change (or not), offer another source of gratification if the student is unsuccessful academically, affect a student's leaving or staying in college, and provide social training and personal ties that may assist students along their career paths.

Throughout the 1960s, sociologists and psychologists offered a fresh look at students and their interaction with the campus environment while student affairs professionals began promoting intentional student development within higher education institutions (Creamer, 1990; Nuss, 2003).

Formal Statements About Student Development

In the late 1960s and 1970s, professional associations, such as the Council of Student Personnel Associations (COSPA) and the American College Personnel Association (ACPA), and private groups, such as the Hazen Foundation, began to reconceptualize the role and mission of student affairs (see Evans, 2001b). The Hazen Foundation created the Committee on the Student in Higher Education (1968), which encouraged colleges and universities to "assume responsibility for the human development of [their] students" (p. 5), something never asked of higher education before. The Committee on the Student in Higher Education went on to proclaim that "our educational procedures rarely take cognizance of what we do know about human development" (p. 5).

At the same time, Tomorrow's Higher Education Project (T.H.E.), initiated by ACPA, explored the viability of student development as a philosophy of the profession (R. Brown, 1972) and specifically examined the student affairs profession's "commitment to student development—the theories of human development applied to the postsecondary education setting—as a guiding theory, and the continued attempt to ensure that the development of the whole student was an institutional priority" (Garland & Grace, 1993, p. 6).

In his influential monograph, *Student Development in Tomorrow's Higher Education—A Return to the Academy,* Brown (1972) challenged college administrators and student affairs professionals to "hold up the mirror" to each other in order to confront the incongruities between the stated goals of higher education and what was happening to students. He questioned whether student affairs professionals should be the only ones on campus concerned about student development and, more important, whether student development can be nurtured without the support and influence of those in the academic domain. A forerunner of "The Student Learning Imperative" (1996) and *Learning Reconsidered* (Keeling, 2004), the T.H.E. project recommended that student affairs educators increasingly emphasize academic outcomes, teaching-learning experiences, reorganizing student affairs offices and functions, being accountable by conducting outcomes assessments, and developing new sets of competencies.

Soon thereafter, the Council of Student Personnel Associations (1975/1994) sought to define the role of the student development specialist and close the gap between theory and practice in the field. Miller and Prince (1976) carried the concept one step closer to implementation by highlighting the developmental tasks of college students and suggesting program options to help students reach their developmental goals.

Later, instruments that focused on measuring student development outcomes (Winston, Miller, & Prince, 1979) and assessing the effect of the institutional environment on students (Pace, 1984) were developed to seek empirical evidence of the student development concept. These statements of philosophy, along with the early research, provided impetus for the student affairs field to redefine itself in ways that helped professionals meet the challenges of intentional student growth.

Major Theories (1950–1970)

In the late 1960s, three major theories were introduced that became the basis for understanding student development for decades to come. Building on Erikson's (1959/1980) ideas about identity development, Arthur Chickering focused specifically on developmental issues facing students in college. His book, *Education and Identity* (1969), quickly became the mainstay for professionals interested in student development. In 1968, William Perry introduced the first theory examining the intellectual development of college students to be used extensively in student affairs practice. Building on Piaget's (1932/1977) study of the moral development of children, Lawrence Kohlberg's (1969, 1976) theory of moral reasoning also gained great popularity in the student affairs field. For several decades, student development educators based their practice largely on these three theories. Extensive discussion of each of these theories, which are still frequently used in student affairs work today, can be found in Part Two of this book.

Alternative Theoretical Perspectives (1970–1990)

Recognizing that development does not happen in a vacuum, counseling psychologists James Banning and Leland Kaiser introduced the campus ecology model in a 1974 article that Banning later expanded into a monograph (1978).

This approach was popularized by work and publications of the Western Interstate Commission on Higher Education (WICHE) and its associates (see Aulepp & Delworth, 1976). Campus ecology focused on the interaction of the student and the campus setting (Banning, 1978). The cube model of Morrill, Oetting, and Hurst (1974), which encouraged counselors and other student affairs educators to consider the campus environment (in the form of primary groups, associational groups, and institutions or communities) as well as individual students as potential targets for interventions, is based on the campus ecology model. Although there is little mention of the campus ecology approach itself in current literature, the importance of considering the impact of the environment on student development is stressed in many current theories. (Ecological approaches are discussed in Chapter Nine.)

While not truly developmental in that they do not consist of stages through which individuals progress, a number of typology theories with implications for student learning and career development gained popularity during the 1980s. Building on the work of Carl Jung (1923/1971), Myers (1980) explored differences in personality type. Student affairs professionals, particularly those who work in the area of career development, also found Holland's (1985/1992) theory of vocational choice helpful. We discuss these two theories further in Chapter Two.

As student affairs educators took a more active role in academic intervention, they sought out theories of learning to assist them. Kolb's (1984) theory, which focused on learning styles, provided a useful way to conceptualize differences in how students learn. Chapter Eight offers an expanded discussion of Kolb's theory.

Later Developmental Theorists

The late 1980s and 1990s saw the introduction of a number of theories that built on earlier foundational psychosocial and cognitive-structural theories. Within the psychosocial tradition, Marcia (1966), using Erikson's (1959/1980) work as a foundation for his research, investigated identity development in adolescence. Josselson (1987a, 1996) then extended Marcia's work to women. The work of Erikson, Marcia, and Josselson is further discussed in Chapter Three. In 1993, to incorporate new research findings related to the order of his developmental vectors and their content, Chickering, in collaboration with Linda Reisser, revised his book, *Education and Identity*. In Chapter Four we cover Chickering and Reisser's revisions in detail.

Several theorists sought to expand Perry's cognitive structural theory. Suggesting that Perry had confused intellectual and psychosocial development in his final stages, King and Kitchener (1994) examined cognitive development beyond relativism, a process they labeled reflective judgment. Also building on Perry's theory, Belenky, Clinchy, Goldberger, and Tarule (1986) were the first researchers to investigate the intellectual development of women. Marcia Baxter Magolda extended the work of Perry (1968) and Belenky and her colleagues (1986) by including both men and women in a longitudinal study of the episte-mological development of individuals whom she originally interviewed when they were students at Miami University (Baxter Magolda, 1992). These three theories have each made a significant contribution to our understanding of student development and are discussed in more detail in Chapter Seven.

Based on twenty-five years of research, James Rest and his colleagues introduced a neo-Kohlbergian theory of moral development (Rest, Narvaez, Thoma, & Bebeau, 2000) that is less rigid and more concrete than Kohlberg's (1976). Gilligan's (1982/1993) identification of care-based rationales for moral decision making also advanced our understanding of moral reasoning. We discuss moral development theories in Chapter Six.

Integrative Approaches

Knefelkamp, Widick, and Parker (1978) argued that attempting to design one "comprehensive model of student development" (p. xi) was futile; nevertheless, current theorists appear to be moving in that direction. Arguing that it is not possible to separate cognitive and affective aspects of development, their theories explore both cognitive and psychosocial dimensions of identity and how these factors are interwoven throughout life.

Robert Kegan (1982, 1994) introduced a life span model of development that also took into account both affective and cognitive processes. Kegan (1982) focused on the evolution of the self and how individuals make sense of their world, particularly their relationships with others. An important outcome of development that Kegan identified is self-authorship—the ability to "internalize multiple points of view, reflect on them, and construct them into one's own theory about oneself and one's experience" (Ignelzi, 2000, p. 8). Following her former students into their adult lives, Baxter Magolda (1999a, 2001, 2007) used Kegan's concept of self-authorship to explain the shift she identified in young adulthood from an identity shaped by external forces and others' viewpoints to an internal identity created by individuals themselves. Theories of self-authorship are presented in Chapter Ten.

Another area receiving increasing attention is spiritual and faith development (Love & Talbot, 1999). Drawing on the ideas of both psychosocial (for example, Erikson, 1950; Levinson, 1978) and cognitive structural (for example, Kohlberg,

1976; Piaget, 1950) theorists, James Fowler (1981, 2000) began the discussion of faith from a developmental perspective. Parks (1986a, 2000) extended Fowler's theory to address faith development during college. Their work is reviewed in Chapter Eleven.

Generally considered a life events theorist within the larger umbrella of adult development theory, Schlossberg, who examined the process of negotiating transitions caused by life events (Schlossberg, 1984; Schlossberg, Waters, & Goodman, 1995; Goodman, Schlossberg, & Anderson, 2006), can also be considered an integrative theorist. We present her theory in Chapter Twelve.

Social Identity Theory

As U.S. society has become more diverse, understanding students from a variety of backgrounds has become increasingly important, and theories focusing on social identities are appearing with greater frequency in the literature. These theories, which are grounded in the sociohistorical context of the United States, in which some groups have privilege and some groups are oppressed, examine the development of both dominant and nondominant identities (McEwen, 2003a). While these identity models all focus on the process of self-definition, many of them also examine how individuals move through stages of increasing cognitive complexity with regard to their self-identification (Helms, 1993a). As such, they can be considered integrative, with qualities similar to theories discussed in the previous section. Helms defined (1993b) racial identity as "a sense of group or collective identity based on one's perception that he or she shares a common racial heritage with a particular racial group" (p. 3). Racial identity theories are predicated on the belief that race is not based in biology but rather is a social construction influenced by cultural norms and understandings about the relative merits of individuals from different heritages. Theories of African American identity development were the earliest theories of racial identity development to appear (see Cross, 1991; B. Jackson, 2001). White identity models, focusing on how white people view race and others from different racial backgrounds, followed (see Helms, 1995; Rowe, Bennett, & Atkinson, 1994). Models of Latino/a (Ferdman & Gallegos, 2001), Asian American (Kim, 2001), and American Indian (Horse, 2001) racial identity, as well as multiracial identity (Root, 1996; 2003a; Renn, 2004), have also been proposed. This body of scholarship is reviewed in Chapters Fourteen and Sixteen.

Ethnic identity has been defined as identification with "a segment of a larger society whose members are thought, by themselves and others, to have a common origin and to share segments of a common culture and who, in addition, participate in shared activities in which the common origin and culture are significant ingredients" (Yinger, 1976, p. 200). Phinney (2003), basing her work on Marcia's (1966) approach to identity development, identified a general model of ethnic identity, while Sodowsky, Kwan, and Pannu (1995), studying Asian Americans, proposed a bidirectional model based on degree of adoption of whiteness and degree of retention of Asianness. Other scholars, such as Torres (1999), have explored the relationship of ethnic identity and acculturation, a concept defined as changes in cultural attitudes, values, and behaviors that result from contact between two cultures (Phinney, 1990). Ethnic identity is discussed in Chapter Fifteen.

Theories of gay, lesbian, and bisexual identity development began to appear in the literature about the same time as the gay liberation movement started in the late 1960s. Cass's (1979) model is probably the best known and most used of these theories. Newer approaches, such as those of Fassinger (1998a) and D'Augelli (1994a), have gained popularity in recent years. Heterosexual identity development has also been discussed recently (see Worthington, Savoy, Dillon, & Vernaglia, 2002). Theories examining the development of sexual identity can be found in Chapter Seventeen.

Gender identity development theories are based on the assumption that gender roles and understanding of what it means to be a gendered person in society are socially constructed rather than determined by one's biological sex. With increasing attention being given to the unique concerns of college students who identify as transgender (that is, individuals whose gender identity does not align with their biological sex; see Carter, 2000; Beemyn, 2005), understanding the role that gender plays in the lives of all students has been highlighted. Bem (1981b, 1983) was one of the first theorists to identify the various ways in which individuals viewed themselves in relation to masculine and feminine traits. More recently, a theory of transgender identity development based on D'Augelli's (1994a) lesbian and gay identity development model has been introduced by Bilodeau (2005, 2009). Gender identity is discussed in Chapter Eighteen.

Other social identities such as class, religion, and ability/disability status have also been studied, and theory in these areas is starting to appear (see McEwen, 2003a). In addition, Jones and McEwen (2000) and Abes, Jones, and McEwen (2007) have reminded us that social identities do not exist independently but rather are intertwined and of varying salience at different times and in different contexts. This work is the focus of Chapter Thirteen.

Specialized Theories of Student Development

A number of other areas of development have been studied and discussed in the literature, many of relevance for educators in their work with students. For example, career development, an early area of interest for student affairs professionals, has an extensive body of theoretical literature (see Brown & Lent, 2005). Theories of learning, including newer approaches such as situated cognition, transformational learning, and critical and postmodern perspectives (see Merriam, 2008; Merriam, Caffarella, & Baumgartner, 2007), are also relevant as they provide another view of how students grow and develop intellectually and gain new knowledge both in and out of the classroom. As an increasing number of college students are adults over the age of twenty-two, student affairs educators must also expand their thinking to consider development across the life span. Adult development theories, including life stage theories, life events theories, life course theories, and integrative adult development theories, are helpful in this process (see Clark & Caffarella, 1999; Hamrick, Evans, & Schuh, 2002). Unfortunately, space limitations preclude further discussion of these important theories.

The Influence of Paradigms

Guba (1990) defined a paradigm as an interpretive framework, a "basic set of beliefs that guides action" (p. 17). McEwen (2003a) noted that theory development can occur as a result of shifting paradigms. When a particular paradigm dominates thinking, its assumptions are unquestioned and implicitly undergird the understanding of phenomena. A paradigm consists of three components: ontology, epistemology, and methodology (Denzin & Lincoln, 1994, p. 99). Ontology explores questions about the nature of reality. Epistemology examines how the inquirer comes to understand the world. Methodology focuses on the process of how information is obtained. Guba and Lincoln (1994) pointed out that since paradigms represent basic beliefs, they cannot be proved; paradigms are human constructions, subject to human error. Guba and Lincoln cautioned that "no construction is or can be incontrovertibly right; advocates of any particular construction must rely on *persuasiveness* and *utility* rather than *proof* in arguing their position" (p. 108).

Paradigms guide both theory and research. New, and often competing, paradigms have emerged to better account for findings when research results cannot be explained within the context of the dominant, positivist paradigm (Kuhn, 1970) that has guided theory and research in psychology, as well as most other fields, for the past four hundred years (Crotty, 1998; Guba & Lincoln, 1994). A positivist interpretation of the world assumes an objective reality exists that is time and context free and can be stated in the form of cause-and-effect laws. A researcher is assumed to be independent of the object investigated and able to study a phenomenon without influencing the outcome or being influenced by the object of study. The methodology used to study phenomena is experimental and manipulative. Hypotheses are formulated and subjected to empirical test for verification. Conditions that could interfere with the results are carefully controlled.

Much of the theory and research reviewed in this book has a positivist perspective. For instance, King and Kitchener (1994) presented stages of cognitive development that they believe are apparent in the thinking of individuals regardless of the situation in which the individuals find themselves. They studied cognitive development using a standardized set of interview questions and trained interviewers to present these questions in a similar manner to all research participants. They then outlined a program of research based on explicitly stated hypotheses, which were then tested in a predetermined manner. This research is used to verify the concepts associated with their theory. King and Kitchener's work is excellent within the context of the positivistic tradition. Others who create and test student development theory predominantly from a positivist perspective (which means the underlying assumptions mirror this perspective) include Perry (1968), Kohlberg (1976), Cross (1971), and Helms (1993a).

In the past decade or so, many researchers have begun to find a linear perspective constraining. Meaning in positivist research is often limited and generalizable findings difficult to apply to all categories (for example, all students in higher education). Student differences are too vast and college experiences too varied to look at developmental phenomena from the universal view of a positivist. Examination of human (and thus student) development in its many complex forms may be more successful if a multitude of paradigmatic lenses is used (Guido, Chávez, & Lincoln, in press). In an attempt to better explain the complexity that exists in the world today and give more meaning to what is found, a number of competing paradigms are emerging. The assumptions of critical cultural paradigms (Guido et al., 2003) and constructivism (Guba & Lincoln, 1994) are outlined here.

Critical paradigms reflect "theoretical foundations that promote the deconstruction and critique of institutions, laws, organizations, definitions and practices to screen for power inequities" (Guido et al., 2003, p. 14). Solidified over time, dominant perspectives are taken as "truth." Adherents of a critical perspective believe that research findings are inevitably influenced by the values of the inquirer. Inquiry is seen as transactional, requiring a dialogue between the researcher and researched. The purpose of inquiry is to raise consciousness and correct injustices resulting from ignorance and mistaken ideas by promoting fundamental social change. The work of many feminist and ethnic scholars can be situated within the critical paradigm. Critical race theory (CRT; Delgado & Stefancic, 2001; Solórzano, 1998), discussed further in Chapter Fourteen, is an excellent example of such an approach. Its goal is to challenge and shift the normative structure with regard to race and racism. Tenets of CRT include a belief that our current understanding of race privileges white people and marginalizes people of color. In addition, because racial dynamics are so ingrained in U.S. culture, they are not recognized by most people. To address inequities experienced by people of color, critical race theorists believe that the unique stories of people of color must be recounted, and researchers must use their findings to create a more just society.

The underlying theoretical foundation of cultural paradigms is that truth is socially constructed based on "invisible gender, culture, sexuality, class, language, and even personality preferences" (Guido et al., in press), to name a few. Cultural paradigms look at the world in congruence with the cultures examined and have a purely descriptive and interpretive goal. Examining phenomena from an anthropological and sociological lens, cultural paradigms study the norms, values, assumptions, beliefs, and meanings undergirding an artifact, population, policy, or organization. Magolda's campus rituals ethnographies (2000, 2002) originated from a cultural paradigm and stand in contrast to Rhoads's (1994, 1997) studies on gay college students and students engaged in service-learning, which offer both cultural description and critical analysis.

One of the most widely used paradigms to emerge in recent decades combines aspects of critical and cultural paradigms (Guido et al., in press). Knowledge from this shared paradigm is subjective, experiential, and transactional. Tenets of this paradigm include emancipation of nondominant groups to alter their oppression, intersections of multiple critical and cultural views (for example, class, race, ethnicity, gender, sexuality, and ability), and the high priority of ethical considerations. Racial/ethnic/border/liminal/postcolonial epistemologies (Beverley, 1999; Denzin, Lincoln, & Smith, 2008; Sandoval, 2000; L. Smith, 1999; Trinh, 1989), and feminist and gender theories, as well as embodied perspectives (Butler, 1993; Denzin et al., 2008), all possess tenets in concert with examination of students' intersecting social identities.

As a paradigm, constructivism is "based on a relative ontology, a subjectivist epistemology, and a hermeneutic (for instance, interpretive) and dialectical (for instance, critical) methodology" (Guido et al., in press). Reality is based on specific individual and group experiences and can change over time. Investigators and participants are viewed as linked, although the researcher carries the most weight in interpreting findings. Findings are created in the context of the investigation; the variable and personal nature of social constructions can be identified only through interaction between the researcher and participants involved in the research. Baxter Magolda's (1992, 1999a, 2001) work is constructivist in nature. She set out to discover how students at Miami University thought about their worlds. While guided by earlier work on cognitive development, she entered her investigation without preconceived ideas about what she would find. Her findings were based on a series of in-depth interviews she conducted with 101 individuals over a period of many years. In the presentation of these research findings, Baxter Magolda allowed her participants to present their interpretations of the world around them in their own words. Other scholars conducting constructivist research include Torres and Hernandez (2007). As a component of a larger mixed-method study, qualitative data were gathered to add Latino student voices to the chorus of student development literature. In doing so, Torres and Hernandez were the first to link student development and racism.

New paradigm thinking is having a profound influence on all fields, including student affairs (Fried & Associates, 1995; Guido et al., in press; Guido-DiBrito et al., 2003; Kuh, Whitt, & Shedd, 1987). Student development is being reconceptualized within these new frameworks. Understanding the paradigmatic assumptions underlying a theory is crucial to using the theory appropriately. To give the reader a sense of the ontological, epistemological, and methodological bases of developmental research, throughout this book we present background about the theories and discuss the context in which they were developed. We also outline the populations and methods used in the construction of the theories reviewed. We offer this information to enhance understanding of student development theory creation, development, and application.

Conclusion

Student affairs professionals appear to be the strongest and most consistent voice in the academy articulating concern for the human growth and development of students. Development of the whole student is more complex than one theory or even a cluster of theories can explain. The rapidly expanding body of literature focusing on various aspects of student development underscores this point. Life was certainly much easier for student affairs professionals and faculty teaching student development when all we needed to learn and teach were the theories of Chickering, Perry, and Kohlberg. The sheer volume of theoretical literature currently being produced is daunting even for scholars in the field. Luckily, the new approaches and complexity of perspectives provides a much stronger foundation for understanding and working with today's diverse college students. The challenge of becoming familiar with and learning to apply student development theory in the twenty-first century is certainly worth the effort. Student affairs educators can know only in hindsight how history will shape the future of student development, but for the sake of students, they must help the academy recognize the value of the whole person concept and the theory that contributes to an understanding of students' growth and change. Student development is far too important to be recognized only as a role for student affairs professionals. Faculty, administrators, and even students, parents, and families can benefit from more clearly understanding how students change over the course of their time in college and the factors that contribute to that process.

CHAPTER TWO

USING STUDENT DEVELOPMENT THEORY

Jana has recently accepted a position as coordinator of returning-adult services at a large research university. Both academic and student affairs at this university focus their attention on serving the large numbers of traditionally aged students who enroll there. In fact, Jana is the only full-time staff person in her unit. Adult students make up approximately 10 percent of the student population, but they are not highly visible on campus. Many attend classes part time while holding full-time jobs or caring for their families. They range in age from twenty-four (the age the university uses to define a returning-adult student) to over sixty. Most live off-campus, although a few live in family and graduate student housing. Jana quickly discovers that very few of these students use the services of her office; indeed, many do not even know of its existence. She has been charged by her vice president to develop a comprehensive and visible program to serve the needs of adult students. Yet she hardly knows where to begin.

◆ ◆ ◆

Knowledge of student development theory can be of great benefit to Jana as she addresses the challenges of her new job, but only if she uses these approaches wisely. Successfully using student development theory requires more than merely memorizing various stages, vectors, and theoretical concepts. In this chapter, we provide a context for understanding and using theory, setting the stage for later chapters that examine specific theoretical approaches. Chapter topics include the role of theory, evaluating theory, the role of research and evaluation, linking theory and practice, the interactionist perspective, environmental factors influencing development, considering individual differences, cautions in using theory, thinking holistically, and a response to critics.

The Role of Theory

Theory is the result of the need people have to make sense out of life. It enables the organization and interpretation of enormous amounts of information existing in the world. Each person has a set of organizing principles, or "informal theory," that is used to make sense of experiences. Parker (1977) defined *informal theory* as "the body of common knowledge that allows us to make implicit connections among events and persons in our environment and upon which we act in everyday life" (p. 420). McEwen (2003a) asserted that each student affairs practitioner has informal theories about students, environments, and human development. Certainly Jana brings to her position a set of ideas about the needs and concerns of adult students. These assumptions may be based on her previous interactions with adult students, her own experiences in college, the values she grew up with concerning education and adulthood, and her formal training and education.

Unfortunately, informal theory is not self-correcting (Parker, 1977). People have no basis on which to determine if their interpretations are accurate. Formal theories validated by research are needed to ascertain whether individuals' perceptions hold for the persons with whom they work and the situations in which they find themselves. Rodgers (1980) defined formal theory as "a set of propositions regarding the interrelationship of two or more conceptual variables relevant to some realm of phenomena" (p. 81). It helps to explain how variables interact and provides a framework for the study of these relationships. Many theorists have examined adult development (for example, Erikson, 1959/1980; Goodman, Schlossberg, & Anderson, 2006; Neugarten, 1979), and Jana will find these theories particularly helpful as she begins to identify the needs of her students in a systematic manner.

Theory has four increasingly powerful uses: description, explanation, prediction, and control (DiCaprio, 1974). At the first level, description, theory provides a conceptualization of what is happening. For instance, Chickering and Reisser (1993) identified a series of developmental issues, such as developing competence and managing emotions, which describe the experiences of college students. At the second level, theory can be used to explain the causes of behavior. For example, Perry's (1968) theory of cognitive development suggests that some students exhibit dualistic, either-or thinking. This information might explain why a student is having trouble in a course that involves a great deal of analysis and evaluation of arguments. At the third level, which very few theories achieve, prediction is the goal. A powerful theory might enable us to predict the developmental outcome of placing a student with a certain learning style in a particular class. For instance, Kolb's (1984) theory suggests that students will perform better in classroom environments that are suited for their learning style. The final level, which developmental theory has yet to accomplish, is control. Hypothetically, if a more comprehensive knowledge base existed, theory would enable us to produce specific developmental outcomes, such as higher levels of moral reasoning.

Evaluating Theory

The number of student development theories has increased significantly since 1965. Not all, however, are of equal value to educators. To be useful, theories must exhibit the following qualities: (1) *comprehensiveness*—a theory should make predictions that account for a wide range of behavior; (2) *clarity and explicitness*—concepts and relationships should be defined precisely; (3) *consistency*—a theory should allow inclusion of findings within a logical framework; (4) *parsimony*—explanations should be concise, simple, and easy to follow; and (5) *heurism*—a theory should generate ideas for research (Walsh, 1973).

Knefelkamp (1978) suggested several questions for evaluating the utility of theory that remain helpful:

1. *On what population is the theory based?* It is important to determine the population on which the theory was based and whether the theory has been tested with individuals who have different characteristics. Some aspects of the theory may be specific to the original population, while other concepts may apply to people more generally.
2. *How was the theory developed?* The assessment instruments or techniques that were used in the original study should be clearly described.
3. *Is the theory descriptive?* Does it provide a comprehensive view of individuals' development and specific aspects of the developmental process?
4. *Is the theory explanatory?* Does it outline how development occurs?
5. *Is the theory prescriptive?* Does it discuss ways in which specific outcomes can be produced and lead to the prediction of events or relationships that can be verified through observation or experimentation?
6. *Is the theory heuristic?* Theory should generate research ideas.
7. *Is the theory useful in practice?* Student development theory should help in understanding students, developing programs to serve them, and evaluating the effectiveness of services provided.

Most theories fall short on one or more of these criteria. For instance, student development theories are largely descriptive, and only rarely explanatory or prescriptive (Parker, Widick, & Knefelkamp, 1978). It is also important to remember that no theory is really objective (McEwen, 2003a). Each reflects the perspective of its author. Nevertheless, existing theories are sources of awareness that serve as a means of organizing one's thinking and guiding the choices that are made in working with students.

The Role of Research and Evaluation

Research plays an important role in both the development and refinement of theory (Terenzini, 1994). While some theories have evolved from informal observation and logic, most student development theories have been based on research specifically designed to determine what factors are important in development, how development occurs, and what environmental conditions facilitate development. After a theory is introduced, additional research using the theory as a foundation can lead to its modification and refinement. Researchers may also examine the applicability of the theory for different populations and explore its utility in various settings.

For example, Kohlberg (1958) conducted an initial study of boys between the ages of ten and sixteen to explore factors related to their moral reasoning. Based on his findings, he developed preliminary hypotheses about how moral development occurs (Kohlberg, 1969). He then systematically formulated an extensive program of research to test hypotheses. The results of his studies led him to modify and refine his theory (Kohlberg, Levine, & Hewer, 1984). Kohlberg and other researchers have extended his theory to both men and women across the life span and from various cultural backgrounds. (See Chapter Six for a complete discussion of Kohlberg's work and the work of others based on his theory.)

When deciding whether a theory is valid (that is, whether it presents an accurate picture of development), practitioners should examine the research on which it was based, as well as later studies that have tested the theory's assumptions, propositions, and transferability. An important criterion of good theory is the extent to which it can be verified by research, as well as its ability to generate new knowledge (McEwen, 2003a).

Evaluation differs from research in that it is used to determine the effectiveness of specific programs or interventions. When used to assess the outcomes of theory-based interventions, evaluation data can contribute to our knowledge base by answering theoretical as well as practical questions. For example, a theoretically grounded evaluation might tell us not only if a program works, but also for whom it works and possibly why it works for some students but not others.

In this way, evaluation contributes to the refinement of theory and its application. Kohlberg (1971) used his theory of moral development to develop moral education programs in schools. His evaluation of these programs, like his earlier validation research, led to modification of his theory. Evaluation is an important component in the design of any educational intervention.

Linking Theory and Practice

Theory is a valuable tool for practitioners, but its use also presents challenges. To be effective, theory must be used responsibly.

The Value of Using Theory

Student development theory can help educators understand and respond to students empathically (Knefelkamp, 1984). It provides a lens through which to view students and helps educators put student behavior in context rather than simply being perplexed by it. It explains and suggests action for working with students, guiding practice in advising, teaching, programming, and facilitating student learning both in and outside the classroom. Student affairs practice without a theoretical base is neither effective nor efficient.

"What guides my practice?" is an important question for practitioners to ponder (Forney et al., 2005). Mandates to apply diverse knowledge bases available to the field in student affairs scholarship are evident in special journal issues produced by both ACPA-College Student Educators International (*Journal of College Student Development*; Carpenter, 2001a) and NASPA-Student Affairs Administrators in Higher Education (*NASPA Journal*; Roper, 2002). For example, scholarly practice has been described as intentional, theory based, and data driven. As Carpenter (2001b) stated, "Being a good person or good with students is not enough to be a student affairs professional any more than doctors or lawyers or mechanics are valued for their affability. A scholarly practitioner has obligations to clients, to peers, and to his or her employing institution" (p. 311).

The scholarship of application, that is, using knowledge to address problems of consequence, is promoted in student affairs (Schroeder & Pike, 2001). Some graduate students and practitioners in student affairs may not feel a connection to the phrase "scholar-practitioner"; perhaps "practitioner-scholar" (Komives, 1998) seems more appropriate. In fact a continuum of practitioner-practitioner, practitioner-scholar, scholar-practitioner, and scholar-scholar suggests that those who fall at either end are limited in their effectiveness (Komives).

Student development theory assists practitioners in their work and can aid in forming connections to faculty, who are pivotal academic partners. Using student development theory can enhance the professionalism of student affairs educators not only in their practice but also with regard to the view of their role within the higher education setting.

Challenges in Using Theory

Practitioners sometimes encounter challenges in regard to using theory in practice. Time can be perceived as an issue when it comes to using theory. Practitioners are busy, with competing priorities. For example, they spend much time responding to emergencies in student affairs, so much so that the urgent can displace the important. Some believe that using theory in practice is time-consuming. In response, one might ask if trial-and-error approaches are likely to take less time or be as effective.

Another obstacle to use of theory is practitioners' lack of knowledge or failure to remember what they previously learned. Practitioners need access to literature that discusses existing and newly introduced theory, as well as ongoing research and innovative uses of theory. Examination of literature should be a regular component of staff training programs, as well as individually initiated by student affairs professionals.

Practitioners may also encounter less than supportive attitudes among other staff members who choose to dismiss the knowledge base. Such attitudes can arise from such factors as lack of understanding of the value of theory or a desire to avoid having to learn new information. Demonstrating the effective use of theory may help to convince others of its value.

Some perceive developmental activity as expensive, perhaps because of the use of costly instruments or expensive labor to analyze evaluation data. However, informal assessments can be substituted where assessment is needed. Again, the question of whether trial and error is likely to be less expensive in the long run deserves to be raised, especially if programs are ineffective or result in unhappy students who decide to leave school. In addition, using theory to better understand students and as a basis for programming and policy decisions costs nothing and can be very helpful.

Some practitioners confuse a developmental perspective with permissiveness. When students behave badly, the question is sometimes asked, "Should we punish them, or should we be developmental?" This question contains a false dichotomy. Holding a developmental view means holding students accountable; a just punishment is developmental (Pavela, 1983). Other issues and challenges that can confront those who seek to use student development theory and to persuade others of its worth are less-than-effective approaches by the would-be translator, such as the "bull in a china shop" (well intentioned but clumsy) and the "savior" ("Hallelujah! I know it all and am here to provide the answers"); the slowness and potentially threatening nature of change; and unfamiliar language (Forney, Eddy, Gunter, & Slater, 1992). Using theory to shape policies, programs, and practices can also contain political elements (Desler, 2000). For example, when a senior administrator's pet program is found lacking in regard to developmental outcomes, even solid evidence demonstrating a need for revision may not result in change.

Several strategies can be used in dealing with the challenges described (Forney et al., 1992). These include providing solid rationales, avoiding jargon, using language and strategies appropriate to the audience (for example, using theory and research to promote ideas with faculty), building alliances, persuading staff members one at a time, being unobtrusive versus blatant, identifying and using windows of opportunity, using pilot programs, demonstrating perseverance, and recognizing and celebrating successes.

Helping others, such as professional staff, faculty, graduate students, and peer helpers, become familiar with the content of theory and its potential uses in a straightforward, down-to-earth manner can render theory more user friendly. Minimizing jargon, helping potential users to see connections between theory and their own experiences, and demonstrating (versus telling) how theory has been used successfully facilitates openness to theory among those who are unfamiliar with the content and its value.

Responsible Use of Theory

Appropriate use of theories requires tentative use rather than prescriptive application, keeping the potential for individual variations in mind. No two students are alike, and no one theory is likely to explain the development of every aspect of any one student. Integrating concepts from several theories can often provide a more comprehensive understanding of development. Translating theory to practice can seem like a complicated process (R. Brown & Barr, 1990). To those who are unfamiliar with the many theories of student development, learning them all in enough detail to effectively use them in practice may seem overwhelming. Terminology that is unfamiliar can prompt a hesitant practitioner to think that learning a new language is a prerequisite to incorporating theory in their work. Those in the teacher role need to be mindful of the legitimate nature of such reservations and present theory to others in an accessible fashion. Educators have an intellectual and ethical responsibility to study theory in order to better understand students, colleagues, and environments (Knefelkamp, 1984), and they have an obligation as well to make appropriate use of their expertise.

A trial-and-error approach sometimes results in beneficial outcomes, but it can result in disaster. Jana can guess what the adult students on campus need based on her experiences or the suggestions of her associates, but there is no guarantee her hunches or her colleagues' anecdotes will be accurate. Using theory provides more assurance that the programs Jana implements will have a supportable rationale and lead to effective outcomes.

Theory, however, cannot meaningfully exist in a vacuum. To be of any utility, it must be related to practical situations found in real-life settings. Jana can study every adult development theory available, but unless she relates the theoretical principles to the specific students and university context in which she is working, she may also miss the mark.

The Interactionist Perspective

The famous equation $B = f (P \times E)$ is one cornerstone on which an understanding of student development is based. Introduced by Kurt Lewin (1936), the formula states that behavior *(B)* is a function *(f)* of the interaction ($\times$) of person *(P)* and environment *(E)*. To understand why people behave as they do and to facilitate their development, such factors as their characteristics, background, and developmental level must be examined. Factors related to the environment in which the person is living, studying, and working also must be explored. Most important, the interaction of these variables must be considered; not every person experiences the same environment in a similar way.

Consider the adult students with whom Jana works. A twenty-five-year-old single mother working in a factory and registered for one evening class a semester may have almost no impression of the campus as a whole. Her class is only one of the many demands on her time and energy. In contrast, a twenty-four-year-old veteran attending classes full time and living in a residence hall is likely to be greatly influenced by his living arrangements, his classes, and the students with whom he regularly interacts. Jana will more likely reach the veteran than the single mother, since the veteran is much more involved in campus life and sees himself primarily as a student. Jana needs to make more of an effort to establish contact with the single mother to let her know what services are available.

Student development theories help to describe the "person" aspect of Lewin's (1936) equation and provide background about issues individuals face and ways in which they think about and process those issues. However, student affairs educators must not neglect the "environment" side of the equation. Environments, in the form of physical surroundings, organizational structures, human aggregates, and individually held constructions about them, present the experiences that retard or facilitate development (Strange, 2003). By intentionally attending to the design of the environment (Strange & Banning, 2001) through implementation of policy, creation of programs, and training and supervision of staff, educators can help to ensure person-environment interaction that is healthy and contributes to development.

Environmental Factors Influencing Development

Several conditions found (or not found) in the college environment can have a major impact on students' growth and development: challenge and support, involvement, marginality and mattering, and validation. These concepts are helpful to consider in relation to their impact on aspects of development that we discuss throughout this book.

Challenge and Support

Nevitt Sanford (1966) was one of the first developmental theorists to pay attention to the idea of student development as a function of person-environment interaction. He proposed three developmental conditions: readiness, challenge, and support. He contended that individuals cannot exhibit certain behaviors until they are ready to do so. Readiness results either because of the internal processes associated with maturation or beneficial environmental factors. To encourage development, determining the range of optimal dissonance for the individual is important (Sanford, 1966). If the environment presents too much challenge, students can regress to earlier, less adaptive modes of behavior; solidify current modes of behavior; escape the challenge; or ignore the challenge if escape is impossible. If there is too little challenge in the environment, students may feel safe and satisfied, but they do not develop.

The amount of challenge a student can tolerate is a function of the amount of support available (Sanford, 1966). The range of optimal dissonance for any particular student varies depending on the quality of the challenge and support provided by the environment, as well as a student's characteristics. For example, adult students such as the single mother described above are already facing many challenges when they enter college and are in need of support to succeed in their educational endeavors. If the university environment fails to provide such support or if the students do not experience the available supports, the additional challenge of taking classes on top of the stresses of work and family life may be too great, leading students to drop out of college. Aware of this possibility, Jana might sponsor a support group for adult students and more vigorously publicize the services her office provides.

Involvement

Alexander Astin (1984) stressed the role of student involvement in development. He defined involvement as "the amount of physical and psychological energy that the student devotes to the academic experience" (p. 297). He further clarified that involvement refers to behavior—what the student actually does—rather than the student's feelings or thoughts. Astin's theory has five postulates (p. 298):

1. "Involvement refers to the investment of physical and psychological energy in various objects." An object can be anything from the student experience as a whole to a specific activity, such as an intramural volleyball game.
2. "Regardless of the object, involvement occurs along a continuum." Some students will invest more energy than other students, and any particular student will be more involved in certain activities than others.
3. "Involvement has both quantitative and qualitative features." A quantitative aspect of involvement would be the amount of time devoted to an activity; a qualitative component would be the seriousness with which the object was approached and the attention given to it.
4. "The amount of student learning and personal development associated with any educational program is directly proportional to the quality and quantity of student involvement in that program." Basically the more that students put into an activity, the more they will get out of it.
5. "The effectiveness of any educational policy or practice is directly related to the capacity of that policy or practice to increase student involvement."

Rather than examining development, Astin focuses on factors that facilitate development. He argued that for student learning and growth to occur, students need to actively engage in their environment, and educators need to create opportunities for in- and out-of-classroom involvement. Astin's theory provides support for Jana's efforts to create programs to further engage adult students by providing opportunities for active involvement.

Marginality and Mattering

Nancy Schlossberg (1989a) pointed to the importance of considering the concepts of marginality and mattering when examining the impact of the college experience on student development. Feelings of marginality often occur when individuals take on new roles, especially when they are uncertain about what the new role entails. Marginality can be defined as a sense of not fitting in and can lead to self-consciousness, irritability, and depression. For members of nondominant groups, marginality is often a permanent condition, while others, such as first-year students from dominant populations, may temporarily experience these feelings.

Individuals who feel marginal worry about whether they matter to anyone (Schlossberg, 1989a). Mattering is defined as "our belief, whether right or wrong, that we matter to someone else" (p. 9). Drawing on the work of Rosenberg and his colleagues (cited in Schlossberg, 1989a), Schlossberg investigated four aspects of mattering: *attention*, the feeling that one is noticed; *importance*, a belief that one is cared about; *ego-extension*, the feeling that someone else will be proud of what one does or will sympathize with one's failures; and *dependence*, a feeling of being needed. Based on her own research, Schlossberg added a fifth dimension: *appreciation*, the feeling that one's efforts are appreciated by others.

Institutions of higher education need to help students feel that they matter as a precursor to students' involvement in activities and academic programs designed to facilitate development and learning (Schlossberg, 1989a). Personal attention in the form of phone calls to individual students might be one way that Jana could create a sense of mattering.

Validation

In a study examining the experiences of students in college (Rendón, 1994), traditional students expressed few concerns about their academic success, while nontraditional students (those from diverse racial/ethnic and cultural backgrounds) were often doubtful of their academic ability. Active intervention in the form of validation was needed to encourage nontraditional students to become involved in campus life and to enhance their self-esteem. Validation can be defined as "an enabling, confirming and supportive process initiated by in- and out-of-class agents that foster academic and interpersonal development" (p. 46). Students who were validated developed confidence in their ability to learn, experienced enhanced feelings of self-worth, and believed they had something to offer the academic community. Validation can occur in a variety of settings, including the classroom, student organizations, or the community. Validating agents can be instructors, classmates, student affairs staff, relatives, friends, or other people who are significant to the student in some way. Validation can be seen as a process rather than an end goal because "the more students get validated, the richer the academic and interpersonal experience" (p. 44). Validation is most powerful when offered during the early stages of the student's academic experience, preferably during the first few weeks of classes.

The need for validation is likely to apply to adult students, who are often first-generation college students, experiencing doubts about their ability to succeed. Jana needs to keep this in mind as she talks with adult students and develops programs to meet their needs. Often a few encouraging words can make an impact on a student who has no other sources of support.

Considering Individual Differences

Students are unique individuals with different personalities, interests, and styles of interaction. These differences are important to consider since they influence how students will react to their environments and develop cognitively, interpersonally, and intrapersonally. These individual stylistic differences are reflected in typology theories, which have great utility when used in conjunction with other theories discussed in this book. We encourage readers to refer to the cited works for more detail about the theories and their applications in student affairs (see also Strange & Banning, 2001).

Carl Jung (1923/1971), a typology pioneer, suggested that human behavior does not vary by chance but rather is caused by innate differences in mental functioning. Found in many aspects of daily life, differences such as how individuals take in and process information, how they learn best, or the types of activities that interest them are apparent. When faced with similar developmental challenges, environmental factors, or living situations, students (and other individuals) respond differently, depending on their type. Type, then, serves as a framework within which individual development occurs and influences the manner in which students address development in various aspects of their lives. Typology theories also provide important information about sources of support and challenge for students who are otherwise developmentally similar.

Typology theories are particularly helpful in providing guidance for the design of classes, workshops, training sessions, and other structured educational experiences. Typologies also can explain interpersonal interactions and are therefore useful when working through conflicts. In the same way, groups can analyze their interactions using typology theory and improve group functioning and cohesion through team-building activities. Finally, typology theories can be of great utility in making effective work assignments. Positive work environments can be created when individuals' strengths are recognized and people learn to value what each individual brings to the work setting. Two of the most widely used typology theories in student affairs are those of Holland (1997) and Myers (1980).

Holland's Person-Environment Theory

Holland (1997) explored satisfaction, achievement, persistence, and degree of fit between persons and the environments in which they find themselves. Although he sought to explain vocational behavior, the concepts he introduced are also useful in explaining behavior in social and educational settings.

Holland's (1997) theory begins with four major assumptions. First, to varying degrees, people resemble each of six personality types. Second, there are also six model environments that parallel qualities and attributes of each personality type. Third, people seek out environments that provide them with opportunities to use their talents and express their values and attitudes. That is, they seek out environments made up of individuals similar to themselves. Finally, behavior results from the interaction of the person and the environment.

Holland's (1997) six personality types are defined by specific interests, behaviors, attitudes, and belief systems, while the environmental types provide opportunities to engage in activities and reward behaviors each type values. Holland provided the following snapshot definitions of the six types:

- *Realistic* people tend to be interested in and prefer activities that involve working with objects, tools, machines, and animals. They value concrete things like money and personal qualities such as power and status. They tend to be conforming, practical, inflexible, and reserved.
- *Investigative* types prefer activities that call for systematic investigation designed to understand and control physical, biological, or cultural phenomena. They can be described as analytical, intellectual, precise, and cautious.
- *Artistic* people prefer spontaneous, creative, unregulated activities that lead to the creation of various art forms. They value aesthetic qualities such as self-expression and tend to be emotional, expressive, imaginative, and impulsive.
- *Social* individuals prefer activities that involve working with others in ways that educate, inform, cure, or enlighten. They value helping others and engaging in social activities. Social types can be described as helpful, friendly, and empathic.
- *Enterprising* types prefer working with other people to achieve organizational goals or material outcomes. They value political and economic achievement and tend to be domineering, extroverted, self-confident, resourceful, and adventurous.
- *Conventional* types like activities that involve working with data in systematic, orderly, and explicit ways. They value business and monetary achievement and can be described as careful, conforming, efficient, inflexible, and practical.

These types combine to form personality profiles consisting of two to six types, but most typically three. The dominant type is listed first, the second most dominant appears second, and so forth. Profiles are used to categorize both people and environments.

Environmental information is important, as behavior is dependent on both personality and the context in which a person lives and works. The environment is the situation or atmosphere created by those who dominate the context and reflects the typical characteristics of its members. Several secondary assumptions apply to both personality types and environments. These assumptions help explain how people and environments interact and how types influence behavior. *Consistency* refers to the degree to which pairs of types are related. Holland (1997) hypothesized that some types are more similar to each other than they are to other types. Consistent people are more predictable and harder to influence than inconsistent people, while consistent environments tend to exert more influence on the people in them than inconsistent environments.

Differentiation refers to the degree to which a person or an environment is well defined. A differentiated person has interests that are characteristic of mainly one type (for example, interests that are associated only with the realistic type), while an undifferentiated person has a variety of interests characteristic of many different types (for example, realistic, social, and enterprising). Environments that are differentiated include a predominance of people of one type. Hypothesized behaviors are more likely to occur and are likely to be of greater strength in differentiated people and environments. *Identity* refers to the "clarity and stability" (Holland, 1997, p. 5) of the person's goals, interests, and abilities or, in an environment, the degree to which goals, tasks, and rewards are stable over time.

Congruence, the most influential of these factors, refers to the degree of match between a person and an environment. Perfect congruence occurs, for example, when a social person finds herself in a social environment. Congruent environments provide opportunities for individuals to use their skills and interests and reward them for doing so. Incongruent environments, however, seem like foreign territory.

Myers-Briggs Theory of Personality Type

Personality type theory, proposed by Jung (1923/1971) and further developed by Myers (1980), examines how individuals orient themselves to the world around them, how they take in information from their environment, how they come to conclusions about what they observe, and how they relate to their environment. With regard to orientation to the world, Myers believed that people differ based on their relative interest in the outer world of people and things (extraversion) versus the inner world of ideas and concepts (introversion). For introverts, interacting with the external world is draining; they tend to be reflective and enjoy solitude since they are stimulated by the subjective world of ideas and concepts (Spoto, 1989). Extraverts, by contrast, are stimulated by the world around them; they enjoy social interaction and activity.

Two perceiving functions describe how people take in information and experience events (Jung, 1923/1971). Myers (1980) explained that intuition consists of perceiving information based on unconscious processes; relying on symbols, imagination, connections, possibilities, and inferred relationships while sensing involves using the five senses to take in information and concretely observing details and facts.

There are also two judging functions—thinking and feeling—which are used to organize information and make decisions (Jung, 1923/1971). When using the thinking function, a person organizes information and makes decisions based on facts, evidence, and logic. When relying on the feeling function, a person focuses on subjective values, likes and dislikes, and individual worth.

Jung (1923/1971) did not explicitly discuss the importance of judgment (J) and perception (P). Myers, however, saw the JP preference as having two uses: (1) describing how individuals relate to the world around them and (2) identifying, in combination with extraversion-introversion, the dominant (strongest) and auxiliary (second strongest) functions (Myers, McCaulley, Quenk, & Hammer, 1998). Myers et al. stated that the JP preference indicates the person's orientation to the outer world. Perceptive types tend to spend more time observing and taking in information, while judging types take in information more quickly and focus on making decisions.

Personality type theory, then, suggests eight preferences arranged along four bipolar dimensions: extraversion-introversion (EI), sensing-intuition (SN), thinking-feeling (TF), or judging-perception (JP). These preferences serve as the basis of the Myers-Briggs Type Inventory (MBTI; Myers et al., 1998), the most recognized measure of personality type. The preferences can be organized into sixteen types (detailed descriptions can be found in both Myers, 1980, and Myers et al., 1998). Individuals will differ from others in ways that are representative of their types. Myers and McCaulley (1985) suggested that "people may reasonably be expected to develop greater skill with the processes they prefer to use and with the attitudes (extraversion or introversion) in which they prefer to use these processes" (p. 3).

Cautions in Using Theory

Using student development theory appropriately takes time and practice. The process of using theory is complex and requires competence and creativity (R. Rodgers & Widick, 1980). Several cautions may assist individuals as they undertake this complex process.

This book introduces a number of important student development theories, and there are others that could also be used to guide educational practice. In the future, new theories will be added to the list, making learning and understanding each of these theories well enough to use them all in practice a challenge. Initially, identifying a few theories that make sense and seem to explain development in a way that is logical and useful is a good strategy for determining which theories to study in depth and use in practice. However, it is important to be aware of the limitations of theories used in practice and consider appropriate populations and settings.

Theory can rarely be "applied" in "whole chunks" (Weith, 1985). Specific concepts and ideas associated with a particular theory can be useful in certain cases while other concepts from the same theory may not apply in practice. The ability to identify theoretical concepts applicable in professional contexts is an important skill to develop.

Labels should be used with caution in student affairs practice (Kuh, Whitt, & Shedd, 1987). Too often terms such as *dualist* or *immersed* are used to describe a person, without much thought to what the concept really implies. *Immersed* is equated with hating white people, *dualist* with being stubborn, and so on. It is important to carefully explain the meaning of terms and to present evidence to support their use. Better yet, educators could forgo the use of labels altogether and talk about individuals' behavior. Once applied, labels are difficult to change. It may be both more respectful and more accurate to emphasize the individual by referring to *students who think dualistically, students who demonstrate characteristics of immersion,* and so forth. Such rephrasing puts the student first and the descriptor second.

Three additional cautions in using theory are important to keep in mind (Parker et al., 1978). First, theories are descriptive and do not indicate what behaviors or changes are best for students. Educators cannot assume that specific kinds of change predicted by theory ought to be encouraged for everyone, particularly in light of the Eurocentric value system on which most of these theories are based.

Second, while theories attempt to describe universal phenomena, students are unique individuals. As Strange and King (1990) noted, "Theory cannot be an accurate description of any specific reality, but only an approximate representation of many" (p. 18). Theoretical concepts must be evaluated in light of individual differences, meaning the student always takes precedence over theory. This caution is particularly important to keep in mind when working with groups of students who may exhibit different levels of development and individually vary from theoretical predictions.

Third, educators must avoid the tendency to view students as inert substances that can be manipulated in desired directions. The role of educators is to provide growth-enhancing conditions that empower students, not to make their decisions for them. Presenting a particularly persuasive argument for recognizing the role students play in their own development, Hunt (1978) first described a way in which theory is too frequently used: "The theorist describes and then prescribes to the practitioner who, in turn, delivers the services to the client who is the passive recipient" (p. 252). When this approach is used, students are not informed about the purpose of interventions or the theory behind them and therefore have no voice in the decision as to whether they want to "be developed" or if they wish to engage in the activities designed to achieve this goal. In contrast, Hunt argued that students need to be treated as responsible people who can, when given information, make decisions about when and how they will challenge themselves in growth-enhancing ways.

In a statement that concluded his final exam in a course on student development theory, Weith (1985) wrote, "Probably because the student development literature has offered us so much, we tend to pick it apart when it fails as an end-all. Was it ever meant as such?" Reality is complex. Student development theory does not explain all behavior. Both its benefits and its limitations must be acknowledged.

Thinking Holistically

The theories discussed in this book are presented under the umbrella of theory families, for example, psychosocial and cognitive. Some have cautioned that such an approach may not convey the complexities of development (Wilson & Wolf-Wendel, 2005). Therefore, it is important to emphasize up front that while we tend to learn about theories individually or as part of theory families, the aspects of development these theories portray are not discrete entities within individual students. Instead, aspects such as the psychosocial and the cognitive interact within the person, leading to a more holistic developmental process.

Baxter Magolda (1999a) has also expressed concern that "this focus on separate aspects of students' development can obscure our view of the student as a whole and complex person" (p. 37). While it is important that we perceive the student as a whole, it is likely we may act in a more specialized manner. For example, student affairs practitioners who interact with students primarily outside the classroom may not automatically give much attention to cognitive development. By understanding the differences in how students make meaning, practitioners can also contribute to students' cognitive development by responding appropriately to the reasoning patterns they display during interaction. Similarly, faculty encountering students primarily in the classroom are not as likely to focus on psychosocial or identity development. By understanding these two dimensions, faculty can see their students more clearly for whom they are and what may be important to them—aspects that can influence classroom learning. Therefore, while educators sometimes act in a more specialized way due to the differing emphases within their institutional roles, a holistic perspective of students and their development is crucial.

A Response to the Critics

Student development theory, particularly its use as a foundation for student affairs practice, has sometimes been under attack. In the 1990s, Bloland, Stamatakos, and Rogers (1994, 1996) presented what some have viewed as a scathing indictment of the student development philosophy (see R. Brown, 1995, 1996). Specifically, they claimed that many student affairs educators have inappropriately elevated student development theory to something resembling icon status. If this has happened or is happening in the student affairs profession, the act deserves to be challenged. No single resource stands alone as *the* foundation for professional practice. Student development theory, for example, is one of several knowledge bases that can inform student affairs practice. Considering additional theoretical bases, areas such as environmental theory and organizational theory are important resources also. Knowledge beyond theory is obviously important as well (for example, awareness of and ability to use ethical principles and codes). Moreover, student development theory has its limitations. Due to student development theory's evolving nature, required updating and intelligent use is not reason to dismiss it but an indication of its relevance. Student development theory does not provide answers to every question educators may have, yet it offers a helpful perspective.

Bloland et al. (1994, 1996) also discussed learning and development as though these are mutually exclusive phenomena. Others have elevated learning above development as the central outcome on which student affairs educators should focus (see Woodard, Love, & Komives, 2000). We view separation of learning and development as a false dichotomy. As will be highlighted throughout this book, several student development theories directly address learning. Students' cognitive complexity and preferred learning style have important implications for their ability to learn. In addition, students' struggles with psychosocial development have bearing on their learning processes. For example, drawing on Chickering's theory (Chickering & Reisser, 1993), developing intellectual competence is intertwined with the learning process, and issues of identity development (particularly those related to gender, sexual orientation, and ethnicity) can become so pronounced as to overshadow and limit participation in the academic enterprise. Clearly, for the individual student, learning and development are not discrete personal dynamics that operate in isolation in easily compartmentalized processes.

Knefelkamp (1982) promoted the value of student development theory as a source of common language. Such language can facilitate empathic listening, a crucial process for anyone in higher education who works with students. From Knefelkamp's work, the following question can be derived: If people cannot hear each other's voices, how can they possibly understand each other's natures? Educators need to honor this language, recognize its limitations, and help this common language evolve, particularly expanding its scope to be inclusive of all students. Educators must help others learn to speak the language and understand it when it is spoken to them. A collaborative spirit is essential if faculty and administrators are to be effective in contributing to the education of today's and tomorrow's students.

Finally, we encourage all educators to consider the truth inherent in the statement that having more information would always seem to be more advantageous than having less. Use of student development theory in a generative fashion is a mutually shared responsibility. Higher education professionals who interact with students in the college environment must nourish this never-ending feedback loop to best serve all students.

PART TWO

FOUNDATIONAL THEORIES

Regina is two weeks into her graduate assistantship in multicultural student affairs. She has spent those two weeks getting to know the sixteen students for whom she is the primary multicultural affairs advisor. To give her a range of experiences, her supervisor has assigned her students in all four undergraduate classes, with majors ranging from art to chemical engineering. She is amazed at the wide range of diverse students with whom she works. Marisela and Vijay, both first-year students, are wondering if they can make it in college and have no idea in what fields they will major, while some of the older students, including Rudolfo and Anita, are already talking about internships to help them decide if the career direction they have chosen is going to work out for them. Two of the seniors, Mariama and André, recently made life commitments to their partners and are considering how they will balance their committed relationships and career plans.

Regina has also noticed that students do not think about these issues in the same way. Luisa expects Regina to tell her what to do and assumes there is one right answer for every question. Paul does not seem to want to have anything to do with her and declares to anyone around him that his answers are as good as anyone else's, including Regina's. A few of the older students, especially Isabel and Mike, appear to be able to weigh the pros and cons of their decisions and are willing to adjust their perspectives when they are offered new information.

Making sense out of moral issues is another area in which Regina has noticed differences among her students. In processing a recent situation in which a student in a first-year seminar was charged with plagiarizing a paper, one student, Nikki, stated that rules are rules, and the student should be punished for his actions. LaToya jumped to the defense of the charged student, feeling sure that he did not mean to hurt anyone through his actions. And Les wanted to know more about the situation before making any judgments.

Regina's students also seemed to approach learning differently. Curtis needs to understand how information is related to his personal experience and is in Regina's office constantly for help in making sense of the concepts he is learning in his sociology class that seem abstract and unrelated to real life. Other students, especially Devon and Yuko, are confused unless they are provided with an overall conceptual framework for the material they are studying.

Regina has read the chapters in Part One of this book and is looking forward to learning some student development theory that will help her work effectively with these different students. She has an overall sense of what theory is about and how to evaluate and use it, but she needs specifics. Regina hopes the chapters in Part Two will give her a better sense of what the theories introduced in Chapter One have to offer her as a student affairs educator.

◆ ◆ ◆

In Part Two, we discuss the foundational theories of student affairs, all but one of which can be categorized as either psychosocial or cognitive structural. The final theory, that of David Kolb, introduces the concept of learning style.

Psychosocial Theories

Psychosocial theorists examine the content of development—that is, the important issues people face as their lives progress, such as how to define themselves, their relationships with others, and what to do with their lives. Not all issues are equally important throughout a person's life. Rather, development takes place across the life span within a series of age-linked sequential stages. In each stage, particular issues, called developmental tasks, arise and present compelling questions that must be resolved (Erikson, 1959/1980). Each new stage occurs when internal biological and psychological changes interact with environmental demands, such as social norms and roles expected of individuals at certain ages in particular cultures. Resolution of developmental tasks is influenced by how successful the individual is in developing appropriate coping skills. Regression to earlier stages, readdressing of developmental tasks, and relearning of coping skills frequently occur when individuals are placed in new and stressful situations (Erikson, 1968).

Psychosocial theories are helpful in understanding the issues facing individuals at various points in their lives. For example, Regina might look to these theories to help her understand the specific issues on which her advisees are focused and why their concerns are so varied. Psychosocial theories can also provide guidance concerning topics for programs and workshops for particular groups of students. As she develops programs for multicultural student affairs to sponsor, Regina will want to take into account the developmental issues that psychosocial theories indicate students will be dealing with during their college years and design workshops and other interventions to address them.

Part Two begins with an examination of Erik Erikson's (1959/1980) pioneering theory of psychosocial development and the work of theorists who followed him, specifically examining the identity development of men (Marcia, 1966) and women (Josselson, 1978/1991, 1996). These three theories are discussed in Chapter Three. In Chapter Four, the first major theory to specifically examine the development of college students, that of Arthur Chickering, is introduced (Chickering, 1969; Chickering & Reisser, 1993).

Cognitive Structural Theories

Rooted in the work of Piaget (1952), cognitive structural theories examine the process of intellectual development during the college years. These theories focus on how people think, reason, and make meaning of their experiences. In this approach, the mind is thought to have structures, generally called *stages*, that act as sets of assumptions by which persons adapt to and organize their environments. They act as filters or lenses for determining how people perceive and evaluate experiences and events. Cognitive structural stages are viewed as arising one at a time and always in the same order. The age at which each stage occurs and the rate of speed with which the person passes through it are variable, however. Each stage derives from the previous one and incorporates aspects of it; thus, each successive stage is qualitatively different and more complex than the stages before it. As individuals are exposed to new information or experiences that create cognitive dissonance, they first attempt to incorporate the new data into their current way of thinking (assimilation). If the new information cannot be fit into their existing structure, they create a new, more complex structure (accommodation; Wadsworth, 1979). Piaget (1952) stressed the importance of neurological maturation in cognitive development but also noted the significant role played by the environment in providing experiences to which the individual must react. Social interaction with peers, parents, and other adults is especially influential in cognitive development.

Knowledge of students' reasoning processes will help student affairs professionals understand students' decision making with regard to their own lives, as well as their interactions with others. For instance, it could help Regina understand why her student Paul is unwilling to listen to her, while Luisa is constantly seeking her advice.

Cognitive structural theories can also help student affairs professionals like Regina understand how students view situations they are experiencing and provide guidance about how to communicate effectively with students. Knowing that students interpret their experiences differently depending on their level of intellectual development can help student affairs professionals understand the variations in feedback they receive from students about activities, classes, and other experiences and will assist them in advising students about available options. For example, a student whose thinking is less complex, like that of Regina's student Luisa, will generally feel more comfortable and may do better in a more highly structured classroom, while students whose cognitive processes are more complex, such as Isabel and Mike, may prefer greater autonomy (Widick, Knefelkamp, & Parker, 1975).

Cognitive structural theories can also be very helpful in the design of workshops and classes (Rodgers & Widick, 1980; Widick et al., 1975). For instance in designing a workshop for first-year students on how to decide on a major, Regina could probably assume that most of the students would be at lower levels of cognitive development and would therefore benefit from detailed instructions and personalized feedback, while a senior-level program to assist students like Mariama and André in making the transition to life after college could be more loosely structured and rely on input from these more cognitively advanced students.

In Chapter Five, we examine the work of William Perry (1968), the first cognitive structural theorist to focus on the intellectual development of college students. Chapter Six includes an overview of the work of Lawrence Kohlberg (1976) as well as a discussion of two theorists who expanded thinking about moral reasoning. James Rest and his colleagues (1999) developed the Defining Issues Test, an instrument to assess moral reasoning level, and refined Kohlberg's theory based on their research. Carol Gilligan (1982/1993) introduced the idea of gender-related moral reasoning based on the concept of care rather than Kohlberg's concept of justice. In Chapter Seven, we review three cognitive structural theories whose authors incorporated and built on the work of Perry, Kohlberg, and Gilligan. We first discuss the work of Belenky and her colleagues (1986), who studied women's ways of knowing, demonstrating that the cognitive development process of women in their study differed from that of the men who served as research participants in Perry's initial study (1968). We then examine Marcia Baxter Magolda's (1992) theory of epistemological development, which was based on interviews with both male and female students over a four-year time frame and included gender-related patterns of meaning making. Finally, we focus on the reflective judgment model of Patricia King and Karen Kitchener (1994), who examined how individuals respond to ill-structured problems—problems, that is, with no clear solution.

Learning Style Theory

Learning style refers to the different ways in which individuals approach learning (Merriam, Caffarella, & Baumgartner, 2007) or process information (Jonassen & Grabowski, 1993). These differences are apparent in how individuals handle everyday learning tasks, both in and out of the classroom. Learning style theories are particularly helpful in designing learning approaches that take into account individual differences among learners. For example, Regina's student Curtis needs to see concrete examples before abstract concepts make sense to him. An instructor might start a discussion with Curtis by asking for several examples from his own experience related to a particular topic and then tie them all together to illustrate a general principle. In contrast, Yuko and Devon would learn more quickly if they were first presented with the big picture and then were given examples.

While relatively stable and consistent, learning styles are influenced by the learning environment and learning experiences in which the individual is engaged (Desmedt & Valcke, 2004). For example, the more a student uses a particular style, the better she will be at using it. Although research is not definitive on this point (P. King, 2003), J. Anderson (1988) also suggested that culture plays a role in learning style development: "It would seem feasible that different ethnic groups, with different cultural histories, different adaptive approaches to reality, and different socialization practices, would differ concerning their respective learning styles" (p. 4). For Regina, this point would be particularly important to keep in mind since she is working with students from a variety of backgrounds.

Each learning style has its own strengths and makes different contributions to learners' understanding of their world (Hamrick, Evans, & Schuh, 2002). Overall, no one style is better than any other, although certain tasks are more easily approached using a particular learning style (P. King, 2003). An appropriate end goal is to help students round out their ability to use various learning approaches rather than relying on the one or two they prefer (P. King, 2003). An effective strategy for educators, then, is to structure learning experiences to take into account various learning styles rather than appealing to only one style. Such an approach will encourage the use of multiple styles as well as provide opportunities for students to use their preferred style at least part of the time.

While there are a number of learning style theories (see P. King 2003), we have chosen to focus on one that is often used in student affairs and educational practice. In the final chapter in Part Two, we examine Kolb's learning style theory (1984), in which he proposed that learning is a cyclical process involving four modes of learning, two refer to how information is received and two explain how it is processed. These modes come together to form four different learning styles.

CHAPTER THREE

PSYCHOSOCIAL IDENTITY DEVELOPMENT

Brian, Caitlyn, and Sara, all first-year students, are participants in one of the Hartford College Learning Communities (HCLC), comprised of commuter and residential students interested in getting adjusted to the campus environment. The students of this learning community convened to meet with their community leader and get to know one another. Each is grappling with life issues of identity and meaning making. The community leader enters the room and engages the group in introductory activities prior to beginning the series of thought-provoking conversations that would continue throughout the semester. His final question of the day was, "Who are you?" An awkward silence fills the room as the participants begin to ponder the seemingly simple yet strikingly difficult question.

Brian, a thirty-seven-year-old man, has decided to attend college after several years in the military, a path he chose to emulate his father, a career officer. He was very successful in the military because it provided an environment where he could easily adhere to a formalized structure. He never questioned his life in the military or why he joined, nor did he think about why he chose to attend college after being discharged. Although a host of other avenues interested him, he looked to his father for guidance about what to do next.

Caitlyn is a twenty-one-year-old free spirit. Her philosophy in life is to go with the flow. Following high school, she went to New York to pursue acting. She moved back home with her parents to start over when she was unsuccessful. She then decided to attend Hartford, because it seemed like a good idea and it gave her something to do. However, she planned to stay only for a semester until she figured out her next steps. Filmmaking and fashion design were potential interests, but she was not ready to commit to a clear career direction.

Sara is nineteen years old and interested in becoming a dance choreographer. She has a close relationship with her family and has never questioned their beliefs until recently. Her parents are deeply religious and hold traditional roles. Her father is the breadwinner, and her mother, who has a college degree but has not worked professionally, manages the household. They want Sara to be a teacher, but she has not shared her occupational desires with her parents and believes they will be upset. Sara is trying to balance what she wants with what her parents want for her.

◆ ◆ ◆

Brian, Caitlyn, and Sara can benefit from participation in the HCLC if they are open to examining the "Who am I?" question with thoughtful introspection. Each exhibits behaviors of one of four identity statuses introduced by James Marcia (1966) and modified for women by Ruthellen Josselson (1978/1991). However, before exploring how the HCLC students' experiences relate to identity statuses, we first situate the discussion by examining the work of foundational psychosocial theorist Erik Erikson. After providing an overview of the theories of Erikson, Marcia, and Josselson, we review related research and student affairs applications, ending with a discussion of implications and possible future directions with regard to this body of work.

Erikson's Identity Development Theory

Erik Erikson (1959/1980, 1963, 1968) was the first clinical psychologist to address the identity development journey from adolescence through adulthood. He described development as spanning a person's entire life as opposed to earlier theories that focused only on childhood. Basing his research on Freud's psycho-analytical perspective of individual development, Erikson deviated from Freud in that he viewed development as being based on the influence of the external environment as well as internal dynamics, while Freud credited only the latter as a factor (Widick, Parker, & Knefelkamp, 1978b). Erikson's perspective on growth and development is grounded in the *epigenetic principle*: "Anything that grows has a ground plan, and . . . out of this ground plan the parts arise, each part having its time of special ascendancy, until all parts have arisen to form a functioning whole" (Erikson, 1968, p. 92).

Erikson (1959/1980) put the developing person in a social and historical context and addressed the influences of significant others and social institutions across the life span by describing eight stages of development. Each stage is distinguished by a psychosocial *crisis*, or "turning point," that must be resolved by balancing the internal self and the external environment (Erikson, 1968). Each crisis must produce a developmental change in order for the person to grapple with later developmental crises. Erikson's model begins with a discussion of the first four stages; these coalesce in childhood to form the basis of identity, which is then fostered through the last five stages during adulthood.

Stage One: Basic Trust Versus Mistrust

This stage occurs during the first year of life. Trust in its most basic form is not readily conscious to infants. Instead, encounters with caregivers (during feeding, holding, bathing) prompt the conceptualization of trust throughout the developmental journey. In an effort "to get" these things from the caregiver, infants learn reciprocity as they become better able to identify with the caregiver. A crisis emerges when the pattern of caregiving changes or becomes inconsistent, which may produce feelings of mistrust. An infant's inability to develop and maintain trust can lead to mistrust of others in the future, as well as an inability to effectively handle the unpredictability of life.

Stage Two: Autonomy Versus Shame and Doubt

In this stage, children must have a firm sense of trust as they begin to distinguish themselves from others and explore the environment. Children participate in acts of exploration to develop autonomy, such as walking, talking, and control of bodily functions. A crisis that may occur is being shamed or penalized for not performing expected skills such as toilet training. Thus, caretakers must be patient yet provide firm encouragement. When this balance is missing, children may behave without considering what their skills or capabilities are (impulsive) or become too focused on ensuring that everything they do is just so or perfect (compulsive; Erikson, 1968). When children are encouraged, they gain more overall confidence in their autonomy and develop self-determination.

Stage Three: Initiative Versus Guilt

Children at this stage begin preschool and exercise initiative through games and activities that promote interactions between themselves and others. They also begin to emulate observed behaviors. This stage is one of imagination in which children work toward making their fantasies a reality. The capacity for moral awareness, or what Erikson called *conscience*, becomes real in this stage. This is particularly true when what children conjure in their imagination may be viewed as wrong or unacceptable in reality. Thus if they choose to do something "wrong," they begin to deal with responsibility and guilt as a result of their decision.

Stage Four: Industry Versus Inferiority

At this stage, children expand beyond the sole influence of their parents. Although parents or caregivers are still highly influential, children have multiple interactions with other adults and children in the school environment. Children work toward developing a sense of industry, where they learn to master different skills to feel useful to others (Erikson, 1959/1980). Without encouragement from adults and peers, they may doubt themselves and develop feelings of inferiority. When children feel appreciated for making a contribution, they develop a sense of competency in their skills.

Stage Five: Identity Versus Identity Diffusion (Confusion)

This watershed stage in Erikson's theory (Marcia, 1993a, 1993b) represents a transition between childhood and adulthood that signals a call to define oneself. Marcia's (1966) identity statuses and Josselson's (1978/1991) theory of women's identity development, which we discuss later in this chapter, flow from this fifth stage, in which adolescents begin to develop their core sense of self, values, beliefs, and goals. They become more independent, begin to deal with the complexities of life, and seek answers to the question, "Who am I?" They may struggle with role confusion as they delineate between how others see them versus how they view themselves. Central to this stage is the "sense of ego identity," which Erikson (1959/1980) defined as "the accrued confidence that one's ability to maintain inner sameness and continuity (one's ego in the psychological sense) is matched by the sameness and continuity of one's meaning for others" (p. 89). In other words, individuals seek congruence between external recognition and internal integration of meanings derived from previous stages. Those who experience struggles with developing their core sense of self may experience confusion and insecurities about themselves and their relationships with others. Erikson (1959/1980) labeled this state *identity diffusion*, which develops when individuals lack a clear sense of self or purpose. When they have no clear understanding of their role in life, they may overidentify with others and demonstrate intolerance toward those they view as different.

Stage Six: Intimacy Versus Isolation

This stage is the first of the three stages that Erikson (1959/1980) identified as making up adulthood. Young adults must decide whether to fuse identity with another to create a union. In this stage, adults work toward intimacy, or establishing committed relationships with others, such as friendships, intimate relationships, or participation as a productive member of a community. This stage may involve *distantiation*, or what Erikson (1959/1980) described as "the readiness to repudiate, to isolate, and if necessary, to destroy those forces and people whose essence seems dangerous to one's own" (pp. 95–96). If adults at this stage lack a strong sense of identity, they may have difficulty building relationships, which may lead to emotional stress or isolation.

Stage Seven: Generativity Versus Stagnation

This stage occurs in midlife when adults actively engage in giving back to society and deciding what legacy to leave behind. They devote their attention toward their professional lives and close loved ones. In their personal lives, adults are concerned with *generativity* or cultivating the next generation, which includes raising children or directing efforts toward providing opportunities for others through mentoring, community involvement, or activism. If they are unable to establish a strong path, understand themselves on that path, or do not feel needed, *stagnation* sets in, leading to withdrawal and failure to engage in productive life activities.

Stage Eight: Integrity Versus Despair

This stage emerges during late adulthood, a time when adults deal with getting older, significant changes in body functioning and thought take place, and the reality of inevitable death arises. These factors prompt them to examine their lives and reflect on their choices, successes, and failures. Adults experience despair, regrets, and a desire to "start over" if they feel that they have failed to take advantage of the opportunities afforded in life. Those pleased with their lives have little regret and experience integrity, which Erikson (1959/1980) defined as "the acceptance of one's own and only life cycle and of the people who have become significant to it as something that had to be and that, by necessity, permitted of no substitutions" (p. 98).

Erikson's View of Identity

Erikson (1959/1980) stressed that identity "connotes both a persistent sameness within oneself (selfsameness) and a persistent sharing of some kind of essential character with others" (Erikson, 1959/1980, p. 109). Identity is ever changing from birth to death, but as each crisis is successfully resolved, commitment to an established identity becomes stronger. Identity formation embodies "commitment to a sexual orientation, an ideological stance, and a vocational direction" (as cited in Marcia, 1980, p. 160). Although Erikson's stages are highly descriptive, they are hard to study empirically.

James Marcia's Ego Identity Statuses

Grounding his research in Erikson's stage theory, psychologist James Marcia (1966) was the first to create a "prototype of needed empirical study" (Widick et al., 1978b, p. 11) on the identity development of young adults. Using Erikson's focus on the role of crisis in identity development in late adolescence, specifically the identity-versus-identity diffusion stage, Marcia (1966, 1975, 1980) introduced identity statuses as a way to explain how young adults experience and resolve crises. There are two critical variables in individual identity formation, *exploration (crisis)* and *commitment*, which occur in the contexts of political, religious, and occupational decision making (Marcia, 1980). Based on their study of women, Schenkel and Marcia (1972) added sexual decisions as a fourth context.

Exploration, often referred to as a crisis (Marcia, 1980), involves the questioning of values and goals defined by parents and weighing various identity alternatives and their potential repercussions. Individuals experiencing crisis seek out resources such as trusted others (teachers, friends) to explore their options, preferably those with knowledge of the crisis (Waterman & Archer, 1990). They also read books, take classes, or engage in journal writing to generate enough knowledge to make an informed decision. This process may begin with excitement and curiosity, but as pressures mount, these emotions can be replaced with fear and anxiety, resulting in the need to reach crisis resolution (Waterman & Archer).

Commitment refers to attaching ownership to pronounced choices, values, and goals (Bilsker, Schiedel, & Marcia, 1988). Individuals who have solidified their commitments have made conscious decisions about which they are confident and optimistic. Not only do they confirm their goals, they also take action toward realizing them.

Marcia (1966) identified four identity states, or ways of balancing crisis and commitment. Although Marcia created the identity statuses, Erikson neither identified nor offered any endorsement of the statuses (Marcia, 1993b). Marcia (1980) stated, "The identity statuses were developed as a methodological device by means of which Erikson's theoretical notions about identity might be subjected to empirical study" (p. 161). The statuses move beyond Erikson's theory and offer additional ways to understand how individuals within the identity-versus-identity diffusion stage resolve identity crisis (Marcia, 1980). Unlike Erikson's stages, Marcia's identity statuses are not necessarily progressive or permanent. A person's identity status may or may not change over a life span. Both healthy and unhealthy choices exist within each status. Marcia's (1966, 1980) identity statuses are foreclosure, moratorium, identity achievement, and diffusion.

Foreclosure (No Crisis/Commitment)

In this status, individuals accept parental values without questioning them. Their commitment to values and goals comes without crisis because authorities direct their path. They were either raised in a homogeneous environment with little exposure to different worldviews and no encouragement to challenge the status quo, or they fear that should they attempt to pursue a different direction, they will end up with no purpose in life (Waterman & Archer, 1990). They can remain comfortably in this status as long as authoritative influences remain consistent. However, individuals in foreclosure will experience a major challenge if a crisis arises due to their inability to adapt to changes in the absence of authority. Essentially they follow the rules, maintain conventional relationships, and typically demonstrate inflexible thinking (Marcia, 1994). Marcia (1994) explained that foreclosure is the most common identity status and usually occurs prior to other statuses. Brian, the older student in the learning community, exhibits foreclosed behavior: he has allowed his father's path to dictate his life and has lived within structures that have not encouraged him to engage in risk taking.

Moratorium (Crisis/No Commitment)

In moratorium, individuals actively question parental values in order to form their identity; however, their crisis comes without commitment. They are seen "either as sensitive or anxiety-ridden, highly ethical or self-righteous, flexible or vacillating" (Marcia, 1980, p. 161). The vacillating occurs as they grapple between resistance and conforming to authority (Marcia, 1994). Individuals in moratorium shift between indecisiveness and ambivalence toward authority on one hand and creativity and engaging style on the other (Orlofsky, Marcia, & Lesser, 1973). Marcia (1989b) noted that individuals in moratorium "can generally be expected to move into Identity Achievement" (p. 289). Out of the four statuses, individuals remain in moratorium for the shortest amount of time, exhibit a high degree of moral sensitivity, and are the "most engaging among the statuses" (Marcia, 1994, p. 75).

Identity Achievement (Crisis/Commitment)

Achievement status comes after an extensive period of crisis in which individuals sort through alternatives and make crucial choices that lead to strong commitments in setting goals and establishing a firm foundation (Orlofsky et al., 1973). Individuals in this status are likely to experience more crises than those in other statuses because the foundation of their identity is secure enough to investigate multiple alternatives and engage in risk taking (Marcia, 1994). They are confident and can clearly articulate their choices and conclusions (Marcia, 1994). Individuals rely on an internal rather than external process to construct identity and contextualize their experiences. They choose their own path in life. Achievement is viewed as the healthiest psychological status one can obtain (Marcia, 1980). Those who reach it have successfully navigated Erikson's Identity versus Identity Diffusion stage (Marcia, 1994).

Diffusion (No Crisis/No Commitment)

People in the state of diffusion either refuse to or are unable to firmly commit. In addition, they have not experienced significant crisis. In this status, individuals exhibit a general lack of concern regarding commitments (Marcia, 1989b). They simply "go with the flow," taking no account of consequences (positive or negative) that may affect them personally. They also tend to conform, have difficulty with intimacy, and at times lack cognitive complexity (Marcia, 1989b). Much of their conformity is a reflection of their submission to external rather than internal authority (Waterman & Archer, 1990). In comparison to the other statuses, individuals in diffusion are the most easily manipulated and the most likely to succumb to conformity (Marcia, 1994).

To place the statuses in context, Marcia (1993b) noted that identity should be examined through three lenses: structural, phenomenological, and behavioral. The structural lens is related to identity as the reference point or central foundation from which humans respond to the complexity of life. Thus, identity development is cumulative, and as people grow, they increase their ability to handle various identity domains, such as relationships and careers. The phenomenological lens pertains to the extent to which an identity is shaped by others versus shaped by self and the qualitative experiences that facilitate the construction of one's identity. For example, in the identity achieved status, people tend to construct their identity as opposed to allowing others to shape their view of whom they are. The behavioral lens focuses on how others view a person's identity as demonstrated by the person's behavior. Thus, deciding on a career path and committing to an intimate interpersonal relationship would be considered behaviors in which identity manifests itself.

Josselson's Theory

In 1971, Ruthellen Josselson (1978/1991) set out "to understand the internal and developmental roots of identity formation in women" (p. 33). Her journey led her to the exploration of the internal differences among the four identity statuses described by Marcia (1966) to explain why some women resolve their identity crisis while others avoid creating identity or fail to move beyond the crisis. Over a three-year period, Josselson gathered data from sixty randomly selected female college seniors between twenty and twenty-two years of age from four different colleges and universities. Josselson became curious about the accuracy of her predictions for these women after ten years of presenting and examining her findings. Thus, she conducted follow-up studies of thirty women from the original study (Josselson, 1996). Her research spanned twenty-two years as she observed their development unfold from age twenty-one to age forty-three. She interviewed the women in three phases: as college seniors, during their thirties, and during their forties. In her follow-up study, she was especially concerned with two issues: how women "revise their lives as they grow from late adolescence to mature adulthood" and how changes in societal ideas regarding gender roles affected "women who were coming of age in the midst of such wrenching changes" (Josselson, 1996, p. 5).

The following are patterns identified in Josselson's two studies. Each identity status reflects the original pathway that she assigned in her 1978 study; the designation given in her 1996 publication follows in parentheses.

Foreclosures: Purveyors of the Heritage (Guardians)

In this pathway, women graduate from college with identity commitment but having experienced no identity crisis. They make choices without doubt, hesitation, or questioning childhood messages. Typically they adopt standards about sexual morality, occupation, and religion based on parental beliefs and will not risk disappointing their parents (Josselson, 1978/1991).

Women interviewed twelve years later still exhibited foreclosure patterns. They experienced little identity change, as they were unable to imagine a life different from that of their childhood. They are described as "hardworking, responsible, and capable" (Josselson, 1978/1991, p. 60). Their careers expressed a "preoccupation with the care of others" but their main focus was "in their private worlds" (p. 59). Even when successful in a career, these women sought security in relationships and chose partners who shared their perception of family life. As devoted mothers and wives, they were psychologically tied to the centrality of family.

When interviewed in their forties, these women had experienced important changes, such as allowing themselves freedom to explore new opportunities, albeit in a restricted manner. Sometimes they did not experience a crisis until their thirties or forties as they reflected on why they did not engage in more exploration and risk taking. Ultimately they were able to find the inner strength to move beyond boundaries without crumbling to pressure (Josselson, 1996).

Identity Achievements: Pavers of the Way (Pathmakers)

In this pathway women break the psychological ties to their childhood and form separate, distinct identities. During adolescence, they create identity in their own way after considering who they were in the past and who they want to become in the future. Rather than experience an intense identity crisis, many test their options silently and internally. What matters is feeling pride in themselves as opposed to seeking external affirmation of their self-worth.

Interaction with others outside the family, such as teachers and peers, results in new ways of experiencing the self without abandoning the old self. As traditional college students, they are likely to be somewhat depressed and sad over the psychological separation from their parents. As adults, they often move through the guilt and sorrow toward maturity. Relationships are primary for women in this status. They establish intimate relationships with individuals whom they consider to be partners and structure relationships based on partnership needs rather than societal expectations. The hallmark of adult women on this pathway is balance among work, relationships, and interests.

By the end of college, some were dissatisfied with their career choices and initiated change by obtaining work opportunities that promoted a more harmonious identity. Although this may seem inconsistent with identity achievers, other research (see Schenkel & Marcia, 1972) has demonstrated "that for women occupational identity is less predictive of overall identity status than is ideological and interpersonal identity" (Josselson, 1978/1991, p. 101). In short, once women commit to whom they are in relationship to others, occupational identity becomes a way to express the self.

The success of women in this status is their ongoing capacity to construct their identity. In effect, women experiencing identity achievement are forever becoming. They move through their lives despite the anxiety engendered by new challenges and continue to use their experiences to revise themselves, while also maintaining a sense of continuity (Josselson, 1996).

Moratoriums: Daughters of the Crisis (Searchers)

The moratorium state is an unstable time of experimenting and searching for a new identity. After internalizing the values of the family, these women are convinced of the rightness of these values, but on learning of other legitimate ways of being, they are pulled into a tailspin. Many who remain in moratorium at the end of college are caught in identity conflict, paralyzed to move beyond it, and need time beyond college to resolve the conflict. Some will continue searching, some will regress to a previously prescribed self-identity, and some will move on to identity achievement (Josselson, 1996).

In college, women on this pathway indicated that they had overprotective mothers who indulged and overvalued them. Most did not consciously want to be like their mothers, yet they were closer to their mothers as adults than any other identity status group. While rejecting identification with their mothers, they idealized their fathers, who represented a romantic notion of strength and success. More than any other group, women in moratorium had daydreams of doing wonderful things in the future, such as discovering a cure for cancer or being an ambassador to Russia. While in college, many of these women behaved in ways that did not win approval of either parent and led to omnipresent guilt. Sara, the student who is interested in pursuing a dance major, is exhibiting behaviors of a woman in moratorium. She has adhered to the values of her family her entire life and is now at a crossroads in which the decision she makes regarding her major can have a tremendous effect on her relationship with her parents. She is stuck between doing what she wants versus meeting her parents' expectations. Sara will need to weigh all her options in order to make a cogent decision.

Following college graduation, these women remained in a state of exploration as they dealt with a host of emotions, among them uncertainty. During the next decade of their lives, they spent time testing the waters in search of a pathway suitable for their lives. By midlife, most had garnered some semblance of a path and slightly resembled identity achieved women. The difference is that women in moratorium maintain a sense of ambivalence and uncertainty about their lives. Many moratorium women revise the impossibly high standards they set for themselves, "in the face of which they could only feel inadequate" (Josselson, 1996, p. 141), over the course of their lives. As they progressed, these women realized that although their lives may not have turned out as they imagined, they appreciated the person they had become.

Identity Diffusions: Lost and Sometimes Found (Drifters)

Marked by lack of crisis and commitment, college women on this path are a varied and complex group. Evidence suggests that they score lowest among the four identity status groups "on all measures of healthy psychological functioning" (Josselson, 1978/1991, p. 140). Little is known about why women in this status have so much difficulty, but a critical review of nearly thirty studies examining the identity diffusion pattern suggests that one commonality among them is a tendency to withdraw from situations (Bourne, 1978a, 1978b).

When interviewed as college seniors, women in identity diffusion were a diverse group who demonstrated one of four different patterns: severe psychopathology, previous developmental deficits, moratorium diffusion, or foreclosed diffusion. Women in the first two groups—severe psychopathology and previous developmental deficits—fell outside the normal range of a healthy personality and were considered to have "borderline personality disorders" (Josselson, 1987b, p. 141). Early emotional scars, such as neglect or loss of a caretaker, caused feelings of powerlessness that excluded women in these two subgroups from forming healthy identities. They were "unable to make identity commitments because of the instability and unreliability of their capacity to organize and integrate their experiences" (Josselson, 1987b, p. 142). Women in the third subgroup, moratorium diffusion, experience crisis in identity but not in areas typical of psychosocial functioning. These women are in severe conflict about the choices in their lives, and philosophical questions about the meaning of life perplex them the most. They try different ways to experience the world, "liberally employing drugs, sex, and fringe religious groups to this end" (Josselson, 1978/1991, p. 142). Although these women do not resign themselves to their impulses, they appear to vacillate between moratorium (seriously searching) and diffusion (drifting) statuses.

Women in the fourth and last subgroup, foreclosed diffusion, drift through life neither in a state of crisis nor able to commit. They appear to lack the will to construct a harmonious direction in their lives. Lack of parental direction from a very early age leaves them disoriented rather than independent. Basically these women feel so little control of their lives that they wait passively for someone else to take over. Caitlyn, the last member of the learning community group, is an example of diffusion. She seems to have no clear direction or understanding of how her past activities will affect her future plans. Her desires are whimsical and will not direct her toward solidifying a path of her own.

As women with diffused identities graduated from college, they were typically lost. Although their reasons differed, they essentially had no sense of direction. Twenty years later, these women remained directionless, feeling as if life had treated them unfairly. As they reached their forties, they had a more stable life due to decisions either that they made or others made for them. However, they were "still very much anticipating that their real lives will yet begin and are starting over, hoping for better outcomes" (Josselson, 1996, p. 144). Their families provided the most stability for them throughout their lives and remained at the core of each new starting point. As they aged, their outlook became more realistic, although they optimistically continued to seek options that would make the difference.

Research

The bulk of research related to psychosocial maturity and identity development is built on Erikson's (1959/1980, 1963, 1968) theoretical framework. Most of the research on identity development in young adults conducted between 1950 and 1970 examined late adolescent men at prestigious colleges from an Eriksonian perspective and generalized the findings to women. While Marcia's identity statuses have been the dominant topic of research on ego identity since the 1970s, with over three hundred studies in existence (Bourne, 1978a; Marcia, 1994), little research has been conducted on women's identity in general, and even less research has been conducted using Josselson's work as a theoretical base. In this discussion of research, we highlight investigations based on Marcia's and Josselson's identity statuses. Because much of the research discussed in this section was conducted so long ago, readers should use caution in applying the results to today's students.

Research Involving Marcia's Identity Statuses

Research on Marcia's identity statuses has extended over forty years (Marcia, 1994). A number of researchers have focused their efforts on determining whether the identity statuses as defined and measured by Marcia are valid. In addition, extensive research has examined the relationship of identity status to other psychological variables and outcomes. According to Marcia (1999), "These four identity statuses have become something like a psychological map for researchers" (p. 395). At least four scholars (see Bourne, 1978a; Marcia, 1980; Matteson, 1975; and Waterman, 1982) have given extensive consideration to the abundance of research on identity statuses. A host of researchers have also used identity statuses to frame research in the following areas noted by Marcia (1993c): "personality characteristics of the identity statuses, developmental aspects of the statuses, gender differences, and cross-cultural studies" (p. 22).

More recent scholarship has emerged regarding identity statuses and their relationship to adult development (Marcia, 2002), barriers that affect ego identity status formation (Yoder, 2000), college drinking behaviors (Bentrim-Tapio, 2004), race and gender (Alberts & Meyer, 1998; Miville, Darlington, Whitlock, & Mulligan, 2005), and ethnicity (Branch, Tayal, & Triplett, 2000; Yip, Seaton, & Sellers, 2006). In particular, Marcia's work has been highly influential in the development of Phinney's (1993) model of ethnic identity development (see Chapter Fifteen).

Josselson's Research on Women's Identity

Much of the research on Josselson's theory was conducted by the researcher herself in earlier work (for example, Josselson, 1973, 1978/1991, 1982, 1987b). Josselson identified what is fundamental to women's experience to produce a uniquely feminine identity and how this may vary within identity statuses. She found that women, in creating their identity, are more likely to focus on "the kind of person to be" (Josselson, 1973, p. 47) rather than their vocational decisions, political views, sexual identifications, religious convictions, or ideological beliefs.

Josselson (1973) also tapped the intricacies of how women relate to others. She found that women are in relationship with others for the sake of the relationship not as a means to something else. By simultaneously merging connectedness and autonomy, women demonstrate a symbiotic internal process.

In a study of personality structure and identity status as examined through college women's early memories, Josselson (1982) found that in contrast to women in foreclosure, those in moratorium show more ego development. Dependency and safety are conflict areas for women in foreclosure, who hold on to the past when forming their identity and current perceptions of self. Women in moratorium concentrate on their own abilities and have tremendous capacity to handle anxiety compared to women in foreclosure. Confirming these findings, Ginsburg and Orlofsky (1981) found that identity achievement and moratorium women possess more advanced ego development than women in foreclosure and diffusion.

During identity achievement, women's inner self integrates the need for relatedness with the need to assert the self. In finding this balance, achievement women "are best characterized as rapprochement, a pattern wherein closeness is maintained to the persons from whom the individual is separating and individuating" (Josselson, 1982, p. 298). Rapprochement is considered by some to be the final step to a healthy identity consolidation. To their credit, achievement women moving toward rapprochement blend moratorium and foreclosure patterns.

Identity Differences Between Women and Men

The literature examining distinct differences between the identity development of women and men college students is fairly dated but worth a mention. In his classic study of psychosocial development in three hundred undergraduate women and men at one university, Constantinople (1969) claimed that men develop a greater degree of psychosocial maturity than women as they matriculate through college. Contradicting Constantinople's findings, several follow-up studies demonstrated that college seniors show greater psychosocial maturity than first-year students and that college women generally score higher in psychosocial development than men do (Whitbourne, Jelsma, & Waterman, 1982; Zuschlag & Whitbourne, 1994). Other research has suggested that women and men in foreclosure and diffusion score lower in achievement motivation and self-esteem than women and men in identity achievement and moratorium (Orlofsky, 1978).

Waterman and Waterman (1971) found that college men progress from developmentally less mature identity statuses to more mature statuses during their first year in college. Maturation in the first year was confirmed by the decrease in men identified as diffusions and the increase in men identified as moratoriums in their occupational decision making. A second study of the same men in their senior year found significantly more students in identity achievement and significantly fewer students in moratorium and foreclosure statuses than in the first year (Waterman, Geary, & Waterman, 1974). These findings suggest that achievement status is likely "the final step in the process of development at this stage of life" (Prager, 1985, p. 32).

Women and men college students appear to resolve the processes of intimacy and identity development differently (Hodgson & Fischer, 1979). Late adolescent males tend to discover their identity through addressing issues of competence and knowledge. Men's competence evolves from choosing a career and securing a stable future, and their knowledge comes about through the confidence gained by development of an ideology. Women find their identity by relating to others and have the capacity to experience higher levels of intimacy than men do.

In a different study of identity status and occupational decision making of college students, men more frequently identified as achievers while women more frequently identified as foreclosed or diffuse (Hodgson & Fischer, 1979). In regard to the religious beliefs of college students, men (Hodgson & Fischer) and women (Orlofsky, 1978) are both likely to be identity achievers. Examination of college students' political ideology suggests that men more often become achievers (Hodgson & Fischer) while women are overrepresented as foreclosures (Adams & Fitch, 1982). College students' attitudes toward premarital sex seem to vary developmentally as well (Schenkel & Marcia, 1972); women more frequently report identity achievement status than men, while men are more frequently foreclosed or diffused (Orlofsky, 1978; Waterman & Nevid, 1977).

Applications

An inclusive review of the literature uncovered a dearth of information related to applying the theories of Josselson and Marcia in practice. With regard to Josselson's theory, Weston and Stein (1977) found that contrary to their expectations, structural factors such as type of housing, type of institution, and academic classification were not related to women's identity achievement status. Yet this research did reveal that women's participation in college activities is related to achieving identity. Three facets of participation were examined: number of organizational memberships, degree of activity, and leadership functions performed. Of these three dimensions, "degree of activity was the most useful in predicting identity achievement of college women" (Weston & Stein, p. 23). Women students heavily involved in campus organizations appear to have already achieved identity and participate to express themselves rather than using involvement to reach identity achievement status.

Marcia (1989a) offered some insight into establishing psychological interventions to promote identity development that are easily adapted to student affairs practice. From his perspective, identity statuses may not be as significant as their underlying components of exploration and commitment. Students face difficult decisions about ideology, occupation, sexuality, and relationships that lead to naturally occurring disequilibrium in their lives. Student affairs professionals can capitalize on this predictability and offer safety, structure, and guidance while students experiment with their choices of becoming. In order to make a commitment, young adults need a safety net to catch them during failure and retreat and a caring environment to nurture them back to psychological health.

Marcia (1989a) stressed that teachers must be nourished in supportive environments where they can address their own identity, intimacy, and generativity issues. Student affairs professionals must be concerned with setting the stage for and taking action on their own identity development as well as that of the students they serve. To do less undermines the learning process and precludes individuals from being the best they can be.

Critique and Future Directions

The psychosocial theories we have reviewed in this chapter are clearly beneficial to educators. Since Erikson was the first psychologist to consider development across the life span, his theory has served as the foundation for others who have explored the psychosocial development of adolescents and adults (Hamrick, Evans, & Schuh, 2002). Erikson's work is also significant in that he recognized the importance of environment and context in human development. Although he did not specifically address the development of college students, the developmental issues he noted are clearly applicable to this population. Since Marcia focused on the resolution of identity in young adulthood, his theory also has great utility for individuals working with college students, although, like Erikson, he did not specifically focus on students. Marcia did identify the various issues that are central to identity development for men and the means they use to resolve these issues, knowledge that is useful to educators as they work with male students. In contrast, Josselson's research provides information about identity resolution among women, particularly the important role of relationships in women's identity formation. Her participants were in college when she began her research, so it is directly applicable. A strength of her work is its longitudinal nature.

A number of critiques of psychosocial identity development theory have been offered. Erikson's initial work is often criticized as being overly general and complex (Rodgers, 1980), as well as biased against women (Gilligan, 1982; Josselson, 1996). It is also essentialist, in that it allows no room for variation in development across the life span, suggesting instead that developmental crises unfold in an invariant, linear way.

Many critiques of Marcia's theory can be found in the literature. Marcia (1975) himself noted, "The problem with the statuses is that they have a static quality and identity is never static" (p. 153). Several major critiques lodged against Marcia's work were offered by Côté and Levine (1983, 1988a, 1988b). First, they challenged the assumption that Marcia's statuses are developmentally ordered on a continuum from a diffused identity to an achieved identity. Although there have been some shifts in this continuum assumption, they asserted that the literature has failed to explicitly correct it. Second, Côté and Levine questioned the accuracy of Marcia's statuses in reflecting the Eriksonian conception of identity formation, contending that the statuses do not operationalize Erikson's theory. Moreover, they noted that while Marcia has implied that the identity statuses do not capture the overall complexity of Erikson's theory, he has not made this limitation clear in his work. Finally, Côté and Levine suggested that Marcia inappropriately used terminology from Erikson's theory within the identity statuses.

The paucity of research related to the identity development of women, particularly research validating Josselson's findings, leaves this area ripe for exploration. As S. Jones (1995) and Kroger (1985) have pointed out, work is needed that addresses the intersection of race and other identity domains with gender. In addition, since psychosocial development is very much influenced by societal conditions and norms, ongoing research is needed to determine if findings from Josselson's earlier studies are still applicable, given how rapidly gender norms have been changing.

The application of identity research, for women and men, is important for student affairs professionals who want to create meaningful developmental experiences to help students form a healthy identity. It is especially important to understand how autonomy, connectedness, and decision making are manifest in an individual's quest (or lack thereof) for identity in late adolescence and early adulthood.

CHAPTER FOUR

CHICKERING'S THEORY OF IDENTITY DEVELOPMENT

Melissa has just been elected educational chairperson for her sorority. This is her first leadership role, and she is anxious to do a really good job of providing programs that will be of benefit to the women in her house. Melissa asks for ideas at the first chapter meeting after her election. Some of the seniors immediately speak up. They want information about putting together résumés and conducting job searches as well as the pros and cons of going to graduate school. Some of the sophomores and juniors are more interested in how to go about deciding on a career direction that is right for them.

Sandy, a second-semester student, is obviously frustrated with these suggestions. She blurts out that she is still struggling with study skills and adjusting to college classes; she is nowhere near ready to think about careers and job searches. The group moves on to discuss another area: establishing meaningful relationships. Many of the women complain that all the guys they have been meeting are superficial and immature. They want help in learning how to develop a relationship that has some depth. A few of the younger members indicate they have not been able to talk comfortably with guys at mixers or in class, let alone establish a relationship. A number of the women also mention that they have been having trouble with their parents, who do not seem ready to let them grow up. They want to remain close to their folks, but they also feel that they are ready to make their own decisions.

Shari hesitates but then goes ahead to mention that she thinks the sorority needs to work on understanding differences. She refers back to last year's rush period when the sorority struggled over whether to accept an African American woman as a new member. Carla mentions that she is really struggling to define "who she is." Other people see her as a "party girl" because she is a member of a sorority. She used to be okay with that image, but she is coming to realize that life needs to be more than parties. Lisa chimes in that she too is trying to decide what she really values in life. She used to go along with what the rest of her sorority sisters thought, but lately she has discovered that some of her ideas are different. She wants to discuss how values affect life decisions. Although Melissa appreciates the honesty of all her sisters, she is a bit overwhelmed. *Wow* she thinks. *This is a big job. Everyone seems to have such different needs. How in the world can I address all these issues?*

◆ ◆ ◆

The issues Melissa's sorority sisters raised during their chapter meeting are similar to those experienced by many college students, particularly individuals between the ages of eighteen and twenty-four. In his theory of psychosocial development, Arthur Chickering (1969) provided an overview of the developmental issues that college students face and went on to examine environmental conditions that influence development. Building on Erikson's discussion of identity and intimacy (1959/1980), Chickering saw the establishment of identity as the core developmental issue with which students grapple during their college years. Resolution of a number of issues contributes to the person's growing sense of identity. Establishment of identity in turn allows the person to successfully address issues that may arise later in the developmental process. Chickering also identified key aspects of the college environment that influence development and suggested ways to enhance student growth.

Chickering's theory, widely used in student affairs since its introduction in 1969, has served as the foundation for extensive research as well as practical application. The original theory, and particularly its revision (Chickering & Reisser, 1993), are the focus of this chapter.

Historical Overview

Chickering's theory was first outlined in his landmark book, *Education and Identity* (1969). The theory is based on research he conducted between 1959 and 1965 while he was employed at Goddard College (Thomas & Chickering, 1984). At Goddard, Chickering was responsible for evaluating the impact of innovative curricular practices on student development. He administered sixteen hours of achievement tests, personality inventories, and other instruments to students at the end of their sophomore and senior years. He also asked selected students to keep diaries of their experiences and thoughts and conducted detailed interviews with other students. He began writing *Education and Identity* in 1963 in an attempt to provide a conceptual framework for his findings, as well as other research that had been conducted on college students.

From 1964 to 1969, Chickering served as director of the Project on Student Development in Small Colleges (Thomas & Chickering, 1984). The data he obtained from studies of thirteen dissimilar small colleges across the country were incorporated into the latter half of *Education and Identity*, which focused on the influences of the college environment on development.

Chickering targeted faculty in the preparation of *Education and Identity*. His goal was to provide them with ideas concerning the organization of educational programs to more systematically enhance student development (Thomas & Chickering, 1984). In fact, Chickering noted, "Student affairs professionals as an audience were not in my mind at all. . . . It was entirely by chance that *Education and Identity* made a significant contribution to those professionals" (p. 393). As a result of invitations during the late 1960s and early 1970s to speak to professionals in student affairs, Chickering learned about the field that would come to have the most impact on his later thinking and would do the most to implement his ideas in practice.

Working with Linda Reisser, Chickering revised his theory to incorporate new findings from research others had conducted, summarize the work of other theorists as it related to his theory, and be more inclusive of various student populations (Reisser, 1995). The revised edition (Chickering & Reisser, 1993) adhered to the basic premises of the original work but included 90 percent new material (Schuh, 1994).

Chickering's Theory

Chickering (1969) proposed seven vectors of development that contribute to the formation of identity. He used the term *vectors of development* "because each seems to have direction and magnitude—even though the direction may be expressed more appropriately by a spiral or by steps than by a straight line" (p. 8). In other words, the progression is not necessarily linear. He called these vectors "major highways for journeying toward individuation" (Chickering & Reisser, 1993, p. 35). Chickering noted that students move through these vectors at different rates, that students may deal with issues from more than one vector at the same time, that vectors can interact with each other, and that students often find themselves reexamining issues associated with vectors they had previously worked through in a process of recycling. Although not rigidly sequential and not intended to be stages, vectors do build on each other, leading to greater complexity, stability, and integration as the issues related to each one are addressed. Chickering's work takes into account emotional, interpersonal, ethical, and intellectual aspects of development.

The Seven Vectors

Chickering's seven vectors, as described in his revised theory (Chickering & Reisser, 1993), present a comprehensive picture of psychosocial development during the college years. For each vector, Chickering and Reisser provided examples in students' own words. Quotes from both traditional and adult learners are included to demonstrate the applicability of the theory to both populations.

Developing Competence. Chickering and Reisser (1993) likened competence to a three-tined pitchfork, with the tines being intellectual competence, physical and manual skills, and interpersonal competence. The handle of the pitchfork, necessary if the tines are to do their work, is "a sense of competence [that] stems from the confidence that one can cope with what comes and achieve goals successfully" (p. 53). Intellectual competence involves acquisition of knowledge and skills related to particular subject matter; development of "intellectual, cultural, and aesthetic sophistication" (Reisser, 1995, p. 506); and increased skill in areas such as critical thinking and reasoning ability. Physical competence comes through athletic and recreational activities, attention to wellness, and involvement in artistic and manual activities. Interpersonal competence includes skills in communication, leadership, and working effectively with others.

Melissa's sorority sisters who indicated that they did not yet feel comfortable with their study skills seem to be dealing with intellectual competence issues, while those who could not talk to men are experiencing interpersonal competence concerns.

Managing Emotions. In this vector, students develop the ability to recognize and accept emotions, as well as to appropriately express and control them. In addition, students learn to act on feelings in a responsible manner. Chickering's (1969) original theory focused on aggression and sexual desire. His more recent work addresses a more inclusive range of feelings, including anxiety, depression, anger, shame, and guilt, as well as more positive emotions such as caring, optimism, and inspiration.

Sandy, the young woman in the scenario who became annoyed at her sorority sisters who wanted information on job searches and career exploration, seems to be having trouble appropriately expressing and controlling her emotions. She is not handling anxiety about her intellectual competence in an effective manner.

Moving Through Autonomy Toward Interdependence. This aspect of development results in increased emotional independence, which is defined as "freedom from continual and pressing needs for reassurance, affection, or approval from others" (Chickering & Reisser, 1993, p. 117). Students also develop instrumental independence that includes self-direction, problem-solving ability, and mobility. Finally, they come to recognize and accept the importance of interdependence, an awareness of their interconnectedness with others. Chickering's revised theory places a greater emphasis on the importance of interdependence. To underscore this change, he and Reisser renamed this vector, which was previously titled *developing autonomy*. The sorority women who indicated that they were having trouble redefining relationships with their parents seem to be wrestling with questions of independence and interdependence. They want to be viewed as adults capable of making their own decisions while still maintaining positive relationships with their families.

Developing Mature Interpersonal Relationships. This vector, which in the original version of the theory was titled *freeing interpersonal relationships* and followed the establishing identity vector, was placed earlier in sequence to acknowledge that experiences with relationships contribute significantly to the development of a sense of self. The tasks associated with this vector include development of intercultural and interpersonal tolerance and appreciation of differences, as well as the capacity for healthy and lasting intimate relationships with partners and close friends. Reisser (1995) noted that both tasks "involve the ability to accept individuals for who they are, to respect differences, and to appreciate commonalities" (p. 509).

Shari's concern about learning to appreciate differences, arising from controversy within the sorority over accepting an African American as a new member, is an example of a task related to developing mature interpersonal relationships. The concern of other sorority women over the lack of depth in their relationships with men is another example.

Establishing Identity. Establishing identity builds on the vectors that come before it. In Chickering's revised theory, this vector took on added complexity to acknowledge differences in identity development based on gender, ethnic background, and sexual orientation. Identity includes comfort with body and appearance, comfort with gender and sexual orientation, a sense of one's social and cultural heritage, a clear self-concept and comfort with one's roles and lifestyle, a secure sense of self in light of feedback from significant others, self-acceptance and self-esteem, and personal stability and integration.

Carla is beginning to address identity issues. She is rejecting an identity given to her by others and looking for a lifestyle and roles that are meaningful to her.

Developing Purpose. This vector consists of developing clear vocational goals, making meaningful commitments to specific personal interests and activities, and establishing strong interpersonal commitments. It includes intentionally making and staying with decisions, even in the face of opposition. The term *vocation* is used broadly to refer to paid or unpaid work within the context of a specific career or, more generally, as a person's life calling. Lifestyle and family influences affect the decision-making and goal-setting processes in developing purpose. The sorority women who were interested in career exploration are dealing with issues of purpose. They are attempting to find a life direction that makes sense for them.

Developing Integrity. This vector includes "three sequential but overlapping stages" (Chickering & Reisser, 1993, p. 51): humanizing values, personalizing values, and developing congruence. First, students progress from rigid, moralistic thinking to the development of a more humanized value system in which the interests of others are balanced with their own interests. Next, a personalized value system is established in which core values are consciously affirmed, and the beliefs of others are acknowledged and respected. Over the course of the development of congruence, values and actions become congruent and authentic as self-interest is balanced by a sense of social responsibility. Lisa is examining integrity issues. She is moving away from a value system dictated by her sorority sisters and beginning to establish a personal value system. She is becoming aware that her values have implications for her actions.

Environmental Influences

Chickering argued that educational environments exert powerful influences on student development (Chickering & Reisser, 1993). He proposed seven factors, which he called *key influences*.

Institutional Objectives. Clear and specific objectives to which personnel pay attention and use to guide the development of programs and services have a powerful impact. They lead to greater consistency in policies, programs, and practices while making evident the values of the institution. Students and other constituencies are then able to agree with or challenge these values. Objectives can influence the emphasis given to each vector and, therefore, the educational outcomes for students. As examples, Chickering and Reisser (1993) noted that competence may be most important at one institution and integrity at another.

Institutional Size. Significant participation in campus life and satisfaction with the college experience are important if development is to occur. Chickering and Reisser (1993) argued that "as the number of persons outstrips the opportunities for significant participation and satisfaction, the developmental potential of available settings is attenuated for all" (p. 269). They express concern about redundancy, which is where people become superfluous because of excessive numbers, resulting in less personal development. Meaningful opportunities for involvement are crucial.

Student-Faculty Relationships. Extensive and varied interaction among faculty and students facilitates development. Students need to see faculty in a variety of situations involving different roles and responsibilities. Such interaction leads students to perceive faculty as real people who are accessible and interested in them beyond the classroom. Chickering and Reisser (1993) identified the following components of positive student-faculty relationships: accessibility, authenticity, knowledge about students, and the ability to communicate with students.

Curriculum. A relevant curriculum is needed that is sensitive to individual difference, offers diverse perspectives, and helps students make sense of what they are learning. The assumptions about student learning that underlie the curriculum and the process by which learning takes place have as much impact on outcomes as the specific curricular content. In regard to selecting content, Chickering and Reisser (1993) recommended making it "relevant to students' backgrounds and prior experiences" (p. 362); recognizing "significant dimensions of individual differences between students" (p. 364); creating "encounters with diverse perspectives that challenge pre-exiting information, assumptions, and values" (p. 365); and providing "activities that help students integrate diverse perspectives, assumptions, value orientations" (p. 367).

Teaching. For development to occur, teaching should involve active learning, student-faculty interaction, timely feedback, high expectations, and respect for individual learning differences. Such teaching strategies affect cognitive development in the form of active thinking and integration of ideas. They also encourage interdependence, cooperation, and interpersonal sensitivity.

Friendships and Student Communities. Chickering and Reisser (1993) noted, "A student's most important teacher is often another student" (p. 392). Meaningful friendships and diverse student communities in which shared interests exist and significant interactions occur encourage development along all seven vectors. Communities may be informal friendship groups or more formal groups such as residence hall floors, student organizations, or classes. To have maximum positive benefit, the community should "[encourage] regular interactions between students," "[offer] opportunities for collaboration," be "small enough so that no one feels superfluous," "[include] people from diverse backgrounds," and "[serve] as a reference group" (Chickering & Reisser, 1993, p. 277).

Student Development Programs and Services. Collaborative efforts by faculty and student affairs professionals are necessary to provide developmental programs and services. Chickering and Reisser (1993) "recommend[ed] that administrators of student programs and services redefine themselves as educators and refer to themselves as 'student development professionals'" (p. 278). They noted the importance of student development staff serving as advocates for "the education of the whole student" (p. 427).

The Admonitions

Chickering and Reisser (1993) also introduced what they termed *three admonitions* (not to be confused with the seven key influences) that underscore the creation of educationally powerful environments.

Integration of Work and Learning. Since most students today work as well as take classes, collaborative relationships are needed among business, the community, and institutions of higher education that will maximize the developmental potential of work and volunteer experiences.

Recognition and Respect for Individual Differences. Chickering and Reisser (1993) stated, "It is clear that diversity will only increase in the years ahead. It is also clear that if we are unable to deal with it, we are likely to face increasing conflict, a two-tier society, and economic stagnation" (p. 473). Educators must be cognizant of the different backgrounds and needs of their students and adjust their interactions and interventions to address these differences.

Acknowledgment of the Cyclical Nature of Learning and Development. Learning involves periods of differentiation and integration, equilibrium and disequilibrium. New experiences and challenges provide opportunities for new perspectives and more complex understanding to occur. Chickering and Reisser (1993) cautioned that "signs of discomfort and upset are not necessarily negative. On the contrary, they often signal that developmentally fruitful encounters are occurring, that stimuli for learning are at work" (p. 479).

Research

Schuh (1994) speculated that since its introduction, Chickering's (1969) theory has generated as much research as any other work in the field of student development. Research has centered on development of methods to assess Chickering's vectors of development, validation of Chickering's theory, investigation of development among specific student populations, the relationship of psychosocial development and aspects of college students' experiences, and ways in which psychosocial development and other forms of development are interconnected.

Assessment

Because psychosocial development is multidimensional and complex, its assessment is not easy (Miller & Winston, 1990). Development is continually occurring in many different arenas, and assessment can provide only a limited evaluation of a particular aspect of that development at a specific point in time, much like taking a snapshot (Miller & Winston). Cognitive development also interacts with psychosocial development in that individuals at different levels of cognitive development will interpret their experiences differently (Mines, 1985). In addition, psychosocial development is influenced by the environmental context in which it occurs (Miller & Winston). Cultural values, setting, and historical time affect development and must be considered in the construction of assessment techniques.

Efforts to assess psychosocial development as outlined in Chickering's (1969) theory and Chickering and Reisser's (1993) revision have been made by teams located at the University of Georgia and the University of Iowa (Miller & Winston, 1990). Instruments currently available include the Student Developmental Task and Lifestyle Assessment (Winston, Miller, & Cooper, 1999a, 1999b) and the Iowa Student Development Inventories (Hood, 1986, 1997).

Validation of the Theory

Using the assessment tools that have been developed, a number of researchers have investigated the extent to which Chickering's theory is valid. White and Hood (1989) examined the validity of Chickering's vectors of development by administering the six Iowa instruments plus an objective measure of cognitive development to 225 students. A factor-analytic procedure provided limited support for Chickering's original theory. Factors that accounted for the majority of the variance were parallels to the vectors of identity, purpose, and integrity. In this case, it is difficult to determine if the theory is failing to accurately capture students' development or if the instrumentation used in the study needs to be refined to better reflect the theory.

Other studies have examined specific aspects of Chickering's theory. For example, in a study investigating only autonomy development as described in the revised theory (Chickering & Reisser, 1993), Mather and Winston's (1998) results supported Chickering's hypothesized developmental process and documented the importance of issues of control in this process. In a single institutional study with 247 student participants, repeated administrations of the STDLI resulted in partial support for Chickering's theory (Foubert, Nixon, Sisson, & Barnes, 2005). Students developed during college in the areas of purpose, mature interpersonal relationships, academic autonomy, and tolerance. However, results contradicted the idea that the developing purpose vector is one experienced later in one's college career. Significant development was identified during the first year of college, prompting the researchers to question the sequential nature of the vectors. Finally, Martin (2000) found some support for Chickering's hypothesized relationship between college experiences and psychosocial development. These contradictory findings suggest that further work is needed to determine the validity of Chickering's theory for today's students.

Research on Specific Student Populations

Researchers have also examined the applicability of Chickering's theory to various institutional contexts and diverse student populations. With regard to context, Rogers (2004) explored the psychosocial development of community college students and found Chickering's theory to be meaningful. The competence and purpose vectors were most relevant in describing development among this student population.

As Evans (2003) noted, gender and cultural differences can have an impact on the ordering and importance of the vectors. Students' experiencing of the vectors can differ based on their social identities, such as gender, race, ethnicity, and sexual orientation, as several researchers have suggested.

Women's Development. Researchers examining the applicability of Chickering's theory to women have found that women's development differs from men's development, particularly regarding the importance of interpersonal relationships in fostering other aspects of development. Based on data from their study of African

American and Caucasian women, Taub and McEwen (1991) concluded that development of mature interpersonal relationships may begin earlier for women than for men, while development of autonomy may occur later than Chickering suggested. In a longitudinal study, Blackhurst (1995) found support for this argument. For many women, developing mature interpersonal relationships seems to precede developing autonomy (Greeley & Tinsley, 1988; Straub, 1987; Taub, 1995), and many women achieve autonomy through the development of healthy relationships (Straub & Rodgers, 1986; Taub, 1995). Taub (1997) also found that increasing autonomy did not result in decreased attachment to parents for traditionally aged undergraduate women.

Female college students also score higher on intimacy than do male college students (Foubert et al., 2005; Greeley & Tinsley, 1988; Utterback, Spooner, Barbieri, & Fox, 1995). Foubert et al. also found women, in regard to the mature interpersonal relationships vector, more developed than men throughout the college experience. Notably, women were more tolerant at the start of their college careers than were men after four years of college.

At historically black colleges, African American women scored higher than African American men on interpersonal relationships, autonomy, and life purpose (Jordan-Cox, 1987). But in a longitudinal study over four years of college, men experienced greater increases in identity development than did women (Hood, Riahinejad, & White, 1986).

Development of Students from Various Racial/Ethnic Groups. Several writers have questioned the applicability of Chickering's theory for students who are not from white, middle-class backgrounds. As Pope (1998) stated, theories such as Chickering's can be "insufficient" (p. 274) in explaining the development of students of color. Attention to racial identity is crucial when attempting to facilitate psychosocial development of such students because the constructs are interrelated (Pope, 2000).

Some scholars have examined aspects of the psychosocial development of African American students. Development of racial/ethnic identity is of particular importance to African American students, and it often delays other aspects of psychosocial development (Taub & McEwen, 1992). McEwen, Roper, Bryant, and Langa (1990), in a conceptual piece, and Gibbs (1974) also suggested that the role of assimilation in relation to a dominant culture, acculturation, and cultural awareness in development must be considered. McEwen et al. (1990) stressed that identity for African Americans has both personal and collective elements that result from social interaction and group identifications. For African Americans, developing independence and autonomy seems to occur within the context of interpersonal relationships; affiliation plays an important role in development, and family and extended family exert a pervasive influence. Religion, spiritual development, and social responsibility also take on significance for African Americans (Branch-Simpson, 1984, as cited in Rodgers, 1990b; Hughes, 1987).

A few researchers have investigated the influence of the college environment on African American development. Generally researchers have found that African American students are better adjusted at historically black institutions than at predominantly white schools (Fleming, 1984; Hughes, 1987). Fleming (1984) found that isolation and loneliness affected the establishment of interpersonal relationships for African American students on white campuses, with African American men being particularly at risk. On predominantly white campuses, black women were found to score lower than white women on intimacy; however, the authors of this study questioned the appropriateness of the measuring instrument for African American students (Taub & McEwen, 1991). Cokley (2001) found gender differences in regard to academic psychosocial development among African American students at historically black institutions, with women being more motivated and racial identity being more important in their academic psychosocial development in contrast to men.

Sedlacek (1987) found that noncognitive variables related to psychosocial development, such as confidence, realistic self-appraisal, and a solid ethnic identity, were crucial to the success of African American students on predominantly white campuses. In contrast to other research, Cheatham, Slaney, and Coleman (1990) found that African American students at a predominantly white institution scored higher on emotional and academic autonomy, as well as cultural participation, than did African American students at a historically black college.

Kodama, McEwen, Liang, and Lee (2001, 2002), from a conceptual perspective, have provided much needed insight into the psychosocial development of Asian American students, noting that Chickering's theory (Chickering & Reisser, 1993) does not adequately address development for this population. They observed that Chickering and Reisser's revision fails to consider fully the nature and impact of an oppressive society. Dealing with the tension between Western values and racism and Asian values regarding family and community influences identity development for these students. These authors concluded that while the content of the vectors paralleled the psychosocial issues that Asian American students experience, the specific tasks did not fit as well. For example, the managing emotions vector does not take into account different cultural values such as emotional restraint. Kodama et al. (2001) suggested that exploring or understanding emotions may be more relevant developmental tasks for this population.

Other racial and ethnic differences have been identified. Caucasians score higher on intimacy than Native Americans, African Americans, and Hispanic Americans (Utterback et al., 1995). Asian international first-year students scored significantly lower than American students, for whom race/ethnicity was not specified, in regard to establishing and clarifying purpose and developing mature interpersonal relationships and intimacy (Sheehan & Pearson, 1995). No differences were found in regard to academic autonomy. Alessandria and Nelson (2005), comparing first-generation American students and non-first-generation American students, found no significant differences in levels of identity development.

Development of Gay, Lesbian, and Bisexual Students. Although Chickering and Reisser (1993) expanded the description of establishing identity to include becoming comfortable with one's sexual orientation, almost no research has been done to examine the suitability of Chickering's theory for nonheterosexual populations. In a small exploratory study, Levine and Bahr (1989) found evidence that development of sexual identity may retard other components of psychosocial development for gay, lesbian, and bisexual students. Certainly vectors such as managing emotions, developing mature interpersonal relationships, establishing identity, and developing purpose would be affected by how one feels about one's sexual orientation (Evans & D'Augelli, 1996). Lesbian, gay, and bisexual students may be at a disadvantage in resolving the developmental tasks of the first four vectors, leading to difficulties in resolving more advanced tasks (Fassinger, 1998a).

Gay, lesbian, and bisexual youth face the added pressure of giving up a majority identity and developing a new minority identity (D'Augelli, 1994a). Coming out (that is, acknowledging and disclosing one's sexual orientation) is another developmental task that heterosexual students do not experience (Wall & Evans, 1991).

Factors Related to Development

Researchers have investigated the relationship of psychosocial development and a number of academic, cocurricular, and life experience variables. With regard to academic factors, confidence has been shown to be significantly correlated with academic satisfaction and classroom performance (Erwin & Delworth, 1982; Erwin & Kelly, 1985).

Involvement on campus is also related to psychosocial development. First-year students who remain on campus on weekends report higher levels of autonomy than students who leave campus (Fox, Spooner, Utterback, & Barbieri, 1996). In addition, several researchers (Hood et al., 1986; Hunt & Rentz, 1994; Williams & Winston, 1985) have demonstrated that students who are more involved in cocurricular activities score higher on scales measuring confidence, developing purpose, developing mature interpersonal relationships, and intimacy.

Involvement is not always positively related to development, however. Students who participated in intercollegiate athletics scored lower than nonathletes in regard to educational plans, career plans, and mature relationships (Sowa & Gressard, 1983). And in a longitudinal study, sophomore men in Greek organizations scored lower in regard to confidence than did non-Greek men (Kilgannon & Erwin, 1992). It may be that development in this area occurs after the sophomore year, as the Hood et al. (1986) study suggested.

Previous life experiences also relate to psychosocial development. Women who reported unwanted childhood sexual experiences scored lower on career planning and intimacy, and women who experienced incest scored lower on sexual identity (White & Strange, 1993). Another study demonstrated that students with divorced parents scored higher on confidence and sexual identity than did students from intact families (Heyer & Nelson, 1993).

Relationships Among Forms of Development

The interconnections of forms of development have also been considered. For instance, higher levels of psychosocial development seem to be related to higher levels of career development. Bowers, Dickman, and Fuqua (2001) found a relationship between psychosocial development and career development, reinforcing Chickering's notion that certain developmental tasks must be resolved before career readiness is evident. In addition, Long, Sowa, and Niles (1995) found a connection between having made a career decision and academic autonomy, sense of purpose, vocational identity, and occupational information.

A relationship also seems to exist between psychosocial development and moral development. Students who viewed themselves as having both a high justice and low care moral orientation had higher scores in regard to psychosocial development (Jones & Watt, 1999). The authors of this study pointed out the need for programs to assist students in balancing self-sacrifice and self-care. Jones and Watt (2001) also reported "increasing psychosocial development across class standing" (p. 10) and connectedness and relationships promoting development of identity and autonomy for women, with separation contributing to the same processes for men. Finally, identity development and moral development appear to be parallel processes (Bruess & Pearson, 2000).

Applications

Chickering's theory has generated a number of student affairs applications, particularly in the area of programming. Interventions to facilitate particular aspects of development have been introduced, as well as general programming strategies. Chickering has also provided examples of ways that several of the key environmental factors can be implemented. While the applications found in the literature remain useful and relevant, it is unfortunate that more recent applications of Chickering's theory have not been introduced.

Programming

Chickering's model is particularly effective in developing overall program priorities and strategies. For instance, Chickering's vectors have been used as a basis for the development of a needs assessment instrument to be used in residence hall program planning (Evans, 1982). In addition, Hurst (1978) suggested that programming on campus be targeted to address each of the seven vectors using a variety of different approaches, including direct service, consultation and training, and media (Morrill, Oetting, & Hurst, 1974).

Chickering's theory can also be used to evaluate and explain the impact of programmatic efforts. Chickering (1977) discussed ways in which college union programs affect various aspects of development, particularly competence, autonomy, interpersonal relationships, and humanitarian concern. Klepper and Kovacs (1978) built on Chickering's ideas to suggest ways that programs offered by student unions across the country connect to each of the seven vectors. Similarly, recreational sports programs can encourage development along each vector (Todaro, 1993).

Programs have also been designed to help students address specific developmental issues. For instance, at Valparaiso University, the Freshman Home Reentry program was designed to help students with the transition of returning home for the summer after their first year in college (Lott, 1986). Developmental issues related to establishing identity and freeing interpersonal relationships were discussed. Lemons and Richmond (1987) went a step further to help students deal with sophomore slump, which the authors related to problems with achieving competence, developing autonomy, establishing identity, and developing purpose. Mentoring and individual counseling interventions were introduced. Cognitive-behavioral counseling techniques, such as assertiveness training and self-mastery techniques, have been suggested for women who are dealing with autonomy issues (McBride, 1990). The unique developmental programming needs of students with disabilities are discussed by Huss (1983) and Perreira and Dezago (1989). Hadley (2006) recommended actions to aid students with learning disabilities in developing competence, establishing autonomy, and managing emotions.

Student affairs professionals should be aware, however, that students do not always take advantage of developmental programs. Hess and Winston (1995) found that students tended to take part in programs focusing on developmental tasks that, for them, were already well developed and that they were unmotivated to attend programs designed to address their less-developed skills. Similarly, students who were most likely to become involved in a mentoring program were those least likely to need it (Rice & Brown, 1990). Students with low self-esteem and less well-developed interpersonal relationships were less likely to enroll in the program. By being aware of the potential for students to fail to participate in programs and activities that are developmentally appropriate, student affairs practitioners can make special efforts to encourage involvement, as Hess and Winston suggested, rather than assuming involvement will occur automatically.

Individual Interactions

An awareness of the developmental issues represented by the vectors can aid student affairs practitioners in their interactions with students on an individual level. For example, knowing that entering students are likely to be concerned about competency issues, practitioners can be prepared to suggest activities and institutional supports that can facilitate intellectual, physical, and social competence. As another example, Moran (2001) suggested various ways student affairs practitioners can support students in developing purpose, such as investing quality time in meaningful activities.

Valentine and Taub (1999) noted particular concerns student athletes are likely to have in relation to each vector, given the intense demands on these individuals. They suggested counseling interventions such as academic advising to counteract the "dumb jock" stereotype. L. Harris (2003) extended the focus on athletes by making recommendations in regard to each vector for working with student-athletes who have been injured.

Environmental Interventions

Chickering introduced the idea of a "residential learning contract" at George Mason University (Krivoski & Nicholson, 1989). As part of the application process, students were asked to outline the learning outcomes they wished to achieve by living in university housing. At the end of the year, both students and staff evaluated the extent to which the developmental goals were achieved, with continued occupancy being contingent on good-faith efforts to accomplish the goals established. Also at George Mason, Chickering assisted in the design of a university learning center (Chickering & O'Connor, 1996). Primary goals of the center included fostering collaboration among faculty and student affairs professionals. Programs awarded space in the center met criteria related to collaboration, addressing needs of diverse learners, linking theory and practice, and learning technologies.

In a book geared to both traditional and nontraditional students about to enter college, Chickering and Schlossberg (1995, 2001) introduced students to the areas of development that should occur during college and ways that they can structure their environment to achieve them. Key environmental factors, such as relationships with faculty, active learning, and collaboration with other students, are stressed. In addition, Schlossberg, Lynch, and Chickering (1989) suggested programs and services designed to meet the needs of adult students in college.

Hamrick, Evans, and Schuh (2002) linked Chickering's theory to work related to college outcomes. The vectors and key influences provide information to aid in creating environments to facilitate student development.

Critique and Future Directions

Chickering's theory provides a comprehensive picture of the developmental tasks college students face. His work not only helps to explain the issues and concerns with which students are dealing but also suggests steps that student development educators can take to foster student growth.

Chickering and Reisser's (1993) revisions do much to update the theory. In his review of *Education and Identity* (2nd ed.), Schuh (1994) applauded Chickering and Reisser for their willingness to revise the definitions and ordering of the seven vectors to reflect recent research findings. He was particularly pleased to see the incorporation of material related to women's development and the development of African American and Hispanic students. Schuh noted, however, that attention to Asian American and Native American students was missing. Schuh was also critical of Chickering and Reisser (1993) for not clearly indicating the sources of the quotations they provided as examples.

Chickering's theory is empirically grounded and comprehensive; however, it lacks specificity and precision. Even in the newer version, definitions of vectors are often quite general. Developing integrity is particularly hard to grasp and therefore to measure. Chickering also failed to address the different motivational levels of students to grapple with issues or the process by which they accomplish developmental tasks.

More research to test the validity of Chickering's theory is warranted. Most of the existing research is correlational in nature and designed to focus on one or two vectors rather than the overall pattern of development. More longitudinal research examining development over time is needed. Factors that influence development also require further examination.

Reisser (1995) acknowledged that more research is needed on the interrelationships of age, gender, sexual orientation, race, culture, and aspects of psychosocial development and called for broad inclusive theories rather than ones that are narrow and group specific. However, much of psychosocial development is culture specific, and it may not be possible to develop a theory that is totally valid for everyone.

Qualitative research approaches show promise for examining psychosocial development, particularly as it occurs for members of different multicultural populations. Torres, Howard-Hamilton, and Cooper (2003) asserted that "the important life question—'Who am I?'—is only partially addressed" (p. 16) in foundational theories such as Chickering's, and Pope, Reynolds, and Mueller (2004), while acknowledging that Chickering's theory has changed to accommodate diverse populations, reiterated the charges others have made that multicultural issues and concerns have not been effectively incorporated. Rather than trying to fit Chickering's theory onto groups different from that on which it is based, researchers need to independently determine what is important in the lives of people from different backgrounds, a goal best accomplished using phenomenological techniques.

Chickering's theory has had a significant impact on the development of proactive and intentional interventions in higher education. Because of the practical approach Chickering has taken, his theory is easy to understand and use. As a result, he has become perhaps the most highly regarded student development theorist to date. Higbee (2002) described the theory as one "that stands the test of time" (p. 33). Valentine and Taub (1999) maintained that despite concerns, this theory "remains arguably the most well known, widely used, and comprehensive model available for understanding and describing the psychosocial development of college students" (p. 166). For now, it remains important to use Chickering's theory with care, acknowledging its limitations while continuing to appreciate its utility when used appropriately.

CHAPTER FIVE

PERRY'S THEORY OF INTELLECTUAL AND ETHICAL DEVELOPMENT

L ee, a junior, is president of the university union's student programming board, having served as a member during his freshman and sophomore years. Recently he has been experiencing some frustration with the board, composed primarily of freshmen and sophomores. He values the group's energy but has difficulty dealing with some of their attitudes and behaviors. For example, although they are eager to do the board's work, members have difficulty making decisions about the types of programs to offer, appropriate marketing strategies, and so on. Some board members have strong opinions about what the group should do, and often these opinions conflict.

A recent meeting became deadlocked when one faction took the stance that programming funds should not be given to the university's Black Student Association for special orientation programming designed for students of color and proposed as a supplement to the university's standard orientation activities. The programming board members who opposed this allocation indicated that they believed the university's orientation activities were for all students, so it would be wrong to fund additional activities designed for only some students. One of these board members tried to call for a vote on the issue before alternate points of view could be presented. When Lee suggested that it seemed only fair to listen to other opinions on the subject, he was cut off by one of the more vocal members of the opposing group: "What's right is right, and what's wrong is wrong, so why waste time talking about it?"

Some of the other board members wanted advice from their advisor, Miriam, who was unable to attend the meeting. Lee found this mind-set frustrating as well.

He saw these students as always wanting Miriam to tell them what to do—what programs to offer, how to advertise them, every detail. Lee wondered, *Can't they ever think for themselves?* Lee was also willing to admit to himself that he felt a bit offended that these students consistently turned to Miriam, and not to him, for advice. He considered his opinions as valid as hers.

◆ ◆ ◆

As an entering student, Audrey felt intimidated by the academic experience. She loved literature and loved to read, but her experience so far with her Introduction to Literature class had been stressful. She enjoyed the class when she could sit and listen to the professor lecture on the lives of famous authors and facts related to the readings. But she had difficulty with the expectation that students would speak regularly in class discussions and offer their interpretations. What could she possibly have to offer? The professor was the expert, and she wanted to hear what he thought. Besides, he knew the correct interpretation, and she would feel dumb if her answer was incorrect. Consequently Audrey often sat in silence, staring down at her notebook, hoping the professor would not call on her.

◆ ◆ ◆

Jordan, a sophomore, was enrolled in the same class to fulfill a distribution requirement. He was not a big fan of literature, but he loved class discussion and was willing to offer his views. After he heard the professor's explanation of the graded assignments—for example, discussion contributions and an interpretive paper—Jordan thought this class would be an easy A. All he would have to do was present his own opinion. Having now received two papers back from the professor, Jordan was angry. Both papers received C grades. The professor indicated that while Jordan made creative interpretations, he failed to offer evidence from the literature to support his perspective. Jordan thought the professor was unfair. How could he give a low grade when it was all just opinion anyway?

◆ ◆ ◆

Jerome, a senior, was also taking the course for a distribution requirement. He knew that most students completed these requirements by the end of their sophomore year, but he was glad he had waited. Initially he thought an introductory course might be too basic for a senior. Instead, Jerome connected with the professor's approach to the course. He was enjoying the literature, but his excitement came from honing his analytical skills. Jerome thought that his written and verbal literature interpretations were good practice for the analytical and persuasive skills he would need to be successful in law school and beyond. Although he thought some students in the class, such as Jordan, just talked for class participation points, Jerome appreciated the feedback he received from the professor: it helped him understand his strengths, as well as areas for improvement, in presenting an effective argument.

◆ ◆ ◆

Clearly, how students make meaning can have a profound impact on themselves and others, both inside the classroom and beyond it. William Perry's theory of intellectual and ethical development (1968) can enhance our understanding of meaning-making processes and serves as a resource for appropriate ways of responding to students' differences in meaning making, including approaches to assisting students with growth in cognitive complexity. In this chapter, we provide a historical overview of Perry's theory, examine the theory, review related research, discuss ways in which the theory has been used in student affairs and academic settings, and provide a critique of the theory as well as suggestions for future directions.

Historical Overview

During the 1950s and early 1960s, while serving as the director of Harvard University's Bureau of Study Counsel, William G. Perry Jr., along with his associates, engaged in research examining how students interpret and make meaning of the teaching and learning process. From this research, he and his colleagues formulated what he has described as "the typical course of development of students' patterns of thought" (1981, p. 77) and "unfolding views of the world" (1968, p. ix). Perry (1968) acknowledged indebtedness to Piaget and other developmental psychologists, such as Kohlberg. Because little work had been done to address the adolescent-to-adulthood transition, Perry made particular mention of the influence of Nevitt Sanford's (1962, 1966) and Roy Heath's (1964) research in the higher education setting.

A somewhat reluctant theorist, Perry (1968) revealed that his "initial intent was purely descriptive, and not even systematically so" (p. 6). Students from both Harvard, a men's college, and Radcliffe, a women's college, formed the sample for Perry's longitudinal study, a series of year-end interviews conducted with these students over the course of their four years at the institution. With few exceptions, he used only the interviews with Harvard men in validating and illustrating the theory.

Perry published two major discussions of his research. The first is a book-length treatment of the theory and contains detailed explanations and examples of the concepts that comprise the theory, along with procedural information about the study (Perry, 1968). The second presents a more condensed, though equally rich, treatment of the theory (Perry, 1981). Both require readers to engage actively with the material and to accept the challenge of understanding some complex cognitive concepts.

The Theory

"Forms" of intellectual and ethical development are the structures that shape how people view their experiences (Perry, 1968). Perry's (1968) scheme begins with simplistic forms in which the individual interprets the world in "unqualified polar terms of absolute right-wrong, good-bad" (p. 3) and concludes with complex forms through which the individual seeks to affirm personal commitments "in a world of contingent knowledge and relative values" (p. 3).

The foundation for Perry's (1968) theory consists of nine positions outlined on a continuum of development. He chose *position* over *stage* for several reasons. First, no assumption about duration is made. Second, since individuals may demonstrate some range in structures at any point in time, *position* can represent "the locus of a central tendency or dominance among these structures" (p. 48). Finally, *position* is consistent with the point of view with which we look at the world. Interestingly, the positions are static, with development occurring not in the positions but during the transitions between them. Perry speculated, "Perhaps development is all transition and 'stages' only resting points along the way" (1981, p. 78). Knefelkamp (1999) noted that Perry "emphasized our need to understand students in motion and not imprison them in stages" (p. xii).

The positions in Perry's (1981) theory of intellectual and ethical development move on a continuum from duality to evolving commitments. The precision and more subtle differences that characterize the nine positions represent more detail than is needed to render Perry's scheme a usable tool for understanding and interacting with students. A simplified version of the theory portraying the basic differences in the primary modes of meaning making, along with an explanation of the deflections that can delay cognitive growth, seems sufficient to facilitate active use of these ideas.

Concepts that represent fundamental differences in the meaning-making process are *duality*, *multiplicity*, and *relativism*. *Commitment* signifies another important idea within the scheme. The following descriptions of basic concepts in the Perry scheme are derived from Perry (1968, 1981), King (1978), and Knefelkamp and Cornfeld (1979).

Dualism represents a mode of meaning making in which the world is viewed dichotomously: good-bad, right-wrong, black-white. Learning is essentially information exchange because knowledge is seen as quantitative (facts), and authorities (including people and books) are seen as possessing the right answers. In one of the scenarios at the start of this chapter, Audrey possessed a view of her instructor as the expert. For Audrey, the professor knows the correct answer and should share it with her.

The essence of dualism is seen in the tongue-in-cheek response of a student affairs graduate student who, when asked by an instructor to explain dualism, retorted, "You're the teacher. You tell us." Dualistic meaning makers believe that right answers exist for everything. The transition to multiplicity begins when cognitive dissonance occurs. For example, when experts disagree or when good teachers or other authority figures do not have all the answers or express uncertainty, disequilibrium is introduced into the meaning-making process. *Multiplicity* is sometimes misunderstood and described as an "anything goes" mode of making meaning. In reality, Perry characterized multiplicity as honoring diverse views when the right answers are not yet known. In such instances, all opinions are equally valid from a multiplistic perspective. As individuals move through multiplicity, their conception of the student role shifts from that of one who works hard to learn to one who learns to think more independently. During this progression, peers become more legitimate sources of knowledge, and individuals are likely to improve their ability to think analytically.

In another of the opening scenarios, Lee demonstrated examples of multiplistic thinking when he pronounced that his opinion was as valid as Miriam's, the advisor. By contrast, board members who looked to Miriam for answers were portrayed as dualistic thinkers. If these students were dualistic in their thought processes, Lee, as a peer, would be unlikely to be seen as an expert. To them, his opinions are not considered as valid as Miriam's. Lee needs to establish himself as an authority figure in their eyes to receive the same regard from them.

For multiplistic thinkers, the transition to *relativism* is initiated by recognition of the need to support opinions. All opinions no longer appear equally valid. Relativistic thinkers acknowledge that some opinions are of little value, yet reasonable people can also legitimately disagree on some matters. Knowledge is viewed more qualitatively; it is contextually defined, based on evidence and supporting arguments.

Also in one of the opening scenarios, Jerome manifested relativistic thinking. He valued developing well-founded arguments and welcomed critical feedback that pointed out flaws in his analysis. By contrast, Jordan had difficulty distinguishing between an opinion and a well-developed argument, which reflects multiplistic thinking.

The oppositional students on the programming board who do not want to hear differing opinions are likely dualistic thinkers. They expressed some dichotomous views—for example, what's right is right and what's wrong is wrong. It seems important, however, to come to such a conclusion tentatively. The oppositional students' views are less inclusive, and their mode of meaning making therefore may be assumed to be less complex. However, the content of individuals' views should not be confused with the degree of complexity of the thought process used to reach conclusions (Knefelkamp, Widick, & Stroad, 1976). In reality, dualistic thinkers and relativistic thinkers can resemble each other on the surface. Both may demonstrate strong views. At issue is the degree of examination and reflection that formulates those views. If ideas are essentially swallowed whole from authorities such as parents, teachers, group advisors, or textbooks, if little or no questioning is part of the process of adopting these beliefs, then the process demonstrates a dualistic mode of thinking. By contrast, relativistic thinkers, when presented with ideas by an authority figure, may adopt them as their own. Along the way, they critically examine ideas and perhaps even reject them for a period. The rationale for current adherence to the beliefs reflects a more complex process of coming to conclusions, a process that includes some questioning and a contextual basis for the stance taken.

The movement from relativism to the process of *commitment in relativism*, which involves making choices in a contextual world, exemplifies a shift away from cognitive development because it does not involve changes in cognitive structures (King, 1978). This movement can be viewed as initiating ethical development rather than increasing cognitive complexity. The commitment process involves choices, decisions, and affirmations that are made from the vantage point of relativism. Affirmation of commitment is a time when "one finds at last the elusive sense of 'identity' one has searched for elsewhere" (Perry, 1981, p. 97). Two aspects characterize students' thinking about commitments: area and style (Perry, 1968). Area refers to social content—decisions about major, career, religion, relationships, politics, and so forth. Style has to do with balancing in regard to both the external (for example, relative time use, nature of relationships) and the subjective (for example, action versus contemplation, and control versus openness).

Consistent with the notion that development does not occur in a linear fashion, Perry (1968) also described three deflections from cognitive growth. Temporizing represents a "time-out" period when movement is postponed. Some temporizing may be needed to allow for horizontal decalage (lateral growth or development within a particular stage) or to provide a rest period. With temporizing, cognitive development is essentially put on hold; a plateau is maintained. For example, a student in a Perry interview alleged, "I'll wait and see what time brings, see if I pass the foreign service exam. Let that decide" (Perry, 1981, p. 90). With temporizing, there is a hesitation to take the next step (King, 1978). Escape, another deflection, involves an abandonment of responsibility characterized by alienation. Often avoidance of responsibility leads to failure to make commitments in relativism. For example, a student in a Perry interview described not having any consuming interest or burning desire. The student continued by saying he was drifting and perhaps leading a hollow life (Perry, 1981). Retreat, the third deflection, is a temporary return to dualism and can result from feelings of being overwhelmed or overly challenged. For example, students feeling overwhelmed about the job search process can look to an authority figure such as a faculty member or a career counselor to tell them what to do.

Research

Much research has been done on Perry's theory. In this section, we mention only the development of assessment methods, as well as early groundbreaking research and studies that have examined outcomes within higher education settings.

Assessment Methods

Several assessment methods, including both production and recognition formats, are available and have been used in research studies. Production formats require respondents to generate their own answers, verbally or in writing, while recognition formats have individuals select a response from alternatives provided. In the original study, Perry (1968) and his colleagues conducted open-ended interviews, beginning with a question such as, "Would you like to say what has stood out for you during the year?" (p. 7), and following up with probes seeking specific examples.

After the scheme was conceptualized from a qualitative analysis of early protocols, a manual was developed and subsequent ratings conducted by independent judges (Perry, 1968). The time and expense in conducting interviews and rating protocols for assessment purposes limited widespread use of the technique. As alternatives to the interview approach, several paper-and-pencil measures of the Perry scheme have been developed.

Knefelkamp (1974) and Widick (1975) developed and refined a production-oriented instrument that came to be known as the Measure of Intellectual Development (MID), which measures Perry's first five positions. Baxter Magolda and Porterfield's Measure of Epistemological Reflection (MER; 1985; Baxter Magolda, 1987), another production instrument, also measures the first five positions of the Perry scheme. Erwin's Scale of Intellectual Development (SID; 1983) represents an early effort to create a Perry measure comprising recognition tasks. Another Perry measure that uses the recognition format is Moore's Learning Environment Preferences Measure (LEP; 1989).

Foundational Research

Perry and his colleagues replicated their original work with the Harvard-Radcliffe entering class of 1971 and again with the class of 1979 (Perry, 1981). Although some variations were noted when comparing these samples to the original, the scheme of cognitive and ethical development seemed to be a constant phenomenon in a pluralistic culture.

James Heffernan was credited as being the first to use the scheme for research purposes by incorporating it into an outcome study of a residential college at the University of Michigan (Perry, 1981). Joanne Kurfiss is also identified by King (1978) and Perry (1981) as a researcher who conducted early work based on the Perry scheme. She examined conceptual properties and the comparative rates of development within individuals. Pierre Meyer (1977), who used Perry's theory in the early years, studied the religious development of students with a common religious preference who attended two small colleges (one private, one public). This study showed that an understanding of religious issues can serve as an indication of intellectual development (King, 1978).

Higher Education Outcomes

Use of Perry's scheme as an outcome measure is also represented in the research literature. For example, the MID was used to assess how a program designed to enhance the professional identity of medical students influenced cognitive development (Swick, 1991); the SID was used to assess the impact of a semester-long career planning course for vocationally undecided students (Jones & Newman, 1993); and the MID was used to measure the impact of a year-long interdisciplinary program at Daytona Beach Community College (Avens & Zelley, 1992). In a later study using the MER, service-learning courses had a positive impact on cognitive development, and those with a social justice emphasis had more impact than those without this emphasis (Wang & Rodgers, 2006).

An early and extensive use of the Perry scheme as an outcomes measure occurred at Alverno College (Mentkowski, Moeser, & Strait, 1983). Perry's scheme was used along with other developmentally oriented instruments as a measure of student growth at this institution, which had an outcome-centered curriculum. Results of a five-year longitudinal study involving 750 women, aged seventeen to fifty-five, suggested that students do change on the Perry scheme during their time in college. Development occurred differentially, depending on the area (for example, career development versus classroom learning).

One study found that student affairs practitioners who use Perry in their work are more likely to be Perry relativists and Myers-Briggs feeling and perceiving types (Piper & Rodgers, 1992). In addition, Myers-Briggs sensing types were more likely to be dualistic, while intuitive types were more likely to be multiplistic or relativistic. Encouraging judging and thinking types to use theory and foster cognitive growth might be necessary for relativistic thinkers to apply complex theory in practice.

Finally, Torres (2003), studying Latino college students, raised the possibility that the deflections of retreat and escape may result from dissonance felt by students in relation to their ethnic identity development. Her interpretation forms a connection between cognitive development and ethnic identity development.

Applications

Perry's theory has been used extensively in higher education settings. In this section, we first examine the concept of informal assessment. Then the developmental instruction model will receive attention, followed by discussions of classroom and student affairs applications.

Informal Assessment

The time, expense, and expertise required to implement production-oriented assessments typically render them impractical for applied uses in the classroom or student affairs settings. By contrast, recognition-oriented assessments are likely to be viewed as more viable when formal assessment is desired in a context other than academic research. However, the option of informal assessment should also be considered. Interactions with students in the classroom, the residence halls, student organizations, counseling relationships, and judicial conferences are likely to provide clues about how students make meaning. Such impressionistic information can be valuable in attempting to understand students' perspectives and work effectively with the differences manifested. It is not necessary to conduct a formal assessment to form tentative impressions of students' cognitive development and to use Perry's theory as a support in responding. Caution is advised, however, as assessors run the risk of error in conducting informal assessments (King, 1990).

Thus, it is important to use such information tentatively and empathically while being willing to recognize the possibility of mistaken impressions.

The Developmental Instruction Model

The developmental instruction (DI) model (Knefelkamp, 1999) provides an invaluable resource to aid in operationalizing Perry's model. As second-generation theorists, Knefelkamp and Widick can be credited with producing a model for instructional design, usable in the classroom and other instructional settings, that is grounded in an analysis of Perry's discussion of student learner characteristics. Four variables of challenge and support characterize the model: structure, diversity, experiential learning, and personalism. Each can be viewed as existing on a continuum, which symbolizes greater or lesser amounts of the variable.

Structure refers to the framework and direction provided to students. The continuum represents the movement from a high degree to a low degree of structure. Examples of ways in which structure can be provided are placing the course in the context of the curriculum, affording an opportunity to rehearse evaluation tasks, giving detailed explanations of assignments, and using specific examples that reflect students' experiences. Students in the earlier positions in Perry's model will value structure as a support, while students who have advanced further may consider structure limiting and prefer a more open-ended approach that gives them latitude.

Diversity has to do with alternatives and perspectives that are presented and encouraged. Two dimensions characterize diversity: quantity, which refers to amount, and quality, which refers to complexity. Consequently the two-dimensional continuum reflects these two dimensions and ranges from a few simple pieces of information to many highly complex concepts or tasks. Diversity can be introduced through variety in readings, assignments, points of view, and instructional methods.

Experiential learning relates to the concreteness, directness, and involvement contained in learning activities. This continuum ranges from direct involvement to vicarious learning. The purpose of experiential learning is to help students make connections to the subject matter. Methods include case studies, role plays, and exercises that facilitate reflection on and application of the material. Students in the early stages of cognitive development are most in need of this form of support, which can be lacking in the traditional college classroom.

The final variable, *personalism*, reflects the creation of a safe environment where risk taking is encouraged. This continuum moves from high to moderate, since an impersonal learning environment is not considered facilitative for any student. Personalism is manifested in an interactive environment in which enthusiasm for the material, instructor availability, and comprehensive feedback are exhibited. While personalism has value throughout the cognitive development process, it is especially important for students in the early stages.

By drawing on these four challenge and support variables, faculty and student affairs educators can create learning activities and environments that connect with and support students' cognitive development process.

Another useful resource in the design process is the analysis of learner characteristics presented by Knefelkamp and Cornfeld (see Knefelkamp, 1999). For dualistic, multiplistic, and relativistic ways of making meaning, they described each perspective's view of knowledge, the role of the instructor, the role of the student and peers in the learning process, as well as evaluation issues, primary intellectual tasks, and sources of challenge and support.

The DI model could aid the instructor working with Audrey, Jordan, and Jerome. For example, for Audrey, the variable of personalism could be an important support. An instructor who is approachable, available, and encouraging of participation rather than demanding of it may help Audrey move toward confidence in the legitimacy of her own opinion. Also, an assignment that would require her to read two dissenting interpretations of a literary passage, both written by individuals perceived to be experts in literary criticism, can represent enough diversity to challenge her appropriately. Asking Audrey to report to the class on her findings reflects experiential learning. Because she was being asked to report the opinions of others, this task would not represent the potentially overwhelming challenge of reporting her own ideas. Drawing on structure by giving detailed instructions for the verbal report can be an effective way to provide support to Audrey, so she can mediate the challenges inherent in speaking before the class and instructor.

An assignment that would require Jordan and Jerome to work together to develop and present an interpretation of symbolism in literature can have the potential to aid Jordan in gaining an increased understanding of the need to support opinions. Jordan's current multiplistic thinking means that he considers peers as legitimate sources of knowledge. Jerome, because of his relativistic thinking, has the potential to have an impact on Jordan because he is likely to unknowingly manifest the plus-one staging concept. Plus-one staging, a concept described by Knefelkamp et al. (1976) and attributed to Kohlberg (Stonewater, 1988), refers to the idea that individuals typically understand and are attracted to reasoning that is slightly more advanced than their own. Jordan's current dissatisfaction with his instructor could also render Jerome a more viable teacher. This assignment can reinforce Jerome's sense of mastery of the intellectual tasks involved. If the instructor presented the assignment as an opportunity for students to share views and practice supporting arguments, Jerome is likely to see its relevance for further skill development needed in his chosen law career.

Classroom Applications

Examples of and arguments for use of Perry's theory to enhance the teaching and learning process in the classroom are abundant. The typical application consists of using Perry's work to design learning experiences that provide a match or a developmental mismatch, given the cognitive complexity represented among the students in the course. The use of plus-one staging can serve as a means of providing a developmental mismatch and facilitating further cognitive growth. Relativistic reasoning used with a dualistic thinker makes little sense: this is a nondevelopmental mismatch since too much challenge is present. By contrast, multiplistic thinking can have an impact on dualistic thinkers who are approaching a point of transition. Given that Perry's positions represent a continuum, movement is fluid rather than sudden. Progress along the continuum requires an appropriate mix of challenge and support. Use of Perry's theory in the classroom has been advocated in teaching specific content areas such as philosophy (Rapaport, 1984), art and art history (Crawford, 1989), writing (Burnham, 1986; Dinitz & Kiedaisch, 1990; Hays, 1988), music (Brand, 1988; Cutietta, 1990), literary analysis (Plummer, 1988), foreign languages (Jacobus, 1989), home economics (T. Mullis, Martin, Dosser, & Sanders, 1988), library instruction (McNeer, 1991), economics (Thoma, 1993), public speaking (Hayward, 1993), abnormal psychology (Van Hecke, 1987), and chemical engineering (Woods, 1990).

In conducting workshops, we have occasionally encountered faculty members who question the need to learn and use models such as Perry's. Skeptical comments can include statements such as, "It's my job to teach, and it's the student's job to learn." Such challenges are countered with the question, "Do you see yourself teaching subject matter, or do you see yourself teaching students?" Instructors genuinely concerned about effective teaching and learning will find that applying Perry's ideas and the DI model can help them form connections with students and, in turn, help students form connections with the subject matter and the learning process. A compelling position for the integration of Perry's work into the teaching and learning process argues that student development theory as a source of a common language assists faculty and students in hearing each other's voices (Knefelkamp, 1982).

Student Affairs Applications

While most of the literature describing applications of Perry's theory was published in the 1970s and 1980s, it remains relevant to current student affairs practice. In one of the first student affairs applications, Perry's research was used to understand how students make meaning in the context of career counseling

(Knefelkamp & Slepitza, 1976). The shift from an external to an internal locus of control that characterizes forward movement in the Perry scheme is particularly noteworthy in understanding the differing expectations students bring to the career development process. For example, dualistic thinkers are likely to believe that one "right" career exists for them and that the career counselor, as the expert, knows what that is. Multiplistic thinkers are more likely to look to the career counselor to provide a process for decision making. The level of cognitive complexity necessary to make commitments helps to explain the reluctance to commit that some students exhibit. The affective component of choice and commitment highlights the need to grieve for the loss experienced in giving up the roads not taken (Perry, 1978). Rewriting vocational theory to address "not . . . how you choose what you are going to do, but . . . how you give up all the other selves you are not going to be" (p. 271) might have value for students. As an example, an undergraduate career planning course deliberately included challenge and support components deemed appropriate for the level of cognitive complexity characterizing the students enrolled in the course (Touchton, Wertheimer, Cornfeld, & Harrison, 1977).

One valuable application of Perry's theory in residence hall settings provided useful descriptions of the different ways in which students who are dualistic, multiplistic, and relativistic thinkers are likely to view the residence hall staff, discipline, and roommate conflicts (Stonewater, 1988). Use of challenge and support strategies involving diversity, direct experience, and structure can foster students' movement to the next developmental position.

Another study applied Perry's theory to staff supervision, describing characteristics related to knowledge, authority, the learning process, peer acceptance, and evaluation for staff members who are dualistic, multiplistic, and relativistic in their thinking (Ricci, Porterfield, & Piper, 1987). Still other research used Perry's model to inform group advisement responsibilities, such as those performed by student activities professionals (Cosgrove, 1987). Since students do not learn differently in student organizations than in the classroom, Perry's theory is useful to advisors trying to hear students and provide learning environments for them. Areas of application include offering feedback, designing and developing programs, diagnosing and managing group conflict, and adjusting advising styles.

Also of relevance to advisors of groups, Saidla (1990) suggested that Perry's theory can be used to better understand how groups progress through Tuckman's (1965) stages of group development. Saidla explained that the increasing cognitive complexity represented in movement through Perry's scheme can affect individual behavior in each stage of the group development process and is relevant to counseling groups as well as task groups (for example, classroom projects, committees) or student organizations.

Perry's model can also be helpful in counseling and advising situations. For example, Perry's theory supports the process of counseling women (Knefelkamp et al., 1976). Counselors who recognize the differences between the content of women students' beliefs and developmental stages, and apply plus-one staging, assist women's intellectual growth. Applying Perry's theory to the process of academic advising (Hillman & Lewis, 1980) and even financial aid (Coomes, 1992) can enhance the effectiveness of work with students.

Most of these applications have in common the recognition of the value of the Perry scheme in creating an understanding of how students interpret their experiences and how practitioners deal constructively with such differences in designing developmental responses. Movement along Perry's scheme is slow and uneven across different content areas (Mines, 1982), factors that are important to consider when designing student affairs applications. A short, one-time program with a goal of increasing students' cognitive complexity is misdirected because sustained interventions are needed to promote growth. Measurement of impact is most revealing when conducted in a specific content area on the microlevel.

Returning to the scenario involving the union programming board, the approaches that Miriam, the advisor, used to support further cognitive growth will differ for each student. For Lee, Miriam can serve as a role model and teacher. She can help him understand the dualistic thinking present among many of the board members. She can model helpful responses as well as advise Lee about appropriate approaches he can pursue. In interacting with the group during meetings and in other situations, Miriam needs to support Lee in this leadership role. The dualistic thinkers in the group will look to her for answers. One approach she can take is to reinforce Lee's legitimacy as a source of knowledge by asking for his thoughts when questions are raised.

Miriam can also assist the group by encouraging them to brainstorm alternatives, an activity likely to result in the viability of more than one approach to board tasks. Sharing information about successful approaches used at other institutions is another way Miriam can introduce the legitimacy of multiple strategies.

Making contextually appropriate choices is likely to be beyond the ability of most board members, given their dualistic thinking. By contrast, Lee might be ready to develop these skills. One approach to encouraging contextually appropriate thinking is to have the group develop a list of items important to consider in relation to the institution when making programming decisions. Individuals are likely to suggest the factors they consider important. The group as a whole may or may not embrace the entire list, depending on how individuals perceive the "rightness" of the items. The absence of more complex thinkers in the group could pose a dilemma for Miriam. As the advisor, does she honor a trial-and-error approach if important institutional considerations are not endorsed, or does she intervene into the decision-making process to try to minimize the potential for failure? Clearly a group composition that includes more students who are further along in their cognitive development would be advantageous to interject more complex views into the mix of ideas. As this group is currently composed, the aspect of giving priority to students' growth and development can come into conflict with the task-oriented nature of the student organization and any related political dynamics, including the expectations of supervisors.

Critique and Future Directions

Both strengths and weaknesses are evident in this review of Perry's theory. Legitimate concern can be expressed about the lack of inclusiveness of Perry's samples. Clearly, attempting to generalize from a study of primarily traditionally aged white males at a prestigious institution is risky. Using Perry's theory tentatively in relation to women, people of color, and other nondominant groups is advisable. At the same time, Perry's ways of making meaning intuitively make sense, and student affairs practitioners readily recognize these modes in the students with whom they interact and even in themselves.

While Knefelkamp (1999) acknowledged limitations in comparing students of the 1950s and 1960s to more contemporary U.S. college students, she also noted that the assessment procedures developed have made possible the measurement of "tens of thousands of students at all types of American colleges and universities" (p. xiv) and that these results indicate that the theory is useful "with a wide range of diverse students" (p. xvi). At the same time, other studies (for example, Durham, Hays, & Martinez, 1994) found differing patterns of sociocognitive development when comparing Chicano and Anglo students, adding to our understanding of similarities and differences among students.

Another concern can be raised about the inclusion of two constructs (intellectual and ethical development) rather than one in Perry's scheme. To combine both can result in confounding notions, particularly in terms of what is perceived as being "more developed." The positions associated with Perry's commitment process are no longer measuring or portraying increased cognitive complexity (King, 1978). Structurally, positions beyond relativism do not represent cognitive change. Instead, these positions reflect the second construct of "ethical" growth or the development of commitment. Relatedly, evidence to support the existence of the most advanced positions, the "committed" positions, is limited (King, 1978). Whether this is a weakness of the measurement instruments or of the theory itself is uncertain. Another possible explanation is that most research has been conducted on undergraduate college students, a population that seldom demonstrates postcontextual relativistic thinking (Moore, 2002).

The heuristic value of Perry's theory deserves mention. Perry's work has influenced Belenky, Clinchy, Goldberger, and Tarule's research on women (1986), Baxter Magolda's examination of the cognitive development of both women and men in the college setting (1992), and King and Kitchener's development of the reflective judgment model (1994). In addition, Perry's influence is seen in theories of faith development such as that of S. Parks (2000). With little doubt, "Nearly all the existing psychological work on epistemological beliefs can be traced to . . . Perry" (Hofer & Pintrich, 1997, p. 90).

Clearly Perry's work is of great value in gaining a basic understanding of how students make meaning. The concepts of dualism, multiplicity, relativism, and commitment in relativism are easy to grasp and to recognize, at least tentatively, in students. The possibility exists that the Perry scheme may be measuring students' socialization into Western liberal education, perhaps into the dominant vision of the faculty, rather than measuring growth (Moore, 1994). However, even if this is true, the theory is not any less valuable as an aid in understanding college students' learning processes (Moore, 1994). Perry's theory presents three visions of learning that "enrich and broaden" (Moore, 1994, p. 59) the way learning is considered in today's colleges and universities: learning as intellectual and ethical development, learning as transformation, and learning as loss. Knefelkamp (1999) concluded, "Perry's thinking contributes significant and fundamental notions to our understanding of the nature of students and the natures of developmental models" (p. xii).

Equally important is Knefelkamp and Widick's (Knefelkamp, 1999) effort to operationalize Perry's theory to go beyond understanding to action. The impact of how students make meaning can be felt in the classroom, interactions with student affairs staff, and their contacts with each other. In turn, Perry's theory can be used to support practice in any of these arenas.

Finally, concerns can be raised that Perry's theory simply labels students and that efforts to facilitate development are misdirected. For example, after a faculty development workshop in which Perry's work was promoted, a colleague commented, "They want us to put numbers on students." In regard to the issue of labeling, if Perry's descriptions are used empathically rather than judgmentally in relation to students, faculty and student affairs practitioners will not pigeonhole students but rather will attempt to understand how they make meaning and respond appropriately. With this knowledge, faculty and student affairs staff can more effectively contribute to students' learning processes.

Faculty and student affairs practitioners need to recognize that students cannot be pulled against their will through a developmental sequence. They are agents on their own behalf and cannot be forced to grow. At the same time, higher education's mission centers on student growth and development. Many institutional mission statements make reference to character development and producing responsible citizens; enhanced cognitive complexity supports such goals. Perry (1978) argued that the world is a complicated place and it is better to function in it with "a matching set of complicated ideas" (p. 269) rather than simple ideas that do not fit. Educators have an obligation to help students equip themselves with complicated ideas that are both self-supporting and inclusive of others.

Finally, it is important to note that all cognitive structural theories, including Perry's, will benefit from continuing research efforts inclusive of the diversity inherent in today's and tomorrow's campus. Along with understanding student differences, understanding more about different contexts and their impact on students, and vice versa, warrants attention (Moore, 2002).

CHAPTER SIX

MORAL DEVELOPMENT THEORY

María, Cosmo, and Debbie eagerly attended the initial class meeting of the first-year humanities course. Looking for teammates for a class project, they turned to one another to form a working group. María, Cosmo, and Debbie divided the components among them on the consensual topic: Hispanics of the Southwest. María, born and raised in a barrio of the Hispanic community in a nearby city, committed to recruit participants and shoot and narrate a video. Cosmo agreed to edit it. Debbie volunteered to write the narrative for the video and the required ten-page paper. All felt their assignment capitalized on their strengths and agreed to contribute equally to the research, content, and form of the visual and written components of the class project.

In weekly meetings during the first month of class, all three students participated eagerly. Then the group stopped meeting. During the first week of November, the group met again to move the project forward. María was behind in her commitment: she had taped only two interviews and needed four more. Her mother had been diagnosed with cancer, and María spent more time at home than she expected her first semester. Cosmo was getting anxious: he needed the footage in order to edit the video. Most of his semester had been spent getting to know the inside of a fraternity house. Debbie was confused by the lassitude her peers portrayed. She was waiting on both so she could write the narration for the video and conduct the library research needed for a substantive paper. Time was running out. Awkwardness filled the room at the meeting.

María quickly apologized for not completing the videos earlier. She expressed relief that her mother was feeling better since the chemotherapy had been stopped for now, and she felt certain she could finish her part just before Thanksgiving break. Cosmo groaned. Debbie offered support and empathy to María for her difficult situation. María agreed to complete two more interviews by the next Friday, although an additional two were still needed. She was disappointed she had not kept her commitment, but felt that her mother's need for emotional support took precedence over her need to be fully engaged in academic life.

Cosmo was not feeling sympathetic to María's story. He was planning a long-awaited trip home over break and did not want to be forced to work on the class project. He also did not want an F in the course. He was losing motivation but did not want to tell his family he might not succeed academically. He suggested the work group stage a video scene for their project, casting two of his fraternity brothers he believed could pretend they were Hispanic. Cosmo did not see how the professor could know and thought that as long as the project team did not get caught, they could dodge the consequences of his hoax.

At this point in the conversation, Debbie displayed appropriate anger at everyone's previous lethargy and Cosmo's ludicrous suggestion. After respectful disagreement, the discussion moved forward. Debbie recommended the group think constructively about how to meet the fast-approaching deadline. In a hopeful way, she asked the group to demonstrate solidarity, while maintaining each other's dignity and completing the assignment in the time allotted.

◆ ◆ ◆

The work of three leading moral development theorists—Lawrence Kohlberg, James Rest, and Carol Gilligan—has relevance for the dilemma the students in this scenario are facing. Kohlberg's theory focuses on moral reasoning, the cognitive component of moral behavior. Kohlberg saw moral development as representing "the transformations that occur in a person's form or structure of thought" (Kohlberg & Hersh, 1977, p. 54) with regard to what is viewed as right or necessary. His research stirred controversy while adding vastly to our knowledge of moral development.

Extending Kohlberg's notion of moral reasoning, Rest (1986b) stressed that moral behavior consists of three additional components: (1) *moral sensitivity*—interpreting a situation involving the welfare of another as a moral problem and identifying possible alternatives, (2) *moral motivation*—deciding to follow the moral path, and (3) *moral action*—implementing and carrying out a moral plan. Rest asserted that an understanding of moral behavior requires investigating each component and the interactions among components. Rest and his colleagues (1999) built on Kohlberg's theory and sculpted the neo-Kohlbergian approach to moral development.

Gilligan (1977, 1982/1993) was one of the first to recognize and document what she perceived as two different moral orientations: care and justice. In the past thirty years of the twentieth century, her research received praise and stirred controversy in academe and the general public over the moral orientations of women and men. Few studies grounded in Gilligan's theory have been conducted in the twenty-first century.

Some reviews of moral development research verify the relationship between moral judgment and moral action (Blasi, 1980; Lapsley & Narvaez, 2004; Rest, 1986b). Since encouraging moral behavior is an important developmental goal of higher education (Evans, 1987), understanding and facilitating the development of moral reasoning is an important first step.

This chapter presents an overview of moral development focusing on the research of theoreticians Kohlberg, Rest, and Gilligan. We frame each theory within the context of its history prior to describing it. We then highlight research and application of these theories in the college context to show ways student affairs educators can contribute to students' moral development. When appropriate, we examine these interconnected theories together. We conclude the chapter with theory critiques and suggestions for future research.

Kohlberg's Theory of Moral Development

Kohlberg's ideas were a dominant force guiding moral development research for over forty years (Rest, Narvaez, Thoma, & Bebeau, 2000). His theory, based on both psychology (Piaget) and moral philosophy (Rawls), is cognitive-developmental in nature. The empirical tie between moral and cognitive development is strong (Pascarella & Terenzini, 2005); thus, a more advanced intellect is likely to reveal more developed moral reasoning. Focusing on the process of how individuals make moral judgments, not the content of these decisions, Kohlberg saw such judgments as having three qualities: an emphasis on value rather than fact, an effect on a person or persons, and a requirement that action be taken (Colby, Kohlberg, & Kauffman, 1987).

Historical Overview

Placing universalism and individualism at the center of his thinking, Kohlberg was one of the first to study the moral development of adolescents and, later, college students. Building on Piaget's (1932/1977) research, Kohlberg (1958) examined the moral reasoning of adolescent boys and found their reasoning proceeded through invariant and qualitatively different stages. He identified three more advanced stages of thinking and revised the definitions of the three earlier stages that Piaget had identified.

Kohlberg and his colleagues then embarked on a series of studies to validate the theory, establish the content and sequence of moral stages in other cultures (Kohlberg, 1979), and demonstrate the hierarchical arrangement of stages

(Rest, 1969). The first comprehensive statement of Kohlberg's (1969) approach to moral reasoning emerged from these later inquiries. Anomalies in stage sequence found in Kohlberg's initial longitudinal study (Kohlberg & Kramer, 1969) led to a reexamination of the stage definitions and how stages were determined based on data from his Moral Judgment Interview (MJI; Kohlberg, 1979).

Kohlberg's Theory

Kohlberg's (1981) stages represent "holistic structures that develop in an invariant sequence and constitute a hierarchy" (Walker, 1988, p. 38) labeled a "hard" stage model (Kohlberg, Levine, & Hewer, 1984). Three criteria frame Kohlberg's stage theory (Walker, 1988). The *structure criterion* is the most fundamental of the three characteristics. At a given stage, individuals exhibit a similar reasoning pattern regardless of the content or situation. The *sequence criterion* indicates that stages appear in a specific order, regardless of setting or experience. Not all individuals advance through all stages, and not all will move through the stages at the same rate. However, the sequence of stages is fixed. The final stage characteristic is the *hierarchy criterion*. It states that each successive stage is more highly developed than the previous one because it incorporates aspects of all earlier stages. Individuals understand and use all stages of thinking below the stage at which they currently function, never at higher stages.

Prerequisites for Moral Stage Development. Two domains of cognition are related to moral reasoning: more general cognitive structures (Piaget, 1947/1950) and social perspective taking (Kohlberg, 1976). The ability to put oneself in another person's place, called perspective taking, means understanding what someone is thinking (Selman, 1980). Kohlberg (1976) hypothesized that perspective taking mediates between cognitive and moral development. Both cognitive structures and social perspective taking are necessary but not sufficient conditions for moral development. Growth in these two domains can, with no guarantee, create "a state of readiness" for such development (Walker, 1988, p. 53).

Conditions Facilitating Moral Stage Development. Two factors appear to contribute to moral stage development: exposure to higher-stage thinking and disequilibrium (Walker, 1988). Earlier statements focusing on moral education (for example, Kohlberg, 1975) promoted the use of reasoning one stage above the thinking exhibited by the individual (plus-one reasoning) to enhance development. Theoretically, reasoning more advanced than plus-one is incomprehensible and therefore has no impact. One review of moral research, however, concluded that exposure to thinking at any stage higher than that presented by an individual is sufficient to foster development (Walker, 1988).

Disequilibrium, or cognitive conflict, occurs when individuals are faced with situations arousing internal contradictions in their moral reasoning structures or when they find their reasoning is different from that of significant others (Kohlberg, 1976). Exposure to conflict, in both opinions and reasoning, leads to moral development (Walker, 1983, 1988). A study of university students living in residence halls found that conflict resulting from exposure to real-life issues, rather than hypothetical situations, was particularly effective in facilitating moral development (Haan, 1985).

Kohlberg's Stages of Moral Reasoning. At the core of Kohlberg's theory is the claim that moral reasoning develops through a six-stage sequence grouped into three levels (Kohlberg, 1976). Each level represents a different relationship between the self and society's rules and expectations. At level 1 (preconventional), individuals have not yet come to understand societal rules and expectations; their perspective is concrete and individually focused. Level 2 (conventional) is called the "member-of-society" perspective: individuals identify with the rules and expectations of others, especially authorities. Level 3 (postconventional or principled) is labeled the "prior-to-society" perspective. Individuals separate themselves from the rules and expectations of others and base their decisions on self-chosen principles. Each level of Kohlberg's theory has two stages. The moral stages center on judgments of rightness and obligation (Colby et al., 1987) and are defined by Colby, Kohlberg, and Kauffman (1987) and Kohlberg (1976) as follows.

Stage 1: Heteronomous Morality. In the first stage of the preconventional level, what is right is defined as obeying rules to avoid punishment and refraining from physical harm to others and their property. Individuals justify actions based on avoidance of punishment and the superior power of authorities. They do not consider the rights or concerns of others.

Cosmo, the student described in the opening scenario, is likely in stage 1. He believes that as long as he is not caught making a deceptive video, he can move forward with a free conscience. Cosmo assumes the professor will not learn of the group's deception, and therefore none of them will suffer negative consequences of his proposed fraudulent actions. Cosmo firmly believes the group should proceed as he suggests to meet their impending time line. From his view, the team faces no dilemma.

Stage 2: Individualistic, Instrumental Morality. Individuals at the second stage in the preconventional level follow rules if it is in their interest to do so. They understand that other people have needs and interests that may conflict with their own, so right is defined by what is fair, an equal exchange, or an agreement. They maintain a pragmatic perspective, that of ensuring satisfaction of their own needs and wants, while minimizing the possibility of negative consequences to themselves.

In order for Cosmo to move to this next stage, he must have more interest and empathy for María's situation and help jointly reconstruct another equitable, doable plan. Continuing to advocate fraud clearly will not advance Cosmo's moral development.

Stage 3: Interpersonally Normative Morality. At this stage, the first in the conventional level, right is defined as meeting the expectations of those to whom one is close and carrying out appropriate, acceptable social roles (for example, son, friend). Concern centers on maintaining a "good person" image and gaining others' approval. Shared feelings, agreements, and expectations take precedence over individual interests, but a generalized social system perspective does not yet exist.

In the introductory scenario, María could be considered at stage 3. She believes it is more important to carry out her role in the family and meet the expectations of her parents by being with her mother than to fulfill her academic role related to this group project. As María listens to Debbie try to make peace and move the group forward during the November meeting, she gains exposure to the social system perspective and commits again to her academic group.

Stage 4: Social System Morality. In this second conventional stage, individuals view the social system as made up of a consistent set of rules and procedures applying equally to all people. Right is defined as upholding the laws established by society and carrying out the duties agreed on. Individuals behave in a way that maintains the system and fulfills societal obligations.

Stage 5: Human Rights and Social Welfare Morality. In this first principled stage, laws and social systems are evaluated based on the extent to which they promote fundamental human rights and values. The social system is understood as a freely entered social contract to protect members' rights and ensure the welfare of all. Moral obligations and social relationships are based on making, and being able to depend on, agreements.

Debbie could be considered at stage 5 as she tried to hold team members accountable for their commitments to collect enough data for the project. She understood how important it was for the group to deal with their conflict first and move forward gracefully to make their deadline.

Stage 6: Morality of Universalizable, Reversible, and Prescriptive General Ethical Principles. In the second principled stage, morality involves equal consideration of the points of view of all involved in a moral situation. Decisions are based on universal generalizable principles that apply in all situations, for example, the equality of human rights. The process by which a contract is made is viewed as equally important to the fairness of the procedures underlying the agreement.

Kohlberg was unsuccessful in empirically demonstrating the existence of stage 6 (Kohlberg et al., 1984) in his longitudinal studies. He maintained, however, that it is a philosophical and theoretical stage necessary to bring his theory to a logical end point. Kohlberg based his definition of stage 6 on a few individuals, such as Martin Luther King Jr., with formal training in philosophy and a demonstrated commitment to moral leadership. His inability to articulate this abstract moral apex and empirically test it reaped major criticism of his theory.

Rest's Neo-Kohlbergian Approach

Rest (1979b, 1986a) developed an objective measure of moral development, the Defining Issues Test (DIT), and undertook a significant program of research. He and his colleagues (for example, Narvaez, 2005; Rest et al., 2000; Thoma & Rest, 1999) adapted Kohlberg's theory to create a neo-Kohlbergian approach to moral thinking. The core aspects of Rest's moral development stages, however, are borrowed directly from Kohlberg. Rest (1979a) examined two elements in a person's thinking: how expectations about actions (rules) are known and shared and how interests are balanced. He identified the following central concepts for determining moral rights and responsibilities:

> Stage 1: Obedience ("Do what you're told."). . . .
> Stage 2: Instrumental egoism and simple exchange ("Let's make a deal."). . . .
> Stage 3: Interpersonal concordance ("Be considerate, nice, and kind, and you'll get along with people."). . . .
> Stage 4: Law and duty to the social order ("Everyone in society is obligated and protected by the law.") . . .
> Stage 5: Societal consensus ("You are obligated by whatever arrangements are agreed to by due process procedures."). . . .
> Stage 6: Nonarbitrary social cooperation ("How rational and impartial people would organize cooperation is moral.") [pp. 22–23].

Assumptions Underlying Rest's Theory

While grounded in many assumptions of Kohlberg's theory, a neo-Kohlbergian perspective differs in several ways (Rest et al., 2000). Rest viewed the moral development framework more broadly than Kohlberg did. First, he (1979a) questioned whether content and structure can be separated in moral reasoning. Rest focused on the kind of consideration an individual uses in making a decision, noting that both content and structural elements might be included. He did not assume the same considerations would be addressed at each stage. Kohlberg limited stage content to social institutions, whereas Rest fashioned his schemas around "institutions and role systems in society" (Rest et al., 2000, p. 387).

Next, Rest (1979a) rejected Kohlberg's hard stage model and proposed a more complex alternative. Based on his conception of development as a continuous process, he suggested that it is more appropriate to consider the percentage of an individual's reasoning at a particular stage of development rather than whether a person is "in" a particular stage. Rest believed a person may use or show forward movement in several stages at the same time. For instance, 20 percent of a person's thinking might rank at stage 3, interpersonal concordance; 50 percent at stage 4, law and duty to the social order; and 30 percent at stage 5, societal consensus. The percentage of thinking at the principled level (stages 5 and 6) is of most concern to researchers.

Third, Rest (1979a) rejected the idea of step-by-step development through the stages and instead "envision[ed] development as shifting distributions rather than as a staircase" (Rest et al., 2000, p. 384). Thus, he referred to the development process as schemas (soft, more permeable stages) rather than hard stages, as Kohlberg proposed.

Rest's Schemas

Rest and his colleagues (2000) proposed three schemas related to structures in moral reasoning development, examined strictly by administration of the DIT.

Personal Interest Schema. Derived from Kohlberg's stages 2 and 3, the personal interest schema develops in childhood and is no longer paramount by the time one acquires the reading level of a twelve year old. In this schema, individuals consider "what each stakeholder in a moral dilemma has to gain and lose if [he or she] did not have to worry about organizing co-operation on a society-wide basis" (Rest et al., 2000, p. 387). What is morally right in this schema is that which appeals to the investment an individual holds in consequences of the action. Both individual concerns and the concerns of those with whom one has close attachment are prevalent in this schema.

In short, the personal interest schema puts focus on the self and recognizes some awareness of the other in making moral decisions. Cosmo, creator of the deception solution in the scenario at the start of the chapter, demonstrates signs of the personal interest schema. He mostly displays self-interest in completing the project and gave little indication he could empathize with María's family situation.

Maintaining Norms Schema. Derived from Kohlberg's stage 4, the maintaining norms schema is a first attempt to envision societal collaboration. The following elements are common: (1) a desire for "generally accepted norms to govern a collective," (2) a belief that norms apply to all who live in a particular society, (3) a need for "clear, uniform, and categorical" norms or rule of law, (4) a view of norms as reciprocal (if I obey the law, others will too), and (5) "establishment of hierarchical role orders, of chains of command and of authority and duty" (Rest et al., 2000, p. 387). Respect for authority is derived not from the authority's personal attributes but from respect for society. Simply put, morality in this schema is "an act prescribed by the law, is the established way of doing things, or is the established Will of God" (Rest et al., 2000, p. 388). Thus, the neo-Kohlbergian approach focuses on a need for societal norms motivated by duty and embraced in uniform application (Narvaez, 2005).

Postconventional Schema. Derived from Kohlberg's stages 5 and 6, the postconventional schema places moral obligation on communal values such as shared ideals, reciprocity, and critical inspection in the form of logical consistency and debate. Incorporating more developmental complexity, the postconventional schema also is "more advanced in a normative ethical sense" (Narvaez, 2005, p. 122). Four elements are critical to the postconventional schema: "primacy of moral criteria, appeal to an ideal, shareable values and full reciprocity" (Rest et al., 2000, p. 388). A feature of late adolescent development, the postconventional schema is a leading indicator of students' development in college (Narvaez; Pascarella & Terenzini, 2005).

Research on Moral Stage Development

Literally thousands of studies based on Kohlberg's theory of moral development can be found in the literature. Over five hundred studies have been identified using the DIT alone (King & Mayhew, 2002; Rest, 1986b). Early studies by both Kohlberg's and Rest's research teams focused on validation of the theory and measurement issues related to their respective instruments (Rest, 1979a). Both the DIT and the MJI have been found to be valid and reliable instruments. In addition, the basic constructs associated with Kohlberg's theory have been demonstrated (Rest, 1979a, 1986b; Walker, 1988, Walker & Taylor, 1991).

Factors Related to the Development of Moral Judgment

Review of the DIT research indicated that moral development increases with age and educational level, with educational level being the more powerful variable (Rest, 1986b). Pascarella and Terenzini (1991, 2005) summarized the quantitative research investigating moral development in college, including studies that used both the MJI and DIT. Research continues to reveal that individuals attending college show a significant increase in the use of principled reasoning (as measured by the DIT) beyond that related just to maturation.

Becoming more aware of the world in general and one's place in it does more to foster moral development than specific experiences (Rest, 1986b). Pascarella and Terenzini (1991) suggested, for example, that college may foster moral development by providing a variety of social, intellectual, and cultural experiences for students. An introduction to higher-stage thinking provided by upper-class students in residence halls, courses providing conflicting perspectives on various issues, exposure to divergent ideas resulting from living away from home, and interactions with roommates are conditions found to be related to moral development (Whiteley, 1982). The extent to which individuals take advantage of such experiences is the most important factor leading to growth in moral reasoning.

Specific experiences also may foster moral development. For example, undergraduate students charged with minor disciplinary infractions at a private college in the Southeast were surveyed to examine their moral development and the likelihood of perceiving their disciplinary experience as fair and with educational merit (Mullane, 1999). Not surprisingly, students involved in disciplinary matters score lower on moral development than their nonoffender peers (Chassey, 1999; Mullane).

The Impact of Educational Interventions

Specific interventions designed to foster moral reasoning do seem to have some impact on principled thinking, particularly those emphasizing discussion of moral dilemmas or overall psychological development (Rest, 1986b). This effect may be conditional (Pascarella & Terenzini, 1991); that is, such interventions may work for certain students (for example, formal reasoners who seek intellectual stimulation) but not for others (for example, concrete reasoners; Pascarella & Terenzini, 2005). Other areas of student development—black identity development (Moreland & Leach, 2001), spiritual development (Power, 2005), and psychosocial development (Jones & Watt, 2001)—also affect moral development.

Cultural Differences

Research findings related to cultural differences in moral development are mixed. Although there is variation in rate of development and stage to which individuals may progress, the universality of Kohlberg's stage model has been demonstrated in various cultures (Snarey, 1985). For example, persons from urban and middle-class cultures demonstrate higher-stage thinking, while those from rural and working-class cultures do not score above the conventional level. Likely reflecting educational achievement, these differences reflect the multitude of values and socialization processes of these diverse cultures.

Conversely, values and principles on which individuals base moral judgments (that is, their moral orientation) are found to vary in different cultures and contexts. People descended from Asian cultures demonstrate more altruism and concern for the law, while those from Western cultures exhibit more individualistic values (Iwasa, 1992; Ma, 1989; Miller & Bersoff, 1992). Some researchers have suggested that Kohlberg's theory may not adequately reflect the range of worldviews and values found in non-Western cultures (Heubner & Garrod, 1993). Kohlberg's dilemmas, for example, may not be meaningful where concerns such as compassion and karma, rather than justice, are paramount. A study of adolescents from Israel, the United States, Taiwan, Turkey, and the Bahamas indicated that there may be cultural differences related to autonomous versus heteronomous judgment (Logan, Snarey, & Schrader, 1990).

Religious Differences

Adherence to a conservative versus a liberal religious ideology is moderately related to moral development, with those holding a liberal perspective scoring higher (Rest, 1986b). In an attempt to explain this finding, Dirks (1988) suggested that the tenets of evangelical belief systems may foster unquestioning allegiance to a higher authority consistent with conventional rather than postconventional thinking. Offering a similar explanation for their findings, Good and Cartwright (1998) found no relationship between moral development and religious orthodoxy, intense religious training, or passionate religious devotion among students enrolled in state and Christian universities.

Relationship Between Moral Reasoning and Behavior and Attitudes

Moral reasoning has been found to be significantly related to a number of behaviors, including cheating, cooperative behavior, voting preferences, and delinquency (Kohlberg & Candee, 1984; Rest, 1986b). Links are evident between principled moral reasoning and moral behaviors such as social activism, adhering to contracts, and helping those in need (Pacarella & Terenzini, 2005). Moral judgment scores are also related to liberal versus conservative belief systems, attitudes toward authority, and attitudes toward capital punishment (Kohlberg & Candee; Rest, 1986b). College indirectly fosters moral behavior by encouraging the development of moral judgment (Pascarella & Terenzini, 2005).

Relatedly, a qualitative study of five students with HIV/AIDS at a small southeastern university facing a moral quagmire expressed strong Kohlbergian ideas of a "clear appreciation for individual rights and responsibilities, personal standards, justice and reciprocity" (Bower & Collins, 2000, p. 434). Prior to becoming infected with this devastating disease, most student participants indicated lacking these qualities.

Applications of Kohlberg's Theory in Higher Education

Throughout his career, Kohlberg was committed to creating and evaluating practical applications of his theory. His major efforts were directed toward development of moral education programs and "just communities" for schools and prisons (Kohlberg, 1971, 1975; Reimer, 1981). His early moral education efforts focused on providing students with opportunities to discuss hypothetical moral dilemmas in a classroom setting. The goal was to encourage development by creating cognitive conflict through the presentation of higher-stage thinking. Strategies for conducting such discussions are presented in Galbraith and Jones (1976).

Many efforts have been made to adapt Kohlberg's educational programs to college settings (Pascarella & Terenzini, 1991, 2005). These efforts include discussions of moral dilemmas in academic courses (for example, Mustapha & Seybert, 1990), as well as programs that focus on personal development and self-reflection, such as group counseling (for example, Clark & Dobson, 1980).

A review of research (Derryberry & Thoma, 2000) revealed connections between having supportive friends in college, compared to having little or no social network, and growth in moral judgment. Sadly, other empirical studies and literature reviews (for example, Baier & Whipple, 1990; Derryberry & Thoma; Mathiasen, 2003; Tripp, 1997) pinpoint Greek organizations on college campuses as making minuscule gains in fostering members' moral development. One exception is Mathiasen's (2005) qualitative study of fraternity men who received covert messages in written fraternity materials about behaving in a moral manner yet never formally discussed the topic as a group.

Evans (1987) presented a framework for intentionally designing interventions to foster moral development on college campuses. This model considers the target of the intervention (individual or institutional), the type of intervention (planned or responsive), and the intervention approach (implicit or explicit). Policy, programming, and individual approaches are suggested.

Gilligan's Theory of Women's Moral Development

Prior to the popular and scholarly success of Gilligan's *In a Different Voice* (1982/1993), human development theorists for the most part did not see women as a group worthy of psychological study. Freud's (1905/1965) research had begun a snowball "portrayal of women as deviants" (Kuk, 1992, p. 26) and set men as the standard by which to judge what was normal. Using a theory based solely on male subjects, Kohlberg (1981) had concluded that women are unable to reach the same developmental pinnacle as their male counterparts. Kohlberg later included women as subjects in his research but continued to find them "underdeveloped" (Gelwick, 1985, p. 29).

Historical Overview

In 1982, Carol Gilligan published her seminal work, *In a Different Voice*, in which she presented her research findings about the moral development of women and disputed the previous models of human growth that did not fit women's experience. The different voice she delineated is distinguished not by gender but by the themes of care and justice. Gilligan contrasted female and male voices by empirical observation to pinpoint "a distinction between two modes of thought and to focus a problem of interpretation rather than to represent a generalization about either sex" (Gilligan, 1982/1993, p. 2).

Gilligan spent thirty years studying girls and their relationships, and her research has changed the way we view women's moral development. She pushed connections to others, not universalism and individualism, into the forefront of moral reasoning. In recent years, she has expanded her inquiry to better understand relationships and what is good about being human (Gilligan, 2004). Fluidly inspecting the concept of love, she described a transformation from a patriarchal paradigm of tragedy to a connected place of psychological pleasure (Gilligan, 2002).

Gilligan's Theory

Gilligan's and Kohlberg's beliefs about how people make meaning of their world are quite different (Linn, 2001). Kohlberg's (1969) justice orientation focused morality on understanding rights and rules. His six-stage hierarchy reflects a progression from lower-order to higher-order moral thinking in which autonomy is prized and universal justice is the goal (Romer, 1991). In contrast, Gilligan (1986) observed "in women's thinking the lines of a different conception, grounded in different images of relationship and implying a different interpretive framework" (p. 326). The central focus of her care orientation is that relationships with others must carry equal weight with self-care when making moral decisions.

Gilligan (1977, 1982/1993) demonstrated that women identify care and responsibility as their moral compass. Derived from responses of twenty-nine women facing an abortion decision, Gilligan (1977) "formed the basis for describing a developmental sequence that traces progressive differentiations" in how women understand and judge "conflicts between self and others" (p. 183). She proposed that women's moral development proceeds through a sequence of three levels and two transition periods, with each level identifying a more intricate relationship between self and others. Each transition represents the achievement of a more sophisticated understanding between selfishness and responsibility. Below is Gilligan's framework, including its application to the introductory scenario.

Level 1: Orientation to Individual Survival. The individual is self-centered, preoccupied with survival, and unable to distinguish between necessity and desire. For instance, one eighteen-year-old respondent in Gilligan's study affirmed that "there was no right decision" to be made when it came to her abortion because she did not want to be pregnant. Growth and transition have potential to occur only if her dilemma compelled her to seek another moral option.

Relationships do not meet expectations for most of these women, who may intentionally isolate themselves as protection against the pain associated with unfulfilled intimacy. The goal at this level is to fulfill individual desires and needs for the purpose of preserving the self.

First Transition: From Selfishness to Responsibility. The most poignant issue in the first transition is one of attachment and connection to others. The criterion used for judging moral dilemmas shifts from independence and selfishness to connection and responsibility. The conflict between necessity and desire is distinguishable, giving the individual more choices for moral judgment. Questioning their self-concept, individuals consider the opportunity for doing the right thing. Responsibility and care are integrated into patterns of moral decision making.

Level 2: Goodness as Self-Sacrifice. As the individual moves from a self-centered, independent view of the world to one of richer engagement with and reliance on others, survival becomes social acceptance. Seeking the paradox of self-definition and care for others, individuals at this level reflect conventional feminine values. In fact, an individual may give up her own judgment in order to achieve consensus and remain in connection with others. Disequilibrium arises over the issue of hurting others. Although conflict exists, it is typically not voiced in public but rather in private.

María, described in the opening scenario, can be identified in level 2. Although she desires to be independent at college and leave her previously familial-connected life behind, circumstances prompt her to demonstrate goodness as self-sacrifice in taking care of her mother during this frightening time. Basically her mother's need for care and support trumps everything else in her life. María has postponed her self-interest to support her mother in this time of emotional need.

Second Transition: From Goodness to Truth. Individuals question why they continue to put others first at their own expense in the second transition. During this time of doubt, individuals examine their own needs to determine if they can be included within the realm of responsibility. However, the struggle "to reconcile the disparity between hurt and care" (Gilligan, 1977, p. 498) continues. At this time, individuals make moral judgment shifts from deciding in accordance with those around them to deciding by inclusion of their own needs on a par with others.

For the first time, the individual views examination of her needs as truth, not selfishness. As with the first transition, the second one is linked to self-concept. Taking responsibility for decisions comes as a result of being honest with herself. At this potentially vulnerable time, a transitional impasse can catch her between selfishness and responsibility—in other words, torn between survival and morality.

Level 3: The Morality of Nonviolence. The individual raises nonviolence, a moral mandate to avoid hurt, to the overriding principle that governs moral judgment and action. She is elevated to the principle of care by a "transformed understanding of self and a corresponding redefinition of morality" (Gilligan, 1977, p. 504). Through this second transformation, which now includes respect for the self, the dichotomization of selfishness and responsibility disappears. Reconciliation opens the door for the individual to recognize her power to select among competing choices and keep her needs within the mix of moral alternatives.

Research on Gilligan's Theory of Women's Moral Development

Carol Gilligan has spent the better part of her career examining the relational aspects of moral reasoning. With continued modification and extension of her original work, she has shifted from examination of primarily white, privileged women's moral development to a more inclusive examination of women and girls' relationships and how cultural differences influence these relationships and their development (Taylor, Gilligan, & Sullivan, 1995). Others have contributed to a better understanding of the care ethic; however, findings on gender-related moral orientation are not always consistent.

Gender Differences. *In a Different Voice* presented research from three studies: one explored the identity and moral development of college students (Gilligan, 1981), another emphasized how women make decisions about abortion (Gilligan & Belenky, 1980), and a rights and responsibilities study examined different ways of moral thinking and their relationship to different ways of thinking about the self (Gilligan & Murphy, 1979). Each study employed similar qualitative methods to reveal how different voices (that is, care and justice) reflect moral life. Results are framed using interview excerpts accompanied by Gilligan's interpretations (Brabeck, 1983).

Lyons (1983) confirmed Gilligan's hypotheses that women and men frame moral judgment in two different ways—care and justice—and that these two patterns are gender related and may be related to self-concept. Building on Gilligan's and Lyons's research, Stiller and Forrest (1990) examined differences between female and male undergraduate residence hall students at a large midwestern university to determine differences in how they self-identify and morally reason. The results supported Gilligan's and Lyons's theoretical constructs. Although the study was limited by a low return rate, the authors found that women showed more diversity than men in their self-descriptions and in their choice of moral reasoning. Men displayed "almost exclusively" a preference for a separate/objective self and a rights orientation.

Others examined Gilligan's gender differences in moral reasoning with different results. Ford and Lowery (1986) found few significant differences in the two moral orientations used by 202 female and male college students. Females were more consistent in their use of a care orientation, and males were more consistent in their justice orientation. Conducting a cross-cultural study of Mexican American and Anglo college students, another study found that females scored higher than males and Mexican Americans scored higher than Anglos on the care measure (Gump, Baker, & Roll, 2000). Interestingly, in these studies, women scored higher than men in the care orientation and similar to men on their justice scores.

Cultural Differences Between Care and Justice Orientations. Research is not consistent in reporting gender-related care and justice orientations in different cultures. One study reported gender differences in moral orientation and found differences recognizable across cultures (Stimpson, Jensen, & Neff, 1992). A questionnaire administered to female and male college students in Korea, Thailand, the People's

Republic of China, and the United States reveal that in all four countries, women showed a preference for an ethic of care. Similarly, a study conducted to explore the ethics of care and justice, using the Measure of Moral Orientation (MMO; Liddell, 1995) among female nursing students at different educational levels, found a propensity toward the ethics of care (F. Wilson, 2000). Although these female nursing students incorporated both care and ethics reasoning, the more education they possessed, the higher their moral reasoning scores climbed.

In contrast, research on the moral orientation of American Indian college students, using the MMO (Liddell, 1995), sought to objectively identify the moral orientations of students from three tribal colleges: Little Big Horn College, Kootenai College, and Southwest Indian Polytechnic Institute (Arvizu, 1995). The findings contrasted with the literature regarding women's care and justice scores in that female American Indian students score "higher on justice than either American Indian men or the Euro-American men in these studies" (p. 11).

The enigma remains regarding why more women than men from various cultures primarily adhere to the ethic of care. Some theorists speculate that the complex answer is linked to historical social roles of women, their lack of diverse experience, and limited representation in positions of social power (Kohlberg, 1984; Liddell, 1990). Conceivably, the high justice scores of the women college students from Arvizu's (1995) research may support this speculation and reflect tribal values for women and women's positions of power within their tribes, thus setting them apart from other cultures. Moreover, care and justice constructs do not have to be polar opposites (Guido-DiBrito, Noteboom, Nathan, & Fenty, 1996). Perhaps care and justice orientations can, and should be, interdependent constructs of a holistic moral fabric (Gilligan, 1982/1993; Liddell, Halpin, & Halpin, 1992).

Applications of Gilligan's Theory to Student Affairs

For most student affairs professionals, the ethic of care is embedded within their personal value system and translated daily into professional practice. Since the profession is premised on a long history of support and care of students, a long-standing relationship exists between moral reasoning based on care and practice in student affairs (Canon & Brown, 1985).

Delworth and Seeman (1984) highlighted Gilligan's ethic of care and suggested helpful ways of integrating moral theory into student affairs practice. Institutional policies and organizational structures can be examined for their underlying assumptions about care and justice. For example, the close family ties of some ethnic groups, such as Native Americans and Hispanics, may be representative of the ethic of care. If so, should students with a predominant care mode be treated differently from those who follow the dominant justice mode?

Gilligan's ideas concerning ethics of care and justice have been applied to counseling (Enns, 1991; Hotelling & Forrest, 1985), residence life (Picard & Guido-DiBrito, 1993; Porterfield & Pressprich, 1988), career planning (Stonewater, 1989), service-learning (Gorman, Duffy, & Heffernan, 1994), and leadership development (Fried, 1994; Picard & Guido-DiBrito). This literature offers insight into and practical suggestions for student affairs professionals who want to understand how gender differences may influence students' moral development. For example, when care and connection are viewed as a strength in human relationships, "both counselors and clients are less likely to view embeddedness in relationships as dependency, and are more likely to convey that intimacy and closeness may lead to more complete self-definitions in both men and women" (Hotelling & Forrest, p. 210).

In residence life, emphasizing one moral orientation over the other when training residence life staff (Porterfield & Pressprich, 1988) is not recommended. Instead, resident assistants are encouraged to understand the differences between justice and care and seek balance in realizing both orientations. Gilligan's theory also can be applied in the contexts of community development, policy enforcement, dealing with conflict, and team building (Porterfield & Pressprich). For example, conflict between female roommates can best be resolved through sensitive negotiation that benefits both parties, while male roommates might best resolve conflict in a sports contest where rules are followed and a clear winner is decipherable (Picard & Guido-DiBrito, 1993).

Gilligan's theory is also applied in ways that give student leaders and student affairs professionals a better understanding of how care and justice shape their role (Fried, 1994; Komives, 1994; Picard & Guido-DiBrito, 1993). For instance, the justice voice emphasizes power, domination, assertiveness, strength, the ability to remain cool, control of emotions, and independence in leader roles. Yet values characteristic of the care voice, such as involvement, interdependence, concern for relationships and process, sharing information, and developing a web of inclusion (Helgesen, 1995; Rogers, 1989), must also be developed for leader effectiveness in our rapidly changing organizations. Ultimately advisors to student organizations "can serve students best by understanding, modeling, and teaching how the voice of care and the voice of justice influence group members" (Picard & Guido-DiBrito, p. 30.)

Critique and Future Directions

A strong case can be made that attendance in college contributes to students' moral development. To return to the introductory scenario, María, Cosmo, and Debbie are all facing a moral dilemma in the classroom, not unlike other college students across the country. Student affairs educators know that the moral development of students is enhanced by appropriate educational practices across the university, yet they are still uncertain about much of the context of how the forward leap in moral growth occurs.

Recommendations for continuing research on the moral development of college students abound. Almost five hundred studies have been conducted using the DIT alone to examine this population (King & Mayhew, 2002), and most present ideas for further inquiry. As the most widely used instrument to measure moral reasoning, the DIT and its validation of the neo-Kohlbergian approach are by far the most popular way of examining students' moral reasoning. Pascarella and Terenzini (2005) made a strong case for using more sophisticated models with large-scale samples at different types of institutions as the next step in our understanding student's moral development. We suggest other areas that are ripe for discovery.

More research is needed on how cultural ideology is transmitted and if it limits or facilitates moral development (Rest et al., 1999). Outside the classroom, students' exposure to diverse social and intellectual climates is likely to create development in higher-level moral thinking. Teasing out the cultural nuances of all student cultural groups (for example, ethnicity, race, gender, social class, and ability) and their impact on moral development would help as we delve into understanding how to facilitate moral growth. Not only is it important to know how these identity groups develop morally but also how moral development influences and is influenced by other student developmental issues as well (cognitive, psychosocial, and so on). Conversely, involvement with homogeneous peers, such as fraternity and sorority members, is not likely to show an increase in moral development. Continued research on the moral development of students connected with relatively homogeneous groups (for example, sororities, fraternities, athletic teams, academic majors, and individual ethnic cultural centers) can help us better serve all students' moral development needs. We need better and varied theories and models to decipher how moral development might occur differently in different students, what climates on campus we can create to stimulate a diversity of ideas, and how professionals can best assist students from all cultural backgrounds to increase their moral development.

Next, further examination of how gender might influence moral reasoning should begin. Gilligan was the first to open the door to a unique way to examine moral development void of universalism. New gender-related moral models will help us better serve the majority of our students: women. Research, using a variety of epistemological underpinnings and methods, that focuses on the many identities women and men hold and their interface with moral and intellectual reasoning would contribute significantly to our knowledge of this intricate connection.

Many areas cry out for action inquiry given the questions that arise daily requiring appropriate institutional response to moral dilemmas on campus. Policies regulating appropriate student behavior, for maximum student development and not control, need careful examination to understand their impact on student moral action. Few interventions in institutional practice have been established to point the way (Rest et al., 1999).

María, Cosmo, and Debbie will soon make a choice about appropriate moral action for the completion of their class project. The decisions these three students make individually will mirror their current moral development. Student affairs professionals must take advantage of the opportunity to contribute to student growth by creating healthy environments for moral development.

CHAPTER SEVEN

LATER COGNITIVE STRUCTURAL THEORIES

Karly, Susána, and Zack, twenty-two-year-old student leaders who were about to graduate, were discussing their future plans and reminiscing about the past four years. Karly started: "Do you remember when we met in the orientation course our first year? I was sure scared that I would never make it in college. I took that course because I thought the teacher would tell me what to do to succeed in college." Susána added, "That first year I spent a lot of time listening to the seniors on my floor to decide what activities I should get involved in and what courses and instructors to take. I tried to follow their advice, but it was confusing when they all gave me different suggestions." Zack thought back to that time as well: "I talked to a lot of people too, that first year. I sure must have aggravated both of you by taking up so much airtime in that orientation class. I figured that the more I talked about stuff with the instructor and people who were older than me, the more I would find out. Then I began to think that no one knew anything and I argued with everyone in class, usually just for the sake of arguing."

Karly laughed but then shared a painful memory: "I can relate to that. When I found out that the hall director I thought so much of was having an affair with one of the RAs, I decided that no authority figure could be trusted and I had to rely on myself." Karly's reflection led Susána to reveal how she resolved her disillusionment with authorities: "When I figured out that authority figures didn't have all the answers, I took a different approach. I worked really hard to share information with my classmates and to at least find out from my instructors how they wanted me to go about learning. I just didn't understand what they meant when they stressed the importance of supporting my arguments."

At this point, Zack added, "I started to understand the importance of supporting my position when I was on the judicial board my junior year. We would hear so many cases where the situation and circumstances made a difference in our decision. I had to think critically about what it all meant." Karly could relate to Zack's experience: "I was on that board too! I learned that listening to all the different perspectives of the board members really made me think about where I stood and why I felt the way I did." Susána shared how an experience in a class helped her to work through this type of situation: "Everything finally started to click for me when I took that class in Latino studies my junior year. Because we had to do so much self-reflection and share our experiences, I learned that not everyone sees things the same way as I do and that that is okay. We all have a lot to learn from each other that can help us to make more informed decisions."

Zack noted the current relevance of what he had learned: "Now that I am interviewing for positions with different companies, I really see how important it is to consider all the different aspects of a decision and to weigh my options. Each job situation has its pros and cons, and I can certainly see that there is no perfect situation. I have to do what seems best for me at this point in my life." Susána had a different view, however: "That may be easier for you than it is for me. My family is urging me to move back home to Texas, and that's appealing since I would be around more of my Mexican American friends and the culture I love. But I have just been offered a graduate fellowship at a university on the east coast that has an excellent program in community health science—the area I really want to study. I know it would only be for a few years, but it's so far from home." Karly ended their discussion, reflecting, "I know these decisions are tough, but the choices we are making now are only tentative. I have decided to attend grad school in California to study microbiology, but once I finish my degree, I'll have a whole new set of choices to make. Life sure is complex, isn't it?"

◆ ◆ ◆

While Perry's theory of intellectual and ethical development (1968) provided important information about how students' thought processes develop over time, researchers who followed Perry added significant new information about cognitive-structural development. These second-order theorists identified some of the limitations of Perry's research and theory and designed their own studies to examine his findings using more diverse student populations in different contexts. Given that Perry (1968) drew almost exclusively on information from men in presenting his theory, Belenky, Clinchy, Goldberger, and Tarule's study (1986) focusing on women was a logical next step. Also in contrast to Perry (1968), whose participants came from one elite institution, they included participants from various types of colleges, as well as community service agencies.

Baxter Magolda (1992) built on the work of both Perry (1968) and Belenky et al. (1986) by comparing the epistemological development of men and women over time in a longitudinal study. Her research also moved the study of cognitive development to the Midwest: her participants were students at Miami University, a public university in Ohio. Concerned that Perry's (1968) scheme confounded intellectual and ethical development, King and Kitchener (1994) sought to determine if intellectual reasoning itself continued beyond stage 5 in Perry's scheme. They were also invested in developing an instrument that would more objectively measure cognitive development than the interview procedures of Perry (1968), Belenky et al. (1986), and Baxter Magolda (1992). In this chapter, we examine the work of these later cognitive-structural researchers, examining their contributions to theory, research, and educational practice.

Belenky, Clinchy, Goldberger, and Tarule's *Women's Ways of Knowing*

Belenky, Clinchy, Goldberger, and Tarule's research began in the late 1970s when they "became concerned about why women speak so frequently of problems and gaps in their learning and so often doubt their intellectual competence" (1986, p. 4). The authors cited the work of both Gilligan (1982) and Perry (1968) as influential in shaping their own efforts. They undertook a study of lengthy interviews with 135 women, some of whom were students in or recent graduates of academic institutions and some of whom were affiliated with human service agencies that provided support to women in parenting. The results of this research are presented in their compelling book, *Women's Ways of Knowing: The Development of Self, Voice, and Mind* (Belenky et al., 1986). Stanton (1996) maintained that their theory "has contributed importantly to liberating women's voices" (p. 45).

The Theory

In presenting their theory, Belenky et al. (1986) referred to the different ways of knowing as "perspectives" rather than stages. They maintained that more work is needed to determine if "stagelike qualities" (p. 15) characterize these perspectives. They also offered several disclaimers about the five perspectives, acknowledging that they may not be exhaustive, fixed, or universal; that by the nature of their abstractness, they do not portray the unique and complex aspects of a given individual's thought process; that similar categories may be found in men's thinking; and that others might organize the observations in a different way. However, the authors did state with conviction their finding that for women, the development of voice, mind, and self is "intricately intertwined" (p. 18). Goldberger (1996b) noted that since the publication of their initial theory, the authors had become "much more alert to the situational and cultural determinants of knowing and to the relationship between power and knowledge" (p. 8), aspects that were only implicit in their earlier work.

From the study of women of "diverse ages, circumstances, and outlooks" (Belenky et al., 1986, p. 13) emerged five "epistemological perspectives from which women know and view the world" (p. 15): silence, received knowledge, subjective knowledge, procedural knowledge, and constructed knowledge. Clinchy (2002) later indicated that the authors came to prefer *knowing* rather than *knowledge* in naming these perspectives.

The perspective of *silence* is characterized as mindless, voiceless, and obedient. In this perspective, women find themselves subject to the whims of external authority. Though rare as a current way of knowing among the women interviewed, the perspective of silence was described in retrospect by some interviewees found through the social service agencies. They were among "the youngest and most socially, economically, and educationally deprived" (pp. 23–24) of the women. Goldberger (1996b) indicated that Belenky later suggested using the term *silenced* to reflect the coercion inherent in the position.

Listening to the voices of others is a predominant trait of *received knowing*. A lack of self-confidence is evident in the belief that one is capable of receiving and reproducing knowledge imparted by external authorities but not of creating knowledge on one's own. In the scenario at the start of this chapter, Karly's desire for the teacher of her orientation class to tell her how to succeed in college suggests that she began college as a received knower.

With the perspective of *subjective knowing*, the pendulum swings, and truth is now seen as residing in the self, a shift that is particularly significant for women (Belenky et al., 1986). A frequently cited contributing element is a failed male authority figure, such as a father who commits incest or an abusive husband. Inherent in the process of subjective knowing for women is a quest for the self, often including the element of "walking away from the past" (p. 76). Karly's shock and disillusionment at her hall director's behavior appears to have moved her into subjective knowing, where she felt she could rely only on herself.

The perspective of *procedural knowing* involves learning and applying objective procedures for taking in and conveying knowledge. Two approaches are evident. The first, separate knowing, uses impersonal procedures for establishing truth. It is characterized by critical thinking; listening to reason, though an adversarial tone is implicit; and separating oneself from the issue (Belenky et al., 1986). Separate knowing often involves doubting. The second approach, connected knowing, is grounded in empathy and care. Truth emerges in the context of personal experience rather than being derived from authorities. Connected knowing often involves believing. Both Karly and Susána appear to have moved on to procedural knowing after their orientation class, Karly as a result of her experiences on the judicial board and Susána during her Latino studies class. Strongly influenced by their peers, they appear to prefer connected knowing. Susána, in particular, is influenced by her personal experiences and empathy for her classmates.

Constructed knowing involves the integration of subjective and objective knowledge, with both feeling and thought present. Belenky et al. (1986) asserted that "it is in the process of sorting out the pieces of the self and of searching for a unique and authentic voice" (p. 137) that women discover the two basic insights of constructivist thought: all knowledge is constructed, and the knower is an intimate part of what is known. The authors characterized constructivists as able to listen to others without losing the ability to hear their own voices. Karly appears to be using constructed knowing, at least tentatively: she has independently decided on a future direction in microbiology while acknowledging that all decisions are open to reconsideration.

Research

Belenky et al.'s research (1986) spawned further research investigating the relationship of cognitive development to other factors and also factors influencing development. As an example of the former, Weinstock and Bond (2000) found a relationship between college women's epistemological perspectives and their conceptions of conflicts with close friends. With regard to the latter, Sax, Bryant, and Harper's (2005) study of student-faculty interaction found support for the importance of validation, support, and sense of connectedness for women's intellectual and personal development.

Based on empirical results, Boatwright, Egidio, and the Kalamazoo College Women's Leadership Research Team (2003) recommended designing teaching strategies for connected knowers to promote the leadership aspirations of college women. Similarly, Cabrera et al. (2002) found that collaborative learning had a positive impact on college students' development. Finally, Chapman (1993) found traditional approaches to teaching mathematics to be biased toward separate knowers; she called for more attention to the connected learning perspective.

Applications

Belenky et al.'s (1986) theory has relevance to both classroom teaching and student affairs. Belenky et al. (1986) concluded their book by advocating "connected teaching" (p. 214) to help women nurture their own voices. This teaching approach emphasizes connection rather than separation, understanding and acceptance rather than assessment, and collaboration rather than debate; respecting and supporting firsthand experience as a source of knowledge; and encouraging student-initiated work patterns rather than imposing arbitrary requirements.

Belenky et al. (1986) suggested the role of teacher as midwife—one who assists students "in giving birth to their own ideas" (p. 217). Class discussions that encourage the expression of diverse opinions represent a means of implementing connected teaching. Connected teachers demonstrate belief and trust in their students' thinking. Ten years later, Stanton (1996) reported that voice and connection were the most widely adapted of the concepts presented by Belenky et al. (1986). The teaching methods that Susána's Latino studies teacher used suggest that the teacher created a connected classroom in which students could grow and critically consider their positions.

Ortman (1993) used principles of connected teaching in an undergraduate learning theory course conducted at a women's college. She included *Women's Ways of Knowing* as a text and used a discussion format, case studies, group presentations, a cooperative evaluation system, and a final paper rather than an exam. Other classroom applications of connected teaching are discussed by Crowley (1989) and Nesbit (2000). Ursuline College, in an institution-wide application, introduced a core curriculum, the Ursuline Studies Program, based on the work of Belenky and her colleagues, which emphasized group discussions and collaborative learning in a freshman seminar (Gose, 1995).

Focusing on student affairs applications, Forrest (1988) and Fried (1988) asserted that development can be supported in any area of student affairs if practitioners emphasize issues of connection when working with women. One way to do so is to adopt the midwife role and help students produce their own ideas. Clearly the experiences that Karly had on the judicial board facilitated her move from a subjective to a procedural knower.

Love and Guthrie (1999) pointed out the importance of recognizing that some women may need to reject their past; that the sexual harassment, abuse, and violence present in many women's lives have an impact on cognitive development; and that some women may experience a disconnect from authority. They also advocated nurturing both separate and connected knowing and their integration. Student affairs professionals should also be aware of Belenky's (1996) and Belenky, Bond, and Weinstock's (1997) call for teaching developmentally oriented leadership. Finally, Egan (1996) cited the work of Belenky et al. (1986) as a resource for providing effective mentoring to women.

Baxter Magolda's Model of Epistemological Reflection

Informed by both her own research and the work of Belenky et al. (1986), Marcia Baxter Magolda was struck by both the similarities and differences that emerged from Perry's (1968) work on men and Belenky et al.'s work on women. Kitchener and King's (1981, 1990) research involving both men and women also influenced Baxter Magolda because of the differing conception of the nature of knowledge that emerged. However, because gender was not at the core of Kitchener and King's research, Baxter Magolda believed she had identified an important gap in the existing research: the need to address gender in a study of cognitive development that would include both men and women. From this realization came the longitudinal study that served as the basis for the most extensive treatment of Baxter Magolda's early work, *Knowing and Reasoning in College: Gender-Related Patterns in Students' Intellectual Development* (1992). We discuss Baxter Magolda's continuing longitudinal research and its theoretical implications in Chapter Ten.

The Theory

Baxter Magolda (1992) presented the results of a five-year longitudinal study of 101 students at Miami University. This volume reflects interviews begun in 1986, during the students' first year, and continuing annually through their first year after graduation. In the random sample of entering students, 51 were women and 50 were men, 3 were from underrepresented groups, and 70 students participated for the entire five-year period, including 2 of the underrepresented students (Baxter Magolda, 2001).

Baxter Magolda (1992) identified six guiding assumptions underlying her model: (1) ways of knowing and patterns within them are socially constructed; (2) ways of knowing can best be examined using naturalistic inquiry; (3) students' use of reasoning patterns is fluid; (4) patterns are related to but not dictated by gender; (5) student stories are context bound; and (6) ways of knowing appear as "patterns," a term suggested by Frye (1990) to "make sense of experience but stop short of characterizing it in static and generalizable ways" (p. 17).

The epistemological reflection model that resulted from Baxter Magolda's (1992) research contains four stages, with gender-related patterns reflected in the first three. Baxter Magolda (2004a) defined epistemological reflection as "assumptions about the nature, limits, and certainty of knowledge" (p. 31). In the first stage, *absolute knowing*, knowledge is viewed as certain. Instructors are seen as authorities with the answers, and the purpose of evaluation is to reproduce what one has learned so that the instructor can determine its accuracy. Two patterns, *receiving knowledge* and *mastering knowledge*, were found within this stage.

Receiving knowledge, a more private approach, was used by more women, and mastering knowledge, a more public approach, was used by more men. Receiving knowledge involves "minimal interaction with instructors, an emphasis on comfort in the learning environment, relationships with peers, and ample opportunities to demonstrate knowledge" (Baxter Magolda, 1992, p. 82). Although receiving knowers have more independent perspectives, these views, perhaps because of socialization, are not expressed. Karly, in the scenario at the start of the chapter, may be a receiving knower; however, she does not seem to acknowledge the value of her own perspective. Mastering knowledge is characterized by a verbal approach to learning, a willingness to be critical of instructors, and an expectation that interactions with peers and instructors will lead to the mastery of knowledge. Mastery knowers rely on logic and demonstrate a competitive style. Zack's approach to learning by talking in his orientation class suggests that he was probably a mastery knower at that point.

The second stage, *transitional knowing*, involves an acceptance that some knowledge is uncertain." A realization that authorities are not all-knowing is a turning point from absolute knowing. Transitional knowers expect instructors to go beyond merely supplying information to facilitate an understanding and application of knowledge. A utilitarian perspective motivates students, with investment in learning determined by perceived future usefulness of the information. Evaluation that focuses on understanding is endorsed over that which deals only with acquisition. All three students in the opening scenario appear to have moved into transitional knowing early in their college careers as it became evident to them that authority figures did not have all the answers and were sometimes unreliable. *Interpersonal knowing* and *impersonal knowing* are the two patterns within this stage.

Interpersonal knowing, used more by women, is characterized by interaction with peers to gather and share ideas, valuing of rapport with instructors to facilitate self-expression, a preference for evaluation geared to individual differences, and resolving uncertainty by employing personal judgment. Susána's cooperative style in class during her first few years in college is indicative of interpersonal knowing. Impersonal knowing, used more by men, involves a desire to be forced to think, a preference for debate as a vehicle for sharing views, an endorsement of evaluation that is fair and practical, and the use of logic and research to resolve uncertainty. Zack's argumentative approach at the end of his orientation class indicates a move into impersonal knowing.

In *independent knowing*, the third stage, knowledge is viewed as mostly uncertain. The preferred role of the instructor shifts to providing the context for knowledge exploration. Students value instructors who promote independent thinking and the exchange of opinions. Independent knowers believe evaluation should reward their thinking and not penalize views that diverge from those presented by instructors or in textbooks. This stage includes *interindividual* and *individual* patterns.

Interindividual knowing, used more by women, places value on one's own ideas as well as the ideas of others. Susána demonstrates interindividual knowing as she struggles to consider her own needs and desires, as well as those of her family, in deciding whether to move back to Texas once she graduates or to accept a fellowship on the east coast. Individual knowing, used more by men, also values interchange with peers and instructors, but more attention is given to the individual's own thinking. Baxter Magolda (1992) noted that sometimes listening to others has an element of struggle for individual knowers. As Zack considers various job options during his senior year, he appears to be exhibiting individual knowing; in weighing his options, he relies on himself to make a decision. Although interindividual knowers lean toward connection and individual learners toward separation, Baxter Magolda (1992) emphasized that they are moving closer together.

Contextual knowing, the final stage, reflects a convergence of previous gender-related patterns. Demonstrated only rarely among undergraduate students, contextual knowing involves the belief that the legitimacy of knowledge claims is determined contextually. While the individual still constructs a point of view, the perspective now requires supporting evidence. Karly may be approaching this stage in the final days of her senior year as she understands that her decision to pursue microbiology is only tentative and that she will have additional decisions to make after graduate school that will be influenced by factors of which she is not yet aware. The role of the instructor now involves the creation of a learning environment that endorses contextual applications of knowledge, discussions that include evaluation of perspectives, and opportunities for mutual critiques by students and instructor. Evaluation that measures competence contextually and permits the mutual involvement of instructor and student is endorsed. Because only 12 percent of the postgraduation interviews contained indications of contextual knowing, Baxter Magolda (1992) considered the data to be insufficient to explore gender patterns. Baxter Magolda (1995) later indicated, in the postcollege phase of her study, that the relational and impersonal patterns of knowing that characterized the preceding stages become integrated in the stage of contextual knowing.

Baxter Magolda (1992) emphasized that she found more similarities than differences in men's and women's ways of knowing. In addition, she stressed that variability exists among members of a particular gender. Therefore, patterns are related to, but not dictated by, gender.

In regard to the evolution of the ways of knowing, Baxter Magolda (1992) found that absolute knowing was most prevalent in the first year of college (68 percent). Among sophomores, 53 percent were transitional knowers. Transitional knowing was also the most prevalent mode among juniors (83 percent) and seniors (80 percent). Independent knowing was most represented in the year following graduation (57 percent).

Quite appropriately, Baxter Magolda (1992) discussed the limitations of her findings for diverse student populations. She noted that her model is based on information supplied by traditionally aged students, typically from white, middle-class families, and living in a student culture where high involvement, academic focus, and tradition are valued. She cautioned that her model may not apply to other young adults.

Baxter Magolda (1992) maintained that three underlying story lines "form the foundation of parallels" (p. 191) between her study participants and other young adults: the development and emergence of voice, changing relationships with authority, and evolving relationships with peers. She also noted that dominance-subordination and socialization can affect voice and relationships. For example, students who are placed in subordinate roles are less likely to express their own voices. In addition, gender-related socialization can encourage the expression of voice for men and the suppression of voice for women. As another example of the effect of these two variables, African American children, who are subordinated in U.S. society, may be taught that their voices are not worth expressing. Baxter Magolda (1992) cautioned, however, that "true transferability can only be judged through dialogue with students" (p. 192).

Baxter Magolda (2004a) referred to her experience in conducting her longitudinal research as a "transformational journey" (p. 31) for both herself and her study participants. She also stated, "My narrow focus on gender led me to overlook the importance of race" (p. 33). In addition, she indicated that she had abandoned her assumption of development as a gradual process that naturally unfolds in a logical sequence. Instead, she now regards existing developmental models as "descriptions of how contexts have shaped young adults" (p. 39).

Research

Baxter Magolda's ongoing longitudinal study led to an evolution of her theory away from an examination of cognitive development exclusively to a more comprehensive focus on how cognitive, affective, and interpersonal development in combination lead to self-authorship. (We discuss this later work in Chapter Ten.) While most researchers have built on Baxter Magolda's self-authorship model, two noteworthy studies based on her epistemological reflection model provide insight into the experiences of diverse student populations. First, Day Shaw (2001) found Baxter Magolda's model to be applicable to black and Latino students. She noted that family and community are especially important in students' decision making throughout their cognitive development process. Second, Morse (2002) found a significant relationship between black racial identity development and epistemological development in college (that is, more complex ways of viewing one's race were linked with more complex ways of knowing).

Applications

Baxter Magolda (1992) devoted the second half of her book to higher education applications. Using the term *educational practice* to include both curricular and cocurricular applications, she discussed implications for academic and student affairs, identifying three major influential factors. First, validating students as knowers is essential to encouraging the development of their voices. Baxter Magolda (1992) found this concept to be consistent with other professional literature, including Belenky et al.'s concept of the teacher as midwife (1986). Second, Baxter Magolda (1992) found that "situating learning in the students' own experience legitimizes their knowledge as a foundation for constructing new knowledge" (p. 378). This concept is important because it provides a link between the world of the student and academic knowledge, and it allows students to be legitimate sources of knowledge. Baxter Magolda (1992) also observed that cocurricular involvements emphasize the student's experience, legitimizing it as a basis for constructing new knowledge. Baxter Magolda's third finding is that "defining learning as jointly constructed meaning empowers students to see themselves as constructing knowledge" (1992, p. 380).

The three factors influencing learning that Baxter Magolda (1992) highlighted are evident in Susána's experience in her Latino studies class. Her instructor clearly validated the students' own learning, centered learning in the students' experiences, and encouraged them to jointly construct meaning by having them relate their experiences and share their perspectives with each other. This setting enabled Susána to move from transitional knowing to independent knowing as she became more secure in her beliefs and able to express them.

Baxter Magolda (1992) cautioned, however, that some issues within higher education can impede implementation of her findings. She discussed six concerns: the need for educators to have a better understanding of diverse student populations, the need for educators to understand the impact of context on learning, the importance of studying specific students in specific contexts, the need for an encouraging environmental structure to enable voice to develop, the perceived conflict between promoting the development of voice and learning content, and the need to address broader educational issues, such as the separation of academic and student affairs, if efforts to promote the development of voice are to succeed.

Baxter Magolda's (1992) suggestions for improving educational practice have at their core the realization that learning is a relational activity and that education is often not relational. She provided many specifics to improve the learning environment, addressing the dimensions of professors' attitudes, professor-student interaction, teaching strategies, classroom structure, evaluation, and knowledge discrepancies.

To develop students' voices, Baxter Magolda (1992) suggested applying Kegan's (1982) concepts of confirmation, contradiction, and continuity in the environment. Confirmation of students' abilities is necessary, as is contradiction of the image of authority (for example, faculty or student affairs staff) as omnipotent. Continuity refers to the need to persevere with students as they work toward constructing knowledge. Baxter Magolda (1992) synthesized implications for student affairs practitioners in the following categories: peer relationships, student organizations, living arrangements, internship or employment experiences, educational advising, general campus environment, and international experiences. She sustained her efforts to promote application of her theory in numerous publications, providing multiple resources to aid in creating facilitative contexts both within and outside the classroom (Baxter Magolda, 1998a, 1999b, 2000, 2003; Baxter Magolda & King, 2004). (See Chapter Ten for further discussion.)

King and Kitchener's Reflective Judgment Model

In their 1994 book, *Developing Reflective Judgment*, King and Kitchener cited several influences in the development of their model: the individuals whom they interviewed about epistemic assumptions, their interest in understanding the process of and rationale for the evolution of different forms of reasoning, and their efforts to identify the differences between their own and other approaches. Dewey's ideas (1933, 1938/1960) related to reflective thinking and Piaget's assumptions (1956/1973) about stage-related development were influential in King and Kitchener's work, as was Kohlberg's (1969) work on cognitive and moral development. Their model also builds on previous theories developed by Perry (1968); Harvey, Hunt, and Schroder (1961); and Loevinger (1976). Central to King and Kitchener's model is the observation that "people's assumptions about what and how something can be known provide a lens that shapes how individuals frame a problem and how they justify their beliefs about it in the face of uncertainty" (1994, p. xvi).

The Theory

In the development of the reflective judgment model (RJM), King and Kitchener (1994) adopted Dewey's (1933, 1938/1960) notion that reflective judgments are made to bring closure to situations that can be characterized as uncertain. Reflective thinking, then, focuses on epistemological assumptions and ill-structured problems. Ill-structured problems have no certain answers, in contrast to well-structured problems, for which single correct answers can be identified. King and

Kitchener (1994) cited hunger, overpopulation, pollution, and inflation as examples of ill-structured problems.

Each of the seven stages characterizing the RJM represents a distinct set of assumptions about knowledge and the process of acquiring knowledge, and each set of assumptions results in a different strategy for solving ill-structured problems. Increasingly advanced stages signify increasing complexity. The seven stages may be clustered into prereflective thinking (stages 1, 2, and 3), quasi-reflective thinking (stages 4 and 5), and reflective thinking (stages 6 and 7).

Prereflective thinkers do not acknowledge or possibly even realize that knowledge is uncertain. Consequently they do not recognize the existence of real problems that lack an absolute, correct answer, nor do they use evidence in reasoning toward a conclusion. The three students in the opening scenario appear to have started college as prereflective thinkers, in that they sought out the "right answers" about how to succeed in college. *Quasi-reflective thinkers* realize that ill-structured problems exist and that knowledge claims about these problems include uncertainty. Consequently, quasi-reflective thinkers can identify some issues as being genuinely problematic. At the same time, although they use evidence, they have difficulty drawing reasoned conclusions and justifying their beliefs. Susána's difficulties in supporting her positions in class a bit later in her college career are illustrative of quasi-reflective thinking. *Reflective thinkers* maintain that knowledge is actively constructed, and claims of knowledge must be viewed in relation to the context in which they were generated. Reflective thinkers maintain that judgments must be based on relevant data, and conclusions should be open to reevaluation.

By the end of their college careers, Zack, Susána, and Karly all appear to have become reflective thinkers. They understand the importance of considering data and context as they make their postcollege decisions. Karly, in particular, understands that the decisions made at this point in their lives will necessarily be reconsidered many times as they encounter new situations. Stages within the RJM are presented as qualitatively different and as building on the skills of previous stages while also providing the groundwork for the increasing complexity of subsequent stages. King and Kitchener (2002) noted that individuals typically display "reasoning that is characteristic of more than one stage at a time" (p. 45). Therefore, individuals should not be portrayed as in a single stage. King and Kitchener (1994) also noted that some interviews with graduate students and college faculty suggested epistemological positions beyond relativism.

Research

King and Kitchener (1994) developed the Reflective Judgment Interview (RJI) to gather information about individuals' assumptions about knowledge and how it is obtained as proposed in the reflective judgment model. The RJI consists of four ill-structured problems and a standard set of follow-up questions. Problems are read by a trained interviewer, and interviewees are asked to explain and justify their own points of view on the issues. King and Kitchener (1994) indicated that more than seventeen hundred people, representing varied student and nonstudent subgroups, had participated in RJIs at that time.

On the basis of a longitudinal study conducted from 1977 to 1987 involving eighty participants at a wide range of ages, King and Kitchener (1994) concluded that "the development of reflective thinking as measured by the RJI evolves slowly and steadily over time among individuals engaged in educational programs" (p. 132). Although they also identified a strong linear relationship between age and RJM stage in this study, they cautioned that the role of age should not be overstated because participants were actively involved in educational pursuits during the study's time period and demonstrated a high level of scholastic aptitude.

Gender differences were also found in the longitudinal study; however, fourteen later studies investigating gender differences produced mixed results (King & Kitchener, 1994). They did indicate that men and women may develop at different rates and that these rates may be different between cohorts of women and men. Data also suggested that differences in timing may characterize developmental changes in men and women. King and Kitchener (2002) cited later studies by Jensen and Guthrie, King, and Palmer that found no gender differences.

King and Kitchener (1994) were careful to note that the sample for their longitudinal study was restricted to white adolescents and adults from the Upper Midwest with the students involved possessing unusually high academic aptitude scores. At the same time, they concluded that there was strong evidence to support the development of reflective thinking and that the observed changes in reasoning were consistent with the RJM. Numerous longitudinal and cross-sectional studies conducted later provided additional evidence that reflective judgment develops slowly and steadily over time and that increases in scores are not based on practice or selective participation (King & Kitchener, 1994). Limited research indicates that the RJM may be applicable in other cultures (King & Kitchener, 1994) and to African American and Latino populations (King & Kitchener, 2002).

Guthrie, King, and Palmer (as cited in King & Kitchener, 2002) found a relationship between reflective judgment and tolerance for diversity, with participants reasoning at quasi-reflective and reflective thinking levels tending to hold tolerant views regarding race and sexual orientation. Finally, Li and Lal (2005) found that service-learning increased students' reflective thinking in multicultural education.

Applications

King and Kitchener (1994) asserted, "Teaching students to engage in reflective thinking and to make reflective judgments about vexing problems is a central goal of higher education" (p. 222). They offered eleven suggestions to support the efforts of both faculty and student affairs practitioners:

1. "Show respect for students as people regardless of the developmental level(s) they may be exhibiting" (p. 231).
2. Understand that students differ in their assumptions about knowledge and that responding to individual differences is important for educators working both within and outside the classroom.
3. Introduce students to ill-structured problems in their areas of study.
4. "Create multiple opportunities for students to examine different points of view on a topic" (p. 237) so that they can practice paying attention to the evidence used and emphasized in various perspectives.
5. "Create opportunities and provide encouragement for students to make judgments and explain what they believe" (p. 238).
6. "Informally assess students' assumptions about knowledge" (p. 240).
7. "Acknowledge that students work within a developmental range of stages, and target expectations and goals accordingly" (p. 242).
8. "Provide both challenges and supports in interactions with students" (p. 244).
9. "Recognize that challenges and supports can be grounded emotionally as well as cognitively" (p. 246).
10. Be aware of which skills are needed for various activities and learning tasks.
11. Nurture a climate that encourages thoughtful analysis of issues the campus is facing.

To aid in facilitating processes supportive of promoting reflective thinking, King and Kitchener (1994) provided exhibits for stages 2 through 6 that describe assumptions of each stage, sample instructional goals, examples of difficult tasks for individuals at this stage, sample assignments (challenges) to stimulate development, and supportive activities that would complement the challenges.

Love and Guthrie (1999) identified several ill-structured problems that exist in student affairs work. These include questions such as: "Which student leader would make the most effective organizational president? Which candidates should be chosen as resident assistants? How should funding be allocated among student organizations?" (p. 50). They recommended that student affairs professionals give students feedback on their responses to such questions, provide input regarding evaluating arguments, and model advanced reasoning about such complex issues. King and Shuford (1996) suggested an approach to promoting reflective thinking in multicultural education by using challenge and support in the classroom, and Spaulding and Wilson (2002) advocated using reflective journal writing to promote reflective thinking.

Critique and Future Directions

The theories presented in this chapter and the research supporting them certainly advanced the knowledge base regarding the cognitive development of students. Important gender-related differences in how students interpret their experiences were outlined by Belenky et al. (1986) and Baxter Magolda (1992). King and Kitchener (1994) identified the existence of more complex thought processes in response to ill-structured problems. The longitudinal and programmatic research conducted by Baxter Magolda and King and Kitchener provided a strong foundation for the theories they introduced. King and Kitchener's Reflective Judgment Interview has also provided a useful means for assessing reasoning processes. All of these researchers expanded the student population base to which cognitive development theory is applicable.

Clearly a strength of the work of these three authors is the attention each has paid to the practical applications of their work in the classroom and in student affairs. Sensitivity to the need for differing instructional methods to facilitate the development of at least some women is a reasonable implication for practice that can be derived from Belenky et al.'s (1986) work. Student affairs practitioners can also benefit from using *Women's Ways of Knowing* as a framework for listening and responding in their interactions with women. Love and Guthrie (1999) pointed out that the theory was important because "it focused on women, social classes, and differences that are significant in our society" (p. 17).

Bock (1999) noted the value of the patterns Baxter Magolda (1992) identified in creating effective learning environments both in and out of the classroom. Certainly the substantial attention Baxter Magolda devoted to implications for educational practice is notable. As McEwen (1994) pointed out, however, this discussion would have been strengthened by devoting some attention to gender patterns. Baxter Magolda (1992) provided suggestions for only the four ways of knowing in general.

King and Kitchener's (1994) discussion of how educational practice, within the classroom and beyond, can foster reflective judgment is important in promoting theory-to-practice connections. At least a fundamental understanding of prereflective, quasi-reflective, and reflective thinking, along with a grasp of how to challenge and support students demonstrating each process, would have value for educators.

Despite these advances, critiques of this body of work can certainly be found, particularly with regard to methodological issues. Examining Belenky et al.'s (1986) study, King (1987) pointed out the lack of detail in the discussion of procedures used and the presentation of the data. Also, Evans (1996) noted that because the study was not longitudinal, the question remains as to whether the perspectives found are sequential and hierarchical. Goldberger (1996a) has indicated that the four authors are not in complete agreement that the ways of knowing represent a developmental sequence.

With regard to Baxter Magolda's work, McEwen (1994) expressed concern that while her stages bear similarities to Perry's positions (1968), and her patterns reflect Belenky et al.'s concepts of separate and connected knowing (1986), these earlier works are not acknowledged as fully as they could be. In addition, the restriction of Baxter Magolda's focus to students from Miami University and the minimal representation of students of color even within that sample pose limitations in terms of traditional generalizability to other groups of students. Baxter Magolda (1992) acknowledged this problem and also provided cautions and suggestions regarding efforts to determine the validity of the information for other students. She suggested (2002a), however, that it is probable, based on the presence of a connected pattern across ways of knowing, that the epistemological reflection model reflects the experiences of students of color, who have been described as "connected" (p. 101). She also called for more research to determine the applicability of her model to diverse populations (2002a, 2004a).

Liddell (1995), in reviewing King and Kitchener's 1994 book, noted that the issue of gender differences in relation to the RJM merits further attention. While more research has been done, continuing efforts to examine potential differences in regard to reflective judgment based on gender, race, and ethnicity would be valuable. King and Kitchener (2002) have endorsed this idea.

In addition to the methodological issues noted, it is important to acknowledge that cognitive development cannot be separated from affective and interpersonal development. It is understandable that early researchers considered these aspects of development separately to gain a better understanding of each process. However, as Baxter Magolda herself recognized in her later work (2001), it is now time to examine the interaction of these components of development and how, together, they affect the college experiences of students.

CHAPTER EIGHT

KOLB'S THEORY OF EXPERIENTIAL LEARNING

April is a first-generation African American college student who has recently begun her first semester of school. Because she would like to major in business, she enrolled in a prerequisite math course. April is concerned about her performance on the course's first two quizzes. Her grades of C and D reflect both her difficulty in understanding the mathematical concepts and the bell-shaped curve that her professor uses to grade test results. April considers her professor to be very intelligent, but she also finds her rather intimidating. The professor has told the class that her job is to teach and their job is to learn. Relatedly, April is scared to ask for help. She is afraid her professor will think that she is not very smart or is just not working hard enough.

By contrast, April really enjoys her introductory sociology class. Her instructor usually comes to class early and walks through the lecture hall talking to students. He also frequently encourages students to come to talk with him if they have questions. April also likes the course assignments. For example, she enjoys reviewing the newspaper to find examples of articles that demonstrate concepts presented in the professor's lectures, and she is looking forward to the field trip planned later in the semester. The members of her small group have already met a few times to begin work on the research project they will conduct and present to the class. April feels she is learning much from this opportunity to discuss the course material with other students, and she is enjoying getting to know these students better.

◆ ◆ ◆

Alex, a junior and a philosophy major, has recently become a resident assistant. He was disappointed in fall training. As a person who likes to think about issues and strategies and consider the possibilities, he found his training to consist almost entirely of nuts and bolts. He spent most of the time listening to others tell him what to do. He wanted to understand more about the rationales for the policies he was responsible for enforcing. When he went to speak with his supervisor about his concerns, the hall director told him that he did not know what the reasons were for some of the policies, but what was really important, anyway, was to get the job done. Alex feels increasingly frustrated with his job. The one bright spot for him is his programming responsibilities, which have given him the opportunity to use his creativity and form meaningful connections with the residents on his floor. The hall director has heard that Alex is doing a good job with programming, but he finds Alex's constant challenging of policies and procedures to be a "pain in the butt." He has been wondering if perhaps Alex was not such a good choice for a resident assistant position.

◆ ◆ ◆

Given the diversity of today's student population, understanding and working with student differences effectively, in the classroom and beyond, is important. David Kolb's theory of experiential learning provides information that can be useful to gain insight into, and respond effectively to, style differences, thereby enhancing educators' ability to provide appropriate challenge and support in the various environments in which student learning and development can occur.

Although Kolb's theory is probably best known for its learning style component, it is conceptually more broadly based as a developmental theory. In fact, Kolb (1984) described his theory as one of adult development. In this chapter, we provide a historical overview of the development of Kolb's theory, outline its major components, discuss research based on Kolb's work, and review applications of the theory that have appeared in the literature. We close with a critique and suggestions for future directions.

Historical Overview

Kolb became interested in academic cultures and the "best" fit for individual students while he was a faculty member at Massachusetts Institute of Technology (Kolb, 1981). This interest and related observations evolved into his theory of experiential learning, which he presented most fully in *Experiential Learning: Experience as the Source of Learning and Development* (1984).

Kolb (1984) chose the term *experiential learning* to link his ideas to their roots in the work of Dewey (1958), Lewin (1951), and Piaget (1971) and to underscore the role of experience in the learning process. He also acknowledged the influences of the "therapeutic psychologies" on the development of his theory (Kolb, 1984, p. 15), especially the work of Jung (1960); the "radical educators" (p. 16) Freire (1973, 1974) and Illich (1972); brain research, particularly left brain–right brain discoveries; and the philosophical literature concerned with metaphysics and epistemology. Clearly Kolb's theory has a strong intellectual foundation and a sophistication that transcends the simplicity of the learning style component if the latter is considered in isolation. Kolb's 1984 book is intricately crafted and conceptually complex. Student affairs practitioners and faculty wishing to gain a more basic understanding of Kolb's theory may find "Learning Styles and Disciplinary Differences," a chapter in *The Modern American College* (Kolb, 1981), more helpful for an initial exposure to the author's own words.

The Theory

Kolb's work focused on a discussion of learning styles, the relationship between learning and development, and implications of learning styles for higher education.

Learning Styles

Kolb (1984) defined learning as "the process whereby knowledge is created through the transformation of experience" (p. 38). Kolb (1981, 1985) regarded learning as a four-stage cycle consisting of *concrete experience* (CE), a feeling dimension; *reflective observation* (RO), a watching dimension; *abstract conceptualization* (AC), a thinking dimension; and *active experimentation* (AE), a doing dimension. Although he used the term *stage* in describing the learning cycle, he was referring to a series of steps rather than developmental stages. Each step provides a foundation for the succeeding one. Concrete experience (CE) forms the basis of observation and reflection (RO). These observations, in turn, are used to develop one's ideas, including generalizations and theories (AC). From this development of ideas, new implications for action can be discerned (AE). To be effective, learners need the abilities represented by each of these four components of the learning cycle. Learners involve themselves fully and without bias in learning experiences (CE), observe and reflect on these experiences from multiple perspectives (RO), formulate concepts that integrate their observations into theories (AC), and put such theories to use in making decisions and solving problems (AE). (See Figure 8.1.)

Mastery of all four components, or adaptive modes, is complicated by Kolb's additional observation that learning requires abilities that are polar opposites.

FIGURE 8.1. KOLB'S CYCLE OF LEARNING

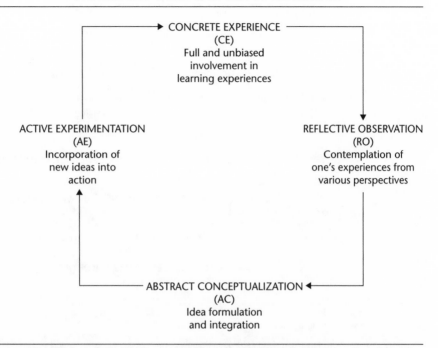

Source: Adapted from Kolb (1981) and Smith and Kolb (1986). © Experience-Based Learning Systems, Inc. 1981, revised 1985. Developed by David A. Kolb. Reproduced with permission from McBer and Company, Inc., 116 Huntington Avenue, Boston, MA 02116.

CE and AC compose a *prehending* or grasping dimension—how one takes in information. AE and RO form a *transforming* or processing dimension—how one makes information meaningful. Learners must therefore choose which learning abilities (CE or AC, AE or RO) they will use each time they encounter a learning situation.

Based on individual preferences for one of the polar opposites in each of these processes, four individual learning styles emerge (see Figure 8.2). Kolb (1981) defined a learning style as a habitual way of responding to a learning environment and offered detailed descriptions of each of the styles (Kolb, 1994). Briefly, *convergers* (AC and AE) are inclined to be good problem solvers and decision makers. They are effective at applying ideas to practical situations. They excel at tasks involving identification of the single best answer when there is only one (for example, conventional intelligence tests) and display deductive reasoning. Convergers would rather deal with technical tasks and problems than social and interpersonal concerns. *Divergers* (CE and RO), in many ways the opposite of convergers, tend to

FIGURE 8.2. KOLB'S LEARNING STYLE MODEL

*CONCRETE EXPERIENCE
(feeling)

Accommodator	**Diverger**
• Action oriented, at ease with people, trial and error problem solving	• People and feeling oriented
• Strengths in carrying out plans, openness to new experiences, and adapting to change	• Strengths in imaginative ability, awareness of meaning and values, and generating and analyzing alternatives

ACTIVE EXPERIMENTATION (AE) ——— ****REFLECTIVE OBSERVATION (RO)
(doing)   (watching)

Converger	**Assimilator**
• Prefers technical tasks over social/interpersonal settings	• Emphasizes ideas rather than people
• Strengths in problem solving, decision making, and practical application	• Strengths in inductive reasoning, creating theoretical models, and integrating observations

*ABSTRACT CONCEPTUALIZATION (AC)
(thinking)

---

*Grasping dimension.
**Processing dimension.

Source: Adapted from Kolb (1984, 1985) and Forney (1994). Kolb, David A. *Experiential Learning: Experience as the Source of Learning and Development,* © 1984, pp. 78–79. Adapted with the permission of Pearson Education, Inc., Upper Saddle River, NJ.

be imaginative and aware of meaning and values. They can view situations from many perspectives and excel at coming up with alternatives and implications. Divergers display an interest in people and are feeling oriented. *Assimilators* (AC and RO) excel at inductive reasoning and display an ability to create theories by integrating disparate ideas. They value ideas for their logical soundness more than for their practical value. Assimilators prefer to focus on ideas and concepts more so than people. Finally, *accommodators* (CE and AE) are doers. They implement plans, complete tasks, and are open to new experiences. Accommodators are willing to take risks and tend to be good at adapting to changing circumstances. They prefer a trial-and-error approach to problem solving over using analytical ability. Accommodators are comfortable with people.

In 1999, Kolb changed the style names to *converging, diverging, assimilating,* and *accommodating* to address his concern that individuals might consider their style to be a static entity. He wanted to convey that learning styles can change (Kolb, 2000).

Learning styles do contain weaknesses (Smith & Kolb, 1986). Individuals with a converging style are prone to premature decision making and solving the wrong problem; those with a diverging style can be indecisive and overwhelmed by alternatives; people with an assimilating style may be impractical; and those who prefer an accommodating style can get caught up in activity for activity's sake. The lack of adequate skills represented by each of the four styles can result in further limitations for the individual. Too little convergence can result in a lack of focus and a failure to test out ideas; too little divergence can result in an absence of both creativity and the ability to recognize opportunities and problems; too little assimilation can result in an unsystematic approach and an inability to learn from mistakes; and too little accommodation can result in impractical plans and a failure to complete work on time. Because Kolb (1984) essentially viewed learning as a person-environment transaction, individuals need flexibility in style in order to have the competencies needed to be contextually adaptive.

Learning styles are influenced by heredity, life experiences, and the demands of the immediate environment. In the environment, Kolb (1984) especially acknowledged the influence of one's undergraduate major, career choice, current job, and current task within the job. Learning styles are therefore viewed not as fixed traits but as current states of mind or of operating that have some long-term stability (Kolb, 2000). Kolb and Kolb (2005b) used the term *dynamic state*.

The four original learning styles can be expanded to nine styles (Kolb & Kolb, 2005b). Citing the work of Hunt (1987), Kolb and Kolb (2005b) discussed the styles of Northerner, Easterner, Southerner, and Westerner. These labels reflect where the styles fall on the learning style grid created by the intersecting lines of the grasping dimension (CE-AC) and the processing dimension (AE-RO). Northerners emphasize CE (feeling) and balance AE and RO. Easterners emphasize RO (reflection) and balance CE and AC. Southerners emphasize AC (thinking) and balance AE and RO. Westerners emphasize AE (action) and balance CE and AC. In addition, citing Mainemelis, Boyatzis, and Kolb (2002), Kolb and Kolb (2005b) discussed a "balancing" learning style that integrates all four learning modes, CE, RO, AC, and AE, and falls at the center of the learning style grid. This potential for nine styles reinforces the idea that learning styles are not "categorical entities" but "continuous positions" (Kolb & Kolb, 2005b, p. 198) on the CE-AC and AE-RO dimensions.

Learning and Development

Viewing learning as a central life task, Kolb (1981) believed that "how one learns becomes a major determinant of the course of personal development" (p. 248). This developmental process is a significant component of Kolb's theory. Development consists of three stages: (1) *acquisition*, in which basic learning

abilities and cognitive structures develop and which occurs from birth until adolescence; (2) *specialization*, in which social, educational, and organizational socialization forces shape the development of a particular learning style and which
extends through formal schooling or career training and the early experiences of
adulthood, both work related and personal; and (3) *integration*, in which the person
emphasizes the expression of his or her nondominant adaptive modes (learning
cycle components) or learning styles in work and personal contexts, and that is
likely to begin at midcareer, though much individual variability characterizes the
timing of this transition (Kolb, 1981, 1984).

Kolb (1981, 1984) posited that development through these stages is characterized by increasing complexity and relativism in dealing with the world and
by increased integration of the dialectical conflicts between concrete experience
(CE) and abstract conceptualization (AC) and between active experimentation
(AE) and reflective observation (RO). Each of these four adaptive modes or
learning cycle components is associated with a major facet of personal growth.
Development in the adaptive mode results in increased complexity in the specified facet. More specifically, development in the mode of concrete experience
increases one's affective complexity (feelings), development in reflective observation increases perceptual complexity (observations), development in abstract
conceptualization increases symbolic complexity (thoughts), and development in
active experimentation increases behavioral complexity (actions). Kolb considered
integrative development, or the ability to adapt by using nondominant modes, to
be important not only for personal fulfillment but also for cultural development.
Mainemalis et al. (2002) found some support for the idea that adaptive flexibility
in regard to learning style is a predictor of complex and highly integrated levels
of adult development.

Higher Education and Learning Styles

Kolb's theory has many implications for higher education environments, both in
and beyond the classroom. His discussion of disciplinary cultures is especially relevant to academic programs, including graduate preparation in student affairs. Kolb
(1981) observed that different academic disciplines are inclined to impose different
kinds of learning demands, as is evidenced in "the variations among their primary
tasks, technologies and products, criteria for academic excellence and productivity,
teaching methods, research methods, and methods for recording and portraying
knowledge" (p. 233). In addition, disciplines demonstrate sociocultural variation,
including differences in faculty and student demographics, personality and apti-
tudes, values, and group norms. From Kolb's perspective, therefore, education in
an academic discipline represents for the individual student a process of socialization

to the norms in that field. These norms are related not only to "truth"—what it is, how it is communicated and used, and so forth—but also to personal styles, attitudes, and social relationships. Kolb (1981) added that over time, an "increasingly impermeable and homogeneous disciplinary culture" (p. 234) is produced, along with "a specialized student orientation to learning" (p. 234). That is, norms within an academic discipline can become exclusionary, and one learning style may be favored.

In relation to the four learning styles, Kolb (1981) indicated, for example, that students with converging styles are often found in the physical sciences and engineering, those with diverging styles in the humanities and liberal arts, individuals with the assimilating style in the basic sciences and mathematics, and people with the accommodating style in practical fields such as business. Kolb (1981) also reported a positive relationship between student-discipline learning style congruence and academic performance, social adaptation, and career commitment; students whose style matched the dominant style were more successful in these areas.

If academic disciplines are to be accessible to students with diverse learning styles, efforts must be made to provide varied methods of instruction and evaluation. Such methods, to offer both support to aid students in connecting with subject matter and challenge to assist them in developing the nondominant aspects of their preferred styles so that they can achieve the level of flexibility needed to respond to differing environmental demands, need to include activities that match as well as mismatch each of the four learning styles. Smith and Kolb (1986) provided examples of preferred learning situations for those with strengths in each of the four components of the learning cycle. For example, those with strengths in concrete experience (CE) would value methods such as games, role plays, peer discussion and feedback, and personalized counseling; students strong in reflective observation (RO) would value lectures, observing, seeing different perspectives, and tests of their knowledge; people who favor abstract conceptualization (AC) would value theory readings, studying alone, and well-organized presentations of ideas; and those inclined toward active experimentation (AE) would value opportunities to practice with feedback, small group discussions, and individualized learning activities. Because individuals prefer either CE or AC and either RO or AE, activities associated with the nonpreferred component can be considered challenging. Each of the four components also represents a different preference for the role of the instructor, with CE seeing the teacher as a coach-helper, RO as a guide-taskmaster, AC as a communicator of information, and AE as a role model for how to do something.

Returning to the introductory scenario, April's positive regard for small group work, finding actual examples of concepts in the newspaper, and a proposed field trip seems to indicate a preference for CE and AE components—a hands-on orientation. By contrast, she is having difficulty with the abstraction of mathematical concepts, an AC component. Her valuing of the instructor who seems to take on the coach-helper role provides another indication that she probably has an accommodating learning style.

Alex's situation as an RA exemplifies how learning style information is relevant to learning environments outside the classroom. Alex's interest in exploring ideas and rationales and his contrasting disregard for "nuts and bolts" implies some valuing of both AC and RO dimensions. At the same time, his interest in having meaningful relations with his residents and his valuing of creativity represent a connection to CE aspects. Although he articulates preferences of a thinker, Alex is also a doer in relation to his programming role, reflecting the AE aspect. Thus, while Alex is likely to prefer a diverging style, his profile illustrates that all four dimensions are likely to be present to some degree in any individual.

Research

Much of the research on experiential learning theory has focused on the learning style concept, particularly assessment of learning styles of individuals (Kolb & Kolb, 2005b). Kolb et al. (2001) stressed the need for more research focused on integrated learning and experiential learning constructs. Kolb maintains and periodically updates a bibliography of research on experiential learning theory and the Learning Style Inventory (available at www.learningfromexperience.com), which reflects a wide array of research based on his work. Most of these studies have been conducted in the field of education, with several done in other cultures (Kolb et al., 2001). Yamazaki (2005) examined the relationship between cultural differences and learning styles and concluded that a country's culture is an important factor in understanding learning styles.

In relation to higher education, the learning styles of several student populations have been researched. These populations include nursing students, accounting students, adult learners, and community college students. Forney (1994) studied a national sample of master's students in student affairs and found the most frequently represented learning style to be that of accommodator and the least frequently represented to be that of assimilator. One implication is the need for program faculty to underscore the relationship between the academic and experiential aspects of the field since the traditional classroom experience (lecturing and note taking) is inconsistent with the accommodators' more active preferred modes of learning. Another implication is the need to encourage those with an accommodating style to slow down and reflect on what they are doing.

Holley and Jenkins (1993), in a study of accounting students, found some relationships between learning style preferences and performance on different test question formats (for example, multiple choice, open ended). These findings suggest a potential for different forms of measurement to favor certain learning styles, which could have implications for how learning is measured across academic disciplines.

Exploring linkages among different aspects of development among first-year students, Baxter Magolda (1989) found that different cognitive structures were accompanied by different learning orientations on the grasping dimension of Kolb's theory; those exhibiting position 2 thinking in Perry's scheme preferred abstract conceptualization, while those in position 3 preferred concrete experience. She also noted that the percentage of men and women preferring each of Kolb's learning styles was almost equal.

In regard to stability versus change in learning styles, Pinto, Geiger, and Boyle (1994) found mixed support for the idea that students' learning styles are likely to change over their college careers. The converging style was the least stable over time in a study of student affairs graduate students (Salter, Evans, & Forney, 2006).

Although a substantial body of research based on Kolb's work exists, most of it addresses the classroom or populations outside higher education. Learning style research conducted within traditional student affairs functional areas represents a potentially valuable and comparatively unexplored direction.

Applications

The most direct application of Kolb's theory may be in the use of the information on learning styles as an empathy and design tool for responding to the increasing diversity represented among the student population as educators seek to provide both challenge and support in learning experiences in the classroom and beyond and in the modes used to deliver services to students. In most groups, it is likely that all learning styles are present. Therefore, particularly in relation to group-based application activities based on Kolb's theory, it is not necessary to know the learning style composition. Using techniques that reflect all four learning cycle components has the potential to form some connection for each participant, as well as to introduce some challenging elements for each. Applications of Kolb's theory have focused on formal and informal methods of assessing learning styles, uses in student affairs settings, and classroom applications.

Learning Style Assessment

The Kolb Learning Style Inventory, Version 3.1 (Kolb, 2005; Kolb & Kolb, 2005a) is the current version of Kolb's assessment instrument. (Regarding previous versions, see Kolb, 1976, 1985, 1993, 1999.) The instrument is most useful for "self-exploration, self-understanding, and self-development" (Smith & Kolb, 1986, p. 8). Kolb (2000) also claimed "cross-cultural applicability" (p. 11).

Two other assessment techniques related to Kolb's theory are also available: the Adaptive Style Inventory (ASI, Boyatzis & Kolb, 1993a) and the Learning Skills Profile (LSP, Boyatzis & Kolb, 1993b). The ASI is designed to assess an individual's ability to adapt to different learning situations. The LSP provides individuals with a means of assessing their personal learning skills and comparing them to job-related skills.

An informal assessment of learning styles can be done by presenting individuals with written descriptions of the styles and having them select the one that seems most like them or having them underline aspects in any of the descriptions that sound like them. Informal assessments may also be done by asking probing questions about how individuals have approached learning tasks (for example, learning to drive, finding one's way around campus) and by asking individuals to select from a list those learning tasks that seem to help them learn.

Student Affairs Applications

Kolb's theory has been used as a foundation for interventions in orientation, academic advising, counseling, career development, and self-exploration, as well as staff development. In orientation, learning style information has been used to aid students in understanding their preferences and strengths in learning and to stimulate the development of new ways of learning needed for classroom success (Claxton & Murrell, 1987). Claxton and Murrell noted similar advantages in using learning style information in both academic advising and study skills assistance. Chickering and Schlossberg (2001), in their guide to succeeding in college, included activities designed to help students analyze courses and interview faculty to determine how different learning style components may be addressed. Kolb's theory has also been used as the foundation for a series of online study skills workshops addressing time management, textbook reading, memory and concentration, and overall academic performance (Lynch & Kogan, 2004).

Sugarman (1985) found links between Kolb's cycle of learning and the implementation of the counseling process. The symbols for the learning style components have been inserted to show the connection. Sugarman stated, "As a counselor, I aspire to approach each client in an open minded way and attempt to involve myself fully and without bias in the experience (CE). . . . I must, however, remain separate from the experience so that I can observe and reflect on it (RO). . . . On the basis of these observations, I develop a theory or hypothesis of how best to intervene next (AC). . . . Finally, I test out my hypothesis by intervening or not intervening (AE)" (p. 267). Sugarman also noted that counselors can use Kolb's model to reflect on their counseling styles. For example, counselors with a converging style can consider whether they tend to be too dominant in the relationship, while those with a diverging style may find that they are often hesitant to share their own views.

Atkinson and Murrell (1988) demonstrated how Kolb's model can be applied to career counseling to aid in providing a variety of techniques to help individuals learn more about both themselves and the world of work. Self-exploration activities can be designed to correspond to each of the four learning style components. For example, talking with a counselor about personal values, needs, and interests corresponds to CE; identifying patterns in previous life and career decisions corresponds to RO; completing and receiving interpretations of career inventories corresponds to AC; and interviewing individuals in careers of interest corresponds to AE. In relation to the world of work, shadowing represents CE, a group-based discussion of personal reactions to careers explored reflects RO, researching careers through print and other resources corresponds to AC, and role playing as a preparation for job interviews represents AE.

Forney (1991a, 1991b) explained how career centers can use learning style information as a support in providing services that are responsive to a diverse student clientele. Diversifying the modes by which a given service is made available represents one alternative. Students who prefer the assimilating style would probably value printed information, information shared by a staff member, and the opportunity to raise questions about their own ideas. Students with an accommodating style are likely to appreciate personal contact, the chance to focus on nuts and bolts, and receiving feedback on their own drafts. Those who prefer the converging style may prefer accessing information on the computer and discussing the best approach for their own résumés, including receiving answers to specific questions. Students with a diverging style would generally appreciate the opportunity to read and reflect on printed materials and follow up with personal contact, individually or in a group.

Meaningful activities for each learning style can also be incorporated into a single instructional session, such as a job hunting workshop (Forney, 1991b). For example, a staff member's providing information on available resources, suggested job hunting strategies, and considerations to think about, along with an opportunity for students to receive feedback on some of their own ideas and plans, supports students with an assimilating style. A group discussion on putting the information to use in relation to personal situations, with accompanying attention to individual questions and concerns, supports those with an accommodating style by giving attention to action, students who prefer a converging style by addressing questions about individual situations, and those who prefer a diverging style through group involvement. Actually showing participants the career library or computerized job vacancy services and how to use them could connect with the accommodating students' desire for hands-on experience and the converging students' inquisitiveness. Diverging students and assimilating students are likely to value knowing that they can schedule a follow-up appointment after they have had more time to think about the job hunting process.

Although these examples focus primarily on career development, any educational function (for example, programming, counseling, and teaching or training) that student affairs departments perform can be rendered more or less accessible to a diverse student clientele by nature of the degree to which learning styles are addressed. For example, Rainey and Kolb (1995) advocated the use of experiential learning theory in diversity education. Moreover, Lea and Leibowitz (1986) maintained that programmers need all four learning style components in order to be effective in different stages of the program development process.

The process of helping students (and others) better understand the concept of learning styles can be aided by Hagberg and Leider's (1982) work. Producing their own adaptation of Kolb's theory, they discuss four styles—imaginative (diverging), logical (assimilating), practical (converging), and enthusiastic (accommodating)—and provide helpful examples in language that is less academic than Kolb's own work. Their material can aid in translating Kolb's important ideas to students in general, such as entering students, as well as to students who occupy leadership positions in which helping others learn is a primary responsibility—for example, peer educators and sorority and fraternity scholarship chairs.

Staff training and supervision represents another area where learning style information can be useful. Alex, the RA, experienced a mismatch in his work setting: lots of nuts and bolts, but no opportunity to explore the more abstract rationales behind the policies and expectations. Providing work environments that both challenge and support a diverse group of individuals is important for attracting and retaining a diverse staff.

Kolb's theory can supply insight into staff dynamics, with implications for both the individual and the organization. For example, individuals with different learning styles display different strengths in relation to their adaptive competencies (Kolb, 1984). Those with a diverging style are likely to excel in valuing skills (for example, being sensitive to people and listening with an open mind); those with an assimilating style in thinking skills (for example, organizing information and conceptualizing); individuals who prefer a converging style in deciding skills (for example, choosing the best solutions and experimenting with new ideas); and individuals who prefer an accommodating style in acting skills (for example, committing to objectives and influencing and leading others). In turn, these differing strengths can result in differing contributions that can be made to the process of problem solving. Relatedly, because of differing strengths in adaptive competencies, some tasks may be best carried out by a homogeneous group (for example, brainstorming by individuals with a diverging style) and some by a heterogeneous group (for example, complex problem solving). It may also be helpful to consider adaptive competencies when making work assignments to individuals. Drawing on individual strengths as well as helping individuals develop nondominant aspects could be considerations. Kolb's theory can be used to support team effectiveness, especially the aspect of team learning, by drawing on learning style information (Kayes, Kayes, & Kolb, 2005a, 2005b; Kayes, Kayes, Kolb, & Kolb, 2004).

Finally, Abbey, Hunt, and Weiser (1985) maintained that supervisors function best when they can draw on all four learning or adaptive modes. In short, learning style information can provide a systematic way of looking at and dealing with individual differences among staff.

Classroom Applications

Smith and Kolb's (1986) efforts to provide examples of learning activities that correspond to the four components of the learning cycle are complemented by the work of Murrell and Claxton (1987), Svinicki and Dixon (1987), and Anderson and Adams (1992). All of these authors provided helpful resources for designing classroom environments and activities that can both challenge and support students with different learning styles. Anderson and Adams also addressed the potential impact of ethnicity and gender on learning styles. For example, African American, Hispanic, and Native American students generally "demonstrate competence in social interactions and peer cooperation, performance, visual perception, symbolic expression, and narrative and therefore are less comfortable with tasks that require independence, competition, or verbal skills" (p. 21). Regarding gender, one example of potential learning style differences is the tendency of white females and African American, Native American, and Hispanic males and females to prefer a relational rather than an analytical style.

Use of Kolb's theory has been advocated in a variety of academic contexts, such as foreign languages (Castro & Peck, 2005), political science (Brock & Cameron, 1999), engineering (Sharp, 2006), and technology subjects (Sutliff & Baldwin, 2001). In addition, Enns (1993) found Kolb's model to be useful in integrating separate and connected knowing (Belenky, Clinchy, Goldberger, & Tarule, 1986; see Chapter Seven).

As noted earlier, academic disciplines tend to have a dominant learning style evidenced among student majors (Kolb, 1981), and career choice is related to learning style (Smith & Kolb, 1986). Although types should not become stereotypes (Kolb, 1981), these tendencies have implications for students whose learning styles deviate from the norm for that discipline or for their chosen career. For example, learning may be more difficult, and feelings of not fitting in may exist.

Instructional methods that take into account learning style differences can serve as an equalizer for students, as can helping students understand their own learning styles and potential supports and challenges.

Considering again the scenario of April, one might conclude that she should switch her major from business to sociology to avoid her difficulties with math. This possible solution maintains the status quo in the math classroom, an environment that is likely to unintentionally, yet systematically, exclude other students like April. However, the classroom could be modified to include the availability of tutorial assistance, encouragement of study groups, and efforts to render the abstract concepts more concrete through the use of examples and simplified language. A more personalized style on the part of the instructor could also be implemented. If such modifications were made, April might become successful, especially since no indication is given that she is not "bright enough" to master math. Even if the environment remained unchanged, if she understood more about her own learning style, April could potentially seek outside supports, such as tutorial assistance or a study group, on her own.

Kolb and Kolb (2005b, 2006) discussed the concept of learning spaces, which can be viewed as looking at Kolb's theory through an environmental lens. Kolb and Kolb's (2005b) intent was to enhance understanding of the interaction between students' learning styles and institutional learning environments. The physical and social environment and quality of relationships as experienced by each student creates a "cheers/jeers experiential continuum" (Kolb & Kolb, 2005b, p. 207). At one end, students feel respected by faculty and colleagues and believe that their experience is taken seriously. At the other end, learners feel "alienated, alone, unrecognized, and devalued" (p. 207). Parallels can be drawn to Schlossberg's concepts of marginality and mattering (see Chapter Two). Kolb and Kolb (2005b) also maintained, "To fully develop the whole person requires an educational culture that promotes diverse learning spaces and locomotion among them" (p. 205).

Another recent focus for Kolb is conversational learning, "a process whereby learners construct meaning and transform experiences into knowledge through conversations" (Kolb, Baker, & Jensen, 2002, p. 51). Conversation is viewed as "a process of interpreting and understanding human experience" (Baker, Jensen, & Kolb, 2002, p. 1). Kolb believes that individuals move through the learning cycle as they "construct meaning from their experiences in conversation" (Kolb et al., 2002, p. 52).

Critique and Future Directions

While most of the early debate concerning Kolb's theory was centered around the psychometric properties of the LSI, "critique . . . focused on the theory . . . examining the intellectual origins and underlying assumptions . . . from what might be called a postmodern perspective, where the theory is seen as individualistic, cognitivist, and technological" (Kolb et al., 2001, p. 240). Focusing on management education, Kayes (2002) believed much of the criticism to be a product of "fundamentally different assumptions about the nature of management learning" (p. 142), particularly in regard to power relations and their impact on learning.

Experiential learning theory provides a foundation for developing strategies to help people learn more effectively. As Kolb et al. (2001) noted, "For those with an interest in learning organizations, it provides a theory and assessment methods for the student of individual differences while addressing learning at many levels in organizations and society" (pp. 244–245).

The learning style component of Kolb's theory provides support in both conceptualizing how students learn and designing experiences that respond to individual differences. Kolb's work aids in understanding that in any classroom or learning environment, students represent multiple realities regarding what it is like to be a learner in that context and what instructional techniques offer challenge and support. Some questions remain unanswered, however. For example, what role does intelligence or cognitive complexity play in the evolution of learning style? More research is also needed to explore relationships among gender, race, culture, and learning styles.

Looking at Kolb's experiential learning theory as a whole also prompts some questions. If one is to consider Kolb's theory a theory of development, a question must be raised as to how adequately he has attended to the personal aspects. While Kolb's theory does address development across the life span, is it more accurate to consider it a learning theory rather than a more full-blown theory of adult development? Also, because of the heavy emphasis within Kolb's theory on formal education and traditional careers, how well does the theory incorporate populations that are not "white collar" or individuals who are "off time," such as adult learners?

In relation to student affairs programs, services, and staffing, as well as the classroom, issues related to alienation and limited performance of those involved can undercut success for the individual as well as for the organization. Learning style information can assist us in providing support by demonstrating our understanding, fostering feelings of connectedness, and building on individual strengths, as well as challenge by supplying developmental mismatches to aid in overcoming weaknesses and by helping individuals to value differences in others. When short-term learning experiences such as a single program are being constructed, providing connections for all learning styles is important so learning can occur relatively quickly. In a semester-long course, matches as well as mismatches to promote further development of nondominant learning style components are appropriate.

Hagberg and Leider (1982) noted that individuals with different learning styles approach the process of growth and change differently. An awareness of this concept seems important in fulfilling a student development function. Moreover, Claxton and Murrell (1987) asserted, "Consideration of styles is one way to help faculty and administrators think more deeply about their roles and the organizational culture in which they carry out their work" (p. 1).

In conclusion, Kolb presented a theory that can be very useful in understanding oneself as learner, service provider, staff member, supervisor, or faculty member. It can also help students gain a level of self-awareness that can support their success in the learning environments of higher education as well as in environments that will characterize their career. Kolb's theory provides the design tools necessary to create learning environments that can be inclusive in relation to both challenging and supporting all participants. Educators seek to respond as a profession to the increasing diversity within the student population and to have that diversity represented among student leaders, student staff, graduate students in professional preparation programs, and professional staff. To make progress in regard to such goals, one must provide services that meet the needs of a variety of students, along with educational and work environments that both challenge and support a diverse group of individuals. Kolb's theory can aid in doing so.

PART THREE

INTEGRATIVE THEORIES

Regina found the theories in Part Two very useful in understanding and working with her students. However, as the semester progresses, she is left thinking that development is far more complex than any of the theories she has studied so far account for. In making decisions, for example, her students often seem to be influenced by their emotions and the people around them rather than just using cognitive reasoning processes to decide what to do. For example, she has had numerous discussions with André regarding his plans for the future. He has been offered a lucrative position in a large company on the east coast that his partner and his parents are urging him to take, but he has had his heart set on working for a nonprofit organization devoted to assisting indigenous people in Central America develop their own businesses. Logical thinking does not appear likely to help André make this decision.

Regina is also wondering why none of the theories she has studied so far have mentioned spirituality and faith, an issue at the forefront for many of her students. As a Muslim, Mariama is constantly questioned about why she wears a hijab and what she believes. Regina has even heard students tell Mariama she will go to hell because she is not a Christian. Yet when she questions some of her Christian students, like Curtis, about why he believes what he does, all he can tell her is that he believes what his parents and pastor tell him is right.

The lockstep nature of many of the stage theories bothers Regina as well. The process for her students just does not seem to be that orderly. "Life" frequently gets in the way of moving smoothly along a clear developmental path. LaToya, for example, just learned that her father lost his job when the small business he worked for declared bankruptcy. This situation is complicated by her unmarried younger sister's pregnancy and her mother's inability to work because of multiple sclerosis. LaToya was set to graduate with honors next year and planned to go on to graduate school in social work, but now she is not even sure if she can return to school next semester. At the beginning of the semester, LaToya seemed to have everything under control; now she often bursts into tears at unexpected moments and cannot seem to concentrate on anything. Regina is at a loss as to how to support her during this difficult time.

Another aspect of the foundational theories that bothers Regina is their strong focus on internal processes. What about the environment? She really liked Lewin's idea that development is the result of the interaction of the person and the environment, but none of the theories she has studied so far talk much about the role that the environment plays in the developmental process. Her student Devon, who is a student-athlete, comes to mind. The athletic department certainly seems to have a strong impact on his decisions, and, in Regina's opinion, they do not always have his best interests in mind. For example, Regina believes that Devon should be doing an internship related to his major next summer, but his coaches are advising him to stay in town and work out with the team. Devon has a shot at starting next year and does not want to displease his coaches. Regina's advice seems to carry little weight in comparison to that of his coaches and teammates.

As Regina opens her text to Part Three, she is encouraged that the title of this part of the book is "Integrative Theories." Perhaps this group of theories will address some of her nagging questions.

◆ ◆ ◆

The chapters in Part Three address theories that expand understanding of student development to include a number of factors that occur simultaneously. Although the theories grouped under this heading are eclectic, they are integrative in the sense that they consider intersections of aspects of development and factors that contribute to change.

Chapter Nine examines ecological approaches to college student development. Based on Kurt Lewin's (1936) ideas, ecological approaches focus on the interaction of the person and the environment in the developmental process and the influence that each has on the other. This chapter covers three types of ecological models: (1) human ecology (Bubolz & Sontag, 1993), which considers the interrelationship of humans with their environments; (2) developmental ecology (Bronfenbrenner, 1979, 1989, 1993), a psychological approach that provides a way of looking at how and why development occurs by examining various aspects of the environment and their influence on the person surrounded by that environment; and (3) campus ecology (Banning & Kaiser, 1974), an approach specifically focused on the reciprocal relationship between the student and the campus environment. Ecological models provide a different lens for Regina as she considers the experiences of each of her students. For example, Devon is being influenced by the environment of the athletic department, as Regina is aware. Bronfenbrenner's developmental ecology approach may help her to understand how and why this is occurring.

A criticism of many of the foundational theories is that they separate the developmental process into discrete categories: cognitive, moral, psychosocial, and so forth. In conducting research and considering this criticism, several researchers recognized that affective, cognitive, and interpersonal processes are intertwined in the process of development. Robert Kegan, whose work is discussed in Chapter Ten, was among the first to take this position. In examining the meaning-making process, he argued that both cognitive and affective components are involved (Kegan, 1982, 1994). He also viewed the evolution of meaning making as involving changing interpretations of the relationship between the self and others, thus bringing the interpersonal dimension into play in the developmental process. Regina may find Kegan's theory helpful in understanding why André is having difficulty deciding on his future, given its consideration of how self and others interact.

Chapter Ten also presents the later work of Marcia Baxter Magolda (for example, 2001, 2007, 2008), whose continuing longitudinal study of development in young adulthood led her to the conclusion that three processes are involved in identity development: (1) an epistemological, meaning-making component; (2) an intrapersonal dimension—how individuals view themselves; and (3) an interpersonal component—how interactions with others influence how individuals see themselves (Baxter Magolda, 2001). The end goal of development in her approach, self-authorship, integrates these factors in a way that enables individuals to take control of their lives and decisions. Regina may want to consider the extent to which André has achieved self-authorship as she seeks reasons for his struggle in making life decisions. Baxter Magolda's theory may also provide some guidance as she works with him to manage the many factors involved.

Consideration of the development of faith and spirituality is also integrative in nature. Leading developmental theorists investigating spirituality are James Fowler and Sharon Daloz Parks. Their approaches are discussed in Chapter Eleven. Influenced by the work of both cognitive structural (for example, Piaget and Kohlberg) and psychosocial theorists (such as Erikson), as well as the integrative theories of Gillian and Kegan, Fowler (1981, 1996) recognized the importance of cognitive meaning making, as well as relational dimensions in how people view faith. Although his theory is cognitive structural in nature, Fowler (1981) acknowledged that cognition and affect cannot be separated, and he incorporated affective influences into his stage model. As Regina works with students dealing with issues of faith and spirituality, examining Fowler's theory may provide her with a conceptual understanding of the different ways in which individuals at various stages of development define and experience faith. For example, Curtis's unquestioning acceptance of the tenets of his parents' and pastor's religious beliefs could be viewed through the lens of Fowler's theory.

Parks (1986a, 2000) specifically examined the development of faith during the college years. In her theory, which expanded that of Fowler, she hypothesized that three forms of development—cognition, dependence, and community—contribute to faith development. Cognition involves how individuals "know," dependence is focused on the extent to which individuals rely on others as a key to the role of emotion in their development, and community refers to individuals' interactions with their social settings and overall environments. Thus, Parks's theory integrates cognitive, affective, and environmental dimensions in considering development. Parks suggested ways in which college campuses can become mentoring communities to students during their faith journeys. Regina may want to consider Parks's suggestions as she searches for ways to support her students.

Schlossberg's transition theory, the topic of Chapter Twelve, departs from the stage models used by theorists reviewed in earlier chapters. Nancy Schlossberg and her colleagues (Schlossberg, 1984; Schlossberg, Waters, & Goodman, 1995; Goodman, Schlossberg, & Anderson, 2006) examined how people react to life events, focusing on the transitions that result in people's lives and how they handle them. This theory is integrative in the sense that it examines both the internal psychological processes that people in transition experience and also the circumstances surrounding them, including the situation itself and the supports available to the individuals experiencing the transition. Clearly, Schlossberg's transition theory will prove helpful to Regina in working with LaToya, who certainly is experiencing a major life transition as a result of several simultaneous life events: her father's layoff, her sister's unwanted pregnancy, and her mother's illness.

While the theories presented in Part Three are a bit more complex than those in Part Two, the added dimensions that they provide in understanding student development are worth the effort it may take to comprehend them.

CHAPTER NINE

ECOLOGICAL APPROACHES TO COLLEGE STUDENT DEVELOPMENT

Bobbi and Lien had been roommates since their first semester. Although both were busy juniors, they made time to eat dinner together every Sunday night at their off-campus apartment. These weekly dinners featured conversations about school, life, love, futures, and everyday matters such as dishes left in the sink and who should shovel the next snow from the sidewalk. Bobbi and Lien could hardly be more different from one another. Bobbi, a white woman attending school on an athletic scholarship supplemented by a generous allowance from her parents, was a finance major and devout Catholic. Lien was a premed general sciences major from a family so poor that she routinely sent home money from the two jobs she worked on and off campus. She was raised by Vietnamese immigrant parents who struggled to make ends meet while their two children were in college and supported an extended family, including Lien's grandparents, an aunt and uncle, and assorted cousins who lived with them while getting their own households in order.

Differences in Bobbi and Lien's backgrounds were overcome by their shared sense of humor, commitment to academic excellence, and passion for personal and professional achievement. After living together for two years on one of the university's residence hall honors floors, they had moved off campus where there was more freedom, which Bobbi craved, and lower costs, which were important to Lien.

One evening, Bobbi talked about how torn she felt about a situation with her boyfriend of two years. He wanted to engage in more sexual activity than Bobbi was comfortable with. She had talked with teammates and with friends from the

Newman Catholic Center, but they were giving her different advice. Looking around campus, it would seem that everyone was sexually active. Ads in the student newspaper touted condoms, residence advisors sponsored programs on safer sex, and the student health center always asked female patients if there was a chance they might be pregnant. Teammates told Bobbi that there was nothing to fear from being sexually active so long as she was careful. Newman Center friends told her to stand her ground, not to cave in to pressure from her boyfriend and other students, and to honor the Catholic prohibition of sex outside marriage. Bobbi was not sure what she would ultimately decide and wanted advice from Lien, whom she trusted as her closest friend at school.

Lien was in a different mood that night. She had just learned that she had been selected for a student manager role in the chemistry lab where her work-study job had been since her first year. The promotion meant more money, both from an increased wage and more hours in the lab. When she told her off-campus employer, a professor for whose children Lien babysat, that she would be leaving at the end of the semester, the professor congratulated her and reminded her that not only was the promotion a financial benefit; it also put Lien in even more contact with scientists, which would be an academic benefit. Now Lien could spend all of her work time in the lab of her favorite professor *and* earn enough money to send some home. Her family did not always understand what Lien was doing at the university, but they were proud of her and insisted that she stay in school as long as it took to reach her goal of completing medical school.

Tonight, though, was for a conversation about relationships, values, faith, and the promotion in the chemistry lab, for a celebration for Lien and a heart-to-heart talk about the conflicting messages Bobbi was getting from various sources.

◆ ◆ ◆

How does theory account for the different developmental contexts in which Bobbi and Lien find themselves? Are the same theories that explain their identity, cognitive, and ethical development useful across their differing contexts? Ecological approaches to understanding human development provide a way to understand how interactions between people and their environments promote growth and development. Ecological approaches also account for how people influence their environments and how some environments favor some people's development more than others.

Based in part on scientific notions of ecology, ecology models explain the processes, but not necessarily the specific outcomes, of human development. They are not intended to explain, for example, the ways that multiracial students identify themselves or how lesbian, gay, bisexual, or transgender (LGBT) identity changes over time. Rather, ecological models provide a way of understanding how students interact with campus environments to promote the development of racial or sexual orientation identities. They do not attempt to determine outcomes, but provide ways to understand how those outcomes may be achieved. Ecological models can be considered integrative in the ways that they account for multifaceted contexts for the development of the whole person. Student affairs educators can use ecological models to understand how student development may occur and also to consider how campus environments can be shaped to promote optimal growth and development.

In this chapter, we introduce three major bodies of ecological approaches: human ecology, developmental ecology, and campus ecology. We present descriptions of each approach and its key assumptions, as well as comparisons across models when appropriate. We also present examples of research and applications in the college context and conclude with a summary and suggestions for future directions.

Human Ecology

Human ecology theory lays the foundation for understanding college students using ecological approaches. Deriving from a general understanding of ecology as "adaptation to environment" (Steward, 1955, p. 30), it represents a way of looking at the "interaction and interdependence of humans (as individuals, groups, and societies) with the environment" (Bubolz & Sontag, 1993, p. 421). Arising from the study of home and family in the late nineteenth century, human ecology introduced a scientific approach to understanding growth and development in context. Social scientists in the early to mid-twentieth century adopted an ecological framework in sociology, geography, anthropology, psychology, political science, and economics (Bubolz & Sontag). It is commonly used in the applied fields of family studies, social work, and the health professions.

The foundation of the theory rests in understanding a family or other social unit as an ecosystem. The family or other unit (for example, a peer friendship group on campus) is located in a nested context of the human-built environment (for example, a residence hall), the social-cultural environment, and the natural physical-biological environment—literally, the climate, soil, water, and so forth (Bubolz & Sontag, 1993). Humans may alter the natural physical-biological environment to survive, but the natural environment exists before, during, and after human intervention. A primary goal of the ecosystem is survival, which is accomplished through adaptations to the environment and adaptations of the environment.

These very basic tenets of human ecology theory—adaptation for survival and ecosystem location in human-built, social-cultural, and natural physical-biological environments—provide a lens through which to understand college students and campus life. Bobbi and Lien's lasting friendship forms an ecosystem that adapts to off-campus living, with its attendant demands on time and communication, after sharing a residence hall room for two years. The human-built characteristics of each living space (double or single bedrooms; physical proximity; the need to cook and the facilities to do so) provide stresses and buffers to the relationship itself. The social-cultural context of the ecosystem is shaped by family income, cultural backgrounds, and commitments to academics, athletics, and work. Even the natural physical environment has an impact on the ecosystem, as Bobbi and Lien argue over whose turn it is to shovel snow and how warm to keep the apartment (Bobbi wants it warm enough to walk around in pajamas; Lien is budget conscious and willing to put on a sweatshirt instead of turning up the heat). Human ecology theory thus emphasizes the interactions between individuals and the environment, considering ways that each influences the other.

Developmental Ecology

Coming from a psychological rather than anthropological perspective, developmental ecology also considers interactions between individuals and their developmental context, but it focuses attention on the individuals rather than the cultures in which they are embedded. Developmental psychologist Urie Bronfenbrenner (1917–2005) was the pioneer in this area, introducing his ecological systems theory (Bronfenbrenner, 1979) to explain growth and development in early childhood. The model evolved over time from introduction of the theory in the 1970s (see Bronfenbrenner, 1974, 1977, 1979) to refinements in the 1980s and 1990s (see Bronfenbrenner, 1989, 1993). Bronfenbrenner published extensively and continued to make adjustments to the theory as empirical studies and sociocultural changes suggested improvements. The posthumous publication of an "ecobiological model of human development" (Bronfenbrenner & Morris, 2006) outlined the evolution of the model over nearly forty years.

Working from the assumption that development cannot be accounted for by individual attributes that can be studied outside the context of the developing individual, Bronfenbrenner adapted Kurt Lewin's equation: *Behavior is a function of the interaction of the person and the environment* to *development is a function of the interaction of the person and the environment*. Such person-environment theories are common in the study of student development (for example, Banning & Kaiser, 1974; Banning & McKinley, 1980; J. Holland, 1966; Moos, 1979; Tinto, 1987/1993; Weidman,

1989) and show connections between individual outcomes (including behaviors, decisions, identity, and learning) and environmental context. What these theories fail to illuminate—and what Bronfenbrenner's developmental ecology model adds to the study of student development—is a way to look inside the interactions between individuals and their environments to see how and why outcomes may occur as they do. For example, whereas racial identity development models focus on the outcome (racial identity), an ecology model may help explain how that outcome occurs as an interaction of person and environment (see Renn, 2003).

Components of Bronfenbrenner's Theory

Four main components (process, person, context, and time, or PPCT) and the interactions among them comprise the model. These four components interact in ways that promote or inhibit development; across Bronfenbrenner's career, he defined the components similarly, but he periodically adjusted his assessment of how the interactions influenced development or the importance of various subcomponents in the developmental process. The model itself therefore evolved (Bronfenbrenner, 2005).

Process. *Process* is at the core of the model and "encompasses particular forms of interaction between organism and environment, called *proximal processes*, that operate over time and are posited as the primary mechanisms producing human development" (Bronfenbrenner & Morris, 2006, p. 795). To achieve optimal development, proximal processes should be progressively more complex and be buffered appropriately so as not to overwhelm the developing individual. Student affairs educators recognize these functions as Astin's (1984) theory of involvement and Sanford's (1966) idea of challenge and support.

Person. Attending to the *person* component in conjunction with process provides a greater understanding of how the PPCT model shines light on what is going on in the how and what of the person-environment interaction. Bronfenbrenner (1993) proposed, "The attributes of the person most likely to shape the course of development, for better or for worse, are those that induce or inhibit dynamic dispositions toward the immediate environment" (p. 11). He called these attributes *developmentally instigative characteristics* and identified four types. Renn and Arnold (2003) summarized them and offered examples for college students. First are those that act to invite or inhibit responses from the environment; different students elicit different responses from administrators, peers, and faculty. Second are those of selective responsivity, which describe how individuals explore and react to surroundings, including such activities as joining student organizations or preferring solitary pursuits. Structuring proclivities are the third type, and these relate to how individuals engage or persist in the increasingly complex activities that are keys to development; so students who consciously seek more difficult courses, leadership positions, and so forth exhibit stronger structuring proclivities than those who limit new challenges. Directive beliefs are the fourth type, including how individuals experience agency in relation to environments. Renn and Arnold (2003) gave the example of high-achieving valedictorians who believe that their accomplishments are the result of hard work directed at appropriate academic targets.

Together, developmentally instigative characteristics influence how an individual will experience an environment and how the environment will respond to that individual. In these person-environment interactions, "developmentally instigative characteristics do not *determine* the course of development; rather, they may be thought of as 'putting a spin' on a body in motion. The effect of that spin depends on other forces, and resources, in the total ecological system" (Bronfenbrenner, 1993, p. 14). The "force-resource" approach again echoes Sanford's (1966) principles of challenge and support. Bronfenbrenner's approach, however, allows student affairs educators to look beyond student demographics, common variables in the study of learning and developmental outcomes, to see what else might be affecting student development.

The developmentally instigative characteristics bring to mind, for example, four of Sedlacek's (2004) eight noncognitive variables: positive self-concept, realistic self-appraisal, successfully handling the system, preference for long-term goals. Though not exactly parallel, Bronfenbrenner's characteristics emerge in Sedlacek's noncognitive variables; given the demonstrated predictive qualities of the noncognitive variables (see, for example, Ransdell, 2001; Sedlacek, 2004; Ting, 2003), it is not too far a stretch to see how the developmentally instigative characteristics might help explain differing college outcomes. As Renn and Arnold (2003) proposed, these characteristics may help explain differential outcomes among students whose demographics and entering academic profiles would predict similar learning and developmental outcomes.

Context. The *context* element of the ecology models often receives the most attention. In the human ecology model, it typically is the focus of empirical and theoretical inquiry. But in developmental ecology, the person remains the focus, with the surrounding context understood as a critical location for interactions (the process) between the individual and the environment. Thus, the context forms an inextricable part of the developmental ecology.

As in human ecology models (for example, Bubolz & Sontag, 1993), Bronfenbrenner proposed a nested series of contexts. In his model, the person is in the center, with four levels of context surrounding her or him: the microsystem, mesosystem, exosystem, and macrosystem. These systems are where the work of development occurs as an individual's developmentally instigative characteristics inhibit or provoke reactions—forces and resources—from the environment in the course of proximal processes.

Microsystems. "A microsystem is a pattern of activities, roles, and interpersonal relations experienced by the developing persons in a given face-to-face setting with particular physical, social, and symbolic features that invite, permit, or inhibit engagement in sustained, progressively more complex interaction with, and activity in, the immediate environment" (Bronfenbrenner, 1993, p. 15). Although Bronfenbrenner did not include computer-mediated contexts in which college students now experience "activities, roles, and interpersonal relations" (p. 16), in the twenty-first century it seems reasonable to include these contexts, which are not face-to-face settings, in the definition of microsystems since they are sites where social, physical, and symbolic features may provoke or retard engagement with the environment, as described by Bronfenbrenner (1993).

It is not hard to imagine how microsystems play a role in the lives of college students and their development. Renn and Arnold (2003) suggested that roommates, friendship groups, work settings, athletic teams, families, and faculty relationships represent potential microsystems for students. Astin's (1984) involvement theory, and the abundant research that it spawned, including the Cooperative Institutional Research Project (CIRP) and National Survey of Student Engagement (NSSE), tends to focus on interactions between specific microsystems and individual students and their engagement, development, and learning. Often this approach is analyzed as though microsystem interactions are additive; that is, the effects of interactions in one microsystem, such as student-faculty interaction, can be added to or subtracted from the effects of interactions in other microsystems (friendship groups, work, athletics) to calculate the total effects of college on students. Yet these additive analyses of microsystems leave out the important interactions between and among microsystems. Bronfenbrenner accounted for these interactions in the mesosystem.

Mesosystems. As defined by Bronfenbrenner (1993), a *mesosystem* "comprises linkages and processes taking place between two or more settings containing the developing person. Special attention is focused on the synergistic effects created by the interaction of developmentally instigative or inhibitory features and processes present in each setting" (p. 22). So it is the synergy across microsystems and webs of mesosystems that creates additional possibilities for proximal processes that promote development. Mesosystems may be consonant, reinforcing developmental effects, or dissonant, sending competing messages or creating inconsistent influences that may provoke or inhibit development (Renn, 2003).

Renn and Arnold (2003) identified the mesosystem as the locus of campus peer culture, where students' multiple microsystems interact to create a web of developmental possibilities. For example, interactions between the roommate relationship and athletic team create a mesosystem; another mesosystem may be created by the roommate and classroom microsystems. Bobbi and Lien's microsystem forms a mesosystem when combined with (for Bobbi) her boyfriend microsystem, the Newman Club microsystem, her family microsystem, and her academic microsystem. Lien's mesosystem includes microsystems interacting across roommate, work, classes, and family.

Renn and Arnold (2003) pointed out that institutions with highly consonant mesosystems—military academies, for example—create ecosystems that favor certain kinds of developmentally instigative characteristics. Students with these characteristics will thrive, while their peers with equal academic ability but unfavored developmentally instigative characteristics may not. The parallels between evolutionary biology and developmental ecology become clear when considering how environmental niches favor some characteristics over others; if developing organisms or individuals cannot adapt to or change the environment, they will not survive. Students do not exist in micro- and mesosystems entirely of their own creation, and they are affected by circumstances outside their control. These activities occur in the exosystem.

Exosystems. Exosystems do not contain the developing individual but exert an influence on his or her environment through interactions with the microsystems (Bronfenbrenner, 1993). Exosystems that may affect students include parents' or partners' workplaces, institutional decision makers who issue tuition and financial aid policies, faculty curriculum committees, federal financial aid policies, immigration and visa agencies, and others (Renn & Arnold, 2003). Lien is affected by her family's circumstances, many of which are influenced by decisions made well outside her immediate setting. National Collegiate Athletic Association (NCAA) regulations regarding recruiting, practice time, and scholarships affect Bobbi's developmental context, even though she has never met anyone from the NCAA. The inclusion of exosystems in considering student development provides a mechanism to examine factors that are often considered beyond the control of the researcher. They also provide a way to address the diversity of student experiences—adult students with full-time jobs and families, as well as younger students who may or may not be financially dependent on their parents—in student development discussions.

Macrosystems. The broadest level of context in the developmental ecology model is the macrosystem, which "consists of the overarching pattern of micro- meso- and exosystems characteristic of a given culture, subculture, or other extended social structure, with particular reference to the developmentally instigative belief systems, resources, hazards, lifestyles, opportunity structures, life course options and patterns of social interchange that are embedded in such overarching systems" (Bronfenbrenner, 1993, p. 25). As such, the macrosystem can be thought of as, if not universal, at least locally encompassing higher education institutions and their inhabitants. Renn and Arnold (2003) claimed that macrosystems encompass "meritocratic notions derived from democratic values and capitalist ideology," as well as "cultural understandings of gender, race, and ethnicity" (p. 273). College going (that is, who goes to college, who goes to what college) is shaped by the macrosystem, as well as by sociohistoric influences related to economics, the workforce, and societal values.

The Systems Together as Context. The four levels of systems—micro-, meso-, exo-, and macrosystems—are inextricable, interactive, and complexly related. What happens in one affects the others as well as the developing individual. They provide stressors and buffers, creating opportunities for increasingly complex activities in which the student can participate, while supporting and rewarding sustained commitment to those increasingly complex endeavors. Renn and Arnold (2003) represented the context component of the PPCT model as nested circles (Figure 9.1).

Although this static depiction of the model cannot capture the dynamic nature of developmental ecology, it provides a snapshot of a hypothetical college student's environment. It is important to remember that the student is constantly exerting forces on the micro- and mesosystems, just as they are exerting forces back on him or her. Missing from this depiction is the fourth component: time. Time is what enables educators to see growth, change, development, and stasis in college students.

Time. The component of time has come and gone from the ecological systems model during its evolution, but it is a clear presence in the last published statement of the model (Bronfenbrenner & Morris, 2006). Bronfenbrenner and Morris described it at three levels: "*Microtime* refers to continuity versus discontinuity in ongoing episodes of proximal process. *Mesotime* is the periodicity of these episodes across broader time intervals, such as days and weeks. Finally, *Macrotime* focuses on the changing expectations and events in the larger society, both within and across generations, as they affect and are affected by, processes and outcomes of human development over the life course" (p. 796, italics in original).

Time thus interacts with process, person, and context to affect the developmental influence of proximal processes. The extent to which proximal processes are continuous, durable, and increasingly complex determines their impact on development (Bronfenbrenner, 1993), and time has a critical role to play.

FIGURE 9.1. AN EXAMPLE OF THE CONTEXT OF COLLEGE STUDENT DEVELOPMENT

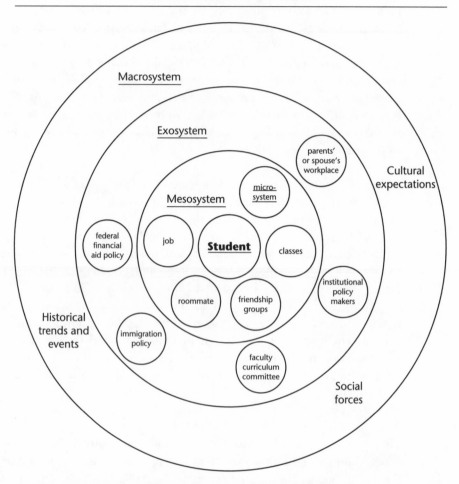

Source: Renn, K. A., & Arnold, K. D. (2003). Reconceptualizing research on college student peer culture. *Journal of Higher Education, 74*(3). © 2003 The Ohio State University. Reprinted with permission.

Time also plays a role across the life span as societal values change. As noted above, questions of who attends college under what circumstances—and the developmental environments thus opened to people of different genders, races, abilities, and socioeconomic statuses—are determined largely in the macrosystem as an outcome of changes over time in societal values and needs. Developmental ecology is concerned with time within individual lives, across the life span (Bronfenbrenner & Morris, 2006).

Renn and Arnold (2003) provided examples of time operating in the developmental ecologies of college students. They pointed to the timing of family events (birth of a sibling, parents' divorce, family move) in a young person's life and the timing of college attendance (for example, immediately after high school, returning after working for a time) as instances of time playing a role in development. Renn and Arnold (2003) also noted that Bronfenbrenner sometimes (see Bronfenbrenner, 1995) opted to call time the *chronosystem*, putting it in a parallel status with the micro-, meso-, exo-, and macrosystems of the context. Bronfenbrenner's return to "time" in later iterations (see Bronfenbrenner & Morris, 2006) helps clarify how it fits into the process-person-context-time model as a core component, not a subcomponent like the four levels of context.

Research Using Developmental Ecology Theory

Unlike human ecology, developmental ecology theory has recently gained traction in research on college students, their experience, and development. Dey and Hurtado (1995) and Renn and Arnold (2003) advocated for the incorporation of developmental ecology frameworks in understanding peer cultures. Renn (2003) used the theory to study bi- and multiracial college students. It has also been used to study topics as divergent as the role of peer support in academic success of ethnic minority, first-generation college students (Dennis, Phinney, & Chuateco, 2005), college drinking (Weitzman, Nelson, Lee, & Wechsler, 2004), rural students' college aspirations (Chenoweth & Galliher, 2004), immigrant community college students in Canada (Kilbride & D'Arcangelo, 2002), the human environment of historically black colleges and universities (Outcalt & Skewes-Cox, 2002), peer group influences in applying to and paying for college (Tierney & Venegas, 2006), and the experiences of Latino fraternity members at a Hispanic-serving university (Guardia & Evans, 2008).

Applications of Developmental Ecology Theory

There are few examples of explicit use of developmental ecology in student affairs practice. Renn and Arnold (2003), however, suggested that the ecology model could be useful in creating interventions to promote student development by, for example, working with individual students to explore their developmental environments through life histories and current ecologies. They suggested intervening at multiple levels of the environment, such as through policy, curriculum, and immediate contexts. And they suggested that the ecology model might be useful in understanding how peer cultures, famously resistant to intervention, might be influenced to improve the campus living and learning environment. They neglected, for the most part, the theoretical and practical tradition of campus *ecology* in student affairs, which is described next.

Campus Ecology

Deriving mainly from the Stanford school of ecological psychology (for example, Barker, 1968; Moos, 1973; Moos & Insel, 1974), campus ecology was introduced to student affairs by James Banning and Leland Kaiser (Banning & Kaiser, 1974). Campus ecology assumed a substantial role in student development theory and student affairs administration through the 1970s and early 1980s, but did not persist as a central theoretical approach (Renn & Arnold, 2003). Recent uses of developmental ecology have drawn attention back to campus ecology as a potentially powerful perspective for understanding student development in college.

Campus ecology, "the study of the relationship between the student and the campus environment, . . . incorporates the influence of environments on students and students on environments," as well as focusing on "the transactional relationship between students and their environment" (Banning, 1978, p. 4). This concern with the reciprocal relationship between people and their environments is consistent with human ecology and developmental ecology. Bringing an ecological perspective to the specialized context of higher education allows campus ecologists to focus on both the individual student, who is often at the center of student development and student affairs work, and his or her surrounding people, places, and policies.

Theoretical Foundations of Campus Ecology

A 1978 National Association of Student Personnel Administrators (NASPA) monograph (Banning, 1978) presented key elements of campus ecology and proposed uses for it in designing learning environments. In the monograph, Walsh (1978) laid out six theoretical foundations for campus ecology. They are summarized here in relation to their role in the campus ecology approach.

First, Barker's (1968) *behavior-setting theory* posited that "people tend to behave in highly similar ways in specific environments, regardless of their individual differences as persons" (Walsh, 1978, p. 7). The environment thus shapes behaviors within specific settings. People seek to maintain settings that they favor or find pleasant and try to change (or vacate) settings that they do not enjoy. Key to the connection between Barker's work and campus ecology is that environments can be considered "behavior settings" (that is, settings or contexts in which somewhat predictable behaviors will occur), and "both the individual and the environment are to be taken into account in predicting behaviors" (p. 8). In theory, if enough is known about students, environments, and the behaviors that those environments elicit, then student affairs educators—"milieu managers" (Helsabeck, 1980) or "campus ecology managers" (Banning, 1980a, 1980b) in the language of the

1970s campus ecologist—might predict student behaviors and take steps to manage the setting to elicit different behaviors.

Second, Walsh (1978) presented the *subculture approach*. This approach "tends to describe the environment in terms of the attitudes, values, behaviors, and roles of its members" (p. 9). As does behavior-setting theory, the subculture approach emphasizes the environment element of the person-environment interaction, assuming that individuals will enter into subcultures that match their values and characteristics. Walsh cited examples of subculture researchers familiar in higher education literature, including Clark and Trow (1966) and Feldman and Newcomb (1969). An updated list might also include Horowitz (1987) and Katchadourian and Boli (1985). Renn and Arnold (2003) also considered subcultures in discussing developmental ecology. Campus ecologists use subculture analyses to understand the broader context of institutional cultures and contexts for student learning and development.

Holland's *personality types* represent Walsh's (1978) third contributing category. Holland (1966) took a clear person-environment approach to individual behavior, but shifted the weight more to the person than to the environment, as did Barker (1968) and the subculture researchers. Rooted in vocational testing models, Holland's six types (realistic, investigative, artistic, social, enterprising, and conventional) are meant to describe personality types that can be measured and used to predict behavior. The degree of match between a person's strongest types and the characteristics of the environment (which can also be measured according to types that correspond with the personality types) may influence, for example, choice of college major or career. Holland's work emphasizes the importance of finding congruent person-environment matches and supports the notion of favorable environmental niches for student development as described by Renn and Arnold (2003), though Renn and Arnold maintained that development may result from the tension experienced in a poor fit as well.

The fourth theory underlying campus ecology is Stern's (1970) *need × press = culture* theory. Based on Lewin's and Murray's work in the 1930s, Stern postulated that "behavior is a function of the relationship between the individual (needs) and the environment (press)" (Walsh, 1978, p. 11). When this idea is extended to a campus level, an accumulation of behaviors across individuals creates a culture, which then contributes to the environmental press on individuals (as in Holland, 1973). A college culture "is defined as a composite of the environmental press and the needs of its inhabitants" (Walsh, p. 11). Campuses tend to be populated by students whose needs match the environmental presses available. Like Holland, Stern focused attention on the individual in the person-environment interaction.

Moos's (1973, 1979) *social ecological approach* constitutes the fifth explanation of campus ecology (Walsh, 1978) and deserves special attention because of its contributions to the broader area of ecology models. Rudolf Moos, a Stanford professor, worked in psychiatric, correctional, and community settings before turning his attention to higher education (Moos, 1979). Although Walsh noted that "Moos (1974) in his approach suggests that environments, like people, have unique personalities" (p. 12), Moos himself moved away from the term "personality of environment" (Moos, 1979, p. vii). He maintained a focus, however, on measuring social contexts and examining physical and architectural settings, organizational settings, and the types of people in them (Moos, 1979).

Based on the assumptions that "psychosocial qualities of environment (perceived climate) can be inferred from behavioral perceptions" and that "the way one perceives his/her surroundings influences the way one behaves in that environment" (Walsh, 1978, p. 12), Moos developed scales to measure specific higher education environments including student living groups and classroom settings. Immersed in student development literature of the time (for example, Astin, 1968; Holland, 1973; Pace & Stern, 1958), Moos examined the process of person-environment interactions as mediated through cognitive appraisal (that is, perceptions of climate), activation or arousal (that is, motivation), and student efforts to adapt or cope (Moos, 1979). Student stability and change, he proposed, depended on the interaction of the environmental system and the personal system, mediated through these factors. Student behavior is thus an outcome of environmental perceptions, personal characteristics, and their interaction in a dynamic system. The inclusion of the physical environment is different from some other ecological theories and makes a key contribution to campus ecology, which concerns itself in part with physical aspects of campus life.

The sixth and final contribution to an understanding of campus ecology is Pervin's (1967, 1968) *transaction approach*. In this approach, "behavior can best be understood in terms of the interactions of transactions between the individual and the environment" (Walsh, 1978, p. 13). Pervin (1968) maintained that people work to reduce discrepancy between their ideal selves and perceived selves, seeking environments that will help them attain ideal self-hood. Using an instrument he developed called TAPE (transactional analysis of personality and environment), Pervin (1967) measured self-reported perceptions of individuals and their environments. It is the emphasis on perceptions and reactions to perceptions that sets this approach apart as phenomenological and different from the other five.

Strange and Banning (2001) integrated these six approaches to advocate for campus design that promoted four goals: inclusion, safety, involvement, and community building. They proposed that these goals are enacted through physical, human aggregate, organizational, and constructed components of campus milieu. Consistent with other ecological approaches, Strange and Banning thus attended to the natural and human-built environments of campus geography and architecture, peer and other group interactions, structural aspects of the organization (such as administration, policy, and campus culture), and the ways individuals perceive, or construct, their environments.

A contribution of campus ecology is the combination of related but distinct threads of theory about college students, their behaviors, and the development that might result from those behaviors. Taken as a group, these theories focus attention on the individual, the environment, and interactions between them, either as measured or as perceived by students themselves. Considering the psychosocial as well as physical environment, campus ecology brings theoretical approaches to understanding college students directly into the classrooms, residence halls, athletic fields, families, and peer groups of college students.

The theoretical bases of campus ecology do not contradict the tenets of human ecology or developmental ecology. Rather, they provide complementary approaches, sometimes with instruments to measure concepts included in the other ecological models. The focus remains on person-environment interactions, though analyses do not always extend beyond the immediate campus environments (as would human ecology and developmental ecology) or across time (as would developmental ecology). They have much to offer when combined into an overall campus ecology approach.

Applications of Campus Ecology

Following the emergence of campus ecology, a flurry of publications proposed research and practical uses for this approach. Student affairs handbooks (for example, Creamer, 1980; Morrill, Hurst, & Oetting, 1980) contained chapters and sections on campus ecology. The 1978 NASPA monograph on campus ecology (Banning, 1978) is now out of print but available online (www .campusecologist.org files/Monograph.pdf), as is Aulepp and Delworth's (1976) *Training Manual for an Ecosystem Model: Assessing and Designing Campus Environments* (www .campusecologist.org/files/tmem/home.htm). A Web site, currently maintained at Indiana State University (www.campusecologist.org/), contains copies of the *Campus Ecologist* newsletter, published regularly from 1983 to 1996, which also provides abundant examples of how campus ecology might be used to improve student affairs practice and research.

Recommended applications tended to be in specific functional areas, for more general use across student affairs, and occasionally for use across the campus environments, often with an emphasis on campus design. Drawing from the Western Interstate Commission for Higher Education project on improving mental health services (1972), Banning and Kaiser (1974) proposed a planning model for designing campus environments to achieve specific educational values. In their model, values are translated into goals, environments are designed to achieve those goals and are fitted to students, student perceptions of those environments are measured, and student behavior resulting from environmental perceptions is monitored (Banning & Kaiser, p. 372). The theoretical underpinnings of campus ecology are apparent in the planning model (environments shape behavior, perceptions matter, and so forth). Though conceived with mental health services in mind, it is easy to see how this model might be used to achieve other desired outcomes, values, and goals. Huebner (1979), Kaiser (1975), and Kaiser and Sherretz (1978) provided additional recommendations for using a campus ecology approach to shape environments to maximize student learning and development.

Campus ecology has potential as a theoretical framework within student affairs functional areas. Williams (1986) proposed using it in admissions to optimize student institutional fit. Banning and Cunard (1996) applied it to student union renovation and construction. Schroeder (1981), Schroeder and Freesh (1977), and Schuh (1979) considered residence halls from a campus ecology perspective. Perhaps because of its roots in the Western Interstate Commission for Higher Education (1972) project, campus ecology literature on student mental health counseling is better developed than literature on most other functional areas (see Conyne, 1975; Conyne & Rogers, 1977; Hurst & McKinley, 1988). Throughout all of this literature on student affairs implementation, the interaction of individuals with their physical and psychosocial environments is at the center.

Other literature puts campus ecology to use in considering how best to provide services to diverse campus populations. Banning and Hughes (1986) proposed ways to design campuses with commuter students in mind. Hispanic/Latino culture (Banning & Luna, 1992), Native American students (St. Clair, 1994), sexism (Banning, 1992), and prejudice against gay men and lesbians (termed *homoprejudice*; Gerst & Fonken, 1995) benefit from consideration through a campus ecology lens. First-year students (Banning, 1989) and general student outcomes (Baird, 1976) can be considered through this lens as well.

Although campus ecology has lost whatever central role it may once have played in research on student development, it has much to offer in the way of understanding how "involving colleges" (Kuh, Schuh, & Witt, 1991) function to involve students, how "student engagement" (Kuh, 2001) happens, how "self-authorship" (Baxter Magolda, 2001) is instigated, and how the learning in *Learning Reconsidered* (Keeling, 2004) actually takes place. By bringing the critical person-environment interaction to the center of analysis, campus ecology focuses attention on the theoretical and practical matters attending how individuals are attracted to and react to particular campuses and campus subcultures.

Implications and Future Directions

Human, developmental, and campus ecologies have at their core a concern with the interactions of humans and their environments. Taken from family studies, anthropology, psychology, geography, and sociology, these approaches add to the study of student development by drawing analytical and practical attention to the settings in which students develop cognitively, morally, interpersonally, and psychosocially. With few exceptions, theories describing development in these domains rely on factors outside the student—though in his or her setting—for instigation of increasingly complex ways of being and knowing. Without the person-environment interactions theorized and analyzed by the ecology models, there might in fact be no student development.

A particular strength of the ecology models is that they are flexible enough to consider equally well the developmental context of residential students, commuters, distance and online learners (though less may be known about their nonacademic contexts than may be known about the contexts of face-to-face students), and students of different ages, backgrounds, and life histories. The ecology models do not presume that engagement in the campus setting is the primary priority of college students and provide lenses through which to understand the forces and resources (challenges and supports) provided by the interacting micro-, meso-, exo-, and macrosystems of students' personal and shared ecologies. Ecology models have as much to say about Bobbi and Lien's developmental contexts as they do about the developmental contexts of their classmates who are part-time students working full-time jobs and raising children of their own. Rather than mark these so-called nontraditional students as somehow not fitting into the campus environment, ecology models, with their emphasis on reciprocity and dynamism, call on student affairs educators to adapt the environment to serve these students, just as nontraditional students must adapt their priorities to fit college into their lives.

It is not clear why ecology models have not been an enduring theoretical force in student development, but some of their characteristics and limitations may provide clues. First, they are not developmental; that is, they do not represent a beginning, a middle, and an end, as many familiar models do. They do not contain trajectories or spirals of development and do not describe stages, levels, or other developmental positions that many graduate students and professionals in student affairs find satisfying. That is not their purpose. Instead, they describe the process of development—the why and how, not the what, of student growth and change. As such, they provide powerful frameworks for analyzing the process of development but not the content of development. In an era of accountability and outcomes assessment, attention is more often on the product (outcome) than on the process or on the environment that promotes or inhibits that process.

Another characteristic that may limit use of these models is the complexity of implementing developmental interventions based on interactions of individuals and environments. Peer cultures are notoriously resilient to intervention by administrators (Renn & Arnold, 2003), and measuring individual interactions in multiple microsystems is challenging at best. Online social networks like FaceBook may open up new ways to study peer groups, as it may be possible to map students' overlapping friendship and peer groups, though there is some concern that online social networks do not reflect face-to-face friendship groups and students' time spent online reduces time spent with peers (Lloyd, Dean, & Cooper, 2007). To truly map an entire campus environment would be impossible for any but the most intrepid researchers or practitioners, and by the time the landscape was mapped, it would already have changed.

The fluid nature of the environments that ecology models propose represents a third potential reason that these models are not in more frequent recent use. Developmental and campus ecologists (for example, Bronfenbrenner & Morris, 2006; Banning, 1978) provide fluidity in the context, indicating campus environments that may change in response to changes in the micro-, exo-, and macro-systems. Mapping a fluid, changing environment in order to attempt to shape it is beyond the interests of many student affairs educators, who work within the constraints and demands of these changes. In a practical sense, using campus ecology for assessment and planning may seem daunting.

Yet with regard to the day-to-day implementation of policy and programs, ecological models make good sense for student affairs educators. Lien's academic advisor may notice how reducing her work time in other settings, and thus reducing her overall number of microsystems, increases her passion for chemistry. The increasingly complex interactions she is able to have not only with chemistry but also with postdocs, faculty, and other students in the lab represent ideal proximal processes (Bronfenbrenner, 1993) for development. The tension Bobbi feels among her family, faith, and boyfriend's values can be seen as a product of her mesosystem. The relationship, which itself had become more complicated and required more cognitive and emotional complexity, between the two women is an important microsystem for each of them. Although they moved off campus, ecology models make clear that they continue to engage in the kinds of interactions that promote learning and development.

Given the relatively long history of ecology models in the study of student development and their recent reemergence as a lens for studying the influences of peer culture, it would seem that these models might have a strong future in student affairs research and practice. Future directions could include revisiting the campus ecology measures of the 1970s to see what they can offer the study of student development in the twenty-first century. The diversity of students and student learning contexts (face-to-face, distance, online) represents a ripe area for the application of ecological models, especially campus ecology. The advent and omnipresence of technology and Internet-enabled communication and community building create important new areas for ecological examination. To what extent these contexts can be considered to contain the developing individual (Bronfenbrenner, 1993) is up for interpretation, as is the question of how reciprocal interactions occur in online environments.

Bobbi and Lien have created a face-to-face microsystem in which reciprocal interactions play a key role. Their regular discussions, their trust, and their working out of increasingly complicated matters between them represent opportunities for optimal development. The developmentally instigative characteristics that drew them together and keep them together put "the spin on the body in motion" (Bronfenbrenner, 1993, p. 14) or, in this case, the two bodies in motion. Their adaptations to the campus environment, and its adaptations to them in response to their behaviors and characteristics, are the other side of the person-environment model. The chemistry lab, the Newman Club, and the athletic team adapt to take in Bobbi and Lien, just as the women adapt to these settings. Ecological models can hold all of these interacting contexts and the people in them, in their individual and collective complexity and fluidity.

CHAPTER TEN

DEVELOPMENT OF SELF-AUTHORSHIP

In response to information they received from their minister, Symone, Laticia, and Rodney have decided to attend a meeting at Midwest Community College for adult students who might be interested in attending college. Each of them is at a crossroads in life and is looking for a new direction. Symone has always done what others, most notably her father and her husband, have told her to do. However, her husband recently left her, and her father died two years ago. She has been overwhelmed by these losses of the two most important people in her life. When her minister handed her the information about this program, it seemed to her that this might be the answer to her prayers.

Laticia has been a waitress all her life and has been increasingly unhappy with this role. She has thought for awhile about going to college and now feels secure enough about her interests and skills to pursue this option. Although many people she works with have derided her decision and told her she will not make it, Laticia really believes that she can succeed and fulfill her dream of becoming a teacher.

Rodney is considering college for purely pragmatic reasons: he knows it will make him eligible for a higher-paying job. He and his older brother are somewhat competitive, and he wants a job that pays better than Randy's. He knows that it will come as a shock to his family if he gives up his current job and starts college. His wife will not be happy about taking on more responsibility to support the family, but he figures that is her problem and he has to look out for himself.

◆ ◆ ◆

These three individuals are all approaching the same situation but are making meaning of it in very different ways. This chapter introduces theories that are categorized as *constructive-developmental*: they focus on "the growth or transformation" of ways people "construct meaning" (Kegan, 1994, p. 199) regarding their life experiences. We examine two important constructive-developmental theories: those of Robert Kegan and Marcia Baxter Magolda.

Kegan's Theory of the Evolution of Consciousness

Kegan introduced his theory of self-evolution in 1982 in his book, *The Evolving Self*. In his later book, *In over Our Heads: The Mental Demands of Modern Life* (1994), he presented a revised version of his theory and further discussion of the implications of his work for society. Kegan (1982) noted that Piaget's work served as inspiration for his own. Pointing out that Piaget had attended very little to emotion or to the process and experience of development, Kegan sought to address these omissions, drawing on the work of object-relation theorists such as Kernberg (1966), who explored how interpretations of self-other relationships evolved over time, and psychosocial theorists, particularly Erikson. Kegan especially valued "building strong intellectual bridges" (Scharmer, 2000, n.p.) to educational practice, leadership, and organizational development.

Kegan's Theory

The focus of Kegan's (1994) theory is the "evolution of consciousness, the personal unfolding of ways of organizing experience that are not simply replaced as we grow but subsumed into more complex systems of mind" (p. 9). Growth involves movement through five progressively more complex ways of knowing, which Kegan referred to as *stages of development* in 1982, *orders of consciousness* in 1994, and *forms of mind* in 2000. The process of growth involves an evolution of meaning that is marked by continual shifts from periods of stability to periods of instability, leading to ongoing reconstruction of the relationship of persons with their environments (Kegan, 1982). Each succeeding order consists of cognitive, intrapersonal, and interpersonal components.

Kegan (1982, 1994) saw the process of development as an effort to resolve the tension between a desire for differentiation and an equally powerful desire to be immersed in one's surroundings (Kegan, 1994). The evolutionary truces evident at each developmental stage of Kegan's (1982) model are "temporary solution[s] to the lifelong tension between the yearnings for inclusion and distinctness" (p. 107). While initially stating that his ways of knowing alternated between favoring autonomy at one stage and favoring embeddedness at the next (Kegan, 1982), he later modified his view, stating that "each order of consciousness can

favor either of the two fundamental longings" (Kegan, 1994, p. 221) and that neither position is better than the other. He suggested that increased differentiation
could mean finding new ways to stay connected. Paradoxically, as people make
meaning in a more differentiated way, they also develop the capacity to become
closer to others.

Kegan (1982) was clear that the process of growth can be painful since
it involves changing one's way of functioning in the world. Borrowing from
Winnicott (1965), Kegan (1982) introduced the idea of the "holding environment" (p. 116) to assist individuals with these changes. The holding environment
has two functions: supporting individuals in their current stage of development
and encouraging movement to the next evolutionary truce. Kegan (1994) equated
a holding environment to an "evolutionary bridge, a context for crossing over"
(p. 43) from one order of consciousness to the next, more developed order.

Descriptions of Kegan's levels of consciousness follow. They have had different names in different iterations of his theory. We provide the numerical orders
used in the 1994 version, as well as the names used for the later orders in the 2000
version. In addition to describing each order, we provide Kegan's (1982) suggestions regarding ways to challenge and support development to the next order.

Order 0. Kegan (1982) described newborn infants as "living in an objectless
world, a world in which everything sensed is taken to be an extension of the
infant" (p. 78). As a result, when the infant cannot see or experience something,
it does not exist. By the time infants are eighteen months old, they begin to recognize the existence of objects outside themselves, propelling them into the next
stage. Parents must remain steadfast as the child pushes against them to determine
where the boundaries are between its self and the environment.

Order 1. Children develop order 1 meaning making at about age two, when
they realize that they have control over their reflexes (Kegan, 1982) and become
aware of objects in their environment as independent from themselves (Kegan,
1994). Their thinking tends to be "fantastic and illogical, their feelings impulsive
and fluid, [and] their social-relating egocentric" (p. 29) in that they are attached
to whatever or whoever is present at the moment. Parents should support their
children's fantasies while challenging them to take responsibility for themselves
and their feelings as they begin to perceive the world realistically and differentiate
themselves from others while moving into order 2.

Order 2: Instrumental Mind. Individuals in order 2 are able to construct "durable categories"—classifications of objects, people, or ideas with specific characteristics (Kegan, 1994). As a result, their thinking becomes more logical and

organized, their feelings are more enduring, and they relate to others as separate and unique beings. Kegan and others (2001) noted that at this time, "rules, sets of directions, and dualisms give shape and structure to one's daily activity" (pp. 4–5). In this order, individuals develop a sense of who they are and what they want. "Competition and compromise" (Kegan, 1982, p. 163) are characteristic themes of the second order and are often played out within peer group settings. Support at this stage requires confirmation of the person the child has become. Challenge to develop further involves encouragement to take into consideration the expectations, needs, and desires of others.

Rodney, in the opening scenario, appears to make meaning using the second order of consciousness. As he considers attending college, he is mostly concerned about his own needs and desires, he is competitive with his brother, and he does not take into consideration the effect that his actions will have on his family.

Order 3: Socialized Mind. Cross-categorical thinking—the ability to relate one durable category to another—is evident in the third order of consciousness. As a result, thinking is more abstract, individuals are aware of their feelings and the internal processes associated with them, and they can make commitments to communities of people and ideas (Kegan, 1994). Kegan and his colleagues (2001) noted that in this order of consciousness, "other people are experienced . . . as sources of internal validation, orientation, or authority" (p. 5). How the individual is perceived by others is of critical importance since acceptance by others is crucial in this order. Support is found in mutually rewarding relationships and shared experiences, while challenge takes the form of resisting codependence and encouraging individuals to make their own decisions and establish independent lives.

In the opening scenario, order 3 meaning making is evident in Symone's thinking and actions. She takes direction from those around her—in the past her father and husband and now her minister. She needs someone to tell her what to think and do.

Order 4: Self-Authoring Mind. Cross-categorical constructing—the ability to generalize across abstractions, which could also be labeled systems thinking—is evident in the fourth order of consciousness (Kegan, 1994). In this order, self-authorship is the focus. Individuals "have the capacity to take responsibility for and ownership of their internal authority" (Kegan & others, 2001, p. 5) and establish their own sets of values and ideologies (Kegan, 1994). Relationships become a part of one's world rather than the reason for one's existence. Support at this stage is evident in acknowledgment of the individual's independence and self-regulation. Individuals are encouraged to develop further when significant others refuse to accept relationships that are not intimate and mutually rewarding.

Laticia seems to be using order 4 meaning making. She has decided on her own that she wants to attend college, despite discouragement from those around her. She is confident in her abilities and seems to have a self-authored sense of the future direction she wishes to pursue: becoming a teacher.

Order 5: Self-Transforming Mind. In this order of consciousness, which is infrequently reached and never reached before the age of forty (Kegan, 1994), individuals see beyond themselves, others, and systems of which they are a part to form an understanding of how all people and systems interconnect (Kegan, 2000). They recognize their "commonalities and interdependence with others" (Kegan, 1982, p. 239). Relationships can be truly intimate in this order, with nurturance and affiliation as the key characteristics. Kegan (1982) noted that only rarely do work environments provide these conditions and that long-lasting adult love relationships do not necessarily do so either.

The Demands of Modern Life. Kegan (1982) argued that modern life, particularly within the contexts of the family and the work environment, places enormous stress on individuals. Kegan's (1994) book, *In over Our Heads*, focused on the demands of modern society, or the "hidden curriculum" (p. 9). He argued that expectations of adult life—parenting, partnering, and working—require fourth-order meaning making, and many adults have not attained that level.

Kegan (1994) went on to hypothesize that postmodern life requires an ever more complex way of knowing, that of the fifth order, which very few people ever reach. He suggested that rather than demand that people think in a way that is impossible for them to do, helping people reach self-authorship, the necessary first step on the path to fifth-order meaning making, would be more realistic.

Research

Several studies have built on Kegan's theory. A four-year longitudinal study of twenty-two adults conducted by Kegan, Lahey, Souvaine, Popp, and Beukema using the Subject-Object Interview (Lahey, Souvaine, Kegan, Goodman, & Felix, 1988) revealed that "at any given moment, around one-half to two-thirds of the adult population appears not to have fully reached the fourth order of consciousness" (Kegan, 1994, pp. 188, 191). Drawing on thirteen other studies conducted mainly by his doctoral students, Kegan (1994) reported that in the composite sample of 282 relatively advantaged adults, 59 percent had not reached the fourth order. Findings from a longitudinal study of identity development of West Point cadets using Kegan's (1982, 1994) theory as a framework indicated that for most cadets, the challenge of college is moving from self-interest (order 2) to thinking in terms of being part of a community (order 3), a goal that must be accomplished before self-authorship can be considered (Lewis et al., 2005).

In a study of adult basic education learners in their twenties, who were mostly nonwhite, nonnative English-speaking, lower-income immigrants, participants interpreted and negotiated learning depending on their developmental level (Kegan et al., 2001). Students in the cohort, partially because of the different ways of knowing they exhibited, played an important role as a holding environment in the learning process by challenging and supporting each other.

Applications

Much of Kegan's 1994 book is devoted to understanding and addressing the demands of modern life using his theory as a framework. With regard to the college learning environment, Kegan (1994) suggested that while most students approach learning from an order 3 perspective, teaching is generally approached through the lens of order 4, creating a developmental mismatch. For instance, instructors expect students to be self-reflective, engaged, independent, self-directed, critical thinkers—skills that become evident only in order 4. Rather than assuming and treating students as if they are already self-authoring, Kegan (1994) stressed the importance of building a "consciousness bridge" (p. 278) between the point at which the student enters the classroom (generally order 3) and the level at which he or she is expected to perform in the classroom (order 4), noting that "the bridge builder must have an equal respect for both ends, creating a firm foundation on both sides of the chasm students will traverse" (p. 278).

Ignelzi (2000) used Kegan's concepts to discuss applications in traditional undergraduate classrooms. Pointing out that most undergraduate students use order 3 meaning making and therefore look to their instructors and classmates to determine how they should think and the conclusions they should draw about the material being examined, Ignelzi suggested the following strategies for encouraging both learning and development: (1) value and support students' current ways of thinking, (2) provide structure and guidance in taking on unfamiliar tasks, (3) encourage students to learn from each other by working together in groups, and (4) acknowledge and reinforce students' successes in moving to a self-authored perspective while recognizing the challenges required to do so. These suggestions reflect Kegan's (1982) idea of an effective holding environment.

King and Baxter Magolda (1996) used Kegan's (1994) model to frame student affairs educational practice. They suggested that the role of student affairs educators is to assist in the creation of the evolutionary bridges Kegan discussed. Assessment and evaluation of student development are important components of this process. Ongoing dialogue with students is needed to help students establish developmental goals and determine ways to achieve them.

To assist students in moving from the second order of consciousness to the third, Love and Guthrie (1999) pointed out the importance of letting students' know what behaviors are expected of them and what their responsibilities are, working with them to understand how others' perspectives compare to their own and when the needs of others take priority, and encouraging self-reflection. The transition from the third to the fourth order of consciousness is often precipitated by a failed relationship around which the individual has constructed his or her life's meaning and the resulting need to develop independent goals and values. Educators must recognize the pain associated with this transition and support students through the process by recognizing them as independent people, acknowledging their achievements, and encouraging them to get involved in activities where their talents will be valued.

Kegan's concept of coaching can easily translate into student affairs practice (Love & Guthrie, 1999). In the challenging college environment, student affairs staff can act as "sympathetic coaches" (p. 74), providing support for students to be who they are while also encouraging them to move beyond their current way of making meaning. Coaching can take the form of programs that keep students' developmental levels in mind by providing appropriate structure and communicating in ways that students understand, while at the same time encouraging them to try new ways of approaching ideas.

Based on Kegan's (1994) ideas, King and Baxter Magolda (2005) introduced a multidimensional model focusing on the development of intercultural maturity, which they described as consisting of a "range of attributes, including understanding (the cognitive dimension), sensitivity to others (the interpersonal dimension), and a sense of oneself that enables one to listen to and learn from others (the intrapersonal dimension)" (p. 574). They identified three levels of development in each dimension that influence each other and are intertwined rather than independent. Educators will be more effective in promoting intercultural maturity if they consider all of the dimensions of development and if the process is viewed as one that evolves, given appropriate experiences (King & Baxter Magolda, 2005).

With Kegan's theory as a framework, Ignelzi (1994) investigated what student affairs graduate students and new professionals were looking for from their work supervisors. He found that expectations fell into three categories paralleling Kegan's order 3, the transition from order 3 to order 4, and order 4, with most first-year professionals falling in the transition where they desired more autonomy yet also struggled with wanting the approval of their supervisors. As such, they needed both structure and support from their supervisors. Professionals at this point of development have trouble sharing problems and concerns with their supervisors because they fear disapproval (Ignelzi, 1994). The first goal of a supervisor must therefore be establishing a strong relationship with the supervisee so that the supervisee will feel comfortable revealing personal and professional issues that may interfere with work performance. Supervisors must be aware of the developmental level of their supervisee rather than assuming it based on age or years in the field (Ignelzi & Whitely, 2004). Since it is unrealistic to expect new professionals to be at the level of self-authorship (order 4), ongoing developmental supervision is critical.

Baxter Magolda's Theory of Self-Authorship

As discussed in Chapter Seven, Marcia Baxter Magolda's early research focused on the epistemological development of 101 Miami University students during the college years. Her later work followed a subset of thirty-nine of these students during their twenties and thirty of the thirty-nine into their thirties. All thirty (eighteen women and eleven men) continuing participants are white; seventeen have advanced degrees, and most work in the fields of business and education. Twenty-seven are married or in committed relationships, and twenty-two have children.

In her postcollege research, Baxter Magolda has used sixty- to ninety-minute informal conversational interviews, mostly conducted by telephone (Baxter Magolda, 1999a). Participants told her that learning was not an appropriate framework to discuss their postcollege development and suggested that they discuss their overall experience instead (Baxter Magolda, 2004a). In these interviews, Baxter Magolda (1998b, 1999a, 2001, 2004a, 2008) found evidence that her participants' epistemological development was intertwined with the development of their sense of self and relationships with others. Based on her research involving young adults in their twenties, Baxter Magolda (1998b, 1999a, 1999c, 2001) extended her theory to explain their development at this point in their lives—development that centered on achieving self-authorship. Drawing on the work of Kegan (1994), Baxter Magolda (2008) defined self-authorship as "the internal capacity to define one's beliefs, identity, and social relations" (p. 269). Her most recent work (Baxter Magolda, 2008) has explored the developmental process her participants experienced in their thirties, a time in which self-authorship becomes solidified.

Baxter Magolda's Theory

Baxter Magolda (2001) highlighted a number of developmental tasks associated with the decade of the twenties, including values exploration, making sense of information gained about the world in previous years, determining the path one will take, and taking steps along that path. During this time, three major questions take precedence: "How do I know?" "Who am I?" and "How do I want to construct relationships with others?" (p. 15). The first question has to do with "the *epistemological* dimension of self-authorship—the evolution of assumptions about the nature, limits, and certainty of knowledge" (p. 15). The "Who am I?" question refers to the intrapersonal dimension—individuals' sense of who they are and what they believe. The relationship question reflects the interpersonal dimension—"how one perceives and constructs one's relationships with others" (p. 15). People soon learn that the answers to these questions are intertwined.

As they attempt to find answers, young adults are bombarded by the fast pace, lack of clarity, and complexity characterizing society. They enter the unfamiliar world outside education with concerns that center around establishing careers, developing meaningful relationships, being able to manage their lives on their own, eventually establishing families, and being satisfied and happy (Baxter Magolda, 2001). To accomplish these tasks, a self-authoring perspective is needed (Baxter Magolda, 2008). Unfortunately, college environments often do not create the conditions necessary for self-authorship to develop, and many students struggle with the challenges they face.

Baxter Magolda (2001) indicated that students in her study were only anticipating self-authorship as they finished their degrees: "They left college with an initial awareness that they would have to make their own decisions, but without internal mechanisms to do so" (p. 36). She also stated, "Higher education has a responsibility to help young adults make the transition from being shaped by society to shaping society in their role as leaders in society's future" (Baxter Magolda, 1999a, p. 630).

In describing the early adult years, Baxter Magolda (2001) discussed both the internal process involved in the development of self-authorship and conditions that foster it. It is important to keep in mind that "developing self-authorship takes time and energy" (Baxter Magolda, 2004c, p. 17).

The Path to Self-Authorship. Baxter Magolda (2001) identified four phases in the journey toward self-authorship involving movement from external to internal self-definition. Cognitive, intrapersonal, and interpersonal dimensions are associated with each phase.

Phase 1: Following Formulas. In the first phase of the "journey toward self-authorship" (Baxter Magolda, 2001, p. 40), young adults follow the plans laid out for them by external authorities about what they should think and how they should accomplish their work, although they frame these formulas to sound as if they are their own ideas. Likewise, they allow others to define who they are. Gaining approval of others is the critical aspect of relationship building. Sources of external formulas include societal expectations, adults with whom they interact, and their peers. Parents, significant others, and mentors are particularly influential. Baxter Magolda (1998b) equated this phase with the third order in Kegan's (1994) theory.

Formulas are carried out in careers and in personal lives. For instance, decisions about careers and jobs "revolved around doing what one was supposed to do to be successful" (Baxter Magolda, 2001, p. 78), which often did not lead to meaningful work since the formulas did not always reflect individuals' actual interests. In taking on adult roles, individuals found it even more difficult to follow external formulas to satisfactory conclusions. Often formulas conflicted, such as "be in a relationship" and "devote yourself to your career." Not having a clear sense of self made it difficult to determine what to do, both personally and in relationships, and thus when one formula did not work out, other formulas were sought.

Both Symone and Rodney seem to be following formulas established by the external world. In Symone's case, the new formula of going to college to find direction is one provided by her minister. Previous formulas established by her father and former husband are no longer available to her. In Rodney's case, his formula for success has been established by society, which sends messages that a person will make more money and get a better job by going to college.

Phase 2: Crossroads. As individuals progress along their journey, they discover that the plans they have followed do not necessarily work well and that they need to establish new plans that better suit their needs and interests. At the same time, they become dissatisfied with how they have been defined by others and see the need to create their own sense of self. They also see that allowing approval of others to dictate their relationships is limiting and that being more authentic would be preferable. In some cases, following external formulas leads to crisis, and in others, the result is a general sense of unhappiness and lack of fulfillment. In each instance, however, young adults are not yet at a point where they can act on their desires to be more autonomous, fearing the reactions of others.

Baxter Magolda (2001) determined that career settings often provided the impetus to question external formulas. In the workplace, her participants' developing inner voices often questioned their career paths. Relationships were also the focus of the crossroads as individuals attempted to resolve tension between what they wanted and what others wanted or expected. Establishing one's own beliefs rather than adopting those of others as they had done in the past was also a difficult experience in this phase for many young adults. A clearer sense of direction and more self-confidence marked the end of the crossroads. Laticia appears to be at the end of her crossroads as she has decided that she will return to college to become a teacher. She is confident that this is a good direction for her, despite the doubts of others.

Phase 3: Becoming the Author of One's Life. Similar to Kegan's (1994) fourth order of consciousness, this phase is characterized by the ability to choose one's beliefs and stand up for them in the face of conflicting external viewpoints (Baxter Magolda, 1998b, 2001). After choosing their beliefs, individuals feel compelled to live them out, which is often difficult. They are also aware that belief systems are contextual, can change, and are never as clear as one would wish. As a result of intensive self-reflection, individuals develop a strong self-concept. In relationships, renegotiation often occurs as young adults weigh their needs and desires, along with those of others around them. Individuals are also more careful in making relationship commitments to ensure that the commitment "honor[s] the self they [are] constructing" (Baxter Magolda, 2001, p. 140). The three dimensions of self-authorship are closely intertwined, and the saliency of each dimension differs depending on life circumstances and experiences.

Phase 4: Internal Foundation. Young adults who successfully negotiate this stage are grounded in their self-determined belief system, in their sense of who they are, and in the mutuality of their relationships. A "solidified and comprehensive system of belief" (Baxter Magolda, 2001, p. 155) now exists. At the same time, individuals are accepting of ambiguity and open to change. They experience feelings of peace, contentment, and inner strength. Although they are aware of external influences, they are not greatly affected by them. They trust their own feelings and act on them rationally. Life decisions are based on their internal foundation. For some individuals, this leads to new directions in their careers; for others, changes are made in their personal lives. At the same time, their responsibilities to others, based on their own sense of those responsibilities, are clearly a part of their internal foundations. For many individuals, spirituality plays a role.

The Elements of Self-Authorship. Interviews with participants in their thirties uncovered three elements of self-authorship: trusting the internal voice, building an internal foundation, and securing internal commitments (Baxter Magolda, 2008). *Trusting the internal voice* involved participants' realizing that while they could not always control events external to them, they did have control over how they thought about and responded to events, which led to their becoming more confident of their internal voices. This process occurred in each of the different dimensions of development (epistemological, interpersonal, and intrapersonal) and in different domains (such as work, relationships, and self-awareness).

Once individuals learned to trust their internal voices, they began *building an internal foundation*, which Baxter Magolda (2008) defined as a personal philosophy or framework to guide their actions. One participant in Baxter Magolda's study called this foundation the "core of one's being" (p. 280). All the dimensions of development merge to create a "cohesive entity" (p. 280). As individuals experience different life events, they may reevaluate and adjust their foundation.

Once the third element of self-authorship, *securing internal commitments*, had been achieved, "participants felt that living their convictions was as natural and as necessary as breathing" (Baxter Magolda, 2008, p. 281). They integrated their internal foundations with the realities of their external worlds, which led to a sense of freedom to live their lives authentically. The development of self-authorship is not a linear process but rather can follow many different paths influenced by personal characteristics of individuals, contexts in which they find themselves, and the challenges and supports they experience along the way. Self-authorship enhances rather than detracts from relationships and interactions with the external world. As people become more confident and clear about who they are, they are able to relate to others in a more honest and open manner.

Learning Partnerships Model. Baxter Magolda was as concerned about the conditions that foster development of self-authorship as she was about the concept itself. Based on the findings of her longitudinal study of young adults and ideas first outlined in her 1992 book, she introduced the learning partnerships model in *Making Their Own Way* (2001) and elaborated on it in her book with Patricia King, *Learning Partnerships* (2004). Baxter Magolda (2001) stated that "environments that were most effective in promoting self-authorship" challenged dependence on authority. Three assumptions guided her approach: (1) "knowledge [is] complex and socially constructed," (2) "self is central to knowledge construction," and (3) "authority and expertise [are] shared in the mutual construction of knowledge among peers" (p. xx). These assumptions address cognitive, intrapersonal, and interpersonal aspects of development (Baxter Magolda, 2004b).

Building on these three assumptions, Baxter Magolda (2001) claimed that educational practice that encourages self-authorship is based on three principles: (1) "validating learners' capacity to know," (2) "situating learning in learners' experience," and (3) "mutually constructing meaning" (p. xxi), the same principles she introduced in relation to her original theory of epistemological development (Baxter Magolda, 1992). She noted that while the assumptions challenged students' meaning-making processes, the principles served as a bridge between their current level of development and self-authorship (Baxter Magolda, 2004b). Uses of the learning partnership model are discussed in the Applications section.

Research

A number of other researchers have explored aspects of Baxter Magolda's theory of self-authorship.

The Concept of Self-Authorship. Several studies have been designed to explore the concept of self-authorship as well as factors associated with its development. Jane Pizzolato is primary among the researchers working in this area.

To learn more about factors associated with self-authorship, Pizzolato (2005) examined narratives written by 613 students in response to her Experience Survey (see Pizzolato, 2007) regarding important decisions they had made. Her findings indicated that experiencing a decision as a "provocative moment" (that is, one creating disequilibrium leading to reevaluation of one's goals or sense of self; Pizzolato, 2005, p. 629) on the path to self-authorship was related to character-istics of both the student and the situation. More important was the student's purpose for making the decision. Pizzolato (2005) suggested that it is possible to create situations that will be provocative moments using principles associated with the learning partnerships model (Baxter Magolda & King, 2004).

In a study validating two measures of self-authorship, Pizzolato (2007) sug-gested that self-authored action may be dependent on whether the individual views the situation as supportive of self-authorship. She proposed four expressions of self-authorship, based on whether reasoning or action is self-authored.

Self-Authorship in Diverse Populations. To extend Baxter Magolda's theory to more diverse populations, several researchers have investigated self-authorship in different settings. In an interview study, Pizzolato (2003) found that high-risk college students often reached self-authorship prior to college as a result of expe-riencing challenging situations early in life that required them to make decisions and take action on their own, such as making the decision to attend college and needing to negotiate the admissions process without any guidance or encourage-ment from parents.

Pizzolato (2004) discovered that although high-risk students entered college at the level of self-authorship (see Pizzolato, 2003), this way of making meaning was challenged by classroom and out-of-classroom experiences that led them to feel incompetent, misunderstood, and different from their peers, which led to high levels of anxiety and dissonance and resulted in students' reconsidering their internal foundations and attempting to meet external expectations. Discomfort with this strategy allowed them to eventually return to a self-authored perspective. Pizzolato (2004) noted that acting in self-authored ways may require not only the ability to reason independently but also feeling supported to take action.

Two studies reported by Pizzolato, Chaudhari, Murrell, Podobnik, and Schaeffer (2008) suggested that ethnic identity development and epistemological development are intertwined processes, with each process having a positive effect on the other. Together, ethnic identity development and epistemological development predicted college grade point average (GPA) almost as well as previous academic performance measured by SAT scores and high school GPA. In particular, capacity for autonomous action made a difference.

In a longitudinal qualitative study involving Latino/a students from seven colleges and universities, Torres and Baxter Magolda (2004) found that ethnic identity development, an intrapersonal dimension of development, was very much interwoven with cognitive and interpersonal dimensions of development, with all three dimensions working together as students developed self-authorship. The challenge of cognitive dissonance caused by experiences of stereotyping and cultural oppression was a key factor in propelling students toward self-authorship, while support to address this dissonance was also a critical factor.

Torres and Hernandez (2007) also reported that for the twenty-nine Latino students they interviewed, recognizing and making meaning of racism was important in developing self-authorship. Studying a different population, Abes and Jones (2004) discovered that where lesbian students were on the path toward self-authorship determined the extent to which external influences, such as family, peer group, social norms, and stereotypes, affected self-perceptions of sexual orientation identity and other dimensions of identity, including religion, race, gender, and social class, as well as the intersections of the dimensions.

Self-Authorship in Context. Research has also suggested relationships between self-authorship and other variables. In a longitudinal study of the relationships among student characteristics, students' academic and living environment, and self-authorship, Wawrzynski and Pizzolato (2006) found that sex, being a transfer student, strong academic performance prior to college, being a student of color, and living on campus significantly predicted several of the subscales on the Self-Authorship Survey (Pizzolato, 2004).

The authors of a study examining the relationship between self-authorship and women's career decision making concluded that early in the process of self-authorship, women still relied heavily on advice from people they trusted, usually parents, even though the women were aware that they were ultimately responsible for their own decisions (Creamer & Laughlin, 2005; Laughlin & Creamer, 2007). This finding supports Baxter Magolda's (2001) description of young adults' reliance on external formulas as they begin the journey to self-authorship.

Pizzolato (2006) determined that students who worked with advisors who encouraged reflection in goal setting and intentional planning and discussed with students their nonacademic life experiences were more likely to develop abilities and perspectives associated with self-authorship. Continuing to explore the developmental experiences of students in advising situations, Pizzolato and Ozaki (2007) investigated early movement toward self-authorship experienced by students who were part of an advising program modeled after the learning partnerships model (Baxter Magolda, 2001) that was designed to help students in academic difficulty stay in school. Their findings suggested that students entered the program using external formulas to make sense of the world. However, external pressures caused them interpersonal and intrapersonal stress, pushing them into the crossroads in Baxter Magolda's (2001) model. As a result of participating in the program, they appeared to experience more rapid development than most other students. They came to believe that they had control over the outcomes they experienced and that they personally played an important role in constructing knowledge and decision making, precursors of self-authorship.

Applications

Much of Baxter Magolda's scholarship has focused on applications of her model to classroom and student affairs settings. She has argued that to adequately prepare students for this century, self-authorship needs to be the basis for advanced learning outcomes in college (Baxter Magolda, 2007). Using the principles for learning and development initially proposed in her 1992 book and outlined in detail in several other books and in numerous articles (see Baxter Magolda, 1998b, 1999a, 2001, 2002b, 2003; Baxter Magolda & King, 2004), Baxter Magolda has suggested methods for measuring and promoting self-authorship in college settings.

Baxter Magolda and King (2007) described two interview strategies to aid educators in assessing self-authorship. The first is the Self-Authorship Interview (see Baxter Magolda, 2001) in which participants share their personal reflections on topics of importance to them. The second is the Wabash National Study of Liberal Arts Education Interview, designed to determine development related to seven liberal arts outcomes, as well as students' paths toward self-authorship.

Pizzolato (2007) introduced a short, quantitative measure of self-authorship, the Self-Authorship Survey (SAS), consisting of four subscales: capacity for autonomous action, problem-solving orientation, perceptions of volitional competence, and self-regulation in challenging situations. The second half of the same instrument is the Experience Survey, which asks participants to write narratives about a significant decision they have made. Essays are scored on each of three dimensions: decision making, problem solving, and autonomy. She recommended using the two instruments together to provide a more complete picture of participants' ability to self-author both their reasoning and their actions.

Baxter Magolda (2002b) stressed the need for students and educators to work together to develop student self-authorship, demonstrating respect for each other and actively sharing ideas and viewpoints. Both classroom and cocurricular settings provide opportunities for this type of exchange. Classroom discussion and course assignments, career and academic advising, campus living situations, student employment, and student organizations are examples.

Opportunities for self-reflection in these settings also assist students in becoming clearer about what they know, why they hold the beliefs they do, and how they want to act on their beliefs (Baxter Magolda, 1999a, 2008). Baxter Magolda and King (2008) introduced the Wabash National Study Conversation Guide as an aid for engaging students in meaningful, reflective conversations. This guide is based on the interview protocol mentioned earlier. The purpose of the conversations for which the guide was constructed is to offer "students an opportunity to reflect on the meaning of their experiences and to help them develop reflective habits" (p. 9). These conversations might be initiated by advisors, faculty, supervisors of student employees, diversity educators, or other student affairs staff.

Active involvement in meaningful activities and leadership positions is another variable needed to foster development of self-authorship (Baxter Magolda, 1999a). Baxer Magolda (1999d) stressed that "students do not learn to behave in mature ways without practice" (p. 4). This process requires identifying situations that are safe and doable for students who are at varying points along the journey to self-authorship (Baxter Magolda, 2003). Support is critical as students assume meaningful responsibility.

Examples of ways in which the learning partnerships model has been used in instructional settings and in student affairs practice have been discussed in numerous books and articles (see Baxter Magolda, 2003; Baxter Magolda & King, 2004; Meszaros, 2007). Some of these applications are mentioned below.

Instructional Applications. Baxter Magolda (1999b) conducted semester-length observations of three classrooms—one each in the fields of mathematics, zoology, and education—and interviewed both faculty and students in the courses to understand different methods for implementing constructive-developmental pedagogy in various classroom settings. Processes used included an interactive lecture format for learning scientific inquiry, an "investigating together" method for approaching mathematics, and a narrative approach to teaching social foundations of education, in which storytelling was used to promote self-authorship. Based on this study, Baxter Magolda (1999b) offered a theory of learning and teaching using a constructive developmental framework and discussed the challenges and opportunities of this type of teaching approach.

Examples of ways in which the learning partnerships model has been used in academic settings include framing faculty development (Wildman, 2004, 2007), undergirding curriculum development (Bekken & Marie, 2007), providing impetus for institutional development (Wildman, 2004), creating an urban leadership internship program designed to promote intercultural maturity (Baxter Magolda, 2007; Egart & Healy, 2004), structuring an international service-learning curriculum (Baxter Magolda, 2007; Yonkers-Talz, 2004), establishing a multicultural education class at a community college (Baxter Magolda, 2003; Hornak & Ortiz, 2004), developing a college honors program (Haynes, 2006), providing a guiding philosophy for student affairs graduate preparation (Baxter Magolda, 1999b, 2007; Rogers, Magolda, Baxter Magolda, & Knight Abowitz, 2004), and creating conditions for self-authorship in graduate education (Baxter Magolda, 1998a).

Student Affairs Applications. The learning partnerships model has also been used in student affairs settings as an overall framework to structure the work of student affairs divisions (Baxter Magolda, 2007; Mills & Strong, 2004), to create community standards in residence halls (Baxter Magolda, 2003, 2007; Piper, 1997; Piper & Buckley, 2004), in conceptualizing developmental academic advising (Baxter Magolda, 2003, 2007), in providing a basis for career advising (Baxter Magolda, 2007), as a focus for training honors councils that adjudicate academic dishonesty cases (Baxter Magolda, 2007), and in professional student affairs staff development (Baxter Magolda, 2007).

In the final chapter of the book *Learning Partnerships*, King and Baxter Magolda (2004) offered a framework for educators to decide whether and how to use the learning partnerships model. It includes questions to ask when considering whether to use the model, as well as offering ten specific steps for its implementation.

Critique and Future Directions

As both Kegan (1994) and Baxter Magolda (2008) have effectively articulated, the complexities of society make self-authorship a necessity. This concept, introduced by Kegan in the 1980s, has gained new life with the ongoing work of Baxter Magolda and later researchers, including Pizzolato and Torres.

Kegan's (1982, 1994) theory offered conceptual breakthroughs, particularly with regard to the interconnection of epistemological, intrapersonal, and interpersonal components of development, as well as the role of the environment in shaping development. However, his writing is often dense and psychoanalytic in tone. Kegan was also vague about the research foundations of his work, which can lead to skepticism about its validity. In his 1994 book, Kegan offered more in the way of suggestions for encouraging development in educational settings than he had earlier. The concepts of holding environments, evolutionary bridges, and sympathetic coaches all have meaning for those who work closely with students.

The importance of Kegan's theory as a description of developmental evolution over the life span cannot be overstated. However, it has been the work of Marcia Baxter Magolda that has popularized it within educational circles. The power of Baxter Magolda's scholarship lies in her longitudinal approach, depth of analysis, and careful attention to application of theory in practice. In each of these areas, her work is exemplary.

No other student development theorist has even considered interviewing the same participants yearly for over twenty years. As one reads their stories as told in Baxter Magolda's books and articles, they become real people facing challenging life experiences. As a result, it is easy to relate to their circumstances and their meaning making. The shifts in perspective over time are clear. The evidence from their narratives definitely validates Baxter Magolda's evolving theory.

Baxter Magolda (1992, 2004a) has described her methodological transformation from a quantitative to a qualitative researcher. In her work with students, she came to see that a qualitative approach enabled her to truly understand and tell their stories in a way that quantitative methodology did not allow. The narratives she provides and her careful grounded theory analysis have led to a carefully conceptualized theory that is easy to understand and therefore to use.

A major strength of Baxter Magolda's work is its utility. She has done a remarkable job of outlining ways in which her theory translates into practice in both student affairs and academic settings. The learning partnerships model has been used in numerous settings and is making a difference in the lives of students, faculty, and student affairs professionals.

The primary weakness of Baxter Magolda's work has been the narrowness of the population on which it is based—white, mostly privileged individuals who were all undergraduate students at Miami University. Recognizing this limitation, Baxter Magolda (2004a) has called for additional studies of self-authorship based on diverse populations of students in different types of settings. Pizzolato and Torres are pursuing this line of research with high-risk students and Latino/a students, respectively. More work is needed to examine the experiences of diverse student populations, particularly those who come from more communally oriented cultures.

Baxter Magolda (2004a) also saw the need for further investigation of the interconnections of the multiple components of self-authorship. Pizzolato's identification of distinctions between self-authored reasoning and self-authored action provides an interesting direction to pursue.

CHAPTER ELEVEN

DEVELOPMENT OF FAITH
AND SPIRITUALITY

Guisela, Amy, Toccara, Yen, Wesley, Mike, and Philip, members of a multicultural learning community, were having a late-night discussion at the local all-night diner after their class, Multicultural Learning in a Global Context. The instructor, Dr. Ruiz, often got them thinking, and tonight was no exception. Tonight's class had focused on the role of spirituality in the learning process. Dr. Ruiz had asked students to pair up with a classmate and discuss their own spiritual belief system and how it influenced them as learners. Although they were used to self-reflection as part of this class, most of the students felt uneasy openly discussing spirituality, a topic not generally talked about in their public university classes. They left the class wanting to process the experience.

Mike started the conversation, noting that he was glad that Dr. Ruiz made a distinction between religion and spirituality because Mike did not view himself as religious. Since coming to State, however, he had been feeling that something was missing in his life, and their class discussion had him thinking about his spiritual base. Wesley jumped in at this point to invite Mike to a meeting of Campus Crusade for Christ, an evangelical group he had recently joined at his older brother's suggestion, assuring Mike that this group would provide the spiritual base he was seeking, as it had for him. Guisela also expressed a deep faith, hers very much steeped in her Mexican Catholic heritage. She had never considered not following the tenets her priest and parents had taught her. Toccara could relate to Guisela's experience, having grown up in an African American family that went to church twice a week. Toccara told the group that she was starting to question what her faith really meant; however, her church community was too important for her to consider ever leaving her church. Philip, who shared Guisela's Mexican cultural background, explained that he had rejected Catholicism when his father was killed trying to cross the border illegally. He could no longer believe in a God who would let this happen. He believed in himself and his ability to make the world a better place without the help of a higher power. Yen, who was Buddhist, found her beliefs quite different from those of other Americans, yet she viewed herself as a spiritual person. Amy chimed in that she really appreciated being part of a learning community where she had found friends with whom she could discuss these matters, since she had started attending a church different from the one in which her parents had raised her and needed support.

◆ ◆ ◆

Spirituality, faith, belief, religion: as can be seen in the scenario just presented, these concepts are confusing and often used interchangeably. For this chapter, we have selected research-based definitions to clarify the differences among these concepts. Based on his study of eight students with different worldviews, Mayhew (2004) described *spirituality* as "the human attempt to make sense of the self in connection to and with the external world" (p. 666). Fowler (1996), whose research is discussed later in this chapter, defined *belief* as conscious intellectual agreement with particular doctrines or ideologies, while *religion* consists of many beliefs and practices of a collective group of people over a period of time. *Faith*, in Fowler's opinion, underlies both belief and religion but is also inclusive of secular worldviews: it "is our way of finding coherence in and giving meaning to the multiple forces and relations that make up our lives" (Fowler, 1981, p. 4).

Although the first colleges in the United States were created to train clergy and ensure that youth received a religiously grounded education (Temkin & Evans, 1998), public higher education in the past century has been reluctant to address the spiritual and faith development of students (Tisdell, 2003). Speck (2005) identified three factors that have contributed to avoidance of spirituality as a topic for discussion in public higher education: (1) the erroneous belief that the constitutional requirement of separation of church and state precludes any mention of matters that could be construed as religious, (2) the emphasis in higher education on objectivity and rationality, and (3) the lack of preparation that most educators have to address the topic of spirituality.

While some students reject the concepts of faith and spirituality altogether (Goodman & Mueller, 2009), research suggests that others are increasingly interested in these concepts (Higher Education Research Institute, 2004). Some follow a traditional path within the context of organized religion, others are attracted to nondenominational evangelical groups, and many choose to pursue spirituality in nontraditional ways unconnected to mainstream religion (Coomes, 2004; Dalton, Eberhardt, Bracken, & Echols, 2006; Hartley, 2004; Kuh & Gonyea, 2005).

Despite the reluctance of public higher education to be involved in activities that focus on spiritual development, a plethora of books and articles addressing the topic of spirituality in higher education settings have appeared in recent years (for example, Chickering, Dalton, & Stamm, 2006; Hoppe & Speck, 2005; Jablonski, 2001; Miller & Ryan, 2001; Rogers & Dantley, 2001; Zajonc, 2003), supporting Tisdell's (2003) assertion that educators are seeing this topic as timely. Each of these writings presented excellent examples for integrating spirituality into the life of colleges and universities. With a few exceptions, however (see Dalton, 2006a; Love, 2001; Stamm, 2006, Strange, 2001), the authors have discussed spirituality generally, failing to provide clear definitions of the concept or theoretical bases for their arguments. In this chapter, we attempt to fill this void by discussing theories of faith and spiritual development that are research based and have applications in student affairs practice, specifically the work of James Fowler and Sharon Daloz Parks.

Fowler's Theory of Faith Development

James W. Fowler is the foremost theorist to address faith using a developmental approach. The author of eleven books on the topic, Fowler presented the primary explication of his theory in 1981 in the book *Stages of Faith*. Iterations of his theory appeared in publications from 1978 through 2000.

Historical Overview

Trained as a Methodist minister, Fowler began to formulate his theory of faith development when he was working at a retreat center for clergy and laypeople. There, he had the opportunity to listen to the life stories of nearly three hundred people and saw connections between what he was hearing and Erikson's model of identity development (Dykstra & Parks, 1986). When he joined the faculty at Harvard in 1969, Fowler went on to more formally study the developmental trajectory he had detected. He became familiar with and was influenced by Kohlberg's (1969) work on moral development, as well Piaget's (1950) study of intellectual development and Selman's (1976) investigations of social perspective taking (Fowler, 1981). Kegan's (1982) exploration of self and others in relationship also influenced Fowler's understanding of faith (Fowler, 1980). Later in his career, other developmental theorists contributed to his thinking, including Gilligan (1982/1993) and Stern (1985).

Fowler's (1981) model was based on interviews with 359 individuals, ranging from three and a half to eighty-four years of age, obtained between 1972 and 1981 in the areas around Boston, Toronto, and Atlanta. The sample was 97.8 percent white and evenly divided between men and women. Protestants constituted 45 percent of the sample, 36.5 percent were Catholic, 11.2 percent were Jewish, 3.6 percent were Orthodox, and 3.6 percent identified other belief systems. As Fowler developed his theory, he vetted it in presentations to religious practitioners and educators, using their feedback in his revisions (Fowler, 1996).

Fowler's Theory

Fowler (1978) made clear that he did not equate faith and religion but rather saw faith as being "both broader and more personal" (p. 18) than religion. Fowler's work rests on the assumption that faith is universal (Fowler, 1981, 2000), but he also noted that each person's faith is unique in the manner in which it is exhibited, as demonstrated by the students in our opening scenario. Fowler (1981) stressed the relational nature of faith; to explain, he used a triangle with energy flowing in both directions along the baselines between self, others, and an agreed-on belief system, each represented as a point of the triangle. In addition, he interpreted faith as a process of imagination, positing that knowing begins and is maintained as internal representations or images of particular situations, events, or information that evolve as one matures and reacts to different experiences.

Faith takes the form of unconscious structures that constitute a series of stages of faith development (Fowler, 2000). Starting with the first iteration of his theory, Fowler (1978) stressed the distinction between content and structure, pointing out that individuals at the same stage can hold beliefs that are vastly different (content) while their ways of thinking about and making sense of their beliefs (process) are similar. As in other cognitive-structural models, although the order in which Fowler's stages of faith arise is invariant, some individuals never reach the more advanced stages (Fowler, 1996). Fowler (1981, 2000) also clarified that movement through the stages is more like a spiral than a step-by-step advancement. Each proceeding stage in his model is a more complex and comprehensive way of understanding one's religious tradition. Influenced by Kegan, and unlike other cognitive-structural theories, Fowler (1981) did not separate cognition and affect in his stages of faith development. He was hesitant to claim universality for his stages but did suggest that their descriptions were generalizable and testable across cultures.

Stages of Faith. The following descriptions of Fowler's stages are based primarily on the delineations of his theory presented in 1981, 1996, and 2000:

Prestage 1: Primal faith (labeled *undifferentiated faith* in earlier versions of the model). A prelinguistic manifestation of faith arises in the person's first years in the context of relationship with primary caretakers. These relationships form the basis of one's first images of God.

Stage 1: Intuitive-projective faith. This stage manifests around age two with the emergence of language; at this time children begin to construct their first images of God, based on "perception, feelings, and imaginative fantasy" (Fowler, 2000, p. 42) that result from stories, pictures, and images shared with the young child by significant others.

Stage 2: Mythic-literal faith. During the early elementary school years (ages six and seven), as children develop the ability to see perspectives other than their own, they are able to follow, make sense of, and remember stories told to them by their family and significant others. Without reflection, they accept these narratives literally and they form the basis of the person's beliefs. Adults as well as children may function at this stage of faith, as well as any of those to follow. In the opening story, Guisela's faith might reflect this stage since she accepts the tenets of her religion without reflection.

Stage 3: Synthetic-conventional faith. During early adolescence, individuals develop the ability to think abstractly and integrate ideas from various sources, including peers, school, media, and perhaps a religious community. Although individuals at this stage find their faith to be meaningful, they are not yet able to consider it critically. External validation is still necessary to affirm one's decisions (Fowler, 1996). Amy might be at this stage, since she is seeking peer support of her decision to change her religion.

Stage 4: Individuative-reflective faith (initially labeled *individuating-reflexive*). This stage is initiated when one's self-definition becomes self-authored, and one's system of beliefs, values, and commitments becomes a coherent and explicit meaning-making system. In his 1981 work, Fowler suggested that stage 4 thinking "most appropriately takes form in young adulthood" (p. 182). However, in later writings (see Fowler, 2000), he indicated that this transition usually occurs between ages thirty and forty, typically resulting from changes in relationships or challenges in one's environment.

Stage 5: Conjunctive faith (labeled *paradoxical-consolidative* initially). Movement into this stage takes place at midlife or beyond. It involves an increasing awareness of the complexity of life and unconscious influences on one's behavior and attitudes.

Symbolism is again appreciated in conjunction with conceptual meanings, and individuals are more deeply aware of their convictions. Individuals are more accepting of other faith traditions while also holding a deep commitment to theirs.

Stage 6: Universalizing faith. Persons who reach this final stage experience a "radical decentration from self," defined as "knowing" the world through the eyes of others different from them, and they value God and other people "from a standpoint more nearly identified with the love of the Creator for creatures" (Fowler, 2000, pp. 55–56). Fowler stated that it was rare to find individuals in the universalizing stage. He cited Gandhi, Martin Luther King Jr., and Mother Teresa of Calcutta as examples. In the face of criticism that little evidence supports the existence of this stage (see Broughton, 1986; G. Moran, 1983), Fowler (2000) modified his theory, stating that conjunctive faith (stage 5) is the end point of a natural progression of development. He went on to suggest, however, that "in partnership with Spirit," any person has the potential to move on to universalizing faith (Fowler, 2000, p. 61).

Faith Development. "Biological maturation, emotional and cognitive development, psychosocial experience, and religio-cultural influences" (Fowler, 1996, p. 57) all affect movement through the stages of faith development. The process is triggered when one's experiences create dissonance that cannot be addressed effectively by one's current way of making meaning (Fowler, 1981, 2000). The result is a new stage consisting of a change in one's belief system and sense-making process.

Three phases are evident during times of transition between stages: endings, the neutral zone, and new beginnings (Fowler, 1996). Endings have four processes: (1) *disengagement* from a particular relational context that has given one's life meaning; (2) *disidentification*, the loss of one's sense of self that accompanies disengagement; (3) *disenchantment*, which involves parting with one's previous view of reality and experiencing feelings of grief, loss, confusion, and, in some cases, liberation; and (4) *disorientation*, "the cumulative impact of the three other aspects of our experience of endings" (Fowler, 1996, p. 73), which leads to the neutral zone. The neutral zone is experienced as "a time out of ordinary time" (Fowler, 1996, p. 74) in which one lives through the disintegration of one's previous way of life and struggles to develop a new way of making sense of the world. Eventually the individual begins to explore new beginnings. Fowler (1996) cautioned that new beginnings should not be rushed, noting that therapy, religious communities, and spiritual guides can create "holding environments" (p. 74) that enable individuals to fully explore the potential new paths they are considering.

Life Span Development and Vocation. While cautioning against "viewing stages as constituting an achievement scale" (Fowler, 1986b, p. 38), Fowler (1986b) stressed that "each stage represents genuine growth toward wider and more accurate response to God and toward more consistently humane care for other human beings" (pp. 38–39). As such, it is the obligation of faith communities to encourage development. Surprisingly, he also reported that most of the participants in his studies had rarely had the opportunity to talk about their faith with others. Fowler saw opportunities for exploration and discussion of faith as being particularly important since faith is an organizer for one's entire life.

In his 2000 work, Fowler took these ideas further, linking his model of faith development to the idea of vocation, which he saw as more than work, occupation, profession, or career. In his view, vocation draws in every aspect of the person's life and is therefore a desired, but not automatic, end goal of development. It is influenced by environmental conditions that the person must address. Fowler (2000) suggested that one's faith community plays an important role in determining the extent to which a sense of vocation is formed and carried out during one's life.

Research

Fowler's initial research (Fowler, 1981) validated aspects of his theory. Stages corresponded to ages as predicted by the model, particularly in the earlier stages. At later ages, individuals exhibited a range of stages from stage 2 to 6. Stage 5 was evident starting in the middle to later years of life, and only one person was at stage 6. A relationship between age, sex, and stage of faith was somewhat evident, with more women than men at stage 3 and fewer women than men at stages 4 and 5 in younger age groups. However, more women than men were in stage 5 in the older age groups. Fowler (1981) stressed that a larger, more representative sample was needed to verify this finding.

Lee (2002) has also contributed to the validation of Fowler's theory. In a qualitative study using a narrative approach to examine how faith developed among Catholic students, she discovered that her participants were progressing toward intuitive-reflective faith, assuming responsibility for their own beliefs and decisions while at the same time being challenged by social and academic aspects of their environments.

Fowler's research was based on semistructured interviews. In an attempt to develop an easier assessment method, Leak, Loucks, and Bowlin (1999) constructed the Faith Development Scale (FDS), a forced-choice measure with one response indicative of stages 2 or 3 in Fowler's model and the other response reflecting stages 4 or 5. In a longitudinal study of students from their first year to their senior year using the FDS, Leak (2003) found that students demonstrated increased faith development as discussed in Fowler's (1981) theory. A cross-sectional study that

Leak conducted also suggested that seniors exhibited higher scores on the FDS than did first-year students.

Applications

Published applications of Fowler's theory within higher education settings focus on counseling and teaching. Lownsdale (1997) and Genia (1992) both found value in Fowler's theory for therapists and counselors in that it provides a framework to understand clients' ideas about faith and to develop therapeutic interventions in line with clients' belief systems, particularly for clients who are experiencing crises of faith. To address spiritual issues, T. M. Erwin (2001) argued that counselor trainees need to understand the role of spirituality in their own lives and suggested supervision interventions for students in each of Fowler's (1981) stages to encourage faith awareness and growth.

Gathman and Nessan (1997) developed an honors course, entitled Religion and Science, designed to help students resolve conflicts between religious and scientific perspectives. They used Fowler's (1981) theory to interpret changes in students' reasoning from the beginning to the end of the course and suggested that it could serve as a basis for determining students' learning in other religion courses.

Critique

While Fowler's theory has stood the test of time and has provided the basis for research and later theory building, his work has also been subject to criticism. With regard to his research methodology, Broughton (1986) and Nelson and Aleshire (1986) pointed out that Fowler's sample was ethnically and religiously biased and that the cross-sectional nature of his research limited conclusions related to development. Broughton, Nelson and Aleshire, and C. Anderson (1994) also pointed out the problem of Fowler's developing his theory a priori and then collecting data to support it.

A number of writers have taken issue with Fowler's definition of faith, finding it too generic and prescriptive (Dykstra, 1986), lacking a core understanding of faith as commitment and thus indistinguishable from other developmental theories (Fernout, 1986), incompatible with some forms of Christian faith (Hiebert, 1992), biased in favor of Protestant Christianity (G. Moran, 1983), or theistic rather than nonreligious (Broughton, 1986). Fowler has been accused of basing his work on conformist, individualistic assumptions associated with a Western cultural perspective (Broughton). In addition, Harris (1986) pointed out that Fowler relied heavily on the writing and thinking of male psychologists such as Piaget,

Kohlberg, and Selman, an observation that Fowler (1986a) found valid. Harris therefore questioned the extent to which Fowler's theory reflected the true experiences of women, a concern that Anderson (1994) echoed. Watt (2003) pointed out that the cognitive focus and lack of attention to the influence of ethnic culture limit the utility of this theory for African American women. A number of writers have criticized assumptions and aspects of Fowler's stage model. For example, Fernout (1986) found little support for the aspects of faith Fowler identified in his stages. And despite Fowler's claim that each stage of faith can lead to a satisfying life, some have argued that he implied that individuals should be pushed toward higher stages (Batson, Schoenrade, & Ventis, 1993; G. Moran, 1983). Batson et al. also suggested that Fowler's stages were in reality styles of faith rather than stages. A major criticism of Fowler's theory has focused on the existence and definition of stage 6, universalizing faith, since few examples exist of individuals who have reached this stage (Broughton, 1986; G. Moran). Parks (1986b), Broughton, and G. Moran were also troubled by the discontinuity between this stage and previous stages, in that it is based on a direct relationship with God, whereas earlier stages focus on the development of increasingly complex cognitive processes that occurs through social interaction.

The Faith Development Theory of Sharon Daloz Parks

The contributions of Sharon Daloz Parks to the faith development literature include two books: *The Critical Years: Young Adults and the Search for Meaning, Faith, and Commitment* (1986a) and *Big Questions, Worthy Dreams: Mentoring Young Adults in Their Search for Meaning, Purpose, and Faith* (2000). Her theory is based on her own experiences as a teacher, counselor, and researcher in college, workplace, and religious environments (Parks, 2000).

Parks's Theory

The premise that underscored Parks's (1986a) work is that young adulthood is the time when a person begins to self-consciously reflect on life's meaning, as the students in the opening scenario were doing. She defined *faith* as "the activity of seeking and discovering meaning in the most comprehensive dimensions of our experience" (Parks, 2000, p. 7). Faith is validated through lived experience, making "itself public in everyday acts of decision, obedience, and courage" (p. 26). Thus, it is a broader concept than religious belief.

Parks (1986a) set out to explore the role higher education plays in the development of faith for young adults. Like Fowler, she drew on the work of developmental psychologists, including Piaget, Erikson, Kohlberg, Gilligan, Perry, and Kegan. While similar to Fowler's theory, Parks's theory (1986a, 2000) differs in two important ways. First, Parks (1986a) focused on the connection between the structure and content of faith, as well as the role of affect and imagination, while Fowler concentrated mainly on structure and symbolism in development.

Second, Parks (1986a, 2000) argued that an important stage was missing from Fowler's theory of faith development: that of young adulthood. In this stage, individuals begin the process of taking responsibility for themselves, including their faith. Parks noted that this stage rarely occurs until at least age seventeen and that many people never reach it at all.

Parks (1986a, 2000) explained that during young adulthood, individuals are consumed with questions regarding purpose, vocation, and belonging. They are also concerned with the world in which they find themselves, desiring to make it a better place but worrying about their ability to do so. A sense of ambivalence pervades this period in life. In the opening story, this ambivalence can be seen in Mike's desire for something more in his life and Toccara's questioning of her beliefs.

Parks (1986a) identified three forms of development—cognition, dependence, and community—that contribute to the process of faith development throughout adulthood. Drawing heavily on Perry's understanding of cognitive development, Kegan's and Gilligan's descriptions of interpersonal development, and Fowler's discussion of community, in her first book Parks (1986a) presented a developmental model in which each form of development consisted of four increasingly complex stages that contribute to a more complex overall understanding of faith. In her later work, Parks (2000) revised and expanded her initial model, identifying four periods associated with development: adolescence or conventional, young adult, tested adult, and mature adult. She also modified and relabeled many of the model's stages.

Forms of Knowing. Parks (2000) identified five forms of knowing that occur within the four periods of development.

Authority-bound. In this early adolescent stage, which parallels Perry's dualistic stage of cognitive development, individuals place their trust in known authorities, such as parents, religious leaders, or teachers—as Guisela did—or impersonal authorities such as media, cultural figures, or custom. Individuals using this form of knowing see life in rigid terms and have little tolerance for ambiguity.

Unqualified relativism. As trusted authorities are found to be fallible, adolescents begin to realize that reality has many forms. This shift can occur gradually or abruptly, in an uncomplicated manner or through more challenging processes. The death of Philip's father may have led to such a shift. Eventually persons come to view all knowledge as relative. As they move through this stage, they begin to see that not all opinions are equally valid but rather that those that are based on evidence tend to have more substance.

Probing commitment. Young adulthood is characterized by tentative commitments that are often short term but based on "serious, critically aware exploration" (Parks, 2000, p. 67). These commitments often center on future plans related to relationships, vocation, and faith. Amy's newly found church home may be a probing commitment that she needs to test further.

Tested commitment. As individuals advance in adulthood, their commitments become more secure.

Convictional commitment. In midlife, a new form of deep commitment may arise that many have labeled wisdom. It results from actively exploring the complexity and mystery of life. At this stage, individuals possess both a deep commitment to their own understanding of truth and the ability to recognize and appreciate the truth of others.

Forms of Dependence. Parks (2000) stressed that emotion plays an important role in the development of faith. She believed that examining changes in dependency on others provides a way to evaluate the role of affect in faith development.

Dependent/counterdependent. In adolescence, individuals rely on authorities to determine how they should feel about events in their worlds. This reliance is challenged when the truth they have been taught is discovered to be fallible or when they begin to be uncomfortable and want to explore other possibilities. Their response, counterdependence, is still a variation of dependence, however, in that they are reacting against the positions of their authorities rather than creating new truth for themselves. As such, authorities still have the power to determine one's reactions. If one is encouraged to explore by benevolent authorities, this process can be relatively smooth, such as Wesley's decision to join Campus Crusade for Christ at the urging of his brother. If the bonds to authorities are tighter or if authorities resent one's pulling away, the process can be more difficult and upsetting.

Fragile inner dependence. In young adulthood, fragile inner dependence develops. Parks made an important distinction between inner dependence and independence, criticizing the overemphasis that Western culture has placed on being able to function completely on one's own without connection to others. She explained that inner dependence balances the views of others with one's own views. Since individuals at this stage are particularly vulnerable and need support, mentors are needed to guide and reinforce their new identities (Parks, 2000). Amy may benefit from finding a mentor to support her as she begins to make her own decisions about her faith.

Confident inner dependence. With the passage of time and as individuals receive encouragement in the process of developing their own sense of self and faith, they become increasingly confident in their ability to shape their destinies. Parks stated that confident inner dependence is a necessary precursor to interiority, that is, inner dialogue. She stressed the importance of inner dialogue and reflection in "the formation of conscience and the ethical life" (Parks, 2000, p. 84). Given his self-confidence, Philip may have reached this stage.

Interdependence. Around midlife, a strong and confident sense of self leads to a new understanding of faith in which individuals come to see the value in others' beliefs and perspectives without experiencing them as a challenge to their own values. They recognize the interconnections among self, others, the world, and "God."

Forms of Community. Parks (2000) explained that individuals need familiar and dependable networks of people, places, and communities in which to explore themselves and their values. Everyone experiences tension between the need to establish a sense of agency and the need to be in relationship with others. At different points in one's life, this tension is resolved in different ways—Parks's forms of community.

Conventional community. In adolescence, when individuals are dependent on others to define themselves and their faith, communities of importance generally consist of face-to-face relationships. Individuals adhere to the values and cultural norms of the significant people and groups in their lives.

Diffuse community. As adolescents begin to explore new ideas and ways of being, their familiar social groups become uncomfortable. Relationships can be difficult to maintain when one's views are constantly changing. As the inadequacy of this position is recognized, individuals search for new relationships to confirm their tentative new choices, which leads them to a new form of community. The friendship group in the opening scenario is such a community.

Mentoring community. Parks stressed the importance of a mentoring community for young adults that recognizes and encourages their potential. Often these communities support young adults as they distance themselves from the conventions and beliefs of their pasts. The multicultural learning community to which the students in the opening narrative belong appears to be a mentoring community.

Self-selected group. Tested adults seek out communities that share their beliefs and make meaning in similar ways, since they prefer relationships with others like themselves.

Open to the other. A deepening awareness of otherness can lead to further transformation. A community that truly values different perspectives is most likely to be sought past midlife.

The Nature of the Model. Parks cautioned that rather than being linear and fixed, as some might perceive from the description, her model is actually dynamic and multidimensional; she suggested that a spiral model might be a more accurate portrayal of her thinking. In her earlier book, Parks (1986a) also pointed out that the three forms of development do not remain separate but rather are interwoven to form a unified whole.

The Content of Faith. Parks (1986a) stressed that young adults are particularly vulnerable to various ideologies, as well as charismatic leaders and communities; therefore, it is important to understand the content of their faith, as well as the structure. Content includes the symbols, images, and ideology that give meaning to faith.

Imagination. Defined as "the highest power of the knowing mind" (Parks, 2000, p. 104), imagination encompasses three components: "a process" (p. 104), "an act of naming" (p. 105) one's experiences, and a way of participating in "the ongoing *creation* of life itself" (p. 105). In explaining the role of imagination in the development of faith, Parks (2000) cited Loder, who described how imagination evolves. In his model, five key elements, which Parks (1986a) called moments, are involved in the process of imagination: conscious conflict, pause, image, repatterning and release of energy, and interpretation.

Conscious conflict. Parks (2000) noted that growth occurs when one begins to feel uncomfortable with one's current situation. This dissonance can cause doubt, restlessness, a desire to explore options, or even a renunciation of previously held beliefs. As a result of the class activity, Mike and Toccara seem to be experiencing conscious conflict. Parks (1986a) explained that "within the moment of disequilibrium lies a threefold task: the conflict must be felt, allowed, made conscious; the conflict must be clarified; the conflict must be suffered with the expectation of a solution" (p. 111). Parks (2000) suggested that individuals experiencing conflict need communities that will sustain and encourage them intellectually, emotionally, and spiritually.

Pause. After clarification of an issue, according to Parks (2000), it is best to let it rest. In this moment of pause, the issue incubates below the surface of consciousness. This "interlude for scanning" (p. 113) may last only a few seconds or as long as several years. The students in the opening scenario might find a period of pause beneficial.

Image. Often referred to as an "aha!" moment, image (or insight) occurs when all the disparate aspects of the conflict come together and the situation becomes clear. Wesley's experience of fitting in at Campus Crusade might have been an image moment.

Repatterning and release of energy. With new insight, the tension associated with the previous conflict is released, and energy is freed up to move ahead. Seeing the previous conflicting situation in a new way, repatterning requires a reordering of one's larger perspective, which often takes time. At the end of the process, one experiences "a sense of having achieved a more adequate orientation to reality" (Parks, 2000, p. 121). Amy may be in a repatterning phase exploring her new religious home.

Interpretation. Proof that a new insight is fully a part of one's life is the ability to verbalize it to others, an act that Parks (2000) referred to as *testimony*. Feedback from one's community tests one's insights. She cautioned, however, that the judgment of communities can be fallible. Thus, the searching students in the opening scenario should not rely solely on the opinions of their community as they test new insights.

Mentoring Communities.

Parks (1986a, 2000) argued that the higher education community is a place in which young adults benefit greatly from mentoring relationships. Mentors provide young adults with recognition, support, challenge, and inspiration (Parks, 2000). According to Parks (2000), mentoring is not always a long-term, face-to-face experience. It can occur at a distance, in a moment, through observation, or using technology. Because one-on-one mentoring may not always meet the needs of young adults, Parks (2000) stressed the importance of mentoring communities, such as the learning community in the narrative, in which trusting relationships can be formed.

A mentoring community is a "network of belonging" (Parks, 2000, p. 135) in which young adults' imaginations are supported. Such a community allows young adults to consider big questions that will shape their future lives: "questions of meaning, purpose, and faith" (p. 138). These questions may be raised by young adults themselves, or they may be posed by members of the mentoring community. Mentoring communities also provide opportunities for young adults to interact with others not like themselves—interactions that can lead to awareness that people who are different from them may nonetheless share similar feelings and responses to various situations, as the students did in the narrative. Within the context of a safe and open mentoring community, young adults develop a willingness to consider different perspectives. To be successful in encouraging faith development, mentoring communities must foster particular "habits of mind" (p. 142): dialogue, critical thought, connective-systemic-holistic thought, and a contemplative mind. Mentoring communities also assist young adults in developing "worthy dreams," which Parks defined as "imagined [possibilities] that [orient] meaning, purpose, and aspiration" (p. 146). A sense of vocation or calling is the most complete and spiritual form of the dream.

Parks (2000) pointed out that young adults need access to appropriate images to develop worthy dreams and that mentoring communities provide young adults with such images. First, they provide "images of truth" (p. 148) about both the world's suffering and its beauty. Second, they offer "images of transformation [and] hope for renewing the world" (p. 150). They also provide young adults "positive images of self" (p. 151), as well as "images of the other as both similar and unique" (p. 152). Finally, mentoring communities offer "images of interrelatedness and wholeness" (p. 153). In addition to being places that support young adult imagination, mentoring communities are "communities of practice" (Parks, 2000, p. 154) that offer a peaceful and welcoming place in which contemplation and dialogue can occur. They also encourage activity and commitment to improve the lives of others.

Higher Education: A Community of Imagination. Parks (2000) listed a number of potential mentoring communities in the lives of young adults, including the workplace, families, religious institutions, the natural world, and travel. Higher education, however, is given an especially prominent role. Parks (2000) viewed faculty as having major responsibility for guiding students' spiritual lives by creating communities of imagination where students' ideas can be both challenged and supported, such as the community that Dr. Ruiz created in his classroom in the narrative. Parks (1986a, 2000) also stressed the responsibility of higher education as a whole to create communities in which students feel welcomed and safe while being provided with experiences that will encourage them to explore and address conscious conflicts, have opportunities for pause, and be supported as they clarify, confirm, and test their new images.

Research

Only a few studies to date have been based on Parks's (2000) theory. Buchko (2004) investigated the faith development of college students, reporting that women, more than men, reported close relationships to God and with spiritual advisors; these results may indicate that the affective dimension of faith Parks (2000) proposed is more important to women than to men. Buchko's use of a measure of religiosity rather than faith, as well as her references to religious practices, does call her interpretations regarding faith into question, however.

Lee (2002) reported that participants in her study of the faith development of Catholic college students described their development in terms similar to Parks's (2000) hypotheses. During college, the students "redefined themselves" (Lee, p. 355) within the context of their previous religious identity rather than giving up that identity completely. Further research is clearly needed to validate Park's (2000) theory.

Applications

More authors have suggested applications of Parks's theory. Love (2001) stressed the importance of student affairs professionals being comfortable with their own spirituality. Using Parks's (2000) theory as a foundation, Love suggested that staff development focus on how student affairs professionals make meaning, the role of relationships in this process, and examination of one's communities, using critical reflection, journaling, and other processes that allow individuals to look inward. He went on to advocate recognition of the importance of spirituality in students' lives, inclusion of theories of spiritual development in the study of student development and use of these theories in settings such as judicial affairs, development of mentoring communities and assessment of existing organizations for their potential as mentoring communities, and bringing spirituality into higher education in an open manner.

Building on Parks's (2000) concept of a mentoring community and Nash's (2002) levels of community, Dalton (2006a) offered a number of suggestions for developing personal, campus, societal, and global communities within higher education settings. Strange (2001) suggested that Parks's (2000) criteria for mentoring communities could be used to guide student affairs graduate programs in developing educational environments that focus on assisting students in making meaning of their experiences. Based on Parks's concepts, Strange stressed the importance of creating networks of belonging, presenting students with "big enough questions" (p. 61), helping students understand cultural differences, encouraging dialogue and critical thinking, assisting students as they develop "worthy dreams" (p. 63), and providing access to images of "truth and goodness" (p. 64) to enhance the "spiritual dimensions of . . . students' lives" (p. 65).

Critique

Reviews of *Big Questions, Worthy Dreams* (Parks, 2000) have been quite positive (Bowman & Wessel, 2002; Brinkman, 2000; Mussi, 2001). Comparing Parks's (2000) theory with other spiritual and cognitive development theories, Love (2002) concluded that Parks's (2000) integration of affective, social, and cognitive processes in her discussion of development made it particularly useful for examining "both the structures and the content of meaning making" (Love, 2002, p. 373).

However, Watt (2003) argued that while claiming to attend to both cognitive and affective aspects of faith development, Parks (2000) in actuality emphasized the cognitive. As such, her theory may not be useful in working with African American women, whose faith development process is often affective in nature (Watt). Watt also criticized Parks for ignoring the role of ethnicity in the faith development process. Anderson (1994) expressed concern that Parks (1986a) failed to consider the unique aspects of women's faith development.

Stamm (2006) noted that by using Fowler's (1981) theory as a foundation for her work, Parks failed to consider whether stage theories are appropriate for understanding development across cultures. Stamm argued that stage theories are based on Western cultural assumptions of independence and individualism, ignoring the values of community and the common good that are found in many other cultures.

Implications and Future Directions

The work of Fowler and Parks has added an important dimension to our understanding of student development. These theories are particularly relevant given the interest in spirituality and faith that students are currently expressing. Having clearer definitions of faith and spirituality, a better sense of the different ways in which students make meaning of these concepts, and factors that contribute to their development will help student affairs professionals work more effectively with students. The theories have some weaknesses, however.

Most of the studies of spiritual and faith development have been cross-sectional in nature. Longitudinal studies are needed to determine the developmental process across the life span (Cartwright, 2001). Hodge (2001) and Cartwright also suggested that qualitative designs be used to explore specific events that contribute to spiritual development and to gain a richer, more individualistic understanding of participants' experiences.

Much more work is needed to explore spirituality outside Western traditions, within specific religious and cultural contexts (Cartwright, 2001), and in relation to the worldview of nonbelievers (Goodman & Mueller, 2009). Love (2002) called for research examining the way in which culture and spiritual development intersect, work that Tisdell (2003) has started. Watt (2003) has conducted initial research on the faith development of African American women that warrants further consideration. Anderson's (1994) examination of the spirituality of feminist women is also important. Finally, Goodman and Mueller (2009) have begun an important line of research examining the experiences of atheist students.

Dalton (2006b) argued that student affairs staff must do a better job of addressing students' spirituality. Dalton et al. (2006) offered a number of suggestions for creating a spiritual context within higher education settings. They include designating space on campus for meditation and reflection; offering programs on spirituality; opportunities for dialogue with individuals of different faiths; incorporation of spirituality into appropriate courses; and art, music, and drama with spiritual themes. They went on to offer strategies for responding to the increasing interest in spirituality on campus: awareness and advocacy of spirituality as an important aspect of student development; creation of supportive environments that encourage spiritual development; education programs; and staff and faculty development to help educators work effectively with students in the area of faith development. Dalton (2006c) took his ideas further, developing a comprehensive set of institutional principles and practices for enhancing the spiritual growth of students.

As educators are called on to focus more on the spiritual development of students, Gilley's (2005) cautions are important to keep in mind. He stressed that educators have a responsibility to "do no harm" (p. 96), which can be accomplished only by actively preparing through reading and study to address spiritual issues with which students may be grappling. He went on to caution that "issues of the spirit may require more preparation than those more temporal" (p. 97). A learning environment in which the meaning making associated with spiritual development can occur must include a careful balance of care, support, and challenge.

CHAPTER TWELVE

SCHLOSSBERG'S TRANSITION THEORY

Marie is a forty-year-old student who has returned to school after a twenty-year absence. She left college at the age of twenty to marry. Recently Marie and her husband divorced. Her return to college was precipitated by a need to secure full-time employment and her desire to achieve her original career goal of becoming a teacher. Marie is concerned about simultaneously maintaining her roles as a mother and a student. She was awarded primary custody of her twelve-year-old daughter and sixteen-year-old son. Financial and time concerns are also on her mind as she anticipates the challenges inherent in continuing her part-time secretarial job and raising her children, while adding the responsibilities of being a full-time student. She is finding that the emotional toll of the divorce is still an issue as well.

◆ ◆ ◆

It has been a difficult semester for Eric, a twenty-one-year-old senior. Within the past two months, his father was killed in an automobile accident, and he failed to gain admission to any of the medical schools to which he had applied. To become a doctor was a lifelong dream for Eric, a dream for him that his family shared. Eric thought things were starting to look a little brighter when he began going out with Jason, but Jason has since indicated that he does not wish to pursue their relationship.

◆ ◆ ◆

College students, whether traditionally or nontraditionally aged, face many changes that can have short- and long-term effects on their lives. Nancy Schlossberg's transition theory provides insights into factors related to the transition, the individual, and the environment that are likely to determine the degree of impact a given transition will have at a particular time. The nature of the supports available to facilitate coping, as well as strategies that can be used to assist those experiencing change, is also addressed.

Schlossberg's theory is typically categorized as a theory of adult development. Given the integrative nature of the work in relation to preexisting theories of adulthood, this classification is appropriate. However, the theory is also relevant to traditionally aged college students. Educators should avoid creating a false dichotomy between "adult development" and "college student development" when identifying theories that can be helpful in understanding and working with students.

In this chapter, we provide an overview of the origins and evolution of Schlossberg's theory, outline its major concepts, discuss research based on the theory, and examine applications of the theory in higher education. We end the chapter with a critique of Schlossberg's theory and suggestions for future directions in its development.

Historical Overview

Schlossberg (1984) described a primary goal of her theory of development as being that of operationalizing variability. In other words, she believed a need existed to develop a framework that would facilitate an understanding of adults in transition and aid them in connecting to the help they needed to cope with the "ordinary and extraordinary process of living" (p. vii). To create this framework, Schlossberg (1981) drew heavily "on the work and ideas of others" (p. 3). Examples of influences are the work of D. J. Levinson (1978), Neugarten (1979), and Lowenthal and Chiriboga (1975). Her theory represents a conceptual integration of and expansion on existing theory and research.

In relation to the traditional body of college student development theory, Schlossberg's work can be viewed as psychosocial in nature and as a counterpoint to age and stage perspectives. Transitions provide opportunities for growth and development, but a positive outcome for the individual cannot be assumed.

Schlossberg's earliest extended treatment of her conceptualizations appeared in *The Counseling Psychologist* in 1981. Describing her model as a vehicle for "analyzing human adaptation to transition" (p. 2), Schlossberg asserted that adaptation was affected by the interaction of three sets of variables: the individual's perception of the transition, characteristics of the pretransition and posttransition environments, and characteristics of the individual experiencing the transition. The perceptions, environmental characteristics, and personal characteristics could each include some components that might be considered assets, liabilities, a mix of the two, or neutral in regard to influence on the ability to cope with a particular transition.

Schlossberg incorporated the feedback received in the critiques that appeared in the same issue and reconceptualized her model as dealing with "response to transition" since adaptation may not always be achieved. Her book-length treatment, *Counseling Adults in Transition*, was published in 1984. Along with chapters that placed her approach in the broader context of adult development theory in general and provided programmatic examples of applications, this more extensive discussion of the theory was accompanied by a chapter linking transition theory to the contemporary version of Egan's helping model (1982). This connection provided substantial support for theory-to-practice efforts of a counseling or programming nature.

Overwhelmed (Schlossberg, 1989b) represented a popular press rendition of Schlossberg's work and was particularly significant for introducing several of the modifications that were later integrated into the theory (Schlossberg, Waters, & Goodman, 1995). In *Overwhelmed*, Schlossberg presented the transition process as having three components: approaching change, taking stock, and taking charge. The taking-stock section introduced the 4 *S*'s: situation, self, support, and strategies. The 4 *S*'s represent a reframing of Schlossberg's (1984) previous discussions of coping resources as variables characterizing the transition, the individual, and the environment. The taking-charge section introduced the terminology of "moving in," "moving through," and "moving out" to describe the phases of transitions.

Schlossberg, Waters, and Goodman produced the second edition of *Counseling Adults in Transition* in 1995. Geared to an audience made up of counselors, this edition is divided into three parts: "What Do We Need to Know?" "What Are We Likely to Hear?" and "What Can We Do with What We Know and Hear?" The first part presented the revised version of transition theory in the context of adult development theory in general; the second part considered individual, relationship, and work transitions; and the third part included an integration of the transition framework with Cormier and Hackney's (1993) counseling model—in lieu of Egan's model (1982)—and related applications. Finally, in 2006, Goodman, Schlossberg, and Anderson produced the third edition of this book. In this edition, the authors noted the increasing importance of the global community, the continuing impact of technology, and the importance of understanding cultural diversity and spirituality—all in regard to supporting adults coping with transitions.

Transition Theory

Schlossberg's theory of transitions includes an examination of what constitutes a transition, different forms of transitions, the transition process, and factors that influence transitions. Schlossberg et al. (1995) also introduced the Cormier and Hackney (1993) counseling model as a means to support individuals in transition.

Transition Defined

Goodman et al. (2006) defined a transition as "any event, or non-event, that results in changed relationships, routines, assumptions, and roles" (p. 33). In the scenario at the start of this chapter, Marie's divorce is an example of an event—something that happened that has changed her life. She has, for example, taken on the new role of student and lost the role of wife. She is concerned about her relationship with her children as her routine has been dramatically changed by the absence of the marriage relationship and the addition of academic responsibilities. Eric's not being accepted into medical school represents a nonevent—something desired and anticipated that did not happen. The reality of not going to medical school requires Eric to rethink the life he had envisioned for himself, including the assumption that he would become a physician.

Goodman et al. (2006) stressed the role of perception in transitions, noting that a transition exists only if it is so defined by the individual experiencing it. Changes may occur without the individual's attaching much significance to them. Such changes would therefore not be considered transitions.

Type, Context, and Impact

Goodman et al. (2006) noted that to understand the meaning that a transition has for a particular individual requires considering the type, context, and impact of the transition. Three nondiscrete types of transitions are described: *anticipated transitions*, which occur predictably, such as Eric's expected graduation from college; *unanticipated transitions*, which are not predictable or scheduled, such as Marie's divorce and the sudden death of Eric's father; and *nonevents*, which are expected to occur but do not, such as Eric's failure to be admitted into medical school. Nonevents can be classified as *personal*—related to individual aspirations; *ripple*—felt due to a nonevent of someone close; *resultant*—caused by an event; and *delayed*—anticipating an event that may still happen. Schlossberg and Robinson (1996) pointed out that nonevents are associated more with probability than possibility. Only when an event is likely to occur but fails to occur does it qualify as a nonevent.

The meaning attached to transitions by different individuals is relative, as is the way in which the transition is categorized by type. Again, the role of perception is important.

Context refers to one's relationship to the transition (one's own or someone else's) and to the setting in which the transition takes place (work, personal relationships, and so forth). *Impact* is determined by the degree to which a transition alters one's daily life. Both positive and negative transitions, as perceived by the individual, produce stress. The presence of multiple transitions, as in the case of Eric's father's death, rejection by medical schools, and loss of a prospective partner, can compound the stress. The impact of such stress is dependent on the ratio of the individual's assets and liabilities at the time.

The Transition Process

While a transition may be precipitated by a single event or nonevent, dealing with a transition is a process that extends over time. Essentially the individual moves from a preoccupation with the transition to an integration of the transition. The time needed to achieve successful integration varies with the person and the transition. Transitions may lead to growth, but decline is also a possible outcome, and many transitions may be viewed with ambivalence by the individuals experiencing them. Building on the work of Schlossberg et al. (1995) in integrating the work of other authors, Goodman et al. (2006) endorsed the concept of transitions consisting of a series of phases, which they termed "moving in," "moving through," and "moving out," using the language initially introduced by Schlossberg (1989b).

The 4 *S*'s

Goodman et al. (2006) presented four major sets of factors that influence one's ability to cope with a transition: situation, self, support, and strategies, known as the 4 *S*'s. The individual's effectiveness in coping with transition depends on his or her resources in these four areas—in other words, his or her assets and liabilities—at that time. The ratio of assets to liabilities helps to explain "why different individuals react differently to the same type of transition and why the same person reacts differently at different times" (Schlossberg et al., 1995, p. 57).

The individual's appraisal of the transition is an important determiner of the coping process (Goodman et al., 2006). Two types of appraisals are made. Primary appraisal has to do with one's view of the transition itself. Is it regarded as positive, negative, or irrelevant? Secondary appraisal is a self-assessment of one's resources for coping with the transition. Both types are subject to change as the individual proceeds through the transition process. The 4 *S*'s provide a framework for an individual's appraisal process.

Situation. In examining an individual's situation, the following factors are considered important:

> *Trigger*—What precipitated the transition?
>
> *Timing*—Is the transition considered "on time" or "off time" in terms of one's social clock, and is the transition viewed as happening at a "good" or "bad" time?

Control—What does the individual perceive as being within his or her control (for example, the transition itself, his or her reaction to it)?

Role change—Is a role change involved, and if so, is it viewed as a gain or a loss?

Duration—Is it seen as permanent, temporary, or uncertain?

Previous experience with a similar transition—How effectively did one cope, and what are implications for the current transition?

Concurrent stress—Are multiple sources of stress present?

Assessment—Who or what is seen as responsible for the transition, and how is the individual's behavior affected by this perception?

Self. Factors considered important in relation to the self are classified into two categories: personal and demographic characteristics and psychological resources. *Personal and demographic characteristics* are described as affecting how an individual views life. This category includes socioeconomic status, gender, age (emphasizing psychological, social, and functional age over chronological), and stage of life, state of health, and ethnicity/culture. *Psychological resources*, aids to coping, include ego development; outlook, in particular optimism and self-efficacy; commitment and values; and spirituality and resiliency.

Support. Support is composed of three facets: types, functions, and measurement. "Support" in this model really refers to social support, and four types are cited: intimate relationships, family units, networks of friends, and institutions and communities. Affect, affirmation, aid, and honest feedback serve as the functions of support. Incorporating the work of Kahn and Antonucci (1980), Goodman et al. (2006) suggested that social support can be measured by identifying the individual's stable supports, supports that are to some degree role dependent, and supports that are most likely to change.

Strategies. In discussing the fourth *S*, strategies, Goodman et al. (2006) endorsed Pearlin and Schooler's (1978) descriptions of coping responses as essentially falling into three categories: those that modify the situation, those that control the meaning of the problem, and those that aid in managing the stress in the aftermath. In relation to the differing goals reflected by these categories, individuals may also employ four coping modes: information seeking, direct action, inhibition of action, and intrapsychic behavior. Goodman et al. emphasized that individuals who cope effectively demonstrate flexibility and use multiple methods. (Exhibit 12.1 provides a summary of the transition model.)

Exhibit 12.1. Schlossberg's Transition Model

Transitions
Events or nonevents resulting in changed relationships, routines, assumptions, and/or roles.

Meaning for the Individual Based on:
Type: anticipated, unanticipated, nonevent
Context: relationship to transition and the setting
Impact: alterations in daily life

The Transition Process
Reactions over time
Moving in, moving through, and moving out

Coping with Transitions
Influenced by ratio of assets and liabilities in regard to four sets of factors:

Situation
Trigger, timing, control, role change, duration, previous experience, concurrent stress, assessment

Self
Personal and demographic characteristics: socioeconomic status, gender, age, health, ethnicity/culture
Psychological resources: ego development, outlook, commitment, values, spirituality and resilience

Support
Types: intimate, family, friends, institutional
Functions: affect, affirmation, aid, honest feedback
Measurement: stable and changing supports

Strategies
Three categories: modify situation, control meaning, manage stress in aftermath
Four coping modes: information seeking, direct action, inhibition of action, intrapsychic behavior

Note: Compiled from information in Goodman, Schlossberg, and Anderson (2006).

Aspects of transition theory can be used to assist the two students in the opening scenario. To help Marie and Eric take stock of their assets and liabilities, a helper could guide them through a consideration of each of the 4 *S*'s. Regarding her situation, Marie may consider the timing of the divorce to be good if she felt control in initiating the process. Eric, by contrast, is unlikely to find the timing to be good since the loss of his father, the rejection by medical school, and the terminated relationship with Jason were all beyond his control. Relatedly, Eric is likely to view his role changes as losses, while Marie has the potential to find something positive in her new role as student. Duration of the transitions may pose challenges for both Marie and Eric. Marie is juggling the multiple roles of student, single parent, and employee, a demanding combination even on a temporary basis, and Eric is confronted by the permanent loss of a parent, along with rejections on the professional and personal levels. He may be able to achieve acceptance to medical school in the future and find a new partner, but most immediately, these are uncertain prospects. Concurrent stress represents a challenge for both students, given Marie's multiple roles and Eric's multiple losses.

In regard to self, physical health can be assumed to be a desirable asset for both Marie and Eric. In addition, a higher socioeconomic status tends to be an asset. Gender, age, and ethnicity represent variables that are open to interpretation. Do Marie and Eric view these as assets, liabilities, or mixed blessings for themselves, and do these aspects have an impact on the options open to them to aid in coping? In considering psychological resources, more advanced levels of ego development imply a maturity that would be an asset in coping. Similarly, a positive outlook—seeing the glass as half full rather than half empty—and a belief in one's own ability to have an impact (self-efficacy) are considered assets. Commitments, which are subject to change, and values and beliefs can also play a role. For example, if Marie saw herself as very committed to her marriage and if she holds religious beliefs that are critical of divorce, her difficulty in dealing with her transition would be heightened. Similarly, Eric presents becoming a doctor as a lifelong dream. Especially if this value was accompanied by a significant commitment to academic achievement, the denial of medical school admission would represent a severe blow.

Examining social supports for Marie and Eric is the next step. The amount of support available to Marie may depend to some degree on how the loss of the marriage relationship affects other relationships. For example, will friends whom she and her ex-husband have in common maintain their relationships with her? At the same time, her resumption of her student status opens the door to a new form of institutional support—from the college itself. Assuming that Eric will be relocating, he will soon lose the supports provided by his college, but he has access to services while he is still enrolled. Similarly, his network of friends is likely to be disrupted by his impending graduation. If Eric returns home, family has the potential to be a source of support. However, more would need to be known about family reactions to the father's death, Eric's medical school situation, and other life circumstances for the likelihood of support to be accurately assessed. Marie's remaining in the same location is likely to afford her access to preexisting and new supports, while Eric's loss of relationships and the pervasive impact of graduation and relocation pose additional challenges in his transition.

Both Marie and Eric may benefit from using strategies that help them manage current stress and control the meaning of the situation. Both could fall into self-defeating thinking ("poor me"). Marie could become discouraged by the weight of her multiple responsibilities, and Eric could become despondent by concluding that he has lost everything important to him. Marie may benefit from reinforcing the message that her situation is temporary and Eric from believing that he will find a career alternative or try for medical school again and that future relationships are possible. Eric may benefit from seeking career information and inhibiting the urge to give up. Marie may benefit from learning more about services available to her and taking action to enhance her time management and stress management skills.

Links to Helping Models

In integrating the transition model with the Cormier and Hackney (1993) counseling model, Schlossberg et al. (1995) provided a useful vehicle for identifying effective actions that can be taken to support individuals in transition, and Goodman et al. (2006) continued to endorse this approach but referred to the later version of the model (Hackney & Cormier, 2005). The 4 S's of situation, self, supports, and strategies supply a structure for considering what helpers can do in each stage of the Cormier and Hackney model to assist individuals in transition. These five stages are (1) relationship building, (2) assessment, (3) goal setting, (4) interventions, and (5) termination and follow-up.

Goodman et al. (2006) presented again the following integration of the two models, originally suggested by Schlossberg et al. (1995). In relationship building, helpers use basic listening skills. In assessment, the second stage, areas to assess include the individual's environment (situation), internal resources (self), external resources (support), and current coping skills (strategies). In stage 3, goal setting, individuals may find it helpful to set goals related to each of the 4 S's. Goodman et al. provided the examples of modifying the environment (situation), regaining a sense of balance or equilibrium (self), increasing support (support), and developing an action plan (strategies). For the fourth stage, interventions, Goodman et al. suggested the following possible helper behaviors: reframing, or changing the individual's interpretation of the meaning of the situation; conducting an assessment of the individual's assets (self); referral to a support group (support); and generating problem-solving strategies (strategies). Finally, in regard to termination and follow-up, the helper can aid the individual in reviewing what has happened so far and planning next steps.

Some of the language in the Cormier and Hackney (1993; Hackney & Cormier, 2005) model may sound more clinical than that used in the Egan (1982) model in the first edition. When sharing the model with paraprofessionals and general student audiences for their use, though, this resource could be adapted by substituting less clinical language, as was done in the previous paragraph, and using examples relevant to students.

The Egan (2007) model remains a helpful tool to be used in conjunction with the transition model. As Schlossberg (1984) discussed, the three stages of Egan's model essentially are exploration, understanding, and coping. Therefore, helpers can assist individuals in transition explore what is happening to them by providing an unbiased relationship as well as listening and responding, understand what is happening by offering a more objective perspective, and cope by influencing appropriate action or inaction.

To summarize, a transition is an event or nonevent that results in change. Dealing with such change is a process that evolves and includes the moving-in, moving-through, and moving-out phases. Perception plays a crucial role in how the transition itself is viewed and how the individual goes about coping. The individual's ratio of assets and liabilities in terms of situation, self, supports, and strategies determines his or her coping effectiveness. The process of providing assistance to individuals in transition can be guided by counseling models such as those provided by Cormier and Hackney (1993), Hackney and Cormier (2005), or Egan (2007).

Research

Research based on Schlossberg's theory is largely absent from the student affairs literature. In this section, we examine some important initial research based on her model in settings outside higher education and briefly mention one study focusing on adult learners in higher education.

Initial Research

Research in support of early theory development included studies such as Schlossberg and Leibowitz's investigation (1980) of men who lost their jobs at the National Aeronautics and Space Administration (NASA) and the resulting impact of a support program and Charner and Schlossberg's study (1986) of university clerical workers, which emphasized an exploration of coping strategies. Schlossberg and Leibowitz's interviews reinforced the importance of institutional supports and also the idea that the transition process often has both positive and negative components for the same individual.

Schlossberg (1981) also conducted a pilot study of transitions related to geographical mobility. Interviews were conducted with couples who had recently relocated. The most important factors related to coping were sex and sex role identification, perceived duration of the move, interpersonal supports, and degree of control. The results also reinforced the concept that transitions often involve both positive and negative aspects for the same person.

In her first published presentation of the model, Schlossberg (1981) discussed the research of Lyons (1980) and Merikangas (1980)—projects that involved the design, implementation, and evaluation of programs to aid in coping with transitions in the workplace. Lyons developed a workshop to facilitate effective entry into the first job, and Merikangas created a planning seminar for employees nearing retirement. Both projects were implemented at NASA's Goddard Space Flight Center.

Higher Education

In relation to higher education, Schlossberg, Lynch, and Chickering (1989) provided support for their conceptual framework through interview information obtained from adult learners. Goodman et al. (2006) pointed out that these interviews also served as another confirmation that transitions often include both positive and negative aspects for the same person.

Applications

Applications of Schlossberg's theory have addressed work with adult learners, as well as traditional undergraduates. In addition, assessment strategies have been proposed for use in helping students understand transitions they are facing.

Assessment Techniques

Informal and formal assessment techniques may be used in relation to Schlossberg's theory. Although psychometrically sophisticated instruments are not available, a fact that may pose some limitations in relation to traditional quantitative research, methods of self-assessment to support individual coping can be readily accessed.

For instance, *The Transition Guide and Questionnaire* is a helpful assessment tool (Kay & Schlossberg, 2003).

Student affairs professionals interested in providing a structure for self-assessment for individuals experiencing transitions could easily create a worksheet by identifying each of the 4 *S*'s and listing under each important aspects for the individual's reflection and discussion. For example, under "situation," factors such as trigger and timing could be included. If desired, a plus and minus system or the "assets/liabilities" labels could be used to help individuals identify supports and challenges or obstacles.

Adult Learners

Schlossberg et al. (1989) provided a detailed approach to how transition theory can be used to support the higher education experiences of adult learners. Using the transition model as a framework for service provision, these authors emphasized the variety of environmental responses needed to accommodate the heterogeneity of adult learners and the different points at which they may find themselves in the transition process. A common theme is transitions as triggers for college attendance. Payoffs for the institution (for example, retention, involvement, and alumni support) also received attention.

Schlossberg's theory can be used as a design tool for developmental interventions for adult learners (Champagne & Petitpas, 1989). Recognizing the need for adult learners to understand and deal with numerous transitions and receive support in the process, Champagne and Petitpas recommended that student affairs staff perform eight functions in relation to adult learners: provide specialized services (adapted for adult needs), education (information and skills related to adult development, transitions, and the college experience), advocacy, a clearinghouse (campus services and resources), referrals (institutional and community), program planning (including support groups), networking and mentoring, and counseling (including outreach and peer support).

General Student Affairs Interventions

Although applications of the theory in support of adult learners are certainly valuable, it is equally important not to pigeonhole Schlossberg's theory as one that is meaningful solely in designing interventions for adults. As in *Improving Higher Education Environments for Adults* (Schlossberg et al., 1989), Chickering and Schlossberg, in *How to Get the Most Out of College* (1995) and *Getting the Most Out of College* (2001), conceptualized the process of college attendance as involving phases of moving in, moving through, and moving out, with certain transitions and accompanying supports being characteristic of each period. These publications, which are packed with self-assessment exercises, show the applicability of transition theory to students of all ages.

Several studies (Schell, 1997; Swain, 1991; Wheeler, Malone, Van Vlack, Nelson, & Steadward, 1996) have used transition theory as a basis for examining and understanding experiences of athletes, especially the aspect of retirement from sports. Pearson and Petitpas's application (1990) of Schlossberg's theory as a support for designing developmental interventions for the anticipated and unanticipated transitions of athletes (for example, not making the team, injury) represents an approach that could be readily adapted to collegiate athletes and provides an example of using the theory to address the needs of a specific population.

Applications of Schlossberg's transition theory can take many forms. Schlossberg et al. (1995) discussed the relevance of the model for program and workshop development, consulting, advocacy, and self-help groups. The approach taken by Schlossberg (1989b) in presenting the theory in *Overwhelmed* also renders it useful as a self-help vehicle. For example, this book served as a support to a student convalescing in a hospital after an automobile accident.

Schlossberg's theory can be easily taught to organization officers, resident assistants (RAs), and other student leaders to support their efforts in assisting their peers as well as to general student audiences to aid them in understanding and responding to their own experiences. For example, for RAs, the model can serve as a general guide for designing programming to support dealing with environmental changes, such as a series of programs planned on buying cooking equipment, preparing low-budget meals, and so on for residents of a hall that had recently been renovated to form suites with kitchens. The links to helping models (Cormier & Hackney, 1993; Egan, 2007; Hackney & Cormier, 2005) can also provide RAs with a way to think about and approach individuals who may have experienced a potentially traumatic transition, such as the loss of a loved one in an automobile accident, as in the example involving Eric.

Orientation programs for entering students can use the transition model, especially the moving-in component, as a design tool. Crissman Ishler (2004) has incorporated transition theory to understand "friendsickness" (caused by moving away from an established network of friends) during the first year of college, and Marks and Jones (2004) have drawn on transition theory to understand the continuities and shifts in students' volunteering behaviors during the transition from high school to college. Transition programs for seniors approaching graduation may also be designed, paying particular attention to the challenges inherent in moving out (for example, Chickering & Schlossberg, 1998; Forney & Gingrich, 1983).

Transition theory has been used in the design of an ongoing transition program intended to provide support to student affairs master's students throughout their graduate experience (Forney & Davis, 2002), and for promoting graduate assistant success (Brown-Wright, Dubick, & Newman, 1997). Transition theory also provides the information necessary to create effective supports at the institutional level, which can result in students' developing valuable life skills for future use (Hamrick, Evans, & Schuh, 2002). In so doing, transition theory can be linked to educational outcomes. Given the constancy of change in the lives of college students, the potential for use of this model for programmatic and counseling purposes far exceeds the examples that have appeared in the literature.

Critique and Future Directions

Schlossberg (1981, 1984), Schlossberg et al. (1995), and Goodman et al. (2006) have evolved an excellent model to facilitate understanding and action with regard to transition. The work reflects their ability to identify, extract, and integrate core ideas from a wide range of sources. The framework is comprehensive in scope, highly integrative of other theoretical contributions, and conceptually and operationally sound. The authors have taken a vast array of writings and gleaned the most important concepts from them, added their insights, and created a dynamic model that can provide a solid foundation for practice that is responsive to both commonalities and idiosyncrasies. Schlossberg's openness to criticism and her willingness to revise and extend her theory since its inception have resulted in a practical resource for assisting college students in dealing with change. Because the structure of the theory places so much emphasis on consideration of the individual's perspective and the specifics of the situation, Schlossberg has provided a tool that readily allows for the integration of individual and cultural differences.

The utility of Schlossberg's theory is supported by the number of applications of her work that have appeared in the student affairs literature. Not only is Schlossberg's theory useful in working with its original audience, adult learners, but it is also helpful when working with traditional-aged students and, indeed, individuals of any age who are dealing with changes in their lives. Significant transitions, such as entering college, graduating from college, addressing relationship issues, and facing career decisions, can all be better understood and approached when using this model, as the illustrations earlier in this chapter show.

Although the literature has demonstrated the utility of Schlossberg's theory in practice, research studies supporting its validity are scant, particularly in higher education. The complexity of the theory, as well as the lack of formal assessment tools, has undoubtedly given researchers pause when considering ways of testing its merits. Until further research is conducted, however, it is impossible to affirm that the transition process occurs in the manner in which Schlossberg and her colleagues have outlined it.

Future directions must focus on expansion of the research base related to Schlossberg's theory. Although the complexity of the model (for example, the number of variables included) may pose some challenges in regard to design, both quantitative and qualitative studies are needed. Quantitative work is contingent on the development of measurement tools to assess the variables related to transition that Schlossberg proposed. Qualitative research might present a better place to start in that transitions could be viewed holistically, as perceived by individuals experiencing them.

In addition, more research related to diverse student populations, such as students of color; students with disabilities; lesbian, gay, bisexual, and transgender students; and international students, has the potential to increase our understanding of, and ability to assist with, various transitions that these students experience while moving into, through, and out of our higher education settings.

PART FOUR

SOCIAL IDENTITY DEVELOPMENT

Regina is certainly learning a lot in her first semester, and she is finding that in many cases, student development theory helps her to understand and work effectively with students. But some dimensions of development that are very important to the students she works with in multicultural student affairs have not yet been addressed: dimensions of social identity. The students Regina advises are diverse. Ethnically, they come from various cultures: Latino, Indian, Japanese, Native American, and African American, to name a few. But even students with similar cultural backgrounds identify differently. Marisela, for example, sees herself as Mexican American and proudly displays her heritage in her daily life, wearing brightly colored clothes and making Mexican food for her friends. Rudolfo identifies as Latino. His mother emigrated from Cuba, but his father comes from Belize. Identifying as Latino makes more sense to him than choosing one aspect of his heritage over another. And Anita, who is of Latino heritage but whose ancestors arrived in the United States in the nineteenth century, knows almost nothing about Latino culture and identifies as Latino only on required official documents.

Race is another matter. Many of Regina's advisees have been greatly affected by institutional and societal racism. Curtis was actively discouraged from going to college by his high school guidance counselor, who believed that someone from an impoverished black high school in Washington, D.C., would never succeed in college. Mike, a member of the Crow Nation in Montana, recounts the constant derogatory remarks he and his friends heard every time they left their reservation.

Yuko, who is of Japanese heritage, has had to deal with the stereotype that she will naturally excel in math and science, because Asian Americans are supposed to be good in these fields. In actuality, Yuko is an accomplished artist who struggles in math and science. And then there is Paul. His heritage is a mix of white, African American, and Latino. Because he is multiracial, he has a difficult time feeling as if he belongs to any racial or ethnic group.

Sexual orientation issues have also come up for Regina's students. Vijay recently confided to Regina that he is gay. He is very frightened of his parents' reaction as he comes from a traditional Indian family and is expected to enter into an arranged marriage. Because he knows that many of his peers do not approve of gays, Vijay has not told anyone other than Regina about his sexual identity. She wants to be of assistance, but she is also experiencing some dissonance with her own personal beliefs in this area. Regina's suggestion that Vijay might want to attend a meeting of the lesbian, gay, bisexual student organization was met with abject fear.

Gender identity issues are also evident for many of Regina's students. Marisela struggles with the traditional gender roles within her Mexican American family, particularly when other students tease her about how often she goes home to see them. She wants to be a good Mexican daughter, but she also wants to fit in at college. And Regina was shocked when Les, the brilliant chemistry student, revealed that he had never really felt comfortable as a male and was considering changing his gender identity.

Regina is relieved that the next part of her student development text focuses on social identity development. She needs some assistance with all the identity issues her students are sharing with her and, she acknowledges to herself, with the impact of her own social identities.

◆ ◆ ◆

Social identity development, the theme of Part Four, is the process by which people come to understand their social identities (ethnicity, race, gender, sexual orientation, and others) and how these identities affect other aspects of their lives (McEwen, 2003b). What makes these aspects of identity "social" is that other people, as well as the individual involved, evaluate a person and make judgments based on these identities. Social identities are very much influenced by time and place and are constantly shifting. For instance, what it means to be African American in the urban North today can be quite different from what it was like to be African American in the rural South of the 1920s. Indeed, how one acts and thinks about being African American can vary depending on whether one is at home in an all-black neighborhood or at school in a predominantly white university.

Underlying interpretations of social identity are the concepts of privilege and oppression. Some identities are privileged in our society, and others are oppressed. Rather than just being different, some identities are more highly valued and have more authority than others by virtue of the attributions that are made about them in society. Individuals' social identities influence how they see themselves, how they interact with others, the decisions they make, and how they live their lives. Ideological, social, and economic decisions are also contingent on how various social identity groups are perceived.

Chapter Thirteen provides an introduction to the ideas underlying social identity and its development, beginning with an in-depth examination of oppression and privilege. The many manifestations of privilege—white privilege, class privilege, heterosexual privilege, ability privilege, and Christian privilege—are then discussed. Multiple identity development—how a person's privileged and oppressed social identities come together and influence each other and the person's overall self-concept, as explained by the theories of S. Jones and McEwen (2000) and Abes, Jones, and McEwen (2007)—follows. In the final section of this chapter, the diversity development model of Chávez, Guido-DiBrito, and Mallory (2003) is introduced. This model focuses on the cognitive, affective, and behavior processes by which individuals become aware of and come to affirm differences in themselves and others. Having an overall understanding of the concepts of privilege and oppression and how social identities are shaped will be of benefit to Regina as she seeks to better understand the diverse students with whom she works and the societal dynamics with which they must live. Learning about these concepts will also help her to better understand herself and how she may be viewed and treated as an African American student affairs professional.

In Chapter Fourteen, the concept of race as a social construction and the tenets of critical race theory (CRT) in which privilege and oppression are embedded (Delgado & Stefanic, 2001) are explored as precursors to an examination of racial identity development theories. Specifically, the chapter includes Sue and Sue's (2003) racial and cultural identity development (RCID) model, which is designed to apply to any minority identity; Cross and Fhagen-Smith's (2001) model of black identity development; Helms's white racial identity development model (1995) and the white racial consciousness model of Rowe, Bennett, and Atkinson (1994); as well as models of Latino identity development (Ferdman & Gallegos, 2001), Asian American identity development (Kim, 2001), and American Indian identity development (Horse, 2001). Regina can use the information presented in this chapter about how race and racism affect people of color in the United States both to empathize with her advisees who have to deal with racial oppression daily and also to address these issues on campus through programming and policy development. For instance, she might work with Yuko to develop a program about the model minority myth with which Asian Americans have to contend. The racial identity theories will offer Regina insight into why some of the students she works with want nothing to do with whites and will only attend activities sponsored by Multicultural Student Affairs, while it is difficult to get other students of color to even consider enrolling in an ethnic studies class.

Chapter Fifteen focuses on ethnic identity development and acculturation as experienced in U.S. society. Defined by Phinney (1995) as "a multicultural construct, involving ethnic feelings, attitudes, knowledge, and behaviors" (p. 58), ethnic identity has both an internal component that involves how individuals see themselves, their values, and their feelings and attitudes about their ethnicity and an external component that includes active involvement in their ethnic community, the language they speak, the foods they eat, and so forth (Isajiw, 1990). Acculturation refers to the process by which members of an ethnic minority group adapt to a dominant culture with which they come in contact (Berry, 1993). This chapter includes a review of Phinney's (1995) model of ethnic identity formation; Torres's model of Hispanic identity development (1999, 2003) the application of the concepts of ethnic identity and acculturation to Native American Indians and Asian Americans; and the ethnic identity of black/African Americans, specifically Caribbean cultural identity (S. Hall, 1995) and womanist identity (Ossana, Helms, & Leonard, 1992). Understanding factors that contribute to ethnic identity and acculturation will be useful to Regina as she works with students who view their ethnic heritage very differently.

Multiracial identity development is gaining more attention in the United States as the number of individuals born to interracial/interethnic couples is increasing. In Chapter Sixteen, we examine how multiracial identity has been historically viewed and treated in the United States, as well as models for explaining how multiracial individuals develop their identities. Included are stage models, such as that of Kerwin and Ponterotto (1995); typology models (Cortés, 2000; Daniel, 2002); and ecological models (Root, 2003a, 2003b). Renn's ecological approach (2004), the first model to specifically address college students, is given particular attention. As Regina has discovered in working with Paul, multiracial identity development is a complex process about which more knowledge is needed as society becomes increasingly complex racially and ethnically. As Regina will learn, different theories present differing views of the process Paul is experiencing.

Chapter Seventeen presents an examination of how individuals come to view themselves as gay, lesbian, bisexual, or heterosexual. Gay and lesbian identity development has been studied systematically since the introduction of Cass's (1979) stage theory. Later researchers included examination of bisexual identity, although much more work in this area is needed. Finding Cass's stage theory too rigid, Fassinger (1998a) and her colleagues introduced a model of gay, lesbian, and bisexual identity development that separated this process into two aspects: internal identification and group identification. D'Augelli (1994a) used a life span approach to suggest that development occurs in six areas of one's life at varying times as a result of how individuals interpret their experiences and the decisions they make, their interactions with others who are important to them, and the cultural, historical, and geographical circumstances in which they find themselves. Only recently has heterosexual identity development been examined. Worthington and his colleagues (2002) considered both the individual and social processes involved in defining sexual needs, values, and behaviors. In their model, they also take into consideration the development of individuals' attitudes and beliefs about those who identify as gay, lesbian, and bisexual. Regina is relieved that she will be studying these theories in her class as she has very little knowledge in this area and has been quite uncomfortable talking with Vijay about it. She is hoping that the reading and class discussion will enable her to talk about her concerns and work through the dissonance she is experiencing between her desire to support and honor all of her students and what her family and religion have taught her about same-sex relationships.

Definitions of the concepts of sex, gender, and gender identity open Chapter Eighteen to provide clarity as to how they interrelate. The ideas of Lev (2004), who questioned the assumption that gender is binary (that one is either a man or a woman), are presented, as is a discussion of what it means to be cisgender (the gender roles one assumes align with one's biological sex) and transgender (one's gender identity does not align with one's biological sex). Bem's (1983) gender schema is introduced in this chapter, as is Bilodeau's (2005, 2009) work on transgender identity development. As Regina has worked with Marisela and other students this semester, she has become increasingly aware of the rigid gender roles to which many individuals, including Marisela, adhere. Regina is interested in reading this chapter to better understand how these roles develop and influence how people see themselves. And she is particularly pleased to see that the chapter includes information on transgender identity, as she has had no exposure to this topic and is very much at a loss as to how to interact with and assist Les in an exploration of how to personally make sense of gender identity.

Part Four introduces many new and complex concepts that may challenge Regina and other readers to reconsider how they understand both people's identities and the dynamics in society by which they are affected. We encourage an open mind and extensive personal reflection as these topics are explored.

CHAPTER THIRTEEN

SOCIAL IDENTITY

Concepts and Overview

In a neighborhood coffee shop, Community Café, the dean of students at Regional State University joined four randomly selected students for a chat over coffee to learn about their lives and how the university could be more responsive to their needs. As the students introduced themselves, they each highlighted aspects of themselves and concerns they had about their university experience. The dean listened carefully as the students shared their stories, which are referred to and extended throughout this chapter.

Sylvia, a first-semester sophomore and a Chicana feminist raised in the slums of Los Angeles, is majoring in secondary education and expressed concerns that her perspective might not be welcome in most public schools. Sylvia preferred serial monogamy to Internet hook-ups, where many of her friends met sexual partners. She hoped the dean could find ways to help her feel more comfortable in a local community not her own.

Tyler, a student who lived with his parents in the university community, studied hard and earned excellent grades while holding down several service jobs. As a first-generation college student, he began his story by describing his parents' working-class roots. Tyler did not recognize his privilege as a white man because his family's financial status overshadowed his other identities. He asked for more student jobs on campus and places for commuter students to study.

Kimberly, a first-semester, first-year student, whose parents were both doctors, volunteered to go next. She grew up with a doorman and a live-in nanny. Her German family values, such as individuality and lack of demonstrative emotion, played a large role in her urban yet cloistered upbringing. Enrolled in an eastern prep school attended almost exclusively by white privileged students, she saw different others only on TV before coming to college. Lacking awareness of her privilege and the dean's lack of power, Kimberly asked for sorority legacies to be granted a guaranteed bid.

Arnold, a senior marketing major from the state's largest metropolitan area, grew up in a socially active Jewish community. Boldly announcing he was gay at a large family gathering in his early teens, in college he advocated for gay rights. Arnold decided to work for a few years before applying to law school, but worried that law would not sustain his soul in the way his activism did. He wanted the dean's advice on the path to pursue.

◆ ◆ ◆

In some way, all of these students have been influenced by the social movements of the past fifty years in the United States. Tracing these developments reveals identity models relevant to college students that parallel the social issues that emerged in different time periods. In this chapter, we provide a brief historical review of the concept of social identity and examine the related concepts, oppression and privilege, including the many forms of privilege (for example, social class, sexual, racial, religious) identified in the growing literature. We then discuss a multiple identity model and its revision and an individual diversity development model. A critique and suggestions for future work in this area close the chapter.

Historical Overview

Social identity became a prominent issue in the United States during the black civil rights movement of the 1960s. Soon after, African American scholars developed models of black identity (for example, Cross, 1971) highlighting the contrast between black identity and white identity. The 1970s spawned the women's movement and models related to gender (Gilligan, 1977; Josselson, 1973; Kimmel, 2003b) and eventually feminism (hooks, 1981). Also during the 1970s, the gay rights movement led to the development of homosexual identity models (Cass, 1979), later identified as lesbian, gay, and bisexual. In the 1980s, theorists sought synthesis of individual cultural group models designed to encompass the experiences of all minority group members, such as the minority development model (Atkinson, Morten, & Sue, 1989) and the multiethnic model (Banks, 1984). As the twentieth century came to a close, white (Helms & Carter, 1990), Latino (Torres, 2003), Asian (Kim, 2001), and ethnic (Phinney, 1990) frames and explanations for the identity development of their respective ethnic groups followed.

During the 1990s and into the twenty-first century, scholars delved deeper into the complexity of multiple identities and their extensive overlapping influences and formations (Abes, Jones, & McEwen, 2007; S. Jones, 1997; Jones & McEwen, 2000; Reynolds & Pope, 1991). As a result of this work, identity is no longer viewed as made up of separate components, but rather as intertwined and unique for each individual.

In the early twenty-first century, the social identity literature exploded, as did foundational knowledge related to privilege, oppression, multiple identities, and diversity development, all outlined in this chapter. This expansion signifies a shift away from the dominance of mostly positivist psychosocial and cognitive structural theories to guide student development toward inclusion of a wider range of research methods and social science disciplines, such as sociology and anthropology. To enhance college students' development, student affairs professionals, especially counselors, have also begun to seek out ways to work with oppression, privilege, and power as they address multifaceted identity issues (Black & Stone, 2005; Hanna, Talley, & Guindon, 2000; Reynolds & Pope, 1991).

Harnessing these overlapping and complicated identity concerns brings both the interpersonal and intrapersonal components of development to the foreground. In addition, much of the foundation of the social identity literature is methodologically grounded in social constructivism and less so in the tradition of the foundational theories previously discussed in this book. How individuals and groups make meaning of the world they occupy is vital to understanding social identity, making social constructivism a worldview and method appropriate to explore these ideas. Recognizing the burgeoning availability of resources on these topics, we first review selected literature tied to the key concepts of oppression and privilege and then examine specific research linked to these and related concepts in the higher education literature.

Oppression

While scholars disagree about the meaning of oppression, inequality of power is a key component of most definitions (New, 2001). Oppression consists of a family of concepts and conditions, one of which is the inability to develop (Young, 2000), making it an important concept in student affairs.

Often thought of as embedded in colonial domination, oppression as "tyranny by a ruling group" (Young, 2000, p. 36) was transformed during the social movements of the 1960s and 1970s. During this time, the meaning of oppression shifted to injustices perpetrated by the privileged (that is, middle class, young, white, Christian, heterosexual, male, and without obvious mental, physical, or emotional impairments), sometimes unconsciously, on the oppressed (basically anyone not in the aforementioned categories). Woven into the fabric of tacit societal assumptions, close examination indicates that oppression is a structural issue, not a political one. Indeed, oppression has long been an element of the dominant culture in the United States (Torres, Howard-Hamilton, & Cooper, 2003), and exposing its invisible, toxic nature heightens awareness and may encourage members of dominant groups to change their perspective and take social action to address more equitable change.

Bohmer and Briggs (1991) defined *oppression* as "those attitudes, behaviors, and pervasive and systemic social arrangements by which members of one group are exploited and subordinated while members of another group are granted privileges" (p. 155). For example, college women of color may be viewed as oppressed by both race and gender in the academy, while gay men in college might be considered oppressed by their sexuality and privileged by their gender.

Oppressed people are "confined and shaped by forces and barriers which are not accidental or occasional and hence avoidable" (Frye, 2003, p. 141), leaving them trapped and immobile as if locked in a bird cage. A silenced culture is created when the dominant culture oppressors ignore oppressed voices and expect conformity to dominant views (Hanna et al., 2000). When the powerless in any culture are not heard, the voiceless oppressed put their future in the hands of their oppressors (Freire, 1974). One obvious illustration is the climate on many college campuses in the South just prior to the civil rights movement. The University of Alabama did not admit African American students until civil rights activists protested for black students' admittance. Prior to this time, black students' futures lay primarily with white state legislators.

Oppression can take many forms, including exploitation, marginalization, powerlessness, cultural imperialism, and violence (Young, 2000). Added to this complexity, research has shown that individuals place themselves in various locations along an oppressed-oppressor continuum, "depending upon the contexts, time, and social and legal relationships involved in their interactions" (Sonn & Fisher, 2003, p. 117). To recognize and eliminate oppression, the visible and invisible interaction of privilege and oppression must be inspected. Basically, "we need more adequate concepts of power, and an analysis of hidden power, in our own relationships and in social structures on the large scale" (Harvey, 2000, p. 187) to take an appropriate first step toward stopping this symbiotic social interaction.

As with anything examined too closely and dissected in small parts, oppression can be hard to recognize when looking at its elements and not focusing on its structure as a whole. Using Afrocentric psychology as a foundation, Reynolds and Pope (1991) examined the complexity of multiple oppressions derived from multiple identities and challenged societal polarization and lack of attention to differences of nondominant identities. Building on Root's (1990) biracial model, these researchers developed the multidimensional identity model (MIM) "to clarify and expand understanding of the existing multiple options for identity resolution for members of more than one oppressed group" (p. 178). Challenging traditional notions of linear development, the model outlines two dimensions: one addresses identification (that is, the individual identifies with just one or with more than one identity), and the other examines an active or passive role in negotiating multiple identities. The MIM presents four possible options for identity resolution: "1) society assigned—passive acceptance; 2) conscious identification; 3) multiple aspects of self in a segmented fashion, or 4) identity intersection" (Reynolds & Pope, p. 179). Individuals may move among the options throughout their lives, depending on their personal needs, reference group, or other environmental factors.

Privilege

In the United States, a centuries-old democracy, the notion of privilege has been ignored until recently, but the myth of meritocracy (McIntosh, 1989, 2003) is making widespread inequities more difficult to ignore. Such inequities might include that only those from the highest economic classes can afford college in the near future; men are still paid more than women for comparable work; white people have more freedom to live where they want than people of color; and so on. Most privileged individuals in U.S. society cannot see the power they hold, making privilege invisible and intact for the possessors (Robinson & Howard-Hamilton, 2000). Many who are privileged unknowingly take advantage of it, often without thought of the inequity or even cruelty they inflict on those without privilege.

McIntosh (1989, 2003) discussed two kinds of privilege: *unearned entitlements*, privileges we should all possess, such as feeling safe in the workplace; and *conferred dominance*, giving one group power over another. Kimberly, introduced earlier and born into privilege, was sure the dean could be instrumental in granting her request for an automatic sorority bid because her mother had served as president of the chapter twenty-eight years ago. Unaware of her social class privilege, Kimberly believed she was entitled to a legacy sorority membership and thought the dean could ensure a bid by arranging preferential treatment.

Not only does conferred dominance bestow privilege on a single group, it also simultaneously makes individuals who are members of this group pivotal as oppressors with power. Some scholars have documented the symbiotic relationship between privilege and oppression in the counseling (Black & Stone, 2005; Croteau, Talbot, Lance, & Evans, 2002; Hanna et al., 2000) and adult education

(Tisdell, 1993) literature, demonstrating how systems of privilege interlock to keep power in the hands of those already privileged and allow them to systematically dominate everyone else. Many people in U.S. society have advantages because of some part of their status (for example, being socioeconomically secure, heterosexual, or male). However, they do not see tackling privilege as their responsibility because they do not see themselves as oppressors or, in some cases, they may not care. Furthermore, some see their privileged status (for example, white, male) outweighed by an oppressed status that is also part of their identity (for example, socioeconomic or sexual orientation) and never recognize the privilege they hold.

Tyler, one of the students at Community Café, felt more oppressed than privileged as a white working-class student living with his parents, working part time, and attending class full time. When he looked around campus, he believed everyone had more than he did, but he used this as a motivator to work harder. He had never considered the privilege he had by virtue of being white and male in U.S. society.

Like a lopsided scale of justice, an unbalanced social structure "bestows privilege in a manner that impacts relationships between people who would otherwise be peers" (Rocco & West, 1998, p. 177). The intricate connection between self, others, and environment shapes the awareness and unawareness of privilege. Privilege comes in many seen and unseen manifestations in U.S. society, including white privilege, class privilege, gender privilege, sexual orientation privilege, ability privilege, Christian privilege, and other forms, such as age and appearance. We discuss many of these types of privilege, followed by a review of selected literature examining privilege in university contexts.

White Privilege

Whether accepted as truth or not, white privilege has dominated North America since the arrival of Columbus, evident in the power assumed by light-skinned people of nearly every culture who lived on the continent then and arrived later. As a shifting social construction, definitions of the white population have varied throughout U.S. history, and no consensus has emerged for "the optimal term one should use to describe American descendants of European and Middle Eastern immigrants" (McDermott & Sampson, 2005, p. 247). *White*, the most common term in use, was coined by the U.S. Census, though other terms, such as *Caucasian, European American*, and *Anglo*, are often used by whites to place themselves in an ethnic or racial category. Ironically, as the nonwhite population increases, a stronger, not weaker, connection will bind whiteness and privilege (McDermott & Sampson). Regardless of any other circumstance, a vast majority of whites fail to recognize and take responsibility for the unhealthy and symbiotic relationship between white privilege and oppression.

As an identity construct, whiteness is "ill-defined, illusory (as an identity marker) and elusive" (R. Jackson, 1999, p. 52). By contrast, white privilege is explicitly defined, but often hard for whites, while easy for nonwhites, to see as a "system of benefits, advantages, and opportunities experienced by white persons" (Donnelly, Cook, Van Ausdale, & Foley, 2005, p. 6) bestowed solely because of skin color.

A fitting metaphor for white privilege describes it as being "like a weightless knapsack of special provisions, assurances, tools, maps, guides, codebooks, passports, visas, clothes, compass, emergency gear, and blank checks" (McIntosh, 1989, p. 2). Today white privilege is rapidly increasing as a topic for discussion in myriad bodies of literature, including counseling (for example, Hays & Chang, 2003), higher education (for example, Hurtado, 2001), and student affairs (for example, Ortiz & Rhoads, 2000).

Rocco and West (1998) pointed out that manifestations of privilege (for example, power, status, credibility, and normality) and determinants of privilege (that is, personal attributes that define who we are) combine to form "polyrhythmic realities" (Sheared, 1994, p. 28). In this case, reality privileges one individual characteristic while disadvantaging others. For example, white women are often advantaged over women of color, while white women are often disadvantaged in comparison to all men in higher education as well as society.

Since the majority of college students are white, they are the group most often used as subjects in all kinds of research conducted on campus. As the majority group in predominantly white institutions, white students also are often the most privileged by the outcomes of this research.

White participants in one study disassociated from racist family, friends, and institutions as they made more connections with people of color, but also experienced race-related guilt (Arminio, 2001). As a method of freeing one's self from the oppression that comes with privilege, white people can move from "acceptance of oppression to naming oppression (the feeling of guilt), to reflection and redefinition (learning from guilt), to multiperspective integration (to act on what one has learned from guilt)" (Arminio, pp. 246–247).

Social Class Privilege

In polite U.S. society, the topic of social (and economic) class is taboo. Many believe the United States is classless or entirely middle class, increasingly rich, and everyone has the same chance to succeed (Mantsios, 2004). Underlying these myths are erroneous assumptions, for example, that differences in U.S. citizens' economic standing are not significant. The truth behind this myth is that "the middle class in the U.S. holds a very small share of the nation's wealth, and its income—in constant dollars—is declining" (Mantsios, p. 196). In addition, "enormous class differences in the lifestyles of the haves, the have-nots, and the have-littles" (p. 201) exist.

For individuals, social class has three components: "a social class of origin, a current felt social class and an attributed social class" (Barrett, 2007, n.p.). When a shift in class occurs, identity can change, and felt and attributed social classes can be at odds with each other. A sharp social class contrast experience in college can lead to working-class students' lack of persistence. Ignoring these inequities and others saturating our economic and social systems perpetuates class privilege and class oppression.

Class privilege is also shaped by intersections with identity, including "race, gender, sexuality, and geography" (Borrego, 2004, p. 4). An individual's social connections and experiences, often referred to as cultural capital, open doors and extend power. Although social class is often measured with criteria like income, occupation, and education, "class rests on other people's evaluation of our presentation of self" (Kimmel, 2003a, p. 7).

Most people think of class as "the kind of work they do, income they earn and their education" (Ostrander, 1984, p. 4). In contrast, the upper class frame their assets as "ownership of wealth, exercise of power, and membership in an exclusive network" (p. 5). Wealth, power, and a closed social network keep class distinctions in the hands of the rich, who preserve class invisibility and maintain the social class status quo. As higher education costs rise, creating a more exclusive environment, more students attending college will occupy the highest social class statuses.

Kimberly and Tyler, at opposite ends of the economic spectrum, were each considering what this meant. Kimberly lived in a condo near campus that her parents had purchased for her. At the meeting with the dean, she began to question her assumptions about the power of social networks. Tyler saw the world from the other extreme. He believed studying hard would lead to stable, well-paying employment. Tyler believed attending college made him privileged, even though he knew his privilege was not the same as Kimberly's.

A paucity of literature exists on how students from different social classes develop in college because no social class developmental model exists. However, one empirical study sheds light on this elusive phenomenon and identified themes, including the importance of social class rules and symbols, the strong influence of cultural and familial messages, the significant role of gender and class in the Latino culture, and hope for their family's future, among self-identified Mexican male students (Schwartz, Donovan, & Guido-DiBrito, 2009). Student affairs practitioners are encouraged to promote community dialogue about the meaning of social class, create more on-campus work for students, encourage Latino family involvement, and provide culturally sensitive mentors and models.

Gender Privilege

Male privilege has been a dominant theme throughout U.S. history and was adamantly challenged during the women's movement of the late twentieth century. Gender privilege is most often invisible to men of all backgrounds and connected to other kinds of privilege. For example, in a mixed-method study of college students' perceptions of privilege and oppression, white men viewed these concepts differently than people of color did (Chizhik & Chizhik, 2005). The study found that "white men are reluctant to see classism as an oppressive force in our society" (p. 137). Three reasons white male students are resistant to discussions of social justice are an unrealistic sense of privilege, denial of its presence, and fear of responsibility for initiating necessary social change (Chizhik & Chizhik).

Studies of the upper class reveal "rigid gender differentiation and stratification more so than any other social class" (Ostrander, 1984, p. 6). Perhaps the upper class's static stratification helps keep our male-dominated society intact and equitable treatment for others at bay. Invisibility is a privilege in that it maintains the power dynamics of inequality (Kimmel, 2003a). Simply put, "It is a luxury that only men have in our society to pretend that gender does not matter" (p. 4).

Women are economically and socially disadvantaged throughout society. Even with the flood of "race and class in feminist analysis" (Hurtado, 2001, p. 153), women with different identities are lumped together in media statistical reporting of the socioeconomic conditions of all women, especially when compared to men. For example, white women are in school longer, earn more bachelor's degrees, earn higher incomes, and are less likely to be heads of households living in poverty than their women of color counterparts (Hurtado). Differences among working-class, middle-class, and upper-class women of all colors are usually ignored.

Heterosexual Privilege

One of the most invisible privileges in U.S. society is heterosexual privilege. Feigenbaum (2007) explained that "heterosexism is not about individuals or how comfortable they are around queers," but rather "about dominance, and the practices that support it are often replicated, reinforced, and reflected by the attitudes, behaviors and practices of even our best-intentioned allies" (p. 7).

Similar to other privileged identities, most people who identify as heterosexual do not think about their sexual orientation until they recognize their relationship to others who do not identify as heterosexual (Evans & Broido, 2005). Most heterosexuals view their sexuality as "normal" and all other sexual identities as deviant (Bieschke, 2002). As such, the dominant culture almost never perceives sexuality as a social identity and takes heterosexual privilege for granted (Evans & Broido, 2005). To interrupt heterosexism and homophobia, we must learn how to recognize and combat its interpersonal and political manifestations.

Simoni and Walters (2001) studied heterosexual identity to expose its privilege and reduce prejudice toward nonheterosexuals. In this study, they proposed that attitudes of whites about their privileged status evolve in a similar manner to heterosexuals' attitudes about their sexual identity, also a privileged status. Results of the inquiry "partially confirmed the hypothesized associations between evolving identity stages and less heterosexist attitudes" (Simoni & Walters, p. 157). Taking responsibility for and acknowledging one's own privilege mediates "between developing a dominant group identity and decreasing prejudicial attitudes towards non-privileged groups" (p. 157).

Ability Privilege

Examining attitudes toward people with disabilities and their treatment throughout history reveals that ability privilege and the psychological, social, emotional, and often economic freedom it bestows on its beholders is very real (see Evans, 2008; Evans, Assadi, & Herriott, 2005; Griffin, Peters, & Smith, 2007). Historically, disability has been viewed as "a sign of spiritual depravity, a cause for ridicule, a genetic weakness to be exterminated, something to be hidden away, a source of pity, a community health problem, and a problem to be fixed" (Evans, 2008, p. 11). Even the language used indicates that able-bodied people view people with disabilities as "less than" normal as it frequently focuses on physical or mental limitations (Marks, 1999). When terms such as *learning disabled, hearing impaired*, or *brain injured* are used, they suggest that the individual so described cannot function at the level or in the way that society expects (Evans & Herriott, 2009). The terms w*heelchair bound, handicapped*, and *afflicted* make assumptions about the experiences of people with disabilities that may not be true. They also disempower individuals and elicit feelings of pity that are neither desired nor needed.

By assuming one normative way to do things (move, speak, learn, and so forth), society privileges those who carry out these functions as prescribed and oppresses those who use other methods (Evans & Herriott, 2009). "Ableism"— the "pervasive system of discrimination and exclusion that oppresses people [with] . . . disabilities on . . . individual, institutional, and societal/cultural levels" (Rauscher & McClintock, 1997, p. 198), is an evident form of privilege in society and on college campuses (Evans, 2008).

In reality, the causes of disability are environmental conditions and attitudes, not physical and mental impairments (Griffin et al., 2007). The physical barriers that prevent people from accessing buildings, separate individuals in educational settings, fail to provide alternative methods of consuming information (for example, visual captioning for those with hearing loss), and so on are situations that put people with disabilities at a disadvantage. Attitudes of able-bodied people that discount the talents and skills of anyone with a disability are equally at fault (Evans & Herriott, 2009).

Christian Privilege

A vast array of religious traditions can be found across the globe. In general, whatever religion predominates in a specific location is privileged, in that it is recognized and honored, while other religious traditions are discriminated against, ignored, or ridiculed. Christian privilege is prevalent in the United States since the majority of its citizens identify as Christians. One scholar defined Christian as anyone who believes in "(a) Jesus as their Lord and Savior, and (b) the teachings of the Old and New Testaments" (Schlosser, 2003, p. 45).

The dominant religions in the United States are Roman Catholics, mainstream Protestant groups (for example, Lutherans, Methodists, Presbyterians), evangelical Christian groups (including Pentecostals, Southern Baptists, Assembly of God), Eastern Orthodox (for example, Greek, Russian), and smaller denominations, including the Church of Jesus Christ of Latter-Day Saints and Seventh-Day Adventists. Non-Christian religious groups (for example, Buddhism, Hinduism, Judaism, and Islam) are relatively small in number in the United States and face oppression and prejudice based on their group membership (Schlosser, 2003). Those with Christian privilege have a responsibility to reflect on their privilege and power and create more equitable religious identification patterns.

Christian privilege is embedded in the academy (Seifert, 2007). Ritual, symbols, and practices representative of Christian privilege in U.S. higher education are clearly delineated examples of assumed Christian "cultural markers" (p. 11), such as religious practices held concurrently with state and federal holidays. In addition, until recently, Christians accepted without question public representations of their religion. Manger scenes in public institutional spaces at Christmas, unwillingness of faculty and others to learn the religious customs of non-Christians, and dress (for example, the wearing of a Christian cross) are obvious examples.

Judaism, and even anti-Semitism, is absent in most college classroom discussions of multiculturalism (Langman, 1995), another sign of Christian privilege. Seen as white by most in the dominant culture, Jews are mostly invisible in our society, as they are likely to project different public and private identities and fear being publicly identified as Jewish. In a study of thirty Jewish gay men in Toronto, Schnoor (2006) discovered that these men did not compartmentalize their identity or choose one identity over the other; rather "these men had the clear expectation that multiple parts of their identities can and should be validated by society at the same time" (p. 58). In post-9/11 U.S. society with its globally touched religious unrest, institutions of higher education should celebrate the variety of worldwide religious traditions tied to the multiple identities of students, staff, and administrators when creating healthy multicultural campuses.

Multiple Identities

Traditional linear stage identity theories, mostly derived from Erikson (1959/1980), are the foundation for understanding how college students identify. Yet social constructions of identity like class, ethnicity, race, gender, sexual orientation, religion, geography, and ability are recognized as playing an important role in understanding identity dimensions (McEwen, 2003b). Some identity dimensions, like geography, are not developmentally grounded yet play a critical role in self-definitions. Not only are the theories and models presented in this book key to understanding identity, but the complex, collective interaction of these dimensions and how they tie to the process of our unique individual identity formation (Robinson, 1999) may be even more significant in an increasingly pluralistic world. Delworth (1989) was one of the first student affairs scholars to raise the issue of the intersection of gender and ethnic identity while raising questions about the lack of consideration given to the convergence of identities.

In the past, the dominant culture controlled the invisibility of the discourse around multiple identities, as well as oppressions and privileges (Dworkin, 2002; Liang & Alimo, 2005). Recently this discourse has become more transparent as research in student affairs (for example, Abes et al., 2007; Abes & Kasch, 2007; Jones, 1997; Jones & McEwen, 2000; Reynolds & Pope, 1991) and related disciplines like psychology (Stanley, 2004) and counseling (C. Williams, 2005) have provided a better illumination of our multiple identities and their corresponding privileges and oppressions. Based on an analysis of the scholarship on multiple identity constructs of race, class, gender, and sexuality, Weber (1998) concluded that the intersection of multiple identities is a socially constructed, contextual phenomenon enacted in everyday life that motivates action to create a more equitable society.

A conceptual model of multiple dimensions of identity was developed by Jones and McEwen (2000) based on their grounded theory study of ten undergraduate women of diverse racial and cultural backgrounds. Portrayed at the center of the three-dimensional model is the core sense of self (one's personal identity), including personal attributes and characteristics, and other factors important to the individual. Surrounding and enveloping the core is the context within which identity occurs; special attention is given to family background, sociocultural conditions, current experiences, and career decisions and life planning. Significant identity dimensions (race, culture, gender, family, education, sexual orientation, social class, and religion) are depicted as intersecting circles surrounding the core identity. Dots located on each of these intersecting circles represent the importance of the identity dimension to the individual. The closer the dot is to the core, the greater the importance of that identity dimension to the individual at that time. Like Reynolds and Pope (1991), Jones and McEwen (2000) added to the research by offering an alternative to linear development, describing and illustrating their model as "a fluid and dynamic one, representing the ongoing construction of identities and the influence of changing contexts on the experience of identity development" (p. 408).

Based on Abes and Jones's (2004) study of lesbian identity development and meaning making, Abes, Jones, and McEwen (2007) reconceptualized Jones and McEwen's (2000) model of multiple identity dimensions, drawing on feminist theoretical conceptualizations of multiple identities (for example, Anzaldúa, 1987/1999) for this model. Feminist narratives demonstrate recognition of the concurrent, nonhierarchical experience of multiple identities, in other words, intersectionality (Abes et al., 2007; Knight, 2002). To add to this complexity, aspects of identity such as class, race, ethnicity, gender, and sexual orientation have no universal understanding, making the varied intricacies of these intersections even less transparent. Choosing from the multiplicity of underlying postmodern frameworks, this study abandoned universal truth and recognized the positive and negative social, political, and cultural differences between and within groups. These student affairs researchers drew on queer theory, which temporarily defers sexual orientation categories and instead suggests that identity is performance (Butler, 1990) where "repetition creates a sense of self, including a core sense of personal values, however fluid that sense of self might be" (Abes et al., p. 15). None of the relationships depicted in this model stand alone, as all dimensions must be understood in relationship to each other.

Unlike Jones and McEwen's (2000) more illustrative model of multiple dimensions of identity, the reconceptualized model is two-dimensional, depicting the interaction of context, meaning making, and identity perceptions. Multiple identity dimensions including race, gender, social class, religion, and sexual orientation are portrayed in an identical manner to the Jones and McEwen model, looking like planets in orbit around earth. On the other side of a meaning-making filter are contextual influences such as peers, family, stereotypes, norms, and sociopolitical conditions that are external to multiple identity dimensions but represented as arrows pointing toward them. The meaning-making filter acts as a sieve, and "depending on complexity, contextual influences pass through to different degrees" (Abes et al., 2007, p. 7), influencing identity self-perceptions. The model portrays this identity development process (see Figure 13.1).

Abes et al. (2007) discussed the model using portraits of three participants who demonstrate multiple dimensions of identity through formulaic meaning making (relatively simple), transitional (conflict within identity, more complex) meaning making, and foundational (relationship between context and perception

FIGURE 13.1. RECONCEPTUALIZED MODEL OF MULTIPLE DIMENSIONS OF IDENTITY

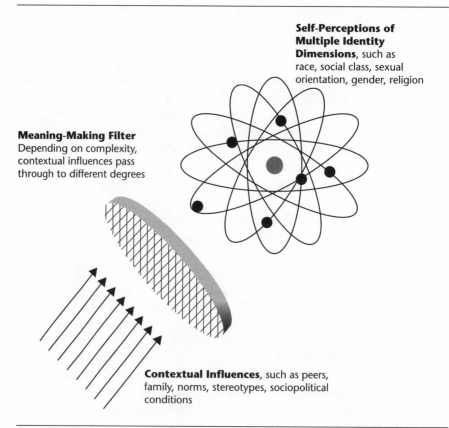

Self-Perceptions of Multiple Identity Dimensions, such as race, social class, sexual orientation, gender, religion

Meaning-Making Filter
Depending on complexity, contextual influences pass through to different degrees

Contextual Influences, such as peers, family, norms, stereotypes, sociopolitical conditions

Source: From Abes, E. S., Jones, S. R., & McEwen, M. K. (2007). Reconceptualizing the model of multiple dimensions of identity: The role of meaning-making capacity in the construction of multiple identities. *Journal of College Student Development, 48*(1), 7.

of identity is complex) meaning making. Reformulating Jones and McEwen's (2000) multiple dimensions model to include meaning making "provides a richer portrayal of not only *what* relationships students perceive among their personal and social identities, but also *how* they come to perceive them as they do" (p. 13). Jones and McEwen's model was the first student development theory in the literature to offer "a conceptual framework for understanding relationships among students' personal and socially constructed identities" (p. 13). By adding meaning making to the Jones and McEwen model, Abes et al. created one of the first holistic models of student development.

Exploration of multiple identities is often not a voluntary activity for students of color because skin color is evident while other identities can appear invisible. Indeed, most students with multiple marginalized identities face the intersections of their complex selves not necessarily as willing participants but for survival in the dominant culture. Arnold, one of the students at Community Café, recognized many identities with which he resonated. Although others consider him white (his skin looks white), he sees himself as a gay Jew. Arnold finds he cannot separate these two interlocking identities but worries he may be forced to live an incongruent life separating and hiding his identities at different times.

The student affairs and development literature is rapidly increasing our understanding of multiple identities (see Poindexter-Cameron & Robinson, 1997; Sanchez & Carter, 2005). Some research has revealed that major influences on the multiple identity development of college students include active coalition building with others who are similar and different; attendance at a historically black, women's, or historically black women's college or university (Poindexter-Cameron & Robinson; Jackson, 1999); and participation in classroom discussions that highlight intersectionality (Knight, 2002). The ways in which individual identities such as race, class, and gender are woven together to create a whole, unique individual, not a person with separate, distinct, unrelated identity categories, demands more study.

Diversity Development

Chávez, Guido-DiBrito, and Mallory (2003) created a model of diversity development that examines how healthy individuals develop organically in ways that make awareness possible and moves toward affirmation of others. This individual diversity development framework details "cognitive, affective, and behavioral growth processes toward consciously valuing complex and integrated differences in others and in ourselves" (Chávez et al., p. 453). The model represents reflection along six dimensions in which developmental movement occurs in a nonlinear fashion from undetermined times of unawareness, dual awareness, questioning and self-exploration, risk taking or other exploration, and integration and validation of others (see Figure 13.2). Cognitively, affectively, and behaviorally, individuals progress at "various ages, simultaneously, or not at all" (p. 458) along these permeable dimensions.

Unawareness/lack of exposure to the other is a dimension an individual experiences prior to knowledge of or contact with others with whom they are unfamiliar. Cognitively, individuals lack consciousness or exposure to difference. Affectively, individuals have no experiential reference point and are void of feeling for this type of otherness. Behaviorally, people do not act in response to differences, even when confronted with them.

FIGURE 13.2. A FRAMEWORK OF INDIVIDUAL DIVERSITY DEVELOPMENT

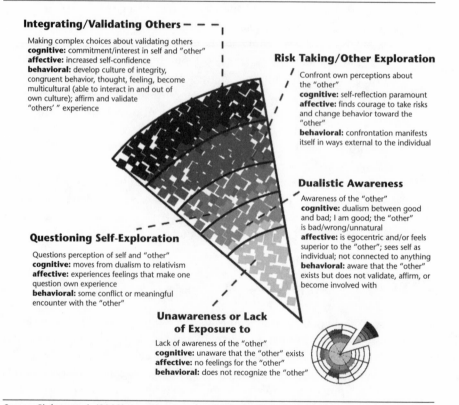

Integrating/Validating Others — — —

Making complex choices about validating others
cognitive: commitment/interest in self and "other"
affective: increased self-confidence
behavioral: develop culture of integrity, congruent behavior, thought, feeling, become multicultural (able to interact in and out of own culture); affirm and validate "others' " experience

Risk Taking/Other Exploration

Confront own perceptions about the "other"
cognitive: self-reflection paramount
affective: finds courage to take risks and change behavior toward the "other"
behavioral: confrontation manifests itself in ways external to the individual

Dualistic Awareness

Awareness of the "other"
cognitive: dualism between good and bad; I am good; the "other" is bad/wrong/unnatural
affective: is egocentric and/or feels superior to the "other"; sees self as individual; not connected to anything
behavioral: aware that the "other" exists but does not validate, affirm, or become involved with

Questioning Self-Exploration

Questions perception of self and "other"
cognitive: moves from dualism to relativism
affective: experiences feelings that make one question own experience
behavioral: some conflict or meaningful encounter with the "other"

Unawareness or Lack of Exposure to

Lack of awareness of the "other"
cognitive: unaware that the "other" exists
affective: no feelings for the "other"
behavioral: does not recognize the "other"

Source: Chávez et al. (2003). Learning to value the "other": An individual framework for diversity development. *Journal of College Student Development, 44*(4), 459.

Prior to college, Kimberly lived in a rich white community with her esteemed professional parents. The prep school she attended enrolled a handful of students of color with whom she had no contact. Even when exposed to the invisibility of her vast, deep privilege, Kimberly did not want to accept it. Lacking awareness of otherness may be dwindling as the Internet gives us exposure to myriad differences, yet often information individuals gain about the other is "incorrect, stereotypical, out of context, or exaggerated" (Chávez et al., 2003, p. 459).

The next dimension, *dualistic awareness*, frames familiar difference as normal and unfamiliar difference as bad. Cognitively, individuals perceive difference dichotomously, do not reflect on it, and interpret others based on instantaneous interpretations. Affectively, individuals are egocentric, do not question their assumptions about "the other," and feel superior. Behaviorally, individuals have little contact outside familiar groups, and when contact does occur, "it may be to point out wrong behavior, to try to correct behavior, or to try to remove others from their environment" (Chávez et al., 2003, p. 460). In this polarizing dimension, behavior is not likely to change without first altering feelings (affective) and then examining inaccurate information (cognitive).

The third dimension along this permeable continuum, *questioning/self-exploration*, perhaps the most critical component of valuing others, is when individuals "reflect on feelings, thoughts and behaviors in relation to others" (Chávez et al., 2003, p. 461). Cognitively, individuals move to relativism as they ponder the meaning of their beliefs originating in religious, familial, or cultural practices. Affectively, they experience trepidation of possible rejection by loved ones and excitement at opening a door to a broader understanding of self, others, and the world. Behaviorally, individuals retreat to internal dialogue and interaction with trusted others. Exploration through journaling and searching for cultural information about a specific "other" produces growth and encourages risk taking.

The *risk taking/exploration of otherness* dimension moves individuals into active engagement and confrontation of their own views of the world and entering the foreign world of unknown others. Individuals often experience a thorny discomfort around family and friends, whose values may be discarded, as the commencement of exploration is delicate. Cognitively, individuals are self-reflective and compare their experiences to what they know about others. Affectively, risk taking is seen as a continual process as individuals wonder at their place in this ocean of diversity. Behaviorally, as individuals risk understanding the other, their feelings, thoughts, and behaviors are modified based on their experience, thus producing more risk taking. Some start to advocate for others in an effort to assist them "rather than considering the more integrated possibility of mutual activism" (Chávez et al., 2003, p. 462).

Finally, the *integration/validation* dimension intertwines concepts of self and other. Individuals see themselves as complex individuals and affirm members of many different groups. After careful consideration, these individuals make reflective choices about individual and group validation of the other. Cognitively, individuals understand their rights and responsibilities as well as those of others and recognize differences and similarities between self and others. Affectively, a balance occurs between self-esteem and comfort with others as the individual develops a healthy self-concept and secure self in relation to others. Behaviorally, individuals create a culture of integrity supportive of congruent feelings, thoughts, and actions.

Though there is no empirical evidence to support this diversity development model, some anecdotal evidence highlights the usefulness of the model in practice. One student affairs faculty member built a syllabus around the model for a graduate multicultural course she taught (V. Torres, personal communication, December 2003), while another colleague used the model as a foundation to facilitate professional development of the board of trustees at a medium-size public university (J. Fried, personal communication, February 1, 2004). As the world becomes smaller and more diverse, we find ourselves surrounded by familiar and unfamiliar difference. Taking the necessary risks to create more acceptance and affirmation for higher education community members can reap valuable benefits.

Critique and Future Directions

Privilege and oppression are studied in most academic disciplines, and sorting through their meaning in light of multiple identities makes the need for more examination critical. The complexity of multiple identities and their growth and change over time enrich and deepen the conversation about social identity and make the boundedness of a generalized single theory of identity seem outdated. Living in postmodernity and recognizing how privilege and oppression intersect our complex lives and those of others helps untangle the systems of injustice perpetuated by those with privilege and power in our diverse higher education institutions. Becoming familiar with the breadth and depth of knowledge necessary to understand all students' individual identities (and, by extension, those of one's colleagues and oneself) can create a more vibrant, interactive campus community focusing on the whole student.

Jones and McEwen (2000) developed one the first holistic models of student development for application in the academy, yet the first clarion call for attention to the whole student was over seven decades ago (American Council on Education, 1937/1994a). A need for additional research from multiple epistemological perspectives can help educators better understand the complicated interlocking of privilege, oppression, diversity, and identity in their expanding manifestations. Opening the door to diverse students' complicated uniqueness is movement toward a campus culture reinforced by genuine community acceptance of difference.

Student affairs educators must uncover language to allow meaningful, respectful dialogue about power between and among individuals with unequal status in the academy. To continue to deny that inequality exists and ignore the voices of oppressed others denies students their full potential (Brown, Hinton, & Howard-Hamilton, 2007). We need a better understanding of how adapting identities shape who students become and how they interact with diverse others. Student affairs professionals can make significant contributions to the creation of college campuses with inspiring visions of equality and social identity in student affairs policy and practice. Educators must create opportunities for students like Sylvia, Tyler, Kimberly, and Arnold to achieve a healthy social identity in today's multifaceted world.

CHAPTER FOURTEEN

RACIAL IDENTITY DEVELOPMENT

It has been ten years since the violent and racist hate crimes occurred at Kando University. An advisory task force of students, staff, and administrators has been convened to continue focused dialogue about racial injustices and implement programming initiatives on campus. Angela, an entry-level student affairs educator, was asked to represent residence life on the task force. Angela prided herself on understanding human differences and possessing the capacity to provide assistance to any student in need. Although she was a white woman who grew up in a small, rural, isolated town in the Midwest, Angela believed her undergraduate experiences and, most recently, her time in a student affairs program had prepared her to have consistent, meaningful interactions with racially diverse people.

The first topic the task force considered was the implementation of a multicultural learning community (MLC) in the residence halls. Angela explained the concept of the MLC and the benefits of the program to the students and the university: "The MLC will demonstrate that our institution is committed to diversity and will give *you* [referring to the students of color present] a chance to interact with other students in a diverse setting." The ideas Angela shared caught the attention of some and engendered concern for others.

Phylicia, the Black Student Union president, shared her concerns: "Angela, I've been a student here for three years, and this institution has been all talk and no action. No offense, but if I didn't know better, I would think this MLC is a ploy by this white school to create a ghetto-like environment for students of color. And why aren't white students involved? If only students of color participate in this MLC, but no white students, how does that promote diversity? White students never have to take ownership for learning about other cultures and addressing their racist behavior, such as the affirmative action bake sale and the blackface incidents at that white fraternity's Halloween party. They seem like the ones who need to be in the MLC!"

David, a Mexican American student and member of the Latino Student Union, added, "I'm tired of people trying to lump us together. Not only do people see Latinos as all the same, they also see students of color as one big group. I'm tired of the discrimination here. 'Catch an Immigrant Day' was so offensive to me, and the administration did nothing. We need to focus on how to educate students to recognize and challenge racism and discrimination. Also, with the MLC, how can we be sure that our diverse needs will be met?"

Richard, a Chinese American student, could hardly understand what the commotion was about. He did not identify with Chinese culture but had joined the Asian Student Organization because it would look good on his résumé. His decision to serve on the task force and deal with "multicultural" issues was out of a desire to be perceived as a student leader. However, he became increasingly uncomfortable as the meeting continued.

Allison, one of the few Native American students at the institution, privately pondered whether the MLC would cater only to black students or if the organizers would take time to recognize the presence of Native American students who were often treated as invisible. She stated, "Angela, you mentioned that the MLC would benefit the university, but can you explain what benefits you see for American Indian students, given our low numbers? As a Cherokee woman and member of the American Indian Union and this task force, I value cooperation, sharing, and consensus building. How can these values be implemented in the MLC? My hope is that this MLC can be more about the students and what they need and less about how Kando looks to others."

Angela and the other task force members listened intently, but were at a loss for words regarding many of the questions and concerns the students raised. Angela began to reflect on some of her own assumptions as the meeting continued and how they may have come across as racist. She assumed that the students would like the idea without question. *After all*, she thought, *who wouldn't want to be a part of the MLC?* She had not really thought about how promoting the idea only to multicultural groups might be perceived, nor had she given thought to her color-blind approach toward thinking about the MLC.

◆ ◆ ◆

W.E.B. Du Bois (1903) accurately predicted, "The problem of the Twentieth Century is the problem of the color line" (p. vii). His prophetic words remain relevant in the twenty-first century. College mascots representing American Indian tribes, images of U.S. immigrants constructed solely around Latino populations, and a white person exclaiming that affirmative action is reverse discrimination represent issues that keep race at the center of public thought.

A number of scholars have noted that race has no biological premise (Cokley, 2007; Ladson-Billings, 1998; Muir, 1993). Omi and Winant (2004) defined *race* as "an unstable and 'decentered' complex of social meanings constantly being transformed by political struggle" (p. 116). The definitions and manifestations of race are social constructions based on an individual's racial and ethnic heritage and reflected in white domination of other racial and ethnic groups. Race is consistently used in politics, education, and everyday interactions. It is a determining factor in how people view the world, how they are treated, and the opportunities to which they are (or are not) exposed.

Racial identity theories focus on the role of race and the extent to which it is incorporated into identity or self-concept. Racial identity is more accurately defined as "a sense of group or collective identity based on one's perception that he or she shares a common racial heritage with a particular racial group" (Helms, 1993b, p. 3). Racial identity theory comes from "the tradition of treating race as a sociopolitical and, to a lesser extent, a cultural construction" (Helms, 1995, p. 181). Thus, an underlying assumption about race in the United States presupposes that racial groups experience either domination or oppression, particularly to preserve whiteness.

Due to the prevailing nature of race in U.S. society, it is important to frame our discussion of the racial identity models presented in this chapter using critical race theory (CRT). CRT is an interdisciplinary movement of scholars committed to challenging and deconstructing the interplay of race, racism, and power based on several key tenets (Delgado & Stefancic, 2001). First, racism is part of everyday life in America, so embedded that it often goes unnoticed (Delgado, 1995; Delgado & Stefancic, 2001). Second, the voices of communities of color are legitimate and central to challenging the privilege of white people in racial discourse (Delgado, 1995; Solórzano, 1998). Third, the dominant culture will concede to advances for people of color only when there is also a benefit for them, referred to as *interest convergence* (Delgado, 1995; Ladson-Billings, 1998). There is some gain to Kando students who participate in the MLC, but if the MLC did not benefit Kando, there is a likelihood that resources would not be extended to establish it. Fourth, notions of color blindness and neutrality must be challenged (Bergerson, 2003; Solórzano, 1998). When color blindness is used as the dominant script, it renders invisible the unique experiences of people of color (Ladson-Billings, 1998).

Racial Identity Development Models

Racial identity development of persons of color and white persons has attracted increasing attention in the student affairs literature (McEwen, 2003b). Building on the work of Erikson (1950, 1968) and Marcia (1966, 1980), researchers began to examine racial identity development (for example, Cross, 1978, 1991; Helms, 1993a; Kim, 1981) and build models to better understand how identity issues are resolved.

The Atkinson, Morten, and Sue (1979, 1989, 1993, 1998) minority identity development model was introduced in the late 1970s. Sue and Sue (2003) revised the model, referring to it as the racial and cultural identity development (RCID) model. It comprises five stages. In *conformity*, individuals identify with white culture, internalize negative stereotypes about themselves or their racial/ethnic group, and have no desire to learn about their cultural heritage. In *dissonance*, individuals' experiences contradict their white worldview. They begin a journey of questioning the dominant culture, and gaining an increased interest in learning more about their own racial/ethnic group. *Resistance and immersion* involves conscious exploration of one's racial/ethnic identity. Individuals reject white culture and immerse themselves in learning as much as possible about themselves and their cultural group, leading to the formation of a new identity. In the *introspection* stage, individuals grapple with finding a balance between the dominant culture and their own cultural heritage and the role of both in shaping their identity. Those who continue this intensive exploration move to *synergistic articulation and awareness* in which they integrate their knowledge and experiences into a new identity where they accept themselves, appreciate contributions of other groups, and can balance their racial/ethnic identity with other aspects of their identity.

The RCID serves as a foundation for understanding the stages and orientations found in other identity development models presented in this chapter, including models of black (Cross & Fhagen-Smith, 2001), white (Helms, 1995; Rowe, Bennett, & Atkinson, 1994), Latino/a (Ferdman & Gallegos, 2001), and American Indian (Horse, 2001) identity development. Literature presenting research and application of most of these racial identity models is largely lacking. As a result, our review of research is limited to the small amount of work related to black identity development, and our discussion of application is brief. To close, we offer a critique and suggestions for future work.

Cross and Fhagen-Smith's Model of Black Identity Development

A host of scholars have created models of black identity development (Helms, 1990; Jackson, 2001; Sellers, Smith, Shelton, Rowley, & Chavous, 1998).

However, Cross's theory of psychological nigrescence is the best known. The French term *nigrescence* refers to the "process of becoming black" (Cross, 1991, p. 147). In 1971, Cross introduced a five-stage nigrescence model, but in 1991 he condensed it to four stages. In this revision, Cross introduced three central concepts: personal identity (PI), reference group orientation (RGO), and race salience. *Personal identity* refers to the traits and characteristics that comprise an individual's personality, whereas *reference group orientation* describes what a person values, how the individual sees the world, and the lens through which the individual's philosophical and political views are filtered. *Race salience* "refers to the importance or significance of race in a person's approach to life" (Vandiver, 2001, p. 168). In recent years, Cross and Fhagen-Smith (2001) have approached black identity development using a life span perspective to reposition the original nigrescence theory within the larger discourse on human development and to take into account racialized experiences during childhood.

The nigrescence life span approach has three patterns. *Nigrescence pattern A* describes a normative process wherein individuals have developed a black identity as a result of "formative socialization experiences" (Cross & Fhagen-Smith, 2001, p. 243). In this pattern, individuals establish their black identity through interaction with parents and significant others from birth toward adulthood. This pattern is representative of the experience of most black people because they have adopted one of several black identities by adulthood. *Nigrescence pattern B* represents the conversion experience described in Cross's (1991) earlier work. African Americans who are not socialized toward blackness or have not formed a healthy black identity usually experience a conversion during adulthood. Whether African Americans experience nigrescence pattern A or B, *nigrescence pattern C* will occur. This pattern involves what Cross and Fhagen-Smith (2001) called *nigrescence recycling*, a process that involves an expansion or modification of black identity throughout adulthood. The Cross and Fhagen-Smith life span model of black identity development (2001) has six sectors encompassing all three nigrescence patterns.

Sector One: Infancy and Childhood in Early Black Identity Development. In sector one, factors including family income, traditions, and practices; social networks such as school and church; and all historical events contribute to the early socialization experiences of black children. These factors make up the human ecologies of black children who are unaware of racism or a racial identity (Cross & Fhagen-Smith, 2001).

Sector Two: Preadolescence. Development is highly contingent on parental teachings and the degree to which others reinforce these teachings outside the home. As a result of parental socialization, three identity types tend to emerge: low race salience, high race salience, and internalized racism. Children with low race salience receive few or no messages from their parents regarding race and place no significance on being black with the exception of knowing that their physical features make them black. High-race-salience children have parents who instill the importance of their race. These children are taught to view black culture as an important aspect of their self-concept. The internalized racism identity develops when children see patterns of negativity toward being black or toward black people in their immediate family. As a result of miseducation, these children adopt negative ideas and believe stereotypes, which can lead to self-hatred. Despite the presence of these three emergent identity types in preadolescence, fully developed identities are not apparent until the onset of adolescence.

Sector Three: Adolescence. Using Marcia's (1996) identity statuses as a framework, Cross and Fhagen-Smith (2001) pointed out that as they enter adolescence, many black children accept without critical reflection the identity they have developed as a result of their socialization to this point (that is, their identity status is foreclosed). Black children move into moratorium as they begin the exploration process necessary to establish a personally created self-concept. Adolescents reach an achieved identity status by determining that their black self-concept is truly based on their own beliefs, rather than the beliefs of others. The authenticated identity adolescents adopt may reflect low race salience, high race salience, or internalized racism.

Cross and Fhagen-Smith (2001) clearly delineated between the black identity changes that occur in adolescence (sector three) and adulthood (sector four). Authentication is related to adolescence, while black identity conversion is related to adult development. The original nigrescence theory assumed black people entered adulthood with no idea of their blackness and had to reconstruct their self-concept into one that placed salience on race and black culture. In the current model, it is assumed that most adolescents possess some awareness of a black self. Black adolescents who enter moratorium with low race salience or internalized racism patterns may have an experience similar to the adult conversion, if they move beyond these patterns and develop a healthy black self-concept with high race salience.

During moratorium, black youth for whom race has low salience may confirm low-race-salience self-concepts. Instead of exploring black identity, these individuals explore the nonrace identities that emerged while they were preadolescents (for example, being American, not African American, or focusing on a nondominant sexual or gender identity). For black youth who approach adolescence with an internalized racism identity pattern, their negative black self-concepts are likely to be maintained and strengthened if the assumptions they have previously internalized are not challenged or dispelled.

Sector Four: Early Adulthood. The three identity types that emerged in pre-adolescence and were potentially explored during adolescence are present in early adulthood. African Americans with high-race-salience identities typically represent the largest number in this sector. These adults have established a clear reference group orientation that values race and black culture. Phylicia, the representative from the Black Student Union, obviously identifies with being an African American and through her understanding of institutionalized racism is mistrusting of the intentions behind the MLC idea, particularly given her previous experiences at Kando University. Individuals like Phylicia who exhibit high race salience do not experience adult nigrescence because they already have a self-concept in which being black is salient. Thus, identitity changes that may result occur during nigrescence recycling (sector six). Persons who failed to examine their reference group orientation critically in adolescence (that is, they maintained a foreclosed identity) may need to involve themselves as young adults in experiences that will expand their understanding of their black self-concept. In short, the nigrescence experience is not a conversion for these individuals because they already have a high race salience, but nigrescence helps them personalize their sense of blackness.

African American young adults with low race salience still see race as nonessential and will have constructed diverse identities across an array of categories. Black adults with low race salience can continue to live in environments where their identities can be maintained and their race never has to be acknowledged. However, they are highly susceptible to adult nigrescence, particularly if they experience a critical event that causes them to examine their race.

Internalized racism continues into adulthood as well. The same prevalent issues that existed in earlier stages of life remain embedded. To move toward a more corrective self-concept, these individuals have to experience adult nigrescence. In other words, a conversion is absolutely necessary in order for them to establish a healthy black identity and race salience.

Black adults who have low race salience or internalized racism may never experience adult nigrescence. Race can potentially remain nonessential, and feelings of self-hatred may persist throughout adulthood. Similarly, those with high race salience may remain stagnant without having renewed or refreshed their black self-concept. Thus, for many black individuals, their identity remains unchanged in adulthood (Cross & Fhagen-Smith, 2001).

Sector Five: Adult Nigrescence. This sector represents Cross's (1991) original model. Nigrescence involves four stages: preencounter, encounter, immersion-emersion, and internalization/internalization commitment. *Preencounter* involves two identity types previously mentioned: low race salience (preencounter assimilation) and internalized racism (preencounter antiblack). The *encounter* stage occurs when black people experience an event that causes a conflict in their understanding of their racial identity. Cross (1991) noted that an encounter is an unexpected situation, which can be one traumatic experience or a series of events that prompts a turning point.

Immersion-emersion has two developmental processes. In discussing the earlier Cross (1971) model, Vandiver (2001) stated, "Individuals immerse themselves in black culture to the point of romanticizing it" (p. 166). They become deeply entrenched in the immersion process and ultimately adopt a black nationalist or pro-black identity, which embraces everything black and strongly opposes white culture. In the updated version of this model, Cross (1991) explained that on entering immersion, individuals have a clear sense of the identity they wish to shed, but have little information about the identity they wish to assume. As a result, individuals go through an in-between phase in which they connect themselves to symbols of black identity (hair style, clothing, music, language; Cross, 1991). In some cases, individuals may take on a "blacker than" attitude. However, as individuals move away from an antiwhite perspective toward a pro-black vision, they begin to focus on nurturing a connection and commitment to black people. In *emersion*, individuals begin their transition toward stage four, internalization, by reexamining, through a more balanced and focused lens, the coalescing of the affective and cognitive aspects of black identity. Moving beyond the superficiality characteristic in the immersion phase, individuals adopt a more altruistic and authentic understanding of black identity.

Although the immersion-emersion stage is the seminal transitional point in this model, Cross (1991) explained that in some cases, negative outcomes can occur, such as regression, continuation or fixation, and dropping out. Regression toward preencounter can occur when individuals have negative experiences that are growth inhibiting. Regression can also occur when individuals unsuccessfully grapple with the push toward a new identity and seek the comfort of the old identity. Individuals who harbor overwhelmingly negative perceptions of white people and hold fast to these ideas exhibit continuation or fixation. Individuals who become exhausted, depressed, and stressed may drop out of dealing with being black. Others may drop out once they have established a comfortable sense of blackness and feel compelled to move on to examine other pressing matters in life.

Internalization represents dissonance resolution and has three perspectives: black nationalist, bicultural, and multicultural. Individuals with a *black nationalist identity* consider being black their most salient identity and commit themselves to political and social platforms to advance the black community. Individuals who have a *bicultural* reference group orientation concern themselves with infusing their black identity and their dominant culture identity into their overall identity. Individuals who accept a *multicultural* perspective focus on a wide range of identities; thus, in addition to being black, they explore other identities and worldviews and may openly serve as social justice advocates.

Black adults who experience a conversion through adult nigrescence represent nigrescence pattern B, a reinterpreted framework of blackness. The nigrescence process can be corrective, particularly for black adults who exhibit self-hatred. Race consciousness and establishing a more authentic, balanced comprehension of being black shape this sector.

Sector Six: Nigrescence Recycling. Cross and Fhagen-Smith reworked Parham's (1989) model of nigrescence recycling to be more applicable to their life span model. *Nigrescence recycling* occurs when an individual's preexisting black self-concept is called into question. Having no explanatory power to resolve the new questions that have emerged regarding their identity, adults reflect on the emerging identity issue and subject it to close scrutiny as they seek resolution. This examination results in an identity that has been enhanced or changed in some way. Throughout adulthood, African Americans will continuously be prompted to address issues or questions of identity and through resolution may reach *wisdom*, or a complex and multidimensional understanding of black identity.

Helms's Model of White Identity Development

Helms introduced two identity development models: one for people of color and one for white people (Helms, 1995). The white identity development model (WIDM) is widely known and the most researched theory of white identity development. It was created to raise the awareness of white people about their role in creating and maintaining a racist society and the need for them to act responsibly by dismantling it (Helms, 1992). Helms (1995) contended that all people in the United States have a racial identity that is experienced within a framework of power and privilege. She noted that U.S. residents experience and respond differently to differential racial socialization and their designated racial group.

According to Helms (1992), white identity development occurs in two sequential phases. *Abandonment of racism*, the first phase, describes the process of moving from oblivious or naive conceptions of race. When encountering a racial dilemma that causes dissonance, individuals grapple with the idea of relinquishing idealized notions of whiteness and acknowledging their complicity in maintaining a racist society. The *evolution of a nonracist identity*, the second phase, involves deeper reflection and attempts to interact with other racial group members that are often superficial or paternalistic. In this phase, people spend a significant amount of time devising a way to "be White without also being bad, evil, or racist" (Helms, 1992, p. 61). Angela, the student affairs educator introduced in the opening scenario, may be able to relate to this phase. She seems to be conscious about being white and the privileges associated with whiteness. She wants to help others, but was left with several questions regarding the assumptions she brought to the meeting. The meeting may serve as an impetus toward further reflection on how she perceives racial groups, as well as the paternalistic attitude she held toward the students in the meeting. This phase progresses as individuals begin a quest toward understanding themselves as racial beings and the racism and privilege associated with being white, as well as redefining for themselves what it means to be white and taking ownership of racial privilege and how it affects others. Individuals continuously work toward abandoning white privilege and learning about other racial groups.

Rowe, Bennett, and Atkinson's White Racial Consciousness Model

Rowe, Bennett, and Atkinson (1994) introduced the white racial consciousness model (WRCM) in response to four key concerns with white racial identity (WRID) models, including Helms's model. They took issue with the fact that many WRID models are structured in a way that suggests white people and people of color have parallel identity development processes. Second, they asserted that rather than focusing on the development of a white identity, WRID models "mainly describe how Whites develop different levels of sensitivity to and appreciation of other racial/ethnic groups (i.e., racial attitudes)" (p. 131). A third problem is that WRID models assume an arbitrarily assigned linear process that has yet to be verified empirically. The fourth concern is that WRID models, namely Helms's theory, are contextualized strictly through a black-white framework with no consideration for other racial groups. Rowe et al. offered an alternative model that explains "the role of White attitudes toward their own and other racial groups . . . and can consequently describe the phenomena more accurately, predict relationships better, and provide a more stable base for assessment" (p. 133).

White racial consciousness involves "one's awareness of being White and what that implies in relation to those who do not share White group membership" (Rowe et al., 1994, pp. 133–134). Rowe et al. assumed that white racial consciousness and racial awareness are related and that dissonance and the manner in which it is resolved is the primary cause for change in racial attitudes. The model, derived from the ethnic identity stage model introduced by Phinney (1989), is described using "types" of attitudes that white individuals may possess. The types are grouped into two categories: *unachieved white racial consciousness* and *achieved white racial consciousness*. It is important to note that the types are not stages and have no linear sequence. Instead, individuals may move from one type to another contingent on the experiences they encounter. Transitions occur as the result of a significant amount of dissonance, needed to move between unachieved and achieved white racial consciousness types. The experience of dissonance, positive or negative, can determine to which type one moves.

Unachieved white racial consciousness is composed of three attitude types: avoidant, dependent, and dissonant. Individuals who possess *avoidant* attitudes have not consciously thought about their race or the racial experiences of other racial groups, often dismissing, ignoring, or avoiding race until forced to address their denial.

Dependent attitudes exist when individuals have committed to a superficial form of white consciousness, taking no ownership of being white and primarily depending on others in order to gauge what views and opinions they should possess. To move beyond dependent attitudes, individuals must engage in a reflective internalization process that holds personal meaning.

Dissonant types are characterized by high levels of uncertainty regarding their white racial consciousness and the experiences of people of color. These individuals, while open to receiving information and alternative perspectives, may experience confusion due to the disconnection between their previous understanding of race and their newly found knowledge. Individuals with dissonant attitudes tend to be in the midst of a transition toward seeking more information and experiences that will allow them to shed their previous racial attitudes and frame new attitudes for the future.

Achieved white racial consciousness comprises four types: dominative, conflictive, reactive, and integrative. Individuals who hold *dominative* type attitudes are ethnocentric and strongly believe they are superior to people of color. If and when they think about other racial groups at all, these individuals rely heavily on negative stereotypical images to frame their knowledge of people of color. Dominative attitudes "might be expressed in more or less passive or active modes" (Rowe et al., 1994, p. 138). Passive dominative attitudes are expressed through avoidance of interaction with people of color. While individuals exhibiting this type possess racist attitudes and beliefs, rarely will they ever admit this to themselves; nor will they recognize the contradictions between their beliefs and their actions. Active dominative attitudes are overtly expressed through the use of racial slurs, violence, and discrimination.

White people who possess *conflictive* attitudes "are opposed to obvious, clearly discriminatory practices, yet are usually opposed to any program or procedure that has been designed to reduce or eliminate discrimination" (Rowe et al., 1994, p. 138). Individuals with these attitudes espouse justice and equality, but disagree with measures that might be taken to achieve these goals. They believe that people of color have equal opportunity now and are therefore responsible for their own problems.

Individuals with *reactive* racial attitudes recognize that inequities and injustices exist and that people of color bear the brunt of these issues in their life experiences. Holding reactive attitudes also leads people to understand that white people are afforded unearned privileges and benefits that perpetuate inequality, and to work toward recognizing and addressing discrimination, while attempting to connect with people of color. Reactive attitudes may be passive or active. Those who consider issues facing people of color on an intellectual level reflect passive attitudes, although they may present themselves as having a keen awareness of and concern for people of color in the presence of other white people, while having no extensive interactions with members of racially dominant groups. Those who actively express reactive attitudes are at times paternalistic in their approach to concerns of people of color, often using a white framework. While they have a genuine concern, these individuals grapple with a tension between creating connections with people of color and challenging the dominance of the white status quo. A host of emotions can result from this tension, including guilt and anger about the way racism and inequalities are perpetuated.

Those whites who see the realities of living in a dominant society demonstrate *integrative* racial attitudes, including understanding the complexities associated with race and having come to terms with being white. Moreover, they have a more integrated view of their own identity in relation to people of color and are committed to social change. The personal lives of whites holding integrative attitudes may include genuine interactions with people of color, or they may engage in social activism. Rowe et al. (1994) warned that "this type of racial awareness should not be construed as a state of racial self-actualization or transcendence, but more as a process" (p. 141).

Ferdman and Gallegos's Model of Latino Identity Development

Ferdman and Gallegos (2001) stated, "The racial constructs that have predominated in the United States do not easily apply to Latinos, and when they are forced to fit, they truncate and distort Latino realities" (p. 44). Ferdman and Gallegos offered three considerations for understanding how Latinos experience race and racism. First, while being Latino involves racial, cultural, and ethnic distinctions, race is secondary for this population. However, skin color remains pertinent among Latinos, and racism may manifest itself in the devaluing of those with darker skin (that is, people with African and indigenous backgrounds). Second, Latinos often come from mixed heritages and represent a wide range of skin colors, making it difficult to place them in finite racial categories. Third, Latinos respond in various ways to the racial categories in which they are placed in the United States. Some identify as white, while others reject this classification and use Latino as a racial and ethnic category. Such distinctions can either be "imposed or self-imposed" (p. 45). A number of factors, including familial reference group, educational experiences, peer interaction, and physical appearance, contribute to how people develop their identities.

Ferdman and Gallegos (2001) offered a model of Latino identity that considers the racial system in the United States. They avoided the use of stages to describe the identity process and instead provided six different orientations that serve as lenses through which Latinos may view themselves. The orientations are constructed based on five factors: "one's 'lens' toward identity, how individuals prefer to identify themselves, how Latinos as a group are seen, how whites are seen, and how 'race' fits into the equation" (p. 49). The model is neither cyclical nor linear in nature. Instead, Latinos may relate to several orientations in their lives, or remain within one orientation throughout the life span. Ferdman and Gallegos's six orientations follow:

Latino-integrated. Persons with this orientation have a holistic self-concept that successfully integrates their Latino identity with other identities. They understand the racial constructs that exist in the United Sates, are willing to challenge racism, and see themselves within a larger multicultural framework inclusive of all people. Among Ferdman and Gallegos's six orientations (2001), integrated Latinos also possess the widest lens.

Latino-identified. Individuals in this orientation assume a pan-Latino identity where race is fluid and the rigidity of U.S. racial constructs is rejected. However, while other racial groups exist in set categories, Latino-identified individuals recognize the entire Latino community as encompassing one Latino race. Based on their actions, white people can be viewed by Latinos in this orientation as a separate race whose members are supportive or not.

Subgroup-identified. Subgroup-identified Latinos solely identify with their specific subgroup of origin and may view other subgroups, including Latino subgroups, as "inferior." Not viewing themselves within a larger pan-Latino framework, subgroup-identified Latinos have "a more narrow and exclusive view of their groupness" (Ferdman & Gallegos, 2001, p. 52). While race is not as significant as culture or ethnicity to individuals in this orientation, they do realize that white people exist and can inhibit full access for their subgroup. David, the Latino Student Union representative in our scenario, might identify with this orientation. He sees himself as Mexican American, is aware of racism and discrimination, and challenged the MLC idea at the meeting.

Latino as other. Persons who identify with this orientation have a mixed identity and view themselves in generic terms because they do not know their specific background or heritage within the Latino community. However, they are likely to connect with other people of color because of their physical attributes (skin color) and the manner in which race is socially constructed. They do not place themselves in a rigid racial category or identify with any particular group, including white and Latino.

Undifferentiated/denial. In this orientation, individuals have a narrow lens and adopt a color-blind ideology in which they claim that race does not matter. Living their lives according to the dominant culture, these Latinos do not connect with other Latinos. Any racism or oppression that they experience is attributed to the individual instead of a racist system.

White-identified. Individuals in this orientation adopt a white racial identity and live their lives as white people. They see other racial groups, including Latinos, as inferior and have minimal association with other Latinos. Their lens is entirely constructed around the white culture, which remains unexamined.

Kim's Asian American Identity Development Model

Based on research examining the experiences of Japanese American women, Jean Kim (1981, 2001) introduced the Asian American identity development model, which addresses how Asian Americans come to terms with their racial identity and resolve racial conflicts in a society dominated by white perspectives. Kim (2001) presented three key assumptions to explain how racialized populations manage their identities in a white racist society. First, Asian American identity and white racism are not mutually exclusive entities. The insidious nature of racism and the press of the external environment influence the development of an Asian American self. Second, Asian Americans must consciously work to unlearn and challenge the negative messages and stereotypes that they previously adopted without question. Third, a positive Asian American identity is contingent on one's capacity to grapple with identity crises and transform previous negative experiences into constructive, growth-enhancing ones (Kim, 2001). Kim's (2001) model has the following "five conceptually distinct, sequential, and progressive stages" (p. 67).

Ethnic awareness. Individuals at this stage view their identity through their families and have not yet had any schooling experiences. As they develop, those who live in predominantly Asian American communities begin to gain a greater awareness of their culture and ethnicity and develop a positive self-concept. Those who live in predominantly white communities experience confusion about being Asian American and feel "neutral" about their ethnicity. The primary factor in this stage is discovery of ethnic heritage (Kim, 2001).

White identification. At this point, children have begun their schooling experiences and may have learned several cultural norms such as enduring suffering quietly, avoiding public shame, and valuing a collective group orientation (Kim, 2001). At a very early age, Asian Americans are exposed to others who may make fun of them or point out how Asian Americans are different. Due to the "collective orientation" (Kim, 2001, p. 74) among Asian American communities, children react by attempting to fit in. The desire to be accepted leads to the rejection of their Asian identity and internalization of white standards, "especially regarding standards of physical beauty and attractiveness" (Kim, 2001, p. 74). This stage is characterized by both active and passive white identification. Asian Americans who experience active white identification usually have grown up in predominantly white environments. As a result they forgo their "Asianness," adopt a white identity, and take measures to erase any trace of an Asian identity (including language and physical features). Asian Americans who exhibit a passive white identification are likely to have had a positive Asian ethnic awareness that extends to middle school. White identifiers do not view themselves as white yet they internalize white culture and experience moments of "fantasizing about being white" (Kim, 2001, p. 75). Richard, the Chinese American student in our case study, could be in this stage of Kim's model given his lack of identification with his culture and adoption of mainstream values. However, the discomfort that he begins to feel at the meeting has the potential to prompt him toward the next stage.

Awakening to social political consciousness. In this stage, Asian Americans no longer blame themselves for being treated differently and realize that their negative experiences are the result of a racist social structure. Because Asian Americans now reject the superiority of whiteness, individuals in this stage no longer consider "passing" for white as acceptable. As individuals realize the political and social implications of racism for Americans of Asian descent, they come to recognize their status as members of an oppressed group and are willing to participate in coalition building with other racially oppressed groups.

Redirection to Asian American consciousness. In this stage, Asian Americans move beyond the oppressed group designation, consciously identify with being an Asian American, and establish a sense of pride in whom they are (Kim, 2001). This transition occurs with the support of family, friends, and the Asian American community, as well as through exploration of themselves and Asian culture and heritage.

Incorporation. The incorporation stage involves establishing a strong level of confidence in one's Asian American identity, accompanied by a positive self-concept (Kim, 2001). As Asian Americans move beyond immersion in familiar homogeneous communities and interact positively with other races, they focus on other aspects of their identity without forsaking their newly redefined racial identity.

Horse's Perspective on American Indian Identity Development

American Indians represent a diverse array of peoples, tribes, and cultures. In order to understand their racial identity, it is important to recognize the role of colonization: "the formal and informal methods (behaviors, ideologies, institutions, policies, and economies) that maintain the subjugation or exploitation of Indigenous Peoples, lands, and resources" (Waziyatawin & Yellow Bird, 2005, p. 2). In the face of colonization, such as efforts by white people to "civilize" them and force them into hegemonic cultural assimilation (Tierney, 1996), Native Americans consistently have fought to preserve their culture. While cautioning against the generalization of American Indian identity (see Chapter Fifteen for further discussion of this point), Horse (2001) offered several factors that often prevail in the establishment of a healthy identity for members of this population.

Horse's (2001) framework for understanding of Indian racial identity is grounded in what he termed individual and group "consciousness" (p. 100). Horse referred to a consciousness that captures both the unique and collective experiences of American Indians through a model in which consciousness is characterized in five ways. First, knowledge of one's native language and culture reinforces a person's sense of consciousness. Language is a core factor in American Indian culture and helps individuals establish a sense of self, while also providing a vehicle through which cultural traditions, values, and behaviors are transmitted (Horse, 2001). Second, consciousness is grounded in the validity of one's genealogical heritage as an Indian. American Indian youth need to not only understand tribal history but also embrace what tribal elders and other members have taught them about the world and what it means to be Indian. Third, consciousness exists through adopting a worldview that respects the traditions and philosophical values of Indian ways (Horse). The extent to which individuals see themselves as Indian people is the fourth aspect of consciousness. Allison, the Cherokee student in the case study, shared her values associated with being an American Indian and wanted to ensure that those values would have a place in the new MLC. The fifth element of consciousness is one's status as a member of an officially recognized tribe.

Research

Research related to racial identity development has largely centered on black identity. With regard to student populations, much of the research on black racial identity examines the phenomenon in counseling situations (Helms, 1993a; Carter, 1993; Bradby & Helms, 1993). Little attention has focused on how racial identity affects students' daily lives and decision making. However, one study examined the relationship between black students' racial identity and their participation in cultural (black-oriented) and noncultural campus organizations (Mitchell & Dell, 1992). As the researchers hypothesized, students whose scores on the RIAS-B (Parham & Helms, 1981; an instrument based on Cross's (1978) early work on black identity) indicated they were in encounter, immersion, or internalization stages and were likely to be involved in cultural organizations, while students in the preencounter stage were not.

Using the RIAS-B and the African American Acculturation scale (AAAS), Pope-Davis, Liu, Ledesma-Jones, and Nevitt (2000) found significant positive correlations between the constructs of acculturation and racial identity among 187 African American students. A study of black college students using Cross's early model provided partial support for the hypothesis that racial identity stage and self-esteem are related (Parham & Helms, 1985). The study found that black college students in the preencounter and immersion stages tend to have low self-esteem, whereas those in the encounter stage tend to have positive self-esteem. In a later study endorsing the theoretical concepts offered by Cross's revised model, racial identity was a significant predictor of the psychological health of 136 African American college students at a predominantly white institution (Pillay, 2005).

Research indicates that racial identity is not a predictor of grades or academic outcomes for college students (Awad, 2007; Lockett & Harrell, 2003). However, Sanchez and Carter (2005) reported significant relationships between racial identity attitudes and religious orientation. Scholars have examined the relationship of racial identity in black college students and several other variables, including moral judgment (Moreland & Leach, 2001), stereotype threat (Davis, Aronson, & Salinas, 2006), perceptions of racial bias (Jefferson & Caldwell, 2002), psychosocial development (Pope, 1998; Taub & McEwen, 1992), college racial composition (Cokley, 1999), coping (Neville, Heppner & Wang, 1997), involvement (Taylor & Howard-Hamilton, 1995), and adjustment to college (Anglin & Wade, 2007).

Applications

A few scholars have encouraged faculty to learn more about their own and their students' racial identity development. Tatum's work (1997) is particularly helpful since she used many examples to explain racial identity theory and its utility. Ortiz and Rhoads (2000) offered an elective multicultural education framework that can be helpful in programming to explore and deconstruct whiteness. These scholars assert that the only way to "displace white racial identity as the universal norm is by challenging ourselves and our students to name it" (p. 82).

Clayton and Jones (1993) recommended workshops that focus on unlearning racism for student affairs administrators and students in graduate preparation programs because these experiences allow white participants to shift from viewing other racial groups as invisible or in a stereotypical way to respecting, appreciating, and celebrating racially different others. Such workshops can contribute to the eradication of racism in the academy.

Critique and Future Directions

While it is encouraging to see a number of racial identity development theories appearing in the literature, the lack of research needed to validate the theories discussed in this chapter, as well as others (for example, Hardiman, 2001; Jackson, 1976, 2001), is problematic (Burrow, Tubman, & Montgomery, 2006). Moreover, the research studies of racial identity that do exist rarely address the applicability of the models to higher education or student affairs specifically. To complicate matters, existing models do not account for the complexity of development and characterize identity "in relationship to other groups and, in particular, the dominant majority" (Casas & Pytluk, 1995, p. 166), with little attention to other factors that can influence development. Not only is there an increased need for theoretical perspectives that address diverse student populations, closer scrutiny of nonwhite racial identity theories is also necessary to better understand the rapidly growing student populations that are increasingly becoming the majority in U.S. institutions of higher education. More must be known about the identity processes of diverse students from a "dynamic perspective—the affective and cognitive manifestations and their implications for an individual's psychological well-being and personality and/or characterological development from both a short- and a long-term perspective" (Casas & Pytluk, p. 176). In addition, the tendency to generalize, particularly African American identity models, across Asian, Hispanic/Latino/Chicano, and American Indian ethnic groups implies that oppression is at the core of identity rather than factors such as language, country of origin, and culture that can also shape identity (Sue & Sue, 1990), as we discuss in Chapter Fifteen.

Racial identity models have highlighted individual differences in our student populations. Yet the theories and models available represent only a tiny portion of what student affairs educators need to know to ease racial tensions prevalent on campuses like Kando University and to create healthy environments that promote racial identity exploration. If we believe that student affairs work should be grounded in theory, the lack of applicable racial identity development theories and accompanying research serves as a call to action to create theories that represent the array of students on campus. While much remains to be learned about black and white racial groups, it is also important to consider other racial groups and validate their unique experiences. Using a critical race lens, the continued focus on black and white creates a binary in which other racial groups remain understudied (Chen & others, 2006; Delgado, 1998). This black/white binary, a result of institutionalized racism, must be challenged in a productive way through scholarly efforts to include other voices. For example, Tippeconnic Fox, Lowe, and McClellan (2005) studied Native American students, drew attention to the lack of knowledge that exists, and encouraged educators to seek knowledge about Native Americans to help these individuals succeed in college. Similarly, McEwen, Kodama, Alvarez, Lee, and Liang (2002) focused on Asian American college students, placing emphasis on issues of race and racism in their lives.

Student affairs professionals who depend on theory to inform their work must proceed with extreme caution given the lack of existing information. Institutions of higher education are increasingly more diverse, and the failure of student affairs educators and faculty to fully understand students' racial identity development "can lead to inappropriate and ineffective responses to volatile racial situations on campus" (Hardiman & Jackson, 1992, p. 21).

Helping white individuals like Angela find avenues for exploring their identity can help curb, and eventually eliminate, racism and other discriminatory practices against people of color as all students move toward cultural pluralism. Educators must recognize their role in providing opportunities for students and staff to explore racial identity. In order to help individuals grow, educators need to participate in their own self-exploration to better understand themselves and then work collectively toward helping others do the same.

CHAPTER FIFTEEN

ETHNIC IDENTITY AND ACCULTURATION

Hope University's director of international studies programs has formed a task force to investigate new ways for students of all ethnic origins to study abroad. She wants to fulfill the university's mission of preparing students for a civil global society and believes Hope's graduates will benefit from exposure to dominant and nondominant ethnic cultural values through study beyond U.S. borders.

The students appointed to the task force demonstrate skills in critical thinking and creativity, while also representing both dominant and nondominant campus ethnic groups. Paul grew up in San Francisco's Chinatown. His parents, both first-generation Chinese immigrants, are proud people who still live in Paul's childhood home. He hopes one day to amass enough wealth to move his parents out of Chinatown and create a rich material life for them. Paul's honor and respect for his parents is transparent, and he also treats others on campus with uncompromising high regard. He hopes his double major in business and technology will enable him to reach his goal of becoming a technology entrepreneur. Paul wants to study in China to meet relatives and make career connections.

Sonya grew up in a black neighborhood of New Orleans; her mother was killed in Hurricane Katrina. Personal trauma and loss motivated Sonya to attend college so she could learn how to prevent the human mayhem of the Katrina disaster from happening again. Now Sonya wants to learn how African societies deal with life-changing upheaval and bring these ideas back to New Orleans.

Raised on a reservation near campus by family who value tradition, Little Eagle has difficulty adapting to the rules and structure of the university while also respecting tribal customs. He returns home as often as possible to participate in tribal rituals, but when he does, his grades suffer. Little Eagle wants to study in New Zealand to learn about how its indigenous peoples overcame white oppression.

Sofia was raised in an Italian neighborhood in western Minnesota by first-generation immigrant Italian parents. When Sofia was a child, her Grandma Lucille taught her to sew, and her mother took her to plays at Minneapolis's Guthrie Theatre, where she was mesmerized by the actors' costumes. Fluent in Italian, she wants to study costume design in Italy.

Lydia grew up in Texas but courageously fled with her two small children because her husband continually abused them. Her mother, Tina, accompanied them. Lydia, both bicultural and bilingual, is first generation in the United States. Tina, a Mexican immigrant who speaks little English, always encouraged her daughter to obtain an education and now provides child care. Every Sunday after mass, Lydia and her mother connect with Spanish speakers from all over the world at the Catholic church. Lydia is fascinated by South America and wants to dig for ancient ruins near Machu Picchu before she graduates.

After introductions, Hope University's director of international studies began the first meeting. All the students in the room wanted to create ways for students like them to study outside the United States. The director expressed optimism that with task force ingenuity, this team could be instrumental in broadening students' experiences and cultural exposure.

◆ ◆ ◆

The breadth and depth of ethnic identity research conducted in the past two decades is too extensive to review in this chapter. The preponderance of literature on ethnic identity resides in four basic areas of social science: anthropology, sociology, psychology, and counseling, although education, the arts, political science, and religion also have begun to address the topic. Some anthropological and sociological perspectives are based on ethnicity and nationalism, often examining how minorities are assimilated into a national identity, but more perspectives, particularly those in psychology and counseling, examine individual or group ethnic identity. There is no universal definition of the concept of ethnic identity in the literature.

In this chapter, we examine ethnic identity, clarifying several of its varied meanings. First, we frame ethnic identity within several academic disciplines to lay a foundation for this often misunderstood, evolving concept. Next, we consider why college students' ethnic identity is difficult to understand and discuss acculturation and its tie to students' ethnicity. We then review universal models of ethnic identity and models related to major ethnic groups. We conclude the chapter with a critique and offer future directions for studying college students' ethnic identity.

Framing Ethnic Identity

Some psychology literature reveals clear evidence that researchers define, measure, and compare ethnic groups to one another or to the dominant culture in different ways (Phinney, 1996). To complicate matters, psychologists and counselors often use the term *ethnic identity* synonymously with *racial identity* (Helms & Talleyrand, 1997). Some defend the interchange of racial and ethnic identity as a natural evolution of language in which popular speech becomes integrated into "official definitions" (Quintana, 2007, p. 259). In contrast, many consider ethnic and racial identity related but different constructs.

Nearly all sociologists examine "ethnicity seeking to understand the forces in society that create, shape, and sustain ethnic identity" (Waters, 1990, p. 17). However, some social science researchers offer rigid, biological justifications for ethnic differences (Bell, 1975). The popular myth in U.S. society that ethnicity is biological leaves no room for personal choice. Proponents of this perspective view ethnicity as consisting of inherited characteristics such as eye color, nose shape, skin color, or other genetic predispositions. In this frame, by virtue of familial ancestors, all individuals can be categorized conveniently into various ethnic groups (Jenkins, 1997; Waters, 1990). In this pervasive misinterpretation, ethnic identity is considered an objective truth rather than the symbolic actions of a group.

Anthropologists and sociologists, moving to a more subjective understanding of ethnicity, theorized cognitive and perceptual notions of the phenomenon (Waters, 1990). In the 1970s and 1980s, Norwegian anthropologist Frederick Barth (1969) suggested that perceptions of ethnicity are socially constructed. Barth shifted anthropology's emphasis away from seeking definition and instead created an inventory of cultural practices delineating clear, sustained ethnic boundaries. Ethnicity develops through difference and ties the individual to the group in important ways: "Ethnicity, when it matters to people, really matters . . . . Ethnicity depends on similarity and difference rubbing up against each other collectively: 'us' and 'them'" (Jenkins, 2004, p. 65).

Ethnic identity seen through a psychosocial lens is grounded primarily in the theoretical concepts of ego identity (Erikson, 1968) and social identity (Tajfel, 1981). Scholars suggest that positive ethnic identity is important for healthy psychological functioning and self-esteem (Umaña-Taylor, 2004; Umaña-Taylor & Shin, 2007). Researchers from this perspective suggest that "ethnic identity is a multidimensional construct, involving ethnic feelings, attitudes, knowledge and behaviors" (Phinney, 1995, p. 58). Some key identifiable elements of the construct are "self identification as a group member; attitudes and evaluations relative to one's group; attitudes about oneself as a member; extent of ethnic knowledge and commitment; and ethnic behaviors and practices" (p. 58).

A specific example illustrates this point. Sofia, in the introductory scenario, is Italian because her ancestors were Italian and because the category Italian exists and has meaning now. However, Italy's history goes back thousands of years and includes people from many parts of the world. During the time of feudal lords, Italians were identified by family, such as the Medicis, and eventually by local geographical region, such as Sicilian, Calabrian, and Venetian. The diversity of these Italians and their opinions made agreement difficult, and not until the second half of the nineteenth century did Italy "unite" and attain a more unified identity.

Sofia chooses to be Italian based on her ancestry and the cultural practices she learned as a child. She demonstrates many cultural manifestations of her ethnic roots: speaking Italian, participating in Catholic rituals, and cooking her grandmother's spaghetti sauce. Yet Sofia has a part-time job at the local Gap and lives in the dominant culture. Because she understands the changing nature of Italian people's history, culture, and migration patterns over time, for her this knowledge logically defies the current socially constructed, rigid categorization of this group that others accept.

Ethnic Identity and College Students

In 1969, Chickering declared that students in college must resolve the developmental task of defining their identity by answering the question, "Who am I?" For students who identify with one or more ethnic groups, addressing this question is more complex and perhaps more urgent as they likely face some form of stereotyping and discrimination on campus. Many privileged, white, dominant-culture students ignore their cultural heritages and do not consider issues unrelated to their homogeneous and nondiscriminatory dominant culture experience (McIntosh, 1989). For example, white students often resist social justice learning for reasons that may include a fear of examining their privilege (Jones, 2008). In contrast, many college students raised outside the dominant culture are highly attuned to their culture and ethnicity in both positive and negative ways.

While racial identity models frame an oppressed group's reactions to the dominant white group's societal race oppression and privilege, ethnic identity models outline how cultural characteristics are acquired and sustained (Helms, 1996). *Ethnic identity* can refer to differences in a multitude of characteristics like "nationality, ancestry, religion, language, culture, and history to which personal and social meanings of group identity are usually attached" (Cokley, 2007, p. 518).

Most research on college students' ethnic identity centers on Latino and Asian Americans across generations. Interestingly, there are no clearly identified black or American Indian ethnic identity models or theories among this burgeoning

falls into race;

literature. Several reasons for this discrepancy exist related to immigration, phenotype, and within-group differences. First, most Latinos and Asians immigrated to the United States, which meant they voluntarily came and could freely choose to maintain their own culture. In contrast, African Americans were forced to leave their country of origin and culture behind for slavery, and American Indians faced genocide at the hands of white men on this continent. Second, skin color is intricately tied to race, and groups with lighter skin (Latinos and Asians) appear to be framed in ethnic terms, while people with darker skin (blacks and American Indians) are referred to most often by their racial identity.

Third, African Americans and American Indians are composed of numerous subgroups whose members hold different values and beliefs, and practice different customs, language, history, and culture. Due to the large variation within each group, ethnic identity cannot be generalized across all American Indian or African American groups.

At the risk of offending some scholars of color and appearing to encourage generalizations to all groups, we present models, not empirically tested, of American Indian and African American worldviews, in addition to empirically derived Latino and Asian ethnic development models. These American Indian and African American perspectives give insight into some underlying beliefs of selected ethnic groups within a larger, often stereotyped group. Understanding a group's worldview offers a glimpse into the values important to the group's identity. Although stereotyping is not our goal, we encourage the reader to examine the transferability of these models and be open to their helpfulness in working with students of diverse ethnic backgrounds.

Components of Ethnic Identity and Acculturation

Ethnic identity can be classified into external and internal components (Breton, Isajiw, Kalbach, & Reitz, 1990). *External ethnic identity* refers to recognizable social and cultural behaviors like ethnic language, media, and traditions; friendship with other ethnic group members; and involvement in ethnic group functions and activities. More complex in nature, *internal ethnic identity* incorporates cognitive, moral, and affective dimensions. The cognitive dimension incorporates ethnic individuals' self-images, images of the group, and knowledge of the ethnic group's heritage and values. The moral dimension encompasses an obligation to the ethnic group resulting in commitment to the group's cohesion (Isajiw, 1990). Finally, individuals' feelings of attachment to a particular ethnic group include an affinity for similar ethnic group members and cultural patterns of the group.

As a bidirectional system, ethnic identity can be examined in two ways: the degree to which individuals adopt whiteness (acculturation) and the strength with which individuals retain their culture of origin (Sodowsky, Kwan, & Pannu, 1995), for example, Asianness (including Japanese, Chinese, Indian, and all their variations). This model, which allows individual movement over time and across contexts, is described later in this chapter.

Acculturation refers to the changes that occur in beliefs, values, and behaviors of ethnic individuals as a result of contact with, and desired or undesired adaptation to, the dominant culture (Berry, 1993). Although there is a relationship between acculturation and ethnic identity, the internal and external components of ethnic identity appear to vary independently (Sodowsky et al., 1995). Visible elements like ethnic behaviors are more affected by acculturation, while invisible elements of ethnic identity like cultural values can resist change over time (Rosenthal & Feldman, 1992; Sodowsky & Carey, 1988). One study of ethnic identity among three generations of U.S. immigrants suggests that some individuals can maintain high levels of internal and external ethnic identity while imparting a white identity, and vice versa (Clark, Kauffman, & Pierce, 1976). Students with strong ethnic ties may find this the case at predominantly white institutions.

The acculturative process begins at the moment of "contact and interaction between two or more autonomous cultural groups" (Mena, Padilla, & Maldonado, 1987, p. 207). Evidence shows that most immigrants create or experience conflict within their group or with other groups in their efforts to minimize cultural differences with unfamiliar others, producing acculturative stress (Born, 1970). One particularly helpful study of acculturative stress among minority college students identified the factors ranked most stressful related to students' perceptions of discrimination and their lack of a sense of belonging (Mena et al.). Paradoxically, the stronger the ethnicity the students exhibited, the more stress and less self-esteem they reported. Planning appropriate action and talking with others are strategies students used to combat acculturative stress.

In his model of acculturation, Berry (1984, 1993) outlined four distinct acculturative strategies ethnic college students can employ to relate to the dominant culture. In relationship to the dominant culture, ethnic students can "*assimilate* (identify solely with the dominant culture and sever ties with their own culture), *marginalize* (reject both their own and the host culture), *separate* (identify solely with their group and reject the host culture), [or] *integrate* (become bicultural by maintaining aspects of their own group and selectively acquiring some of the host culture)" (Farver, Xu, Bhadha, Narang, & Lieber, 2007, p. 187).

Ethnic identity and acculturation are related but separate concepts. Both are nonlinear processes requiring contact with unfamiliar and unknown others.

Familiarity with each concept is necessary for understanding immigrants across several generations. Higher education must create healthy environments to support integration of all students' ethnic identities. Descriptions of helpful models follow.

Models of Ethnic Identity Development

Ethnic identity constructs focus on what people learn about their culture from family and community (Torres, 1999) passed down from one generation to the next (Spencer & Markstrom-Adams, 1990). Ethnic identity develops from sharing culture, religion, geography, and language with individuals who are often connected by strong loyalty and kinship. Theories of ethnic identity formation examine how students "understand the implications of their ethnicity and make decisions about its role in their lives, regardless of the extent of their ethnic involvement" (Phinney, 1990, p. 64).

As part of the process of committing to an ethnic identity, minority youth must resolve two basic conflicts: stereotyping and prejudice on the part of the majority white population toward the minority group and clashing value systems between majority and minority groups, which require minority adolescents to negotiate a bicultural value system (Torres, 1999). These issues influence minority adolescents' self-concept and sense of ethnic identity. One of the earliest theorists to develop and test a general ethnic identity development model was Jean Phinney.

Phinney's Model of Ethnic Identity Development

Phinney (1990) maintained that the issue of ethnic identity is important to the development of a positive self-concept for minority adolescents. Based on Erikson's (1964, 1968) theory, Phinney's model is consistent with Marcia's identity model (1980). In her seminal article, Phinney (1990) described the development of her theoretical model of ethnic identity based on growing evidence that revealed commonalities across ethnic groups, instead of placing each group (for example, Latino, Asian American, white) and their dissimilarities under a microscope. Phinney's (1995) three-stage model of ethnic identity formation is outlined next.

Stage 1: Unexamined Ethnic Identity (Diffusion-Foreclosure). Individuals in the first stage of ethnic identity development have not explored feelings and attitudes regarding their own ethnicity. Ethnicity may be seen as a nonissue, which leads to diffusion, or individuals may have acquired attitudes about ethnicity in childhood from significant others, leading to foreclosure. Adolescents who accept negative attitudes displayed by the majority group toward the minority group are at risk of internalizing these values. However, for the most part, this stage is marked by disinterest in ethnicity.

Stage 2: Ethnic Identity Search/Moratorium. During the second stage of ethnic identity development (Phinney, 1990, 1993), students become increasingly aware of ethnic identity issues as they face situations that cause exploration. This new awareness causes students to examine the significance of their ethnic background. The experience may be harsh, such as an encounter with overt racism, or it may be more indirect, such as gradual recognition (as a result of less dramatic incidents) that their ethnicity is perceived as "less than" by the dominant culture. As a result of this awakening, adolescents begin an ethnic identity search or moratorium, where they seek more information about their ethnic group while attempting to understand the personal significance of ethnic identity. Characterized by emotional intensity, this stage encompasses anger toward the dominant group and guilt or embarrassment about one's own past lack of knowledge of racial and ethnic issues.

Before college, Paul's tightly knit Chinese community protected him from the racism he initially faced at college. In college, he became angry, and in his sophomore year, he refused to trust or have much contact with students from the dominant culture. Lydia too felt racism growing up in Texas and was embarrassed by some of her family's cultural practices, which she hid from her dominant-culture friends.

Stage 3: Ethnic Identity Achievement. In the final stage of ethnic identity development, students achieve a healthy bicultural identity. They resolve their identity conflicts and come to terms with ethnic and racial issues. As students accept membership in minority culture, they gain a sense of ethnic identification while being open to other cultures. The intense emotions of the previous stage give way to a more confident and calm demeanor.

The students of color in the introductory scenario, Paul, Lydia, Sonya, and Little Eagle, fit stage 3 of Phinney's (1990) ethnic identity theory: to varying degrees, all have reached an achieved identity status. In some cases, dramatic incidents of discrimination and oppression caused change in these students' ethnic perception, and in other cases awareness occurred gradually. After moving through identity moratorium, these students accepted their struggle and now feel confident in themselves as ethnic minority members and accepting of others from different ethnic groups. In the task force meeting, all of these students admitted they would not be ready for study abroad had they not resolved their ethnic identity conflicts.

A prolific researcher, Phinney continues to shed light on a pivotal developmental issue for college students: the process of ethnic identification. Phinney's research has examined a number of issues relevant to ethnic college students, including acculturation and self-esteem (Phinney, 1995; Phinney, Chavira, & Williamson, 1992), parental support and academic achievement (Ong, Phinney, & Dennis, 2006), positive intergroup attitudes and intercultural thinking (Phinney, Jacoby, & Silva, 2007), reasons ethnic students choose to attend college (Phinney, Dennis, & Osorio, 2006), ethnicity as an important identity issue in minority students' lives (Phinney, 1993), and the link between ethnic identity achievement and positive intergroup attitudes and mature intercultural thinking (Phinney et al.).

Ethnic Identity of Latinos/Hispanics/Chicanos

In the past fifteen years, research on the ethnic identity of Latinos (a term used in this chapter to include Latinas and Latinos) has rapidly increased. Just the notion of naming this identity is controversial and more complex than it may appear (Torres, Howard-Hamilton, & Cooper, 2003). Researchers have identified these individuals as Chicano, Latino, Hispanic, and Mexican American, often seeking one term to define this diverse group of people, whose families of origin come from parts of the Caribbean and Latin and Central America, with the majority from Mexico (Torres, 2004). Today individuals with these ancestral roots living in the United States are often identified simply by geographical location—Puerto Rican, Cuban, Chilean, or the like—not always hyphenated with "American."

Keefe and Padilla (1987) surveyed Mexican American students to examine cultural awareness (that is, awareness of Mexican people and culture), ethnic loyalty (attitudes and feelings about Mexican culture), and ethnic social orientation (preference for interacting with those who identify as Mexican and for Mexican food) as aspects of a Chicano identity. Four-generation families in the United States demonstrated a steady decrease in cultural awareness, with the biggest shift occurring between the first and second generations. Only a slight decease in ethnic loyalty was identified between the first and second generations. Third- and fourth-generation participants scored higher on ethnic loyalty than cultural awareness, which may have meaning for current students, as many have lost the language of their ancestors but maintain a sense of pride in their heritage.

Torres's Model of Hispanic Identity Development. Vasti Torres is amassing an impressive program of methodologically diverse research on the ethnic identity development of Hispanic (her term) college students. One of her first studies (Torres, 1999) validated the bicultural orientation model (BOM), demonstrating a correlation between acculturation and ethnic identity among Hispanic college students using demographic data and other ethnic scales and measures (for example, Marin, Sabogal, Marin, Otero-Sabogal, & Perez-Stable, 1987; Phinney, 1992; Ramirez, 1983). Four cultural orientation quadrants frame this model. Individuals demonstrating high levels of acculturation and ethnic identity are categorized as bicultural, signifying a preference for both Hispanic and Anglo cultures. High-level acculturation and low-level ethnic identity represent an Anglo orientation, signifying a preference for Anglo culture. Low-level acculturation and high-level ethnic identity embody the Hispanic orientation, indicating a preference for the Hispanic culture. Finally, low-level acculturation and ethnic identity point to a marginal orientation, describing the inability to function effectively in either the Anglo or Hispanic cultures.

In a grounded theory study, Torres (2003) explored the influences on Latino students' ethnic identity development during their first two years in college. Two salient categories emerged from this study: situating identity and influences on change. Conditions for situating identity are the environment where students grew up, family influence and generational status, and self-perception of status in society. Influences on change include cultural dissonance and relationship changes within the environment.

Based on this research, Torres (2003) introduced a conceptual model that captures the influences of ethnic identity through the sophomore year in college. In the first year of college, three influences were apparent:

Environment where they grew up. Considered a continuum, this dimension ranges from having been raised in a diverse environment to having been raised in a predominantly white environment. Latino students at the latter end of the continuum are secure in their ethnicity and open to those from other cultures. Students at the former end prefer the company of those from the dominant culture, though they are not likely to discard the culture of their ancestors.

Family influence and generational status. Two dimensions encompass this category. Initially first-year Latino students likely use the same label their parents assign to their culture of origin. Parents' level of acculturation also tags students as first or second generation in the United States or beyond. Torres (2003) found that less acculturated parents of first-generation Latino students expected their children to consider parental desires, which sometimes conflicted with collegiate expectations. Not surprisingly, second-generation Latino students and beyond with more acculturated parents found less stress in the collegiate environment as the students' two worlds more smoothly intertwined.

Self-perception and status in society. This condition centers on Latino students' perceived privilege in their culture of origin. Though a correlation may exist, this privilege is not necessarily related to socioeconomic status. Students who grew up feeling some privilege often believed the negative stereotypes about Latinos, but these students did not apply the stereotypes to their own lives. In contrast, Latino students voicing no perceived privilege in their youth were more open to the experiences of others and recognized racism in their everyday lives.

Two processes are possible that can signal change in a student's ethnic identity: conflict with the culture or a shift in relationships within the environment. Positive and negative changes are associated with both processes:

Cultural dissonance. Behaviors reflecting cultural dissonance reveal "conflict between one's own sense of culture and what others expect" (Torres, 2003, p. 540). Depending on the student's issue and how it is approached and resolved, different outcomes can occur. For example, exploration of the Spanish language can resolve a cultural conflict for one student, while another may retreat from her or his culture of origin when in conflict with parental cultural expectations.

Changes in relationships. Shifts in relationships, mainly with peer group members, appear to produce a comparable interaction. If Latino students find congruence between their old and new beliefs within their peer groups, positive relationship outcomes are possible. If conflicts are not resolved, relationships will likely be negative.

A number of follow-up studies have been based on Torres's (2003) model. In a grounded theory study, college students who reconstructed their identity in more complex ways to reduce their vulnerability to stereotypes developed a stronger ethnic identity (Torres & Baxter Magolda, 2004). Examining the results of this study led the authors to conclude that although derived from white samples, the holistic foundation of self-authorship theory makes it an appropriate lens for examining Latino ethnic identity change.

Qualitative findings from a study conducted to examine Latino college students' ethnic identity and its influence on holistic development (Torres & Hernandez, 2007) also found characteristics similar to those Baxter Magolda (2001) identified in research on white student self-authorship. Additional developmental tasks revealed a matrix of holistic development, adding Latino cultural choices, which included cognitive, intrapersonal (ethnic identity), and interpersonal (cultural orientation) factors. Latino students exploring their ethnic identity moved from external formulas traced through geography, family, and a belief in negative stereotypes, to a comfort with cultural difference and demonstration of cultural choice and behavior as students moved to a solid internal foundation. At the crossroads, students cognitively recognized expansion of views, including racism, as well as stereotypes about the group, and made intentional choices related to their feelings of discrimination. Becoming an author of one's life required integrated daily cultural choices—in other words, creating an informed Latino identity, as well as advocating for others of similar ethnic origin, before moving to an integrated sense of self in a diverse environment. Latino students need meaningful support as they face the developmental tasks associated with confronting racism, so their growth will not stagnate or regress (Torres & Hernandez). A profound contribution to the student affairs literature, this study was the first empirical research to identify the experience of racism and its meaning in students' lives as a significant developmental task.

Environmental Influences on Ethnic Identity. Guardia and Evans (2008) conducted a phenomenological study to examine the ethnic identity development of Latino fraternity members at a Hispanic-serving institution (HSI). Applying a more fluid racial identity orientations model (Ferdman & Gallegos, 2001) examined through the lens of Bronfenbrenner's (2005) bioecological theory of human development, this study revealed six influences: family, the HSI campus, other Greeks and Greek affairs policies, gender, language, and involvement. The study also found that students engaged in Latino fraternity life view the environment of the fraternity as multicultural; providing members with *hermandad*—"a family atmosphere and Latino unity" (Guardia & Evans, p. 177), and find many aspects of the HSI, such as interactions with Hispanic faculty, conducive to enhancing ethnic identity.

Ethnic Identity of Asians in the United States

Thirty-seven percent of U.S. immigrants are of Asian descent, with the bulk coming from Vietnam, the Philippines, China, and India (Sodowsky et al., 1995), yet uniform categories with agreed-on definitions of Asian Americans and Pacific Islanders do not exist (Kawaguchi, 2003). Asian American panethnicity, which is referred to by some as "a collective identity organized around broad commonalities rooted in a variety of particular ethnicities traceable to points in Asia (i.e., Chinese American, Japanese American, Indian American, Taiwanese American, Vietnamese American, etc.)" (Rhoads, Lee, & Yamada, 2002, p. 877), complicates any categorization.

Asian Americans are the most ethnically diverse group in the country (Huang, 1997), making examination of their ethnic identity complicated (Torres et al., 2003). Linear ethnic models previously applied to most groups are not applicable to Asian Americans (Yeh & Huang, 1996). Ethnic identity for Asian Americans, including students, is not a psychosocial journey (internal process), but one heavily influenced by others (external process; Yeh & Huang). Like other ethnic groups referred to in this chapter, we do not condone generalization of the experiences of any one Asian group or the population as a whole. For example, the myth that Asian American college students are the model minority (Omatsu, 1994) and forced to live up to unrealistic stereotypes bestowed on them must be exposed.

One model points out the important role of ethnic identity for South Asian Americans (Ibrahim, Ohnishi, & Sandhu, 1997), a group often ignored when Asian Americans are discussed. South Asian immigrants possess a strong sense of ethnic pride and accept the differences between their culture of origin and host country. Some of the cultural values and beliefs of South Asians that may or may not overlap the beliefs of other Asian Americans include self-respect, dignity, and self-control; respect for family and age; awareness and respect for community; fatalism; and humility (Ibrahim et al). Most of these values can be placed at one end of a continuum with dominant culture values at the opposite end (see Guido-DiBrito & Chávez, 2003).

Ethnic Identity of Native Americans/American Indians

Native American scholars do not appear to agree on a single self-definition of their group of origin; most identify either as Native American (see Jackson, Smith, & Hill, 2003; Lundberg, 2007) or American Indian (see Brown & Robinson Kurpius, 1997; Cajete, 2005). Recently, some Native scholars have used the term *indigenous scholars* to identify themselves within the academy (Mihesuah & Wilson, 2004). *Indigenous Americans* is an appealing term to those who tie their heritage to the land and to other Native peoples around the globe (Mihesuah & Wilson). In this section, we refer to indigenous people living in the United States as Native American and American Indian.

Identifying the ethnic identity of American Indians as one population is not viable, and not desirable, as they are victims of a violent, genocidal history perpetuated by whites who have for too long dictated how American Indians should be identified. The broad diversity among tribes also precludes generalization of ethnic characteristics to the entire population, as each tribe has its own customs, traditions, language, history, myths, religion, culture, and symbols. Yet being Native American may reflect at least one sign, cultural pride, of sharing a similar ethnic heritage: "In the context of ethnicity—as opposed to race—Indian people are intensely proud of their respective cultures" (Horse, 2001, p. 105). Although Native tribes' beliefs and values share similarities and differences, customs and traditions are tribe specific and frame "Indianness" for each group (Choney, Berryhill-Paapke, & Robbins, 1995), making a universal description unlikely due to "the missing homogenous worldview" (p. 75). By one count, over 2.3 million American Indians are part of 280 tribes and numerous nations (for example, Apache, Sioux, Cherokee, Navajo, and Tewa) that speak over 252 languages (Herring, 1990).

As a minority group, most American Indians are expected to reflect dominant culture values as they acculturate (Keefe, 1980). By contrast, Cajete (2005) explored the "origins, nature, and methods of coming to know" (p. 69) and found at the heart of nearly every Native way of knowing symbolic constructs reflecting mythic metaphors that "present the Nature-centered orientation of indigenous epistemologies in the Americas" (p. 73). These myths, which appear in almost every Native American language, include Tree of Life, Earth Mother, Sun Father, and Sacred Directions. A deep understanding of the tribe's place in the world is marked by combining the physical and spiritual. These concepts are imperative to understanding the differences between individualism, embraced by the dominant culture, and communalism, lived in American Indian cultures.

Higher education's dominant culture and discriminatory practices are at odds with the underlying cultural beliefs of American Indian students and likely interfere with students' development. The reasons institutions are unsuccessful at recruiting and retaining Native students include potential issues related to development, such as transparent racist treatment (Brown & Robinson Kurpius, 1997; Jackson et al., 2003) and structures and philosophies of higher education embedded with cultural bias (Garrett & Pichette, 2000; Mihesuah, 2004; Pewardy & Frey, 2004; Tierney, 1992).

Ethnic Identity of African Americans/Blacks

Black Americans who can trace their ancestral origins to the African continent draw from a cornucopia of custom, language, history, tradition, religion, and other cultural legacies too numerous to address. Colonialism and slavery stripped blacks of their identity, causing deep psychological trauma (Fanon, 1967), and blocked their education for generations. The long-term effects of these conditions still prevent most blacks from identifying many of the particulars of their ethnic heritage. For purposes of this chapter, the terms *African American* and *blacks* are used interchangeably.

There is no universal ethnic identity model for all African Americans, a fact linked to a variety of worldviews and perspectives and traced to the heart of each African tribe or kinship, and white man's theft of African Americans' past. Within this frame, the concept of "identity is always a question of producing in the future an account of the past, it is always about narrative, the stories which cultures tell themselves about who they are and where they came from" (S. Hall, 1995, p. 5). Linked to stories that were altered over time, "identity shifts with the way we think and hear them and experience them" (p. 8). For many U.S. blacks of African descent, these stories are their only tangible inheritance, and many of these precious life fragments were silenced and became lost legacies.

Some of the literature on the ethnic identity of African American students has examined the relationship of ethnic identity to racial identity and self-esteem

(Phelps, Taylor, & Gerard, 2001), encouragement and ethnicity (Phelps, Tranakos-Howe, Dagley, & Lyn, 2001), and the impact of diasporic travel on ethnic identity development (Day-Vines, Barker, & Exum 1998). Much of this research uses the labels *racial* and *ethnic identity* interchangeably, which makes understanding these concepts difficult and context specific. West Indian immigrant students defined themselves in one study by their nationality (Cuban, Haitian, Jamaican, and so on), but when with other West Indians, blacks, or white Americans, they used the term *West Indian* to identify themselves (McLaughlin, 1981).

Ethnic identity concepts are evident in the following two models. The first is framed within the context of a specific geographical region of the Diaspora (Caribbean), while the second is related to gender identity (womanist identity). As a reminder, these models are not meant to be generalized to African Americans as a group. The numerous, varied places of origin of blacks in the United States make identifying a single ethnic identity model inconsistent with the underlying assumptions of ethnicity.

Caribbean Cultural Identity. Finding an origin of U.S. blacks from the Caribbean is not likely due to the broad, diverse composition of each group's history, geography, practices, language, customs, and other ethnic identifiers within the context of different colonizing cultures. Reinterpretation of these many cultures to produce a single culture is called *bricolage* (Knepper, 2006). In the process of borrowing and accepting culture from one another, the fragments of many cultures combine to produce a newly formed distinctive culture, a process known as *creolization*. The islands' archipelago is used as a metaphor for Caribbean identity (S. Hall, 1995), a string of related, but not necessarily connected, geographical and social pods in physical proximity, some tracing roots back to British, Spanish, Dutch, and French colonizers. Each island has also been influenced by additional ethnic cultures, like those originating in China and Portugal.

This quintessential Caribbean Diaspora was seen as a place where the most influential values originated in some other place (S. Hall, 1995). The survival and assimilation of the Caribbean peoples, particularly those enslaved, were set in the context of "the retention of old customs, the retention of cultural traits from Africa; customs and traditions which were retained in and through slavery, in plantation, in religion, partly in language, in folk customs, in music, in dance" (p. 7). These Caribbean cultural practices were built within "Victorian and pre-Victorian" British culture and Christian traditions, and "always surrounded by the colonizing culture" (p. 7). The cultural revolution of the late 1960s brought a shift in religion from Christianity to the language and rituals of Rastafarianism (S. Hall). A return to religious roots and creolization meant that those with no voice could be heard in a language understood by most people on the islands.

This nationalist perspective of a liberated Caribbean identity is one way of understanding the black ethnic identity of some students.

Womanist Identity. A form of identity created by black women for themselves, womanist theory "is specific in articulating personal insights from a Black female perspective" (Heath, 2006, p. 160) related to the intersectionality of sexism, racism, and classism, and obliteration of these "isms" in black women's lives. Based on this assumption, one model illuminates the transition from women defining themselves through external characterization to an internal standard of womanhood (Ossana, Helms, & Leonard, 1992). In this stepwise developmental process, women move from compliance with societal expectations about gender to define their identity (stage 1: preencounter) to a self-affirming positive definition of womanhood and powerful associations with women (stage 4: internalization). In between, women question their previously unquestioned values (stage 2: encounter), while the next stage (stage 3: immersion-emersion) involves "ideation of women" and "active rejection of male supremacist definitions of womanhood (regardless of their source)" (Ossana et al., p. 403) before accepting broader meanings of womanhood.

Sonya, the student from New Orleans who lived through Hurricane Katrina but her mother did not, identifies with a womanist identity in that she believes black women can accomplish anything. After Katrina, Sonya reclaimed her roots with female family in New Orleanian culture. As a woman activist, she wants to help black women rebuild their lives after a disaster.

Critique of Models and Future Directions

The ethnic identity of college students continues to be an area of study ripe with research possibility as college and university campuses' student demographics shift. Educators need to know more about how ethnicity and its development enhance identity in all ethnic groups during the college years (Phinney & Ong, 2007). Research on ethnic identity is in its infancy, and its variations and applications to college students are necessary to help students know themselves better. Increased research can aid in enhancing students' development and creating diverse campus environments that encourage it.

First, the vast individual cultural differences of those identifying with the large numbers of specific black and American Indian ethnic groups leave the door open for rich research opportunities to better serve the needs of these two groups. In fact, further research regarding each ethnic group's identity is needed. For example, more examination of Asian American ethnic identity development is clearly warranted. The many identification labels of those of Asian descent (for example, Chinese American, Japanese American, Indian American, and Southeast Asian American, to name a few), like the diversity among Latino groups, highlights a need to examine each group and its diversity separately. Research is also needed on the development of a pan-Asian identity resulting from intermarriage among individuals from various Asian backgrounds (Tuan, 2002).

Next, longitudinal studies of ethnic identity change are long overdue. Researchers need to examine the functional form of "trajectories of ethnic identity . . . over the adolescent and early adult years" (Phinney & Ong, 2007, p. 279). To do so, more sophisticated methodological tools to conduct longitudinal studies are needed to explain in greater detail the process of ethnic identity development during late adolescence.

Third, ethnic identity's intersectionality with other social identities such as race, class, gender, sexuality, and religion, to name a few (McCall, 2005), is cutting-edge investigation. The ways in which social identities intersect and demonstrate behavioral preferences reveal a major component of shifting identity development and are underresearched, particularly with regard to college students.

Complex ethnic identity development models better reflect the whole student. Instead of components of the student's identity studied in isolation, ethnic identity examined from the intersections with other social identities gives a broader snapshot of growth. We need to know more about how these identities interact and mold the individuals our students become so that programs and policies can enhance their development. Sonya, Lydia, Little Eagle, Paul, and students like them deserve our attention and an opportunity to celebrate their ethnic identity and that of the students around them.

CHAPTER SIXTEEN

MULTIRACIAL IDENTITY DEVELOPMENT

Sitting in her residence hall room reading the campus newspaper, Danae almost jumped out of her chair. In the paper was an announcement of an interest meeting for students of mixed-race heritage. Having been at her mid-western university for over a year, she had thought she must be the only student of mixed-race background there. She was eager to meet other people who might have had similar experiences of isolation and lack of acceptance that she had had throughout her life. Danae's mother was white and her father was black; her own appearance was that of a light-skinned black woman. She had grown up in a predominantly black community where she felt constantly tested to "prove" her blackness. Now at college, she was not totally accepted by the black student orga-nization she had joined during her first year and did not really fit with the white students in her residence hall either. She saw herself as a unique combination of black and white and referred to herself as biracial. She had been really frustrated that the application form she completed when she applied to college did not give her the option to select this choice. She reluctantly checked the black box because that was what most people labeled her. When forced to identify as black, she felt that she was selling out her white mother, to whom she felt very close.

In another residence hall, Thomas was also excited about the new mixed-race group. He was of Vietnamese and black heritage and was also looking for a place he could feel at home. He was not accepted by his Vietnamese extended family, who looked down on his father for marrying a non-Vietnamese woman. Thomas was usually labeled as black by others, although this identity did not feel totally comfortable to him either, as his family lived in a middle-class predominantly white neighborhood and he had attended a mostly white high school. In reality, race did not seem as important to him as other aspects of his identity, especially his academic and musical abilities. He was tired of people trying to put him in a box racially and was looking forward to talking with other mixed-race people in this new group whom he hoped would accept him for who he was.

◆ ◆ ◆

Danae and Thomas are representative of the many mixed-heritage students now attending U.S. colleges and universities. Their stories underscore the importance of student affairs educators' understanding the identity development processes multiracial students experience, the challenges they face, and the support they need as they negotiate their identities.

Nearly 7 million people (2.4 percent of the population) indicated on the 2000 U.S. Census that their ancestry included more than one race (Jones & Smith, 2003). Based on data from that census, Jones and Smith described the multiracial population of the United States as young, reflecting an increase in multiracial births and more mixed-heritage individuals claiming multiracial identities. The mixed-race population is also diverse, with the largest percentage (32.3 percent) indicating they are white and "some other race" (p. 5).

As the number of mixed-heritage individuals in the United States has grown, research examining their identity development has also increased. In this chapter, we provide an overview of the history of mixed-heritage people in this country, followed by a review of theories of multiracial identity development, related research, and student affairs applications. We close by discussing implications for future research and practice.

Many terms have been used interchangeably in the literature to refer to individuals whose racial and/or ethnic heritage is mixed. While *biracial, multiracial, mixed race,* and *blended* commonly appear, Stephan (1992) correctly pointed out that *mixed heritage* is actually the accurate term to represent this population since it avoids the biological assumption underlying the use of the term *race*. In this chapter, we retain the terms used by the various authors we examine, with the caveat that *mixed heritage* is a more accurate label.

Historical Perspective

In many parts of the world, mixed-race identities are commonplace. For example, in many Latin American countries the majority of the population identifies as *mestizo* (Trianosky, 2003). In the United States, however, societal and legal steps to ensure that whites maintain power over those of other racial and ethnic backgrounds have slowed recognition and acceptance of mixed identities. In addition, many people inaccurately assume that most mixed-race people have black and white ancestry (Root, 1995). Although the claiming of a multiracial identity is relatively recent, sexual unions (both voluntary and involuntary) between people of different races have resulted in mixed children since colonists arrived in North America (Douglass, 2003; T. Wilson, 1992), despite laws forbidding mixed-race marriages that existed until 1967, when the Supreme Court declared them unconstitutional (Renn, 2004; Sullivan, 2006).

The first sexual unions between people of different races in the United States involved white European colonists and Native American Indian people (Douglass, 2003; T. Wilson, 1992). After the introduction of slavery, black people also partnered with Native American Indian people. As a result of these pairings, there are high numbers of "mixed blood" individuals among Native groups, as well as blacks and whites who possess Native heritage (Douglass; T. Wilson). Whites also paired with Asian immigrants, who were recruited to build the western railroads in the nineteenth century (Takaki, 1993). Numbers of mixed Asian children increased significantly after World War II, when American soldiers brought home war brides, and especially since the war in Vietnam, after which many refugees came to the United States (Takaki). Latinos, who have lived in the United States since before the founding of the country and whose immigration from Latin America has increased dramatically over the past several decades (Takaki), have also contributed to the mixed-heritage population of the United States. Indeed, multiracial births are now much higher among those of Asian or Latino descent than among blacks (Jones & Smith, 2003; Root, 2003a), perhaps because of greater acceptance of unions between whites and members of these ethnic groups than of partnerships between whites and blacks (Zack, 1997).

From the early 1700s until 1989, biracial babies with a white parent were, first by custom and later by law, assigned to the subordinate race (Davis, 1995; Root, 1996) since the importance of keeping the white race "pure" was paramount (Pinderhughes, 1995). The "hypodescent or 'one-drop' rule," which was used to categorize mixed individuals as black "regardless of the proportion of black ancestry or the person's physical appearance" (Davis, p. 115), was also intended to prevent children of white slave masters born to black slave women from having any of the privileges associated with their paternity (Root, 1995). Categorization of mixed-race individuals as nonwhite was a way to keep the white male power structure intact, as it ensured that property, voting, and inheritance rights stayed in white hands (Wijeyesinghe, 1995). The United States also extended the hypodescent rule to individuals of other nonwhite races. During World War II, for instance, individuals with as little as one-sixteenth Japanese ancestry were sent to Japanese internment camps (Spickard, 1989).

Acceptance of *multiracial* as an identity is difficult for those who want to consider—and maintain—"the races" as discrete (Zack, 1995). People who have been led to believe in the "purity" of race often cannot fathom the idea that individuals can legitimately belong in more than one category (Root, 2003a). In the minds of many people, mixed-race people are, first and foremost, not white (Gordon, 2004; Root, 1990). Because of the one-drop rule, to be considered white in this country, a person must have only white ancestors (Renn, 2004). As a result, mixed-race people experience oppression in ways similar to other nonwhite people (Root, 1990; Zack, 1995).

Furthermore, lack of acceptance of multiracial individuals by nonwhite persons is also common (E. Brown, 2006; Root, 1990; Song, 2003). A worry, particularly among African Americans, is that multiracial identification will lead to diminishing numbers of individuals from specific racial groups being counted for official purposes, the result of which could be decreased resources for nondominant populations and a lessening of political power (DeBose & Winters, 2003; Pinderhughes, 1995; Wu, 2006). Opponents of multiracial identification argue that such identification would obscure important racial differences and make it impossible to track progress on efforts to eliminate racial discrimination (Staples, 2007; Wu).

While attitudes toward interracial relationships and the offspring thereof have improved in recent years, particularly among whites (Root, 1996), it can still be difficult, as the students in the opening scenario found, for people from mixed backgrounds to develop a secure identity because they do not fit into a specific racial group and have few role models (DeBose & Winters, 2003). As Danae discovered in the opening scenario, multiracial individuals often find themselves in the untenable position of simultaneously being expected to identify solely as a member of the least dominant community represented in their heritage and not being accepted by that community because they are not black enough, Asian enough, and so forth (Song, 2003). As a result of their lack of acceptance by monoracial communities and the unique developmental issues and experiences they share, mixed-heritage people such as Danae have increasingly been asserting their distinct identity by labeling themselves biracial, multiracial, or mixed (Song). Two activist multiracial organizations, the National Association of MultiEthnic Americans and the MAVIN Foundation, have been created to increase awareness of issues facing multiracial people (Douglass, 2003; Renn, 2008). Nakashima (1996) identified three goals advocated by proponents within the mixed-race movement: "inclusion and legitimacy" (p. 81), creation of a new multiracial community, and deconstruction of race ideology and creation of a human community.

Approaches to Multiracial Identity Development

Identity development is a complex process for individuals from mixed-race backgrounds (Kerwin & Ponterotto, 1995). Not only must they deal with prejudice similar to that experienced by people who are members of nonwhite ethnic and racial groups, but they must also decide "how to reconcile the heritages of both parents in a society that categorizes individuals into single groups" (p. 200). In this section, we present an overview of the types of approaches that have been used to explain the process of identity development that mixed-heritage individuals experience. A separate section follows, presenting in detail Renn's (2004) theory, which examines the identity development of multiracial college students.

Deficit Approaches

Early explanations of biracial development (for example, Gibbs, 1987; Stonequist, 1937) were based on the assumption that the end point of development was a marginal personality. Biracial and multiracial people were presented as "confused, distraught, and unable to fit in anywhere in the American racial landscape" (Wijeyesinghe, 2001, p. 131). In these approaches, identity problems were viewed as internal to biracial individuals (Poston, 1990) rather than the result of pressure placed on them by society to identify only with one specific race/ethnicity, regardless of their actual ancestry (Pinderhughes, 1995). Thus, the two students in the opening scenario would be viewed as experiencing inner conflict about their identity because of their inability to fit into existing society. Countering this "problem approach" (Thornton, 1996, p. 108), Poston cited research by Hall (1980) and Herman (1970) in which biracial persons reported that they saw their multiracial backgrounds as an asset rather than a liability.

Stage Theories

In response to the early research cited by Poston (1990), theorists began to explain multiracial identity development as a normal developmental process (Wijeyesinghe, 2001). Some suggested that the end point of multiracial development was assimilation to white culture, while others argued that multiracial individuals could never assimilate because of environmental factors over which they had little control (Thornton, 1996). Proponents of the latter perspective saw the end point of development for multiracial people as identifying as biracial and being able to draw on both aspects of their heritage (Thornton, 1996; Wijeyesinghe, 2001). Patterned after stage theories of black and white identity development (for example, those of Cross, Jackson, Helms, and Hardiman), these approaches included an immersion-like stage, strong emotional content, and greater self-awareness and self-appreciation in later stages (Wijeyesinghe, 2001). Returning to the opening scenario, stage theorists would suggest that Danae, who identifies as biracial, would be further along in her development than Thomas, who is uncomfortable with any type of racial identification.

Examples of stage theories include those of Poston (1990), who presented a five-stage theory, the end point of which was a stable and integrated racial identity; Kich (1992), who introduced a three-stage theory with the end point being self-acceptance and assertion of an interracial identity; and Collins (2000), who identified four phases of development leading to resolution and acceptance of a biracial identity.

Based on their empirical research examining the identity development of children of mixed black and white heritage (Kerwin, 1991; Kerwin, Ponterotto, Jackson, & Harris, 1993), Kerwin and Ponterotto (1995) proposed a more complex stage theory of biracial identity development that paralleled periods in the individual's life from preschool through adulthood. Miville, Constantine, Baysden, and So-Lloyd (2005) reported that their interviews with five men and five women of diverse mixed-race backgrounds, in which they investigated critical time periods in identity development, supported Kerwin and Ponterotto's theory.

Critics have pointed out that stage theories are not as appropriate for multiracial people as they might be for people whose background is monoracial, since multiracial individuals have more than one heritage to reconcile, a process that is varied and complex rather than linear (Renn, 2004). In addition, Standen (1996) suggested that the choice of a single multiracial identity could be viewed as a "forced choice" (p. 247) and therefore not necessarily positive.

Typology Approaches

Cortés (2000) and Daniel (2002) both rejected the idea that an integrated multiracial identity is the only healthy identity for mixed-race individuals. They proposed that, depending on background and environmental influences, a number of options exist for how an individual may choose to identify. In reference to the opening scenario, they would see the identity choices Danae and Thomas have made as both being valid. The focus of these approaches, which can be considered typology theories, is the various identity choices mixed-race individuals might make.

Cortés (2000) identified five identity patterns among mixed-race individuals of various backgrounds: single racial identity, where one aspect of the individual's heritage is favored; multiple racial identity, in which individuals identify with each race that makes up their heritage (for example, black and white); multiple racial-multiracial identity, where individuals identify with each aspect of their heritage while also viewing themselves as multiracial; multiracial identity (Danae's choice), in which this identity is the primary one chosen rather than one or more specific racial identities; and nonracial identity (Thomas's choice), where a person has no sense of racial identity (for example, a recent immigrant from a country in which race has little or no meaning).

Daniel (2002) also proposed different outcomes of identity development. He hypothesized a continuum of identity for individuals with mixed black and white heritage, ranging from integrative to pluralistic. On this continuum, Daniel (2002) saw three identity types: synthesized identity, functional identity/ European American orientation, and functional identity/African American orientation.

A weakness of the approaches introduced by Cortés (2000) and Daniel (2002) is that both are based on anecdotal data only. Also, while Cortés and Daniel (2002) expanded how multiracial identity is conceptualized, neither theorist examined factors that influence the identity choices individuals make.

Ecological Approaches

Critics have argued that the assumed universality and linearity inherent in stage models do not hold for multiracial individuals because changing social and environmental influences across the life span are ignored (Wijeyesinghe, 2001). Taking the position that ethnic and racial identities are not fixed, but rather influenced by the environment in which individuals find themselves, ecological models include an examination of external factors that affect how individuals decide to identify racially or ethnically, as well as how and why an initially chosen identity may change over time and place (Root, 2003a). To explain how Danae and Thomas have chosen to identify, these theorists would examine influential personal and environmental factors, such as Thomas having lived in a white neighborhood and Danae not wanting to "sell out" her mother.

A number of theorists writing about multiracial identity development adopted an ecological perspective, including Stephan (1992), Wijeyesinghe (2001), Root (1996, 2003a, 2003b), and Renn (2004). Stephan (1992) suggested that exposure to ethnic cultural customs, appearance, socialization, identification with a parent, and geographical location were some of the factors that influenced identity choice. Wijeyesinghe (2001) identified eight factors that may contribute to the racial identity choices of multiracial individuals: racial heritage, cultural attachment, early experiences and socialization, physical appearance, social and historical context, political awareness and orientation, other social identities, and spirituality.

A weakness of these three approaches is that the theorists did not conduct follow-up research to validate their findings. They also failed to consider the various identities individuals chose. In her ecological model, Root (1996, 2003a, 2003b) addressed these issues by outlining the variety of identity choices that mixed-heritage individuals make, in addition to delineating factors that influence identity development. Her model is based on empirical research conducted during the 1990s.

Root (1996) first described four ways that mixed-race individuals negotiate their identities as "border crossings" (p. xx): (1) accept the identity assigned by society, (2) choose a monoracial identity, (3) choose a mixed-race identity (Danae's decision), or (4) create a new racial identity. Later she added a fifth identity type: select a white identity (Root, 2003a, 2003b). This choice, which Thomas could decide on in the future, might be made by individuals who are immersed in the white community and have little contact with their families of color or ethnic community. According to Root (2003a), persons understand themselves within the context of their environments, which change over the course of their lives and can lead them to alter how they identify. Root (2003a) also noted that people may label themselves in more than one way depending on where they are or with whom they are interacting.

Root (1995, 2003a, 2003b) identified a number of external factors that influence the ethnic and racial identity development of mixed-race individuals. The first five influences are contextual and therefore may not be obvious: the history of race within one's geographical region, generation, sexual orientation, gender, and class. More apparent factors are family functioning, family socialization, community, personal attributes, and physical appearance.

A number of studies (U. M. Brown, 2001; Hall, 1992; Kilson, 2001; Mass, 1992; Rockquemore & Brunsma, 2002; Wallace, 2001) have found that mixed-heritage individuals choose a variety of labels when identifying themselves, as Root (2003a) suggested, and that the identity choices of these individuals change over time and are contingent on the social context (U. M. Brown, 2001; Kilson; Standen, 1996). Researchers have also determined that Root's (1995, 2003a, 2003b) personal and contextual factors (U. M. Brown, 2001; Hall, 1992; Hall & Cooke Turner, 2001; Korgen, 1998; Mass; Pinderhughes, 1995; Rockquemore, 2002; Rockquemore & Brunsma; Root, 1997, 2001; Talbot, 2008; Twine, 1996), as well as family and community influences (DeBose & Winters, 2003; Hall & Cooke Turner; Kilson; Miville et al., 2005; Rockquemore & Brunsma; Shih, Bonam, Sanchez, & Peck, 2007; Wallace, 2003; T. Williams, 1996), are influential in the identity development process. Few of these studies, other than those conducted by Root herself, were explicitly designed to validate Root's theory, and a limited number have been based on the experiences of college students (Kilson; Rockquemore; Rockquemore & Brunsma; Twine; Wallace, 2001, 2003). While Root's theory has been supported by a reasonable amount of research, no specific applications to higher education could be found. Renn's ecological theory of mixed-race identity development addressed these concerns.

Renn's Ecological Theory of Mixed-Race Identity Development

Noting that very little research on biracial identity had been completed in college settings, Kristen Renn (2000, 2003, 2004) conducted three increasingly complex studies examining both the identity development process and outcomes experienced by mixed-race college students of various racial/ethnic backgrounds, coming up with her own ecological model of mixed-race identity. She interviewed fifty-six mixed-race students at six colleges and universities in the eastern and midwestern United States and analyzed data obtained from written responses from participants, focus groups, observations, and archival sources. In her 2004 book, Renn presented an in-depth analysis and theoretical explanation for her findings.

Aspects of the Theory

Renn's theory focuses on both ecological factors that influence multiracial identity development and the various labels individuals with mixed heritages use to identify themselves.

Ecological Influences. Renn's (2000) study revealed the importance of space and peer culture on multiracial identity development. The concept of space included both physical and psychological elements. Students were influenced by the extent to which they found places where they saw themselves fitting in, either in formal organizations or in informal peer groups. Seeing parallels between her findings and Bronfenbrenner's (1979, 1993) ecology model of human development (see Chapter Nine), Renn (2003, 2004) used the four components of Bronfenbrenner's (1979, 1993, 1995) person-process-context-time (PPCT) model as a framework to discuss her mixed-race participants' experiences. The experiences of Danae and Thomas in the opening scenario fit well into this framework.

Renn (2003) found that for biracial individuals, the following aspects of the *person* component of the model applied: family background and heritage, extent of cultural knowledge, degree of experience with individuals of one's own heritage and other cultural backgrounds, and physical appearance. Second, Renn (2003) noted that in Bronfenbrenner's model the "key to development is the increasing complexity of interactive *processes* [italics added] in which the individual is engaged" (p. 392). The college environment provides many such options for multiracial students to grapple with the cognitive demands of making sense of race (Renn, 2003, 2004).

Within the *context* of the college environment, Renn (2003, 2004) identified the following settings that influenced the identity development of mixed-race students: (1) microsystems that encouraged face-to-face interactions with either positive or negative racial overtones, including monoracial and multiracial student organizations; (2) mesosystems of campus culture that sent positive or negative messages, including the "permeability of group boundaries and the desirability of identifying with various groups within the campus environment" (Renn, 2003, p. 394); (3) the exosystem that affected students' awareness of racial identity, including policies for identifying one's race/ethnicity on forms required by the college and attention paid in the curriculum to racial issues; and (4) the aspects of the macrosystem that were influential in the students' development, including how the students viewed race and culture and their own roles in these systems as influenced by the existing belief systems about individuals with mixed-race backgrounds. *Time*—the sociohistorical context—greatly influenced the macrosystem, in that debates about the racial and ethnic categories to be included on the 2000 census were very prevalent during these students' formative years. Renn (2003) correctly pointed out that Bronfenbrenner's model does not provide a sense of individual development over time.

Identity Patterns. Renn (2004) illustrated the variability and fluidity of identity among mixed-race college students. Her participants chose various ways of identifying racially, and many presented different identities depending on the situation and context. Indeed, Taylor (2005) suggested that the most important finding from Renn's (2004) study is that a single identity may be neither possible nor desirable for mixed-race students. Renn (2004) described five fluid and non-exclusive "identity patterns" (p. 67), all of which she viewed as healthy: monoracial, multiple monoracial, multiracial, extraracial, and situational. Different life experiences may lead individuals to change how they identify at various times in their lives. Following is a discussion of each of these patterns.

Monoracial Identity. Close to half (48 percent) of Renn's (2004) participants claimed a monoracial identity; if one of their parents was white, the identity they chose generally represented their nondominant ancestry. Claiming a monoracial identity was easiest for students whose appearance and cultural knowledge were congruent with that identity. Cultural knowledge was greatly influenced by the presence or absence of family representing that heritage. Once in college, peer microsystems affected the degree to which students could easily assume a monoracial identity and have it accepted.

Multiple Monoracial Identity. Almost half (48 percent) of the students Renn (2004) interviewed identified using multiple monoracial identities, most representing their parental heritages (for example, white and Latino; African American and Asian). These students often were equally knowledgeable about each aspect of their heritage or sought out more information in college. They exhibited a strong desire to label themselves rather than be labeled by others. Students' ability to successfully identify with more than one monoracial group was contingent on how accepting their peers were of such a label.

Multiracial Identity. Along with Danae, most of the students (89 percent) in Renn's (2004) study identified using a term that represented their unique mixed-race background (for example, *multiracial, biracial, hapa, mixed*). They saw themselves as "existing outside of the monoracial paradigm" (Renn, 2004, p. 156) and sharing common experiences with other mixed-race students regardless of heritage. For some students, this was a privately held identity, while others used it openly. On campuses that had formal or informal groups where mixed-race students interacted, public identification as mixed was more common. Being exposed to racial identity issues in classes and other educational settings also contributed to identification as multiracial.

Extraracial Identity. Students in this pattern either opt out of racial categorization completely, as Thomas did, or do not adhere to the categories used in the United States (Renn, 2004). About one-quarter of Renn's (2004) interviewees fit this pattern. Many had been raised outside the United States, and about half attended an institution where they were exposed to postmodern perspectives and the idea that race is a social construction rather than a biological reality, ideas that contributed to their decision not to identify racially. All but one of the students who chose this identity were juniors and seniors. None of the students solely identified in this manner, which might suggest that "holding such an approach to racial identity is a difficult stance to maintain in the face of powerful forces on campuses that are organized in part around racial identities" (Renn, 2004, p. 78).

Situational Identity. Over half (61 percent) of Renn's (2004) participants identified differently in different contexts, including all of the students who identified extraracially. They considered racial identification fluid and contextually driven. Shifting among identities was sometimes unconscious and other times quite deliberate. For some students, this process was easy; for others, it was stressful. The rigidity of racial boundaries on campus was a factor. Renn (2004) argued that rather than being problematic as stage theorists would suggest, "the ability to read contexts and construct identity in relation to specific contexts is a highly evolved skill requiring emotional maturity and cognitive complexity" (p. 80).

Research

Renn (2004) identified trends with regard to identity choice among various student populations. In addition, researchers have found patterns of identity labeling similar to Renn's. Factors influencing identity choice have also been investigated. In particular, the importance of the college years for multiracial identity development has been documented.

Trends in Identity Choice. Renn (2004) reported some trends with regard to the five identity patterns. Women identified with more patterns (on average, 3.03) than men, who reported 2.10 patterns. Men were more likely than women to select only one monoracial identity. Students whose parents were both people of color were less likely than students with a white parent to identify monoracially, more likely to select multiple monoracial identities, and very much more likely to select situational identities. Students with one white parent and one black parent were less likely to select an extraracial identity, perhaps because of peer pressure to identify racially.

Identity Patterns. While not directly based on Renn's (2004) theory, a number of research studies support some or all of the identity patterns that Renn found. These include Wallace's (2001) study of high school and college students of mixed-race background, Kilson's (2001) study of biracial youth, and Rockquemore and Brunsma's (2002) study of 177 black and white mixed-heritage college students. Wallace (2001) found that 14 of the 15 students in her study used at least two labels to identify themselves, consistent with Renn's (2004) finding that many students identify in more than one way. However, fewer of Kilson's (2001) participants (10 of 52) chose more than one label. Participants in a study conducted by Miville et al. (2005) reported both a private multiracial identity and a public identity that was most often monoracial. They also exhibited an ability to adapt their identities to their social surroundings and expectations of others, as Renn (2004) suggested.

Factors Influencing Identity Development. Identity development for the individuals in Miville et al.'s (2005) study was influenced by significant others, particularly parents; specific places, especially school environments; and critical time periods, especially elementary school years, high school years, and college, findings that support Renn's (2004) ecological perspective. Renn (2004) also found differences in identification based on the specific institution the students attended, indicating that the culture and curriculum of the institution had an influence on how students saw themselves. In their study of forty-seven racially mixed college students of various heritages at two state universities in California, one more racially diverse than the other, Phinney and Alipuria (1996) discovered that 80 percent of the students chose a monoracial identity label when asked for their race on an open-ended question. Students with a white parent were more likely to identify as white, rather than mixed or the race of their other parent, on the predominantly white campus (45.5 percent) than on the ethnically diverse campus (5.9 percent), demonstrating the influence of context on identity, similar to Renn's (2003, 2004) findings concerning the differential impact of campus environments.

The Impact of College. Paralleling Renn's (2004) findings, researchers have found that college is a particularly challenging time for biracial individuals (U. M. Brown, 2001; A. King, 2008a; Korgen, 1998; Twine, 1996; Wallace, 2003). College is a major transition for mixed-heritage students in that they leave the direct influence of their families and enter an environment in which peer interaction and friendships become especially important. U. M. Brown (2001) found that since her black and white biracial participants were not given an opportunity to identify as biracial on application forms and therefore indicated that they were black, they were recruited into black organizations, where many found a home, but others felt pushed to be something they were not and to choose between black and white cultures. The black and white biracial students at the University of California, Berkeley who participated in Twine's (1996) study reported that the politicized racial environment pressured students who had any black ancestry to assume a black identity, date black partners, and join black student organizations. Korgen's (1998) respondents also felt pressured to choose between the black and white communities on campus, particularly by monoracial black students, and to "act black" to be accepted (p. 58).

In the college setting, "cultural legitimacy and loyalty" (Wallace, 2003, p. 89) are key factors in acceptance and greatly influence the identity development of mixed-heritage students. If their appearance is ambiguous or their name or language does not reflect their ethnic identity, students may have a particularly difficult time being accepted by monoracial groups of color (Wallace, 2003). At the same time, biracial students are assumed by whites to be "of color" and are therefore excluded from white peer groups. The degree of fluency mixed-heritage students have with their racial/ethnic cultures greatly influences the extent to which they are eventually accepted by and see themselves as belonging to groups reflecting their background (Wallace, 2003).

A. King's (2008b) findings supported those of Wallace (2003). She identified the two major challenges facing multiracial students in her study to be how other students perceived their racial identities based on the multiracial student's appearance and pressure from peers to conform to specific ways of being based on their perceived racial heritage. A. King (2008a) reflected that "as a light-skinned multiracial woman with a racially ambiguous appearance and no knowledge of what [her] actual racial identity is because [she is] adopted" (pp. 35–36), finding an answer to the question, "What are you?" was an ongoing concern. A. King (2008a) also reported another poignant example of being spoken to in Spanish because individuals perceived that she was Latina and the awkward result when she was unable to understand them.

College experiences led many individuals in U. M. Brown's (2001) study to reconsider and modify how they identified racially, and they left college "more firmly grounded about who they were" (p. 92). The women in Twine's (1996) study noted that taking courses in black and ethnic studies helped them to learn about their heritage and influenced their identity decisions. In addition, the establishment of multiracial groups on campuses provided a critical space for mixed students to explore identity issues (A. King, 2008a, 2008b; Wallace, 2003).

Applications

A strength of Renn's (2004) work is the number of implications she offered for higher education practice. Her suggestions relate to assessment, policy changes, programs, structural diversity, curriculum, and boundary crossing.

Assessment. Renn (2004) stressed the need to accurately determine the numbers of mixed-race students enrolled in colleges and universities and the various ways in which they identify. She also pointed out the importance of assessing the campus climate as experienced by mixed-race students.

Policy. Institutional policy on how racial and ethnic data are collected must be reviewed and changed (Renn, 2004). For multiracial students like Danae, being able to indicate their mixed heritage, either by selecting more than one race/ethnicity or being able to choose "multiracial" as a way of identifying, gave students in Renn's (2004) study a feeling of inclusion, while having to "check one box only" was viewed as exclusionary. Renn and Lunceford (2002) reported that only 17.3 percent of the 127 randomly sampled institutions provided students the option to indicate more than one race/ethnicity. Not only does limiting students to only one racial/ethnic choice result in inaccurate data, but it also unfairly forces students to negate part of their heritage—an arbitrary decision with significant emotional ramifications for many (Cortés, 2000). Beginning in the 2010–2011 academic year, institutions will be required to offer the opportunity to indicate more than one race, with reporting to the U.S. Department of Education including an unduplicated head count of students in two ethnic categories (Hispanic/Latino or Not Hispanic/Latino), five races (American Indian/Alaska Native, Asian, Black/African American, Native Hawaiian or Other Pacific Islander, White), and a combined "two or more races" category (Kellogg & Niskodé, 2008).

Programs. Renn (2004) stressed the importance of creating welcoming spaces for multiracial students on campus. One way to achieve this goal is by establishing a specific student organization for mixed-heritage students. Williams, Nakashima, Kich, and Daniel (1996), as well as Cortés (2000), also stressed the importance of organizations for mixed-race students on college campuses. Cortés reported the existence of twenty-seven such organizations in 1999; certainly more have been started since then. Such organizations help mixed-race students to find other people who have common experiences, a variable that Renn (2000, 2004) identified as important in identity development. Ozaki and Johnston (2008) delineated issues facing multiracial student organizations and their advisors, offering suggestions for creating effective environments in which multiracial students can explore their identities and bond with others who have similar backgrounds.

Addressing multiracial issues through orientation presentations, speakers' series, and awareness workshops, as well as providing opportunities for multiracial students to participate in cultural events, are other ways of creating a feeling of inclusion among mixed-race students (Renn, 2003, 2004). Wong and Buckner (2008) provided an overview of emerging student services and practices for working with multiracial students, as well as case studies of three leading programs. The Internet is providing an important means for multiracial students to find each other and communicate. Gasser (2008) discussed the role played by social networking sites, wikis, blogs, and other technology in supporting this population.

Structural Diversity. Having individuals with whom to interact who have had similar experiences is critical to the identity development process (Renn, 2004). Multiracial faculty and staff should be visible and available to interact with multiracial students. At the same time, faculty must protect their time to accomplish the work demands they face, particularly if they are not yet tenured (Cuyjet, 2008). Increasing the numbers of students of color on campus also increases the likelihood that the number of mixed-race students will increase to the critical mass necessary to create informal and formal networks.

Curriculum. Renn (2000, 2003) pointed out the importance of including information about multiracial issues and identity in classes to enable all students to learn more about this increasingly important topic, as well as create a more inclusive environment for students of mixed heritage. Renn (2003) noted that being able to discuss identity issues with others in classes assisted multiracial students in developing a sense of their own identity. In addition, Williams et al. (1996) stressed that courses on multiracial topics are important for social and political purposes in that they legitimize multiracial identity.

Introducing a social constructionist view of race in and out of the classroom, while challenging the idea of race as a biological reality, also provides support for students from mixed-race backgrounds. In Renn's (2004) study, exposure to postmodern theories of race provided multiracial students with language and concepts to understand their experiences. She found that exposure to postmodern thinking was more valuable to students than more traditional diversity initiatives.

Encouraging Boundary Crossing. Finally, Renn (2004) argued for environmental design that allows students to cross boundaries between peer cultures. Ensuring that student groups over which the university has some control, such as orientation groups, advising groups, and course sections, are diverse and physical space is used in ways that promote interaction among students of different backgrounds can assist in this process. Faculty and student affairs staff can also encourage boundary crossing in one-on-one conversations, leadership education programs, and student group advising.

Conclusions and Future Directions

Multiracial identity development underscores the social construction of race (Rockquemore & Brunsma, 2002). As research has suggested, mixed-race identity is fluid, contingent on context and social influences, and changeable over time. As such, mixed-race identities challenge the traditional perceptions of race to which U.S. society has adhered for centuries. To support multiracial students and help monoracial students understand the experiences of these students, educators have an obligation to raise awareness of how the concept of race was constructed historically and present alternative constructionist perspectives that better represent reality.

There is no one path that individuals follow in forming their identities and presenting themselves as mixed-heritage people. And as Funderburg (1994) reflected in her collection of essays based on interviews with forty-six biracial individuals, "no single factor that influences identity can be examined in isolation from any other" (p. 377). The lives of her interviewees, like those of multiracial people studied by other researchers, were shaped by parents and family, neighborhood, school, friends and strangers, work, love and romance, and other forces. All of these influences combine in different ways to shape individuals' belief systems, sense of themselves, and how they choose to present themselves in various settings.

Given this complexity, ecological theories of multiracial identity development seem to provide a closer representation of reality than other theories found in the literature. Further research is needed, however, to validate these approaches. Existing research, while supportive of the ecological theories of Root and Renn, is mostly atheoretical (Miville, 2005; Miville et al., 2005).

Existing research has a number of other limitations. Most of it has been based on biracial individuals of mixed black and white heritage; studies have used small, regional, self-identified samples; methodologies have been mostly qualitative and therefore are not generalizable; consistent definitions of racial identity variables have been lacking; and data analysis procedures have not been clearly discussed (Miville, 2005; Miville, et al., 2005; Rockquemore & Brunsma, 2002; Spencer, 2006). Also, most of the studies have focused on children and adolescents rather than college students or adults (Miville).

It is also important to keep in mind that society's treatment of, and reaction to, individuals of different racial and ethnic combinations are not the same (Thornton, 2004). While there are some similarities in experience (for example, not being totally accepted by monoracial groups that make up one's heritage), specific combinations of heritages also create different dynamics. Most notably, Rockquemore and Brunsma (2002) argued persuasively that assimilation of any racial or ethnic population into white culture is possible and even desired, except for African Americans. Rockquemore and Brunsma pointed out that people "with one quarter or less Native American, Mexican, Chinese, or Japanese ancestry are treated as assimilating Americans [sic]" (p. 110). In contrast, whites, blacks, and biracial individuals with black ancestry have consistently adhered to the one-drop rule, a norm that keeps undesired assimilation from occurring. By challenging this rule, the recent multiracial movement has contributed to increasing tension among these groups over the identity of mixed-race individuals. Rockquemore and Brunsma argued that the one-drop rule will not disappear until prejudice and discrimination are significantly reduced. However, multiracial individuals who resist using a single racial category to identify themselves are pushing against this norm and the racial biases associated with it (Rockquemore & Brunsma). To fully understand the identity development process among mixed-race individuals, this important difference based on racial heritage must be kept in mind.

CHAPTER SEVENTEEN

SEXUAL IDENTITY DEVELOPMENT

The Lesbian, Gay, Bisexual, Queer, and Questioning Alliance (LGBQQA) faces a dilemma. Its advisor has just announced that he has taken a new job and will be leaving the university. To remain an active student organization, LGBQQ needs a member of the university faculty or staff to serve as their advisor. So far, they have had no luck finding a suitable LGBQQ person for this position, as members of the community are either already overburdened or are reluctant to take on this public role because it might jeopardize their careers in a rather conservative university setting. The alliance president, John, has decided to ask a relatively new student activities advisor, Andrea, who has been supportive of the LLBQQ community, if she would be willing to take on this responsibility. John believes that a strong ally such as Andrea might have a positive impact on the organization as well as the straight community. The Alliance advocacy director, Travis, is up in arms about this possibility, arguing that no "het" can provide the support and active voice the group needs. The social director, Allison, likes Andrea and finds her accepting, a factor that is important to Allison, who is still getting comfortable disclosing her identity to heterosexuals. Younger members of the group are mostly indifferent to the issue; they are mainly concerned with their own comfort level in the group.

Word has gotten out within the student government association (SGA), which Andrea advises, that there is a possibility that Andrea will become the LGBQQA advisor. The SGA president, Jeremy, views this possibility positively, as he would like more collaboration between student government and the LGBQQ community in order to provide learning opportunities and break down stereotypes on campus. Blaire, the SGA vice president, is shocked. She is now questioning Andrea's sexual orientation since she does not know why Andrea would be asked if she was not a lesbian and Blaire does not want any association with someone who may be "homosexual."

Andrea herself is interested in working with the alliance, as it would allow her to demonstrate that she is a strong ally to the LGBQQ community, but she is concerned about maintaining a good rapport with the student government officers.

◆ ◆ ◆

The scenario just presented illustrates in part the complexity of sexual identity in the lives of college students. Many students begin or accelerate exploration of their sexual identities during college (Evans & D'Augelli, 1996). For gay, lesbian, or bisexual students who have known they are not heterosexual earlier in their lives, college is often seen as a safer environment in which to explore and "come out" than their home environment. Since research indicates that as many as 10 percent of all college students identify as gay, lesbian, or bisexual and that others may be questioning their sexuality (Ellis, 1996), student affairs educators must understand the developmental challenges these students face and provide appropriate supports to assist them in navigating what is often a hostile environment (Evans & Rankin, 1998; Rankin, 2003).

Heterosexual students also find college an opportune time to explore and solidify their sexual values, needs, and attitudes (Chickering & Reisser, 1993), as well as their feelings about same-sex attraction and nonheterosexual individuals (Sullivan, 1998). However, heterosexuality has only recently received attention in the developmental literature. Bieschke (2002) stressed the importance of bringing sexual identity development into the awareness of heterosexuals to clarify important aspects of their sexuality as well as the privilege bestowed on heterosexuals by society.

In this chapter, we present an overview of lesbian, gay, and bisexual (LGB) identity development in the first section and of heterosexual development in the second section. Each section begins with a brief review of the evolution of theory and research, followed by a discussion of prominent models of gay, lesbian, and bisexual identity development and heterosexual identity development, respectively. We then discuss research and applications in the college setting specific to each model. We close the chapter with implications and suggestions for future directions. Although sometimes included in discussion of lesbian, gay, and bisexual identities, *transgender* identity is gender based and discussed with gender theories in Chapter Eighteen.

Gay, Lesbian, and Bisexual Identity Development

The first important studies of same-sex attraction, which in the past was considered pathological, focused on identifying its "cause" in order to find a "cure" (L. S. Brown, 1995). Another major debate in the literature has centered around the question of whether sexual orientation is innate (the essentialist argument) or fluid and changeable over time in response to context and interpersonal experiences (the constructionist position; Broido, 2000; L. S. Brown; Kitzinger, 1995). Broido, citing work by Epstein (1987) and Rhoads (1994), suggested that there may be a middle ground between these two positions that recognizes "that people experience and make meaning of their sexual orientation in a variety of ways, some experiencing it as a central, stable, and fundamental part of who they are and others experiencing more fluid identities" (p. 24).

In the early 1970s, the focus shifted away from the etiology of sexual orientation and viewing same-sex attraction as an illness to the development of a gay or lesbian identity (Cass, 1990; Fox, 1995). Gay and lesbian identity was distinguished from sexual acts between individuals of the same sex since many people engage in same-sex sexual behavior without identifying themselves as gay or lesbian (Cass, 1983–1984). Cass (1990) defined gay or lesbian identity as "the sense that a person has of *being* a homosexual/gay man/lesbian" (p. 246).

The term *homosexual identity* is found in earlier literature and generally refers only to sexual behavior. Klein (1990) stressed that sexual identity encompasses much more than sexual activity. He noted that emotional preference, social preference, lifestyle, and self-identification, as well as sexual attraction, fantasy, and behavior, must all be considered to provide a complete picture of sexual identity. Later theorists examined gay, lesbian, and bisexual identities encompassing emotional, lifestyle, and political aspects of life, as well as sexual aspects. This broader perspective is usually preferred in the LGB community since it has a more positive, comprehensive, and less clinical connotation (Levine & Evans, 1991).

Early models of identity development can be loosely grouped into two categories: sociological, which focus on the impact of community, development of social roles, and managing stigma, or on the coming-out process (Coleman, 1981–1982; DuBay, 1987; Lee, 1977); and psychological theories, including those of Plummer (1975) and Troiden (1989), which concentrate on internal changes, such as growing self-awareness, formation of a gay/lesbian/bisexual self-image, and personal decisions about identity management, experienced by individuals as they come to identify as nonheterosexual. Levine and Evans (1991) identified four general developmental levels common to these models: first awareness, self-labeling, community involvement and disclosure, and identity integration. The first model to remain in use over a period of time is the gay and lesbian identity model of Vivienne Cass (1979, 1996).

Cass's Model of Sexual Orientation Identity Formation

Cass's (1979) model (originally called homosexual identity formation) was based on her clinical work with gays and lesbians in Australia. Cass identified six stages of perception and behavior, moving from minimal awareness and acceptance of a gay or lesbian identity to a final stage in which gay or lesbian identity is integrated with other aspects of the self. She expanded her discussion of these stages in her later revision (Cass, 1996). The process of movement through these six stages is multifaceted, based on the interaction of personal needs, desires, and behaviors with biological factors (such as sex drive) and contextual variables (including the person's social class, geographical location, and race).

Cass (1983–1984) cautioned that not all gays and lesbians progress through all the stages, stressing that individuals make choices and play an active role in the development of their identities. In 1996, Cass introduced possible pathways leading to either movement to the next stage or foreclosure at the current stage. Earlier, she also indicated that sex-role socialization might result in differences in how males and females negotiate the developmental process (Cass, 1979). Cass (1990) argued that because societal norms view identity as fixed, and this belief also finds support in the gay and lesbian community, most people view their identity as essential rather than variable.

Cass's (1979, 1996) stages include both a cognitive component, reflecting how individuals view themselves, and an affective component, indicating how they feel about their own and others' perceptions. The stages are defined as follows:

- *Prestage 1.* Prior to the first stage, individuals perceive themselves as heterosexual and recognize this as a preferred state of being (Cass, 1996). As their perceptions change, increased conflict occurs between self-concept, behavior, and the perceptions of others, resulting in either movement to a new stage or identity foreclosure at this stage (Cass, 1979).
- *Stage 1: Identity confusion.* This stage begins with individuals' first awareness that their behavior or feelings could be labeled gay or lesbian (Cass, 1996). These perceptions may be accompanied by curiosity, confusion, or anxiety. Reducing discomfort is the primary focus of this stage.
- *Stage 2: Identity comparison.* Movement from stage 1 to stage 2 occurs once individuals have accepted the possibility that they might be gay or lesbian (Cass, 1979). Individuals must now determine how to manage the social alienation that accompanies a nonheterosexual identity. Their reactions may range from intense feelings of ostracism and pain to relief that previously unexplained feelings of difference are now clearer (Cass, 1996).
- *Stage 3: Identity tolerance.* Individuals entering stage 3 have acknowledged that they are probably gay or lesbian and seek out other gay and lesbian people to reduce their feelings of isolation (Cass, 1979). The nature of this contact can determine how individuals come to feel about themselves and their newly

determined identity. Some of the newer members of the LGBQQA in the opening scenario might be at this level.

- *Stage 4: Identity acceptance.* Although one's self-perception is clearly gay or lesbian at this stage, Cass (1996) noted that the person's "inner sense of self is still tenuous" (p. 244). Contacts with other gay and lesbian people are frequent, and friendships develop (Cass, 1990). Selective disclosure to heterosexual individuals also occurs. The greater commitment to a gay or lesbian identity made at this stage leads to a more stable sense of self (Cass, 1996). The norms and behavior of individuals' social groups influence how they choose to present themselves, particularly in mainstream heterosexual society. The LGBQQA's social director, Allison, may be at this stage since she is not always comfortable coming out to heterosexual individuals.

- *Stage 5: Identity pride.* In this stage, individuals focus on gay issues and activities and minimize contact with heterosexuals (Cass, 1979, 1996). Feelings of both pride in things gay and anger at things not gay propel individuals into activism and confrontation with an oppressive society. The angry reaction of the advocacy director, Travis, to the possibility of a straight ally serving as the LGBQQA advisor suggests he may be in stage 5.

- *Stage 6: Identity synthesis.* In the final stage of development, gay/lesbian and heterosexual worlds are less dichotomized, and individuals judge others on the basis of their personal qualities rather than solely on the basis of their sexual identity (Cass, 1979, 1996). Public and private identities become more congruent as individuals become comfortable and secure with who they are. Sexual identity is now seen as just one aspect of self rather than one's entire identity. The LGBQQA president, Steve, who is able to see that a straight advisor has much to offer the organization, appears to be in this stage.

Research. To validate her model, Cass (1984) developed two measures, the Homosexual Identity Questionnaire (HIQ) and the Stage Allocation Measure (SAM). She found that stage identification on the HIQ, a multiple-choice and checklist instrument describing feelings, thoughts, and actions that she categorized as indicative of specific stages in her model, generally corresponded to the one-paragraph descriptions of the stages presented on the SAM. Six stages were identifiable in her data; however, there was a great deal of overlap between stages 1 and 2 and stages 5 and 6, suggesting that a four-stage model might be a better fit (Eliason, 1996a). Eliason (1996a) also noted that the cross-sectional nature of the study made validation of the stage sequence impossible.

In 1983, Brady independently developed a measure of Cass's (1979) model for gay men called the Gay Identity Questionnaire (GIQ), which he later refined (Brady & Busse, 1994). Brady and Busse found significant relationships between stage and assessments of psychological well-being and adjustment to a gay or lesbian identity, as predicted by Cass's (1979) model. Levine (1997) demonstrated the utility of Brady's instrument for measuring the last three stages of lesbian identity development. A later validity study of the GIQ (Marszalek, Cashwell, Dunn, & Heard Jones, 2004) suggested that a two-stage approach in which gay identity is categorized at concrete (lower stages) versus abstract (upper stages) might be more appropriate than Cass's six-stage model.

Criticism of Cass's (1979, 1996) model of lesbian and gay identity development argued against her assumption that all individuals pass through the same six stages in order as they form their identities. Many studies examining whether the linear stage progression Cass (1979, 1996) proposed was evident in the lives of gay men and lesbians have provided evidence of a number of patterns rather than one linear, universal progression (Degges-White, Rice, & Myers, 2000; Kahn, 1991).

Cass's assumption that individuals must pass through an activist stage (stage 5) to achieve identity synthesis (stage 6) was rejected by Eliason (1996a) and Morris (1997) after their reviews of the research literature on the coming-out process, as well as by Degges-White et al. (2000), who conducted a qualitative study of adult lesbians to determine the validity of Cass's model for women in the twenty-first century. In addition, Whitman, Cormier, and Boyd (2000) suggested an additional stage beyond stage 6 that they would label "living out" (p. 17) because for many women in their study, disclosing their identity was no longer a choice but rather an aspect of who they were and how they lived.

The applicability of Cass's model to women has been especially challenged, as women tend to demonstrate more variability in identity formation than do men (Degges-White et al., 2000; Morris, 1997). Cass's failure to include participants who were diverse in age, race, and ethnicity has also been noted as a limitation (Morris).

Applications. In her 1996 chapter, Cass offered a number of implications directed at counselors and psychotherapists that are valuable for student affairs educators as well. She pointed out that individuals' behaviors may not be a true reflection of their internal feelings and that listening to how they describe their identities is important. Other literature on counseling gay, lesbian, and bisexual students also stresses the importance of being familiar with the issues students face at different stages of development (Mobley & Slaney, 1996). Ritter and Terndrup (2002) introduced stage-specific counseling interventions that include exploring and validating feelings associated with each stage.

Cass (1996) pointed out that sexual identity development intersects with other aspects of development. For example, Levine and Bahr (1989) found that students in the middle stages of Cass's (1979) model scored lower on the three scales of the SDTI-2 (developing purpose, developing autonomy, and developing mature interpersonal relationships) than those in either the earlier or later stages of sexual identity development, suggesting that sexual identity issues take precedence over other issues during the emotional middle period of sexual identity development.

Cass's (1996) model also underscores the importance of peer group interaction. As students' sexual identity develops, contacts with other lesbian and gay individuals influence how students come to see themselves (Cass, 1996). Thus, providing opportunities and encouragement for students to interact with other gay and lesbian persons, as in the LGBQQA, is helpful.

Critique. Several problems exist with the early sexual identity development models, most notably Cass's model (Frable, 1997; Levine & Evans, 1991). First, most of the models reflect the social and political forces of the 1970s when they were developed and may not reflect current social realities. For example, recent research has demonstrated that an integrated sense of identity can be achieved without moving through the period of anger and opposition toward heterosexuals that is included in most models developed during the early years of the gay rights movement when such feelings were prevalent in the face of strong societal homophobia and harassment (Eliason, 1996b).

Another perceived weakness in early models of gay and lesbian identity development is the failure to differentiate personal identity development from development of identity as a member of the gay and lesbian community (McCarn & Fassinger, 1996; Reynolds & Hanjorgiris, 2000). Cass and other theorists assumed that to be mentally healthy, a person must publicly identify as gay or lesbian and be active in the community.

Third, many of the early models lack a strong research base to support their suppositions (Eliason, 1996b; Frable, 1997; Reynolds & Hanjorgiris, 2000), and longitudinal studies that are necessary to really map development are rare (Frable). Recent studies of milestone events in the lives of gay men and lesbians, such as first awareness of same-sex attraction, labeling self as gay or lesbian, and becoming involved in the gay/lesbian community, have found great variability in the timing and ordering of these experiences rather than the clear linear progression Cass and others outlined (see Diamond & Savin-Williams, 2000; Maguen, Floyd, Bakeman, & Armistead, 2002; Parks, Hughes, & Matthews, 2004; Rosario, Schrimshaw, & Hunter, 2004).

Finally, because most of the early work on sexual identity development centered on gay men and white Eurocentric populations, many writers (Bilodeau & Renn, 2005; Levine & Evans, 1991; Frable, 1997; Reynolds & Hanjorgiris, 2000) have criticized its lack of generalizability to women, bisexuals, and people of color. Feminist theorists argued that the process of development is much more contextually determined for women than it is for men (Reynolds & Hanjorgiris). Bisexual identity, which has often been viewed as a form of foreclosed identity or a transitional stage between heterosexual and gay or lesbian identification (Fox, 1995, 1996), has more recently been legitimized as a separate sexual identity, the development of which is complex and variable (Ritter & Terndrup, 2002; Robin & Hamner, 2000; Rust, 2002). Finally, Fukuyama and Ferguson (2000) noted that a white Eurocentric bias is evident in most existing models of gay, lesbian, and bisexual identity development. They provided a number of examples, including these:

- Sexual orientation itself is a Western concept not found in all cultures (see also Bilodeau & Renn, 2005). For instance, Latino/as more often identify as bisexual than as gay or lesbian; the latter concepts are seen in the Latino culture as applying to whites only (Cintrón, 2000; Morales, 1989).
- The assumption that gay, lesbian, or bisexual people are always stigmatized does not hold in some cultures. For example, in some Native American cultures (particularly among those that have not been acculturated to white values), "two-spirit persons" are accepted and valued (W. Williams, 1996; A. Wilson, 1996).
- Models that suggest that coming out is necessary to achieve a positive lesbian, gay, or bisexual identity conflict with the community and family values of many cultures. In some Asian cultures, for example, the idea of sexual identity beyond the familial expectation for procreation is nonexistent, and same-sex attraction can be expressed only if it does not interfere with the person's prescribed role within the family (Chan, 1995).
- Integrating two central identities makes the process of identity formation more complex for people of color than it is for white individuals (Jones & Hill, 1996; Wall & Washington, 1991). For example, African Americans must negotiate both racial/ethnic identity development and sexual identity development, processes that are often in conflict given the norms and values of each community (Greene, 2000; Parks et al., 2004). In addition to ethnic and racial identities, the interaction of other social identities with gay, lesbian, and bisexual identity is important to acknowledge. For example, Harley, Nowak, Gassaway, and Savage (2002) stressed that "LGBT college students with disabilities have been relegated to a status of invisibility" (p. 525), in part because "persons with disability have been desexualized" (p. 527). Also, Valocchi (1999) argued that social class has played a significant role in how gay and lesbian identities have been formulated. Fukuyama and Ferguson (2000) stressed that cultural context, privilege and oppression, and social group memberships contribute significantly in gay, lesbian, and bisexual identity development. They also argued that intersection of multiple social identities—gender, ability status, social class, spiritual identity, race, and ethnicity, in addition to sexual identity—is critical in overall identity construction (see also Bilodeau & Renn, 2005; Eliason, 1996b; Poynter & Washington, 2005).

To overcome some of the criticisms of the earlier models of gay, lesbian, and bisexual identity development, Fassinger and D'Augelli proposed alternative models.

Fassinger's Model of Gay and Lesbian Identity Development

McCarn and Fassinger (1996) attempted to provide a more accurate model of lesbian identity development than that provided by earlier models. Their model was later validated for men as well (Fassinger & Miller, 1997). Fassinger and her colleagues (Fassinger & Miller; McCarn & Fassinger; Mohr & Fassinger, 2000) sought to address the criticism that Cass and other stage theorists equated identity disclosure and activism with higher stages of identity development. Their work also took into account cultural and contextual influences on development to a greater extent than many earlier stage theories, particularly those developed by psychologists (Fassinger, 1998a).

The Theory. Fassinger and her colleagues hypothesized two parallel processes of identity development: one related to individual sexual identity and the other focusing on group membership identity (Fassinger, 1998a). The former process involves internal awareness and acceptance of being lesbian or gay, while the latter centers around what it means to be gay or lesbian in society and one's role in the gay/lesbian community.

Each of the two processes consists of a four-phase sequence of development: awareness, exploration, deepening/commitment, and internalization/synthesis (Fassinger, 1998a). With regard to the development of individual identity, awareness involves perceiving oneself as different from other people. In the second phase, exploration, one begins to actively investigate feelings of attraction for individuals (or a particular person) of the same sex. In the deepening/commitment phase, one's sense of self as a gay or lesbian person is strengthened, and one's sexual identity becomes more secure and internalized. In the last phase of the individual identity process, one's sexual identity becomes a part of one's overall identity.

In the group membership identity process of the model introduced by Fassinger and her colleagues (Fassinger, 1998a), the first phase centers on awareness of the existence of people with different sexual orientations. In phase two, individuals begin to explore their relationship to the gay and/or lesbian community. In the opening scenario, members of the LGBQQA are doing this by being involved in the organization. In phase three, individuals make a personal commitment to the lesbian and gay community and accept the potentially negative consequences of being part of this group. The LGBQQA officers, who are often called on to speak for the group, are likely at this stage or the next one. The final phase of group membership identity is internalization of a minority group identity across contexts.

Fassinger (1998a) pointed out that a person could be in different phases of development with regard to each of these two processes but that development in one branch of the model could influence development in the other. Recycling through phases could also occur, particularly as individuals experience new environmental contexts. Unlike in other stage models, coming out to others is not assumed to be a prerequisite for identity integration in Fassinger's (1998a) model.

Research. Research conducted by Fassinger and her colleagues supports the validity of their model. McCarn (1991) studied identity development among a group of thirty-eight lesbians who were diverse with respect to age, education, race, ethnicity, and occupation, while Fassinger and Miller (1997) explored the applicability of the model for a similarly diverse group of thirty-four gay men. In both studies, support was found for each of the two processes as well as the four-phase sequence within each process. Degges-White et al. (2000) provided indirect support for Fassinger's model in their examination of the validity of Cass's (1979) model. Based on the findings of their qualitative study, they stated, "Perhaps [stage 4 of Cass's model] would be a better representation of the experience of lesbians if it was divided into two stages, one stage representing the more reflective inner process . . . and the second stage being a more external process where lesbians seek out community with each other" (p. 328). In their longitudinal study of two first-year students, Evans and Herriott (2004) also reported evidence of separate internal and external developmental processes similar to those in Fassinger's model. However, Stevens (2004) failed to find two processes of development among the gay men he interviewed.

Abes and Jones (2004) explored lesbian identity development in a diverse group of college women, focusing on the intersection of various dimensions of identity, including race, social class, and religion, with sexual identity. They also considered the influence of cognitive and interpersonal development on the manner in which students made meaning of their identities. As Fassinger (1998a) hypothesized, increased cognitive complexity appeared to be related to lesbian identity development. The multidimensionality of identity was evident in Abes and Jones's study, and they argued for a more complex understanding of identity development than that proposed by Fassinger (1998a).

Applications. Fassinger (1998a) stressed the importance of recognizing that gay and lesbian individuals may be in different places with regard to their individual and group identities. Because a student is not active in an organization such as the LGBQQA does not mean that he or she does not have a secure sense of self as gay or lesbian. Factors such as parental attitudes, level of support in the student's academic department, or partner's comfort with being out can all affect how open and involved a person is in the larger community. Conversely, a high level of community involvement does not necessarily mean that a student is personally secure with his or her individual identity. Understanding the two separate processes of development is important when working with gay and lesbian students.

Tomlinson and Fassinger (2003) explored the relationship of lesbian identity development, perceived campus climate, and career development for 192 lesbian and questioning college women. Their findings indicated that vocational development is influenced by campus climate and, to a lesser degree, by lesbian identity development status. They suggested that lesbian and questioning students might feel freer to explore both their sexual and vocational identities in an environment that is supportive. Thus, career counselors need to create a visibly welcoming environment for gay and lesbian students.

D'Augelli's Model of Lesbian, Gay, and Bisexual Development

Arguing against the essentialist notion of a linear identity development process, D'Augelli (1994a) introduced a life span model of gay, lesbian, and bisexual identity development based on the idea that identity is a "social construction," shaped to varying degrees by social circumstances and environment and changeable throughout life. D'Augelli (1994a) pointed out that the social invisibility of sexual orientation and the social and legal penalties associated with same-sex sexual expression represent two unique and powerful barriers to self-definition as gay, lesbian, or bisexual. Societal oppression can lead to feelings of panic, anxiety, and denial when individuals first become aware of thoughts and desires indicating same-sex attraction. Because of oppression and the feelings it elicits, developing a gay, lesbian, or bisexual identity takes time.

The Theory. D'Augelli's (1994a) life span model of lesbian, gay, and bisexual identity development takes into account "the complex factors that influence the development of people in context over historical time" (p. 317). Three sets of interrelated variables are involved in identity formation: personal actions and subjectivities, interactive intimacies, and sociohistorical connections.

Personal subjectivities and actions include individuals' perceptions and feelings about their sexual identities, as well as actual sexual behaviors and the meanings attached to them. In the opening scenario, for instance, Travis, the advocacy director, perceives that no heterosexual advisor could be supportive of the LGBQQA and actively opposes Andrea's selection.

Interactive intimacies include the influences of family, peer group, and intimate partnerships and the meanings attached to experiences with significant others. In the scenario, the officers of the LGBQQA are aware of the influence their new advisor can have on them; they are also influenced by each other in the group setting.

Sociohistorical connections are defined as the social norms, policies, and laws found in various geographical locations and cultures, as well as the values existing during particular historical periods. Certainly students today have greater opportunities to come together and live in a society that is more open about sexual orientation than did students in earlier decades of the twentieth century, when an organization such as LGBQQA could never have existed.

Assumptions of D'Augelli's Model. Accepting the assumptions of more general life span models (for example, Baltes, 1987), D'Augelli (1994a, 1994b) viewed development of sexual orientation as a life-long developmental process. Multiple changes can occur over time in attitudes, feelings, and behavior.

"Developmental plasticity," a concept that refers to human responsiveness to environmental and biological changes, is important in D'Augelli's (1994a) model. At certain times, sexual identity may be very fluid, while at other times, it will be more solidified. Hormonal changes, social circumstances, and peer relationships at different life stages are three factors that may influence development.

Another idea that D'Augelli (1994a, 1994b) borrowed from the life span perspective is that the developmental path of each individual is different. D'Augelli suggested that there may be more similarities in sexual self-definition in certain periods of life, such as late adulthood; in certain kinds of families, such as those that do not value difference; in certain communities, such as those that are highly homogeneous; and in certain historical periods, such as the 1950s. The degree of difference tends to increase in late adolescence and adulthood as persons are exposed to more models of behavior and have more choices about how to live their lives.

Finally, D'Augelli (1994a, 1994b) stressed the impact that individuals have on their own development. People not only react to social circumstances, they make choices and take action. Lesbian, gay, and bisexual people, particularly, shape their own identity, since our heterosexist culture provides little or no socialization for how to be gay, lesbian, or bisexual. In the LGBQQA, the students are defining for themselves what it means to be gay, lesbian, and bisexual personally and on their campus.

The Identity Development Process. D'Augelli (1994a) identified six interactive processes (not stages) involved in lesbian, gay, and bisexual identity development:

- *Exiting heterosexual identity* requires recognition that one's feelings and attractions are not heterosexual as well as telling others that one is lesbian, gay, or bisexual.

Attending a meeting of a group such as the LGBQQA is often a first step for college students in this process.

- *Developing a personal lesbian / gay / bisexual identity status* involves determining for oneself the unique meaning being gay, lesbian, or bisexual will have in one's life. One must also challenge internalized myths about what it means to be gay, lesbian, or bisexual. Developing a personal identity status must be done in relationship with others who can confirm ideas about what it means to be nonheterosexual. Members of groups such as the LGBQQA often do this for each other.

- *Developing a lesbian / gay / bisexual social identity* consists of creating a support network of people who know and accept one's sexual orientation. Determining people's true reactions can take time. Reactions may also change over time and with changing circumstances, such as whether an individual is involved in an intimate relationship. To some extent, all of the students attending the LGBQQA come seeking a support network. This need is more salient for students like Allison, the social director, who are less ready to be publicly out than others.

- *Becoming a lesbian / gay / bisexual offspring* involves disclosing one's identity to parents and redefining one's relationship after such disclosure. D'Augelli (1994a) noted that establishing a positive relationship with one's parents can take time but is possible with education and patience. This developmental process can be particularly troublesome for many college students who depend on their parents for financial as well as emotional support. Some of the LGBQQA members may be struggling with the issue of how to be themselves in their home environments without risking their parents' love and acceptance.

- *Developing a lesbian / gay / bisexual intimacy status* is a more complex process than achieving an intimate heterosexual relationship because of the relative invisibility of lesbian and gay couples in society. D'Augelli (1994a) noted, "The lack of cultural scripts directly applicable to lesbian/gay/bisexual people leads to ambiguity and uncertainty, but it also forces the emergence of personal, couple-specific, and community norms, which should be more personally adaptive" (p. 327). The college years are often a time when individuals establish their first meaningful relationships (Evans & D'Augelli, 1996). In addition to their other reasons for existence, groups like the LGBQQA serve as places to meet potential romantic partners or to see models of same-sex couples.

- *Entering a lesbian / gay / bisexual community* involves making varying degrees of commitment to social and political action. Some individuals never take this step, while others do so only at great personal risk, such as losing their jobs or housing. Some members of the LGBQ faculty and staff were reluctant to serve as the LGBQQA advisor because of the risks they perceived.

In summarizing his theory, D'Augelli (1994a) stated, "A revision of our operational definition of 'sexual orientation' must occur, allowing for the study of the continuities and discontinuities, of the 'flexibilities' and 'cohesiveness,' of sexual and affectional feelings across the lifespan, in diverse contexts, and in relationship to culture and history" (p. 331).

Research. In support of a life span perspective, researchers have documented many different patterns of gay, lesbian, and bisexual identity development and provided evidence that such development occurs over a wide age range (D'Augelli, 1994b; Savin-Williams, 1995). Environment has also been found to influence development. Because urban youth, for example, have more opportunity to meet gay, lesbian, and bisexual individuals and to be exposed to LGB culture, they also tend to come out earlier than youth living in rural communities (D'Augelli, 1991; Savin-Williams, 1995; Sears, 1991). Finally, Kahn (1991) and Rhoads (1994) reported that supportive family and friends facilitate formation of a positive LGB identity and self-disclosure.

In a study of identity development of lesbian, gay, and bisexual college students living in residence halls, Evans and Broido (1999) found that students' coming-out process was affected by the three factors D'Augelli (1994a) hypothesized as being involved: personal subjectivities and behaviors (the ways in which they perceived their experiences and how they chose to act on them), interactive intimacies (the attitudes, values, and behaviors of peers), and sociohistorical connections (past settings and specific residence hall environments in which the students lived). A second study, which examined the effect of first-year students' participation in an ethnographic investigation of the campus climate for lesbian, gay, and bisexual students, also revealed that involvement with the sociocultural environment of a college campus; interactions with significant others, including peers and mentors; and the students' actions and reflections on their experiences in the form of journals and debriefing sessions influenced the identity development of a gay student and a student questioning her sexual identity (Evans & Herriott, 2004).

In a study investigating aspects of gay students' identities and factors that influenced identity development, Stevens (2004) confirmed D'Augelli's (1994a) belief that sexual identity development is nonlinear and varies depending on context and the sense that gay men make of their situations. In particular, interactions with different people (peers, staff, faculty) led to revisions in the participants' identity. Critical incidents reported by the participants "centered around disclosure of their gay identity and assessment of their surroundings" (p. 201). The men reported that incidents of heterosexism and homophobia in the campus environment, as well as supportive statements and actions, had a significant effect on their willingness to disclose.

Love, Bock, Jannarone, and Richardson (2005), examining the link between lesbian and gay identity development and spiritual development among college students, found that the twelve lesbian and gay students in their study had all addressed four of the six developmental processes that D'Augelli (1994a) suggested as part of the identity development of lesbian and gay students. A significant majority had also dealt with the other two processes: developing intimacy status and coming out to parents. Their study validated the role of past experiences and environment (sociohistorical connections), the values and beliefs of parents and peers (interactive intimacies), and the meaning that the individuals made of their experiences (personal subjectivities) in the extent to which students were able to reconcile their sexual and spiritual identities. Love et al. stressed that nonlinear models of identity development, such as D'Augelli's (1994a), are more helpful than stage models when considering the interaction of multiple aspects of identity.

Applications. As D'Augelli's (1994a) theory suggested, environmental factors play a major role in the development of a positive gay, lesbian, or bisexual identity. Strategies for creating more supportive campus environments for lesbian, gay, and bisexual students can be found in Cramer (2002), Wall and Evans (2000), Sanlo (1998), D'Augelli (1996), Evans and D'Augelli (1996), and Evans and Wall (1991). An inclusive approach that addresses campus policies; provision of campus support services and resources specifically for lesbian, gay, and bisexual students; programming for heterosexual as well as gay, lesbian, and bisexual students; inclusion of content about gay, lesbian, and bisexual topics in the curriculum; supportive faculty and staff who are willing to act as advocates and role models; and active intervention to address homophobic acts are critical (D'Augelli, 1996; Evans & D'Augelli, 1996). "Safe zone" programs (Evans, 2002)—networks of individuals who identify themselves as available to provide support and information to gay, lesbian, and bisexual students—provide personal support that D'Augelli (1994a) viewed as important in identity development. They also provide visible signs of support that can make the climate appear more positive to gay, lesbian, and bisexual people.

Based on the findings of Evans and Broido's (1999) study of the coming out process for students in residence halls, Evans (2001), Evans and Broido (2002), and Evans, Reason, and Broido (2001) made specific recommendations designed to enhance the climate of college residence halls. Strategies included hiring LGB-affirmative staff and training them so they can effectively address homophobia and provide support to gay, lesbian, and bisexual students. The importance of developing policies to support lesbian, gay, and bisexual students and actively confronting acts of harassment was also stressed. Visible programming, curricular changes to educate students, and support groups and social activities where lesbian, gay, and bisexual students can meet other members of the community were recommended. Bourassa and Shipton (1991) and Schreier (1995) provide examples of affirming programming.

Heterosexual Identity Development

Perhaps because of the assumption that heterosexuality is normative, almost no attention has been given to heterosexual identity development (Bieschke, 2002). As Kitzinger and Wilkinson (1993) noted, normative identities "are always less well theorized, less articulated, less self-conscious, than are oppositional or oppressed identities; lack of reflectiveness is the privilege of power" (p. 32).

Early Views of Heterosexuality

While Freud did view heterosexuality as a constructed identity, with the gender of individuals to whom persons are attracted being influenced by children's interactions with their parents, most theorists who followed Freud took an essentialist position, viewing heterosexual identity as innate and fixed (Eliason, 1995). By the end of the twentieth century, theorists again began arguing that sexual identity development was a fluid process influenced by historical period, societal norms, and culture (Katz, 1995; Wilkinson & Kitzinger, 1993). Feminist writers (Hyde & Jaffee, 2000; Rich, 1980) contributed to the constructivist position, arguing that social forces such as family, peers, the media, and the educational system played a significant, though often unconscious, role in pushing women to adopt a heterosexual identity.

Recently some efforts have been made to explain heterosexual identity formation from a developmental standpoint. For example, using Marcia's (1980) identity development model, Eliason (1995) found evidence of identity exploration and commitment in heterosexual students' written explanations of how their sexual identity was formed and how it affected their lives. Worthington, Savoy, Dillon, and Vernaglia (2002) pointed out limitations of this model, including its failure to account for variation in commitment and exploration across time.

Stage models of heterosexual identity development have also been introduced. Sullivan (1998) modified Hardiman and Jackson's (1992) racial identity development model to describe both lesbian/gay/bisexual and heterosexual identity. Sullivan's model consisted of five stages of increasing awareness and complexity regarding sexual identity. Suggesting that heterosexual identity development parallels white identity development, Simoni and Walters (2001) also proposed a five-stage model starting with a complete lack of awareness of heterosexism progressing to full acknowledgment of the heterosexual bias in society. Worthington et al. (2002) pointed out the limitations of stage models of heterosexual identity development, particularly noting their inability to allow variation and fluidity in the developmental process.

Using a somewhat different approach, Mohr (2002) proposed that heterosexual identity derives from the interaction of individuals' "working models of sexual orientation" (p. 539) and their "core motivations" (p. 539). Individuals' working models (beliefs) about heterosexual identity are determined by their sexual attractions, fantasies, and behavior, as well as their exposure to information about sexual orientation from external sources such as the media, significant others, and societal institutions. The roles played by individuals' core motivations—to be accepted by others and to maintain an internally consistent self-concept—suggest that individuals' ideas about sexual identity are influenced by both the views of people who are important to them and their own need for congruence between how they experience heterosexuality internally and express it publicly. In a qualitative study, Mueller and Cole (2009) found evidence of Mohr's working models of sexual orientation among the fourteen self-identified heterosexual students interviewed.

The Multidimensional Model of Worthington and His Colleagues

Worthington, Savoy, Dillon, and Vernaglia (2002) have introduced the most comprehensive model of heterosexual identity development to date. Unlike most other models that focus primarily on psychological processes in development, their model also considers social aspects of identity, such as the roles played by group affiliation and privilege. Worthington et al. (2002) defined heterosexual identity development as "the individual and social processes by which heterosexually identified persons acknowledge and define their sexual needs, values, sexual expression, and characteristics of sexual partners" (p. 510). They also stressed that understanding of the privilege and oppression associated with majority and minority group status was important in heterosexual identity development. They included attitudes, values, and beliefs about lesbian, gay, and bisexual individuals as part of their model.

Worthington et al. (2002) identified six interactive factors as influential in the development of sexual identity: (1) biology, particularly physical maturation; (2) microsocial context, including the values and attitudes held by significant others; (3) gender norms and socialization; (4) culture, including place and time; (5) religious orientation, including the extent to which one adheres to a fundamentalist belief system and the importance of religion in one's life; and (6) systemic homonegativity, sexual prejudice, and privilege; that is, the discrimination and negativity targeted at gays, lesbians, and bisexuals and the benefits society awards to heterosexuals.

The Theory. As in Fassinger's (1998a) model of lesbian/gay identity formation, Worthington et al. (2002) included two interactive processes in their model of heterosexual identity development: (1) an internal process of identity development related to one's growing awareness and acceptance of "one's sexual needs, values, sexual orientation and preferences for activities, partner characteristics, and modes of sexual expression" (p. 510); and (2) an external process of developing a social identity in which one sees oneself as belonging to a specific sexual identity group (predominantly heterosexual, but possibly having other identities, such as celibate, voyeuristic, swinging, and so forth). A person's social identity also includes seeing oneself as part of a group with specific attitudes toward those whose sexual identities are nonheterosexual.

Drawing on concepts from Marcia's (1980) identity development model, Worthington et al. (2002) proposed five developmental statuses applicable to individual and group identity. These statuses are not rigid, can be revisited at different points in the individual's life, and may be arrived at consciously or unconsciously as a result of both cognitive and behavioral learning experiences. As such, there are many different paths and outcomes associated with the heterosexual identity development process.

The first status discussed by Worthington et al. (2002) is *unexplored commitment*. Similar to Marcia's (1980) foreclosed identity status, unexplored commitment is characterized by unconscious acceptance of a sexual identity largely defined by the expectations of society and important people in one's life; individuals are minimally, if at all, cognizant of their dominant status and, because of the heterosexist assumptions and biases of society, usually exhibit negative attitudes toward individuals who are not heterosexual. It is likely that Blaire, the SGA vice president in the opening scenario, is in this stage of development, as her attitudes about sexuality appear quite rigid. Because movement out of unexplored commitment requires conscious choice, one cannot later return to this status.

Worthington et al.'s (2002) second status, *active exploration*, which is similar to Marcia's (1980) moratorium identity status, consists of careful consideration of one's sexual desires, values, and preferred sexual activities and involves both cognitive and behavioral exploration; it may lead the individual into either of two statuses: deepening and commitment or diffusion. At the group level, the individual becomes aware of the privilege that is automatically ascribed to individuals who profess a heterosexual identity—either questioning these benefits or more actively asserting one's rights to them. Views of nonheterosexual individuals will vary widely in this status but are likely to be somewhat more positive than in unexplored commitment. Given the openness that the SGA president, Jeremy, demonstrated in the opening scenario, it is possible that he is actively exploring his heterosexuality.

Worthington et al.'s (2002) third status, *diffusion,* is similar to Marcia's (1980) identity diffusion status in which the individual does not engage in either exploration or commitment. Diffusion is often the result of crisis and may be associated with psychological distress. Persons in this status may actively reject the heterosexual identity expected by others and exhibit a willingness to try new behaviors without considering the implications of their choices. Individuals may enter diffusion from any of the other identity statuses, but the only path out of diffusion is through active exploration.

In the fourth status of Worthington et al.'s (2002) model, *deepening and commitment,* individuals have a more thoughtful and complex understanding of their individual and group sexual identities, as well as a heightened awareness of oppression and privilege. While their attitudes toward lesbian, gay, and bisexual individuals may vary, their positions are carefully considered, self-chosen, and coherent. Although similar in many ways to identity achievement in Marcia's (1980) model, *deepening and commitment* is different from Marcia's achievement status in that it is often the result of developmental maturation rather than active exploration because of the strong societal norms that accept a very narrow range of sexual behaviors. Andrea, the potential LGBQQA advisor, certainly seems to have a strong commitment to her identity that would indicate she is in this status. Individuals may move out of this status into synthesis or back into active exploration or diffusion.

In the final status of Worthington et al.'s (2002) model, *synthesis,* "individual sexual identity, group membership identity, and attitudes toward sexual minorities merge into an overall self-concept, which is conscious, volitional, and (hopefully) enlightened" (p. 519). As such, this status is the most sophisticated and adaptive. In this status, other social identities, such as gender, race, ethnicity, and religious beliefs, are compatible with the individual's sexual identity. It is possible for individuals to move out of synthesis and back into either active exploration or diffusion if faced with significant challenges to their belief systems.

Research. In an ongoing program of research, Worthington and his colleagues have developed two instruments based on their model that show great promise for further exploration of two components of heterosexual identity development: the Lesbian, Gay, and Bisexual Knowledge and Attitudes for Heterosexuals (LGB-KASH), which measures attitudes toward lesbian, gay, and bisexual people

(Worthington, Dillon, & Becker-Schutte, 2005), and the Measure of Sexual Identity Exploration and Commitment (MoSIEC), a measure of sexual identity development (Worthington, Navarro, Savoy, & Hampton, 2008). Both instruments need further validation.

Initial studies based on Worthington et al.'s (2002) model support its validity. For instance, Worthington et al. (2005) demonstrated a strong relationship between positive attitudes toward lesbian, gay, and bisexual people and the extent to which individuals had explored their own sexual identities. In a later study involving 178 practicing psychotherapists and therapists in training, Dillon, Worthington, Soth-McNett, and Schwartz (2008) found that individuals who reported sexual identity exploration and commitment on the MoSIEC also reported being more confident of their ability to work effectively with LGB clients than those who had less fully explored their sexual identity.

Worthington et al.'s (2008) MoSIEC offers great potential for comparing the sexual identity development processes of gay, lesbian, bisexual, and heterosexual individuals. Preliminary research suggests that they are different. For example, in a study using a measure of Marcia's (1966) ego identity statuses, Konik and Stewart (2004) found that heterosexually identified college students scored higher on identity foreclosure and moratorium than students who identified as gay, lesbian, or bisexual, while the former scored higher on identity achievement. Heterosexual students were also less likely than LGB students to see sexual identity formation as a process requiring effort and intentionality. In a qualitative study, Mueller and Cole (2009) found that heterosexual students had rarely considered their sexual identity. Their data suggested that exploration related to sexual identity was subtle and less conscious than Worthington et al. (2002) proposed. A study comparing LGB and heterosexual identity development using the MoSIEC is needed.

Applications. Several implications can be derived from Worthington et al.'s (2002) model. As these authors pointed out, sexual identity is often an issue that clients bring up in counseling sessions. Worthington et al.'s (2002) heterosexual identity development model can provide guidance in working with clients who identify as heterosexual. Heterosexual counselors and student affairs educators would also benefit from having a clearer understanding of their own sexual identity development process in order to more clearly understand the sexual diversity of individuals with whom they work (Hoffman, 2004).

Mohr's (2002) model suggests that LGB-affirmative environments are influential in shaping positive working models of heterosexual orientation. Being around others who are secure in their sexual identity and affirmative of sexual diversity provides the necessary context and motivation for the self-exploration and commitment Worthington et al. (2002) have suggested as precursors to achievement of a synthesized heterosexual identity. Thus, focusing on development of an affirmative environment in which individuals can explore and grow is as important as working with the individuals themselves.

Critique and Future Directions

In recent years, research and theory about sexual identity development has increased in quantity and quality. Models are much more sophisticated and inclusive than were initial attempts to describe the formation of sexual identity.

The four theories reviewed in depth in this chapter—those of Cass, Fassinger, D'Augelli, and Worthington et al.—explore the interaction of psychological and sociological variables in formation of identity and the differential outcomes that result. D'Augelli, in particular, took issue with the rigidity of earlier stage models and presented an alternative that allows fluidity and variation in identity development. His theory has generated more research in college settings than the other models and has led to theory-to-practice applications.

Problems remain, however. First, too few attempts have been made to validate the theoretical propositions that have been advanced. Study of identity and factors related to identity development is preliminary at best. Retrospective self-report does not always present a reliable picture of reality, and it is difficult to draw any firm conclusions about developmental processes based on cross-sectional studies; almost no longitudinal research has been reported. More effort needs to be focused on development of assessment techniques and research designs to validate models of sexual identity development. The work of Worthington and his colleagues is a good start.

Researchers also need to consider the interaction of sexuality and other social identities. Developmental theorists, particularly Jones and McEwen (2000) and Abes, Jones, and McEwen (2007), have demonstrated the importance of considering identity development as an integrated process; researchers need to explore the roles that gender, ethnicity, religion, race, disability, class, and other identities play in sexual identity formation.

Sociocultural influences on development also warrant further exploration. Historical time, geography, and cultural norms all contribute to the sexual identity development process. A typology model (Dilley, 2002, 2005) based on an analysis of the lives of gay men in college between 1945 and 1999 shows promise for explaining the different ways in which gay men see themselves at different historical times and how they live out their identities. The influences of societal values at particular times are worthy of consideration as well.

Of particular interest is the effect of acculturation on development of sexual identity for second- and third-generation Americans. Exploration of sexual identity development in non-Western cultures is also important for an overall understanding of the role of culture in identity development.

Bieschke (2002) pointed out the need for an integrated model of sexual identity development that would explain the development of both gay/lesbian/bisexual and heterosexual identities. Theory development along this line would lessen the dichotomization of sexuality and further understanding of the process of identity formation for all people. The development by Worthington and his colleagues (2008) of the MoSIEC, a general measure of sexual identity development applicable across sexual orientation identities, is a step forward in this area.

In addition, as Broido (2000) argued, a resolution to the essentialist/constructionist debate is needed. It seems likely that sexual feelings are innate and sexual identity is constructed in interaction with the environment. This idea deserves further exploration. What is most important, however, as Broido reminded us, are the personal definitions individuals use to describe their sexual identities. The implications of personal identity definitions for other outcomes, such as self-esteem and decision making, require further study.

This chapter underscores the limited number of studies that have examined sexual identity development in college settings or ways that sexual identity development theory can contribute to intentional design of strategies to enhance identity formation. We encourage higher education scholars to build on the research that is available and to develop and evaluate interventions to facilitate the sexual identity development of students.

CHAPTER EIGHTEEN

GENDER AND GENDER IDENTITY DEVELOPMENT

Prema, Ayeesha, and Kim left their first gender studies class and walked across the street to the coffee shop. There they met up with friends Gabe and Sanjay, who greeted them, "Hey ladies. How was class? Are you going to learn everything you need to know to be women of the twenty-first century?"

"Come on, guys, lay off. It's about power and politics, not hair and makeup!" replied Prema. "Besides, it's not a class *for women*, it's a class *about gender*. And there are two guys in it. You should think about it. You might learn something, and it's not too late to do a drop/add."

"Thanks, but I've got a full schedule of engineering classes. They're killing us now that we're seriously into the major. Come to think of it, now that we're juniors, there are hardly any girls left in my lab section. I wonder what happened to them? Maybe they couldn't handle the pressure?"

"Or didn't like the profs," Gabe added. "Some of them are pretty tough on the girls, or just ignore them. Dr. Sharp looked really surprised when that one girl showed up for class today."

Kim joined in, "Guys, has it ever occurred to you that people in college might be *women*, not *girls*? We don't call you *boys*, you know."

"Gosh, Kim, one class and already you're a feminist! Touchy, touchy," replied Gabe. "What? Are you going to join the Lesbian Alliance next?"

"No, seriously, Gabe. I'm starting to think about all the ways that this campus centers around men, with 'the girls' kind of tagging along. There's football, of course, with the dance team and cheerleaders on the sidelines. And the mascot— who thought up that 'Bombardiers' thing, with the 'Lady Bombardiers' as an afterthought, like who would have imagined that we'd have women athletes? Men run the student newspaper and student government. Women do the caretaking—as RAs, community service leaders, campus tour guides, all that stuff. And don't get me started on how my sorority sisters treat the fraternity guys. I love them to death, but when it's time for pairing up for parties, they seem to forget that they're smart, strong women."

Sanjay paused, then said, "I don't know, Kim. I see what you're saying, but I also think that you're making a big deal out of stuff that just is the way it is. Do you think it's about guys and girls—sorry, men and women—or about the way the world is? Aren't there real differences between me and you, based on our genes? I'm not saying things like intelligence—I'm pretty sure that you're way smarter than me!—but things like size and strength and how guys like to be rougher and more competitive. And women are more nurturing and pay more attention to relationships, at least in my family. My sisters were always playing 'house,' while my brother and I were out building forts. Maybe some of these things are built in."

Ayeesha had been quiet throughout the conversation. "It's possible. I had a boy cousin who wanted to play with my dolls, and that didn't go over so well with the family. But I wonder," she said, "if some of this is also about culture. Being black is what matters first and foremost. When it comes down to it, it doesn't matter if you're a guy or a girl, a man or a woman; being black is what other people see first. Of course, *within* the black community, we see the distinctions really clearly between men and women. I feel like on campus there's only one way to be a black woman if you want to be accepted in the group. And our black men have to represent, you know what I mean? So I'm not into breaking down gender like you are, Kim, but I am really curious about how black men and women can support each other, even though we're really different in some ways."

"Yeah," Prema added. "I feel Indian first, then female. But also 'Indian-female' in a way that can't be separated out."

"Really?" asked Kim. "You don't feel like a woman first and foremost? Maybe because I don't have to think about being white, I think more about gender first."

"Now that, Kimberly Ann, is another subject. We'd better save that for next class!" laughed Ayeesha. "Let's get some coffee and see if we can convince these guys—no, men—that they should drop their engineering lab and join us in our gender studies class for some enlightenment!"

◆ ◆ ◆

Like race, gender is a concept so deeply embedded in U.S. culture that it can be almost invisible, even as it shapes everyday decisions, first impressions, self-concept, and academic, career, and social aspirations. When Kim, Ayeesha, and Prema have their awareness of gender as a framing concept raised, they begin to see how it shapes their life on campus. Gabe and Sanjay wonder where the women have gone in their engineering major, and Kim identifies several gendered contexts of student life. As women of color, Ayeesha and Prema point to the interaction of gender and race in their lives, and the students recognize that their ideas about gender were shaped in childhood, through games of "house," building forts, and dolls. Words that convey gender, such as *ladies, guys, girls,* and *women,* are part of the collegiate patois, as are gendered icons (mascots, athletic teams) and activities (sororities and fraternities, leadership roles, activities). These students also wonder about the ways that gender and sex differences are built in biologically, and how much might be shaped by expectations of, for example, who plays with dolls or becomes an engineer. While their ideas about gender may have been shaped years before they came to college, the ways that gender influences their lives remain profound.

This chapter provides an introduction to important concepts related to sex, gender, and gender identity. It introduces research and theories related to how individuals come to understand their gender identity, whether they are cisgender (that is, their gender identity matches the sex observed at birth; see Green, 2006) or transgender (their gender identity is different from their observed sex at birth). Applications of research to college students are presented and suggestions for future directions offered.

Foundational Concepts: Sex, Gender, and Gender Identity

Although sometimes the words are used interchangeably, *sex* and *gender* are distinct concepts. *Sex* is biological, and *gender* refers to the "culturally shaped expression of sexual differences: the masculine way in which men should behave and the feminine way in which women should behave" (Gender, n.d.). *Sex* and *gender* are thus very closely related, but they are not synonymous, and an individual's gender cannot be assumed in all cases to match what is expected based on his or her sex. Research over several decades (see Bem, 1981b, 1983; Deaux, 1985; Kohlberg, 1966; Stiver, 1991) provides evidence that in most cases, one's *gender identity,* or sense of self as male, female, or in between (Lev, 2004; Wilchins, 2002), is fixed in childhood, and perhaps intensified in early adolescence (Galambos, Almeida, & Petersen, 1990), well before students enter college. For the small percentage of the population for whom gender identity does not align with biological sex (that is, a female who does not identify as being a woman or a male who does not identify with being a man), some of whom may identify as *transgender,* college can be a time of identity exploration and expression, and sometimes also a time of isolation and harassment (Beemyn, 2005; Bilodeau, 2005, 2009; Bilodeau & Renn, 2005; McKinney, 2005; Pusch, 2005).

The relationships between and among the concepts of sex, gender, and gender identity are important to understand before knowing more about how gender identity is experienced by cisgender and transgender students. Queer theorists (for example, Bornstein, 1994; Butler, 1990, 2004; Jagose, 1997) have pointed out the ways that these categories, as well as sexual orientation, have been posed as binaries; that is, common understandings of sex and gender, for example, have been framed around the binaries of male/female and masculine/feminine. Gender identity in a binary system is either "man" or "woman," and sexual orientation is "heterosexual" or "homosexual" (based on one's sex, gender, and gender identity in relation to the sex, gender, and gender identity of the persons to whom one is attracted). According to Lev (2004), in such a binary system, sex, gender identity, gender role (the enactment of gender), and sexual orientation are assumed to align and to lead to the next, as in Figure 18.1.

In Lev's (2004) binary model, "If a person is a male, he is a man; if a person is a man, he is masculine; if a person is a masculine male man, he will be attracted to a feminine female woman; if a person is a female, she is a woman; if a person is a woman, she is feminine; if a person is a feminine female woman, she will be attracted to a masculine male man" (p. 94).

Lev was not the first to question this binary construction. Sandra Bem, creator of the widely used Bem Sex-Role Inventory (Bem, 1974, 1981a), proposed that masculinity and femininity were not opposites to be measured against one another, but characteristics that could be measured in two spheres, with a low-to-high scale for each. Bem (1983, 1993) called the process by which sex-based socialization affects the development of behaviors considered gender appropriate "gender schema theory" and raised the question of "dismantling gender polarization and compulsory heterosexuality" (Bem, 1995, p. 329).

As an alternative to a set of binary categories, linked to one another by assumptions of causal relationships (sex causes gender, which leads to appropriate gender role and sexual orientation), Lev (2004) proposed a model (Figure 18.2) in which each element is on a continuum and exists in interaction but not causation with other elements. Such a model provides for the reality that some people are born "intersex," or having biological (for example, genetic, physical) traits of males and females (Fausto-Sterling, 1993), that one's internal sense of gender may not be exclusively as a man or as a woman, that gender role may be—as Bem (1981b, 1993) proposed—both masculine and feminine, and that sexual orientation may be toward individuals of more than one sex, gender, and gender role (for example, bisexual). Lev proposed as well that "in any category people can change their behavior, presentation, or identity and none of these categories represents an

FIGURE 18.1. LEV'S (2004) CONCEPTUALIZATION OF BINARY SYSTEMS OF SEX, GENDER IDENTITY, GENDER ROLE, AND SEXUAL ORIENTATION

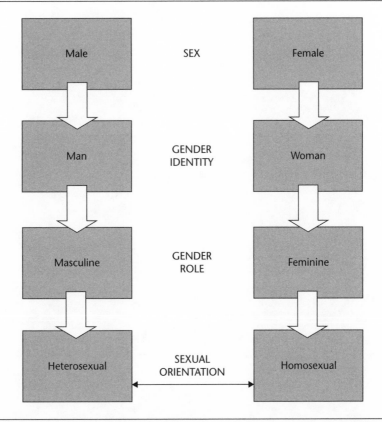

Source: Transgender Emergence: Therapeutic Guidelines for Working with Gender-Variant People and Their Families by A. I. Lev. © 2004 by Haworth Press/Taylor & Francis Books. Reproduced with permission of Haworth Press/Taylor & Francis Books.

immutable entity" (p. 96). This fluidity within and across categories, in the present and across time, represents a different way of thinking about gender identity and its relationship to sex, gender, and sexual orientation.

Gender Identities

If one's socialized gender roles align as expected with one's biological sex, one's gender identity can be considered cisgender, sometimes called "traditionally gendered" or "nontransgender" (Bilodeau, 2009; Green, 2006). A person whose

FIGURE 18.2. RELATIONSHIP AMONG SEX, GENDER, GENDER ROLE, AND SEXUAL ORIENTATION WHEN ALL ARE FLUID AND ON A CONTINUUM

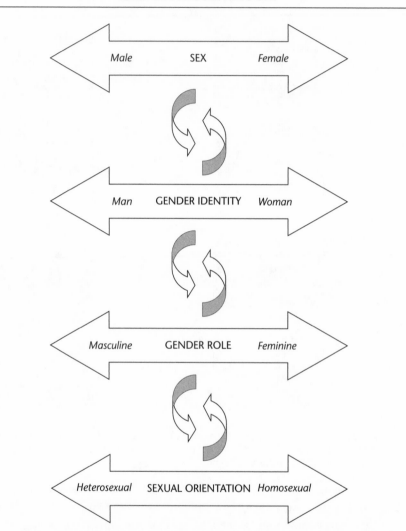

gender identity and gender roles do not align as expected with biological sex may be considered transgender (Bornstein, 1994; Lev, 2004; Wilchins, 2002). It is important to note that not everyone would call himself or herself by these terms, and there may be additional ways of considering gender identity that fall between or beyond these categories. In the cisgender/transgender approach to gender identity, individuals who are male and identify as men or who are female and identify as women are cisgender; individuals who are male but do not identify as men (they may identify as women or somewhere else on the gender identity continuum from man to woman), or are female but do not identify as women, are transgender.

Scholars have pointed out that there is more variation within than across gender categories (Deaux, 1985). Masculinity and femininity, for example, vary widely among men, as they do among women (Bem, 1981b). Masculinity and femininity, then, are not wholly reliable predictors of an individual's gender identity. A female student with strong masculine traits may identify as a cisgender woman, just as a feminine male student may identify as a man. Decoupling gender roles from sexual orientation, as Lev (2004) would suggest, these students may be heterosexual, lesbian, gay, or bisexual. Their gender identity does not determine their sexual orientation.

Transgender Students

In the college experience of students who identify as transgender, gender identity and sexual orientation may be more complicated matters than they are for cisgender students. As in much of the rest of society, college campuses are governed by a set of assumptions that Bilodeau (2009) called "genderism," which call on all members of a community to express their gender identities in ways that align as expected with their observed sex and subscribe to a gender binary that allows for masculine (male) men and feminine (female) women. Students whose gender expression—the ways in which they publicly enact gender roles through clothing, grooming, speech, posture, and other behaviors—does not conform to the expectations of peers and faculty report being subject to alienation, harassment, and violence (Beemyn, 2005; Bilodeau, 2005, 2009). Even allowing for within-gender variation, the penalties for stepping beyond the boundaries of what is considered acceptable can be harsh.

Yet transgender students are increasingly visible in U.S. higher education, and their experiences are the subject of an increasing empirical, theoretical, and practical literature (for example, Beemyn, 2005; Bilodeau, 2005, 2009; Bilodeau & Renn, 2005; Carter, 2000; McKinney, 2005; Pusch, 2005). According to this literature, transgender students may find college a place for identity exploration or for expression of a gender identity that they had not previously named or expressed publicly. For the first time, transgender students may find a community of other trans people, and they may experiment with gender expression, trying on masculine or feminine expression.

The operation of genderism (Bilodeau, 2009), however, may constrict opportunities for students' gender identity exploration. The ongoing separation of men and women on athletic teams, in some campus activities (for example, fraternities and sororities), and in public facilities (locker rooms, restrooms) may pose challenges to transgender students who are exploring new modes of gender expression. Some features of campus life, such as residence hall rooms assigned by sex, may be unavoidable, even if other single-sex/gender venues are managed through avoidance (by, for example, changing at home instead of using a locker room designated for males or females).

Cisgender Students

Genderism's twin values—gender expression conforming to expectations based on observed sex and a firmly etched gender binary—also influence the college experiences and identities of cisgender students. Historically "college men" and "college women" fulfilled clear gender and social roles (see Horowitz, 1987). Abundant and persistent evidence on gender-related phenomena including college, academic major, and career choices (Harris & Harper, 2008; Sax & Bryant, 2004), dating and socialization (Handler, 1995; Holland & Eisenhart, 1990), body image and eating disorders (Cash, Morrow, Hrabosky, & Perry, 2004; Feingold & Mazzella, 1998), alcohol use (Harper, Harris, & Mmeje, 2005; Wechsler, Dowdall, Davenport, & Rimm, 1995), and attitudes related to rape (Hinck & Thomas, 1999; Nagel, Matsuo, McIntyre, & Morrison, 2005) supports the claim that traditional gender roles and expectations continue to play a central role in the lives of undergraduate students.

For cisgender students, violating gender norms by being a "too masculine" woman or too "feminine" man has consequences. For example, harassment of and violence against lesbian, gay, and bisexual (LGB) students, regardless of their gender identities, are attributed in part to outwardly directed reactions of hatred and fear generated by LGB students' apparent lack of conformity to expected sex/gender identity/gender role/sexual orientation linkages (Kimmel, 1994; Rankin, 2003). Antigay epithets, invoking female body parts to insult men, and the use of *bitch* as an all-purpose put-down (implying that the worst thing to call a man is a demeaning term for a woman and that the worst thing to call a woman is an assertive, gender-nonconforming woman) provide additional evidence of the ways that gender—and commenting on others' gender—operate on campus to reinforce expected roles and norms (Davis, 2002; Hamilton, 2007; Handler, 1995; Kimmel, 1994). Although gender roles and norms are reinforced on campus, students by and large come to campus with gender identities well established (Harris & Harper, 2008). There is some evidence, however, that the college experience may also influence perceptions of gender roles. The next section describes how gender identity develops before and, to a certain extent, in college.

Gender Identity Development

Gender identity development has been shown to begin in early childhood and is believed to be well established before even traditional-age college students arrive on campus (see Bem, 1981a, 1983; Davis, 2002; Deaux, 1985; Galambos et al., 1990; Harris & Harper, 2008; Kohlberg, 1966; Stiver, 1991). Yet aspects of student life may challenge the identities students bring to campus, or reinforce existing gender identities. There is no predominant model of gender identity development that applies to college students, especially to cisgender students. Much of the literature on gender identity development relates to clinical populations of transgender-identified youth and adults. The complexity of the sex/gender identity/gender role triad and the lack of a unified language (some authors use *sex* and *gender* interchangeably; some use different terms from others for the same concept) confound attempts to identify a single model that describes gender identity development in college students. Yet theories converge on the idea that one's sense of one's masculinity and femininity and the person-environment interactions related to gender roles and expression are key components of gender identity, and gender identity is related to other aspects of overall psychosocial identity. Thus, this section describes Bem's (1981b) gender schema, gender schema on campus, transgender identity development, and gender as a domain within emerging models of multidimensional identity development.

Bem's Gender Schema as Cognitive-Developmental and Social Learning Theory

Sandra Bem (1983) eschewed Freudian theories of sex typing in favor of gender schema theory, which incorporates elements of cognitive-developmental theory and social learning theory. Bem (1983) claimed that this combination of individual/agentic and person-environment approaches accounts for cross-cultural aspects of self-identity and sex differences, as well as socially constructed gender expectations that are reinforced (or punished, in the breach) as the individual interacts with his or her environment. Bem (1983) wrote:

> In particular, gender schema theory proposes that sex typing derives in large measure from gender-schematic processing, from a generalized readiness on the part of the child to encode and to organize information—including information about the self—according

to the culture's definitions of maleness and femaleness. Like cognitive-developmental theory, then, gender schema theory proposes that sex typing is mediated by the child's own
cognitive processing. However, gender schema theory further proposes that gender-schematic
processing is itself derived from the sex-differentiated practices of the social community.
Thus, like social learning theory, gender schema theory assumes that sex typing is a learned
phenomenon and, hence, that it is neither inevitable nor un-modifiable. (pp. 117–118)

This attention to interpersonal, intrapersonal, and epistemological development is not unique to Bem or unheard of among student development researchers; the concept of self-authorship (Kegan, 1984) and some theories about
multiple dimensions of identity development (Abes & Jones, 2004; Abes, Jones, &
McEwen, 2007) also relate these three areas to one another. Bem (1981b, 1983)
claimed that these gender schemas are developed in early childhood, by age three
or four, a period in human development not well attended to by most student
development theories involving the emergence of self-authorship or multiple
dimensions of identity.

Bem's (1981b, 1983) theory rests on three key research findings. First, gender schema theory is based on the "observation that the developing child invari-
ably learns his or her society's cultural definitions of maleness and femaleness"
(p. 603), including anatomy, family and work roles played by members of different sexes, and emotional characteristics of various community members. Then,
in accordance with cognitive-developmental theory, the child learns to recognize
and organize incoming information in gender-based categories. As a cognitive
structure, a gender schema comprises networks of ideas and information that
filter perceptions, before the child is even aware of this process. Gender thus
becomes a cross-categorical sorting mechanism for items as apparently disparate as colors (pink for girls, blue for boys), personality traits (gentle for women,
aggressive for men), career aspirations (teacher, nurse, professional football player,
firefighter), and hobbies (dance, sports). The cognitive process predetermines
what will be perceived and then categorizes perceptions into existing categories
of girl/woman/female/feminine and boy/man/male/masculine. Bem (1983)
noted, "Like schema theories generally, gender schema theory thus construes
perception as a constructive process in which the interaction between incoming
information and an individual's preexisting schema determines what is perceived"
(p. 604). The centrality of gender, as opposed, for example, to eye color or height,
in children's social learning rests on the strength and resilience of masculine and
feminine categories in the environment (Bem, 1983).

The third key element of gender schema theory is that individuals construct
and experience their self-concept within the framework of these gender-based
categories. Children learn which elements of their environments and cultures

belong in male and female categories, and then link those elements to themselves based on the category in which they feel they belong, leaving behind elements that do not fit into the "appropriate" gender category (for example, nurturing is included for girls but not boys; competitive is included for boys but not girls). Children—and then adolescents and adults—evaluate themselves according to how well they conform to the gender schemas they have created.

Bem (1983) noted that as these three processes work together, they create motivations for individuals to conform to cultural criteria of maleness and femaleness. She wrote, "Thus do cultural myths become self-fulfilling prophecies, and thus, according to gender schema theory, do we arrive at the phenomenon known as sex typing" (Bem, 1983, p. 605). Though Bem's gender schema theory has been much discussed and critiqued, empirical evidence strongly supports the existence of this process of developing masculine and feminine gender schemas (see Bem, 1983, 1993).

Bem (1974, 1981a) designed the Bem Sex Role Inventory (BSRI) to measure the extent to which individuals report subscribing to what may be viewed as socially desirable, stereotypically masculine or feminine characteristics. The BSRI asks respondents to indicate on a seven-point scale the degree to which sixty characteristics describe them. Twenty items are stereotypically masculine (for example, ambitious, independent, assertive), twenty are feminine (affectionate, understanding, gentle), and twenty are "filler" (happy, truthful, conceited). Masculinity and femininity are considered within an orthogonal—not binary— array. If masculinity and femininity are not opposite ends of one scale but crossed in a matrix where an individual can range from low to high on a masculinity scale and a separate femininity scale, then an individual's measurements could result in placement on the matrix as follows (Figure 18.3):

- High on masculinity and femininity: Androgynous
- Low on masculinity and femininity: Undifferentiated
- High on masculinity and low on femininity: Masculine
- Low on masculinity and high on femininity: Feminine

Comparing a person's results to his or her reported sex, a woman who scored "feminine" would be considered "sex-typed" and a woman who scored "masculine" would be considered "cross-sex-typed."

To be clear, being anything other than sex-typed does not indicate a transgender identity, nor does being sex-typed mean that an individual is necessarily cisgender. But understanding how individuals develop gender schemas and how these schemas operate to influence identity, decisions, and behaviors may elucidate college students' gender identities and gender-related decisions.

FIGURE 18.3. BEM'S SEX ROLE TYPES

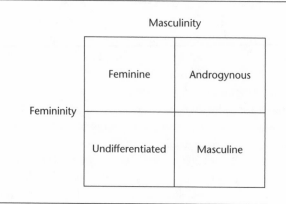

Research Related to Gender Schemas on Campus

If Bem's (1981b) gender schema theory is taken as a guide to understanding environmental influences on gender identity, aspects of campus life can be considered in light of how they challenge or reinforce the gender schemas that students may bring with them to college. Assuming that students of all ages have long since developed gender schemas that shape their perceptions and that social learning theory predicts that individuals will attempt to conform to the gender schemas that they hold (Bem, 1983), students' decisions, behaviors, and attitudes indicate the power of gender in their lives. Research provides evidence of gender interactions in academic (for example, majors, faculty mentoring), career planning, and student life (for example, social, cocurricular, athletic, leadership, judicial) contexts, among others. Gender schema theory would predict these interactions to be mutually reinforcing, with students' perceptions shaping, and being shaped by, the gender schemas they hold. Students would then act in ways that would positively reinforce their own and others' conformity to the expected gender norms and inhibit behaviors and attitudes that were gender nonconforming. As noted earlier, heterosexism and homophobia are part of the reinforcement/inhibition mechanism.

Academic and Curricular. Women became the majority of college students in 1979 and have remained so. Yet they remain the minority in science, technology, engineering, and mathematics (STEM) fields. Men are underrepresented in teaching, nursing, social work, and allied health fields (National Center for Education Statistics, 2008). Given assertions that all of these fields are expected to be essential to the twenty-first-century workforce and that many of them are experiencing personnel shortages (Goodin, 2003; Murphy, DeArmond, & Guin,

2003), why is it that gender imbalance persists? If, for example, women pursued engineering majors at the rate that men do, the supply of U.S. engineers would likely be robust; the same can be said for teachers and nurses if men pursued these majors at the rate that women do.

Gender schema theory suggests that students come to college with predetermined ideas about what majors are appropriate for which gender. Students who go against schemas to enroll in an academic program where they are in the gender minority find themselves one of a few men or women in class. Faculty are disproportionately of a different gender from these nonconforming students (National Center for Education Statistics, 2008), and even textbooks may reinforce gender stereotypes of who belongs in an education, nursing, or engineering classroom (Bell-Scriber, 2008). Evidence suggests that persistence of the minority gender in these majors is lower than persistence of students of the majority gender, so in upper-level classes the effects may be exaggerated, as observed by Sanjay and Gabe in the case study. As Bem (1983) noted, the stereotypes have become "self-fulfilling prophecies" (p. 605).

Faculty mentors have been cited as a buffer against the effects of gender stereotyping in academic majors. There is some debate about whether same-gender mentors are necessary to maximize buffering effects (see Burke & McKeen, 1996; Fassinger & Hensler-McGinnis, 2005), but the dearth of female STEM faculty and male education, nursing, and human service faculty renders the debate less meaningful. The question often comes down to whether having any faculty mentor is more effective than no mentor, and the answer is a resounding endorsement of the role of mentoring and role models in the academic success and persistence of students who are gender minorities in their academic majors (Chandler, 1996; Herzig, 2004; Smith, 2007). The exact operation of the mentoring effect is not clear, but some evidence (Benishek, Bieschke, Park, & Slattery, 2004; Chandler, 1996; Fassinger & Hensler-McGinnis, 2005) points to the power of mentors and role models to challenge—directly, by example, or both—students' gender schema: if Professor Tina (or José) can be a physicist (or elementary educator), then maybe I can too. Students who are in the majority gender in their academic majors may have their gender schemas reinforced as they find themselves among similar others, just as they expected to be (Bryant, 2003).

Career Planning. Just as gender schemas factor into choices of academic majors, they factor into career planning for women and for men. Phillips and Imhoff (1997) reviewed ten years of research on women and career development, concluding that females have more flexible self-concepts and consider a wider domain of life contexts than do males; women's vocational aspirations can be traced to both individual and social factors, including race, class, and gender; women have higher self-efficacy (belief that they will be successful) in sex-typed careers than in cross-sex-typed careers; and reducing children's gender stereotypes produces higher aspirations among girls and boys. Scholarship in the subsequent decade has not produced different results (see Coogan & Chen, 2006). The role of gender schemas in shaping women's and men's career aspirations appears for now to be durable. Harris and Harper (2008) extended this work by positing the ways men's gender socialization and racial/ethnic identities intersected with their educational and career aspirations, leading some to community colleges on their way to—or from—four-year institutions.

Student Life. Research has repeatedly shown peer culture to be one of the most powerful influences on student development and college outcomes (see Astin, 1977; Kaufman & Feldman, 2004; Kuh, 1995). The residential, cocurricular, student employment, athletic, and other student life contexts in which peer culture operates play critical roles in reinforcing and challenging gender schema and sex-role stereotypes. As Kim noted in the coffee shop, women may choose campus involvement that is consistent with their sense of self as nurturing, caretaking, and relational, while men may choose involvement that reinforces a masculine self-concept that is assertive, competitive, and independent. Of course, these are broad stereotypes, but there is evidence that nearly twice as many female than male students are interested in community service and study abroad (Desoff, 2006; Hurtado et al., 2007), areas that draw on "feminine" characteristics such as concern for community and cross-cultural awareness.

Social life and dating are areas that are particularly gendered. In 1990, Holland and Eisenhart wrote that college women were being "educated in romance," a phrase they coined to describe highly heterosexualized campus climates where women's concern about how they ranked as desirable to men outweighed their concern about friendships, academic life, and personal development. A decade later Bank and Yelon (2003) found that even at a single-sex institution, gender roles and heterosexual desirability were powerful influences on women students' decisions. Davis (2002) found evidence that gender role conflict occurred for men as they interacted in the social milieu of campus life at the turn of the twenty-first century. The fraternity and sorority system has been singled out as a context in which gender is particularly salient (Hamilton, 2007; Handler, 1995; Rhoads, 1995); involvement in fraternities and sororities has been shown to increase the strength of previously held ideas about gender and sex roles (Pascarella & Terenzini, 2005).

Men are accused of and found responsible for student misconduct at much higher rates than women (Harper et al., 2005). Their overrepresentation in campus judicial systems has been attributed in part to "arrested emotional development"

(Ludeman, 2004) that can be traced directly from traditionally held gender schemas that inhibit expressions of emotion by boys and men. Harper et al. (2005) proposed a theoretical model to explain the overrepresentation of men among students who misbehave on campus. Their person-environment model included six factors: precollege socialization, male gender role conflict, developing competence and self-efficacy, social construction of masculinities, context-bound gendered social norms, and environmental ethos and corresponding behaviors. Taken as a set, these factors illustrate how the persistent effects precollege gender schemas can have a profound impact on attitudes and behaviors of college men.

Intersectionality. Gender is a key component of several models and theories of multidimensional identity and identity development in college students, including those of Abes, Jones, and McEwen (2007) and Chávez, Guido-DiBrito, and Mallory (2003; see Chapter Thirteen for further discussion of these models). Perhaps because gender schemas are shaped so early, they may play a role in other domains of identity development, as illustrated by Prema and Ayeesha's claims that gender and race are inextricable in their experiences and identities.

Overall Effect of College on Gender Schemas. Evidence over three decades confirms that college attendance has a generally liberalizing—that is, less constricting—effect on students' gender role attitudes (see Bryant, 2003; Pascarella & Terenzini, 1991, 2005). The specific constellations of student experiences (their environment or ecology), including work, major, course-taking patterns, and involvement in activities, mediate this effect (Bryant). For example, taking women studies courses and participating in diverse friendship groups are likely to increase egalitarian attitudes toward women, while playing football, being in a sorority or fraternity, and being in a major that matches one's sex type are likely to decrease egalitarianism (Bryant). Comparing these findings to gender schema theory, then, it could be said that students whose gender schemas lead them to sex-typed academic and cocurricular activities may be more likely to have those schemas reinforced; students who operate outside gender schemas are more likely to move toward a less clearly defined masculine or feminine view. This proposition has not been tested, though studies like Bryant's that use egalitarian attitudes toward women as a dependent variable offer promising models for how to go about doing so. Men's gender socialization before and during college is a growing area of study, with results indicating that gender role conflict may play some role in men's higher attrition rates (see Harper et al., 2005; Harris & Harper, 2008). It is important to remember also that there appears to be more variation within sex (male or female) than between the two groups, so gender schemas and sex typing must not be considered categorical characteristics of men and women.

There is also no empirical evidence addressing gender schemas, and college effects on them, of transgender students.

Transgender Identity Development

The majority of work on transgender identity has come from medical and clinical psychological perspectives addressing transgender identity described as Gender Identity Disorder (GID) in the American Psychiatric Association's (2000) *Diagnostic and Statistical Manual of Mental Disorders, Fourth Edition, Text Revision (DSM-IV-TR)*. The *DSM-IV-TR* defines GID according to four major criteria, summarized as:

1. Evidence of a strong and persistent cross-gender identification, described as the desire to be, or the insistence that one is, of the other sex.
2. Evidence of persistent discomfort about one's biological (birth) sex or sense of inappropriateness in the gender role of that sex.
3. The individual is not intersex.
4. Evidence of significant distress or impairment in social, occupational, or other important areas of functioning.

Individuals who meet these criteria may be diagnosed with GID and thus become eligible for medical and psychological treatment as their health insurance allows.

Transgender activists and educators typically resist the medical/clinical perspective, in favor of one that does not posit transgender individuals as having a mental illness on the basis of their gender identity (see Carter, 2000; Wilchins, 2004). Postmodern, feminist, and queer theoretical perspectives on gender and gender identity provide alternatives (see Bilodeau & Renn, 2005), and the identity development of transgender college students has recently received modest attention from researchers and student affairs educators who subscribe to nonmedical approaches. Recent studies of transgender identity in college students (Bilodeau, 2009; McKinney, 2005; Pusch, 2005) take a human development perspective that emphasizes the person-environment interactions in the higher education context.

Brent Bilodeau (2005), for example, adapted the six identity processes that Anthony D'Augelli (1994a) proposed as a life span model for lesbian, gay, and bisexual (LGB) development to describe the experiences of transgender college students. Bilodeau thus framed transgender identity development in this way:

1. "*Exiting a traditionally gendered identity* [by] recognizing that one is gender variant, attaching a label to this identity, and affirming oneself as gender variant through coming out to others."

2. "*Developing a personal transgender identity* [by] achieving the stability that comes from knowing oneself in relation to other transgender people and challenging internalized transphobia."
3. "*Developing a transgender social identity* [by] creating a support network of people who know and accept that one is gender variant."
4. "*Becoming a transgender offspring* [by] coming out as transgender to family members and reevaluating relationships that may be disrupted by this disclosure."
5. "*Developing a transgender intimacy status* [by] creating intimate physical and emotional relationships."
6. "*Entering a transgender community* [by] making a commitment to political and social action . . . through challenging transphobia [and genderism]. (p. 26)

Viewing the identities of transgender college students through these six processes allows a multidimensional, fluid model for how identities are context specific and influenced by reciprocal relationships with others in the context. Another strength is that it emphasizes a life span approach, maintaining the possibility that gender schemas are not fixed and immovable by the time a student enters college. A weakness of scholarship on transgender identity is that it is typically based on very small samples on one or a few campuses. Further empirical studies of the experiences and identities of transgender college students could provide much needed support for improving educational practices for this population.

Applications

As is clear throughout this chapter, gender identity is formed well before college, influences the college experience, and may modestly be able to be influenced by the college environment. For cisgender students, a challenge may lie in getting them to see gender as a central shaping force in their lives and to reconsider long-held gender stereotypes. For transgender students, challenges may already be abundant; the role of the educator may lie more in providing adequate support through programs, services, and policies. Yet in many areas of campus life, gender and its implications for all campus constituents provide opportunities to apply theory to practice to promote healthy development.

Whether or not a campus has a women's center or similar office dedicated to educational and academic programming related to women's and gender issues, programs and services that address the curriculum, cocurricular activities, and career exploration can provide venues for students to explore their ideas about gender and sex roles. Research (for example, Bryant, 2003; Pascarella & Terenzini, 1991, 2005) has shown that academic and cocurricular interactions can have an impact on gender-related attitudes. Thoughtful programming presented in the classroom and in appealing nonacademic settings could help students uncover tacit expectations they hold for themselves and others. Explicit use of the Bem Sex Role Inventory (Bem, 1981a) or another tool that measures gender expectations could enrich career exploration, values clarification, and academic advising with language related to gender and gender roles. Programs that introduce role models and provide peer support for students in nontraditional majors and careers for their gender have the potential to provide buffers against negative reactions they may receive in those settings or about their decision to enter those majors and careers. In short, though Bem's (1983) gender schema model may have some limitations, it also provides a way to introduce students to the unseen operation of gender in their lives on and off campus.

Supporting transgender students may take more active attention, in part because they are a small population only recently becoming visible on some campuses and in part because higher education operates, as Bilodeau (2009) pointed out, in a system of genderism that reinforces a gender binary to which all members are expected to subscribe. Beemyn (2005) recommended educational programs for and about transgender students to raise awareness and visibility; support services such as discussion groups in resource centers for lesbian, gay, bisexual, and transgender students; campus nondiscrimination policies that include gender identity and expression as protected categories; gender-neutral housing options that do not assume that all students are male or female, or that they remain the same gender throughout their time at the university; locker room and restroom facilities that provide adequate privacy (for example, single stall, lockable, unisex) for transgender individuals who do not choose to undress and shower in full view of other facility users, for fear of discrimination, harassment, or violence; counseling and health care that are trans-inclusive and sensitive to the needs of transgender people; and record keeping that permits changing gender in institutional systems in ways that are not unduly burdensome on the individual.

As is often the case when recommendations are made to improve the quality of life for a minority population, several of these recommendations could benefit cisgender people as well. For example, gender-neutral housing could benefit mixed-gender friendship groups that wish to share residence hall suites. Convenient, unisex, single-stall bathrooms benefit anyone who lives or works near that facility who does not have to go farther to locate a designated men's or women's restroom, as well as anyone seeking more privacy than is available in shared public restrooms. Many locker room users might prefer the privacy of shower curtains and changing room stalls to the "gang shower" model prevalent in university recreation centers built in the mid-1900s. And education about human diversity can be seen as a benefit to all community members, not only to those who fall into the group about whom the educational program is happening. By viewing the campus environment—physical, social, and policy—through the lens of gender, as Kim was beginning to at the opening of the chapter, educators may discover other ways that genderism operates on their campuses to constrain the gender identities and life decisions of all community members.

Critique and Future Directions

Researchers have not articulated a clear, full understanding of how gender identity develops during college in cisgender or transgender students. Gender schema theory (Bem, 1983) provides one way to frame the identities that students bring with them to college, and then a rich literature explores the ways that gender is reinscribed during college. Sex differences between college men and women are explored through student outcomes research (see Pascarella & Terenzini, 2005), in which sex (sometimes labeled as gender) is frequently used as a binary independent variable. Perhaps there is no unified gender identity theory for college students because none is needed. Yet ongoing gender differences in majors and career choices point to the persistent, unspoken power of gender to shape students' lives; understanding more clearly how gender does so could benefit educators and students.

Additional studies of transgender identity development in college are also warranted. The few studies that exist provide some guidance for practice, but they are based on limited samples, are not longitudinal, and cannot be assumed to apply broadly. Locating representative samples of a population that is small and widely dispersed is not easy but will be important as educators seek to provide evidence-based support to transgender students.

As is evident in the coffee shop conversation among five friends presented at the beginning of this chapter, gender is at once ever-present and largely invisible in the lives of college students. Gender schemas formed and intensified long before students come to campus operate to filter what possibilities student see for themselves and what expectations they place on others for conforming to gender norms. Students who violate those norms face correction in the form of teasing, discrimination, harassment, and violence. Whether they are cisgender or transgender, students are expected to fall in line and hold others in line in higher education institutions that mirror society's powerful system of genderism (Bilodeau, 2009).

PART FIVE

CONCLUDING REFLECTIONS

R egina has come to the end of her course on student development theory. Throughout the semester she has studied a number of foundational, integrative, and social identity theories. She read Perry's original work and wrote a critique of his book. She has considered the implications of each theory for diverse student populations and has interviewed several Asian American students to determine if the theories fit their experiences. She has examined research related to each theory and has even designed a study to investigate whether lesbian identity development is similar for African American and white women. She has considered how theory can be used in practice and has designed an orientation program for transfer students based on Schlossberg's transition theory. Yet as she reflects on her experience, Regina is unsettled. She has been exposed to a lot of material and experiences designed to provide her with a comprehensive background in student development theory and its uses in practice. But it is not all coming together. Maybe the final take-home exam will help. It requires that she analyze a scenario and discuss ways in which various theories can be used in combination to understand and intervene in the situation. In addition, she is asked to critique the knowledge base with regard to student development theory and make recommendations concerning future directions. The exam is due in a week. Regina decides she better get busy!

◆ ◆ ◆

Like Regina, our work is drawing to a close. Parts One through Four included consideration of the concept of student development, review of the historical and philosophical underpinnings of the student development movement, discussion of the uses of student development in practice, and review of the major foundational, integrative, and social identity theories. A step back from the details and a look at the big picture is now necessary. How do these ideas and theories come together to guide educational practice? What can be gained from all this knowledge?

In many respects, student development theories are like a kaleidoscope. When the kaleidoscope is turned, the design changes. Likewise, when different theories are used to interpret the same situation, the results of the analysis vary. Thinking about situations through many different theoretical lenses helps to provide a more comprehensive understanding of what is going on and points to a variety of possible strategies for addressing issues. Depending on the particular situation, some theories will fit better than others. Having a repertoire of theories to consider is helpful in finding the ones that are of most value. Nor can theory always lead us to the best solution. In some instances, theory is not sophisticated enough to be of much assistance. In other cases, it does not apply to the population under consideration. Sometimes it helps in describing the situation but does not provide guidance in terms of how to proceed. Users of theory must recognize its limitations as well as the positive contributions it has made to educational practice.

All professionals are obligated to reflect on the current state of their profession and the knowledge base that underpins it. Furthermore, they must challenge themselves and their colleagues to test, refine, and extend that knowledge base. As educators, it is particularly important to critically examine student development theory and constantly seek out opportunities to add to the information that already exists about how students change and grow during the college years, for it is through such efforts that educational practice is improved, and society, in the long run, is benefited.

The final two chapters present possible responses to Regina's final exam. Chapter Nineteen addresses ways in which theories can be used in combination to understand and approach issues on college campuses. We also introduce two models that can be used to guide practical application of theory to frame this discussion: Knefelkamp's (1984) practice to theory to practice model and Evans's (1987) developmental intervention model. Three scenarios are discussed. In the first, a student's dilemma concerning the future is presented, and ways of thinking about the situation are reviewed through various theoretical lenses. In the second situation, an instructor uses Knefelkamp's model to redesign a class for peer counselors. Finally, the developmental intervention model is used to consider a variety of ways in which theory can guide practice in student affairs.

Chapter Twenty presents final thoughts and recommendations for future work related to student development. It begins with a review of the current status of developmental theory, research, and practice, looking at both its accomplishments and its limitations. We then provide a list of recommendations to extend the student development knowledge base and enhance the work of student development educators.

CHAPTER NINETEEN

USING THEORIES IN COMBINATION

Having examined a large number of student development theories in the past chapters, it is now time to consider how they can be used effectively and systematically to enhance student affairs practice. In each previous chapter, we offered examples of how particular theories can be helpful in understanding specific students and situations they may face in college. Rarely, however, is an issue in student affairs so straightforward that one theory will adequately explain it or provide sufficient guidance to address it. Looking at concerns from a variety of perspectives can assist practitioners to more fully understand the dynamics in situations they face and come up with a number of possible strategies to consider. In this chapter, we draw on numerous theories to explain and address various scenarios that student affairs educators are likely to face when working with individual students as well as designing interventions that will have an impact on students in groups, classrooms, and the campus as a whole.

Making meaningful theory to practice connections at these various levels can be challenging. Links are needed to connect students' everyday reality and the conceptual frameworks provided by developmental theory. Models are designed to provide this developmental bridge between theory and practice (Evans, Bradley, & Bradley, 1985). Models do not define phenomena or explain relationships; they provide guidance in using theory. Two types of models exist: process models, which consist of a recommended series of action steps for connecting theory to practice, and procedural models, which present a particular way of accomplishing some aspect of student affairs practice. Process models are grounded in theory; procedural models are not necessarily theory based. Several writers have proposed models that help educators use theory effectively in practice. The process model developed by Knefelkamp (1984), with Golec and Wells, and the procedural model introduced by Evans (1987) can be particularly helpful to student affairs professionals and other educators. Each of these models is discussed in this chapter, along with examples that illustrate its use in making theory to practice connections. To begin our analysis, we examine ways in which theories can be used in combination to better understand a student's challenging situation and work with the student to address the issues.

Advising a Student

A senior student, Pat, comes to talk with the hall director near the conclusion of the final semester and shares this story.

I have a lot of decisions that I feel I have to make soon. You've known me for the past three years I have been living in the hall. I thought maybe you could help me sort things out. For quite a while now, I've wanted to go into the ministry. My father is a minister. But there are some things going on with me personally that are making me wonder if I should forget about going to seminary. This is kind of hard to talk about, but for the past six months I've been in a relationship that has become very important to me. Chris and I have become very close. I've never been in a homosexual relationship before, but this relationship just feels right—much better than the relationship I had with Terry, even though Terry and I almost became engaged.

Anyway, my church teaches that homosexuality is wrong. So I don't know what to do about the seminary. I have my interview next week. I don't know whether to be open about my sexual orientation or not. Chris thinks I should be honest and tell. Chris may be right. On the one hand, I hate the idea of not being who I am. On the other hand, if I am open about my homosexuality, I think my chances of being admitted are zip! And what if my parents find out? They would be so hurt and disappointed in me. I feel caught between people I care about very much. If I'm open about who I am, I hurt my parents. If I'm not open, I hurt Chris. I don't want to harm anyone.

And if I don't get to go into the ministry, what will I do? Some of my professors in my major department, English, have been pushing grad school in that area, but that idea just doesn't feel right. Besides, I've been a good student, but not a great one in terms of my grades. I don't think I'd really like being an egghead professor. I love the theatre and I've done some acting on campus, but I don't think I have anywhere near enough talent to be a professional. Why can't I be who I am and be a minister in my church, too? I am so frustrated! That feels so unfair!

Sometimes I just wish the semester would never end. I feel comfortable here. The pressure about what to do next feels overwhelming. Sometimes I think I'd just like to disappear, to get away from all the stress for a while, but I guess that would be too irresponsible. Sometimes I feel like I can't even think straight. Please help me.

Clearly, Pat is facing a number of challenges. Several developmental theories, used in combination, can be helpful in understanding and responding to students like Pat. First, psychosocial theory can serve as a useful resource. For example, Pat is struggling simultaneously with several of the developmental issues described in Chickering's vectors (Chickering & Reisser, 1993). Identity concerns are paramount, particularly in relation to sexual orientation, making social identity theory relevant. The question of "Who am I?" and the resulting ramifications of the response represent a complex process of struggling and coming to terms for Pat. These identity issues also have an impact on Pat's ability to resolve aspects of developing purpose. Intrapersonal and career aspects are somewhat at odds because of the conflict between aspects of Pat's identity and the church's lack of acceptance of homosexuality. Conflicts between Pat's religious values and sexuality have also made developing integrity a challenge, because of the perceived lack of congruence between Pat's values and actions. Pat could be at a point of desperation. The fact that Pat has chosen to talk with the hall director demonstrates the value of one of Chickering's key influences, student developmental programs and services. Over a three-year period, the hall director has formed a relationship with Pat that gives Pat an important environmental support in a time of personal crisis and difficult decision making.

Pat's self-identification with homosexuality makes clear the potential value of both Cass's (1979) and D'Augelli's (1994a) models. Pat may be in the middle stages of developing a homosexual identity. Characterizing involvement in a same-sex relationship as a new experience, Pat expresses the desire to "be who I am" as well as the frustration of having to deal with disapproving others (for example, church leadership) who render the identity illegitimate and consider it a basis for denying the opportunity to pursue a career in the church. Coming-out issues for Pat can become even more difficult because of the career goal of becoming a minister in a church not supportive of Pat's sexual identity. From the perspective of D'Augelli's model, while Pat seems to have established an intimacy status, the process of "becoming a lesbian-gay-bisexual offspring" remains. Pat views the hall director as an individual who can be trusted to hear and not judge the concern, which is an advantage. The hall director also needs to display sensitivity to the challenges inherent in the decisions related to coming out to parents and to seminary personnel and the related impact of such decisions on Pat's relationship with Chris.

Pat's gender and race are not specified in this scenario. Both characteristics are relevant, and social identity theory could be helpful here as well. For example, if Pat is African American, or Latino/a, multiple issues of oppression are likely to exist (Wall & Washington, 1991). The role of the family and of the church may also take on heightened importance. Gender has implications for sexual identity development since the process can differ for gay men and lesbians (Reynolds & Hanjorgiris, 2000).

Schlossberg's theory (Goodman, Schlossberg, & Anderson, 2006) provides insight related to the transition issues that Pat is experiencing. For example, the shift in sexual identity for Pat and the upcoming graduation represent major transitions. In relation to Schlossberg's 4 *S*'s (situation, self, support, and strategies), the situation Pat faces involves several events that combine to form multiple transitions that are producing a great deal of stress for Pat. Major role changes are involved: a view of self as heterosexual to a view of self as homosexual and a shift from the role of undergraduate student to what is currently an unknown role in terms of education or career. As graduation rapidly approaches, pressure on Pat to figure out where to go and what to do next is stressful. The need to address sexual identity matters must take place in the context of an environment that must soon be vacated.

Descriptive information related to the "self" aspect of the 4 *S*'s is limited. Identifying as a member of a minority may be a new experience if Pat has not previously done so in regard to other personal or demographic characteristics. If Pat is a person of color, increased feelings of marginalization (Schlossberg, 1989b) can occur based on multiple issues of oppression.

Support, the third of the 4 *S*'s, could be a difficult aspect for Pat since the intimate relationship with Chris has the potential to conflict with the possibility of receiving support from family. For now, Pat has the opportunity to use the hall director as a source of institutional support. Since the semester will soon end, Pat is likely to lose this resource in the near future. For strategies, the last of the 4 *S*'s, Pat could benefit from assistance in developing all three types: modifying the situation where possible, controlling the meaning of the situation, and managing related stress.

Cognitive-structural theories also provide insight into how Pat is making meaning and what types of approaches may be useful. Early on in the conversation with the hall director, Pat asks for help with sorting things out. This request, quite different from asking to be told what to do, would seem to imply a high level of cognitive complexity. Issues of connection, found in Belenky, Clinchy, Goldberger, and Tarule's model (1986), as well as in Baxter Magolda's (1992) and Kegan's (1994), seem to be reflected in Pat's meaning making. Gilligan's care voice (1977, 1982/1993) can be heard in Pat's desire to avoid doing harm to anyone—parents or Chris. Kohlberg's justice voice (1976) can also be heard in Pat's challenging the fairness of having to choose between becoming a minister and having a same-sex partner. Clearly Pat is experiencing dissonance and may be dealing with what Parks (2000) described as a probing commitment to enter the ministry. Pat's wish for the semester to never end and the desire to disappear may signal the need for one of the deflections that Perry (1968) described. Pat is snared in a web of dilemmas, and coming to conclusions seems like an overwhelming task. Pat may genuinely need to take some time out.

Kolb's (1981) discussion of fit with academic cultures seems to apply to Pat's reluctance to consider going to graduate school in English to become a professor.

Pat may benefit from visiting the career planning office to gain greater insight into options currently under consideration, as well as additional possibilities for meaningful work. Having a greater understanding of Pat's learning style strengths is helpful to the career counselor as well as to Pat.

A focus on Pat's situation reinforces the value of using multiple theoretical filters to aid in understanding and attempting to provide assistance. As described in the analysis, the hall director can provide various forms of support, such as serving as a sounding board for exploration of identity issues, including aiding Pat with decision making and planning regarding communicating with others about these issues. The hall director can also serve as a helper who can collaborate in analyzing Pat's transitions and developing an approach to using and enhancing current coping strategies. The staff member's understanding of cognitive development can be used to discuss the possibility of Pat taking time out to sort through what is happening and consider future alternatives more fully. Because it would appear that faith is important to Pat, based on Pat's desire to enter the ministry, the hall director may consider spirituality as an area for exploration. As a final example from the scenario, the hall director can act as a referral agent for more information gathering about Pat's learning style and perhaps more in-depth counseling.

Rarely is a single theory likely to be sufficient in making meaning of students' experiences and supplying appropriate challenges and supports. As illustrated in this scenario, practice can be enhanced by drawing on a combination of theories. Models designed to connect theory to practice can be helpful in the intentional structuring of programs and interventions to facilitate student development. We turn our attention next to a particularly useful process model and provide a scenario in which it is used to redesign a developmentally appropriate undergraduate counseling course.

The Practice-to-Theory-to-Practice Model

Knefelkamp (1984), with Golec and Wells, proposed an eleven-step model for relating theory to the practical problems of student affairs practice. This model guides users to identify an issue, tie the issue to relevant theories, analyze the issue through a theoretical lens, design an intervention to facilitate development, and implement the intervention in practice:

Step 1: Identify concerns or enhancement opportunities that need to be addressed. These could be problems or issues or opportunities to enhance existing programs.

Step 2: Determine desired educational goals and outcomes.

Step 3: Identify which theories may be helpful in understanding the issue or enhancement opportunity and achieving the desired goals.

Step 4: Analyze relevant student characteristics from the perspective of each of the theories identified.

Step 5: Analyze characteristics of the environment associated with the issue from the perspective of each identified theory.

Step 6: Identify potential sources of challenge and support, taking into account both student and environmental characteristics, and recognizing factors that produce a balance.

Step 7: Reexamine goals and outcomes in light of the theoretical analysis. Modify if needed.

Step 8: Design the intervention using methods that will encourage achievement of goals.

Step 9: Implement the intervention.

Step 10: Evaluate the outcomes of the intervention.

Step 11: Redesign the intervention if necessary.

The practice-to-theory-to practice (PTP) model (Knefelkamp, 1984) can provide a structured approach to using developmental theory to provide insight and possible guidelines for action. It works equally well in designing classroom strategies, developing programming, and determining services to be provided by various student services units. Redesign of a counseling course will be used as an example to demonstrate how the PTP model can provide support.

Using the PTP Model

An instructor was concerned about addressing two issues in an undergraduate counseling course. First, although the course is described as being a peer counseling course, the texts are geared to a professional audience, particularly the case examples used. Second, the instructor wanted to help students value and respond to individual differences while also being able to see commonalities shared with others. The design of the course, however, emphasized difference in that students lacked connection to others who are in some ways different, and they even displayed prejudice toward those differences.

These two identified problematic components of the course represent the concern identified in step 1 of the PTP model. The issues represent both problem and enhancement aspects. Risks could include uncovering a multitude of problems related to the complexity involved in trying to address the peer component of the course more effectively, especially valuing difference. Potential benefits could be a greater connectedness among the students, instructor, and course material and more effective peer counselors.

In considering step 2, desired educational goals and outcomes, the students who took the course were typically juniors and seniors who were majoring in a field related to counseling and had an interest in helping. Typical classes included more women than men, more whites than nonwhites, and more traditional-aged than nontraditional-aged students, whose cognitive development typically displayed characteristics of multiplistic thinking, such as viewing the teacher as the source of the right process for finding the answer, valuing fairness, and giving attention to quantity issues (for example, time, effort, and number of pages to be read or written). Students often demonstrated some regard for their peers as potential contributors to the learning process.

The course design followed Knefelkamp and Widick's developmental instruction model (Knefelkamp, 1984), discussed in Chapter Five, with varied methods of learning and evaluation. The basic premise for the course was that knowledge of self, others, and the environment, along with skill development, would result in effective peer counseling. Two goals that emerged from a consideration of the issues described were to help students develop a conception of peer counseling and expand the sphere of people and concerns toward which they could demonstrate empathy.

In step 3, investigating theories that might be helpful, several had the potential to be of use. Psychosocial and social identity theories can be useful in understanding and addressing identity issues and ramifications related to relationships and tolerance. Cognitive-structural theories can give insight into how the students make meaning, as well as provide assistance in designing approaches that appropriately challenge and support students.

In analyzing student characteristics for step 4, Chickering's theory (Chickering & Reisser, 1993) provides insight into the heightened challenge of relating to others when both the helpee's and helper's identities may be in flux. If I am not quite sure who I am and you are not quite sure who you are, do we experience obstacles when attempting to connect? Perry's theory (1968) can be helpful in anticipating who may be likely to use peer helpers as well as who may be likely to enroll in a peer counseling course. As mentioned earlier, students in the course tended to be multiplistic thinkers. It seems unlikely that students demonstrating dualistic thinking would use peer counselors or enroll in a peer counseling course since peers would not be considered legitimate contributors to learning.

Gilligan's work (1977, 1982/1993) contains useful elements in trying to promote linkages among students. For example, her message that different does not equal deficient can be helpful in raising consciousness and helping students understand issues of invisibility and misrepresentation.

In examining environmental characteristics, step 5, it is also important to consider student characteristics. To aid students in exploring identity issues, an open environment for discussion is important, as Baxter Magolda's (2001) self-authorship theory suggests. Similarly, the developmental instruction model provides guidance in designing environmental supports and challenges. Ecology theory can aid in understanding person-environment fit issues, and Kolb's (1984) theory is useful in addressing different learning styles.

In regard to developmental challenges and supports, step 6, the DI model and attention to learning styles are both helpful, as is an understanding of the relationship between psychosocial issues, such as those represented in Chickering's seven vectors and the key influences in colleges, as described by Chickering and Reisser (1993), that can affect student development.

In step 7, reanalyzing educational goals and outcomes, it can be determined that a developmental mismatch is desirable. Timing and approach are both important, and the nonthreatening nature of the classroom environment provides support. An overriding goal becomes challenging students' narrow definition of *peer*, in the sense of who can help whom, to reduce exclusionary tendencies that may be based as much on feelings of inadequacy as on prejudice.

Several revisions were made in the design of the learning process, step 8. One example is the creation of activities designed to get a preliminary indication of how students are conceptualizing peer counseling. These exercises were done during the first class. To add to the knowledge-of-self component of the course, an instrument was designed to solicit information on what types of issues students anticipated they would and would not relate to as peer counselors. The instrument could be used in a pre/post fashion at the beginning and conclusion of the course. The "pre" component was not to be administered until after students had received back at least one written assignment with instructor comments in order to allow some time for the establishment of trust. In relation to the skill development component, the texts were supplemented with literature geared to peer counseling, and the cases used were changed so that they described scenarios likely to be more typical of those encountered by peer helpers. The knowledge-of-others component was modified to go beyond counseling theories and include readings and discussions geared to various student populations, and the cross-cultural counseling component was moved to an earlier position in the syllabus.

Using the PTP model as a support, substantial redesign work was done by the instructor. Use of process models such as this one provides an opportunity to be thorough, deliberate, and thoughtful in better understanding and addressing developmental concerns of students. Models have also been introduced to assist educators in considering various possibilities for developmental intervention.

Labeled procedural models, these models encourage big-picture thinking about how developmental outcomes can be achieved. We next discuss a procedural model and consider how it could be used to frame a variety of developmental outcomes.

The Developmental Intervention Model

Evans (1987), drawing on Morrill, Oetting, and Hurst's (1974) cube model, presented a framework for facilitating development that encourages student affairs professionals to use a variety of strategies. Developmental interventions are targeted at either the individual or the institution, they are either planned or responsive, and the approach used is either explicit or implicit. These three components are defined as follows:

Target of intervention. Individual interventions focus on the attitudes, knowledge, behavior, or concerns of specific students. The advising scenario at the beginning of this chapter is a good example of an individual intervention in which the student affairs professional used knowledge of theory to understand and assist a specific student. Institutional interventions are designed to create a developmental environment on campus. Attention to the developmental implications of university policy is a particularly powerful way to affect the climate by focusing on the educational experience and not only the bottom line (Coomes, 1994). Formally assessing the overall campus climate using a model such as that proposed by Rankin (2003) is another institutional approach. Since oppressive environments have the potential to restrict development of identity for members of nondominant groups (Evans & D'Augellli, 1996), having accurate information on campus climate is important as a precursor to intervention.

Type of intervention. Planned interventions are intentional, proactive, and structured. Such interventions are designed in anticipation of challenges or developmental needs that college students are expected to face. Using Chickering and Reisser's psychosocial theory (1993) to identify specific developmental issues of students in a residence hall and designing a programming series to intentionally address these issues would be a planned intervention. Baxter Magolda's (2004b) learning partnerships model can be used to structure experiential learning activities in this setting. Responsive interventions are reactive and make use of, or respond to, opportunities or challenges as they arise. Specific events on campus or in society may trigger certain issues. For instance, an economic downturn may create more concern among students about career options that will be available to them (that is, concerns associated with Chickering and Reisser's developing purpose vector). Specific programming can be developed in reaction to this heightened interest.

Intervention approach. Explicit interventions address developmental issues directly; those involved make very clear what the developmental issue is and how the intervention is designed to advance development in the targeted area. For instance, a program might be designed to assist students in the transition from college to full-time employment using Schlossberg's model (Goodman, Schlossberg, & Anderson, 2006) as a guide. Each of the 4 *S*'s—self, situation, support, and strategies—would be examined in light of this impending transition to assist students in better preparing for the future. Implicit interventions approach developmental issues indirectly. While the specific issue is not necessarily mentioned, the intervention will have an effect on it. An academic advisor might, for example, attempt to enhance self-authorship (Baxter Magolda, 2001) by encouraging a student to study abroad for a semester. While the advisor does not necessarily mention this potential outcome, being immersed in another culture certainly may result in the student's independent decision making and assuming greater personal responsibility, qualities associated with self-authorship.

Consideration of various combinations of target, type, and approach leads to a comprehensive program of interventions having a powerful developmental impact on students. The developmental intervention model encourages student affairs professionals to think in intentional, purposeful, and creative ways as they consider applications of theoretical concepts and approaches.

Conclusion

With each of the examples, the use of theory and models for its application is intended to be representative rather than exhaustive in regard to approaches that can be taken. Readers may identify viable alternate approaches. Other helpful discussions of how various student development theories can be used in a comprehensive manner are provided in sources such as Hamrick, Evans, and Schuh (2002), Fried and Associates (1995), Rodgers (1990a), and Ricci, Porterfield, and Piper (1987). Using theories in combination can afford a more holistic focus on both students and the college environments they inhabit.

CHAPTER TWENTY

FINAL THOUGHTS AND FUTURE DIRECTIONS

The previous chapters in this book represent the ever expanding range of student development theory from stage theory to multidisciplinary social identity models to integrated multiple identity theory. Although fifty years have passed since the concept was first presented, student development is a relatively young idea now coming into its own with a vast array of theories and models to examine college students' development. In a world filled with conflict, the need for a humanistic approach is critical and offers the backdrop for an expansion of the student development knowledge base.

The theory and research presented in this book embody the bulk of available knowledge on the topic, yet there is much more to learn about students and how they develop and grow. If a theory is not included here, it does not necessarily mean it is not worthy or credible for research or practice. Fortunately, the student development research is quickly expanding exponentially, although this growth is making it increasingly difficult to capture all of it in one volume. This book, however, is a good source for reviewing the state of the art regarding student development theory, research, and practice. As is readily evident, significant progress has been made in the past half-century toward understanding the growth and development that students experience during college. Yet even with an expanding theory base, the complexity of students' development and how higher education can influence it is only a snapshot of the big picture. In this concluding chapter, a glimpse at what has been achieved and some challenges to student development theory as presented in the literature are followed by an overall evaluation of the current status of student development theory, research, and practice. Recommendations are made regarding future efforts to better understand students and the impact of their experiences in college.

What Has Been Achieved

In the 1980s, student affairs educators who were familiar with the work of Chickering, Perry, and Kohlberg considered themselves well versed in developmental theory. Today the theory base of the field has grown to include many important perspectives that challenge educators to expand their thinking, particularly related to gender, class, race, sexuality, ethnicity, age, geography, religion, and so on, and how these identities intersect and influence one another. Student development is also about cognitive, psychosocial, moral, and spiritual development, and how these aspects of identity intersect with each other and social identities too. Ultimately the intersection of these developmental perspectives best describes who students are and who they can become.

Indeed, student affairs educators who teach student development theory are faced with the challenging task of determining which theories to include and which to omit from their syllabi. Many master's-level student affairs preparation programs have expanded their offerings to include at least two classes examining student development theory (for example, Iowa State University, Western Illinois University, and the Ohio State University), and at least one offers a course on designing developmental interventions (University of Georgia).

Likewise, significant research has been conducted to examine the propositions associated with existing theories, explore the applicability of theories to different populations of students, and develop new theories. As a result, some theories or models are receiving less attention in the field (for example, the work of Douglas Heath, 1968; Jane Loevinger, 1976; and many of the studies that rely on positivistic assumptions, such as Perry, 1968; and Kohlberg, 1958, 1976), while others have been modified to take into account new information (the work of Chickering and Reisser, 1993, and Baxter Magolda, 2001, are good examples), and new theories, with primarily constructivist assumptions, are being introduced as a basis for student affairs practice (for example, the work of Abes, Jones, & McEwen, 2007; and Torres & Hernandez, 2007).

The application of student development theory to student affairs practice also has become more sophisticated and intentional over the past two decades. Theory-to-practice models, such as those of Knefelkamp (1984) and Evans (1987) discussed in Chapter Nineteen, have provided guidance for practitioners in using theories as a foundation for their work. Examples reported in the literature and at professional conferences suggest that student affairs practitioners are using theory creatively as a tool for understanding the issues students face and for intervening to structure a more positive campus environment to enhance student development. Theories provide insights for working effectively with individual students, advising and training student groups and organizations, designing classroom experiences, and evaluating and developing policy and procedures on college campuses. To this end, Chávez, Guido-DiBrito, and Mallory's (2003) diversity development model has been implemented successfully in diversity training with an active board of trustees at a large east coast research university, as well as used as the foundation and outline for a graduate diversity course syllabus at a major midwestern research university. The message of student development and learning can have influence campuswide in helping to meet the long held goal of educating the whole student (American Council on Education, 1937/1994a).

Limitations of the Existing Knowledge Base

The knowledge base subsumed under the label of "college student development theory" is rich and informative, although limitations exist. Most of the foundational theories reviewed in this book fit contextually within the positivist tradition that assumes the existence of an objective reality that holds regardless of time or situation. As a result, developmental processes are assumed to be similar for every individual in any environment or culture. Research evidence and observation suggest that generalization of developmental processes to all individual students is a narrow and probably inaccurate view.

Epistemology is paramount to understanding theory, and knowledge of it gives the researcher a wider view of ways to examine the world. With or without intention and embedded in every paradigm, the epistemological roots declare the researcher's perspective in carrying out the inquiry. Student development research in the past was not considered credible unless it was based in the positivist paradigm with linear thinking, deductive reasoning, and researcher-subject objectivity as key features. Currently more constructivist research is being conducted to add to the knowledge base, but an even larger view is needed to identify the whole of student development from a wide range of epistemological and methodological lenses (Abes, 2009). Student development research lacks critical/postmodern perspectives and suffers from an unbalanced academic "paradigm dialog" (Guba, 1990, p. 27) in which the gatekeepers of our knowledge choose one, maybe two, related epistemological traditions to deem legitimate for publication over many others (Lincoln & Cannella, 2004). In challenging the research status quo, Abes (2009) explored the use of multiple contradictory theoretical perspectives to reveal "how inequitable power structures have shaped student development theory" (p. 141). Her research highlights what she called the "theoretical borderlands" (p. 142) of combining queer theory and constructivism in studies of lesbian identity. Abes defended "theoretical borderland" student development research as an effective way to best "describe diverse college students' complex understandings and experiences with their identity" (p. 143). The array of methods used in gathering, interpreting, and analyzing research and assessment data from all paradigms is also sadly missing from the student development literature. More emphasis placed on new approaches, such as more visual mediums and those that involve the senses (Banks, 2001; Pink, 2006; Stanczak, 2007), and methods that consider cultural others (Denzin, Lincoln, & Smith, 2008) broadens our scope in understanding development.

In addition, existing developmental theories, for the most part, are based on the values of white, middle-class, and educated people, predominantly men. Such values may contribute to a limited sense of what is important in the lives of students, especially those from other traditions or cultural heritage. As more research on marginalized college populations is conducted, many identity research boundaries have expanded. For example, A. King (2008b) explored self-identified multiracial/biracial-bisexual/pansexual female college students' racial and sexual identity development. As cutting-edge developmental inquiry, this research expands our understanding of identity intersectionality and broadens the research on student groups not often studied.

Another important point to recall is that developmental theory has its base in the field of psychology. As such, internal developmental processes tend to be emphasized, while insufficient attention is paid to the role of environmental forces that influence development. In addition, student development theory is now based in more academic disciplines (for example, sociology and anthropology) and epistemological frameworks (for example, constructivism and feminism), making research on holistic development of college students complex but necessary for a more complete view of student development.

Finally, existing theories tend to fragment development rather than view it holistically. For example, P. King and Kitchener (1994) discussed reflective judgment; Kohlberg (1976) studied moral development; Cross and Faghen-Smith (1971) examined African American identity development. Little is known about how these various aspects of development interrelate.

Stage theories, in particular, suffer from the problems noted. Underlying assumptions on which these theories are based imply that the developmental path is similar for all individuals, leading to an end point, at which time the individual has achieved maximum growth. The descriptions of various stages reflect dominant white culture values and perspectives relevant at the time of their inception. Adaptation of these models may have value for future student development researchers, but generalizing theory to all individuals is a disservice.

Environmental influences are given little attention by most stage theorists. While these theorists discuss conditions in the environment that may facilitate or restrain development through the stages, these influences never change the developmental process itself. For example, a white student attending Harvard in 1960 is assumed to have faced the same developmental challenges as a Native American student attending a tribal college in 2010. And each theory, as noted above, outlines only one particular aspect of development (for example, moral reasoning or racial identity development). More attention to some of the less well-known ecological models (for example, Banning, 1989, and Bronfenbrenner, 2005) using diverse epistemological and methodological underpinnings gives a fuller picture of how the higher education environment shapes students' development.

Limitations of Student Development Research

Several problem areas must also be noted with regard to student development research. First, although it is growing, the research base is limited. Since most existing research grows out of the positivist tradition, it is quantitative in nature. Such an approach limits phenomena that can be examined and ways in which data are interpreted. Much energy goes into testing predetermined hypotheses and controlling experimental conditions, often with a relatively small sample and not necessarily using large, generalizable databases. It is difficult to describe and understand, much less predict and control, all the concepts and variables that contribute to or interfere with human growth and development. As a result, bits and pieces of development are examined, and it is often difficult to see how the obtained information contributes to the bigger picture. All too often what is studied is what is easiest to study rather than what is important to study. Universities exacerbate the situation with unbalanced enthusiasm and reward for faculty with high publication numbers, sometimes without regard to quality. At the other end of the publication pipeline, the most prestigious nationally refereed journals in higher education and student affairs more often favor positivist research, leaving little incentive for a wider sweep of faculty research from various epistemological (such as critical theory and feminism) and methodological (for example, photoethnography) perspectives.

Research findings are often based on small, homogeneous samples that preclude generalization to other populations. Unfortunately, sufficient caution in interpreting the results of such studies is often missing. More such studies are appearing in the literature, but too little research to date has investigated developmental processes for students of color; older students; students from different cultural backgrounds; students with disabilities; gay, lesbian, bisexual, and transgender students; and students from various religious traditions, geographical regions, and socioeconomic classes, or how these identities intersect for diverse students.

Instrumentation remains a significant problem in developmental research. Very few reliable and valid instruments are available to measure any aspect of development. Those that do exist frequently require specialized training to administer, score, and interpret. Often they must be individually administered and hand-scored, costly and time-intensive procedures that limit the number of participants in studies. For many theories, no standardized instruments exist to test related propositions and hypotheses. For other theories, such as that of Chickering and Reisser (1993), existing instruments relate to only certain components of the theory. Obviously the lack of instrumentation limits how research is conducted and what can be studied.

Most studies reported in the literature are cross-sectional in nature. (For example, such a study might compare the developmental level of first-year and fourth-year students.) It is difficult to determine much about the process of development over time and the factors that contribute to it without longitudinal studies (for example, studies that follow the same group of students from the first through the fourth year). Torres and Baxter Magolda are two of only a few student development theorists who conduct longitudinal research.

While the literature presents some elegant applications of theoretical principles to student affairs practice (such as McEwen, 2003a; Rodgers, 1990a), too few comprehensive examples are available. Those that do exist are most likely to be hypothetical rather than reports of actual interventions. In addition, most reported applications of theory have been in the area of programming. While important, programming is only one aspect of student affairs and higher education practice that is informed by theory. Nonprogramming examples in higher education and student affairs are woven throughout the pages of this book.

Finally, few discussions of actual theory-to-practice efforts have included systematic evaluation data. While discussions of ways that theory can be used in practice are helpful in providing ideas, solid evidence from well-designed evaluation studies demonstrating the effectiveness of an intervention is much more persuasive in convincing student affairs administrators of the utility of an approach. It also does much to further the theoretical knowledge base by demonstrating that hypotheses drawn from theory can be validated in practice. In addition, qualitative data can add more meaning to what is found.

Recommendations for the Future

Based on the critique of the student development knowledge base and research presented in the previous sections, we offer recommendations for integrating student development theory, research, and practice. Even with the ever increasing body of literature emanating from numerous disciplines, we make many of the same recommendations suggested in the first edition of the book with updates to acknowledge the expanding body of literature and more fluid research paradigms:

1. *Development must be considered in a more holistic and less linear manner.* In a conference presentation, Kathy Allen (1989) suggested that assumptions about development need to be modified in a number of ways. Her ideas reflect a constructivist perspective and include the following modifications of traditional thought: (a) There are multiple pathways to development rather than a single developmental path. Not everyone will get from point A to point B in the same way. (b) Development consists of themes and patterns rather than stages. Certain themes may be more or less reflective of individuals from different backgrounds. (c) Development is triggered both internally and externally. While maturation certainly plays a role in determining what issues will become salient at particular times and how the individual will respond to them, environmental conditions also contribute to this process in significant ways. (d) Cohort patterns exist with regard to development. Culture, gender, and generation all play a role in how development occurs and what it looks like. Developmental patterns and themes would be more similar for individuals from the same cohort than for persons from different cohorts. For example, developing a life's purpose would be a different process for women born in 1990 than for women born in 1950 because opportunities and values related to the roles of women in society have changed over time. Cultural experiences and worldviews are also likely to be different for African American women and white women. Differing societal expectations of women and men can also affect the developmental paths of each gender group. (e) Aspects of development are interconnected. It is impossible to separate cognitive development from psychosocial development and personality style. As such, development must be studied in a holistic manner. Allen's propositions are as intriguing today as they were in the late 1980s and certainly worthy of continued exploration. These propositions influence many of the recommendations that follow.

2. *Researchers must examine what development looks like for various student populations independent of dominant culture models.* A student in a student development class offered the following comment in a critique of Chickering and Reisser's (1993) theory: "I wonder how we would think about development if the students upon which Chickering based his theory had all been African American?" A good question indeed! Although the knowledge base is expanding to consider the generalizability of developmental theories to students from different backgrounds, most often researchers and practitioners still start from the existing theoretical base and examine how students of color, women, and other groups differ from that base. Implicitly, as Gilligan (1977) suggested, difference is viewed as deficient, and the white dominant culture male experience is still considered the norm. Although

this book is evidence of the expanding nature of the literature, researchers need to explore the development of students from various racial/ethnic groups; gay, lesbian, bisexual students; transgender students; students with disabilities; and other students whose life experiences have shaped them in ways different from students from dominant cultures. Qualitative research approaches, including phenomenological interviews, participant observation, visual methods including photoethnography and video, and other techniques used in anthropology and sociology, are particularly appropriate for determining what development is like over time for students from diverse backgrounds.

3. *Unacknowledged and underacknowledged representatives of groups in our theory base must be given appropriate voice.* Related to recommendation 2, student affairs professionals need to become more aware of the missing voices in the student development literature (see Madrid, 1988). How often do educators read about or consider the developmental experiences of students with disabilities, Jewish students, Islamic students, Mormon students? What about transgender students? What about students raised in poverty and those raised with extreme wealth and privilege? What about the children of migrant workers, veterans, or displaced factory workers returning to college? What about first, second, third, and fourth generation students with strong ethnic and cultural heritages? What about international students who come from nearly every country on the globe? Greater understanding of the role played by background and culture in the lives of students from diverse populations is crucial if student affairs professionals are to be inclusive in creating meaningful experiences to facilitate development for all students. In reality, addressing issues of invisibility and voicelessness in the theory base may be the most pressing need. Educators cannot assume that development is the same process for all students or that the concepts derived from a narrowly defined group of students work equally well for others. Identifying what influences development by learning from students who have been previously overlooked will help in determining what makes students unique and special, as well as the commonalities all students share.

4. *Development must be studied across the life span.* No longer are all college students eighteen to twenty-two years old. Nor does development end at age twenty-two. If educators are truly to understand student development, they must learn more about the changes that occur in later life and the impact of those changes on the ways in which older students negotiate the college environment. Understanding development across the life span is also crucial if student affairs professionals are to understand their own life experiences and effectively work with staff to enhance personal as well as professional development.

5. *Longitudinal research is needed that examines development over time.* Development is not a static variable. It cannot be studied in the same way researchers study

things like who gets admitted to college and who graduates. Researchers must follow people as they move through their lives and see what unfolds in the process. While such research is time-consuming and difficult, the benefits are great. Baxter Magolda (2008), who has now followed her previously interviewed college students into their careers and lives after college, tells us much about not only the process of development during college but also the impact of college experiences on later development. More longitudinal studies with students of color (such as Torres & Baxter Magolda, 2004) are needed to understand the holistic development of diverse college students.

6. *The impact of the environment on development must be considered.* As Lewin (1936) stated long before the advent of the student development movement, behavior is a function of the interaction of the person and the environment. For too long, researchers and theorists have focused on the person by concentrating on internal maturational processes and downplayed the role of the environment in the determination of developmental outcomes. Investigators must balance their efforts more evenly so that environmental forces are given their just due.

Environment has many meanings. It can be the familial, cultural, and social circumstances of a person's life before college. The most significant determinants of students' success in college are their experiences prior to college (Pascarella & Terenzini, 2005). Environment can be the type of institution in which a student is enrolled. For example, liberal arts colleges are more likely than other types of educational institutions to focus attention and resources on student development efforts because faculty and student affairs professionals more easily make the personal connections with students that are so important for their development (Hirt, 2006). Also, research has indicated that the development of African American students attending predominantly white universities is quite different from the development of their counterparts in historically black universities (Fleming, 1984). Particular settings on college campuses must also be considered when examining the environment. In a study of the development of gay, lesbian, and bisexual students in residence halls (Evans & Broido, 1999), students reported very different experiences in various hall settings that either facilitated or retarded the development of their identities.

7. *Influences on development must be examined.* Developmental theory as it currently exists is mainly descriptive (P. King, 1994). More information is needed about movement in developmental processes. Researchers must identify and describe factors and experiences that contribute to growth and learn more about how development can be facilitated. Educators also need to understand more about forces that inhibit development and how those forces might be countered in a higher education environment. Ethnography, case study, photography, and in-depth interviewing are effective methods for conducting such research.

8. *The ways in which various aspects of development intersect and are interconnected must be investigated.* Exploratory research has indicated that various components of development and individual difference are interconnected. For example, level of cognitive development and personality type as measured by the MBTI both appear to influence how developmental tasks are approached and mastered (Anchors & Robinson, 1992; Polkosnik & Winston, 1992). Cognitive style as defined by Belenky, Clinchy, Goldberger, and Tarule (1986) and MBTI personality type were found to correlate in another study (Carter, 1990). And gay and lesbian identity development appears to interact in complex ways with other dimensions of identity (Abes & Kasch, 2007) and other developmental tasks (Levine & Evans, 1991). Researchers must continue to explore ways in which different aspects of development influence each other.

Researchers must also search for new approaches to the study of development that look at processes holistically. Baxter Magolda (2001, 2008) and Torres and Hernandez (2007) have conducted in-depth interviews over extended time periods, which may be one answer to exploring the complexity of development in a more comprehensive manner. Abes, Jones, and McEwen's (2007) model of multiple dimensions of identity is one clear example of a comprehensive examination of the content and context of students' development. Cutting-edge research in student development examines identity intersections. A study of Latino feminist masculinities and intersectionality (Hurtado & Sinha, 2008) and another focused on the ways in which college women who identify as both bisexual and biracial negotiate their identities (A. King, 2008b) demonstrate the multifaceted layers of intersecting student social identities.

9. *Better methods to assess development must be developed.* More accessible and inexpensive assessment techniques are needed, particularly for large-scale evaluation studies. If educators are to determine if programs, services, and other interventions are having an impact on students, they must have ways of measuring development. Programmatic efforts to develop and refine instrumentation, such as the work of Worthington and his colleagues (2005, 2008) and Fassinger (1998b) and Fassinger and Miller (1997), are crucial if progress is to be made in this area. Too many studies use home-grown assessment tools that may have face validity but have not been thoroughly examined for reliability or validity in any systematic way.

Educators must also respect the validity of qualitative approaches to assess development. Such approaches are particularly appropriate when building new theory and extending theory to previously unconsidered populations. Researchers must, of course, hold themselves to high standards in the use of qualitative techniques, recognizing that qualitative research methodology involves much more than just "talking to people."

10. *Educators must challenge themselves to be creative in the use of theory.* Developmental interventions, as Evans (1987) noted, can be targeted at the individual or the institution. Too often practitioners think only of programming when they ponder ways to use theory in practice. While programming is important, theory is also extremely helpful when advising or counseling students, advising student organizations, designing classroom instruction and training initiatives, and formulating policy. The cube model (Morrill, Oetting, & Hurst, 1974) and the developmental intervention model (Evans, 1987), discussed in Chapter Nineteen, are particularly helpful tools for stretching one's thinking about ways in which theory can guide practice.

11. *Educators must intelligently design interventions that are sensitive to the unique needs of specific environments.* The following scenario is played out far too often in student affairs. A practitioner attends a student affairs conference presentation in which the presenters outline a program they have implemented successfully on their campus. The practitioner is impressed. She believes that this program is just what they need to address a similar issue on her campus. She comes home and sells the new program. They implement it the next year. It fails. What the practitioner and her fellow staff members failed to recognize is that each campus is unique. The issue may seem the same, but the environment is different (for example, institutional size, type, mission, culture, history, and so on create unique higher education environments). Programs cannot be transplanted without a careful assessment of the environment and modifications to adapt the program to each particular situation.

12. *Assessment and evaluation must be included as a part of every intentionally designed developmental intervention.* Interventions need to be intentionally planned and based on sound assessment data reflecting the needs of the student community. They also need to be carefully evaluated to determine their effectiveness. Focus groups, targeted interviewing based on purposive sampling, examination of archival data, and other qualitative means of assessment can be used effectively in program evaluation, along with more traditional quantitative approaches (Upcraft & Schuh, 1996).

13. *More effort must be made to publish reports of studies evaluating developmental interventions.* Few evaluative studies of theory-based interventions are available in the literature. Such work is extremely important for advancing the field. Evaluation studies provide information to practitioners about what efforts are worthy of continuation and where resources should be allocated. Well-designed evaluation studies can also lead to refinement of theory and provide direction for future investigation. Student affairs practitioners and faculty can gain from collaborative efforts to evaluate developmental interventions for students.

14. *The use of theory in educational practice must be encouraged.* In an applied field such as student affairs, a knowledge base would seem to be valuable only to the

extent that it informs practice. In the same way, theoretical information that can enhance the teaching and learning process is of limited value if it does not find a home in the classroom. More must be done to disseminate information about how student development theory informs educational practice. As Baxter Magolda's body of work makes clear (see Chapter Ten), collaborative efforts between student affairs educators and faculty are particularly powerful in enhancing the climate for learning and development on college campuses. In this book, case studies and practical scenarios have been systematically included to demonstrate ways in which theory informs practice in a variety of student affairs and classroom settings. Further efforts in this vein are needed.

15. *Educators must remember that all theory reflects the values of its authors and the times in which they live.* In both research and practice, educators need to remain sensitive to the implications of theory as a social construction (McEwen, 2003a), peeling away layers to discover "hidden and unstated bases and intentions" (p. 172). The role of power and oppression in theory development and use must be identified and understood if theory is to be used with wisdom and caring.

16. *Student affairs faculty teaching student development must be aware of the complexity of the broad range of student development theory, encourage their students' fluency in the language and concepts of the knowledge base, and be enthusiastic models for studying student development theory over an entire professional student affairs career.* With an ever increasing developmental knowledge base, it is important for faculty teaching student development to update constantly and be knowledgeable about the various theories related to college students. Faculty will be more proficient in teaching language, concepts, and ideas specific to developmental theory if they continually gain expertise through participation in professional development activities targeted at expanding knowledge of the vast range of traditional and contemporary student development theories. The complexity of student development theory is revealed through some of the more contemporary theories and models; online faculty blogs and study groups, independent learning, and professional development can help faculty gain greater expertise and expand their knowledge of these more sophisticated theories. Although staying current in the field is time-consuming, it is crucial that student affairs educators teaching student development theory to graduate or undergraduate students do so. We encourage faculty and students alike to read widely and explore original sources of student development theory. Faculty and practitioners who engage in the study of student development over their careers will be better able to serve the diverse students entering our institutions.

17. *Educators must take a both-and approach as well as an evolutionary approach to theory.* The study of student development has moved from focus on several theories derived primarily from psychology to many theories derived from a host of academic disciplines and epistemologies. Although it is much easier to be familiar

with and favor a handful of theories, usually those with more linear patterns and a structured developmental path, many theories contribute to knowledge of student development, and educators must not limit their students to only a few. One example of coming to a both-and perspective of student development theory relates to moral development research. In the mid-1980s when Gilligan's (1982/1993) research was becoming popular and seen by some as a threat to studies conducted by Kohlberg (1976), these two theories were seen as gender specific, and controversy ensued over which theorist had accurately described the moral development process of college students. Ultimately as these theories were deemed gender related rather than gender specific, they were viewed as complementary and not exclusive of one another (Liddell, 1990).

18. *Development is a trajectory with contextual influences.* In some ways, this idea suggests that student development has features of both the positivist (in reference to a trajectory or path) and constructivist (in reference to the contextual influences) paradigms. In college, the trajection of students' developmental path can resemble a line, curve, or arc, but in all cases it is influenced by the environment. As student development research moves forward, the context of higher education needs more investigation, particularly as it pertains to the shape of the path for the development of diverse students.

19. *Various theories describe different facets of the entire developmental process picture.* The student development theories discussed in this book (for example, spiritual, cognitive, ethnic identity development, and so on) make up the whole of a student's development. To date, no one theory connects all facets of development, although this kind of single, grandiose vision is not likely the goal to seek. How different social identities intersect and how all student development theories are integrated are areas being examined in some of the cutting-edge research in the field and are most worthy of attention.

20. *The whole of students' development is bigger than its parts.* In 1937, the American Council on Education offered a report that acknowledged the necessity of institutions of higher education to attend to the needs of the whole student (American Council on Education, 1937/1994a). Since that time, and with the advent of the professionalization of student affairs, attention to the developmental needs of all students has been paramount. In order to continue this tradition, researchers and practitioners must find a space to converse about the complexity involved in developing the whole student for the many diverse students who attend institutions of higher education. Thorough examination of students' developmental needs and the institution's environment is likely to uncover that the whole of student development is greater than the sum of its parts. Student development advocates' mission is to continue looking at the parts and their sum for a never-ending current assessment, as students change rapidly in our global village.

Final Thoughts

The many student development models and theories available to practitioners and researchers interested in students' development can be a guide to students' growth processes. As more is learned, some theories receive more attention than others. For instance, Abes, Jones, and McEwen's (2007) model is cited more than any other in this book. As developmental research based in constructivism, its popularity may signal a move away from stage models toward more intersection and integration of student development theory. Limitations in stage theories are evident in theories such as those that are purely cognitive because affect and cognition cannot be separated; the two should be studied in tandem. Linear models are rigid and static, no longer reflecting the rhythms of daily postmodern life.

Since the beginning of the twenty-first century, much student development research and theory has reflected the integration of theory and intersection of identity through a constructivist lens. Future research is needed focusing on ecological approaches (such as that of Bronfenbrenner, 2005), which are so powerful in enhancing understanding of student-institution interaction. As our population ages and numbers of traditional-age students decline, research based on life span theory will expand the knowledge base regarding our student populations. As institutions with predominantly white cultures seek to increase the diversity of their student populations, there is a need to learn more about racial and ethnic identity (such as the work of Phinney, 2007; Torres, 1999, 2003). Self-authorship as a developmental outcome increasingly finds its way into the literature (see Baxter Magolda, 2001, 2008; Pizzolato, 2004, 2006), creating a need to reexamine and extend Kegan's (1994) seminal work. As students' lives continue to become more complicated, further examination of spirituality is needed for students' success and development. As students come from clearly distinguishable lower, middle, and upper social classes (Schwartz, Donovan, & Guido-DiBrito, 2009), more research can shed light on how student identity is shaped by class status and how class shapes other identities. Finally, student development educators must recognize the need to investigate learning theory, particularly Mezirow's (2000) transformational learning, situated cognition (Wilson, 1993), and other theories mainly found in the literature of adult development and education.

A consideration of integration and intersection of all parts of student development provides a warrant for new and creative ways to examine the whole. Student development studied from constructivist, postmodern, and critical lenses with new methodologies opens investigators to a wide-angle view that captures multiple, overlapping images of the development of the whole student. We owe our students nothing less.

REFERENCES

Abbey, D. S., Hunt, D. E., & Weiser, J. C. (1985). Variations on a theme by Kolb: A new perspective for understanding counseling and supervision. *Counseling Psychologist, 13,* 477–501.

Abes, E. S. (2009). Theoretical borderlands: Using multiple theoretical perspectives to challenge inequitable power structures in student development theory. *Journal of College Student Development, 50,* 151–156.

Abes, E. S., & Jones, S. R. (2004). Meaning-making capacity and the dynamics of lesbian college students' multiple dimensions of identity. *Journal of College Student Development, 45,* 612–632.

Abes, E. S., Jones, S. R., & McEwen, M. K. (2007). Reconceptualizing the model of multiple dimensions of identity: The role of meaning-making capacity in the construction of multiple identities. *Journal of College Student Development, 48,* 1–22.

Abes, E. S., & Kasch, D. (2007). Using queer theory to explore lesbian college students' multiple dimensions of identity. *Journal of College Student Development, 48,* 619–636.

Adams, G. R., & Fitch, S. A. (1982). Ego stage and identity status development: A cross-sequential analysis. *Journal of Personality and Social Psychology, 43*(3), 574–583.

Alberts, C., & Meyer, J. J. (1998). The relationship between Marcia's ego identity statuses and selected personality variables in an African context. *International Journal for the Advancement of Counseling, 20,* 277–288.

Alessandria, K. P., & Nelson, E. S. (2005). Identity development and self-esteem of first-generation American college students: An exploratory study. *Journal of College Student Development, 46,* 3–11.

Allen, K. E. (1989, June). *A non-linear model of student development: Implications for assessment.* Paper presented at the American Association for Higher Education Assessment Forum.

American Council on Education. (1994a). The student personnel point of view. In
    A. L. Rentz (Ed.), *Student affairs: A profession's heritage* (2nd ed., pp. 66–77). Lanham, MD:
    University Press of America. (Original work published 1937)

American Council on Education. (1994b). The student personnel point of view. In
    A. L. Rentz (Ed.), *Student affairs: A profession's heritage* (2nd ed., pp. 108–123). Lanham, MD:
    University Press of America. (Original work published 1949)

American Psychiatric Association. (2000). *Diagnostic and statistical manual of mental disorders* (4th
    ed.). Washington, DC: Author.

Anchors, W. S., & Robinson, D. C. (1992). Psychological type and the accomplishment of
    student development tasks. *NASPA Journal, 29,* 131–135.

Anderson, C. (1994, November 11). *"How can my faith be so different?": The emergence of religious
    identity in college women.* Paper presented at the annual meeting of the Association for the
    Study of Higher Education, Tucson, AZ. (ERIC Document Reproduction Service No.
    ED375724)

Anderson, J. A., & Adams, M. (1992). Acknowledging the learning styles of diverse student
    populations: Implications for instructional design. In L.L.B. Border & N.V.N. Chism
    (Eds.), *Teaching for diversity* (pp. 19–33). New Directions for Teaching and Learning, No. 49.
    San Francisco: Jossey-Bass.

Anderson, J. R. (1988). Cognitive styles and multicultural populations. *Journal of Teacher
    Education, 39*(1), 2–9.

Anglin, D. M., & Wade, J. C. (2007). Racial socialization, racial identity, and black students'
    adjustment to college. *Cultural Diversity and Ethnic Minority Psychology, 13*(3), 207–215.

Anzaldúa, G. (1999). *Borderlands, la frontera: The new mestiza.* San Francisco: Aunt Lute Books.
    (Original work published 1987)

Arbuckle, D. S. (1953). *Student personnel services in higher education.* New York: McGraw-Hill.

Arminio, J. (2001). Exploring the nature of race-related guilt. *Journal of Multicultural Counseling
    and Development, 29,* 239–252.

Arvizu, D. R. (1995). The care voice and American Indian college students: An alternative
    perspective for student development professionals. *Journal of American Indian Education, 34,*
    1–17.

Astin, A. W. (1968). *The college environment.* Washington, DC: American Council on
    Education.

Astin, A. W. (1977). *Four critical years.* San Francisco: Jossey-Bass.

Astin, A. W. (1984). Student involvement: A developmental theory for higher education.
    Journal of College Student Personnel, 25, 297–308.

Atkinson, D. R., Morten, G., & Sue, D. W. (1979). *Counseling American minorities.* Dubuque, IA:
    William C. Brown.

Atkinson, D. R., Morten, G., & Sue, D. W. (1989). *Counseling American minorities: A cross-cultural
    perspective* (3rd ed.). Dubuque, IA: Brown.

Atkinson, D. R., Morten, G., & Sue, D. W. (1993). *Counseling American minorities: A cross-cultural
    perspective* (4th ed.). Madison, WI: Brown and Benchmark.

Atkinson, D. R., Morten, G., & Sue, D. W. (1998). *Counseling American minorities: A cross-cultural
    perspective* (5th ed.). San Francisco: McGraw-Hill.

Atkinson, G., Jr., & Murrell, P. H. (1988). Kolb's experiential learning theory: A meta-model
    for career exploration. *Journal of Counseling and Development, 66,* 374–377.

Aulepp, L., & Delworth, U. (1976). *Training manual for an ecosystem model: Assessing campus
    environments.* Boulder, CO: Western Interstate Commission for Higher Education.

Avens, C., & Zelley, R. (1992). *QUANTA: An interdisciplinary learning community (four studies)*. Daytona Beach, FL: Daytona Beach Community College. (ERIC Document Reproduction Service No. ED349073)

Awad, G. H. (2007). The role of racial identity, academic self-concept, and self-esteem in the prediction of academic outcomes for African American students. *Journal of Black Psychology, 33*(2), 188–207.

Baier, J. L., & Whipple, E. G. (1990). Greek values and attitudes: A comparison with independents. *NASPA Journal, 28*(1), 43–53.

Baird, L. L. (1976). Structuring the environment to improve outcomes. In O. T. Lenning (Ed.), *Improving educational outcomes* (pp. 1–23). New Directions for Higher Education, No. 16. San Francisco: Jossey-Bass.

Baker, A. C., Jensen, P. J., & Kolb, D. A. (2002). Learning and conversation. In A. C. Baker, P. J. Jensen, & D. A. Kolb (Eds.), *Conversational learning: An experiential approach to knowledge creation* (pp. 1–13). Westport, CT: Quorum Books.

Baltes, P. B. (1987). Theoretical perspectives on life-span developmental psychology: On the dynamics between growth and decline. *Developmental Psychology, 23*, 611–626.

Bank, B. J., with Yelon, H. M. (2003). *Contradictions in women's education: Traditionalism, careerism, and community at a single-sex college.* New York: Teachers College Press.

Banks, J. A. (1984). *Teaching strategies for ethnic studies* (3rd ed.). Needham Heights, MA: Allyn & Bacon.

Banks, M. (2001). *Visual methods in social research.* London: Sage.

Banning, J. H. (Ed.). (1978). *Campus ecology: A perspective for student affairs.* Washington, DC: National Association of Student Personnel Administrators.

Banning, J. H. (1980a). Campus ecology: Its impact on college student personnel work. In D. G. Creamer (Ed.), *Student development in higher education: Theories, practices, and future directions* (pp. 129–137). Cincinnati, OH: American College Personnel Association.

Banning, J. H. (1980b). The campus ecology manager role. In U. Delworth & G. R. Hanson (Eds.), *Student services: A handbook for the profession* (pp. 209–227). San Francisco: Jossey-Bass.

Banning, J. H. (1989). Impact of college environments on freshman students. In M. L. Upcraft & J. N. Gardner (Eds.), *The freshman year experience* (pp. 53–63). San Francisco: Jossey-Bass.

Banning, J. H. (1992). Visual anthropology: Viewing the campus ecology for messages of sexism. *Campus Ecologist, 10*(1), 1–4.

Banning, J. H., & Cunard, M. (1996). An ecological perspective of buildings and behavior: Implications for the renovation and construction of the college union. *College Services Administration, 19*(4), 38–42.

Banning, J. H., & Hughes, B. M. (1986). Designing campus environments with commuter students. *NASPA Journal, 24*(1), 17–24.

Banning, J. H., & Kaiser, L. (1974). An ecological perspective and model for campus design. *Personnel and Guidance Journal, 52*, 370–375.

Banning, J. H., & Luna, F. C. (1992). Viewing the campus ecology for messages about Hispanic/Latino culture. *Campus Ecologist, 10*(4), 1–4.

Banning, J. H., & McKinley, D. L. (1980). Conceptions of the campus environment. In W. H. Morrill, J. Hurst, & G. Oetting (Eds.), *Dimensions of intervention for student development* (pp. 39–57). Hoboken, NJ: Wiley.

Barker, R. G. (1968). *Ecological psychology: Concepts and methods for studying the environment of human behavior.* Stanford, CA: Stanford University Press.

Barrett, W. (2007, April 25). Talking about social class on campus. *NASPA's NetResults*. Retrieved May 25, 2009, from http://wbarratt.indstate.edu/documents/talking_about_social_class.htm.

Barth, F. (Ed.). (1969). *Ethnic groups and social boundaries: The social organization of culture difference.* London: George Allen and Unwin.

Batson, C. D., Schoenrade, P., & Ventis, W. L. (1993). *Religion and the individual: A social psychological perspective.* New York: Oxford University Press.

Baxter Magolda, M. B. (1987). Comparing open-ended interviews and standardized measures of intellectual development. *Journal of College Student Personnel, 28,* 443–448.

Baxter Magolda, M. B. (1989). Gender differences in cognitive development: An analysis of cognitive complexity and learning styles. *Journal of College Student Development, 30,* 213–220.

Baxter Magolda, M. B. (1992). *Knowing and reasoning in college: Gender-related patterns in students' intellectual development.* San Francisco: Jossey-Bass.

Baxter Magolda, M. B. (1995). The integration of relational and impersonal knowing in young adults' epistemological development. *Journal of College Student Development, 36,* 205–216.

Baxter Magolda, M. B. (1998a). Developing self-authorship in graduate school. In M. S. Anderson (Ed.), *The experience of being in graduate school: An exploration* (pp. 41–54). New Directions for Higher Education, No. 101. San Francisco: Jossey-Bass.

Baxter Magolda, M. B. (1998b). Developing self-authorship in young adult life. *Journal of College Student Development, 39,* 143–156.

Baxter Magolda, M. B. (1999a). Constructing adult identities. *Journal of College Student Development, 40,* 629–644.

Baxter Magolda, M. B. (1999b). *Creating contexts for learning and self-authorship: Constructive-developmental pedagogy.* Nashville, TN: Vanderbilt University Press.

Baxter Magolda, M. B. (1999c). The evolution of epistemology: Refining contextual knowing at twentysomething. *Journal of College Student Development, 40,* 333–344.

Baxter Magolda, M. B. (1999d). Learner-centered practice is harder than it looks. *About Campus, 4*(4), 2–4.

Baxter Magolda, M. B. (2000). Interpersonal maturity: Integrating agency and communion. *Journal of College Student Development, 41,* 141–156.

Baxter Magolda, M. B. (2001). *Making their own way: Narratives for transforming higher education to promote self-development.* Sterling, VA: Stylus.

Baxter Magolda, M. B. (2002a). Epistemological reflection: The evolution of epistemological reflection assumptions from age 18–30. In B. K. Hofer & P. R. Pintrich (Eds.), *Personal epistemology: The psychology of beliefs about knowledge and knowing* (pp. 89–102). Mahwah, NJ: Erlbaum.

Baxter Magolda, M. B. (2002b). Helping students make their own way to adulthood: Good company for the journey. *About Campus, 6*(6), 2–9.

Baxter Magolda, M. B. (2003). Identity and learning: Student affairs' role in transforming higher education. *Journal of College Student Development, 44,* 231–247.

Baxter Magolda, M. B. (2004a). Evolution of a constructivist conceptualization of epistemological reflection. *Educational Psychologist, 39*(1), 31–42.

Baxter Magolda, M. B. (2004b). Learning partnerships model: A framework for promoting self-authorship. In M. Baxter Magolda & P. M. King (Eds.), *Learning partnerships: Theory and modes of practice to educate for self-authorship* (pp. 37–62). Sterling, VA: Stylus.

Baxter Magolda, M. B. (2004c). Self-authorship as the common goal of 21st-century education. In M. Baxter Magolda & P. M. King (Eds.), *Learning partnerships: Theory and modes of practice to educate for self-authorship* (pp. 1–35). Sterling, VA: Stylus.

Baxter Magolda, M. B. (2007). Self-authorship: The foundation for twenty-first-century education. In P. S. Meszaros (Ed.), *Self-authorship: Advancing students' intellectual growth* (pp. 69–83). New Directions for Teaching and Learning, No. 109. San Francisco: Jossey-Bass.

Baxter Magolda, M. B. (2008). Three elements of self-authorship. *Journal of College Student Development, 49*, 269–284.

Baxter Magolda, M. B., & King, P. M. (Eds.). (2004). *Learning partnerships: Theory and models of practice to educate for self-authorship.* Sterling, VA: Stylus.

Baxter Magolda, M. B., & King, P. M. (2007). Interview strategies for assessing self-authorship: Constructing conversations to assess meaning making. *Journal of College Student Development, 48*, 491–508.

Baxter Magolda, M. B., & King, P. M. (2008). Toward reflective conversations: An advising approach that promotes self-authorship. *Peer Review, 10*(1), 8–11.

Baxter Magolda, M. B., & Porterfield, W. D. (1985). A new approach to assess intellectual development on the Perry scheme. *Journal of College Student Personnel, 26*, 343–350.

Beemyn, B. G. (2005). Making campuses more inclusive of transgender students. *Journal of Gay and Lesbian Issues in Education, 3*(1), 77–89.

Bekken, B., & Marie, J. (2007). Making self-authorship a goal of core curricula: The Earth Sustainability Pilot Project. In P. S. Meszaros (Ed.), *Self-authorship: Advancing students' intellectual growth* (pp. 53–67). New Directions for Teaching and Learning, No. 109. San Francisco: Jossey-Bass.

Belenky, M. F. (1996). Public homeplaces: Nurturing the development of people, families, and communities. In N. Goldberger, J. Tarule, B. Clinchy, & M. Belenky (Eds.), *Knowledge, difference, and power* (pp. 393–430). New York: Basic Books.

Belenky, M. F., Bond, L. A., & Weinstock, J. S. (1997). *A tradition that has no name: Nurturing the development of people, families, and communities.* New York: Basic Books.

Belenky, M. F., Clinchy, B. M., Goldberger, N. R., & Tarule, J. M. (1986). *Women's ways of knowing: The development of self, voice, and mind.* New York: Basic Books.

Bell, D. (1975). Ethnicity and social change. In N. Glazer & D. P. Moynihan (Eds.), *Ethnicity, theory and experience* (pp. 141–174). Cambridge, MA: Harvard University Press.

Bell-Scriber, M. J. (2008). Warming the nursing education climate for traditional-age learners who are male. *Nursing Education Perspectives, 29*(3), 143–150.

Bem, S. L. (1974). The measurement of psychological androgyny. *Journal of Consulting and Clinical Psychology, 42*(2), 155–162.

Bem, S. L. (1981a). *Bem Sex-Role Inventory: Professional manual.* Palo Alto, CA: Consulting Psychologists Press.

Bem, S. L. (1981b). Gender schema theory: A cognitive account of sex typing. *Psychological Review, 88*(4), 354–364.

Bem, S. L. (1983). Gender schema theory and its implications for child development: Raising gender-aschematic children in a gender-schematic society. *Signs, 8*(4), 598–616.

Bem, S. L. (1993). *The lenses of gender: Transforming the debate on sexual inequality.* New Haven, CT: Yale University Press.

Bem, S. L. (1995). Dismantling gender polarization and compulsory heterosexuality: Should we turn the volume down or up? *Journal of Sex Research, 32*(4), 329–333.

Benishek, L. A., Bieschke, K. J., Park, J., & Slattery, S. M. (2004). A multicultural feminist model of mentoring. *Journal of Multicultural Counseling and Development, 32*, 428–442.

Bentrim-Tapio, E. M. (2004). Alcohol consumption in undergraduate students: The role of ego-identity status, alcohol expectancies, and drinking refusal self-efficacy. *NASPA Journal, 41*(4), 728–741.

Bergerson, A. A. (2003). Critical race theory and white racism: Is there room for white scholars in fighting racism in education? *Qualitative Studies in Education, 16*(1), 51–63.

Berry, J. W. (1984). Cultural relations in plural societies: Alternatives to segregation and their socio-psychological implications. In N. Miller & M. B. Brewer (Eds.), *Groups in contact* (pp. 11–27). Orlando, FL: Academic Press.

Berry, J. W. (1993). Ethnic identities in plural societies. In M. E. Bernal & G. P. Knight (Eds.), *Ethnic identity: Formation and transmission among Hispanics and other minorities* (pp. 271–296). Albany: State University of New York Press.

Beverley, J. (1999). *Subalternity and representation: Arguments in cultural theory.* Durham, NC: Duke University Press.

Bieschke, K. J. (2002). Charting the waters. *Counseling Psychologist, 30*, 575–581.

Bilodeau, B. L. (2005). Beyond the gender binary: A case study of two transgender students at a midwestern university. *Journal of Gay and Lesbian Issues in Education, 3*(1), 29–46.

Bilodeau, B. L. (2009). *Genderism: Transgender students, binary systems, and higher education.* Saarbrücken, Germany: Verlag.

Bilodeau, B. L., & Renn, K. A. (2005). Analysis of LGBT identity development models and implications for practice. In R. L. Sanlo (Ed.), *Gender identity and sexual orientation: Research, policy, and personal perspectives* (pp. 25–39). New Directions for Student Services, No. 111. San Francisco: Jossey-Bass.

Bilsker, D., Schiedel, D., & Marcia, J. (1988). Sex differences in identity status. *Sex Roles, 18*(3/4), 231–236.

Black, L., & Stone, D. (2005). Expanding the definition of privilege: The concept of social privilege. *Journal of Multicultural Counseling and Development, 33*, 243–255.

Blackhurst, A. B. (1995). The relationship between gender and student outcomes in a freshman orientation course. *Journal of the Freshman Year Experience, 7*, 63–80.

Blasi, A. (1980). Bridging moral cognition and moral action: A critical review of the literature. *Psychological Bulletin, 88*, 1–45.

Bloland, P. A., Stamatakos, L. C., & Rogers, R. R. (1994). *Reform in student affairs: A critique of student development.* Greensboro, NC: ERIC Counseling and Student Services Clearinghouse.

Bloland, P. A., Stamatakos, L. C., & Rogers, R. R. (1996). Redirecting the role of student affairs to focus on student learning. *Journal of College Student Development, 37*, 217–226.

Boatwright, K. J., Egidio, R. K., & Kalamazoo College Women's Leadership Research Team. (2003). Psychological predictors of college women's leadership aspirations. *Journal of College Student Development, 44*, 653–669.

Bock, M. T. (1999). Baxter Magolda's epistemological reflection model. In P. G. Love & V. L. Guthrie (Eds.), *Understanding and applying cognitive development theory* (pp. 29–40). New Directions for Student Services, No. 88. San Francisco: Jossey-Bass.

Bohmer, S., & Briggs, J. L. (1991). Teaching privileged students about gender, race and class oppression. *Teaching Sociology, 19*, 154–163.

Born, D. (1970). Psychological adaptation and development under acculturative stress: Toward a general model. *Social Science and Medicine, 3*, 529–547.

Bornstein, K. (1994). *Gender outlaw: On men, women and the rest of us.* New York: Routledge.

Borrego, S. E. (2004). *Class matters: Beyond access to inclusion.* Washington, DC: National Association of Student Personnel Administrators.

Bourassa, D., & Shipton, B. (1991). Addressing lesbian and gay issues in residence hall environments. In N. J. Evans & V. A. Wall (Eds.), *Beyond tolerance: Gays, lesbians and bisexuals on campus* (pp. 79–96). Alexandria, VA: American College Personnel Association.

Bourne, E. (1978a). The state of research on ego identity: A review and appraisal. Part I. *Journal of Youth and Adolescence, 7*(3), 223–251.

Bourne, E. (1978b). The state of research on ego identity: A review and appraisal. Part II. *Journal of Youth and Adolescence, 7*(4), 371–392.

Bower, B. L., & Collins, K. (2000). Students living with HIV/AIDS: Exploring their psychosocial and moral development. *NASPA Journal, 37,* 428–443.

Bowers, P. J., Dickman, M. M., & Fuqua, D. R. (2001). Psychosocial and career development related to employment of graduating seniors. *NASPA Journal, 38,* 326–347.

Bowman, J., & Wessel, R. (2002). [Review of the book *Big questions, worthy dreams: Mentoring young adults in their search for meaning, purpose, and faith*]. *Journal of College Student Development, 43,* 420–421.

Boyatzis, R. E., & Kolb, D. A. (1993a). *The adaptive style inventory.* Boston: McBer.

Boyatzis, R. E., & Kolb, D. A. (1993b). *Learning skills profile workbook.* Boston: McBer.

Brabeck, M. (1983). Moral judgment: Theory and research on differences between males and females. *Developmental Review, 3,* 274–291.

Bradby, D., & Helms, J. E. (1993). Black racial identity attitudes and white therapist cultural sensitivity in cross-racial therapy dyads: An exploratory study. In J. E. Helms (Ed.), *Black and white racial identity: Theory, research, and practice* (pp. 165–175). Westport, CT: Praeger.

Brady, S. (1983). The relationship between differences in stages of homosexuality identity formation and background characteristics, psychological well-being and homosexual adjustment. *Dissertation Abstracts International, 45,* 3328 (10B).

Brady, S., & Busse, W. J. (1994). The Gay Identity Questionnaire: A brief measure of homosexual identity formation. *Journal of Homosexuality, 26*(4), 1–21.

Branch, C. W., Tayal, P., & Triplett, C. (2000). The relationship of ethnic identity and ego identity status among adolescents and young adults. *International Journal of Intercultural Relations, 24,* 777–790.

Brand, M. (1988, Fall). Toward a better understanding of undergraduate music education majors: Perry's perspective. *Bulletin of the Council for Research in Music Education,* 22–31.

Breton, R., Isajiw, W. W., Kalbach, W. E., & Reitz, J. G. (Eds.). (1990). *Ethnic identity and equality.* Toronto: University of Toronto Press.

Brinkman, A. (2000). [Review of the book *Big questions, worthy dreams: Mentoring young adults in their search for meaning, purpose, and faith*]. *Library Journal, 125*(19), 85.

Brock, K. L., & Cameron, B. J. (1999). Enhancing political science courses with Kolb's learning preference model. *PS: Political Science and Politics, 32,* 251–256.

Broido, E. M. (2000). Constructing identity: The nature and meaning of lesbian, gay and bisexual identities. In R. P. Perez, K. A. DeBord, & K. Bieschke (Eds.), *Handbook of counseling and therapy with lesbians, gays, and bisexuals* (pp. 13–33). Washington, DC: American Psychological Association.

Bronfenbrenner, U. (1974). Developmental research and public policy and the ecology of childhood. *Child Development, 45,* 1–5.

Bronfenbrenner, U. (1977). Toward an experimental ecology of human development. *American Psychologist, 32*, 513–531.

Bronfenbrenner, U. (1979). *The ecology of human development: Experiments by nature and design.* Cambridge, MA: Harvard University Press.

Bronfenbrenner, U. (1989). Ecological systems theory. In R. Vasta (Ed.), *Six theories of development* (pp. 187–249). Greenwich, CT: JAI Press.

Bronfenbrenner, U. (1993). The ecology of cognitive development: Research models and fugitive findings. In R. H. Wozniak & K. W. Fischer (Eds.), *Development in context: Acting and thinking in specific environments* (pp. 3–44). Mahwah, NJ: Erlbaum.

Bronfenbrenner, U. (1995). Developmental ecology through space and time: A future perspective. In P. Moen & G. H. Elder, Jr. (Eds.), *Examining lives in context: Perspectives on the ecology of human development* (pp. 619–647). Washington, DC: American Psychological Association.

Bronfenbrenner, U. (Ed.). (2005). *Making human beings human: Bioecological perspectives on human development.* Thousand Oaks, CA: Sage.

Bronfenbrenner, U., & Morris, P. A. (2006). The bioecological model of human development. In W. Damon & R. M. Lerner (Eds.), *Handbook of child psychology* (6th ed., pp. 793–828). Hoboken, NJ: Wiley.

Broughton, J. M. (1986). The political psychology of faith development theory. In C. Dykstra & S. Parks (Eds.), *Faith development and Fowler* (pp. 90–114). Birmingham, AL: Religious Education Press.

Brown, E. (2006). The multiracial classification is necessary. In E. Stanford (Ed.), *Interracial America: Opposing viewpoints* (pp. 31–36). Farmington Hills, MI: Greenhaven.

Brown, L. L., & Robinson Kurpius, S. E. (1997). Psychosocial factors influencing academic persistence of American Indian college students. *Journal of College Student Development, 38*, 3–12.

Brown, L. S. (1995). Lesbian identities: Concepts and issues. In A. R. D'Augelli & C. J. Patterson (Eds.), *Lesbian, gay, and bisexual identities over the lifespan: Psychological perspectives* (pp. 3–23). New York: Oxford University Press.

Brown, O. G., Hinton, K. G., & Howard-Hamilton, M. (Eds.). (2007). *Unleashing suppressed voices on college campuses: Diversity issues in higher education.* New York: Peter Lang.

Brown, R. D. (1972). *Student development in tomorrow's higher education—A return to the academy.* Alexandria, VA: American College Personnel Association.

Brown, R. D. (1995). Reform in student affairs: A counterpoint comment. *ACPA Developments, 4,* 12.

Brown, R. D. (1996). We've been there. We've done that. Let's keep it up. *Journal of College Student Development, 37,* 239–241.

Brown, R. D., & Barr, M. J. (1990). Student development: Yesterday, today, and tomorrow. In L. V. Moore (Ed.), *Evolving theoretical perspectives on students* (pp. 83–92). New Directions for Student Services, No. 51. San Francisco: Jossey-Bass.

Brown, S. D., & Lent, R. W. (2005). *Career development and counseling: Putting theory and research to work.* Hoboken, NJ: Wiley.

Brown, U. M. (2001). *The interracial experience: Growing up black/white racially mixed in the United States.* Westport, CT: Praeger.

Brown-Wright, D. A., Dubick, R. A., & Newman, I. (1997). Graduate assistant expectation and faculty perception: Implications for mentoring and training. *Journal of College Student Development, 38,* 410–416.

Bruess, B. J., & Pearson, F. C. (2000). A study of the relationship between identity and moral development. *College Student Affairs Journal, 19*(2), 61–70.

Bryant, A. N. (2003). Changes in attitudes toward women's roles: Predicting gender-role traditionalism among college students. *Sex Roles, 48*(3–4), 131–142.

Bubolz, M. M., & Sontag, M. S. (1993). Human ecology theory. In P. Boss, W. J. Doherty, R. LaRossa, W. R. Schumm, & S. K. Steinmetz (Eds.), *Sourcebook of family theories and methods: A contextual approach* (pp. 419–447). New York: Plenum Press.

Buchko, K. J. (2004). Religious beliefs and practices of college women as compared to men. *Journal of College Student Development, 45,* 89–98.

Burke, R. J., & McKeen, C. A. (1996). Gender effects in mentoring relationships. *Journal of Social Behavior and Personality, 11,* 91–104.

Burnham, C. C. (1986). The Perry scheme and the teaching of writing. *Rhetoric Review, 4,* 152–158.

Burrow, A. L., Tubman, J. G., & Montgomery, M. J. (2006). Racial identity: Toward an integrated developmental psychological perspective. *Identity: An International Journal of Theory and Research, 6*(4), 317–339.

Butler, J. (1990). *Gender trouble: Feminism and the subversion of identity.* New York: Routledge.

Butler, J. (1993). *Bodies that matter: On the discursive limits of "sex."* New York: Routledge.

Butler, J. (2004). *Undoing gender.* New York: Routledge.

Cabrera, A. F., Crissman, J. L., Bernal, E. M., Nora, A., Terenzini, P. T., & Pascarella, E. T. (2002). Collaborative learning: Impact on college students' development and diversity. *Journal of College Student Development, 43,* 20–34.

Cajete, G. (2005). American Indian epistemologies. In M.J.T. Fox, S. C. Lowe, & G. S. McClellan (Eds.), *Serving Native American students* (pp. 69–78). New Directions for Student Services, No. 109. San Francisco: Jossey-Bass.

Canon, H. J., & Brown, R. D. (1985). How to think about professional ethics. In H. J. Canon & R. D. Brown (Eds.), *Applied ethics in student services* (pp. 81–87). New Directions for Student Services, No. 30. San Francisco: Jossey-Bass.

Carpenter, D. S. (1996). The philosophical heritage of student affairs. In A. Rentz (Ed.), *Student affairs functions in higher education* (2nd ed., pp. 3–27). Springfield, IL: Thomas.

Carpenter, S. (Ed.). (2001a). Scholarship in student affairs reconsidered [Special issue]. *Journal of College Student Development, 42*(4).

Carpenter, S. (2001b). Student affairs scholarship (re?)considered: Toward a scholarship of practice. *Journal of College Student Development, 42,* 301–318.

Carter, J. A. (1990). A comparison of personality types as determined by the Myers-Briggs Type Indicator with the process of separate-knowing and connected-knowing procedural processing among female, undergraduate, and non-traditional students. *Dissertation Abstracts International, 51*(05), 1475A.

Carter, K. A. (2000). Transgenderism in college students: Issues of gender identity and its role on our campuses. In V. A. Wall & N. J. Evans (Eds.), *Toward acceptance: Sexual orientation issues on campus* (pp. 261–283). Lanham, MD: University Press of America.

Carter, R. T. (1993). Does race or racial identity attitudes influence the counseling process in black and white dyads? In J. E. Helms (Ed.), *Black and white racial identity: Theory, research, and practice* (pp. 145–163). Westport, CT: Praeger.

Cartwright, K. B. (2001). Cognitive developmental theory and spiritual development. *Journal of Adult Development, 8,* 213–220.

Casas, J. M., & Pytluk, S. D. (1995). Hispanic identity development: Implications for research and practice. In J. G. Ponterotto, J. M. Casas, L. A. Suzuki, & C. M. Alexander (Eds.), *Handbook of multicultural counseling* (pp. 155–180). Thousand Oaks, CA: Sage.

Cash, T. F., Morrow, J. A., Hrabosky, J. I., & Perry, A. A. (2004). How has body image changed? A cross-sectional investigation of college women and men from 1983 to 2001. *Journal of Consulting and Clinical Psychology, 72*(6), 1081–1089.

Cass, V. C. (1979). Homosexual identity formation: A theoretical model. *Journal of Homosexuality, 4,* 219–235.

Cass, V. C. (1983–1984). Homosexual identity: A concept in need of definition. *Journal of Homosexuality, 9*(2–3), 31–43.

Cass, V. C. (1984). Homosexual identity formation: Testing a theoretical model. *Journal of Sex Research, 20,* 143–167.

Cass, V. C. (1990). The implications of homosexual identity formation for the Kinsey model and scale of sexual preference. In D. P. McWhirter, S. A. Sanders, & J. M. Reinisch (Eds.), *Homosexuality/heterosexuality: Concepts of sexual orientation* (pp. 239–266). New York: Oxford University Press.

Cass, V. C. (1996). Sexual orientation identity formation: A Western phenomenon. In R. P. Cabaj & T. S. Stein (Eds.), *Textbook of homosexuality and mental health* (pp. 227–251). Washington, DC: American Psychiatric Press.

Castro, O., & Peck, V. (2005). Learning styles and foreign language learning difficulties. *Foreign Language Annals, 38,* 401–409.

Champagne, D. E., & Petitpas, A. (1989). Planning developmental interventions for adult students. *NASPA Journal, 26,* 265–271.

Chan, C. S. (1995). Issues of sexual identity in an ethnic minority: The case of Chinese American lesbians, gay men, and bisexual people. In A. R. D'Augelli & C. J. Patterson (Eds.), *Lesbian, gay, and bisexual identities over the lifespan: Psychological perspectives* (pp. 87–101). New York: Oxford University Press.

Chandler, C. (1996). Mentoring and women in academia: Reevaluating the traditional model. *NWSA Journal, 8,* 79–101.

Chapman, O. (1993). Women's voice and the learning of math. *Journal of Gender Studies, 2,* 206–220.

Charner, I., & Schlossberg, N. K. (1986). Variations by theme: The life transitions of clerical workers. *Vocational Guidance Quarterly, 34,* 212–224.

Chassey, R. A. (1999). *A comparison of moral development of college student behavioral offenders and non-offenders* (Research Report No. 143). U.S. Department of Education: Office of Educational Research and Improvement. (ERIC Document Reproduction Service No. ED435943)

Chávez, A. F., Guido-DiBrito, F., & Mallory, S. (2003). Learning to value the "other": An individual framework for diversity development. *Journal of College Student Development, 44,* 453–469.

Cheatham, H. E., Slaney, R. B., & Coleman, N. C. (1990). Institutional effects on the psychosocial development of African-American college students. *Journal of Counseling Psychology, 37,* 453–458.

Chen, G. A., Lephuoc, P., Guzman, M. R., Rude, S. S., & Dodd, B. G. (2006). Exploring Asian American racial identity. *Cultural Diversity and Ethnic Minority Psychology, 12*(3), 461–476.

Chenoweth, E., & Galliher, R. V. (2004). Factors influencing college aspirations of rural West Virginia high school students. *Journal of Research in Rural Education, 19*(2). Retrieved April 25, 2008, from www.jrre.psu.edu/articles/19–2.pdf.

Chickering, A. W. (1969). *Education and identity.* San Francisco: Jossey-Bass.

Chickering, A. W. (1977). Potential contributions of college unions to student development. In W. M. Kiepper (Ed.), *The impact of college unions and their programs on today's student* (pp. 23–27). Stanford, CA: Association of College Unions-International.

Chickering, A. W., Dalton, J. C., & Stamm, L. (2006). *Encouraging authenticity and spirituality in higher education.* San Francisco: Jossey-Bass.

Chickering, A. W., & O'Connor, J. (1996). The university learning center: A driving force for collaboration. *About Campus, 1*(4), 16–21.

Chickering, A. W., & Reisser, L. (1993). *Education and identity* (2nd ed.). San Francisco: Jossey-Bass.

Chickering, A. W., & Schlossberg, N. K. (1995). *How to get the most out of college.* Needham Heights, MA: Allyn & Bacon.

Chickering, A. W., & Schlossberg, N. K. (1998). Moving on: Seniors as people in transition. In J. N. Gardner, G. Van der Veer, & Associates, *The senior year experience* (pp. 37–50). San Francisco: Jossey-Bass.

Chickering, A. W., & Schlossberg, N. K. (2001). *Getting the most out of college* (2nd ed.). Upper Saddle River, NJ: Prentice Hall.

Chizhik, E. W., & Chizhik, A. W. (2005). Are you privileged or oppressed? Students' conceptions of themselves and others. *Urban Education, 40*(2), 116–143.

Choney, S. K., Berryhill-Paapke, E., & Robbins, R. R. (1995). The acculturation of American Indians: Developing frameworks for research and practice. In J. G. Ponterotto, J. M. Casas, L. A. Suzuki, & C. M. Alexander (Eds.), *Handbook of multicultural counseling* (pp. 73–92). Thousand Oaks, CA: Sage.

Cintrón, R. (2000). Ethnicity, race, and culture: The case of Latino gay/bisexual men. In V. A. Wall & N. J. Evans (Eds.), *Toward acceptance: Sexual orientation issues on campus* (pp. 299–319). Lanham, MD: American College Personnel Association.

Clark, A. J., & Dobson, J. E. (1980). Moral development: A factor in the group counseling process. *Journal for Specialists in Group Work, 5,* 81–86.

Clark, B. R., & Trow, M. (1966). The organizational context. In T. M. Newcomb & E. K. Wilson (Eds.), *College peer groups: Problems and prospects for research* (pp. 17–70). Chicago: Aldine.

Clark, M., Kaufmann, S., & Pierce, R. C. (1976). Explorations of acculturation: Toward a model of ethnic identity. *Human Organizations, 3,* 231–238.

Clark, M. C., & Caffarella, R. S. (Eds.). (1999). *An update on adult development theory: New ways of thinking about the life course.* New Directions for Adult and Continuing Education, No. 84. San Francisco: Jossey-Bass.

Claxton, C. S., & Murrell, P. H. (1987). *Learning styles: Implications for improving educational practice* (ASHE-ERIC Higher Education Report No. 4). Washington, DC: Association for the Study of Higher Education.

Clayton, S. A., & Jones, A. (1993). Multiculturalism: An imperative for change. *Iowa Student Personnel Association Journal, 8,* 35–49.

Clinchy, B. M. (2002). Revisiting *Women's Ways of Knowing.* In B. K. Hofer & P. R. Pintrich (Eds.), *Personal epistemology: The psychology of beliefs about knowledge and knowing* (pp. 63–87). Mahwah, NJ: Erlbaum.

Cokley, K. (1999). Reconceptualizing the impact of college racial composition on African American students' racial identity. *Journal of College Student Development, 40*(3), 235–246.

Cokley, K. (2001). Gender differences among African American students in the impact of racial identity on academic psychosocial development. *Journal of College Student Development, 42,* 480–487.

Cokley, K. (2007). Critical issues in the measurement of ethnic and racial identity: A referendum on the state of the field. *Journal of Counseling Psychology, 54*(3), 224–234.

Colby, A., Kohlberg, L., & Kauffman, K. (1987). Theoretical introduction to the measurement of moral judgment. In A. Colby & L. Kohlberg (Eds.), *The measurement of moral judgment: Vol. 1. Theoretical foundations and research validation* (pp. 1–67). New York: Cambridge University Press.

Coleman, E. (1981–1982). Developmental stages of the coming out process. *Journal of Homosexuality, 7,* 31–43.

Collins, J. F. (2000). Biracial-bisexual individuals: Identity coming of age. *International Journal of Sexuality and Gender Studies, 5*(1), 221–253.

Committee on the Student in Higher Education. (1968). *The student in higher education.* New Haven, CT: Hazen Foundation.

Constantinople, A. (1969). An Eriksonian measure of personality development in college students. *Developmental Psychology, 1,* 357–372.

Conyne, R. K. (1975). Environmental assessment: Mapping for counselor action. *Personnel and Guidance Journal, 54,* 151–154.

Conyne, R. K., & Rogers, R. (1977). Psychotherapy as ecological problem solving. *Psychotherapy: Theory, Research and Practice, 14*(3), 298–305.

Coogan, P. A., & Chen, C. P. (2006). Career development and counseling for women: Connecting theories to practice. *Counseling Psychology Quarterly, 20*(2), 191–204.

Coomes, M. D. (1992). Understanding students: A developmental approach to financial aid services. *Journal of Financial Aid, 22*(2), 23–31.

Coomes, M. D. (1994). Using student development to guide institutional policy. *Journal of College Student Development, 35,* 428–437.

Coomes, M. D. (2004). Understanding the historical and cultural influences that shape generations. In M. D. Coomes & R. DeBard (Eds.), *Serving the millennial generation* (pp. 17–31). New Directions for Student Services, No. 106. San Francisco: Jossey-Bass.

Cormier, L. S., & Hackney, H. (1993). *The professional counselor: A process guide to helping* (2nd ed.). Needham Heights, MA: Allyn & Bacon.

Cortés, C. E. (2000). The diversity within: Intermarriage, identity, and campus community. *About Campus, 5*(1), 5–10.

Cosgrove, T. J. (1987). Understanding how college students think. *Campus Activities Programming, 20*(3), 56–60.

Côté, J. E., & Levine, C. (1983). Marcia and Erikson: The relationships among ego identity status, neuroticism, dogmatism, and purpose in life. *Journal of Youth and Adolescence, 12*(1), 43–83.

Côté, J. E., & Levine, C. (1988a). A critical examination of the ego identity status paradigm. *Developmental Review, 8,* 147–184.

Côté, J. E., & Levine, C. (1988b). On critiquing the identity status paradigm: A rejoinder to Waterman. *Developmental Review, 8,* 209–218.

Council of Student Personnel Associations in Higher Education. (1994). Student development workers in postsecondary education. In A. Rentz (Ed.), *Student affairs: A profession's heritage* (American College Personnel Association Media Publication No. 40, 2nd ed., pp. 428–437). Lanham, MD: University Press of America. (Original work published 1975)

Cramer, E. P. (Ed.). (2002). *Addressing homophobia and heterosexism on college campuses.* New York: Harrington Park.

Crawford, J. S. (1989, May). *Perry's levels and Belenky's findings: The possibilities in the teaching of art and art history.* Paper presented at the Getty Conference on Discipline-Based Art Education, Austin, TX. (ERIC Document Reproduction Service No. ED310698)

Creamer, D. G. (Ed.). (1980). *Student development in higher education: Theories, practices, and future directions.* Cincinnati, OH: American College Personnel Association.

Creamer, D. G. (Ed.). (1990). *College student development: Theory and practice for the 1990s.* Alexandria, VA: American College Personnel Association.

Creamer, E. G., & Laughlin, A. (2005). Self-authorship and women's career decision making. *Journal of College Student Development, 46,* 13–27.

Crissman Ishler, J. L. (2004). Tracing "friendsickness" during the first year of college through journal writing: A qualitative study. *NASPA Journal, 41*(3). Retrieved January 15, 2005, from http://publications.naspa.org/naspajournal/vol41/iss3/art8.

Cross, W. E., Jr. (1971). Toward a psychology of black liberation: The Negro-to-black conversion experience. *Black World, 20*(9), 13–27.

Cross, W. E., Jr. (1978). The Thomas and Cross models of psychological nigrescence: A review. *Journal of Black Psychology, 5,* 13–31.

Cross, W. E., Jr. (1991). *Shades of black: Diversity in African American identity.* Philadelphia: Temple University Press.

Cross, W. E., Jr., & Fhagen-Smith, P. (2001). Patterns in African American identity development: A life span perspective. In C. L. Wijeyesinghe & B. W. Jackson, III (Eds.), *New perspectives on racial identity development: A theoretical and practical anthology* (pp. 243–270). New York: New York University Press.

Croteau, J. M., Talbot, D. M., Lance, T. S., & Evans, N. J. (2002). A qualitative study of the interplay between privilege and oppression. *Journal of Multicultural Counseling and Development, 30,* 239–258.

Crotty, M. (1998). *The foundations of social research: Meaning and perspective in the research process.* Thousand Oaks, CA: Sage.

Crowley, P. M. (1989). Ask the expert: A group teaching tool. *Journal for Specialists in Group Work, 14,* 173–175.

Cutietta, R. A. (1990). Adapt your teaching style to your students. *Music Educators Journal, 76*(6), 31–36.

Cuyjet, M. J. (2008). Bicultural faculty and their professional adaptation. In K. A. Renn & P. Shang (Eds.), *Biracial and multiracial college students* (pp. 73–82). New Directions for Student Services, No. 123. San Francisco: Jossey-Bass.

Dalton, J. C. (2006a). Integrating spirit and community in higher education. In A. W. Chickering, J. C. Dalton, & L. Stamm (Eds.), *Encouraging authenticity and spirituality in higher education* (pp. 165–185). San Francisco: Jossey-Bass.

Dalton, J. C. (2006b). The place of spirituality in the mission and work of college student affairs. In A. W. Chickering, J. C. Dalton, & L. Stamm (Eds.), *Encouraging authenticity and spirituality in higher education* (pp. 145–164). San Francisco: Jossey-Bass.

Dalton, J. C. (2006c). Principles and practices for strengthening moral and spiritual growth in college. In A. W. Chickering, J. C. Dalton, & L. Stamm (Eds.), *Encouraging authenticity and spirituality in higher education* (pp. 272–282). San Francisco: Jossey-Bass.

Dalton, J. C., Eberhardt, D., Bracken, J., & Echols, K. (2006). Inward journeys: Forms and patterns of college student spirituality. *Journal of College and Character, 7*(8), 1–21.

Daniel, G. R. (1996). Black and white identity in the new millennium: Unsevering the ties that bind. In M.P.P. Root (Ed.), *The multiracial experience: Racial borders as the new frontier* (pp. 121–139). Thousand Oaks, CA: Sage.

Daniel, G. R. (2002). *More than black? Multiracial identity and the new racial order.* Philadelphia: Temple University Press.

D'Augelli, A. R. (1991). Gay men in college: Identity processes and adaptations. *Journal of College Student Development, 32,* 140–146.

D'Augelli, A. R. (1994a). Identity development and sexual orientation: Toward a model of lesbian, gay, and bisexual identity development. In E. J. Trickett, R. J. Watts, & D. Birman (Eds.), *Human diversity: Perspectives on people in context* (pp. 312–333). San Francisco: Jossey-Bass.

D'Augelli, A. R. (1994b). Lesbian and gay male development: Steps toward an analysis of lesbian's and gay men's lives. In B. Greene & G. M. Herek (Eds.), *Lesbian and gay psychology: Theory, research, and clinical implications* (Psychological Perspectives on Lesbian and Gay Issues, Vol. 1, pp. 118–132). Thousand Oaks, CA: Sage.

D'Augelli, A. R. (1996). Enhancing the development of lesbian, gay, and bisexual youths. In E. D. Rothblum & L. A. Bond (Eds.), *Preventing heterosexism and homophobia* (pp. 124–150). Thousand Oaks, CA: Sage.

Davis, C., III, Aronson, J., & Salinas, M. (2006). Shades of threat: Racial identity as a moderator of stereotype threat. *Journal of Black Psychology, 32*(4), 399–417.

Davis, F. J. (1995). The Hawaiian alternative to the one-drop rule. In N. Zack (Ed.), *American mixed race: The culture of microdiversity* (pp. 115–131). Lanham, MD: Rowman & Littlefield.

Davis, T. L. (2002). Voices of gender role conflict: The social construction of college men's identity. *Journal of College Student Development, 43,* 508–521.

Day Shaw, J. (2001). *An application of Baxter Magolda's epistemological reflection model to black and Latino students.* Unpublished doctoral dissertation, Florida State University.

Day-Vines, N., Barker, J. M., & Exum, H. (1998). Impact of diasporic travel on ethnic identity development of African American college students. *College Student Journal, 32,* 463–471.

Deaux, K. (1985). Sex and gender. *Annual Review of Psychology, 36,* 49–81.

DeBose, H. L., & Winters, L. I. (2003). The dilemma of biracial people of African American descent. In L. I. Winters & H. L. DeBose (Eds.), *New faces in a changing America: Multiracial identity in the 21st century* (pp. 127–157). Thousand Oaks, CA: Sage.

Degges-White, S., Rice, B., & Myers, J. E. (2000). Revisiting Cass' theory of sexual identity formation: A study of lesbian development. *Journal of Mental Health Counseling, 22,* 318–333.

Delgado, R. (Ed.). (1995). *Critical race theory: The cutting edge.* Philadelphia, PA: Temple University Press.

Delgado, R. (1998). The black/white binary: How does it work? In R. Delgado & J. Stefancic (Eds.), *The Latino condition: A critical reader* (pp. 369–375). New York: New York University Press.

Delgado, R., & Stefancic, J. (2001). *Critical race theory: An introduction.* New York: New York University Press.

Delworth, U. (1989). Identity in the college years: Issues of gender and ethnicity. *NASPA Journal, 26,* 162–166.

Delworth, U., & Seeman, D. (1984). The ethics of care: Implications of Gilligan for the student services profession. *Journal of College Student Personnel, 25,* 489–492.

Dennis, J. M., Phinney, J. S., & Chuateco, L. I. (2005). The role of motivation, parental support, and peer support in the academic success of ethnic minority first-generation college students. *Journal of College Student Development, 46,* 223–236.

Denzin, N. K., & Lincoln, Y. S. (1994). *Handbook of qualitative research.* Thousand Oaks, CA: Sage.

Denzin, N. K., Lincoln, Y. S., & Smith, L. T. (Eds.). (2008). *Handbook of critical and indigenous methodologies.* Thousand Oaks, CA: Sage.

Derryberry, W. P., & Thoma, S. J. (2000). The friendship effect: Its role in the development of moral thinking in students. *About Campus, 5,* 13–18.

Desler, M. K. (2000). Translating theory and assessment results to practice. In M. J. Barr & M. K. Desler (Eds.), *Handbook of student affairs administration* (2nd ed., pp. 285–310). San Francisco: Jossey-Bass.

Desmedt, E., & Valcke, M. (2004). Mapping the learning styles "jungle": An overview of the literature based on citation analysis. *Educational Psychology, 24,* 446–464.

Desoff, A. (2006). Who's NOT going abroad? *International Educator, 15*(2), 20–27.

Dewey, J. (1933). *How we think: A restatement of the relation of reflective thinking to the educative process.* Lanham, MD: Heath.

Dewey, J. (1958). *Experience and nature* (2nd ed.). La Salle, IL: Open Court.

Dewey, J. (1960). *Logic: The theory of inquiry.* New York: Holt, Rinehart, & Winston. (Original work published 1938)

Dey, E. L., & Hurtado, S. (1995). College impact, student impact: A reconsideration of the role of students within American higher education. *Higher Education, 30*(2), 207–223.

Diamond, L. M., & Savin-Williams, R. C. (2000). Explaining diversity in the development of same-sex sexuality among young women. *Journal of Social Issues, 56,* 297–313.

DiCaprio, N. S. (1974). *Personality theories: Guides to living.* Philadelphia: Saunders.

Dilley, P. (2002). *Queer man on campus: A history of non-heterosexual college men, 1945–2000.* New York: Routledge Falmer.

Dilley, P. (2005). Which way out? A typology of non-heterosexual male collegiate identities. *Journal of Higher Education, 76*(1), 56–88.

Dillon, F. R., Worthington, R. L., Soth-McNett, A. M., & Schwartz, S. J. (2008). Gender and sexual identity–based predictors of lesbian, gay, and bisexual affirmative counseling self-efficacy. *Professional Psychology: Research and Practice, 39*(3), 353–360.

Dinitz, S., & Kiedaisch, J. (1990). Persuasion from an eighteen-year-old's perspective: Perry and Piaget. *Journal of Teaching Writing, 9,* 85–97.

Dirks, D. H. (1988). Moral development in Christian higher education. *Journal of Psychology and Theology, 16,* 324–331.

Donnelly, D. A., Cook, K. J., Van Ausdale, D., & Foley, L. (2005). White privilege, color blindness, and services to battered women. *Violence Against Women, 11*(1), 6–37.

Douglass, R. E. (2003). The evolution of the multiracial movement. In M.P.P. Root & M. Kelley (Eds.), *The multiracial child resource book: Living complex identities* (pp. 13–17). Seattle: MAVIN Foundation.

DuBay, W. H. (1987). *Gay identity: The self under ban.* Jefferson, NC: McFarland.

Du Bois, W.E.B. (1903). *The souls of black folk: Essays and sketches* (3rd ed.). Chicago: McClurg.

Durham, R. L., Hays, J., & Martinez, R. (1994). Socio-cognitive development among Chicano and Anglo American college students. *Journal of College Student Development, 35,* 178–182.

Dworkin, S. (2002). Biracial, bicultural, bisexual: Bisexuality and multiple identities. *Journal of Bisexuality, 2*(4), 93–108.

Dykstra, C. (1986). What is faith? In C. Dykstra & S. Parks (Eds.), *Faith development and Fowler* (pp. 45–64). Birmingham, AL: Religious Education Press.

Dykstra, C., & Parks, S. (1986). Introduction. In C. Dykstra & S. Parks (Eds.), *Faith development and Fowler* (pp. 1–12). Birmingham, AL: Religious Education Press.

Egan, G. (1982). *The skilled helper* (2nd ed.). Monterey, CA: Brooks/Cole.

Egan, G. (2007). *The skilled helper* (8th ed.). Belmont, CA: Thomson Brooks/Cole.

Egan, K. S. (1996). Flexible mentoring: Adaptations in style for women's ways of knowing. *Journal of Business Communication, 33,* 401–425.

Egart, K., & Healy, M. P. (2004). An urban leadership internship program: Implementing learning partnerships "unplugged" from campus structures. In M. Baxter Magolda & P. M. King (Eds.), *Learning partnerships: Theory and modes of practice to educate for self-authorship* (pp. 125–149). Sterling, VA: Stylus.

Eliason, M. J. (1995). Accounts of sexual identity formation in heterosexual students. *Sex Roles, 32,* 821–834.

Eliason, M. J. (1996a). Identity formation for lesbian, bisexual, and gay persons: Beyond a "minoritizing" view. *Journal of Homosexuality, 30*(3), 31–58.

Eliason, M. J. (1996b). An inclusive model of lesbian identity development. *Journal of Gay, Lesbian, and Bisexual Identity, 1*(1), 3–19.

Ellis, L. (1996). Theories of homosexuality. In R. C. Savin-Williams & K. M. Cohen (Eds.), *The lives of lesbians, gays, and bisexuals: Children to adults* (pp. 11–34). Fort Worth, TX: Harcourt Brace.

Enns, C. Z. (1991). The new relationship models of women's identity: A review and critique for counselors. *Journal of Counseling and Development, 69,* 209–217.

Enns, C. Z. (1993). Integrating separate and connected knowing: The experiential learning model. *Teaching of Psychology, 20*(1), 7–13.

Epstein, S. (1987). Gay politics, ethnic identity: The limits of social constructionism. *Socialist Review, 17*(3/4), 9–54.

Erikson, E. H. (1950). *Childhood and society.* New York: Norton.

Erikson, E. H. (1963). *Childhood and society* (2nd ed.). New York: Norton.

Erikson, E. H. (1964). *Insight and responsibility.* New York: Norton.

Erikson, E. H. (1968). *Identity: Youth and crisis.* New York: Norton.

Erikson, E. H. (1980). *Identity and the life cycle.* New York: Norton. (Original work published 1959)

Erwin, T. D. (1983). The Scale of Intellectual Development: Measuring Perry's scheme. *Journal of College Student Personnel, 24,* 6–12.

Erwin, T. D., & Delworth, U. (1982). Formulating environmental constructs that affect students' identity. *NASPA Journal, 20*(1), 47–55.

Erwin, T. D., & Kelly, K. (1985). Changes in students' self-confidence in college. *Journal of College Student Personnel, 26,* 395–400.

Erwin, T. M. (2001). *Encouraging the spiritual development of counseling students and supervisees using Fowler's stages of faith development.* (ERIC Document Reproduction Service No. ED4457473)

Evans, N. J. (1982). Using developmental theory in needs assessment. *Journal of the National Association for Women Deans, Administrators, and Counselors, 45*(3), 34–39.

Evans, N. J. (1987). A framework for assisting student affairs staff in fostering moral development. *Journal of Counseling and Development, 66,* 191–194.

Evans, N. J. (2001a). The experiences of lesbian, gay, and bisexual youths in university communities. In A. R. D'Augelli & C. J. Patterson (Eds.), *Lesbian, gay, and bisexual identities and youth: Psychological perspectives* (pp. 181–198). New York: Oxford University Press.

Evans, N. J., with Reason, R. D. (2001b). Guiding principles: A review and analysis of student affairs philosophical statements. *Journal of College Student Development, 42,* 359–377.

Evans, N. J. (2003). Psychosocial, cognitive, and typological perspectives on student development. In S. K. Komives, D. B. Woodard, Jr., & Associates, *Student services: A handbook for the profession* (4th ed., pp. 179–202). San Francisco: Jossey-Bass.

Evans, N. J. (2008). Theoretical foundations of Universal Instructional Design. In J. L. Higbee & E. Goff (Eds.), *Pedagogy and student services for institutional transformation: Implementing universal design in higher education* (pp. 11–23). Minneapolis: University of Minnesota, Center for Research on Developmental Education and Urban Literacies.

Evans, N. J., Assadi, J. L., & Herriott, T. K. (2005). Encouraging the development of disability allies. In R. D. Reason, E. M. Broido, T. L. Davis, & N. J. Evans (Eds.), *Developing social justice allies* (pp. 67–79). New Directions for Student Services, No. 110. San Francisco: Jossey-Bass.

Evans, N. J., Bradley, R., & Bradley, J. (1985, March). *An overview and comparison of student development theory to practice models.* Paper presented at the annual meeting of the American College Personnel Association, Boston.

Evans, N. J., & Broido, E. M. (1999). Coming out in college residence halls: Negotiation, meaning making, challenges, supports. *Journal of College Student Development, 40,* 658–668.

Evans, N. J., & Broido, E. M. (2002). The experiences of lesbian and bisexual women in college residence halls: Implications for addressing homophobia and heterosexism. In E. P. Cramer (Ed.), *Addressing homophobia and heterosexism on college campuses* (pp. 29–42). New York: Harrington Park Press.

Evans, N. J., & Broido, E. M. (2005). Encouraging the development of social justice attitudes and actions in heterosexual students. In R. D. Reason, E. M. Broido, T. L. Davis, & N. J. Evans (Eds.), *Developing social justice allies* (pp. 43–54). New Directions for Student Services, No. 110. San Francisco: Jossey-Bass.

Evans, N. J., & D'Augelli, A. R. (1996). Lesbians, gay men, and bisexual people in college. In R. C. Savin-Williams & K. M. Cohen (Eds.), *The lives of lesbians, gays, and bisexuals: Children to adults* (pp. 201–226). Fort Worth, TX: Harcourt Brace.

Evans, N. J., & Herriott, T. K. (2004). Freshmen impressions: How a campus climate study shaped the perceptions, self-awareness, and behavior of four first-year students. *Journal of College Student Development, 45,* 316–332.

Evans, N. J., & Herriott, T. K. (2009). Philosophical and theoretical approaches to disability. In J. L. Higbee & A. A. Mitchell (Eds.), *Making good on the promise: Student affairs professionals with disabilities* (pp. 27–40). Lanham, MD: American College Personnel Association.

Evans, N. J., & Rankin, S. (1998). Heterosexism and campus violence: Assessment and intervention strategies. In A. M. Hoffman, J. H. Schuh, & R. H. Fenske (Eds.), *iolence on campus: Defining the problems, strategies for action* (pp. 169–186). Gaithersburg, MD: Aspen.

Evans, N. J., Reason, R. D., & Broido, E. M. (2001). Lesbian, gay, and bisexual students' perceptions of resident assistants: Implications for resident assistant selection and training. *College Student Affairs Journal, 21,* 82–91.

Evans, N. J., & Wall, V. A. (Eds.). (1991). *Beyond tolerance: Gays, lesbians and bisexuals on campus.* Alexandria, VA: American College Personnel Association.

Fanon, F. (1967). *Black skin: White masks.* New York: Grove Press.

Farver, J. M., Xu, Y., Bhadha, B. R., Narang, S., & Lieber, E. (2007). Ethnic identity, acculturation, parenting beliefs, and adolescent adjustment: A comparison of Asian Indian and European American families. *Merrill-Palmer Quarterly, 53*(2), 184–215.

Fassinger, R. E. (1998a). Lesbian, gay, and bisexual identity and student development theory. In R. L. Sanlo (Ed.), *Working with lesbian, gay, bisexual, and transgender college students: A handbook for faculty and administrators* (pp. 13–22). Westport, CT: Greenwood Press.

Fassinger, R. E. (1998b). *Lesbian Identity Questionnaire* (Rev. ed.). Unpublished instrument, University of Maryland, College Park.

Fassinger, R. E., & Hensler-McGinnis, N. F. (2005). Multicultural feminist mentoring as individual and small-group pedagogy. In C. Z. Enns & A. L. Sinacore (Eds.), *Teaching and social justice: Integrating multicultural and feminist theories in the classroom* (pp. 143–161). Washington, DC: American Psychological Association.

Fassinger, R. E., & Miller, B. A. (1997). Validation of an inclusive model of homosexual identity formation in a sample of gay men. *Journal of Homosexuality, 32*(2), 53–78.

Fausto-Sterling, A. (1993). The five sexes: Why male and female are not enough. *Sciences, 33*(2), 20–25.

Feigenbaum, E. F. (2007). Heterosexual privilege: The political and the personal. *Hypatia, 22*(1), 1–9.

Feingold, A., & Mazzella, R. (1998). Gender differences in body image are increasing. *Psychological Science, 9*(3), 190–195.

Feldman, K. A., & Newcomb, T. M. (1969). *The impact of college on students* (2 vols.). San Francisco: Jossey-Bass.

Ferdman, B. M., & Gallegos, P. I. (2001). Racial identity development and Latinos in the United States. In C. L. Wijeyesinghe & B. W. Jackson, III (Eds.), *New perspectives on racial identity development: A theoretical and practical anthology* (pp. 32–66). New York: New York University Press.

Fernout, J. H. (1986). Where is faith? Searching for the core of the cube. In C. Dykstra & S. Parks (Eds.), *Faith development and Fowler* (pp. 65–89). Birmingham, AL: Religious Education Press.

Fleming, J. (1984). *Blacks in college: A comparative study of students' success in black and white institutions.* San Francisco: Jossey-Bass.

Ford, M. R., & Lowery, C. R. (1986). Gender differences in moral reasoning: A comparison of the use of justice and care orientations. *Journal of Personality and Social Psychology, 50,* 777–783.

Forney, D. S. (1991a). Learning style information: A support for service delivery, Part I. *Career Waves: Leading Ideas for Career Development Professionals, 4*(1), 2–3.

Forney, D. S. (1991b). Learning style information: A support for service delivery, Part II. *Career Waves: Leading Ideas for Career Development Professionals, 4*(2), 1, 7.

Forney, D. S. (1994). A profile of student affairs master's students: Characteristics, attitudes, and learning styles. *Journal of College Student Development, 35,* 337–345.

Forney, D. S., & Davis, T. L. (2002). Ongoing transition sessions for student affairs master's students. *Journal of College Student Development, 43,* 288–293.

Forney, D. S., Eddy, W. L., Gunter, G. S., & Slater, R. E. (1992, March). *Student development as a subversive activity.* Paper presented at the annual meeting of the American College Personnel Association, San Francisco.

Forney, D. S., & Gingrich, D. D. (1983, March). *Transitions: Making the break to life after college.* Paper presented at the American College Personnel Association National Conference, Houston, TX.

Forney, D., McEwen, M., Reisser, L., Baxter Magolda, M., Hernandez, J., Jones, S., et al. (2005). Student development theory as a foundation for professional practice: A call to the profession. *ACPA Developments.* Retrieved January 26, 2007, from www.my-elf.org/pdfs/stud_dev_pract.pdf.

Forrest, L. (1988). [Review of the book *Women's ways of knowing: The development of self, voice, and mind*]. *Journal of College Student Development, 29,* 82–84.

Foubert, J. D., Nixon, M. L., Sisson, V. S., & Barnes, A. C. (2005). A longitudinal study of Chickering and Reisser's vectors: Exploring gender differences and implications for refining the theory. *Journal of College Student Development, 46,* 461–471.

Fowler, J. (1978). Life/faith patterns: Structures of trust and loyalty. In J. Berryman (Ed.), *Lifemaps: Conversations on the journey of faith* (pp. 14–104). Waco, TX: Word.

Fowler, J. W. (1980). Faith and the structuring of meaning. In *Toward moral and religious maturity: The first international conference on moral and religious development* (pp. 51–85). Morristown, NJ: Silver Burdett.

Fowler, J. W. (1981). *Stages of faith: The psychology of human development and the quest for meaning.* New York: HarperCollins.

Fowler, J. W. (1986a). Dialogue toward a future in faith development studies. In C. Dykstra & S. Parks (Eds.), *Faith development and Fowler* (pp. 275–301). Birmingham, AL: Religious Education Press.

Fowler, J. W. (1986b). Faith and the structure of meaning. In C. Dykstra & S. Parks (Eds.), *Faith development and Fowler* (pp. 15–42). Birmingham, AL: Religious Education Press.

Fowler, J. W. (1996). *Faithful change: The personal and public challenges of postmodern life.* Nashville, TN: Abingdon.

Fowler, J. W. (2000). *Becoming adult, becoming Christian: Adult development and Christian faith.* San Francisco: Jossey-Bass.

Fox, N. S., Spooner, S. E., Utterback, J. W., & Barbieri, J. A. (1996). Relationships between autonomy, gender, and weekend commuting among college students. *NASPA Journal, 34,* 19–28.

Fox, R. C. (1995). Bisexual identities: In A. R. D'Augelli & C. J. Patterson (Eds.), *Lesbian, gay, and bisexual identities over the lifespan: Psychological perspectives* (pp. 48–86). New York: Oxford University Press.

Fox, R. C. (1996). Bisexuality: An examination of theory and research. In R. P. Cabaj & T. S. Stein (Eds.), *Textbook of homosexuality and mental health* (pp. 147–171). Washington, DC: American Psychiatric Press.

Frable, D. E. (1997). Gender, racial, ethnic, sexual, and class identities. *Annual Review of Psychology, 48,* 139–162.

Freire, P. (1973). *Education for critical consciousness.* New York: Continuum.

Freire, P. (1974). *Pedagogy of the oppressed.* New York: Continuum.

Freud, S. (1965). *Three essays on the theory of sexuality* (J. Strachey, Trans.). New York: Basic Books. (Original work published 1905)

Fried, J. (1988). Women's ways of knowing: Some additional observations. [Review of the book *Women's ways of knowing: The development of self, voice, and mind*]. *Journal of College Student Development, 29,* 84–85.

Fried, J. (Ed.). (1994). *Different voices: Gender and perspective in student affairs administration.* Washington, DC: National Association of Student Personnel Administrators.

Fried, J., & Associates. (1995). *Shifting paradigms in student affairs: Culture, context, teaching, and learning.* Lanham, MD: American College Personnel Association.

Frye, M. (1990). The possibility of feminist theory. In D. L. Rhode (Ed.), *Theoretical perspectives on sexual difference* (pp. 174–184). New Haven, CT: Yale University Press.

Frye, M. (2003). Oppression. In M. S. Kimmel & A. L. Ferber (Eds.), *Privilege: A reader* (pp. 13–20). Cambridge, MA: Westview Press.

Fukuyama, M. A., & Ferguson, A. D. (2000). Lesbian, gay, and bisexual people of color: Understanding cultural complexity and managing multiple oppressions. In R. P. Perez, K. A. DeBord, & K. Bieschke (Eds.), *Handbook of counseling and psychotherapy with lesbian, gay, and bisexual clients* (pp. 81–105). Washington, DC: American Psychological Association.

Funderburg, L. (1994). *Black, white, other: Biracial Americans talk about race and identity.* New York: William Morrow.

Galambos, N. L., Almeida, D. M., & Petersen, A. C. (1990). Masculinity, femininity, and sex role attitudes in early adolescence: Exploring gender intensification. *Child Development, 61*(6), 1905–1914.

Galbraith, R. E., & Jones, T. M. (1976). *Moral reasoning: A teaching handbook for adapting Kohlberg to the classroom.* Minneapolis: Greenhaven Press.

Garland, P. H., & Grace, T. W. (1993). *New perspectives for student affairs professionals: Evolving realities, responsibilities, and roles* (ASHE-ERIC Higher Education Report No. 7). Washington, DC: George Washington University, School of Education and Human Development.

Garrett, M. T., & Pichette, E. F. (2000). Red as an apple: Native American acculturation and counseling with or without reservation. *Journal of Counseling and Development, 78*(1), 3–13.

Gasser, H. S. (2008). Being multiracial in a wired society: Using the Internet to define identity and community on campus. In K. A. Renn & P. Shang (Eds.), *Biracial and multiracial college students* (pp. 63–71). New Directions for Student Services, No. 123. San Francisco: Jossey-Bass.

Gathman, A. C., & Nessan, C. L. (1997). Fowler's stages of faith development in an honors science-and-religion seminar. *Zygon, 32*, 407–414.

Gelwick, B. P. (1985). Cognitive development of women. In N. J. Evans (Ed.), *Facilitating the development of women* (pp. 29–44). New Directions for Student Services, No. 29. San Francisco: Jossey-Bass.

Gender. (n.d.). *The Oxford dictionary of philosophy.* Retrieved May 16, 2008, from Answers.com Web site: www.answers.com/topic/gender.

Genia, V. (1992). Transitional faith: A developmental step toward religious maturity. *Counseling and Values, 37*(1), 15–23.

Gerst, J., & Fonken, M. A. (1995). Homoprejudice within the campus ecology. *Campus Ecologist, 13*(3), 1–2.

Gibbs, J. T. (1974). Patterns of adaptation among black students at a predominantly white university: Selected case studies. *American Journal of Orthopsychiatry, 44*, 728–740.

Gibbs, J. T. (1987). Identity and marginality: Issues in the treatment of biracial adolescents. *American Journal of Orthopsychiatry, 57*, 265–278.

Gilley, D. V. (2005). Whose spirituality? Cautionary notes about the role of spirituality in higher education. In S. L. Hoppe & B. W. Speck (Eds.), *Spirituality in higher education* (pp. 93–99). New Directions for Teaching and Learning, No. 104. San Francisco: Jossey-Bass.

Gilligan, C. (1977). In a different voice: Women's conception of self and morality. *Harvard Educational Review, 47*, 481–517.

Gilligan, C. (1981). Moral development in the college years. In A. Chickering (Ed.), *The modern American college* (pp. 139–157). San Francisco: Jossey-Bass.

Gilligan, C. (1982). *In a different voice: Psychological theory and women's development.* Cambridge, MA: Harvard University Press.

Gilligan, C. (1986). Reply (to critics). *Signs: Journal of Women in Culture and Society, 11,* 324–333.

Gilligan, C. (1993). *In a different voice: Psychological theory and women's development.* Cambridge, MA: Harvard University Press. (Original work published 1982)

Gilligan, C. (2002). *The birth of pleasure.* New York: Knopf.

Gilligan, C. (2004). Recovering psyche. *Annual of Psychoanalysis, 32,* 131–147.

Gilligan, C., & Belenky, M. F. (1980). A naturalistic study of abortion decisions. In R. Selman & R. Yando (Eds.), *Clinical-developmental psychology* (pp. 69–90). New Directions for Child Development, No. 7. San Francisco: Jossey-Bass.

Gilligan, C., & Murphy, J. M. (1979). Development from adolescence to adulthood: The philosopher and the "dilemma of the fact." In D. Kuhn (Ed.), *Intellectual development beyond childhood* (pp. 85–99). New Directions for Child Development, No. 5. San Francisco: Jossey-Bass.

Ginsburg, S. D., & Orlofsky, J. L. (1981). Ego identity status, ego development, and locus of control in college women. *Journal of Youth and Adolescence, 10*(4), 297–307.

Goldberger, N. R. (1996a). Cultural imperatives and diversity in ways of knowing. In N. Goldberger, J. Tarule, B. Clinchy, & M. Belenky (Eds.), *Knowledge, difference, and power* (pp. 335–371). New York: Basic Books.

Goldberger, N. R. (1996b). Introduction: Looking backward, looking forward. In N. Goldberger, J. Tarule, B. Clinchy, & M. Belenky (Eds.), *Knowledge, difference, and power* (pp. 1–21). New York: Basic Books.

Good, J. L., & Cartwright, C. (1998). Development of moral judgment among undergraduate university students. *College Student Journal, 32,* 270–277.

Goodin, H. J. (2003). The nursing shortage in the United States of America: An integrative review of the literature. *Journal of Advanced Nursing, 43*(4), 335–343.

Goodman, J., Schlossberg, N. K., & Anderson, M. L. (2006). *Counseling adults in transition* (3rd ed.). New York: Springer.

Goodman, K. M., & Mueller, J. A. (2009). Invisible, marginalized and stigmatized: Understanding and addressing the needs of atheist students. In S. K. Watt, E. F. Fairchild, & K. M. Goodman (Eds.), *Intersections of religious privilege: Difficult dialogues and student affairs practice* (pp. 55–63). New Directions in Student Affairs, No. 125. San Francisco: Jossey-Bass.

Gordon, L. R. (2004). Race, biraciality, and mixed race—In theory. In L. Heldke & P. O'Connor (Eds.), *Oppression, privilege, and resistance: Theoretical perspectives on racism, sexism, and heterosexism* (pp. 422–439). New York: McGraw-Hill.

Gorman, M., Duffy, J., & Heffernan, M. (1994). Service experience and the moral development of college students. *Religious Education, 89,* 422–431.

Gose, B. (1995, February 10). "Women's ways of knowing" form the basis of Ursuline curriculum. *Chronicle of Higher Education,* p. A25.

Greeley, A., & Tinsley, H. (1988). Autonomy and intimacy development in college students: Sex differences and predictors. *Journal of College Student Development, 29,* 512–520.

Green, E. R. (2006). Debating trans inclusion in the feminist movement: A trans-positive analysis. *Journal of Lesbian Studies, 10*(1/2), 231–248.

Greene, B. (2000). African American lesbian and bisexual women. *Journal of Social Issues, 56,* 239–249.

Griffin, P., Peters, M. L., & Smith, R. M. (2007). Ableism curricular design. In M. Adams, L. A. Bell, & P. Griffin (Eds.), *Teaching for diversity and social justice* (2nd ed., pp. 335–358). New York: Routledge.

Guardia, J. R., & Evans, N. J. (2008). Factors influencing the ethnic identity development of Latino fraternity members at a Hispanic serving institution. *Journal of College Student Development, 49,* 163–181.

Guba, E. G. (1990). The alternative paradigm dialog. In E. G. Guba (Ed.), *The paradigm dialog* (pp. 17–30). Thousand Oaks, CA: Sage.

Guba, E. G., & Lincoln, Y. S. (1994). Competing paradigms in qualitative research. In N. K. Denzin & Y. S. Lincoln (Eds.), *Handbook of qualitative research* (pp. 105–117). Thousand Oaks, CA: Sage.

Guido, F. M., Chávez, A. F., & Lincoln, Y. S. (in press). Underlying paradigms in student affairs research and practice. *Student Affairs Journal of Research and Practice.*

Guido-DiBrito, F., & Chávez, A. F. (2003). Understanding the ethnic self: Learning and teaching in a multicultural world. *Journal of Student Affairs, 12,* 11–21.

Guido-DiBrito, F., Chávez, A. F., & Lincoln, Y. S. (2003). *Student affairs scholarship in a new universe: Beyond Newton to a quantum age.* Unpublished manuscript.

Guido-DiBrito, F., Noteboom, P. A., Nathan, L. E., & Fenty, J. (1996). Traditional and new paradigm leadership: The gender link. *Initiatives, 58*(1), 27–38.

Gump, L. S., Baker, R. C., & Roll, S. (2000). Cultural and gender differences in moral judgment: A study of Mexican Americans and Anglo-Americans. *Hispanic Journal of Behavioral Sciences, 22,* 78–93.

Haan, N. (1985). Processes of moral development: Cognitive or social disequilibrium? *Developmental Psychology, 21,* 996–1006.

Hackney, H., & Cormier, S. (2005). *The professional counselor: A process guide to helping* (5th ed.). Boston: Pearson.

Hadley, W. M. (2006). L.D. students' access to higher education: Self-advocacy and support. *Journal of Developmental Education, 30*(2), 10–16.

Hagberg, J., & Leider, R. (1982). *The inventurers: Excursions into life and career renewal.* Reading, MA: Addison-Wesley.

Hall, C.C.I. (1980). *The ethnic identity of racially mixed people: A study of black-Japanese.* Unpublished doctoral dissertation, University of California, Los Angeles.

Hall, C.C.I. (1992). Please choose one: Ethnic identity choices for biracial individuals. In M.P.P. Root (Ed.), *Racially mixed people in America* (pp. 250–264). Thousand Oaks, CA: Sage.

Hall, C.C.I., & Cooke Turner, T. I. (2001). The diversity of biracial individuals: Asian-white and Asian-minority biracial identity. In T. Williams-León & C. L. Nakashima (Eds.), *The sum of our parts: Mixed-heritage Asian Americans* (pp. 81–91). Philadelphia: Temple University Press.

Hall, S. (1995). Negotiating Caribbean identities. *New Left Review, 209,* 2–14.

Hamilton, L. (2007). Trading on heterosexuality: College women's gender strategies and homophobia. *Gender and Society, 21*(2), 145–172.

Hamrick, F. A., Evans, N. J., & Schuh, J. H. (2002). *Foundations of student affairs practice: How philosophy, theory, and research strengthen educational outcomes.* San Francisco: Jossey-Bass.

Handler, L. (1995). In the fraternal sisterhood: Sororities as gender strategy. *Gender and Society, 9*(2), 236–255.

Hanna, F. J., Talley, W. B., & Guindon, M. H. (2000). The power of perception: Toward a model of cultural oppression and liberation. *Journal of Counseling and Development, 78,* 430–441.

Hardiman, R. (2001). Reflections on white identity development theory. In C. L. Wijeyesinghe & B. W. Jackson, III (Eds.), *New perspectives on racial identity development: A theoretical and practical anthology* (pp. 108–128). New York: New York University Press.

Hardiman, R., & Jackson, B. W. (1992). Racial identity development: Understanding racial dynamics in college classrooms and on college campuses. In M. Adams (Ed.), *Promoting diversity in college classrooms: Innovative responses for the curriculum, faculty, and institutions* (pp. 21–37). New Directions for Teaching and Learning, No. 52. San Francisco: Jossey-Bass.

Harley, D. A., Nowak, T. M., Gassaway, L. J., & Savage, T. (2002). Lesbian, gay, bisexual, and transgender college students with disabilities: A look at multiple cultural minorities. *Psychology in the Schools, 39,* 525–538.

Harper, S. R., Harris, F., III, & Mmeje, K. A. (2005). A theoretical model to explain the overrepresentation of college men among campus judicial offenders: Implications for campus administrators. *NASPA Journal, 42,* 565–588.

Harris, F., III, & Harper, S. R. (2008). Masculinities go to community college: Understanding male identity socialization and gender role conflict. In J. Lester (Ed.), *Gendered perspectives on community colleges* (pp. 25–35). New Directions for Community Colleges, No. 142. San Francisco: Jossey-Bass.

Harris, L. L. (2003). Integrating and analyzing psychosocial stage theories to challenge the development of the injured collegiate athlete. *Journal of Athletic Training, 38*(1), 75–82.

Harris, M. (1986). Completion and faith development. In C. Dykstra & S. Parks (Eds.), *Faith development and Fowler* (pp. 115–133). Birmingham, AL: Religious Education Press.

Hartley, H. V., III. (2004). How college affects students' religious faith and practice: A review of research. *College Student Affairs Journal, 23*(2), 111–129.

Harvey, J. (2000). Social privilege and moral subordination. *Journal of Social Philosophy, 31*(2), 177–188.

Harvey, L. J., Hunt, D. E., & Shroder, H. M. (1961). *Conceptual systems and personality organization.* Hoboken, NJ: Wiley.

Haskins, C. H. (1957). *The rise of the universities.* Ithaca, NY: Cornell University Press.

Haynes, C. (2006). The integrated student: Fostering holistic development to advance learning. *About Campus, 10*(6) 17–23.

Hays, D. G., & Chang, C. Y. (2003). White privilege, oppression, and racial identity development: Implications for supervision. *Counselor Education and Supervision, 43,* 134–145.

Hays, J. N. (1988). Socio-cognitive development and argumentative writing: Issues and implications from one research project. *Journal of Basic Writing, 7*(2), 42–67.

Hayward, P. A. (1993, November). *The intersection of critical pedagogy and developmental theory for public speaking.* Paper presented at the annual meeting of the Speech Communication Association, Miami Beach, FL. (ERIC Document Reproduction Service No. ED372423)

Heath, C. D. (2006). A womanist approach to understanding and assessing the relationship between spirituality and mental health. *Mental Health, Religion, and Culture, 9*(2), 155–170.

Heath, D. (1968). *Growing up in college.* San Francisco: Jossey-Bass.

Heath, D. (1977). *Maturity and competence: A transcultural view.* New York: Gardner.

Heath, R. (1964). *The reasonable adventurer.* Pittsburgh, PA: University of Pittsburgh Press.

Heath, R. (1973). Form, flow, and full-being. *Counseling Psychologist, 4,* 56–63.

Helgesen, S. (1995). *The web of inclusion.* New York: Doubleday Currency.

Helms, J. E. (1990). *Black and white racial identity: Theory, research, and practice.* Westport, CT: Greenwood Press.

Helms, J. E. (1992). *A race is a nice thing to have: A guide to being a white person or understanding the white persons in your life.* Topeka, KS: Content Communications.

Helms, J. E. (Ed.). (1993a). *Black and white racial identity: Theory, research and practice.* Westport, CT: Praeger.

Helms, J. E. (1993b). Introduction: Review of racial identity terminology. In J. E. Helms (Ed.), *Black and white identity: Theory, research and practice* (pp. 3–8). Westport, CT: Praeger.

Helms, J. E. (1995). An update of Helms's white and people of color racial identity models. In J. G. Ponterotto, J. M. Casas, L. A. Suzuki, & C. M. Alexander (Eds.), *Handbook of multicultural counseling* (pp. 181–198). Thousand Oaks, CA: Sage.

Helms, J. E., & Carter, R. T. (1990). Development of the white racial identity inventory. In J. E. Helms (Ed.), *Black and white racial identity: Theory, research and practice* (pp. 67–80). Westport, CT: Greenwood Press.

Helms, J. E., & Talleyrand, R. (1997). Race is not ethnicity. *American Psychologist, 52,* 1246–1247.

Helsabeck, R. (1980). The student personnel administrator as milieu manager: Reducing destructive conflict through social science research. *Journal of College Student Personnel, 21,* 264–268.

Herman, S. N. (1970). *Israelis and Jews: A continuity of an identity.* New York: Random House.

Herring, R. D. (1990). Understanding Native-American values: Process and content concerns for counselors. *Counseling and Values, 34*(2), 134–138.

Herzig, A. H. (2004). Becoming mathematicians: Women and students of color choosing and leaving doctoral mathematics. *Review of Educational Research, 74,* 171–214.

Hess, W. D., & Winston, R. B., Jr. (1995). Developmental task achievement and students' intentions to participate in developmental activities. *Journal of College Student Development, 36,* 314–321.

Heubner, A. M., & Garrod, A. C. (1993). Moral reasoning among Tibetan monks: A study of buddhist adolescents and young adults in Nepal. *Journal of Cross-Cultural Psychology, 24,* 167–185.

Heyer, D. L., & Nelson, E. S. (1993). The relationship between parental marital status and the development of identity and emotional autonomy in college students. *Journal of College Student Development, 34,* 432–436.

Hiebert, D. W. (1992). The sociology of Fowler's faith development theory. *Studies in Religion, 21,* 321–335.

Higbee, J. L. (2002). The application of Chickering's theory of student development to student success in the sixties and beyond. *Research and Teaching in Developmental Education, 18*(2), 24–26.

Higher Education Research Institute. (2004). *The spiritual life of college students: A national study of college students' search for meaning and purpose.* Retrieved January 3, 2007, from www .spirituality.ucla.edu/spirituality/reports/FINAL%20REPORT.pdf.

Hillman, L., & Lewis, A. (1980). *The AER model of effective advising.* Unpublished manuscript, University of Maryland, College Park.

Hinck, S. S., & Thomas, R. W. (1999). Rape myth acceptance in college students: How far have we come? *Sex Roles, 40*(9–10), 815–832.

Hirt, J. B. (2006). *Where you work matters: Student affairs administration at different types of institutions.* Lanham, MD: American College Personnel Association and University Press of America.

Hodge, D. R. (2001). Spiritual assessment: A review of major qualitative methods and a new framework for assessing spirituality. *Social Work, 46,* 203–214.

Hodgson, J. W., & Fischer, J. L. (1979). Sex differences in identity and intimacy development in college youth. *Journal of Youth and Adolescence, 8,* 37–50.

Hofer, B. K., & Pintrich, P. R. (1997). The development of epistemological theories: Beliefs about knowledge and knowing and their relationship to learning. *Review of Educational Research, 67*(1), 88–140.

Hoffman, R. M. (2004). Conceptualizing heterosexual identity development: Issues and challenges. *Journal of Counseling and Development, 82*(3), 375–380.

Holland, D. C., & Eisenhart, M. A. (1990). *Educated in romance: Women, achievement, and college culture*. Chicago: University of Chicago Press.

Holland, J. L. (1966). *The psychology of vocational choice: A theory of personality types and model environments*. Waltham, MA: Blaisdell.

Holland, J. L. (1973). *Making vocational choices: A theory of careers*. Upper Saddle River, NJ: Prentice Hall.

Holland, J. L. (1992). *Making vocational choices: A theory of vocational personalities and work environments* (2nd ed.). Odessa, FL: Psychological Assessment Resources. (Original work published 1985)

Holland, J. L. (1997). *Making vocational choices: A theory of vocational personalities and work environments* (3rd ed.). Odessa, FL: Psychological Assessment Research.

Holley, J. H., & Jenkins, E. K. (1993). The relationship between student learning style and performance on various test question formats. *Journal of Education for Business, 68,* 301–308.

Hood, A. B. (Ed.). (1986). *The Iowa Student Development Inventories*. Iowa City, IA: Hitech Press.

Hood, A. B. (1997). *The Iowa Student Development Inventories* (2nd ed.). Iowa City, IA: Hitech Press.

Hood, A. B., Riahinejad, A. R., & White, D. B. (1986). Changes in ego identity during the college years. *Journal of College Student Personnel, 27,* 107–113.

hooks, b. (1981). *Ain't I a woman: Black women and feminism*. Boston: South End Press.

Hoppe, S. L., & Speck, B. W. (Eds.). (2005). *Spirituality in higher education*. New Directions for Teaching and Learning, No. 104. San Francisco: Jossey-Bass.

Hornak, A. M., & Ortiz, A. M. (2004). Creating a context to promote diversity education and self-authorship among community college students. In M. Baxter Magolda & P. M. King (Eds.), *Learning partnerships: Theory and modes of practice to educate for self-authorship* (pp. 91–123). Sterling, VA: Stylus.

Horowitz, H. L. (1987). *Campus life: Undergraduate cultures from the end of the eighteenth century to the present*. New York: Knopf.

Horse, P. G. (2001). Reflections on American Indian identity. In C. L. Wijeyesinghe & B. W. Jackson, III (Eds.), *New perspectives on racial identity development: A theoretical and practical anthology* (pp. 91–107). New York: New York University Press.

Hotelling, K., & Forrest, L. (1985). Gilligan's theory of sex-role development: A perspective for counseling. *Journal of Counseling and Development, 64,* 183–186.

Huang, L. N. (1997). Asian American adolescents. In E. Lee (Ed.), *Working with Asian Americans: A guide for clinicians*. New York: Guilford Press.

Huebner, L. A. (Ed.). (1979). *Redesigning campus environments*. San Francisco: Jossey-Bass.

Hughes, M. S. (1987). Black students' participation in higher education. *Journal of College Student Personnel, 28,* 532–545.

Hunt, D. E. (1978). Theorists are persons, too: On preaching what you practice. In C. A. Parker (Ed.), *Encouraging the development of college students* (pp. 250–266). Minneapolis: University of Minnesota Press.

Hunt, D. E. (1987). *Beginning with ourselves*. Cambridge, MA: Brookline.

Hunt, S., & Rentz, A. L. (1994). Greek-letter social group members' involvement and psychosocial development. *Journal of College Student Development, 35,* 289–295.

Hurst, J. C. (1978). Chickering's vectors of development and student affairs programming. In C. A. Parker (Ed.), *Encouraging the development of college students* (pp. 113–126). Minneapolis: University of Minnesota Press.

Hurst, J. C., & McKinley, D. L. (1988). An ecological diagnostic classification plan. *Journal of Counseling and Development, 66*(5), 228–233.

Hurtado, A. (2001). The color of privilege. In P. S. Rothenberg (Ed.), *Race, class and gender in the United States: An integrated study* (5th ed., pp. 152–163). New York: Worth.

Hurtado, A., & Sinha, M. (2008). More than men: Latino feminist masculinities and intersectionality. *Sex Roles, 59,* 337–349.

Hurtado, S., Sax, L. J., Saenz, V., Harper, C. E., Oseguera, L., Curley, J., et al. (2007). *Findings from the 2005 administration of Your First College Year.* Los Angeles: University of California, Higher Education Research Institute.

Huss, J. K. (1983). Developing competence and autonomy for disabled students. *AHSSPPE Bulletin, 1,* 81–92.

Hyde, J. S., & Jaffee, S. R. (2000). Becoming a heterosexual adult: The experiences of young women. *Journal of Social Issues, 56,* 283–296.

Ibrahim, F., Ohnishi, H., & Sandhu, D. S. (1997). Asian American identity development: A culture specific model for South Asian Americans. *Journal of Multicultural Counseling and Development, 25,* 34–50.

Ignelzi, M. G. (1994). *A description of student affairs professional development in the supervisory context and an analysis of its relation to constructive development.* Unpublished doctoral dissertation, Harvard University, Cambridge, MA.

Ignelzi, M. (2000). Meaning-making in the learning and teaching process. In M. B. Baxter Magolda (Ed.), *Teaching to promote intellectual and personal maturity: Incorporating students' worldviews and identities into the learning process* (pp. 5–14). New Directions for Teaching and Learning, No. 82. San Francisco: Jossey-Bass.

Ignelzi, M. G., & Whitely, P. A. (2004). Supportive supervision for new professionals. In P. M. Magolda & J. E. Carnaghi (Eds.), *Job one: Experiences of new professionals in student affairs* (pp. 115–135). Lanham, MD: American College Personnel Association.

Illich, I. (1972). *Deschooling society.* New York: Harrow Books.

Isajiw, W. W. (1990). Ethnic-identity retention. In R. Breton, W. W. Isajiw, W. E. Kalbach, & J. G. Reitz (Eds.), *Ethnic identity and equality* (pp. 34–91). Toronto: University of Toronto Press.

Iwasa, N. (1992). Postconventional reasoning and moral education in Japan. *Journal of Moral Education, 21,* 2–16.

Jablonski, M. A. (Ed.). (2001). *The implications of student spirituality for student affairs practice.* New Directions for Student Services, No. 95. San Francisco: Jossey-Bass.

Jackson, A. P., Smith, S. A., & Hill, C. L. (2003). Academic persistence among Native American college students. *Journal of College Student Development, 44,* 548–565.

Jackson, B. W. (1976). Black identity development. In L. H. Golubchick & B. Persky (Eds.), *Urban social and educational issues* (pp. 158–164). Dubuque, IA: Kendall Hunt.

Jackson, B. W., III. (2001). Black identity development: Further analysis and elaboration. In C. L. Wijeyesinghe & B. W. Jackson, III (Eds.), *New perspectives on racial identity development: A theoretical and practical anthology* (pp. 8–31). New York: New York University Press.

Jackson, R. L., II. (1999). White space, white privilege: Mapping discursive inquiry into the self. *Quarterly Journal of Speech, 85,* 38–54.

Jacobus, E. F., Jr. (1989). *The relationship between cognitive development and foreign language proficiency.* Unpublished manuscript. (ERIC Document Reproduction Service No. ED313894)

Jagose, A. (1997). *Queer theory: An introduction.* New York: New York University Press.

Jefferson, S. D., & Caldwell, R. (2002). An exploration of the relationship between racial identity attitudes and the perception of racial bias. *Journal of Black Psychology, 28*(2), 174–192.

Jenkins, R. (1997). *Rethinking ethnicity: Arguments and explorations.* Thousand Oaks, CA: Sage.

Jenkins, R. (2004). *Social identity* (2nd ed.). London: Routledge.

Jonassen, D. H., & Grabowski, B. L. (1993). *Handbook of individual differences, learning, and instruction.* Mahwah, NJ: Erlbaum.

Jones, B. E., & Hill, M. J. (1996). African American lesbians, gay men, and bisexuals. In R. P. Cabaj & T. S. Stein (Eds.), *Textbook of homosexuality and mental health* (pp. 549–561). Washington, DC: American Psychiatric Press.

Jones, C. E., & Watt, J. D. (1999). Psychosocial development and moral orientation among traditional-aged college students. *Journal of College Student Development, 40,* 125–131.

Jones, C. E., & Watt, J. D. (2001). Moral orientation and psychosocial development: Gender and class standing differences. *NASPA Journal, 39,* 1–13.

Jones, H. J., & Newman, I. (1993, April). *A mosaic of diversity: Vocationally undecided students and the Perry scheme of intellectual and ethical development.* Paper presented at the annual meeting of the American Educational Research Association, Atlanta. (ERIC Document Reproduction Service No. ED360488)

Jones, N. A., & Smith, A. S. (2003). A statistical portrait of children of two or more races in Census 2000. In M.P.P. Root & M. Kelley (Eds.), *Multiracial child resource book: Living complex identities* (pp. 3–10). Seattle: MAVIN Foundation.

Jones, S. R. (1995). *Voices of identity and difference: A qualitative exploration of the multiple dimensions of identity development in women college students.* Unpublished doctoral dissertation, University of Maryland.

Jones, S. R. (1997). Voices of identity and difference: A qualitative exploration of the multiple dimensions of identity development in women college students. *Journal of College Student Development, 38,* 376–386.

Jones, S. R. (2008). Student resistance to cross-cultural engagement: Annoying distraction or site for transformative learning? In S. R. Harper (Ed.), *Creating inclusive campus environments for cross-cultural learning and student engagement* (pp. 67–85). Washington, DC: National Association of Student Personnel Administrators.

Jones, S. R., & McEwen, M. K. (2000). A conceptual model of multiple dimensions of identity. *Journal of College Student Development, 41,* 405–413.

Jordan-Cox, C. A. (1987). Psychosocial development of students in traditionally black institutions. *Journal of College Student Personnel, 28,* 504–511.

Josselson, R. E. (1973). Psychodynamic aspects of identity formation in college women. *Journal of Youth and Adolescence, 2*(1), 3–52.

Josselson, R. E. (1982). Personality structure and identity status in women as viewed through early memories. *Journal of Youth and Adolescence, 11*(4), 293–299.

Josselson, R. E. (1987a). *Finding herself: Pathways to identity development in women.* San Francisco: Jossey-Bass.

Josselson, R. E. (1987b). Identity diffusion: A long term follow-up. *Adolescent Psychology, 14,* 230–258.

Josselson, R. E. (1991). *Finding herself: Pathways to identity development in women.* San Francisco: Jossey-Bass. (Original work published 1978)

Josselson, R. (1996). *Revising herself: The story of women's identity from college to midlife.* New York: Oxford University Press.

Jung, C. G. (1960). *The structure and dynamics of the psyche.* New York: Bollingen Foundation.

Jung, C. G. (1971). *Psychological types* (R.F.C. Hull, Ed.; H. G. Baynes, Trans.). *The collected works of C. G. Jung* (Vol. 6). Princeton, NJ: Princeton University Press. (Original work published 1923)

Kahn, M. J. (1991). Factors affecting the coming out process for lesbians. *Journal of Homosexuality, 21*(3), 47–70.

Kahn, R. L., & Antonucci, T. C. (1980). Convoys over the life course: Attachment, roles, and social support. In P. B. Baltes & C. O. Brim (Eds.), *Life-span development and behavior* (pp. 383–405). Orlando, FL: Academic Press.

Kaiser, L. R. (1975). Designing campus environments. *NASPA Journal, 13*(1), 33–39.

Kaiser, L. R., & Sherretz, L. (1978). Designing campus environments: A review of selected literature. In J. H. Banning (Ed.), *Campus ecology: A perspective for student affairs* (pp. 72–111). Cincinnati, OH: National Association of Student Personnel Administrators.

Katchadourian, H., & Boli, J. (1985). *Careerism and intellectualism among college students.* San Francisco: Jossey-Bass.

Katz, J. N. (1995). *The invention of heterosexuality.* New York: Dutton.

Kaufman, P., & Feldman, K. A. (2004). Forming identities in college: A sociological approach. *Research in Higher Education, 45*(5), 463–496.

Kawaguchi, S. (2003). Ethnic identity development and collegiate experience of Asian Pacific American students: Implications for practice. *NASPA Journal, 40*(3), 13–29.

Kay, S., & Schlossberg, N. K. (2003). *The transition guide and questionnaire.* Available from www .transitionguide.com.

Kayes, A. B., Kayes, D. C., & Kolb, D. A. (2005a). Developing teams using the Kolb team learning experience. *Simulation and Gaming, 36,* 355–363.

Kayes, A. B., Kayes, D. C., & Kolb, D. A. (2005b). Experiential learning in teams. *Simulation and Gaming, 36,* 330–354.

Kayes, A. B., Kayes, D. C., Kolb, A. Y., & Kolb, D. A. (2004). *The Kolb team learning experience: Improving team effectiveness through structured learning experiences.* Boston: Hay Resources Direct.

Kayes, D. C. (2002). Experiential learning and its critics: Preserving the role of experience in management learning and education. *Academy of Management Learning and Education, 1,* 137–149.

Keefe, S. E. (1980). Acculturation and the extended family among urban Mexican Americans. In A. M. Padilla (Ed.), *Acculturation: Theory, models and some new findings* (pp. 85–110). Boulder, CO: Westview.

Keefe, S. E., & Padilla, A. M. (1987). *Chicano ethnicity.* Albuquerque: University of New Mexico Press.

Keeling, R. P. (Ed.). (2004). *Learning reconsidered: A campus-wide focus on the student experience.* Washington, DC: American College Personnel Association and National Association of Student Personnel Administrators.

Kegan, R. (1982). *The evolving self.* Cambridge, MA: Harvard University Press.

Kegan, R. (1994). *In over our heads: The mental demands of modern life.* Cambridge, MA: Harvard University Press.

Kegan, R. (2000). What "form" transforms? A constructive-developmental approach to transformative learning. In J. Mezirow (Ed.), *Learning as transformation* (pp. 35–69). San Francisco: Jossey-Bass.

Kegan, R., Broderick, M., Drago-Severson, E., Helsing, D., Popp, N., & Portnow, K. (2001). *Toward a new pluralism in ABE/ESOL classrooms: Teaching to multiple "cultures of mind."*

Cambridge, MA: Harvard University Graduate School of Education, National Center for the Study of Adult Learning and Literacy.

Kellogg, A., & Niskodé, A. S. (2008). Student affairs and higher education policy issues related to multiracial students. In K. A. Renn & P. Shang (Eds.), *Biracial and multiracial college students* (pp. 93–102). New Directions for Student Services, No. 123. San Francisco: Jossey-Bass.

Kernberg, O. (1966). Structural derivatives of object relationships. *International Journal of Psychoanalysis, 47,* 236–253.

Kerwin, C. (1991). Racial identity development in biracial children of black/white racial heritage (Doctoral dissertation, Fordham University). *Dissertation Abstracts International, 52,* 2469-A.

Kerwin, C., & Ponterotto, J. G. (1995). Biracial identity development: Theory and research. In J. G. Ponterotto, J. M. Casas, L. A. Suzuki, & C. M. Alexander (Eds.), *Handbook of multicultural counseling* (pp. 199–217). Thousand Oaks, CA: Sage.

Kerwin, C., Ponterotto, J. G., Jackson, B. L., & Harris, A. (1993). Racial identity in biracial children: A qualitative investigation. *Journal of Counseling Psychology, 40,* 221–231.

Kich, G. K. (1992). The developmental process of asserting a biracial, bicultural identity. In M.P.P. Root (Ed.), *Racially mixed people in America* (pp. 304–317). Thousand Oaks, CA: Sage.

Kilbride, K. M., & D'Arcangelo, L. (2002). Meeting immigrant community college students' needs on one greater Toronto area college campus. *Canadian Journal of Higher Education, 32*(2), 1–26.

Kilgannon, S. M., & Erwin, T. D. (1992). A longitudinal study about the identity and moral development of Greek students. *Journal of College Student Development, 33,* 253–259.

Kilson, M. (2001). *Claiming place: Biracial young adults of the post-civil rights era.* Westport, CT: Bergin & Garvey.

Kim, J. (1981). *The process of Asian-American identity development: A study of Japanese American women's perceptions of their struggle to achieve positive identities.* Unpublished doctoral dissertation, University of Massachusetts, Amherst.

Kim, J. (2001). Asian American identity development theory. In C. L. Wijeyesinghe & B. W. Jackson, III (Eds.), *New perspectives on racial identity development: A theoretical and practical anthology* (pp. 67–90). New York: New York University Press.

Kimmel, M. (1994). Masculinity as homophobia: Fear, shame and silence in the construction of gender identity. In H. Brod & M. Kaufman (Eds.), *Theorizing masculinities* (pp. 119–141). Thousand Oaks, CA: Sage.

Kimmel, M. S. (2003a). Introduction: Toward a pedagogy of the oppressor. In M. S. Kimmel & A. L. Ferber (Eds.), *Privilege: A reader* (pp. 1–10). Boulder, CO: Westview Press.

Kimmel, M. S. (2003b). Masculinity as homophobia: Fear, shame and silence in the construction of gender identity. In M. S. Kimmel & A. L Ferber (Eds.), *Privilege: A reader* (pp. 51–82). Boulder, CO: Westview Press.

King, A. R. (2008a). Student perspectives on multiracial identity. In K. A. Renn & P. Shang (Eds.), *Biracial and multiracial students* (pp. 33–41). New Directions for Student Services, No. 123. San Francisco: Jossey-Bass.

King, A. R. (2008b). *Uncertainty and evolution: Contributions to identity development for female college students who identify as multiracial/biracial-bisexual/pansexual.* Unpublished doctoral dissertation, Iowa State University.

King, P. M. (1978). William Perry's theory of intellectual and ethical development. In L. L. Knefelkamp, C. Widick, & C. A. Parker (Eds.), *Applying new developmental findings* (pp. 35–51). New Directions for Student Services, No. 4. San Francisco: Jossey-Bass.

King, P. M. (1987). [Review of the book *Women's ways of knowing: The development of self, voice, and mind*]. *Journal of Moral Education, 16*, 249–251.

King, P. M. (1990). Assessing development from a cognitive developmental perspective. In D. G. Creamer (Ed.), *College student development: Theory and practice for the 1990s* (pp. 81–98). Alexandria, VA: American College Personnel Association.

King, P. M. (1994). Theories of college student development: Sequences and consequences. *Journal of College Student Development, 35*, 413–421.

King, P. M. (2003). Student learning in higher education. In S. R. Komives, D. B. Woodard, Jr., & Associates, *Student services: A handbook for the profession* (4th ed., pp. 234–268). San Francisco: Jossey-Bass.

King, P. M., & Baxter Magolda, M. B. (1996). A developmental perspective on learning. *Journal of College Student Development, 37*, 163–173.

King, P. M., & Baxter Magolda, M. B. (2004). Creating learning partnerships in higher education. In M. Baxter Magolda & P. M. King (Eds.), *Learning partnerships: Theory and modes of practice to educate for self-authorship* (pp. 303–332). Sterling, VA: Stylus.

King, P. M., & Baxter Magolda, M. B. (2005). A developmental model of intercultural maturity. *Journal of College Student Development, 46*, 571–592.

King, P. M., & Kitchener, K. S. (1994). *Developing reflective judgment: Understanding and promoting intellectual growth and critical thinking in adolescents and adults.* San Francisco: Jossey-Bass.

King, P. M., & Kitchener, K. S. (2002). The reflective judgment model: Twenty years of research on epistemic cognition. In B. K. Hofer & P. R. Pintrich (Eds.), *Personal epistemology: The psychology of beliefs about knowledge and knowing* (pp. 37–61). Mahwah, NJ: Erlbaum.

King, P. M., & Mayhew, M. J. (2002). Moral judgment development in higher education: Insights from the defining issues test. *Journal of Moral Education, 31*, 247–270.

King, P. M., & Shuford, B. C. (1996). A multicultural view is a more cognitively complex view: Cognitive development and multicultural education. *American Behavioral Scientist, 40*, 153–164.

Kitchener, K. S., & King, P. M. (1981). Reflective judgment: Concepts of justification and their relationship to age and education. *Journal of Applied Developmental Psychology, 2*, 89–116.

Kitchener, K. S., & King, P. M. (1990). The reflective judgment model: Ten years of research. In M. L. Commons, C. Armon, L. Kohlberg, F. A. Richards, T. A. Grotzer, & J. D. Sinnott (Eds.), *Adult development: Vol. 2. Models and methods in the study of adolescent and adult thought* (pp. 63–78). Westport, CT: Praeger.

Kitzinger, C. (1995). Social constructionism: Implications for lesbian and gay psychology. In A. R. D'Augelli & C. J. Patterson (Eds.), *Lesbian, gay, and bisexual identities over the lifespan: Psychological perspectives* (pp. 136–161). New York: Oxford University Press.

Kitzinger, C., & Wilkinson, S. (1993). The precariousness of heterosexual feminist identities. In M. Kennedy, C. Lubelska, & V. Walsh (Eds.), *Making connections: Women's studies, women's movements, women's lives* (pp. 24–36). London: Taylor & Francis.

Klein, F. (1990). The need to view sexual orientation as a multivariate dynamic process: A theoretical perspective. In D. P. McWhirter, S. A. Sanders, & J. M. Reinisch (Eds.), *Homosexuality/heterosexuality: Concepts of sexual orientation* (pp. 277–282). New York: Oxford University Press.

Klepper, W. M., & Kovacs, E. (1978, December). What is the impact of the college union program on today's students? *Association of College Unions-International Bulletin*, 17–20.

Knefelkamp, L. L. (1974). *Developmental instruction: Fostering intellectual and personal growth in college students.* Unpublished doctoral dissertation, University of Minnesota, Minneapolis.

Knefelkamp, L. L. (1978). *A reader's guide to student development theory: A framework for understanding, a framework for design.* Unpublished manuscript.

Knefelkamp, L. L. (1982). Faculty and student development in the '80s: Renewing the community of scholars. In H. E. Owens, C. H. Witten, & W. R. Bailey (Eds.), *College student personnel administration: An anthology* (pp. 373–391). Springfield, IL: Thomas.

Knefelkamp, L. L. (1984). *A workbook for the practice to theory to practice model.* Unpublished manuscript, University of Maryland, College Park.

Knefelkamp, L. L. (1999). Introduction. In W. G. Perry, Jr., *Forms of ethical and intellectual development in the college years: A scheme* (pp. xi–xxxvii). San Francisco: Jossey-Bass.

Knefelkamp L. L., & Cornfeld, J. L. (1979, March). *Combining student stage and style in the design of learning environments.* Paper presented at the annual meeting of the American College Personnel Association, Los Angeles.

Knefelkamp, L. L., Parker, C. A., & Widick, C. (1978). Roy Heath's model of personality typologies. In L. L Knefelkamp, C. Widick, & C. A. Parker (Eds.), *Applying new developmental findings* (pp. 93–105). New Directions for Student Services, No. 4. San Francisco: Jossey-Bass.

Knefelkamp, L. L., & Slepitza, R. (1976). A cognitive-developmental model of career development: An adaptation of the Perry scheme. *Counseling Psychologist, 6*(3), 53–58.

Knefelkamp, L. L., Widick, C., & Parker, C. A. (1978). Editors' notes: Why bother with theory? In L. L. Knefelkamp, C. Widick, & C. A. Parker (Eds.), *Applying new developmental findings* (pp. vii–xvi). New Directions for Student Services, No. 4. San Francisco: Jossey-Bass.

Knefelkamp, L. L., Widick, C., & Stroad, B. (1976). Cognitive-developmental theory: A guide to counseling women. *Counseling Psychologist, 6*(2), 15–19.

Knepper, W. (2006). Colonization, creolization, and globalization: The art and ruses of bricolage. *Small Axe: A Caribbean Journal of Criticism, 21,* 70–86.

Knight, M. (2002). The intersections of race, class and gender in the teacher preparation of an African American social justice educator. *Equity and Excellence in Education, 35*(3), 212–224.

Kodama, C. M., McEwen, M. K., Liang, C., & Lee, S. (2001). A theoretical examination of psychosocial issues for Asian Pacific American students. *NASPA Journal, 38,* 411–437.

Kodama, C. M., McEwen, M. K., Liang, C.T.H., & Lee, S. (2002). An Asian American perspective on psychosocial student development theory. In M. K. McEwen, C. M. Kodama, A. Alvarez, S. Lee, & C.T.H. Liang (Eds.), *Working with Asian American college students* (pp. 45–59). New Directions for Student Services, No. 97. San Francisco, Jossey-Bass.

Kohlberg, L. (1958). *The development of modes of moral thinking and choice in the years ten to sixteen.* Unpublished doctoral dissertation, University of Chicago.

Kohlberg, L. (1966). A cognitive-developmental analysis of children's sex-role concepts and attitudes. In E. E. Maccoby (Ed.), *The development of sex differences* (pp. 82–173). Stanford, CA: Stanford University Press.

Kohlberg, L. (1969). Stage and sequence: The cognitive developmental approach to socialization. In D. A. Goslin (Ed.), *Handbook of socialization theory and research* (pp. 347–480). Skokie, IL: Rand McNally.

Kohlberg, L. (1971). Stages of moral development as a basis for moral education. In C. Beck, B. S. Crittenden, & E. V. Sullivan (Eds.), *Moral education: Interdisciplinary approaches* (pp. 23–92). Toronto: University of Toronto Press.

Kohlberg, L. (1975). The cognitive-developmental approach to moral education. *Phi Delta Kappan, 56,* 670–677.

Kohlberg, L. (1976). Moral stages and moralization: The cognitive-developmental approach. In T. Lickona (Ed.), *Moral development and behavior: Theory, research, and social issues* (pp. 31–53). New York: Holt.

Kohlberg, L. (1979). Foreword. In J. R. Rest, *Development in judging moral issues* (pp. vii–xvi). Minneapolis: University of Minnesota Press.

Kohlberg, L. (1981). *Essays on moral development: Vol. I. The philosophy of moral development.* San Francisco: Harper & Row.

Kohlberg, L. (1984). *Essays on moral development: Vol. II. The psychology of moral development.* San Francisco: HarperSanFrancisco.

Kohlberg, L., & Candee, D. (1984). The relationship of moral judgment to moral action. In L. Kohlberg (Ed.), *Essays on moral development: Vol. II. The psychology of moral development* (pp. 498–581). San Francisco: HarperSanFrancisco.

Kohlberg, L., & Hersh, R. H. (1977). Moral development: A review of the theory. *Theory into Practice, 16,* 53–59.

Kohlberg, L., & Kramer, R. (1969). Continuities and discontinuities in childhood and adult moral development. *Human Development, 12,* 93–120.

Kohlberg, L., Levine, C., & Hewer, A. (1984). The current formulation of the theory. In L. Kohlberg (Ed.), *Essays on moral development: Vol. II. The psychology of moral development* (pp. 212–319). San Francisco: HarperSanFrancisco.

Kolb, A. Y., & Kolb, D. A. (2005a). *The Kolb Learning Style Inventory—Version 3.1 2005 technical specifications.* Available from www.haygroup.com or www.learningfromexperience.com.

Kolb, A. Y., & Kolb, D. A. (2005b). Learning styles and learning spaces: Enhancing experiential learning in higher education. *Academy of Management Learning and Education, 42,* 193–212.

Kolb, A. Y., & Kolb, D. A. (2006). Learning styles and learning spaces: A review of the multidisciplinary application of experiential learning theory in higher education. In R. R. Sims & S. J. Sims (Eds.), *Learning and learning styles* (pp. 45–91). New York: Nova Science.

Kolb, D. A. (1976). *The Learning Style Inventory: Technical manual.* Boston: McBer.

Kolb, D. A. (1981). Learning styles and disciplinary differences. In A. W. Chickering (Ed.), *The modern American college: Responding to the new realities of diverse students and a changing society* (pp. 232–255). San Francisco: Jossey-Bass.

Kolb, D. A. (1984). *Experiential learning: Experience as the source of learning and development.* Upper Saddle River, NJ: Prentice Hall.

Kolb, D. A. (1985). *The Learning Style Inventory.* Boston: McBer.

Kolb, D. A. (1993). *LSI-IIA Learning Style Inventory.* Boston: McBer.

Kolb, D. A. (1999). *Learning Style Inventory—Version 3.* Boston: Hay/McBer.

Kolb, D. A. (2000). *Facilitator's guide to learning.* Boston: Hay/McBer.

Kolb, D. A. (2005). *Kolb Learning Style Inventory—Version 3.1.* Boston: Hay Group.

Kolb, D. A., Baker, A. C., & Jensen, P. J. (2002). Conversation as experiential learning. In A. C. Baker, P. J. Jensen, & D. A. Kolb, *Conversational learning: An experiential approach to knowledge creation* (pp. 51–66). Westport, CT: Quorum Books.

Kolb, D. A., Boyatzis, R. E., & Mainemelis, C. (2001). Experiential learning theory: Previous research and new directions. In R. J. Sternberg & L. Zhang (Eds.), *Perspectives on thinking, learning, and cognitive styles* (pp. 227–247). Mahwah, NJ: Erlbaum.

Komives, S. R. (1994). New approaches to leadership. In J. Fried & Associates, *Different voices: Gender and perspective in student affairs administration* (pp. 46–61). Washington, DC: National Association of Student Personnel Administrators.

Komives, S. R. (1998). Linking student affairs preparation with practice. In N. J. Evans & C. E. Phelps Tobin (Eds.), *The state of the art of preparation and practice in student affairs: Another look* (pp. 177–200). Lanham, MD: University Press of America.

Konik, J., & Stewart, A. (2004). Sexual identity development in the context of compulsory heterosexuality. *Journal of Personality, 72,* 815–844.

Korgen, K. O. (1998). *From black to biracial: Transforming racial identity among Americans.* Westport, CT: Praeger.

Krivoski, J. F., & Nicholson, R. M. (1989). An interview with Arthur Chickering. *Journal of College and University Student Housing, 19*(2), 6–11.

Kroger, J. (1985). Separation-individuation and ego identity status in New Zealand university students. *Journal of Youth and Adolescence, 14*(2), 133–147.

Kuh, G. D. (1995). Cultivating "high-stakes" student culture research. *Research in Higher Education, 36,* 563–576.

Kuh, G. D. (2001). Assessing what really matters to student learning: Inside the national survey of student engagement. *Change, 33*(3), 10–17, 66.

Kuh, G. D., & Gonyea, R. M. (2005, July 11). *Exploring the relationships between spirituality, liberal learning, and college student engagement.* A special report for the Teagle Foundation. Retrieved January 12, 2007, from www.teaglefoundation.org/learning/pdf/20050711_kuh_gonyea .pdf.

Kuh, G. D., Schuh, J., & Whitt, E. J. (1991). *Involving colleges: Successful approaches to fostering student learning and development outside the classroom.* San Francisco: Jossey-Bass.

Kuh, G. D., Whitt, E. J., & Shedd, J. D. (1987). *Student affairs work, 2001: A paradigmatic odyssey.* Alexandria, VA: American College Personnel Association.

Kuhn, T. S. (1970). *The structure of scientific revolutions* (2nd ed.). Chicago: University of Chicago Press.

Kuk, L. (1992). Perspectives on gender differences. In L. V. Moore (Ed.), *Evolving theoretical perspectives on students* (pp. 25–36). New Directions for Student Services, No. 51. San Francisco: Jossey-Bass.

Ladson-Billings, G. (1998). Just what is critical race theory and what's it doing in a *nice* field like education? *Qualitative Studies in Education, 11*(1), 7–24.

Lahey, L., Souvaine, E., Kegan, R., Goodman, R., & Felix, S. (1988). *A guide to the Subject-Object Interview: Its administration and interpretation.* Cambridge, MA: The Subject-Object Workshop.

Langman, P. F. (1995). Including Jews in multiculturalism. *Journal of Multicultural Counseling and Development, 23*(4), 222–236.

Lapsley, D., & Narvaez, D. (Eds.). (2004). *Moral development, self, and identity.* Mahwah, NJ: Erlbaum.

Laughlin, A., & Creamer, E. G. (2007). Engaging differences: Self-authorship and the decision-making process. In P. S. Meszaros (Ed.), *Self-authorship: Advancing students' intellectual growth* (pp. 43–51). New Directions for Teaching and Learning, No. 109. San Francisco: Jossey-Bass.

Lea, H. D., & Leibowitz, Z. (1986). The program developer as learner. In Z. Leibowitz & D. Lea (Eds.), *Adult career development: Concepts, issues, and practices* (pp. 50–62). Alexandria, VA: American Association for Counseling and Development.

Leak, G. K. (2003). Validation of the Faith Development Scale using longitudinal and cross-sectional designs. *Social Behavior and Personality, 31,* 637–641.

Leak, G. K., Loucks, A. A., & Bowlin, P. (1999). Development and initial validation of a global measure of faith development. *International Journal for the Psychology of Religion, 9,* 105–124.

Lee, J. A. (1977). Going public: A study in the sociology of homosexual liberation. *Journal of Homosexuality, 3*(1), 49–78.

Lee, J. J. (2002). Changing worlds, changing selves: The experience of the religious self among Catholic collegians. *Journal of College Student Development, 43,* 341–356.

Lemons, L. J., & Richmond, D. R. (1987). A developmental perspective on the sophomore slump. *NASPA Journal, 24*(3), 15–19.

Lev, A. I. (2004). *Transgender emergence: Therapeutic guidelines for working with gender-variant people and their families.* New York: Haworth Clinical Practice Press.

Levine, H. (1997). A further exploration of the lesbian identity development process and its measurement. *Journal of Homosexuality, 34*(2), 67–78.

Levine, H., & Bahr, J. (1989). *Relationship between sexual identity formation and student development.* Unpublished manuscript.

Levine, H., & Evans, N. J. (1991). The development of gay, lesbian, and bisexual identities. In N. J. Evans & V. A. Wall (Eds.), *Beyond tolerance: Gays, lesbians and bisexuals on campus* (pp. 1–24). Alexandria, VA: American College Personnel Association.

Levinson, D. J., with Darrow, C. N., Klein, E. B., Levinson, M. G., & McKee, B. (1978). *The seasons of a man's life.* New York: Ballantine.

Lewin, K. (1936). *Principles of topological psychology.* New York: McGraw-Hill.

Lewin, K. (1951). *Field theory in the social sciences.* New York: HarperCollins.

Lewis, P., Forsythe, G. B., Sweeney, P., Bartone, P., Bullis, C., & Snook, S. (2005). Identity development during the college years: Findings from the West Point longitudinal study. *Journal of College Student Development, 46,* 357–373.

Li, X., & Lal, S. (2005). Critical reflective thinking through service-learning in multicultural teacher education. *Intercultural Education, 16,* 217–234.

Liang, C.T.H., & Alimo, C. (2005). The impact of white heterosexual students' interactions on attitudes toward lesbian, gay and bisexual people: A longitudinal study. *Journal of College Student Development, 46,* 237–250.

Liddell, D. L. (1990). *Measure of moral orientation: Construction of an objective instrument measuring care and justice, with an investigation of gender differences.* Unpublished doctoral dissertation, Auburn University.

Liddell, D. (1995). [Review of the book *Developing reflective judgment: Understanding and promoting intellectual growth and critical thinking in adolescents and adults*]. *Journal of College Student Development, 36,* 94–96.

Liddell, D. L., Halpin, G., & Halpin, W. G. (1992). The measure of moral orientation: Measuring the ethics of care and justice. *Journal of College Student Development, 33,* 325–330.

Lincoln, Y. S., & Cannella, G. S. (2004). Dangerous discourses, methodological conservatism and governmental regimes of truth. *Qualitative Inquiry, 10*(1), 5–14.

Linn, R. (2001). The heart has its reason and the reason has its heart: The insight of Kohlberg and Gilligan in moral development and counseling. *Social Behavior and Personality, 29,* 593–600.

Lloyd, J. M., Dean, L. A., & Cooper, D. L. (2007). Students' technology use and its effects on peer relationships, academic involvement, and healthy lifestyles. *NASPA Journal, 44,* 481–495.

Lockett, C. T., & Harrell, J. P. (2003). Racial identity, self-esteem, and academic achievement: Too much interpretation, too little supporting data. *Journal of Black Psychology, 29*(3), 325–336.

Loevinger, J. (1976). *Ego development: Conceptions and theories.* San Francisco: Jossey-Bass.

Logan, R., Snarey, J., & Schrader, D. (1990). Autonomous versus heteronomous moral judgment types. *Journal of Cross-Cultural Psychology, 21,* 71–89.

Long, B. E., Sowa, C. J., & Niles, S. G. (1995). Differences in student development reflected by the career decisions of college seniors. *Journal of College Student Development, 36,* 47–52.

Lott, J. K. (1986). Freshman home reentry: Attending to a gap in student development. *Journal of Counseling and Development, 64,* 456.

Love, P. G. (2001). Spirituality and student development: Theoretical connections. In M. A. Jablonski (Ed.), *The implications of student spirituality for student affairs practice* (pp. 7–16). New Directions for Student Services, No. 95. San Francisco: Jossey-Bass.

Love, P. G. (2002). Comparing spiritual development and cognitive development. *Journal of College Student Development, 43,* 357–373.

Love, P. G., Bock, M., Jannarone, A., & Richardson, P. (2005). Identity interaction: Exploring the spiritual experiences of lesbian and gay college students. *Journal of College Student Development, 46,* 193–209.

Love, P. G., & Guthrie, V. L. (Eds.). (1999). *Understanding and applying cognitive development theory.* New Directions for Student Services, No. 88. San Francisco: Jossey-Bass.

Love, P., & Talbot, D. (1999). Defining spiritual development: A missing consideration for student affairs. *NASPA Journal, 37,* 361–375.

Lowenthal, M. F., & Chiriboga, D. (1975). *Four stages of life: A comparative study of men and women facing transitions.* San Francisco: Jossey-Bass.

Lownsdale, S. (1997). Faith development across the life span: Fowler's integrative work. *Journal of Psychology and Theology, 25,* 49–63.

Ludeman, R. B. (2004). Arrested emotional development: Connecting college men, emotions, and misconduct. In G. E. Kellom (Ed.), *Developing effective programs for college men* (pp. 75–86). New Directions for Student Services, No. 107. San Francisco: Jossey-Bass.

Lundberg, C. A. (2007). Student involvement and institutional commitment to diversity as predictors of Native American student learning. *Journal of College Student Development, 48,* 405–417.

Lynch, S. K., & Kogan, L. R. (2004). Designing online workshops: Using an experiential learning model. *Journal of College Counseling, 7,* 170–176.

Lyons, J. (1980). *The effect of a structural group experience in the transition from the role of college student to the role of working professional.* Unpublished master's thesis, University of Maryland, College Park.

Lyons, N. P. (1983). Two perspectives: On self, relationships, and morality. *Harvard Educational Review, 53,* 125–145.

Ma, H. K. (1989). Moral orientation and moral judgment in adolescents in Hong Kong, mainland China, and England. *Journal of Cross-Cultural Psychology, 20,* 152–177.

Madrid, A. (1988). Missing people and others: Joining together to expand the circle. *Change, 20*(3), 54–59.

Magolda, P. M. (2000). The campus tour ritual: Exploring community discourses in higher education. *Anthropology and Education Quarterly, 31*(1), 24–46.

Magolda, P. M. (2002, April). *Saying goodbye: An anthropological examination of campus exiting rituals.* Paper presented at the annual meeting of the American Educational Research Association, New Orleans, LA.

Maguen, S., Floyd, F. J., Bakeman, R., & Armistead, L. (2002). Developmental milestones and disclosure of sexual orientation among gay, lesbian, and bisexual youths. *Applied Developmental Psychology, 23*, 219–233.

Mainemelis, C., Boyatzis, R. E., & Kolb, D. A. (2002). Learning styles and adaptive flexibility: Testing experiential learning theory. *Management Learning, 33*(1), 5–33.

Mantsios, G. (2004). Class in America: Myths and realities—2003. In P. S. Rothenberg (Ed.), *Race, class, and gender in the United States: An integrated study* (6th ed., pp. 193–207). New York: Worth.

Marcia, J. E. (1966). Development and validation of ego-identity status. *Journal of Personality and Social Psychology, 3*, 551–558.

Marcia, J. E. (1975). Identity six years after: A follow-up study. *Journal of Youth and Adolescence, 5*(2), 145–160.

Marcia, J. E. (1980). Identity in adolescence. In J. Adelson (Ed.), *Handbook of adolescent psychology* (pp. 159–187). Hoboken, NJ: Wiley.

Marcia, J. E. (1989a). Identity and intervention. *Journal of Adolescence, 12*, 401–410.

Marcia, J. E. (1989b). Identity diffusion differentiated. In M. A. Luszcz & T. Nettelbeck (Eds.), *Psychological development: Perspectives across the life-span* (pp. 289–295). Amsterdam: North-Holland Elsevier.

Marcia, J. E. (1993a). The relational roots of identity. In J. Kroger (Ed.), *Discussions on ego identity* (pp. 101–120). Mahwah, NJ: Erlbaum.

Marcia, J. E. (1993b). The ego identity status approach to ego identity. In J. E. Marcia, A. S. Waterman, D. R. Matteson, & S. L. Archer (Eds.), *Ego identity: A handbook for psychosocial research* (pp. 2–21). New York: Springer-Verlag.

Marcia, J. E. (1993c). The status of the statuses: Research review. In J. E. Marcia, A. S. Waterman, D. R. Matteson, & S. L. Archer (Eds.), *Ego identity: A handbook for psychosocial research* (pp. 22–41). New York: Springer-Verlag.

Marcia, J. E. (1994). The empirical study of ego-identity. In H. A. Bosma, T.L.G. Graafsma, H. D. Grotevant, & D. J. de Levita (Eds.), *Identity and development: An interdisciplinary approach* (pp. 67–80). Thousand Oaks, CA: Sage.

Marcia, J. E. (1999). Representational thought in ego identity, psychotherapy, and psychosocial developmental theory. In I. E. Siegel (Ed.), *Development of mental representation: Theories and applications* (pp. 391–414). Mahwah, NJ: Erlbaum.

Marcia, J. E. (2002). Identity and psychosocial development in adulthood. *Identity: An International Journal of Theory and Research, 2*(1), 7–28.

Marin, G., Sabogal, F., Marin, B. V., Otero-Sabogal, R., & Perez-Stable, E. J. (1987). Development of a short acculturation scale for Hispanics. *Hispanic Journal of Behavioral Sciences, 9*(2), 183–205.

Marks, D. (1999). *Disability: Controversial debates and psychosocial perspectives.* London: Routledge.

Marks, H. M., & Jones, S. R. (2004). Community service in transition: Shifts and continuities in participation from high school to college. *Journal of Higher Education, 75*, 307–339.

Marszalek, J. F., III, Cashwell, C. S., Dunn, M. S., & Heard Jones, K. (2004). Comparing gay identity development theory to cognitive development: An empirical study. *Journal of Homosexuality, 48*(1), 103–123.

Martin, L. M. (2000). The relationship of college experiences to psychosocial outcomes in students. *Journal of College Student Development, 41*, 292–301.

Mass, A. I. (1992). Interracial Japanese Americans: The best of both worlds or the end of the Japanese American community? In M.P.P. Root (Ed.), *Racially mixed people in America* (pp. 265–279). Thousand Oaks, CA: Sage.

Mather, P. C., & Winston, R. B., Jr. (1998). Autonomy development of traditional-aged students: Themes and processes. *Journal of College Student Development, 39*, 33–50.

Mathiasen, R. E. (2003). Moral development of fraternity and sorority members: A research review. *Iowa Student Personnel Association Journal, 14*(1), 34–50.

Mathiasen, R. E. (2005). Moral development in fraternity members: A case study. *College Student Journal, 39*, 242–252.

Matteson, D. R. (1975). *Adolescence today: Sex roles and the search for identity.* Homewood, IL: Dorsey.

Mayhew, M. J. (2004). Exploring the essence of spirituality: A phenomenological study of eight students with eight different worldviews. *NASPA Journal, 41*, 647–674.

McBride, M. C. (1990). Autonomy and the struggle for female identity: Implications for counseling women. *Journal of Counseling and Development, 69*, 22–26.

McCall, L. (2005). The complexity of intersectionality. *Signs: Journal of Women in Culture and Society, 30*, 1171–1800.

McCarn, S. R. (1991). *Validation of a model of sexual minority (lesbian) identity development.* Unpublished master's thesis, University of Maryland, College Park.

McCarn, S. R., & Fassinger, R. E. (1996). Revisioning sexual minority identity formation: A new model of lesbian identity and its implications for counseling and research. *Counseling Psychologist, 24*, 508–534.

McDermott, M., & Sampson, F. L. (2005). White racial and ethnic identity in the United States. *Annual Review of Sociology, 31*, 245–261.

McEwen, M. M. (1994). [Review of the book *Knowing and reasoning in college: Gender-related patterns in students' intellectual development*]. *NASPA Journal, 31*, 153–157.

McEwen, M. K. (2003a). The nature and uses of theory. In S. K. Komives, D. B. Woodard, Jr., & Associates, *Student services: A handbook for the profession* (4th ed., pp. 153–178). San Francisco: Jossey-Bass.

McEwen, M. K. (2003b). New perspectives on identity development. In S. R. Komives, D. B. Woodard, Jr., & Associates, *Student services: A handbook for the profession* (4th ed., pp. 203–233). San Francisco: Jossey-Bass.

McEwen, M. K., Kodama, C. M., Alvarez, A. N., Lee, S., & Liang, C.T.H. (Eds.). (2002). *Working with Asian American college students.* New Directions for Student Services, No. 97. San Francisco: Jossey-Bass.

McEwen, M. K., Roper, L., Bryant, D., & Langa, M. (1990). Incorporating the development of African American students into psychosocial theories of student development. *Journal of College Student Development, 31*, 429–436.

McIntosh, P. (1989, July/August). White privilege: Unpacking the invisible knapsack. *Peace and Freedom*, 10–12.

McIntosh, P. (2003). White privilege, male privilege: A personal account of coming to see correspondences through work in women's studies. In M. S. Kimmel & A. L Ferber (Eds.), *Privilege: A reader* (pp. 147–160). Boulder, CO: Westview Press.

McKinney, J. S. (2005). On the margins: A study of the experience of transgender college students. *Journal of Gay and Lesbian Issues in Education, 3*(1), 63–76.

McLaughlin, M. E. (1981). *West Indian immigrants: Their social networks and ethnic identification.* New York: Columbia University Press.

McNeer, E. J. (1991). Learning theories and library instruction. *Journal of Academic Librarianship, 17,* 294–297.

Mena, F. J., Padilla, A. M., & Maldonado, M. (1987). Acculturative stress and specific coping strategies among immigrant and later generation college students. *Hispanic Journal of Behavioral Sciences, 9*(2), 207–225.

Mentkowski, M., Moeser, M., & Strait, M. J. (1983). *Using the Perry scheme of intellectual and ethical development as a college outcomes measure: A process and criteria for judging student performance* (2 vols.). Milwaukee, WI: Alverno College Productions.

Merikangas, M. (1980). *The next step: A retirement planning seminar.* Unpublished master's thesis, University of Maryland, College Park.

Merriam, S. B. (Ed.). (2008). *Third update on adult learning theory.* New Directions for Adult and Continuing Education, No. 119. San Francisco: Jossey-Bass.

Merriam, S. B., Caffarella, R. S., & Baumgartner, L. M. (2007). *Learning in adulthood: A comprehensive guide* (3rd ed.). San Francisco: Jossey-Bass.

Meszaros, P. S. (Ed.). (2007). *Self-authorship: Advancing students' intellectual growth.* New Directions for Teaching and Learning, No. 109. San Francisco: Jossey-Bass.

Meyer, P. (1977). Intellectual development: Analysis of religious content. *Counseling Psychologist, 6*(4), 47–50.

Mezirow, J. (Ed.). (2000). *Learning as transformation.* San Francisco: Jossey-Bass.

Mihesuah, D. A., & Wilson, A. C. (Eds.). (2004). *Indigenizing the academy: Transforming scholarship and empowering communities.* Lincoln: University of Nebraska Press.

Mihesuah, J. K. (2004). Graduating indigenous students by confronting the academic environment. In D. A. Mihesuah & A. C. Wilson (Eds.), *Indigenizing the academy: Transforming scholarship and empowering communities* (pp. 191–199). Lincoln: University of Nebraska Press.

Miller, J. G., & Bersoff, D. M. (1992). Culture and moral judgment: How are conflicts between justice and interpersonal responsibilities resolved? *Journal of Personality and Social Psychology, 62,* 544–554.

Miller, T. K., & Prince, J. S. (1976). *The future of student affairs: A guide to student development for tomorrow's higher education.* San Francisco: Jossey-Bass.

Miller, T. K., & Winston, R. B., Jr. (1990). Assessing development from a psychosocial perspective. In D. G. Creamer & Associates, *College student development: Theory and practice for the 1990s* (pp. 99–126). Alexandria, VA: American College Personnel Association.

Miller, V. W., & Ryan, M. M. (2001). *Transforming campus life: Reflections on spirituality and religious pluralism.* New York: Peter Lang.

Mills, R., & Strong, K. L. (2004). Organizing for learning in a division of student affairs. In M. Baxter Magolda & P. M. King (Eds.), *Learning partnerships: Theory and modes of practice to educate for self-authorship* (pp. 269–302). Sterling, VA: Stylus.

Mines, R. A. (1982). Student development assessment techniques. In G. R. Hanson (Ed.), *Measuring student development* (pp. 65–91). New Directions for Student Services, No. 20. San Francisco: Jossey-Bass.

Mines, R. A. (1985). Measurement issues in evaluating student development programs. *Journal of College Student Personnel, 26,* 101–106.

Mitchell, S. L., & Dell, D. M. (1992). The relationship between black students' racial identity attitude and participation in campus organizations. *Journal of College Student Development, 33,* 39–43.

Miville, M. L. (2005). Psychological functioning and identity development of biracial people: A review of current theory and research. In R. T. Carter (Ed.), *Handbook of racial-cultural psychology and counseling: Vol. 1. Theory and research* (pp. 295–319). Hoboken, NJ: Wiley.

Miville, M. L., Constantine, M. G., Baysden, M. F., & So-Lloyd, G. (2005). Chameleon changes: An exploration of racial identity themes of multiracial people. *Journal of Counseling Psychology, 52*(4), 507–516.

Miville, M. L., Darlington, P., Whitlock, B., & Mulligan, T. (2005). Integrating identities: The relationships of racial, gender, and ego identities among white college students. *Journal of College Student Development, 46*(2), 157–175.

Mobley, M., & Slaney, R. B. (1996). Holland's theory: Its relevance for lesbian women and gay men. *Journal of Vocational Behavior, 48*, 125–135.

Mohr, J. J. (2002). Heterosexual identity and the heterosexual therapist: An identity perspective on sexual orientation dynamics in psychotherapy. *Counseling Psychologist, 30*, 532–566.

Mohr, J., & Fassinger, R. (2000). Measuring dimensions of lesbian and gay male experience. *Measurement and Evaluation in Counseling and Development, 33*, 66–90.

Moore, L. V., & Upcraft, M. L. (1990). Theory in student affairs: Emerging perspectives. In L. V. Moore (Ed.), *Evolving theoretical perspectives on students* (pp. 3–23). New Directions for Student Services, No. 51. San Francisco: Jossey-Bass.

Moore, W. S. (1989). The learning environment preferences: Exploring the construct validity of an objective measure of the Perry scheme of intellectual development. *Journal of College Student Development, 30*, 504–514.

Moore, W. S. (1994). Student and faculty epistemology in the college classroom: The Perry scheme of intellectual and ethical development. In K. W. Prichard & R. M. Sawyer (Eds.), *Handbook of college teaching: Theory and application* (pp. 43–67). Westport, CT: Greenwood Press.

Moore, W. S. (2002). Understanding learning in a postmodern world: Reconsidering the Perry scheme of intellectual and ethical development. In B. K. Hofer & P. R. Pintrich (Eds.), *Personal epistemology: The psychology of beliefs about knowledge and knowing* (pp. 17–36). Mahwah, NJ: Erlbaum.

Moos, R. (1973). Conceptualizations of human environments. *American Psychologist, 28*, 652–665.

Moos, R. H. (1979). *Evaluating educational environments: Procedures, measures, findings, and policy implications.* San Francisco: Jossey-Bass.

Moos, R. H., & Insel, P. (Eds.). (1974). *Issues in social ecology.* Palo Alto, CA: National Press Books.

Morales, E. S. (1989). Ethnic minority families and minority gays and lesbians. *Marriage and Family Review, 14*, 217–239.

Moran, C. D. (2001). Purpose in life, student development, and well-being: Recommendations for student affairs practitioners. *NASPA Journal, 38*, 269–279.

Moran, G. (1983). *Religious education development: Images for the future.* Minneapolis: Winston.

Moreland, C., & Leach, M. M. (2001). The relationship between black racial identity and moral development. *Journal of Black Psychology, 27*, 255–271.

Morrill, W. H., Hurst, J., & Oetting, G. (Eds.). (1980). *Dimensions of intervention for student development.* Hoboken, NJ: Wiley.

Morrill, W. H., Oetting, E. M., & Hurst, J. C. (1974). Dimensions of counselor functioning. *Personnel and Guidance Journal, 52*, 354–359.

Morris, J. F. (1997). Lesbian coming out as a multidimensional process. *Journal of Homosexuality, 33*(2), 1–22.

Morse, R. E. (2002). *Racial identity development and epistemological development in college.* Unpublished doctoral dissertation, University of Virginia.

Mueller, J. A., & Cole, J. (2009). A qualitative examination of heterosexual consciousness among college students. *Journal of College Student Development, 50,* 320–336.

Muir, D. E. (1993). Race: The mythic root of racism. *Sociological Inquiry, 63*(3), 339–350.

Mullane, S. P. (1999). Fairness, educational value, and moral development in the student disciplinary process. *NASPA Journal, 36*(2), 86–95.

Mullis, R. L., Martin, R. E., Dosser, D. A., & Sanders, G. F. (1988). Using cognitive developmental theory to teach home economics courses. *Journal of Home Economics, 80*(1), 35–39.

Murphy, P., DeArmond, M., & Guin, K. (2003). A national crisis or localized problems? Getting perspective on the scope and scale of the teacher shortage. *Education Policy Analysis Archives, 11*(23). Retrieved May 24, 2008, from http://epaa.asu.edu/epaa/v11n23/.

Murrell, P. H., & Claxton, C. S. (1987). Experiential learning theory as a guide for effective teaching. *Counselor Education and Supervision, 27,* 4–14.

Mussi, J. M. (2001, March 2). [Review of the book *Big questions, worthy dreams*]. *Journal of College and Character.* Retrieved December 22, 2006, from www.collegevalues.org/spirit .cfm?id=448&a=1.

Mustapha, S. L., & Seybert, J. A. (1990). Moral reasoning in college students: Effects of two general education courses. *Education Research Quarterly, 14,* 32–40.

Myers, I. B. (1980). *Gifts differing.* Palo Alto, CA: Consulting Psychologists Press.

Myers, I. B., & McCaulley, M. H. (1985). *MBTI manual: A guide to the development and use of the Myers-Briggs Type Indicator.* Palo Alto, CA: Consulting Psychologists Press.

Myers, I. B., McCaulley, M. H., Quenk, N. L., & Hammer, A. L. (1998). *MBTI manual: A guide to the development and use of the Myers-Briggs Type Indicator* (3rd ed.). Palo Alto, CA: Consulting Psychologists Press.

Nagel, B., Matsuo, H., McIntyre, K. P., & Morrison, N. (2005). Attitudes toward victims of rape: Effects of gender, race, religion, and social class. *Journal of Interpersonal Violence, 20,* 725–737.

Nakashima, C. L. (1996). Voices from the movement: Approaches to multiraciality. In M.P.P. Root (Ed.), *The multiracial experience: Racial borders as the new frontier* (pp. 79–97). Thousand Oaks, CA: Sage.

Narvaez, D. (2005). The Neo-Kohlbergian tradition and beyond: Schemas, expertise and character. *Nebraska Symposium on Motivation, 51,* 119–163.

Nash, R. J. (2002). *Spirituality, ethics, religion, and teaching.* New York: Lang.

National Center for Education Statistics. (2008). *Digest of education statistics, 2007.* Washington, DC: U.S. Department of Education. Retrieved May 15, 2008, from http://nces.ed.gov/programs/digest/d07/.

Nelson, C. E., & Aleshire, D. (1986). Research in faith development. In C. Dykstra & S. Parks (Eds.), *Faith development and Fowler* (pp. 180–201). Birmingham, AL: Religious Education Press.

Nesbit, M. (2000). Connected knowing and developmental theory. *ReVision, 22*(4), 6–14.

Neugarten, B. L. (1979). Time, age, and the life cycle. *American Journal of Psychiatry, 136,* 887–894.

Neville, H. A., Heppner, P. P., & Wang, L. (1997). Relations among racial identity attitudes, perceived stressors, and coping styles in African American college students. *Journal of Counseling and Development, 75*(4), 303–311.

New, C. (2001). Oppressed and oppressors? The systematic mistreatment of men. *Sociology, 35*(3), 729–748.

Newcomb, T. M., & Wilson, E. K. (Eds.). (1966). *College peer groups: Problems and prospects for research.* Chicago: Aldine.

Nuss, E. M. (2003). The development of student affairs. In S. K. Komives, D. B. Woodard, Jr., & Associates, *Student services: A handbook for the profession* (4th ed., pp. 65–88). San Francisco: Jossey-Bass.

Omatsu, G. (1994). The "four prisons" and the movements of liberation: Asian American activism from the 1960s to the 1990s. In D. H. Hwang & K. Aguilar-San Juan (Eds.), *The state of Asian America: Activism and resistance in the 1990s* (pp. 19–69). Boston: South End Press.

Omi, M., & Winant, H. (2004). Racial formation. In L. Heldke & P. O'Connor (Eds.), *Oppression, privilege, and resistance: Theoretical perspectives on racism, sexism, and heterosexism* (pp. 115–142). New York: McGraw-Hill.

Ong, A. D., Phinney, J. S., & Dennis, J. (2006). Competence under challenge: Exploring the protective influence of parental support and ethnic identity in Latino college students. *Journal of Adolescence, 29*, 961–979.

Orlofsky, J. (1978). Identity formation, achievement, and fear of success in college men and women. *Journal of Youth and Adolescence, 7*, 49–62.

Orlofsky, J. L., Marcia, J. E., & Lesser, I. M. (1973). Ego identity status and the intimacy versus isolation crisis of young adulthood. *Journal of Personality and Social Psychology, 27*(2), 211–219.

Ortiz, A., & Rhoads, R. A. (2000). Deconstructing whiteness as part of a multicultural educational framework: From theory to practice. *Journal of College Student Development, 41*, 81–93.

Ortman, P. E. (1993). A feminist approach to teaching learning theory with educational applications. *Teaching of Psychology, 20*, 38–40.

Ossana, S. M., Helms, J. E., & Leonard, M. M. (1992). Do "womanist" identity attitudes influence college women's self-esteem and perceptions of environmental bias? *Journal of Counseling and Development, 70*, 402–408.

Ostrander, S. A. (1984). *Women of the upper class.* Philadelphia, PA: Temple University Press.

Outcalt, C. L., & Skewes-Cox, T. E. (2002). Involvement, interaction, and satisfaction: The human environment at HBCUs. *Review of Higher Education, 25*, 331–347.

Ozaki, C. C., & Johnston, M. (2008). The space in between: Issues for multiracial student organizations and advising. In K. A. Renn & P. Shang (Eds.), *Biracial and multiracial college students* (pp. 53–61). New Directions for Student Services, No. 123. San Francisco: Jossey-Bass.

Pace, C. R. (1984). *Measuring the quality of college student experience: An account of the development and use of the College Student Experiences Questionnaire.* Los Angeles: University of California, Higher Education Research Institute.

Pace, C. R., & Stern, G. G. (1958). An approach to the measurement of psychological characteristics of college environments. *Journal of Educational Psychology, 49*, 269–277.

Parham, T. A. (1989). Cycles of psychological nigrescence. *Counseling Psychologist, 17*(2), 187–226.

Parham, T. A., & Helms, J. E. (1981). The influence of black students' racial identity attitudes on preference for counselor's race. *Journal of Counseling Psychology, 28,* 250–257.

Parham, T. A., & Helms, J. E. (1985). Attitudes of racial identity and self-esteem of black students: An exploratory investigation. *Journal of College Student Personnel, 26,* 143–147.

Parker, C. A. (1974). Student development: What does it mean? *Journal of College Student Personnel, 15,* 248–256.

Parker, C. A. (1977). On modeling reality. *Journal of College Student Personnel, 18,* 419–425.

Parker, C. A., Widick, C., & Knefelkamp, L. L. (1978). Why bother with theory? In L. L. Knefelkamp, C. Widick, & C. A. Parker (Eds.), *Applying new developmental findings* (pp. vii–xvi). New Directions for Student Services, No. 4. San Francisco: Jossey-Bass.

Parks, C., Hughes, T. L., & Matthews, A. K. (2004). Race/ethnicity and sexual orientation: Intersecting identities. *Cultural Diversity and Ethnic Minority Psychology, 10*(3), 241–254.

Parks, S. D. (1986a). *The critical years: Young adults and the search for meaning, faith, and commitment.* New York: HarperCollins.

Parks, S. D. (1986b). Imagination and spirit in faith development: A way past the structure-content dichotomy. In C. Dykstra & S. Parks (Eds.), *Faith development and Fowler* (pp. 137–156). Birmingham, AL: Religious Education Press.

Parks, S. D. (2000). *Big questions, worthy dreams: Mentoring young adults in their search for meaning, purpose, and faith.* San Francisco: Jossey-Bass.

Parsons, F. (1909). *Choosing a vocation.* Boston: Houghton Mifflin.

Pascarella, E. T., & Terenzini, P. T. (1991). *How college affects students.* San Francisco: Jossey-Bass.

Pascarella, E. T., & Terenzini, P. T. (2005). *How college affects students: A third decade of research* (2nd ed.). San Francisco: Jossey-Bass.

Pavela, G. (1983, January 26). Sanctions for student misbehavior: Let the punishment fit the crime. *Chronicle of Higher Education,* p. 32.

Pearlin, L. I., & Schooler, C. (1978). The structure of coping. *Journal of Health and Social Behavior, 19,* 2–21.

Pearson, R. E., & Petitpas, A. J. (1990). Transitions of athletes: Developmental and preventative perspectives. *Journal of Counseling and Development, 69,* 7–10.

Perreira, D. C., & Dezago, J. L. (1989). College student development: Is it different for persons with disabilities? *Proceedings of the 1989 AHSSPPE Conference,* 51–54.

Perry, W. G., Jr. (1968). *Forms of intellectual and ethical development in the college years: A scheme.* New York: Holt, Rinehart, & Winston.

Perry, W. G., Jr. (1978). Sharing in the costs of growth. In C. A. Parker (Ed.), *Encouraging development in college students* (pp. 267–273). Minneapolis: University of Minnesota Press.

Perry, W. G., Jr. (1981). Cognitive and ethical growth: The making of meaning. In A. W. Chickering (Ed.), *The modern American college* (pp. 76–116). San Francisco: Jossey-Bass.

Pervin, L. A. (1967). A twenty-college study of student x college interaction using TAPE (transactional analysis of personality and environment): Rationale, reliability, and validity. *Journal of Educational Psychology, 58,* 290–302.

Pervin, L. A. (1968). The college as a social system: Student perception of students, faculty, and administration. *Journal of Educational Research, 61,* 281–284.

Pewardy, C., & Frey, B. (2004). American Indian students' perceptions of racial climate, multicultural support services, and ethnic fraud at a predominately white university. *Journal of American Indian Education, 43*(1), 32–60.

Phelps, R. E., Taylor, J. D., & Gerard, P. A. (2001). Cultural mistrust, ethnic identity, racial identity, and self-esteem among ethnically diverse black university students. *Journal of Counseling and Development, 79,* 209–216.

Phelps, R. E., Tranakos-Howe, S., Dagley, J. C., & Lyn, M. K. (2001). Encouragement and ethnicity in African American college students. *Journal of Counseling and Development, 79,* 90–97.

Phillips, S. D., & Imhoff, A. R. (1997). Women and career development: A decade of research. *Annual Review of Psychology, 48,* 31–59.

Phinney, J. (1989). Stages in ethnic identity development in minority group children. *Journal of Early Adolescence, 9*(1–2), 34–49.

Phinney, J. S. (1990). Ethnic identity in adolescents and adults: Review of research. *Psychological Bulletin, 108,* 499–514.

Phinney, J. S. (1992). The multigroup ethnic identity measure. *Journal of Adolescent Research, 7*(2), 156–176.

Phinney, J. S. (1993). A three-stage model of ethnic identity development in adolescence. In M. E. Bernal & G. P. Knight (Eds.), *Ethnic identity: Formation and transmission among Hispanics and other minorities* (pp. 61–79). Albany: State University of New York Press.

Phinney, J. S. (1995). Ethnic identity and self-esteem: A review and integration. In A. M. Padilla (Ed.), *Hispanic psychology: Critical issues in theory and research* (pp. 57–70). Thousand Oaks, CA: Sage.

Phinney, J. S. (1996). When we talk about American ethnic groups, what do we mean? *American Psychologist, 31,* 918–927.

Phinney, J. S. (2003). Ethnic identity and acculturation. In K. M. Chun, P. B. Organista, & G. Marin (Eds.), *Acculturation: Advances in theory, measurement, and applied research* (pp. 63–81). Washington, DC: American Psychological Association.

Phinney, J. S. (2007). Conceptualization and measurement of ethnic identity: Current status and future directions. *Journal of Counseling Psychology, 54*(3), 271–281.

Phinney, J. S., & Alipuria, L. L. (1996). At the interface of cultures: Multiethnic/multiracial high school and college students. *Journal of Social Psychology, 136*(2), 139–158.

Phinney, J. S., Chavira, V., & Williamson, L. (1992). Acculturation attitudes and self-esteem among high school and college students. *Youth and Society, 23*(3), 299–312.

Phinney, J. S., Dennis, J., & Osorio, S. (2006). Reasons to attend college among ethnically diverse college students. *Cultural Diversity and Ethnic Minority Psychology, 12*(2), 347–366.

Phinney, J. S., Jacoby, B., & Silva, C. (2007). Positive intergroup attitudes: The role of ethnic identity. *International Journal of Behavioral Development, 31*(5), 478–490.

Phinney, J. S., & Ong, A. D. (2007). Conceptualization and measurement of ethnic identity: Current status and future directions. *Journal of Counseling Psychology, 54*(3), 271–281.

Piaget, J. (1950). *The psychology of intelligence.* Orlando, FL: Harcourt Brace Jovanovich.

Piaget, J. (1952). *The origins of intelligence in children.* New York: International Universities Press.

Piaget, J. (1971). *Psychology and epistemology.* Harmondsworth, UK: Penguin.

Piaget, J. (1973). *The child and reality* (A. Rosin, Trans.). New York: Viking. (Original work published 1956)

Piaget, J. (1977). *The moral judgment of the child* (M. Gabain, Trans.). Harmondsworth, UK: Penguin. (Original work published 1932)

Picard, I. A., & Guido-DiBrito, F. (1993). Listening to the voice of care: Women's moral development and implications for student affairs practitioners. *Iowa Student Personnel Association Journal, 8,* 21–34.

Pillay, Y. (2005). Racial identity as a predictor of the psychological health of African American students at a predominantly white university. *Journal of Black Psychology, 31*(1), 46–66.

Pinderhughes, E. (1995). Biracial identity—Asset or handicap? In H. W. Harris, H. C. Blue, & E.E.H. Griffith (Eds.), *Racial and ethnic identity: Psychological development and creative expression* (pp. 73–93). New York: Routledge.

Pink, S. (2006). *The future of visual anthropology: Engaging the senses.* London: Routledge.

Pinto, J. K., Geiger, M. A., & Boyle, E. J. (1994). A three-year longitudinal study of changes in student learning styles. *Journal of College Student Development, 35,* 113–119.

Piper, T. D. (1997). Empowering students to create community standards. *About Campus, 2*(3), 22–24.

Piper, T. D., & Buckley, J. A. (2004). Community standards model: Developing learning partnerships in campus housing. In M. Baxter Magolda & P. M. King (Eds.), *Learning partnerships: Theory and modes of practice to educate for self-authorship* (pp. 185–212). Sterling, VA: Stylus.

Piper, T. D., & Rodgers, R. F. (1992). Theory-practice congruence: Factors influencing the internalization of theory. *Journal of College Student Development, 33,* 117–123.

Pizzolato, J. E. (2003). Developing self-authorship: Exploring the experiences of high-risk college students. *Journal of College Student Development, 44,* 797–811.

Pizzolato, J. E. (2004). Coping with conflict: Self-authorship, coping, and adaptation to college in first-year high-risk students. *Journal of College Student Development, 45,* 425–442.

Pizzolato, J. E. (2005). Creating crossroads for self-authorship: Investigating the provocative moment. *Journal of College Student Development, 46,* 624–641.

Pizzolato, J. E. (2006). Complex partnerships: Self-authorship and provocative academic-advising practices. *NACADA Journal, 26*(1), 32–45.

Pizzolato, J. E. (2007). Assessing self-authorship. In P. S. Meszaros (Ed.), *Self-authorship: Advancing students' intellectual growth* (pp. 31–42). New Directions for Teaching and Learning, No. 109. San Francisco: Jossey-Bass.

Pizzolato, J. E., Chaudhari, P., Murrell, E. D., Podobnik, S., & Schaeffer, Z. (2008). Ethnic identity, epistemological development, and academic achievement in underrepresented students. *Journal of College Student Development, 49,* 301–318.

Pizzolato, J. E., & Ozaki, C. C. (2007). Moving toward self-authorship: Investigating outcomes of learning partnerships. *Journal of College Student Development, 48,* 196–214.

Plummer, K. (1975). *Sexual stigma: An interactionist account.* London: Routledge & Kegan Paul.

Plummer, T. G. (1988). Cognitive growth and literary analysis: A dialectical model for teaching literature. *Unterrichtspraxis, 21*(1), 68–80.

Poindexter-Cameron, J., & Robinson, T. L. (1997). Relationships among racial identity attitudes, womanist attitudes, and self-esteem in African American college women. *Journal of College Student Development, 38,* 288–296.

Polkosnik, M. C., & Winston, R. B., Jr. (1992). Relationships between students' intellectual and psychosocial development: An exploratory investigation. *Journal of College Student Development, 30,* 10–19.

Pope, R. L. (1998). The relationship between psychosocial development and racial identity of black college students. *Journal of College Student Development, 39,* 273–282.

Pope, R. L. (2000). The relationship between psychosocial development and racial identity of college students of color. *Journal of College Student Development, 41,* 302–312.

Pope, R. L., Reynolds, A. L., & Mueller, J. (2004). *Multicultural competence in student affairs.* San Francisco: Jossey-Bass.

Pope-Davis, D. B., Liu, W. M., Ledesma-Jones, S., & Nevitt, J. (2000). African American acculturation and black racial identity: A preliminary investigation. *Journal of Multicultural Counseling and Development, 28*(2), 98–112.

Porterfield, W. D., & Pressprich, S. T. (1988). Carol Gilligan's perspectives and staff supervision: Implications for the practitioner. *NASPA Journal, 25,* 244–248.

Poston, W.S.C. (1990). The biracial identity development model: A needed addition. *Journal of Counseling and Development, 69,* 152–155.

Power, R. C. (2005). Motivation and moral development: A trifocal perspective. *Nebraska Symposium on Motivation, 51,* 197–249.

Poynter, K. J., & Washington, J. (2005). Multiple identities: Creating community on campus for LGBT students. In R. L. Sanlo (Ed.), *Gender identity and sexual orientation: Research, policy, and personal perspectives* (pp. 41–47). New Directions for Student Services, No. 111. San Francisco: Jossey-Bass.

Prager, K. J. (1985). Identity development, age and college experience in women. *Journal of Genetic Psychology, 147*(1), 31–36.

Pusch, R. S. (2005). Objects of curiosity: Transgender college students' perception of the reactions of others. *Journal of Gay and Lesbian Issues in Education, 3*(1), 45–61.

Quintana, S. M. (2007). Racial and ethnic identity: Developmental perspectives and research. *Journal of Counseling Psychology, 54*(3), 259–270.

Rainey, M. A., & Kolb, D. A. (1995). Using experiential learning theory and learning styles in diversity education. In R. R. Sims & S. J. Sims (Eds.), *The importance of learning styles: Understanding the implications for learning, course design, and education* (pp. 129–146). Westport, CT: Greenwood Press.

Ramirez, M., III. (1983). *Psychology of the Americas Mestizo perspective on personality and mental health.* New York: Pergamon Press.

Rankin, S. R. (2003). *Campus climate for gay, lesbian, bisexual, and transgender people: A national perspective.* Washington, DC: National Gay and Lesbian Task Force Policy Institute.

Ransdell, S. (2001). Predicting college success: The importance of ability and non-cognitive variables. *International Journal of Educational Research, 35*(4), 357–364.

Rapaport, N. J. (1984). Critical thinking and cognitive development. *Proceedings and Addresses of the American Philosophical Association, 57,* 610–615.

Rauscher, L., & McClintock, M. (1997). Ableism curricular design. In M. Adams, L. A. Bell, & P. Griffin (Eds.), *Teaching for diversity and social justice* (pp. 198–229). New York: Routledge.

Reimer, J. (1981). Moral education: The just community approach. *Phi Delta Kappan, 62,* 485–487.

Reisser, L. (1995). Revisiting the seven vectors. *Journal of College Student Development, 36,* 505–511.

Rendón, L. I. (1994). Validating culturally diverse students: Toward a new model of learning and student development. *Innovative Higher Education, 19,* 33–51.

Renn, K. A. (2000). Patterns of situational identity among biracial and multiracial college students. *Review of Higher Education, 23*(4), 399–420.

Renn, K. A. (2003). Understanding the identities of mixed race college students through a developmental ecology lens. *Journal of College Student Development, 44,* 383–403.

Renn, K. A. (2004). *Mixed race students in college: The ecology of race, identity, and community on campus.* Albany: State University of New York Press.

Renn, K. A. (2008). Research on biracial and multiracial identity development: Overview and synthesis. In K. A. Renn & P. Shang (Eds.), *Biracial and multiracial students* (pp. 13–21). New Directions for Student Services, No. 123. San Francisco: Jossey-Bass.

Renn, K. A., & Arnold, K. D. (2003). Reconceptualizing research on peer culture. *Journal of Higher Education, 74,* 261–291.

Renn, K. A., & Lunceford, C. J. (2002, November). *Because the numbers matter: Transforming racial/ethnic reporting data to account for mixed race students in postsecondary education.* Paper presented at the annual meeting of the Association for the Study of Higher Education, Sacramento, CA.

Rest, J. R. (1969). *Hierarchies of comprehension and preference in a developmental stage model of moral thinking.* Unpublished doctoral dissertation, University of Chicago.

Rest, J. R. (1979a). *Development in judging moral issues.* Minneapolis: University of Minnesota Press.

Rest, J. R. (1979b). *Revised manual for the Defining Issues Test: An object test of moral development.* Minneapolis: Minnesota Moral Research Project.

Rest, J. R. (1986a). *The Defining Issues Test* (3rd ed.). Minneapolis: University of Minnesota, Center for the Study of Ethical Development.

Rest, J. R. (1986b). *Moral development: Advances in research and theory.* New York: Praeger.

Rest, J., Narvaez, D., Bebeau, M. J., & Thoma, S. J. (1999). *Postconventional moral thinking: A Neo-Kohlbergian approach.* Mahwah, NJ: Erlbaum.

Rest, J., Narvaez, D., Thoma, S. J., & Bebeau, M. J. (2000). A Neo-Kohlbergian approach to morality research. *Journal of Moral Education, 29,* 381–395.

Reynolds, A. L., & Hanjorgiris, W. F. (2000). Coming out: Lesbian, gay, and bisexual identity development. In R. P. Perez, K. A. DeBord, & K. Bieschke (Eds.), *Handbook of counseling and psychotherapy with lesbian, gay, and bisexual clients* (pp. 35–55). Washington, DC: American Psychological Association.

Reynolds, A. L., & Pope, R. L. (1991). The complexities of diversity: Exploring multiple oppressions. *Journal of Counseling and Development, 70,* 174–180.

Rhatigan, J. J. (2000). The history and philosophy of student affairs. In M. J. Barr, M. K. Dresler, & Associates, *The handbook of student affairs administration* (pp. 3–24). San Francisco: Jossey-Bass.

Rhoads, R. A. (1994). *Coming out in college: The struggle for a queer identity.* Westport, CT: Bergin & Garvey.

Rhoads, R. A. (1995). Whales tales, dog piles, and beer goggles: An ethnographic case study of fraternity life. *Anthropology and Education Quarterly, 26,* 403–412.

Rhoads, R. A. (1997). *Community service and higher learning: Explorations of the caring self.* Albany: State University of New York Press.

Rhoads, R. A., Lee, J. J., & Yamada, M. (2002). Panethnicity and collective action among Asian American students: A qualitative case study. *Journal of College Student Development, 43,* 876–891.

Ricci, J. P., Porterfield, W. D., & Piper, T. D. (1987). Using developmental theory in supervising residential staff members. *NASPA Journal, 24*(4), 32–41.

Rice, M. B., & Brown, R. D. (1990). Developmental factors associated with self-perceptions of mentoring competence and mentoring needs. *Journal of College Student Development, 31,* 293–299.

Rich, A. (1980). Compulsory heterosexuality and lesbian existence. *Journal of Women in Culture and Society, 5,* 631–660.

Ritter, K. Y., & Terndrup, A. I. (2002). *Handbook of affirmative psychotherapy with lesbians and gay men.* New York: Guilford.

Robin, L., & Hamner, K. (2000). Bisexuality: Identities and community. In V. A. Wall & N. J. Evans (Eds.), *Toward acceptance: Sexual orientation issues on campus* (pp. 245–259). Washington, DC: American College Personnel Association.

Robinson, T. L. (1999). The intersections of dominant discourses across race, gender and other identities. *Journal of Counseling and Development, 77,* 73–79.

Robinson, T. L., & Howard-Hamilton, M. (2000). *The convergence of race, ethnicity and gender: Multiple identities in counseling.* Upper Saddle River, NJ: Merrill.

Rocco, T. S., & West, W. G. (1998). Deconstructing privilege: An examination of privilege in adult education. *Adult Education Quarterly, 48*(3), 171–184.

Rockquemore, K. A. (2002). Negotiating the color line: The gendered process of racial identity construction among black/white biracial women. *Gender and Society, 16*(4), 485–503.

Rockquemore, K. A., & Brunsma, D. L. (2002). *Beyond black: Biracial identity in America.* Thousand Oaks, CA: Sage.

Rodgers, R. F. (1980). Theories underlying student development. In D. G. Creamer (Ed.), *Student development in higher education* (pp. 10–95). Cincinnati, OH: American College Personnel Association.

Rodgers, R. F. (1990a). An integration of campus ecology and student development: The Oletangy project. In D. G. Creamer & Associates, *College student development: Theory and practice for the 1990s* (pp. 155–180). Alexandria, VA: American College Personnel Association.

Rodgers, R. F. (1990b). Recent theories and research underlying student development. In D. G. Creamer & Associates, *College student development: Theory and practice for the 1990s* (pp. 27–79). Alexandria, VA: American College Personnel Association.

Rodgers, R. F. (1990c). Student development. In U. Delworth, G. R. Hanson, & Associates, *Student services: A handbook for the profession* (2nd ed., pp. 117–164). San Francisco: Jossey-Bass.

Rodgers, R. F., & Widick, C. (1980). Theory to practice: Using concepts, logic and creativity. In F. B. Newton & K. L. Ender (Eds.), *Student development practice: Strategies for making a difference* (pp. 5–25). Springfield, IL: Thomas.

Rogers, J. L. (1989). New paradigm leadership: Integrating the female ethos. *Initiatives, 57*(4), 1–8.

Rogers, J. L., & Dantley, M. E. (2001). Invoking the spiritual in campus life and leadership. *Journal of College Student Development, 42,* 589–603.

Rogers, J. L., Magolda, P. M., Baxter Magolda, M. B., & Knight Abowitz, K. (2004). A community of scholars: Enacting the learning partnerships model in graduate education. In M. Baxter Magolda & P. M. King (Eds.), *Learning partnerships: Theory and modes of practice to educate for self-authorship* (pp. 213–244). Sterling, VA: Stylus.

Rogers, M. S. (2004). An exploration of psychosocial development in community college students. *Dissertation Abstracts International,* A65/06, 2070.

Romer, N. (1991). A feminist view of moral development: Criticisms and applications. *Initiatives, 54*(3), 19–32.

Root, M.P.P. (1990). Resolving "other" status: Identity development of biracial individuals. In L. S. Brown & M.P.P. Root (Eds.), *Complexity and diversity in feminist theory and therapy* (pp. 185–205). New York: Haworth.

Root, M.P.P. (1995). The multiracial contribution to the psychological browning of America. In N. Zack (Ed.), *American mixed race: The culture of microdiversity* (pp. 231–236). Lanham, MD: Rowman & Littlefield.

Root, M.P.P. (1996). The multiracial experience: Racial borders as a significant frontier in race relations. In M.P.P. Root (Ed.), *The multiracial experience: Racial borders as the new frontier* (pp. xiii–xxviii). Thousand Oaks, CA: Sage.

Root, M.P.P. (1997). Mixed-race women. In N. Zack (Ed.), *Race/sex: Their sameness, difference, and interplay* (pp. 157–172). New York: Routledge.

Root, M.P.P. (2001). Factors influencing the variation in racial and ethnic identity of mixed-heritage persons of Asian ancestry. In T. Williams-León & C. L. Nakashima (Eds.), *The sum of our parts: Mixed-heritage Asian Americans* (pp. 61–70). Philadelphia: Temple University Press.

Root, M.P.P. (2003a). Five mixed-race identities. In L. I. Winter & H. L. DeBose (Eds.), *New faces in a changing America: Multiracial identity in the 21st century* (pp. 3–20). Thousand Oaks, CA: Sage.

Root, M.P.P. (2003b). Racial identity development and persons of mixed race heritage. In M.P.P. Root & M. Kelley (Eds.), *Multiracial child resource book: Living complex identities* (pp. 34–41). Seattle: MAVIN Foundation.

Roper, L. D. (Ed.). (2002). The scholarship of student affairs [Special issue]. *NASPA Journal, 39*(2).

Rosario, M., Schrimshaw, E. W., & Hunter, J. (2004). Ethnic/racial differences in the coming-out process of lesbian, gay, and bisexual youths: A comparison of sexual identity development over time. *Cultural Diversity and Ethnic Minority Psychology, 10*(3), 215–228.

Rosenthal, D. A., & Feldman, S. S. (1992). The nature and stability of ethnic identity in Chinese youth: Effects of length of residence in two cultural contexts. *Journal of Cross-Cultural Psychology, 23*, 214–227.

Rowe, W., Bennett, S. K., & Atkinson, D. R. (1994). White racial identity models: A critique and alternative proposal. *Counseling Psychologist, 22*, 129–146.

Rust, P. C. (2002). Bisexuality: The state of the union. *Annual Review of Sex Research, 13*, 180–240.

Saidla, D. D. (1990). Cognitive development and group stages. *Journal for Specialists in Group Work, 15*(1), 15–20.

Salter, D. W., Evans, N. J., & Forney, D. S. (2006). A longitudinal study of learning style preferences on the Myers-Briggs Type Indicator and Learning Style Inventory. *Journal of College Student Development, 47*, 173–184.

Sanchez, D., & Carter, R. T. (2005). Exploring the relationship between racial identity and religious orientation among African American college students. *Journal of College Student Development, 46*, 280–295.

Sandoval, C. (2000). *Methodology of the oppressed: Theory out of bounds.* Minneapolis: University of Minnesota Press.

Sanford, N. (1962). Developmental status of the entering freshmen. In N. Sanford (Ed.), *The American college student* (pp. 253–282). Hoboken, NJ: Wiley.

Sanford, N. (1966). *Self and society.* New York: Atherton Press.

Sanford, N. (1967). *Where colleges fail: The study of the student as a person.* San Francisco: Jossey-Bass.

Sanlo, R. L. (Ed.). (1998). *Working with lesbian, gay, bisexual, and transgender college students: A handbook for faculty and administrators.* Westport, CT: Greenwood.

Savin-Williams, R. C. (1995). Lesbian, gay male, and bisexual adolescents. In A. R. D'Augelli & C. J. Patterson (Eds.), *Lesbian, gay, and bisexual identities over the lifespan: Psychological perspectives* (pp. 165–189). New York: Oxford University Press.

Sax, L. J., & Bryant, A. N. (2004). Undergraduates and science. In A. M. Martinez Aleman & K. A. Renn (Eds.), *Women in higher education: An encyclopedia* (pp. 363–366). Santa Barbara, CA: ABC-CLIO.

Sax, L. J., Bryant, A. N., & Harper, C. E. (2005). The differential effects of student-faculty interaction on college outcomes for women and men. *Journal of College Student Development, 46*, 642–657.

Scharmer, C. O. (2000, March 23). Grabbing the tiger by the tail: Conversation with Robert Kegan. *Dialog on Leadership.* Retrieved May 22, 2008, from www.dialogonleadership.org/docs/Kegan-1999.pdf.

Schell, L. A. (1997). Adaptation to transition: The woman athlete's experience with intercollegiate athletic retirement. *Research Quarterly for Exercise and Sport, 68*(1), A115.

Schenkel, S., & Marcia, J. E. (1972). Attitudes toward premarital intercourse in determining ego identity status in college women. *Journal of Personality, 40*, 472–482.

Schlossberg, N. K. (1981). A model for analyzing human adaptation to transition. *Counseling Psychologist, 9*(2), 2–18.

Schlossberg, N. K. (1984). *Counseling adults in transition.* New York: Springer.

Schlossberg, N. K. (1989a). Marginality and mattering: Key issues in building community. In D. C. Roberts (Ed.), *Designing campus activities to foster a sense of community* (pp. 5–15). New Directions for Student Services, No. 48. San Francisco: Jossey-Bass.

Schlossberg, N. K. (1989b). *Overwhelmed: Coping with life's ups and downs.* Lanham, MD: Lexington Books.

Schlossberg, N. K., & Leibowitz, Z. B. (1980). Organizational support systems as a buffer to job loss. *Journal of Vocational Behavior, 18*, 204–217.

Schlossberg, N. K., Lynch, A. Q., & Chickering, A. W. (1989). *Improving higher education environments for adults: Responsive programs and services from entry to departure.* San Francisco: Jossey-Bass.

Schlossberg, N. K., & Robinson, S. P. (1996). *Going to plan B.* New York: Simon & Schuster.

Schlossberg, N. K., Waters, E. B., & Goodman, J. (1995). *Counseling adults in transition* (2nd ed.). New York: Springer.

Schlosser, L. Z. (2003). Christian privilege: Breaking a sacred taboo. *Journal of Multicultural Counseling and Development, 31*, 44–51.

Schnoor, R. F. (2006). Being gay and Jewish: Negotiating intersecting identities. *Sociology of Religion, 67*(1), 43–60.

Schreier, B. (1995). Moving beyond tolerance: A new paradigm for programming about homophobia/biphobia and heterosexism. *Journal of College Student Development, 36*, 19–26.

Schroeder, C. C. (1981). Student development through environmental management. In G. Blimling & J. Schuh (Eds.), *Increasing the educational role of residence halls* (pp. 35–49). San Francisco: Jossey-Bass.

Schroeder, C. C., & Freesh, N. (1977). Applying environmental management strategies in residence halls. *NASPA Journal, 15*(1), 51–57.

Schroeder, C. C., & Pike, G. R. (2001). The scholarship of application in student affairs. *Journal of College Student Development, 42*, 342–355.

Schuh, J. H. (1979). Assessment and redesign in residence halls. In L. Huebner (Ed.), *Redesigning campus environments* (pp. 23–36). San Francisco: Jossey-Bass.

Schuh, J. H. (1994). [Review of the book *Education and identity* (2nd ed.)]. *Journal of College Student Development, 35,* 310–312.

Schwartz, J. L., Donovan, J., & Guido-DiBrito, F. (2009). Stories of social class: Self-identified male Mexican students crack the silence. *Journal of College Student Development, 50,* 50–66.

Sears, J. T. (1991). *Growing up gay in the South: Race, gender, and journeys of the spirit.* New York: Harrington Park Press.

Sedlacek, W. E. (1987). Black students on white campuses: 20 years of research. *Journal of College Student Personnel, 28,* 484–495.

Sedlacek, W. E. (2004). *Beyond the big test: Noncognitive assessment in higher education.* San Francisco: Jossey-Bass.

Seifert, T. (2007). Understanding Christian privilege: Managing the tensions of spiritual plurality. *About Campus, 12*(2), 10–17.

Sellers, R. M., Smith, M., Shelton, N. J., Rowley, S. J., & Chavous, T. M. (1998). Multidimensional model of racial identity: A reconceptualization of African American racial identity. *Personality and Social Psychology Review, 2,* 18–39.

Selman, R. L. (1976). Social cognitive understanding. In T. Lickona (Ed.), *Moral development and behavior: Theory, research, and social issues* (pp. 299–316). New York: Holt, Rinehart, & Winston.

Selman, R. (1980). *Growth of interpersonal understanding: Developmental and clinical analysis.* Orlando, FL: Academic Press.

Sharp, J. E. (2006). Rationale and strategies for using Kolb learning style theory in the classroom. In R. R. Sims & S. J. Sims (Eds.), *The importance of learning styles: Understanding the implications for learning, course design, and education* (pp. 93–113). Westport, CT: Greenwood Press.

Sheared, V. (1994). Giving voice: An inclusive model of instruction—A womanist perspective. In E. Hayes & S.A.J. Collins, III (Eds.), *Confronting racism and sexism* (pp. 27–38). New Directions for Adult and Continuing Education, No. 61. San Francisco: Jossey-Bass.

Sheehan, O.T.O., & Pearson, F. (1995). Asian international and American students' psychosocial development. *Journal of College Student Development, 36,* 523–530.

Shih, M., Bonam, C., Sanchez, D. T., & Peck, C. (2007). The social construction of race: Biracial identity and vulnerability to stereotypes. *Cultural Diversity and Ethnic Minority Psychology, 13,* 125–133.

Simoni, J. M., & Walters, K. L. (2001). Heterosexual identity and heterosexism: Recognizing privilege to reduce prejudice. *Journal of Homosexuality, 41*(1), 157–172.

Smith, B. (2007). Accessing social capital through the academic mentoring process. *Equity and Excellence in Education, 40*(1), 36–46.

Smith, D. M., & Kolb, D. A. (1986). *User's guide for the Learning Style Inventory.* Boston: McBer.

Smith, L. T. (1999). *Decolonizing methodologies: Research and indigenous peoples.* London: Zed Books.

Snarey, J. R. (1985). Cross-cultural universality of social-moral development: A critical review of Kohlbergian research. *Psychological Bulletin, 97,* 202–232.

Sodowsky, G. R., & Carey, J. C. (1988). Relationships between acculturation-related demographics and cultural attitudes of an Asian-Indian immigrant group. *Journal of Multicultural Counseling and Development, 16,* 117–133.

Sodowsky, G. R., Kwan, K. K., & Pannu, R. (1995). Ethnic identity of Asians in the United States. In J. G. Ponterotto, J. M. Casas, L. A. Suzuki, & C. M. Alexander (Eds.), *Handbook of multicultural counseling* (pp. 123–154). Thousand Oaks, CA: Sage.

Solórzano, D. G. (1998). Critical race theory, race and gender microaggressions, and the experience of Chicana and Chicano studies. *International Journal of Qualitative Studies in Education, 11*(1), 121–136.

Song, M. (2003). *Choosing ethnic identity.* Malden, MA: Blackwell.

Sonn, C. C., & Fisher, A. T. (2003). Identity and oppression: Differential responses to an in-between status. *American Journal of Community Psychology, 31,* 117–128.

Sowa, C. J., & Gressard, C. F. (1983). Athletic participation: Its relationship to student development. *Journal of College Student Development, 24,* 236–239.

Spaulding, E., & Wilson, A. (2002). Demystifying reflection: A study of pedagogical strategies that encourage reflective journal writing. *Teachers College Record, 104,* 1393–1421.

Speck, B. W. (2005). What is spirituality? In S. L. Hoppe & B. W. Speck (Eds.), *Spirituality in higher education* (pp. 3–13). New Directions for Teaching and Learning, No. 104. San Francisco: Jossey-Bass.

Spencer, M. B., & Markstrom-Adams, C. (1990). Identity processes among racial and ethnic minority children in America. *Child Development, 61,* 290–310.

Spencer, R. (2006). *Challenging multiracial identity.* Boulder, CO: Lynne Rienner.

Spickard, P. R. (1989). *Mixed blood: Intermarriage and ethnic identity in twentieth-century America.* Madison, WI: University of Wisconsin Press.

Spoto, A. (1989). *Jung's typology in perspective.* Boston: SIGO Press.

Stamm, L. (2006). The dynamics of spirituality and the religious experience. In A. W. Chickering, J. C. Dalton, & L. Stamm (Eds.), *Encouraging authenticity and spirituality in higher education* (pp. 37–65). San Francisco: Jossey-Bass.

Stanczak, G. C. (Ed.). (2007). *Visual research methods: Image, society and representation.* Thousand Oaks, CA: Sage.

Standen, B.C.S. (1996). Without a template: The biracial Korean/white experience. In M.P.P. Root (Ed.), *The multiracial experience: Racial borders as the new frontier* (pp. 245–259). Thousand Oaks, CA: Sage.

Stanley, J. (2004). Biracial lesbian and bisexual women: Understanding the unique aspects and interactional processes of multiple minority identities. *Women and Therapy, 27,* 159–171.

Stanton, A. (1996). Reconfiguring teaching and knowing in the college classroom. In N. Goldberger, J. Tarule, B. Clinchy, & M. Belenky (Eds.), *Knowledge, difference, and power* (pp. 25–56). New York: Basic Books.

Staples, B. (2007, February 5). On race and the census: Struggling with categories that no longer apply. *New York Times.* Retrieved February 5, 2007, from www.nytimes .com/2007/02/05/opinion/05mon4.html?th=&emc=th&pagewanted=print.

St. Clair, D. (1994). The drum: Improving the campus ecology for Native American students. *Campus Ecologist, 12*(2), 1–4.

Stephan, C. W. (1992). Mixed-heritage individuals: Ethnic identity and trait characteristics. In M.P.P. Root (Ed.), *Racially mixed people in America* (pp. 50–63). Thousand Oaks, CA: Sage.

Stern, D. N. (1985). *The interpersonal world of the infant: A view from psychoanalysis and developmental psychology.* New York: Basic Books.

Stern, G. G. (1970). *People in context.* Hoboken, NJ: Wiley.

Stevens, R. A. (2004). Understanding gay identity development within the college environment. *Journal of College Student Development, 45,* 185–206.

Steward, J. H. (1955). *Theory of culture change: The methodology of multilinear evolution.* Urbana: University of Illinois Press.

Stiller, N. J., & Forrest, L. (1990). An extension of Gilligan's and Lyons' investigation of morality: Gender differences in college students. *Journal of College Student Development, 31,* 54–63.

Stimpson, D., Jensen, L., & Neff, W. (1992). Cross-cultural gender differences in preference for a caring morality. *Journal of Social Psychology, 132,* 317–322.

Stiver, I. P. (1991). Beyond the Oedipus complex: Mothers and daughters. In J. V. Jordan, A. G. Kaplan, J. B. Miller, I. P. Stiver, & J. L. Surrey (Eds.), *Women's growth in connection: Writings from the Stone Center* (pp. 97–121). New York: Guilford Press.

Stonequist, E. V. (1937). *The marginal man: A study in personality and culture conflict.* New York: Russell & Russell.

Stonewater, B. B. (1988). Informal developmental assessment in residence halls: A theory to practice model. *NASPA Journal, 25,* 267–273.

Stonewater, B. B. (1989). Gender differences in career decision making: A theoretical integration. *Initiatives, 52*(1), 27–34.

Strange, C. C. (1994). Student development: The evolution and status of an essential idea. *Journal of College Student Development, 35,* 399–412.

Strange, C. C. (2001). Spiritual dimensions of graduate preparation in student affairs. In M. A. Jablonski (Ed.), *The implications of student spirituality for student affairs practice* (pp. 57–67). New Directions for Student Services, No. 95. San Francisco: Jossey-Bass.

Strange, C. C. (2003). Dynamics of campus environments. In S. R. Komives & D. B. Woodard, Jr. (Eds.), *Student services: A handbook for the profession* (4th ed., pp. 297–316). San Francisco: Jossey-Bass.

Strange, C. C., & Banning, J. H. (2001). *Educating by design: Creating campus learning environments that work.* San Francisco: Jossey-Bass.

Strange, C. C., & King, P. M. (1990). The professional practice of student development. In D. G. Creamer (Ed.), *College student development: Theory and practice for the 1990s* (pp. 9–24). Alexandria, VA: American College Personnel Association.

Straub, C. (1987). Women's development of autonomy and Chickering's theory. *Journal of College Student Personnel, 28,* 198–205.

Straub, C., & Rodgers, R. F. (1986). An exploration of Chickering's theory and women's development. *Journal of College Student Personnel, 27,* 216–224.

Student Learning Imperative: Implications for student affairs. (1966). *Journal of College Student Development, 37,* 118–122.

Sue, D. W., & Sue, D. (1990). *Counseling the culturally different: Theory and practice.* Hoboken, NJ: Wiley.

Sue, D. W., & Sue, D. (2003). *Counseling the culturally diverse: Theory and practice* (4th ed.). Hoboken, NJ: Wiley.

Sugarman, L. (1985). Kolb's model of experiential learning: Touchstone for trainers, students, counselors, and clients. *Journal of Counseling and Development, 64,* 264–268.

Sullivan, A. (2006). Interracial marriage should be encouraged. In E. Stanford (Ed.), *Interracial America: Opposing viewpoints* (pp. 153–157). Farmington Hills, MI: Greenhaven.

Sullivan, P. (1998). Sexual identity development: The importance of target or dominant group membership. In R. L. Sanlo (Ed.), *Working with lesbian, gay, bisexual, and transgender college students: A handbook for faculty and administrators* (pp. 3–12). Westport, CT: Greenwood Press.

Sutliff, R. I., & Baldwin, V. (2001). Learning styles: Teaching technology subjects can be more effective. *Journal of Technology Studies, 27*(1), 22–27.

Svinicki, M. D., & Dixon, N. M. (1987). The Kolb model modified for classroom activities. *College Teaching, 35,* 141–146.

Swain, D. A. (1991). Withdrawal from sport and Schlossberg's model of transitions. *Sociology of Sport Journal, 8,* 152–160.

Swick, H. M. (1991, April). *Fostering the professional development of medical students.* Paper presented at the annual meeting of the American Educational Research Association, Chicago. (ERIC Document Reproduction Service No. ED330283)

Tajfel, H. (1981). *Human group and social categories.* Cambridge, UK: Cambridge University Press.

Takaki, R. T. (1993). *A different mirror: A history of multicultural America.* New York: Little, Brown.

Talbot, D. M. (2008). Exploring the experiences and self-labeling of mixed-race individuals with two minority parents. In K. A. Renn & P. Shang (Eds.), *Biracial and multiracial students* (pp. 23–31). New Directions for Student Services, No. 123. San Francisco: Jossey-Bass.

Tatum, B. D. (1997). *Why are all the black kids sitting together in the cafeteria?* New York: Basic Books.

Taub, D. J. (1995). Relationship of selected factors to traditional-age undergraduate women's development of autonomy. *Journal of College Student Development, 36,* 141–151.

Taub, D. J. (1997). Autonomy and parental attachment in traditional-age undergraduate women. *Journal of College Student Development, 38,* 645–654.

Taub, D. J., & McEwen, M. K. (1991). Patterns of development of autonomy and mature interpersonal relationships in black and white undergraduate women. *Journal of College Student Development, 32,* 502–508.

Taub, D. J., & McEwen, M. K. (1992). The relationship of racial identity attitudes to autonomy and mature interpersonal relationships in black and white undergraduate women. *Journal of College Student Development, 33,* 439–446.

Taylor, C. M., & Howard-Hamilton, M. F. (1995). Student involvement and racial identity attitudes among African American males. *Journal of College Student Development, 36,* 330–336.

Taylor, J. M., Gilligan, C., & Sullivan, A. M. (1995). *Between voice and silence: Women and girls, race and relationship.* Cambridge, MA: Harvard University Press.

Taylor, L. (2005). [Review of the book *Mixed race students in college: The ecology of race, identity and community on campus*]. *Teachers College Record, 107*(7), 1467–1474.

Temkin, L., & Evans, N. J. (1998). Religion on campus: Suggestions for cooperation between student affairs and campus-based religious organizations. *NASPA Journal, 36,* 61–69.

Terenzini, P. T. (1994). Good news and bad news: The implications of Strange's proposals for research. *Journal of College Student Development, 35,* 422–427.

Thoma, G. A. (1993). The Perry framework and tactics for teaching critical thinking in economics. *Journal of Economic Education, 24,* 128–137.

Thoma, S. J., & Rest, J. R. (1999). The relationship between moral decision making patterns of consolidation and transition in moral judgment development. *Developmental Psychology, 35,* 323–334.

Thomas, R., & Chickering, A. W. (1984). *Education and Identity* revisited. *Journal of College Student Personnel, 25,* 392–399.

Thornton, M. C. (1996). Hidden agendas, identity theories, and multiracial people. In M.P.P. Root (Ed.), *The multiracial experience: Racial borders as the new frontier* (pp. 101–120). Thousand Oaks, CA: Sage.

Thornton, M. C. (2004). Race and multiraciality: Multiracial challenges to monoracialism. In P. Spickard & G. R. Daniel (Eds.), *Racial thinking in the United States: Uncompleted independence* (pp. 308–340). Notre Dame, IN: University of Notre Dame Press.

Tierney, W. G. (1992). An anthropological analysis of student participation in college. *Journal of Higher Education, 63*, 603–618.

Tierney, W. G. (1996). The college experience of Native Americans: A critical analysis. In C. Turney, N. M. Garcia, & L. I. Rendón (Eds.), *Racial and ethnic diversity in higher education* (pp. 302–311). Boston: Pearson.

Tierney, W. G., & Venegas, K. M. (2006). Fictive kin and social capital: The role of peer groups in applying and paying for college. *American Behavioral Scientist, 49*, 1687–1702.

Ting, S. R. (2003). A longitudinal study of non-cognitive variables in predicting academic success of first-generation college students. *College and University, 78*(4), 27–31.

Tinto, V. (1993). *Leaving college: Rethinking the causes and cures of student attrition.* Chicago: University of Chicago Press. (Original work published 1987)

Tippeconnic Fox, M. J., Lowe, S. C., & McClellan, G. S. (Eds.). (2005). *Serving Native American students.* New Directions for Student Services, No. 109. San Francisco: Jossey-Bass.

Tisdell, E. J. (1993). Interlocking systems of power, privilege and oppression in adult higher education classes. *Adult Education Quarterly, 43*(4), 203–226.

Tisdell, E. J. (2003). *Exploring spirituality and culture in adult and higher education.* San Francisco: Jossey-Bass.

Todaro, E. (1993). The impact of recreational sports on student development: A theoretical model. *NIRSA Journal, 17*(3), 23–26.

Tomlinson, M. J., & Fassinger, R. E. (2003). Career development, lesbian identity development, and campus climate among lesbian college students. *Journal of College Student Development, 44*, 845–860.

Torres, V. (1999). Validation of a bicultural orientation model for Hispanic college students. *Journal of College Student Development, 40*, 285–298.

Torres, V. (2003). Influences on ethnic identity development of Latino college students in the first two years of college. *Journal of College Student Development, 44*, 532–547.

Torres, V. (2004). The diversity among us: Puerto Ricans, Cuban Americans, Caribbean Americans, and Central and South Americans. In A. Ortiz (Ed.), *Addressing the unique needs of Latino American students* (pp. 5–16). New Directions for Student Services, No. 105. San Francisco: Jossey-Bass.

Torres, V., & Baxter Magolda, M. B. (2004). Reconstructing Latino identity: The influence of cognitive development on the ethnic identity process of Latino students. *Journal of College Student Development, 45*, 333–347.

Torres, V., & Hernandez, E. (2007). The influence of ethnic identity on self-authorship: A longitudinal study of Latino/a college students. *Journal of College Student Development, 48*, 558–573.

Torres, V., Howard-Hamilton, M. F., & Cooper, D. L. (2003). *Identity development of diverse populations: Implications for teaching and administration in higher education.* San Francisco: Jossey-Bass.

Touchton, J. G., Wertheimer, L. C., Cornfeld, J. L., & Harrison, K. H. (1977). Career planning and decision-making: A developmental approach to the classroom. *Counseling Psychologist, 6*(4), 42–47.

Trianosky, G. V. (2003). Beyond mestizaje: The future of race in America. In L. I. Winters & H. L. DeBosse (Eds.), *New faces in a changing America: Multiracial identity in the 21st century* (pp. 176–193). Thousand Oaks, CA: Sage.

Trinh, T. M. (1989). *Woman native other.* Bloomington: Indiana University Press.

Tripp, R. (1997). Greek organizations and student development: A review of the literature. *College Student Affairs Journal, 16*(2), 31–39.

Troiden, R. R. (1989). The formation of homosexual identities. *Journal of Homosexuality, 17,* 43–74.

Tuan, M. (2002). Second-generation Asian American identity: Clues from the Asian ethnic experience. In P. G. Min (Ed.), *Second generation: Ethnic identity among Asian Americans* (pp. 209–237). Walnut Creek, CA: Alta Mira.

Tuckman, B. W. (1965). Developmental sequence in small groups. *Psychology Bulletin, 63,* 384–399.

Twine, F. W. (1996). Brown skinned white girls: Class, culture and the construction of white identity in suburban communities. *Gender, Place and Culture, 3*(2), 205–224.

Umaña-Taylor, A. J. (2004). Ethnic identity and self-esteem: Examining the role of social context. *Journal of Adolescence, 27,* 139–146.

Umaña-Taylor, A. J., & Shin, N. (2007). An examination of ethnic identity and self-esteem with diverse populations. *Cultural Diversity and Ethnic Minority Psychology, 13*(2), 178–186.

Upcraft, M. L., & Moore, L. V. (1990). Evolving theoretical perspectives of student development. In M. J. Barr, M. L. Upcraft, & Associates, *New futures for student affairs: Building a vision for professional leadership and practice* (pp. 41–68). San Francisco: Jossey-Bass.

Upcraft, M. L., & Schuh, J. H. (1996). *Assessment in student affairs: A guide for practitioners.* San Francisco: Jossey-Bass.

Utterback, J. W., Spooner, S. E., Barbieri, J. A., & Fox, S. N. (1995). Gender and ethnic issues in the development of intimacy among college students. *NASPA Journal, 32,* 82–89.

Valentine, J. J., & Taub, D. J. (1999). Responding to the developmental needs of student athletes. *Journal of College Counseling, 2,* 164–179.

Valocchi, S. (1999). The class-inflected nature of gay identity. *Social Problems, 46,* 207–224.

Vandiver, B. J. (2001). Psychological nigrescence revisited: Introduction and overview. *Journal of Multicultural Counseling and Development, 29,* 165–173.

Van Hecke, M. L. (1987, May). *Cognitive development during the college years.* Paper presented at the annual meeting of the Midwest Psychological Association, Chicago. (ERIC Document Reproduction Service No. ED288477)

Veblen, T. B. (1946). *The higher learning in America: A memorandum on the conduct of universities by business men.* New York: Hill & Wang. (Original work published 1918)

Wadsworth, B. J. (1979). *Piaget's theory of cognitive development* (2nd ed.). New York: Longman.

Walker, L. J. (1983). Sources of cognitive conflict for stage transition in moral development. *Developmental Psychology, 19,* 103–110.

Walker, L. J. (1988). The development of moral reasoning. *Annals of Child Development, 5,* 33–78.

Walker, L. J., & Taylor, J. H. (1991). Stage transitions in moral reasoning: A longitudinal study of developmental processes. *Developmental Psychology, 27,* 330–337.

Wall, V. A., & Evans, N. J. (1991). Using psychosocial development theories to understand and work with gay and lesbian persons. In N. J. Evans & V. A. Wall (Eds.), *Beyond tolerance: Gays, lesbians and bisexuals on campus* (pp. 25–38). Alexandria, VA: American College Personnel Association.

Wall, V. A., & Evans, N. J. (Eds.). (2000). *Toward acceptance: Sexual orientation issues on campus.* Washington, DC: American College Personnel Association.

Wall, V. A., & Washington, J. (1991). Understanding gay and lesbian students of color. In N. J. Evans & V. A. Wall (Eds.), *Beyond tolerance: Gays, lesbians and bisexuals on campus* (pp. 67–78). Alexandria, VA: American College Personnel Association.

Wallace, K. R. (2001). *Relative/outsider: The art and politics of identity among mixed heritage students.* Westport, CT: Ablex.

Wallace, K. R. (2003). Contextual factors affecting identity among mixed heritage college students. In M.P.P. Root & M. Kelley (Eds.), *Multiracial child resource book: Living complex identities* (pp. 87–93). Seattle: MAVIN Foundation.

Walsh, W. B. (1973). *Theories of person-environment interaction: Implications for the college student.* Iowa City, IA: American College Testing Program.

Walsh, W. B. (1978). Person/environment interaction. In J. H. Banning (Ed.), *Campus ecology: A perspective for student affairs* (pp. 7–18). Washington, DC: National Association of Student Personnel Administrators.

Wang, Y., & Rodgers, R. (2006). Impact of service-learning and social justice education on college students' cognitive development. *NASPA Journal, 43,* 316–337.

Waterman, A. S. (1982). Identity development from adolescence to adulthood: An extension of theory and a review of research. *Developmental Psychology, 18*(3), 341–358.

Waterman, A. S., & Archer, S. L. (1990). A life-span perspective on identity formation: Developments in form, function, and process. In P. B. Baltes, D. L. Featherman, & R. M. Lerner (Eds.), *Life-span development and behavior* (pp. 29–57). Hillsdale, NJ: Erlbaum.

Waterman, A. S., Geary, P. S., & Waterman, C. K. (1974). A longitudinal study of changes in ego identity status from the freshman to the senior year at college. *Developmental Psychology, 10,* 387–392.

Waterman, A. S., & Waterman, C. K. (1971). A longitudinal study of changes in ego identity status during the freshmen year at college. *Developmental Psychology, 5,* 167–173.

Waterman, C. K., & Nevid, J. (1977). Sex differences in the resolution of the identity crisis. *Journal of Youth and Adolescence, 6,* 337–342.

Waters, M. C. (1990). *Ethnic options: Choosing identities in America.* Berkeley: University of California Press.

Watt, S. K. (2003). Come to the river: Using spirituality to cope, resist, and develop identity. In M. F. Howard-Hamilton (Ed.), *Meeting the needs of African American women* (pp. 29–40). New Directions for Student Services, No. 104. San Francisco: Jossey-Bass.

Wawrzynski, M., & Pizzolato, J. E. (2006). Predicting needs: A longitudinal investigation of the relation between student characteristics, academic paths, and self-authorship. *Journal of College Student Development, 47,* 677–691.

Waziyatawin, A. W., & Yellow Bird, M. (2005). *For indigenous eyes only: A decolonization handbook.* Santa Fe, NM: School of American Research Press.

Weber, L. (1998). A conceptual framework for understanding race, class, gender and sexuality. *Psychology of Women Quarterly, 22,* 13–32.

Wechsler, H., Dowdall, G. W., Davenport, A., & Rimm, E. B. (1995). A gender-specific measure of binge drinking among college students. *American Journal of Public Health, 85*(7), 982–985.

Weidman, J. C. (1989). Undergraduate socialization: A conceptual approach. In J. C. Smart (Ed.), *Higher education: Handbook of theory and research* (Vol. 5, pp. 289–322). New York: Agathon.

Weinstock, J. S., & Bond, L. A. (2000). Conceptions of conflict in close friendships and ways of knowing among young college women: A developmental framework. *Journal of Social and Personal Relationships, 17,* 687–696.

Weith, R. (1985). *A student development scenario.* Unpublished manuscript.

Weitzman, E. R., Nelson, T. F., Lee, H., & Wechsler, H. (2004). Reducing drinking and related harms in college: Evaluation of the "A Matter of Degree" program. *American Journal of Preventive Medicine, 27*(3), 187–196.

Western Interstate Commission for Higher Education. (1972). *The ecosystem model: Designing campus environments.* Boulder, CO: Author.

Weston, L. C., & Stein, S. L. (1977). The relationship of identity achievement of college women and campus participation. *Journal of College Student Personnel, 18,* 21–24.

Wheeler, G. D., Malone, L. A., Van Vlack, S., Nelson, E. R., & Steadward, R. D. (1996). Retirement from disability sport: A pilot study. *Adapted Physical Activity Quarterly, 13,* 382–399.

Whitbourne, S. K., Jelsma, B. M., & Waterman, A. S. (1982). An Eriksonian measure of personality development in college students: A reexamination of Constantinople's data and a partial replication. *Developmental Psychologist, 18,* 369–371.

White, D. B., & Hood, A. B. (1989). An assessment of the validity of Chickering's theory of student development. *Journal of College Student Development, 30,* 354–361.

White, K., & Strange, C. C. (1993). Effects of unwanted childhood sexual experiences on psychosocial development of college women. *Journal of College Student Development, 34,* 289–294.

Whiteley, J. (1982). *Character development in college students* (Vol. 1). Schenectady, NY: Character Research Press.

Whitman, J. S., Cormier, S., & Boyd, C. J. (2000). Identity management at various stages of the coming out process: A qualitative study. *International Journal of Sexuality and Gender Studies, 5,* 3–18.

Widick, C. (1975). *An evaluation of developmental instruction in a university setting.* Unpublished doctoral dissertation, University of Minnesota, Minneapolis.

Widick, C., Knefelkamp, L. L., & Parker, C. A. (1975). The counselor as developmental instructor. *Counselor Education and Supervision, 14,* 286–296.

Widick, C., Parker, C. A., & Knefelkamp, L. L. (1978a). Douglas Heath's model of maturing. In L. Knefelkamp, C. Widick, & C. A. Parker (Eds.), *Applying new developmental findings* (pp. 79–91). New Directions for Student Services, No. 4. San Francisco: Jossey-Bass.

Widick, C., Parker, C. A., & Knefelkamp, L. L. (1978b). Erik Erikson and psychosocial development. In L. Knefelkamp, C. Widick, & C. A. Parker (Eds.), *Applying new developmental findings* (pp. 1–17). New Directions for Student Services, No. 4. San Francisco: Jossey-Bass.

Wijeyesinghe, C. L. (1995). Multiracial identity in a monoracial world. *Hispanic Outlook in Higher Education, 6*(8), 16.

Wijeyesinghe, C. L. (2001). Racial identity in multiracial people: An alternative paradigm. In C. L. Wijeyesinghe & B. W. Jackson, III (Eds.), *New perspectives on racial identity development* (pp. 129–152). New York: New York University Press.

Wilchins, R. A. (2002). Queerer bodies. In J. Nestle, C. Howell, & R. A. Wilchins (Eds.), *Genderqueer: Voices from beyond the sexual binary* (pp. 33–46). Los Angeles: Alyson.

Wildman, T. M. (2004). Framing faculty and institutional development. In M. Baxter Magolda & P. M. King (Eds.), *Learning partnerships: Theory and modes of practice to educate for self-authorship* (pp. 245–268). Sterling, VA: Stylus.

Wildman, T. M. (2007). Taking seriously the intellectual growth of students: Accommodations for self-authorship. In P. S. Meszaros (Ed.), *Self-authorship: Advancing students' intellectual growth* (pp. 15–30). New Directions for Teaching and Learning, No. 109. San Francisco: Jossey-Bass.

Wilkinson, S., & Kitzinger, C. (Eds.). (1993). *Heterosexuality: A feminism and psychology reader.* Thousand Oaks, CA: Sage.

Williams, C. B. (2005). Counseling African American women: Multiple identities—Multiple constraints. *Journal of Counseling and Development, 83*, 278–283.

Williams, M. E., & Winston, R. B., Jr. (1985). Participation in organized student activities and work: Differences in developmental task achievement of traditional-aged college students. *NASPA Journal, 22*(3), 52–59.

Williams, T. E. (1986). Optimizing student institutional fit: An interactive perspective. *College and University, 61*(2), 141–152.

Williams, T. K. (1996). Race as process: Reassessing the "What Are You?" encounters of biracial individuals. In M.P.P. Root (Ed.), *The multiracial experience: Racial borders as the new frontier* (pp. 191–210). Thousand Oaks, CA: Sage.

Williams, T. K., Nakashima, C. L., Kich, G. K., & Daniel, G. R. (1996). Being different together in the university classroom: Multiracial identity as transgressive education. In M.P.P. Root (Ed.), *The multiracial experience: Racial borders as the new frontier* (pp. 359–379). Thousand Oaks, CA: Sage.

Williams, W. L. (1996). Two-spirit persons: Gender nonconformity among Native American and Native Hawaiian youths. In R. C. Savin-Williams & K. M. Cohen (Eds.), *The lives of lesbians, gays, and bisexuals: Children to adults* (pp. 416–435). Fort Worth, TX: Harcourt Brace.

Wilson, A. (1996). How we find ourselves: Identity development and two-spirit people. *Harvard Educational Review, 66*, 303–317.

Wilson, A. L. (1993). The promise of situated cognition. In S. B. Merriam (Ed.), *An update on adult learning theory* (pp. 71–79). New Directions for Adult and Continuing Education, No. 57. San Francisco: Jossey-Bass.

Wilson, F. L. (2000). Measuring morality of justice and care among associate, baccalaureate and second career female nursing students. *Journal of Social Behavior and Personality, 14*, 597–606.

Wilson, M. E., & Wolf-Wendel, L. E. (2005). *ASHE reader on college student development theory.* Boston: Pearson.

Wilson, T. P. (1992). Blood quantum: Native American mixed bloods. In M.P.P. Root (Ed.), *Racially mixed people in America* (pp. 108–125). Thousand Oaks, CA: Sage.

Winnicott, D. W. (1965). *The maturational processes and the facilitating environment.* New York: International Universities Press.

Winston, R. B., Jr., Miller, T. K., & Cooper, D. L. (1999a). *Student developmental task and lifestyle assessment (SDTLA).* Athens, GA: Student Development Associates.

Winston, R. B., Jr., Miller, T. K., & Cooper, D. L. (1999b). *Technical manual for the student developmental task and lifestyle assessment.* Athens, GA: Student Development Associates.

Winston, R. B., Jr., Miller, T. K., & Prince, J. S. (1979). *Student developmental task inventory* (Rev. 2nd ed.). Athens, GA: Student Development Associates.

Wong, M.P.A., & Buckner, J. (2008). Multiracial student services come of age: The state of multiracial student services in higher education in the United States. In K. A. Renn & P. Shang (Eds.), *Biracial and multiracial college students* (pp. 43–51). New Directions for Student Services, No. 123. San Francisco: Jossey-Bass.

Woodard, D. B., Jr., Love, P., & Komives, S. R. (Eds.). (2000). *Leadership and management issues for a new century.* New Directions for Student Services, No. 92. San Francisco: Jossey-Bass.

Woods, D. R. (1990). Nurturing intellectual development. *Journal of College Science Teaching, 19*, 250–252.

Worthington, R. L., Dillon, F. R., & Becker-Schutte, A. M. (2005). Development, reliability, and validity of the lesbian, gay, and bisexual knowledge and attitudes scale for heterosexuals (LGB-KASH). *Journal of Counseling Psychology, 52*(1), 104–118.

Worthington, R. L., Navarro, R. L., Savoy, H. B., & Hampton, D. (2008). Development, reliability, and validity of the measure of sexual identity exploration and commitment (MoSIEC). *Developmental Psychology, 44*(1), 22–33.

Worthington, R. L., Savoy, H. B., Dillon, F. R., & Vernaglia, E. R. (2002). Heterosexual identity development: A multidimensional model of individuals and social identity. *Counseling Psychologist, 30,* 496–531.

Wu, F. H. (2006). The multiracial classification can be detrimental. In E. Stanford (Ed.), *Interracial America: Opposing viewpoints* (pp. 37–43). Farmington Hills, MI: Greenhaven.

Yamazaki, Y. (2005). Learning styles and typologies of cultural differences: A theoretical and empirical comparison. *International Journal of Intercultural Relations, 29,* 521–548.

Yeh, C. J., & Huang, K. (1996). The collectivist nature of ethnic identity development among Asian American college students. *Adolescence, 31,* 645–661.

Yinger, J. M. (1976). Ethnicity in complex societies. In L. A. Coser & O. N. Larsen (Eds.), *The uses of controversy in sociology* (pp. 197–216). New York: Free Press.

Yip, T., Seaton, E. K., & Sellers, R. M. (2006). African American racial identity across the lifespan: Identity status, identity content, and depressive symptoms. *Child Development, 77*(5), 1504–1517.

Yoder, A. E. (2000). Barriers to ego identity status formation: A contextual qualification of Marcia's identity status paradigm. *Journal of Adolescence, 23,* 95–106.

Yonkers-Talz, K. (2004). A learning partnership: U.S. college students and the poor in El Salvador. In M. Baxter Magolda & P. M. King (Eds.), *Learning partnerships: Theory and modes of practice to educate for self-authorship* (pp. 151–184). Sterling, VA: Stylus.

Young, I. M. (2000). Five faces of oppression. In M. Adams, W. J. Blumenfeld, R. Castaeda, H. W. Hackman, M. L. Peters, & X. Zuñiga (Eds.), *Reading for diversity and social justice: An anthology on racism, anti-Semitism, sexism, heterosexism, ableism, and classism* (pp. 35–49). New York: Routledge.

Zack, N. (1995). Life after race. In N. Zack (Ed.), *American mixed race: The culture of microdiversity* (pp. 297–307). Lanham, MD: Rowman & Littlefield.

Zack, N. (1997). The American sexualization of race. In N. Zack (Ed.), *Race/sex: Their sameness, difference, and interplay* (pp. 145–155). New York: Routledge.

Zajonc, A. (2003). Spirituality in higher education: Overcoming the divide. *Liberal Education, 89*(1), 50–58.

Zuschlag, M. K., & Whitbourne, S. K. (1994). Psychosocial development in three generations of college students. *Journal of Youth and Adolescence, 23*(5), 567–577.

INDEX

Note to index: An *e* following a page number denotes an exhibit on that page; an *f* following a page number denotes a figure on that page; a *t* following a page number denotes a table on that page.